D1759583

THE
CONFIRMATION OF EXECUTORS
IN SCOTLAND

THE
CONFIRMATION OF EXECUTORS
IN SCOTLAND

by
The Late James G. Currie
Depute Commissary Clerk, Edinburgh

EIGHTH EDITION

by
Eilidh M. Scobbie
Solicitor, Burnett & Reid, Aberdeen

W. GREEN/SWEET & MAXWELL
EDINBURGH
1995

First published 1995

© 1995
W. Green & Son Ltd

ISBN 0 414 01006 X

A catalogue record for this book
is available from the British Library

Typeset by Wyvern Typesetting, Bristol
Printed in Great Britain by The Headway Press, Reading

PREFACE TO THE EIGHTH EDITION

In his preface to the first edition of this work, James G. Currie stated that "the purpose of this book is to afford practical guidance in the preparation of Inventories and in expeding Confirmation". That aim holds true for this, the eighth edition.

In the 20-odd years since the seventh edition was published, Scots private law has developed at an unparalleled pace. This has necessitated the complete rewriting of the text. I have endeavoured to state the law as at December 31, 1994, but I have incorporated some discussion of significant subsequent developments—such as the Requirements of Writing (Scotland) Act 1995. I have omitted any detailed discussion of the law and practice applicable where the deceased died prior to September 10, 1994 (when the Succession (Scotland) Act 1964 came into force), and a practitioner faced with a pre-1964 confirmation problem must therefore refer to the seventh edition of this work.

As I write, it is understood that a new Act of Sederunt will be promulgated early in 1996, to deal with the changes to commissary practice brought about by the Requirements of Writing (Scotland) Act 1995. A Supplement to this volume is to be produced to incorporate that Act of Sederunt and the Appendix of Styles, including those required in light of the 1995 Act.

Most of the previous editions have been written by practising members of staff of the Commissary Office in Edinburgh. As a solicitor in private practice, that perspective is denied to me, and I have to thank the staff of the Commissary Department in Edinburgh (and in particular Marilyn Riddell and Alan Nicol) for sharing with me their expertise in commissary matters, and in commenting on early drafts of the text. A very special thanks is also due to Evelyn Laing of Scottish Courts Administration for her timely assistance.

I have also to thank those of my fellow practitioners who have shared with me their practical solutions to the many and various problems which real life throws up. I would especially mention Messrs. Biggar (Edinburgh), Liddell (Pitlochry), Ion (Dunblane) and Purdie (Turriff).

Responsibility for the final text is my own, but I am indebted to the following for the time and care which they have taken in commenting on particular sections: Barbara Watts, of the Centre for Legal Studies at Nottingham University; William Young and Mrs. E. McKinnell of the Capital Taxes Office, Edinburgh; members of the legal staff of the Auditor of Court's Office and of the Crown Office; Ian H. L. Miller, Advocate; Diane Robertson of Abertay University; Professor A. E. Anton of Aberdeen; Professors George L. Gretton and Kenneth C. G. Reid of Edinburgh University; and Professor Kenneth Norrie of Strathclyde University. Thanks are also due to friends and colleagues who have helped check citations—I would especially mention Bruce Craig, Charles Sandison, Alison Mitchell and Morna Graham—and to my secretary, Carol-Anne Phimister, who showed great patience in converting my unreadable hieroglyphics into printed text.

At this stage, I am most conscious of the tolerance and forbearance shown to me by two groups of people—the editorial team at Greens who have humoured me through many trials and tribulations, and my partners at Burnett and Reid who have made it possible for me to have the time to complete this project.

Eilidh M. Scobbie

PREFACE TO THE FIRST EDITION

The purpose of this book is to afford practical guidance in the preparation of Inventories and in expeding Confirmation. The only work dealing specially with the subject is the Treatise of Mr. Alexander on *The Practice of the Commissary Courts in Scotland*, published in 1859. Since that date there have been important statutory changes affecting the contents of the inventory, the execution of wills, the forms of process, and the payment of inventory duty: several questions under the Intestate Moveable Succession Act which were then in doubt have been settled by the Supreme Court; and on many points, especially those relating to foreign domicile and foreign law, the rules of procedure have become more clearly determined. It is believed, therefore, that a statement of the present practice may not be unacceptable.

During the last twenty-five years notes have been taken by the Author of the procedure in all cases in the Commissariot of Edinburgh involving any specialty, and of the decisions and instructions given by the Commissaries and Sheriffs in regard thereto. The cases quoted within brackets in the text are selected from these notes, and from the earlier records of the Court, and are not otherwise reported.

The Author feels bound gratefully to acknowledge the aid he has received in preparing this work from Mr. John Smith and Mr. George Adam, senior assistants in the Commissary Office, Edinburgh.

Edinburgh, *2nd April*, 1884.

CONTENTS

TABLE OF CASES

Table of Cases

TABLE OF STATUTES

All references are to paragraph numbers

CHAPTER 1

INTRODUCTION

Introduction

1.01   This chapter explores a number of preliminary matters, such as the nature of the commissary jurisdiction, and the rights, powers and duties of the persons involved in the confirmation process—the clerks, the agents and the executors.

NATURE OF COMMISSARY JURISDICTION

1.02   The jurisdiction is essentially of an administrative and tentative nature. In *Hamilton* v. *Hardie*,[1] Lord Shand said:

> "The effect of confirmation is merely to give a title to the executors to administer the estate of the deceased, and that they are liable to an action . . . to have the deed set aside . . . In this country the practice is to give confirmation— subject to any challenge of the will at a future time."

1.03   In commissary cases, findings beyond this limited jurisdiction are to be avoided: a decision on the validity of a testamentary writing is not part of the jurisdiction. This is seen in the judgments in *Martin* v. *Ferguson's Trustees*,[2] a case where two parties had executed a mutual will appointing the survivor to be sole trustee, and one of the testators subsequently executed a codicil appointing other administrators. The sheriff issued findings that the mutual will was irrevocable, and that the codicil, so far as purporting to revoke it, was inept and invalid. Lord President Robertson said:

> "I cannot say that I am surprised that the appellants should feel uneasy at the pronouncing of these findings . . . in any view I should not be inclined to adhere to findings such as those. The duty of the Sheriff as Commissary is to determine who is entitled to the office of executor on the face either of the deeds which are put before the Court, or of the relation to the deceased which is set out as the title of the applicant."[3]

---

[1] (1888) 16 R. 192 at p. 198.
[2] (1892) 19 R. 474.
[3] *Ibid.*, at p. 478.

1

And Lord McLaren, concurring in holding the appointment of
executors in the codicil as valid, stated: "In coming to [this]
conclusion I, of course, give no opinion as to the validity of
this codicil in so far as it deals with the estate for testamentary
purposes."[4]

1.04   This view is repeated by Lord Kinnear in *MacHardy* v. *Steele*.[5]
There a mother and daughter made a mutual will, appointing
executors of the survivor, which was declared to be irrevocable.
After the mother's death, the daughter made a new will
appointing different executors. The sheriff found that the
mutual will was valid and contractual in its terms, and that,
therefore, it was incompetent for the survivor to supersede the
executors appointed therein. Lord Kinnear viewed these findings with disapprobation:

> "I am not prepared to dispose of the merits of the question
> between the rival deeds in this competition, and if the Sher-
> iff is right in saying he could not have pronounced the
> interlocutor which he has pronounced without deciding the
> merits, that is a reason for saying that he ought not to
> have pronounced that interlocutor . . . I think that . . . the
> administration must be committed to the executors who
> have a good title to administer until it is set aside in some
> competent process."[6]

1.05   While this view has been repeated by many distinguished
judges, there are a number of cases where the court has refused
to grant confirmation, or to issue warrant to the commissary or
sheriff clerk to issue confirmation, in favour of a person who
has been nominated as executor in a testamentary writing which
is *ex facie* validly executed.[7]

The Clerks

1.06   Originally, commissary business in Scotland was dealt with in
a separate court—the commissary court—in which the commissary presided, attended by the commissary clerk. However, in
the nineteenth century, the commissary jurisdiction passed to
the sheriff court, and the sheriff thereafter acted as commissary,[8] with the administration handled by the sheriff clerks,[9]
although the office of commissary clerk was retained in
Edinburgh.[10]

[4] *Ibid.*, at pp. 480–481.
[5] (1902) 4 F. 765.
[6] (1902) 4 F. 765 at pp. 769–770.
[7] *e.g.Trs. of XY*, 1939 S.L.T. (Sh. Ct.) 10.
[8] Sheriff Courts (Scotland) Act 1876 (39 & 40 Vict. c. 70), s. 35.
[9] *Ibid.*, ss. 36 and 38.
[10] *Ibid.*, ss. 37 and 38.

1.07 Except in the case of contentious applications (see Chapter 19), all commissary business is dealt with by the sheriff clerk or, in Edinburgh, the commissary clerk, without the sheriff being involved.

1.08 It should be noted that a commissary or sheriff clerk is debarred from being a law agent,[11] and he cannot act in a case in which he is involved as party.[12] In these circumstances, the course is to apply to the court to appoint a wholly independent clerk to act *pro hac vice*,[13] and where the sheriff clerk is himself an applicant for confirmation, the practice is to apply by petition to the sheriff for warrant to the depute to act and sign the confirmation.

1.08A One of the functions of the commissary or sheriff clerk is to issue confirmation in the format set out in the Act of Sederunt.[13a] Under the Act of Sederunt dated February 3, 1933[13b] the commissary or sheriff clerk may issue a certificate of confirmation in respect of an individual item of estate. The Act of Sederunt provided that *quoad* the particular item of estate, the certificate would be valid—just as if the confirmation (to which the certificate related) had been exhibited. Although originally a certificate could be issued only in respect of an item of moveable estate, it may now be issued in respect of an item of heritable property or interest therein in Scotland,[13c] or in an item of real or personal estate in England and Wales or in Northern Ireland.[13d] Irrespective of any provision in a company's articles, a certificate of confirmation will be accepted as sufficient evidence of the grant.[13e]

THE AGENTS

1.09 A petition for appointment of an executor-dative, special warrant, etc. is to be subscribed by the petitioner, or his agent[14]

---

[11] Sheriff Courts & Legal Officers (Scotland) Act 1927 (17 & 18 Geo. 5, c. 35), ss. 3 and 10.

[12] *Manson* v. *Smith* (1871) 9 M. 492.

[13] *Macbeth* v. *Innes* (1873) 11 M. 404.

[13a] Act of Sederunt (Confirmation of Executors) 1967, (S.I. 1967 No. 789) as amended by Sheriff Courts (Scotland) Act 1971 (c.58), s.4.

[13b] Act of Sederunt anent certain Forms of Procedure in the Sheriff's Ordinary and Small Debt Courts and for the Confirmation of Executors (S.I. 1933 No. 48), s. 2, para. 5.

[13c] Act of Sederunt (Confirmation of Executors) 1964 (S.I. 1964 No. 1143), para. 77.

[13d] Act of Sederunt (Confirmation of Executors) (Amendment) 1971 (S.I. 1971 No. 1164).

[13e] Companies Act 1985 (c. 6), s. 187.

[14] Confirmation of Executors (Scotland) Act 1858 (21 & 22 Vict. c. 56), s. 2 as amended by Statute Law Revision Act 1892 (55 & 56 Vict. c. 19). An "agent"

or, in due course,[15] by an executry practitioner or a recognised financial institution providing executry services within the meaning of section 23 of the Law Reform (Miscellaneous Provisions) (Scotland) Act 1990.[16]

The Notary Public

1.10 There are three circumstances in which a notary public may become involved in the process leading up to confirmation. First, prior to August 1, 1995 he may have been called upon to notarially execute a document for someone who was blind or unable to write (see para. 3.135). Secondly, a person may make an affidavit before him—for instance, that a holograph writing and signature is truly the handwriting of the deceased. Thirdly, he may be the person before whom the deponing executor takes the oath or makes affirmation (see para. 10.14).

1.11 The privileged position of a notary public depends upon "his disinterested independence of the transactions which he records or the judicial acts which he performs."[17] Paragraph 1(3) of the Act of Sederunt of July 19, 1933 provides that "affidavits that the writing and signature of a testamentary writing are in the proper handwriting of the deceased person should not be sworn before the magistrate, commissioner for oaths, justice of the peace or notary public who is a solicitor for the pursuer, or a partner or servant of such solicitor." A notary public should not authenticate deeds in which he has a personal interest. For instance, prior to August 1, 1995, he could not, in any circumstances, make a valid notarial execution of a testamentary writing which appointed him a trustee or executor or the law agent of the trust,[18] or which named one of his partners as a trustee and enabled the trustees to appoint one of their own number as law agent of the estate, and to charge the usual professional remuneration[19]: such a purported will is void.[20] Similarly, a

for this purpose presumably includes a solicitor enrolled in pursuance of the Solicitors (Scotland) Act 1980 (see Solicitors (Scotland) Act 1980 (c. 46), s. 65(1) & (2)(*a*)).

[15] Pt. II (ss. 16–23) of the Law Reform (Miscellaneous Provisions) (Scotland) Act 1990 (c. 40) (covering, *inter alia*, the provision of executry services by executry practitioners and recognised financial institutions) will come into force on a date to be determined by statutory instrument.

[16] Law Reform (Miscellaneous Provisions) (Scotland) Act 1990 (c. 40), s. 74(1) and Sched. 8, Pt. II, para. 22(1).

[17] *Per* Lord President Cooper in *Finlay* v. *Finlay's Trs.*, 1948 S.C. 16 at p. 24, approved by Lord Justice-Clerk Thomson in *Gorrie's Tr.* v. *Stiven's Exrx.*, 1952 S.C. 1 at pp. 10–11.

[18] *Newstad* v. *Dansken*, 1918 1 S.L.T. 136.

[19] *Chisholm* v. *Macrae* (1903) 41 S.L.R. 300; *Wall's Exrs.* (1938) 55 Sh. Ct. Rep. 53, reported as *Trs. of XY*, 1939 S.L.T. (Sh. Ct.) 10; *Finlay* v. *Finlay's Trs.*, 1948 S.C. 16; *Gorrie's Tr.* v. *Stiven's Exrx.*, 1952 S.C. 1.

[20] See, further, paras. 3.136–3.137.

notary public cannot take evidence when he is the petitioner's solicitor.[21]

NATURE OF THE OFFICE OF EXECUTOR

1.12 Although originally a benefit,[22] the office of an executor is now an administrative appointment: an executor is simply an administrator of the estate, for all interested in the succession,[23] but not for creditors.[24]

1.13 It has been said that:

> "All that we know . . . . of the office of executor points to this, that it is an appointment which—on whatever ground or in whatever character it may be given—will subsist until the administration of the entire estate has been completed."[25]

1.14 While in England it is possible for an executor to be appointed for a limited period only (*e.g.*, pending the outcome of litigation), in Scotland there is no such thing as a limited appointment of an executor: all executors will go on to complete the entire administration of the estate,[26] unless their appointment is recalled by the court,[27] or, in the case of executors-nominate, they resign from office.[28]

1.15 While the original appointment subsists, no one else may be confirmed as executor to the same deceased.[29] The office is personal, and does not transmit to the executor's representatives on his death or incapacity,[30] or to his trustee in bankruptcy.[31]

---

[21] *Barr, Petr.*, 1960 S.L.T. (Sh. Ct.) 7.

[22] See, for instance, Lord Sands in *Smart* v. *Smart*, 1926 S.C. 392 at p. 402.

[23] *Smart* v. *Smart*, 1926 S.C. 392.

[24] He is merely a debtor to the deceased's creditors, with liability limited to the amount of the deceased's estate (*Stewart's Tr.* v. *Stewart's Exrx.* (1896) 23 R. 739; *Mitchell* v. *Mackersy* (1905) 8 F. 198).

[25] *Per* Lord McLaren in *Johnston's Exr.* v. *Dobie*, 1907 S.C. 31 at p. 34.

[26] *Per* Lord Ardmillan in *Whiffin* v. *Lees* (1872) 10 M. 797 at p. 802; and Lord Kinloch, *ibid.*, at p. 803.

[27] See paras. 19.15–19.17.

[28] See paras. 1.38–1.39.

[29] *Johnston's Exr.* v. *Dobie*, 1907 S.C. 31.

[30] Executors (Scotland) Act 1900 (63 & 64 Vict. c. 55), s. 7 as amended by Succession (Scotland) Act 1964 (c. 41), s. 34(1) and Sched. 2, para. 14; *per* Lord Morison in *Hutcheson & Co.'s Administrator* v. *Taylor's Exrx.*, 1931 S.C. 484 at p. 492.

[31] Bankruptcy (Scotland) Act 1985 (c. 66), s. 33(1)(*b*).

1.16   The executor may, but need not have, a beneficial interest in the estate—an executor-dative invariably has, whereas an executor-nominate often does not. Since the office of executor is an administrative appointment, and not a benefit, a person who has been appointed executor does not have to choose whether to accept the appointment, or to claim legal rights[32]:

> "It is not a ground for displacing executors that they have personal interests conflicting with their duty as executors. The law supposes that they are able to reconcile their interest and their duty until the contrary is proved."[33]

Duties of an executor

Obtaining confirmation

1.17   One of the first duties of any executor is to confirm to the deceased's estate, for it is the confirmation which vests the estate in the executor for the purposes of administration.[34] In order to obtain confirmation, the executor must exhibit[35] to the appropriate court[35a]:

1. a full and true inventory of the deceased's estate and effects—both his heritable[36] and moveable estate in Scotland and, provided that the deceased died domiciled in Scotland, his real and personal estate in England and Wales or Northern Ireland[37]—distinguishing what is in Scotland from what is elsewhere,[38] to which the executor must make oath or affirmation[39];

2. any testament or other writing disposing of such estate and effects—see paragraphs 10.66 *et seq*; and

3. in appropriate cases a bond of caution—see Chapter 9.

---

[32] *Smart* v. *Smart*, 1926 S.C. 392.

[33] *Per* Lord McLaren in *Birnie* v. *Christie* (1891) 19 R. 334 at p. 338.

[34] Succession (Scotland) Act 1964 (c. 41), s. 14(1).

[35] Requirements are set out in the Probate and Legacy Duties Act 1808 (48 Geo. 3, c. 149), s. 38 (as amended by Finance Act 1949 (12 & 13 Geo. 6, c. 47), s. 52 and Sched. 11, Pt. V and Finance Act 1975 (c. 7), Sched. 13, Pt. 1 and *prosp.* Law Reform (Miscellaneous Provisions) (Scotland) Act 1990 (c. 40), s. 74 and Sched. 8, Pt. II, para. 19 and Sched. 9) unless otherwise indicated.

[35a] See paras. 1.57–1.69.

[36] Succession (Scotland) Act 1964 (c. 41), s. 14(1).

[37] Administration of Estates Act 1971 (c. 25), s. 6(1).

[38] Confirmation of Executors (Scotland) Act 1858 (21 & 22 Vict. c. 56), s. 9 as amended by Statute Law Revision Act 1892 (55 & 56 Vict. c. 19), Administration of Estates Act 1971 (c. 25), ss. 6(1), 12(1), Sched. 2, Pt. 1 and Finance Act 1975 (c. 7), ss. 50, 52(2), (3), 59(3) and Sched. 13, Pt. 1.

[39] See paras. 10.10–10.12. From a date to be determined by statutory instrument, the executor will instead make a simple declaration (Law Reform (Miscellaneous Provisions) (Scotland) Act 1990 (c. 40), Sched. 8, Pt. II, para. 19).

The executor is required to apply for confirmation within six months of assuming possession and management of the estate.

Paying the deceased's creditors

1.18   An executor is not a trustee for the deceased's creditors, but simply the representative of the deceased:

> "Towards the creditors of the deceased it appears to me that [the executor] is simply *eadem persona cum defuncto*, standing to the creditors in no other relation than the deceased stood, except that he is a debtor with limited liability, *viz.*, a liability limited by the amount of the deceased's estate. An executor is not a trustee for the deceased's creditors. He is no more so than an heir entering *cum beneficio inventarii*. He is, in a question with creditors, the proprietor of the estate, under burden of payment of their debts. He is not a depositary. He is a debtor, and the equities which result from the position of a depositary—that is to say, of a trustee—are wholly inapplicable."[40]

1.19   Being in the position of a debtor, an executor is not bound to account to creditors for profits which he may make from using the assets.[41] He is not bound to segregate the assets. It is enough if he retains funds of the value of the deceased's estate at the date of his death and is ready to pay claims to that amount.[42]

> "The limit of [the executor's] liability is the amount of the estate to which he has confirmed, and the inventory of the estate is conclusive on this subject unless it is alleged either that the executor has concealed estate or has negligently failed to ingather it, and then the liability is personal and not *qua* executor."[43]

1.20   Since the executor is standing in the deceased's shoes, a third party may set off debts due to him by the deceased against debts due by him to the deceased's executor *qua* executor.[44]

1.21   The executor of a person who was executor-nominate of a deceased debtor is under no obligation to account for the latter's intromissions, as executor, with the debtor's estate.[45]

---

[40] *Per* Lord Kyllachy in *Stewart's Tr. v. Stewart's Exrx.* (1896) 23 R. 739 at p. 743; see also Lord President Inglis in *Jamieson v. Clark* (1872) 10 M. 399 at p. 405.

[41] *Stewart's Tr. v. Stewart's Exrx.* (1896) 23 R. 739.

[42] *Ibid.*

[43] *Per* Lord Morison in *Hutcheson & Co.'s Administrator v. Taylor's Exr.*, 1931 S.C. 484 at p. 492 and in *Macdonald, Fraser & Co. v. Cairns's Exrx.*, 1932 S.C. 699 at p. 711.

[44] *Mitchell v. Mackersy* (1905) 8 F. 198 (where it was held that a law agent, instructed by the executor to ingather the deceased's estate, could set moneys so ingathered against a legal account run up by the deceased).

[45] *Hutcheson & Co.'s Administrator v. Taylor's Exrx.*, 1931 S.C. 484.

1.22   **General principles regarding payment of debts** The executor's position with regard to settling claims made against the estate is as follows. Unless the testamentary writing provides otherwise, he is entitled to pay debts due by the deceased, without requiring the creditor to constitute the debts if he is satisfied that they are proper debts of the estate.[46] If he is not satisfied that they are proper debts of the estate, he must let the matter be determined in court, and should only pay once the court decree has been taken against him. In the case of an executor-nominate, he may be sued before he has been confirmed.[47] Unless the testamentary writing provides otherwise, an executor may even compromise or submit and refer all claims connected with the executry estate[48]: no executor "requires to apply to the Court for special powers to perform such an act of what must normally be ordinary . . . administration e.g. where an (executor) accepts a composition payment from a debtor, or buys off a doubtful litigation by a settlement."[49] If it transpires that the executry is absolutely insolvent (*i.e.*, the debts exceed the assets), the executor must apply for sequestration.[50]

1.23   **Payment of privileged debts** Since the Act of Sederunt of February 28, 1662 gives an equality of ranking on the executry estate to creditors who use legal diligence within half a year of the death, the practice is that for the first six months after the death, the executor should only pay privileged debts. Privileged debts now comprise the death bed[51] and funeral expenses[52] reasonably incurred[53] (including a mourning allowance for the widow and such children as attend the funeral),[54] and any preferred debts, including taxes which the deceased collects on behalf of the Crown, and arrears of wages up to £800[55] due to employees for up to four months before the death.[56] An executor cannot be obliged to pay other debts until the expiry of the

---

[46] Trusts (Scotland) Act 1921 (11 & 12 Geo. 5, c. 58), s. 4(1)(*l*) .
[47] *Emslie* v. *Tognarelli's Exrs. & Ors.*, 1967 S.L.T. (Notes) 66.
[48] Trusts (Scotland) Act 1921 (11 & 12 Geo. 5, c. 58), s. 4(1)(*i*).
[49] Lord President Cooper in *Tennent's J.F.* v. *Tennent*, 1954 S.C. 215 at p. 226.
[50] See paras. 1.54–56.
[51] Death bed expenses include the cost of medicines supplied (*Douglas* v. *Queensberry's Creditors* (1674) Mor. 11826) and the charges for a doctor's attendance during the deathbed sickness, probably limited to the last 60 days (*Russell* v. *Dunbar* (1717) Mor. 11419; *Park* v. *Reps. of Langlands* (1755) Mor. 11421 and *Sanders* v. *Hewat* (1822) 1 S. 333).
[52] Presumably including the cost of a gravestone (*c. f. Prentice* v. *Chalmers*, 1985 S.L.T. 168—a claim under s. 1(3) of the Damages (Scotland) Act 1976).
[53] Bankruptcy (Scotland) Act 1985 (c. 66), s. 51(1)(*c*), retaining this preferred debt at common law (see Bell, *Prin.*, §§ 1402–3). At common law, the claim was limited to debts contracted in Scotland (*Lawson* v. *Maxwell* (1784) Mor. 4473).
[54] *Hall* v. *McAulay & Lindsay* (1753) Mor. 4854; *Sheddon* v. *Gibson* (1802) Mor. 11855; *Griffiths' Trs.* v. *Griffiths*, 1912 S.C. 626.
[55] S.I. 1986 No. 1914.
[56] Bankruptcy (Scotland) Act 1985 (c. 66), s. 51(1)(*e*).

six-month period, and if he pays ordinary debts without providing for privileged debts, or pays the beneficiaries without providing for debts, he is personally liable.[57]

1.24 **Payment of ordinary debts** Only after the six-month period has expired, may the executor pay claimants in full without regard to possible liabilities upon which no claims have been intimated.[58] After the six-month period has expired, any creditor or creditors of the deceased, whose unsettled debts total £750 or more, may petition for the sequestration of the deceased's estate.[59]

1.25 **Preference** Creditors may acquire preferences by diligence after the death of the deceased,[60] though the preference will fall if the estate is subsequently sequestrated within 12 months of the death.[61]

1.26 **Future claims for aliment on the estate** Where the deceased was liable to aliment his children, spouse or divorced spouse, the order is believed to terminate on the deceased's death.[62] Where a child has inadequate means to support himself, he may even up to the age of 25 years claim aliment from his parent's estate.[63] A widow (and presumably also a widower) has an independent claim for aliment against the deceased spouse's estate—both temporary (*i.e.* for perhaps the six months immediately after the death)[64] and permanent,[65] where inadequate provision has been made for the surviving spouse. Since the claim may be met out of the capital of the executry estate if the income is insufficient,[66] and transmits against those who succeed to the estate, the executors are not bound to hold up the distribution of the estate because a claim for aliment may materialise.[67]

Paying inheritance tax
1.27 An executor is liable for U.K. inheritance tax attributable to the value of property transferred on death (excluding property

---

[57] *Lamond's Trs.* v. *Croom* (1871) 9 M. 662; *Heritable Securities Investment Association* v. *Miller's Trs.* (1893) 20 R. 675.

[58] *Laird* v. *Hamilton*, 1911 1 S.L.T. 27; *Taylor & Ferguson Ltd.* v. *Glass's Trs.*, 1912 S.C. 165; *Stewart's Trs.* v. *Evans* (1871) 9 M. 810.

[59] Bankruptcy (Scotland) Act 1985 (c. 66), ss. 5(4) (as amended by Criminal Justice (Scotland) Act 1987 (c. 41), s. 45(5) and Criminal Justice Act 1988 (c. 33), Sched. 15, para. 107) and 8(3).

[60] *Globe Insurance Co.* v. *Scott's Trs.* (1850) 7 Bell's App. 296.

[61] Bankruptcy (Scotland) Act 1985 (c. 66), s. 37(9).

[62] Clive, *Husband and Wife* (3rd ed.), p. 171; Wilkinson and Norrie, *Parent and Child*, p. 282.

[63] Wilkinson and Norrie, *Parent and Child*, p. 286 *et seq.*

[64] Clive, *Husband and Wife* (3rd ed.), pp. 659–662.

[65] *Ibid.*, pp. 662–663.

[66] *Anderson* v. *Grant* (1899) 1 F. 484 at pp. 486–487.

[67] *Howard's Exr.* v. *Howard's C.B.* (1894) 21 R. 787; *Edinburgh Parish Council* v. *Couper*, 1924 S.C. 139.

which was comprised in a settlement before the death),[68] for the tax due where the deceased died within seven years of making a lifetime chargeable transfer,[69] and for the tax due on a gift made by the deceased "with reservation."[70] Since foreign taxes cannot be recovered in an action in the Scottish courts, a Scottish executor need not normally pay foreign inheritance tax.[70a]

Paying the beneficiaries

1.28 Only after the deceased's debts, the funeral expenses and the inheritance tax due on his estate have been paid can the executors in safety distribute the estate to beneficiaries: "the rights of beneficiaries are entirely postponed to those of creditors."[71]

1.29 Where the deceased died testate, his directions must be carried out meticulously. Any beneficiary may bring an action of accounting against an executor in order to obtain his entitlement. Where a bequest of residue included a solicitor's business books, the executors refused to hand them over to the residuary beneficiary, on the ground of their confidentiality. The beneficiary brought an action of delivery of the books, and decree was granted.[72]

1.30 Where the deceased died intestate, the executor is required to make appropriate investigations in order to ascertain who are those in right to share the deceased's estate in terms of the Succession (Scotland) Act 1964.

1.31 Whether the deceased died testate or intestate, the executor must pay out to the deceased's surviving spouse and issue their rights to *jus relictae, jus relicti* or legitim. The rights of legitim, *jus relicti* and *jus relictae* and the prior rights of a surviving spouse under section 8 or 9 of the Succession (Scotland) Act 1964 are subject to the long negative prescription.[73] In such cases the 20–year period during which the claim must be made, or the subsistence of the obligation acknowledged, normally

---

[68] Inheritance Tax Act 1984 (c. 51), s. 200(1)(*a*).

[69] *Ibid.*, s. 199(2), as substituted by Finance Act 1986 (c. 41), s. 103(3) and Sched. 19, para. 26.

[70] Applying Finance Act 1986 (c. 41), s. 102(3) and (4) to IHTA 1984.

[70a] Anton and Beaumont, *Private International Law* (2nd ed.), pp. 662–663.

[71] Lord President Robertson in *Heritable Securities Investment Association Ltd.* v. *Miller's Trs.* (1893) 20 R. 675 at p. 691.

[72] *Robertson* v. *Robertson's Exrs.*, 1925 S.C. 606 (although the court opined that confidentiality would continue to attach to the papers in the beneficiary's hands).

[73] Prescription and Limitation (Scotland) Act 1973 (c. 52), s. 7 (as amended by Prescription and Limitation (Scotland) Act 1984 (c. 45), s. 5 and Sched. 1, para. 2 and Consumer Protection Act 1987 (c. 43), s. 6 and Sched. 1, para. 8: *c. f.* Sched. 1, para. 2(*f*) of 1973 Act).

begins with the date of death.[74] An executor is consequently at risk of a claim by the surviving spouse or issue of the deceased for 20 years after the death, and he should take strenuous steps to ascertain all falling within this category, and to obtain a discharge from them before paying out the estate to other parties.

1.32 In view of the succession rights now afforded to adopted and illegitimate children, an executor may be faced with a difficult task of identifying the heirs—be they the intestate heirs under the Succession (Scotland) Act 1964 or the potential claimants of legal rights. For instance, if a person died aged 90 in the 1990s, few will be around who can give an accurate account of goings-on of 60 or more years ago, and it would be impractical to suggest that a search should always be made in the Register of Births and in court records for possible actions of affiliation and aliment. However, statute affords the executor some protection: the executor may distribute the estate without investigating whether there are any illegitimate persons who could claim on the estate, whether there ever were any illegitimate persons who would have provided the link to others claiming, or whether there are any claimants who are paternal relatives of an illegitimate person.[75] An executor is also protected from claims if he, in good faith, pays out the estate without checking whether an adoption order has been made.[76]

Powers of the executor

1.33 Once confirmation has been obtained, an executor has full power to take possession of, make up title to, uplift or receive the deceased's estate and effects to which he has been confirmed[77]; to administer and dispose of the same, and to grant discharges thereof; to sue for the estate where necessary and extract decree; and generally to do everything concerning the estate which belongs to the office of executor-dative or executor-nominate as appropriate—subject to the provision that the executor shall render just count and reckoning for his intromissions with the executry estate when legally required.

[74] *Sanderson* v. *Lockhart-Mure*, 1946 S.C. 298 (the starting date for a claim to legitim was the parent's death); *Campbell's Trs.* v. *Campbell's Trs.*, 1950 S.C. 48 (the starting date for a claim for *jus relictae* was the spouse's death) and *Mill's Trs.* v. *Mill's Exrs.*, 1965 S.C. 384 (the starting date was the date intestacy supervened).

[75] Law Reform (Miscellaneous Provisions) (Scotland) Act 1968 (c. 70), s. 7, as amended by Law Reform (Parent and Child) (Scotland) Act 1986 (c. 9), Sched. 1, para. 10 and Sched. 2.

[76] Succession (Scotland) Act 1964 (c. 41), s. 24(2).

[77] Revenue Act 1884 (47 & 48 Vict. c. 62), s. 11, as amended by Inland Revenue Act 1889 (52 & 53 Vict. c. 42), s. 19 and Succession (Scotland) Act 1964 (c. 41), s. 14(1).

Exercise of powers where there is more than one executor

1.34   Where there is more than one executor, all the executors hold office jointly,[78] and must act jointly, although decisions may be made by a quorum, comprising a majority of the executors unless one executor has been appointed *sine qua non* or the testamentary writing provides that a quorum shall be constituted differently.[79]

1.35   Accordingly, when sued, executors must answer as one body, and if they make separate submissions, it is competent only to consider those which are unanimous.[80] Similarly, one out of a body of executors cannot sue for the deceased's debts.[81] Exceptionally, one of three executors has been held entitled to raise an action—this against one of her co-executors, in respect of a debt due by the co-executor to the deceased.[82] If an action is raised by all the executors, and settled by a majority, those not party to the settlement have only exceptionally title to continue with the action.[83]

Death of executor
1.36   Where several executors had been confirmed, on the death of one, the office accrues to the survivors.[84] If all die except one, the office survives in him, and he may sue alone.[85]

Detailed Powers of the executor-nominate

1.37   Unless the contrary is expressed in the testamentary writing,[86] an executor-nominate has all the powers, privileges and immunities conferred on a trustee by the Trusts (Scotland) Act 1921.[87] These are set out at paragraphs 1.38–1.41.

Power of resignation (section 3)
1.38   An executor-nominate has power to resign office, unless:

   1. the contrary is expressed in the testamentary writing; or

---

[78] Ersk., III.ix.40.

[79] Trusts (Scotland) Act 1921 (11 & 12 Geo. 5, c. 58), s. 3(c).

[80] *Campbell* v. *Campbell's Trs.*, 1957 S.L.T. (Sh. Ct.) 53.

[81] Stair, III.viii.59; *Inglis* v. *Mirrie & Lockhart* (1738) Mor. 16115.

[82] *Torrance* v. *Bryson* (1841) 14 Scot. Jur. 30.

[83] *Scott* v. *Craig's Reps.* (1897) 24 R. 462.

[84] Ersk. III.ix.38; *Marjoribanks* v. *Balfour* (1575) Mor. 14686; Executors (Scotland) Act 1900 (63 & 64 Vict., c.55), s. 4.

[85] *Earl of Morton* v. *The Duke* (1557) Mor. 14685.

[86] On whether the contrary has been expressed, see for instance *Reid's Exrs.* v. *Reid*, 1954 S.L.T. (Notes) 20.

[87] Executors (Scotland) Act 1900 (63 & 64 Vict. c. 55), s. 2 and definition of "trustee" in Trusts (Scotland) Act 1921 (11 & 12 Geo. 5, c. 58), s. 2.

2. he is sole executor, and has not assumed a new executor[88] or executors who have accepted office; or

3. he had received a legacy or bequest which had been given on condition that he accepted office as executor, and the testamentary writing did not specifically authorise him to resign; or

4. he had been appointed executor on the basis of receiving remuneration for his services, and the testamentary writing did not specifically authorise him to resign.

1.39 The form of the resignation may be either[89]:

1. by minute entered in the sederunt book of the executry, signed by the resigning executor, and by the other executors still acting; or

2. by signing a minute of resignation in the form of Schedule A to the Trusts (Scotland) Act 1921 which, to be effective, must be intimated to the co-executor or executors.

Power to assume a new executor (section 3)

1.40 Unless the contrary is expressed in the testamentary writing,[90] an executor-nominate has power to assume new executors, and where there are more than two executors-nominate, the new executor may be assumed by a quorum (*i.e.* a majority of those accepting and surviving). The deed of assumption may be in the form of Schedule B to the 1921 Act[91] or may be to like effect.

General powers (section 4)

1.41 Unless "at variance with the terms or purposes" of the testamentary writing,[92] an executor-nominate has power:

(*a*) To sell the executry estate or any part thereof, whether heritable or moveable. The sale may be by public roup or private bargain.[93] In the sale of heritage, it is lawful to reserve the mines and minerals.[94]

(*b*) To grant feus of the heritable estate or any part thereof.

---

[88] Notwithstanding the wording of proviso (1) to s. 3, the assumption of one executor is sufficient (*Kennedy, Petr.*, 1983 S.L.T. (Sh. Ct.) 10).

[89] Trusts (Scotland) Act 1921 (11 & 12 Geo. 5, c. 58), s. 19(1).

[90] See para. 5.98.

[91] Trusts (Scotland) Act 1921 (11 & 12 Geo. 5, c. 58), s. 21.

[92] Interpreted by Lord President Cooper in *Tennent's J.F.* v. *Tennent*, 1954 S.C. 215 at p. 225 as meaning "involving a variation of the purposes."

[93] Trusts (Scotland) Act 1921 (11 & 12 Geo. 5, c. 58), s. 6.

[94] *Ibid.*

(c) To grant leases of any duration (including mineral leases) of the heritable estate or any part thereof and to remove tenants.

(d) To borrow money on the security of the executry estate or any part thereof, heritable as well as moveable.

(e) To excamb any part of the executry estate which is heritable.

(ee) To acquire with the funds of the executry estate any interest in residential accommodation (whether in Scotland or elsewhere) reasonably required to enable the executor to provide a suitable residence for occupation by any of the beneficiaries.[95]

(f) To appoint factors and law agents and to pay them suitable remuneration: the concept of *auctor in rem suam* ensures that an executor may not charge for his services, unless the testator had expressly authorised him to charge,[96] or all the beneficiaries had authorised him to charge.[97] If there is no authorisation, the executor may be reimbursed for his outlays only.[98]

(g) To discharge an executor who has resigned and the representatives of an executor who has died.

(h) To uplift, discharge or assign debts due to the executry estate.

(i) To compromise or to submit and refer all claims connected with the executry estate.

(j) To refrain from doing diligence for the recovery of any debt due to the testator which the executor may reasonably deem irrecoverable.

(k) To grant all deeds necessary for carrying into effect the powers vested in the executor.

(l) To pay debts due by the deceased or by the executry estate without requiring the creditors to constitute such debts where the executor is satisfied that the debts are proper debts of the executry.

---

[95] *Ibid*, s. 4.

[96] Where the testator merely authorised the trustees to appoint one of their number as agent or factor, the right to charge may be inferred: *Goodsir* v. *Carruthers* (1858) 20 D. 1141.

[97] *Lang* v. *Lang's Trs.* (1889) 16 R. 590.

[98] *Lauder* v. *Millars* (1859) 21 D. 1353.

(*m*) To make abatement or reduction, either temporary or permanent, of the rent, lordship, royalty, or other consideration stipulated in any lease of land, houses, tenements, minerals, metals or other subjects, and to accept renunciations of leases of any such subjects.

(*n*) To apply the whole or any part of the executry funds which the executor is empowered or directed by the testamentary writing to invest in the purchase of heritable property in the payment or redemption of any debt or burden affecting heritable property which may be destined to the same series of heirs and subject to the same conditions as are by the testamentary writing made applicable to heritable property directed to be purchased.[99]

(*o*) To concur, in respect of any securities of a company (being securities comprised in the executry estate) in any scheme or arrangement—
  (i)   for the reconstruction of the company;
  (ii)   for the sale of all or any part of the property and undertaking of the company to another company;
  (iii) for the acquisition of the securities of the company, or of the control thereof, by another company;
  (iv)   for the amalgamation of the company with another company; or
  (v)   for the release, modification, or variation of any rights, privileges or liabilities attached to the securities or any of them,
in like manner as if the executor was entitled to such securities beneficially; to accept any securities of any denomination or description of the reconstructed or purchasing or new company in lieu of, or in exchange for, all or any of the first mentioned securities; and to retain any securities so accepted as aforesaid for any period for which the executor could have properly retained the original securities.[1]

(*p*) To exercise, to such extent as the executor thinks fit, any conditional or preferential right to subscribe for any securities in a company (being a right offered to him in respect of any holding in the company), to apply capital money of the executry estate in payment of the consideration,

---

[99] See paras. 10.104–10.107 for discussion of allocation of a debt between heritable and moveable property.
[1] Trustee Investments Act 1961 (c. 62), s. 10.

and to retain any such securities for which he has subscribed for any period for which he has power to retain
the holding in respect of which the right to subscribe for
the securities was offered (but subject to any conditions
subject to which he has that power); to renounce, to such
extent as he thinks fit, any such right; or to assign, to
such extent as he thinks fit and for the best consideration
that can reasonably be obtained, the benefit of such right
or the title thereto to any person, including any beneficiary under the executry.[2]

(*q*) To enter into forestry dedication agreements relating to
the executry estate or any part thereof.[3]

(*r*) To enter into access agreements with Scottish Natural
Heritage or a planning authority relating to the executry
estate or any part thereof.[4]

(*s*) To execute a deed, give consent or make an application
for a farm amalgamation scheme, farm capital grant, etc.[5]

(*t*) To enter into or execute a guardianship deed, deed of
servitude or agreement in relation to an ancient
monument.[6]

(*u*) To enter into an agreement with a roads authority regarding cattle-grids or by-passes.[7]

(*v*) To enter into an agreement with Scottish Natural Heritage
to manage the executry estate or any part thereof as a
nature reserve.[8]

(*w*) To enter into management agreements with Scottish Natural Heritage or a planning authority relating to the
executry estate or any part thereof.[9]

1.42 Even if one of the powers listed is at variance with the terms or
purposes of the testamentary writing, the executors-nominate
may petition the court for authority to use the particular
power.[10]

---

[2] *Ibid.*
[3] Forestry Act 1967 (c. 10), s. 5(4) and Sched. 2, para. 4(2).
[4] Countryside (Scotland) Act 1967 (c. 86), s. 13(1)–(4) and (5) as amended.
[5] Agriculture Act 1970 (c. 40), s. 33(3).
[6] Ancient Monuments and Archaeological Areas Act 1979 (c. 46), s. 18(5).
[7] Roads (Scotland) Act 1984 (c. 54), s. 46(3).
[8] National Parks and Access to the Countryside Act 1949 (12, 13 & 14 Geo. 6
c. 97), s. 16(5)(*b*) as amended.
[9] Countryside (Scotland) Act 1967 (c. 86), s. 49A(6) (inserted by Countryside
(Scotland) Act 1981 (c. 44), s. 9) as amended.
[10] Trusts (Scotland) Act 1921 (11 & 12 Geo. 5, c. 58), s. 5.

Powers of the executor-dative

1.43 An executor-dative, once decerned, enjoys the same powers, privileges and immunities as an executor-nominate (see paras. 1.37 and 1.41), except:

1. he cannot resign office; and

2. he cannot assume a new executor.[11]

Powers of an executor to sue the deceased's debtors

1.44 An executor has, under statute, the general power to "uplift, discharge or assign debts" due to the estate.[12] Where the debtor does not willingly pay, the executor may sue. Even before confirmation is obtained, an executor (whether nominate or dative) has title to sue for the estate,[13] but he must confirm the debt before extract.[14] However, a party eligible to be decerned executor-dative, but who has not yet been decerned, has no title to sue.[15] A grant of probate or of letters of administration from a foreign court is sufficient title to sue, but its authenticity must be attested by, for example, the signatory of a notary, or British consul.[16]

1.45 Without confirmation, an executor can neither enforce payment[17] nor can he grant a discharge.

Right to claim legal rights and to grant discharges therefor

1.46 An executor may claim legal rights on behalf of the deceased person.[18] Indeed, an executor who has personally accepted the conventional provisions in his own favour in the testamentary writing may, on behalf of the deceased person, claim legal rights, instead of accepting the conventional provisions—even

---

[11] Succession (Scotland) Act 1964 (c. 41), s. 20.

[12] Trusts (Scotland) Act 1921 (11 & 12 Geo. 5, c. 58), s. 4(1)(*h*).

[13] See *obiter dicta* of Lord Adam in *Symington* v. *Campbell* (1894) 21 R. 434 at 437 and Lord President Clyde in *Bentley* v. *Macfarlane*, 1964 S.C. 76 at p. 79.

[14] McLaren, *Wills and Succession* (3rd ed.), ii, 878, para. 1616; *Stevenson* v. *Maclaren* (1800) Hume 171; *Reid* v. *Turner* (1830) 8 S. 960; *Chalmers' Trs.* v. *Watson* (1860) 22 D. 1060; *Bones* v. *Morrison* (1866) 5 M. 240; *Mackay* v. *Mackay*, 1914 S.C. 200.

[15] *Malcolm* v. *Dick* (1866) 5 M. 18.

[16] *Disbrow* v. *Mackintosh* (1852) 15 D. 123.

[17] Inland Revenue Act 1884 (47 & 48 Vict. c. 62), s. 11, as amended by Inland Revenue Act 1889 (52 & 53 Vict. c. 42), s. 19.

[18] *e.g. Mill's Trs.* v. *Mill's Exrs.*, 1965 S.C. 384; *Campbell's Trs.* v. *Campbell's Trs.*, 1950 S.C. 48.

where this will result in some personal benefit to the executor.[19] Similarly, he may discharge such a claim, or enter into a deed of family arrangement (within the meaning of section 142 of the Inheritance Tax Act 1984) whereby the rights of the deceased person in another executry estate are altered.

Right of executor to give good title to beneficiary, purchaser or lender

1.47   Any person or body may rely on a confirmation granted under the Confirmation and Probate Act 1858[20] in making any payment or any transfer bona fide upon such confirmation. Such person or body shall be indemnified and protected in so doing, notwithstanding any defect or circumstance whatsoever affecting the validity of such confirmation.[21] The 1858 Act originally applied to personal estate only,[22] but has since been extended to cover heritable securities[23] and debts secured by heritable securities and any interest in heritable property in Scotland held by the deceased and described in the confirmation.[24] Where a person has acquired, in good faith and for value, title to heritable property or a security over heritable property which has vested in an executor, the title will not be challengeable on the ground that the confirmation was reducible or has been reduced.[25]

Agricultural lease

1.48   A lease of an agricultural holding held by the deceased tenant on tacit relocation must be confirmed to[26] before the executor can validly transfer the lease under section 16 of the Succession

---

[19] *MacGregor's Exrx.* v. *MacGregor's Trs.*, 1935 S.C. 13.

[20] 21 & 22 Vict. c. 56.

[21] Confirmation and Probate Amendment Act 1859 (22 Vict. c. 30), s. 1 as amended by Administration of Estates Act 1971 (c. 25), Sched. 1, para. 1.

[22] Both in Scotland and, provided that the deceased died domiciled in Scotland and the confirmation was resealed in England or Ireland, to estate there (Confirmation and Probate Act 1858 (21 & 22 Vict. c. 56), ss. 9 (as repealed by Finance Act 1975 (c. 7), s. 59(5) and Sched. 13), 12 and 13).

[23] The confirmation may be used as a link in title for conveyancing purposes (Conveyancing (Scotland) Act 1924 (14 & 15 Geo. 5, c. 27), s. 5(2) as amended by Succession (Scotland) Act 1964 (c. 41), s. 34(2) and Sched. 3 and in the case of standard securities, Conveyancing and Feudal Reform (Scotland) Act 1970 (c. 35), s. 12(3)) or produced to the Keeper for land registration purposes (Land Registration (Scotland) Act 1979 (c. 33), s. 15(3)).

[24] Succession (Scotland) Act 1964 (c. 41), s. 15(1) (as amended by Law Reform (Miscellaneous Provisions) (Scotland) Act 1968 (c. 70), s. 19) and Act of Sederunt (Confirmation of Executors) 1964, s. 1 (S.I. 1964 No. 1143) (as amended by Act of Sederunt (Confirmation of Executors Amendment) 1966, s. 1 (S.I. 1966 No. 593)).

[25] Succession (Scotland) Act 1964 (c. 41), s. 17.

[26] *Rotherwick's Trs.* v. *Hope*, 1975 S.L.T. 187.

(Scotland) Act 1964. However, where confirmation is granted after such nominee has intimated to the landlord his acceptance of the bequest in terms of section 12(1) of the Agricultural Holdings (Scotland) Act 1991, this will validate the transfer retrospectively.[27]

Executors and vitious intromission[28]

1.49   What constitutes vitious intromission is far from clearly defined. The early cases indicate that originally the removal of any of the deceased's effects without title amounted to vitious intromission.[29] Today, it would appear that merely continuing to hold items of the deceased's estate,[30] or even taking possession of them to preserve them, or for some other necessary or equitable purpose, does not constitute vitious intromission. There must be something from which fraud or misappropriation is or may be presumed.[31]

1.50   The Vitious Intromitters Act 1696 provided that:

> "the nearest of kin and other intromitters with the moveables of any defunct who are not executors confirmed to them . . . are and shall be liable as vitious intromitters notwithstanding that there is a third party confirmed executor to a particular debt or subject."

1.51   Accordingly, if a person who had intromitted with the deceased's moveable estate confirmed to the estate before he was charged as a vitious intromitter, he has a complete defence. The law recognises that it is not possible to obtain confirmation immediately on the death, and allows the "intromitter" time to be confirmed: vitiosity may be purged by the executor expeding confirmation after the action is raised, but within a year of the death.[32-33] It would appear that the misappropriation of the deceased's foreign estate does not amount to vitious intromission.[34]

1.52   Only creditors (and not legatees or those claiming legal rights) can plead vitious intromission.

---

[27] *Garvie's Trs.* v. *Garvie's Tutors*, 1975 S.L.T. 94.

[28] See generally, Ersk. III.ix.49–55; Bell, *Prin.*, §1921; Bell, *Comm.*, III.ii.5; *Stair Memorial Encyclopaedia*, vol. 25, paras. 1061–1064.

[29] *Archibald* v. *Lawson* (1705) Mor. 9829; *Scott* v. *Lord Belhaven* (1821) 1 S. 33; *Cuningham & Bell* v. *McKirdy* (1827) 5 S. 315.

[30] *Thomson* v. *Jones* (1834) 13 S. 143.

[31] Per Lord Justice-Clerk Hope in *Adam* v. *Campbell* (1854) 16 D. 964 at p. 972.

[32-33] Ersk., III.ix.52; *Stevenson* v. *Ker* (1663) Mor. 9873; *Drummond* v. *Campbell* (1709) Mor. 14414; see also *Urquhart* v. *Dalgairno* (1680) Mor. 9875.

[34] *Archbishop of Glasgow* v. *Bruntsfield* (1683) Mor. 4449; misappropriation of estate in England and Wales or in Northern Ireland, belonging to a person who died domiciled in Scotland, would presumably now amount to vitious intromission, since confimation now gives title to such property.

1.53 The extent of the liability of a vitious intromitter is no more than the deceased's debts. Vitious intromission was "formerly . . . a penal consequence of having neglected to preserve a proper check for ascertaining the amount of the deceased's funds. The tendency of late years has been to push the responsibility no further than a fair reckoning of the amount of the funds may justify."[35] A vitious intromitter is also liable for the inheritance tax due on the funds which he has possessed.[36]

Executry estate insolvent[37]

1.54 Where the deceased, at any time within a year of his death,[38] either had been habitually resident in Scotland, or had an established place of business there,[39] or had been a partner in a firm which is being sequestrated under Scots law,[40] the provisions set out in paragraphs 1.55 and 1.56 apply: the deceased need not have had a Scottish domicile.

1.55 If, at the time of the death, it is clear that the estate is absolutely insolvent (*i.e.* the deceased's liabilities are greater than his assets[41]), a person who could be appointed an executor on the deceased's estate may instead petition for sequestration.[42]

1.56 If the absolute insolvency of the estate appears at a subsequent stage, the executor should not continue to act, but must petition for the sequestration of the deceased's estate in terms of section 5(3)(*a*) of the Bankruptcy (Scotland) Act 1985 or for the appointment of a judicial factor.[43] If the executor continues to act for some time after it should have been clear to him that the estate was absolutely insolvent, he will be denied the protection of the confirmation in his favour,[44] and will be treated as a vitious intromitter.

Sheriff court districts with commissary departments

1.57 All sheriff courts have jurisdiction to consider petitions for the appointment of executors-dative [45] and all other commissary

---

[35] Bell, *Comm.*, (7th ed.), II, p. 81, citing *Barbour* v. *Kelvie* (1824) 3 S. 299.
[36] Inheritance Tax Act 1984 (c. 51), s. 199(1) and (4)(*a*).
[37] See generally, W.W. McBryde, *Bankruptcy*, pp. 32–33.
[38] Bankruptcy (Scotland) Act 1985 (c. 66), s. 9(5).
[39] *Ibid.*, s. 9(1).
[40] *Ibid.*, s. 9(3).
[41] *Ibid.*, s. 73(2).
[42] *Ibid.*, s. 8(3)(*a*).
[43] *Ibid.* s. 8(4).
[44] *Ibid.*
[45] Act of Sederunt (Commissary Business) (S.I. 1975 No. 539), amended by S.I. 1978 No. 1509, 1979 No. 267, 1979 No. 969, 1979 No. 1405 and 1984 No. 969.

business may be dealt with only at certain sheriff courts within a particular sheriffdom.[46] The court in Edinburgh has exclusive jurisdiction where the deceased died domiciled outwith Scotland or "without any fixed or known domicile except the same was in Scotland". In other cases, while the question of which sheriffdom is appropriate is determined by the domicile of the deceased, the question of which court within that sheriffdom is determined by the last ordinary residence of the deceased.[47] The sheriffdoms and courts are as follows[48]:

Grampian, Highland and Islands

1.58   Commissary business can be dealt with as follows:

Aberdeen	for Districts of City of Aberdeen and of Gordon
Banff	for District of Banff and Buchan, except that part comprised in the Court District of Peterhead
Dingwall	for District of Ross and Cromarty except that part comprised in the Sheriff Court District of Tain; and in the District of Skye and Lochalsh, the parishes of Lochalsh, Glenshiel and Kintail
Dornoch	for District of Sutherland
Elgin	for District of Moray
Inverness	for Districts of Badenoch and Strathspey, of Inverness and of Nairn
Kirkwall	for The Islands Area of Orkney
Lerwick	for The Islands Area of Shetland
Peterhead	for that part of the District of Banff and Buchan comprising the parishes of Aberlour, Crimond, Cruden, Fraserburgh, Longside, Lonmay, New Deer, Old Deer, Peterhead, Pitsligo, Rathen, St Fergus, Strichen and Tyrie

---

[46] *Ibid.*

[47] See, for instance, Act of Court for Sheriffdom of Lothians and Borders 1990 No. 1, r. 15 (reproduced 1990 S.L.T. (News) 173).

[48] Sheriffdoms Reorganisation Order 1974 (S.I. 1974 No. 2087, amended by S.I. 75 No. 637); Sheriff Court Districts Reorganisation Order 1975 (S.I. 1975 No. 637, amended by S.I. 1975 No. 1539, 1977 No. 672, 1978 No. 152, 1983 No. 1028 and 1986 No. 267).

Stonehaven	for District of Kincardine and Deeside
Wick	for District of Caithness.

Tayside, Central and Fife

1.59 Commissary business can be dealt with as follows:

Alloa	for District of Clackmannan
Arbroath	for that part of the District of Angus comprising the parishes of Arbirlot, Arbroath and St Vingeans, Barry, Carmyllie, Craig, Dun, Guthrie, Inverkeilor, Kinnell, Kirkden, Logie Pert, Lunan, Maryton, Monikie, Montrose and Panbride
Cupar	for District of North East Fife
Dundee	for District of City of Dundee
Dunfermline	for District of Dunfermline
Falkirk	for District of Falkirk
Forfar	for District of Angus except that part comprised in the Sheriff Court District of Arbroath
Kirkcaldy	for District of Kirkcaldy
Perth	for District of Perth and Kinross
Stirling	for District of Stirling.

Lothian and Borders

1.60 Where the deceased had his last place of residence within a sheriff court district, all commissary business (including executor-dative petitions) must be directed to the sheriff court of that district.[49] Commissary business is dealt with as follows:

Edinburgh	for Districts of City of Edinburgh and of Midlothian
Haddington	for District of East Lothian
Jedburgh	for Districts of Berwickshire and Roxburgh
Linlithgow	for District of West Lothian
Peebles	for District of Tweeddale
Selkirk	for District of Ettrick and Lauderdale.

[49] Act of Court (Consolidation, etc.) 1990 No. 1, r. 15 (reproduced 1990 S.L.T. 173).

Glasgow and Strathkelvin

1.61   Commissary business is dealt with as follows:
Glasgow   for Districts of City of Glasgow and of Strathkelvin.

North Strathclyde

1.62   Commissary business is dealt with as follows:
Dumbarton   for Districts of Bearsden and Milngavie, of Clydebank and of Dumbarton, and the part of the District of Argyll and Bute within the Sheriff Court District of Campbeltown[50] and Oban[51]
Greenock   for District of Inverclyde, and the part of Argyll and Bute District within the Sheriff Court Districts of Dunoon[52] and Rothesay[53]
Kilmarnock   for Districts of Cunninghame and of Kilmarnock and Loudoun
Paisley   for Districts of Renfrew and Eastwood.

1.63   Dative petitions may be made at any sheriff court in the sheriffdom.

1.64   In all commissary papers, it will be sufficient to refer to the deceased's domicile as being within the Sheriffdom of North Strathclyde in Scotland.[54]

1.65   Petitions for the appointment of executors-dative should be

[50] District of Argyll and Bute except the parts comprised in the Sheriff Court Districts of Dunoon, Oban and Rothesay.

[51] That part of Argyll and Bute District comprising the parishes of Ardchattan and Muckairn, Coll, Colonsay and Oronsay, Craignish, Glenorchy and Innishael, Kilbrandon and Kilchattan, Kilchrenan and Dalavich, Kilfinichen and Kilvicheon, Kilmartin, Kilmore and Kilbride, Kilninian and Kilmore, Kilninver and Kilmelford, Lismore and Appin, Tiree, Torosay and that part of the parish of Jura consisting of the islands north of the Gulf of Corrievreckan.

[52] That part of the District of Argyll and Bute comprising the parishes of Dunoon and Kilmun, Inveraray, Inverchaolain, Kilfinan, Kilmartin, Kilmichael-Glassary, Kilmodan, Lochgoilhead and Kilmorich, North Knapdale, Strachur and Strathlachlan and that part of South Knapdale north of the B8024 road from Clachbreck on Loch Caolisport in the west to the junction of the B8024 road with the A83 road in the east.

[53] That part of the District of Argyll and Bute comprising the parishes of Rothesay, Kingarth and North Bute.

[54] Act of Court (Consolidation, etc.) 1992, r. 3.05.

lodged and published in the sheriff court of the district in which the deceased last ordinarily resided.[55]

1.66   Inventories should be presented in the sheriff court of the district in which the deceased was last ordinarily resident, with the exception of the sheriff court districts of Dunoon and Rothesay (which are dealt with at Greenock) and of Campbeltown and Oban (which are dealt with at Dumbarton).

1.67   In any commissary application, the sheriff may:

  (*a*) remit the application to another court; and

  (*b*) require an applicant who has applied as executor-dative in any other court within the sheriffdom to produce an extract decree of the appointment.[56]

1.68   All additional and corrective inventories, inventories *ad non executa*, inventories *ad omissa* and additional oaths are considered as steps in the original confirmation, and are to be lodged in the sheriff court of the commissariot in which the confirmation was granted or the sheriff court which holds the records of the original application for confirmation.[57]

South Strathclyde

1.69   Commissary business can be dealt with as follows:

Airdrie	for Districts of Cumbernauld and Kilsyth and of Monklands
Ayr	for Districts of Cumnock and Doon Valley and of Kyle and Carrick
Dumfries	for Districts of Nithsdale and of Annandale and Eskdale
Hamilton	for Districts of East Kilbride, Hamilton and Motherwell
Kirkcudbright	for District of Stewartry
Lanark	for District of Lanark
Stranraer	for District of Wigtown.

---

[55] *Ibid.*, r. 3.02.
[56] *Ibid.*, r. 3.04.
[57] *Ibid.*, r. 3.03.

CHAPTER 2

DOMICILE

Introduction

2.01   "Domicile" is a concept which is fundamental to executry practice (see paras. 2.03–205) and here the law applies what may be called the traditional concept of domicile, rather than the special residence-based concept of domicile which is employed for the purposes of civil jurisdiction and the recognition and enforcement of judgments by the Civil Jurisdiction and Judgments Act 1982.[1] The general approach taken by a Scottish court in determining a person's domicile is set out at paragraphs 2.06–2.13, with paragraphs 2.19–2.21 concentrating on the specialities of commissary cases. Decisions where domicile was in issue are not discussed in any detail since, at the time of writing, there is some prospect that the Government may adopt a variation on the proposals contained in the joint report of the Law Commission and the Scottish Law Commission entitled "Private International Law: The Law of Domicile".[1a] Readers with a particular problem on domicile should refer to the fuller commentary provided in A.E. Anton's *Private International Law*.[2]

2.02   Finally, the consequences of domicile *vis-à-vis* commissary jurisdiction is considered at paragraphs 2.25–2.32 and paragraph 2.34 *et seq* explain who may be confirmed when the deceased was domiciled in a country other than Scotland.

The importance of domicile in executry practice

2.03   Many aspects of executry practice hinge on the domicile of the deceased. For instance, the law of the deceased's domicile

1.   will determine whether the deceased had testamentary capacity in respect of his worldwide moveable estate (see para. 3.12);

2.   will determine what restraints there were on him testing;

3.   is one basis for determining under the Wills Act 1963[3] whether his testamentary writings are properly executed (see paras. 3.07–3.08); and

---

[1] See in particular Civil Jurisdiction and Judgments Act 1982 (c. 27), ss 41 and 44; Anton and Beaumont, *Civil Jurisdiction in Scotland* (2nd ed.), Chap. 4.

[1a] (1987) Law Com. No. 168 and Scot. Law Com. No. 107 (Cm. 200).

[2] Chap. 6 of 1st edition and Chap. 7 of 2nd edition.

[3] (c. 44).

4.   will determine who may make claims on the estate (for instance the widow and children of a person who died domiciled in Scotland may claim legal rights).

2.04   Further, the deceased's domicile

1.   will determine the items of the deceased's estate on which liability to UK inheritance tax is calculated (see para. 12.02); and

2.   will determine in which Scottish court the petition for the appointment of an executor-dative should be raised, the inventory recorded and application made for confirmation (see paras. 7.04–7.07, 7.18–7.29 and 10.44–10.45), and who may be confirmed to the office.

2.05   Further, the sheriff or commissary clerk's note of Scottish domicile is sufficient to have the confirmation accepted as a valid title to estate in England and Wales or Northern Ireland, though it does not have effect for other purposes.[4]

Domicile: only one domicile[5]

2.06   The Scots law of domicile presupposes that at any given time, every person has one operative domicile.

Domicile: domicile of origin[6]

2.07   On birth, a person acquires a domicile of origin. The domicile of origin is the father's domicile at the time of the birth, if the child was born legitimate, or that of the mother, if the child was born illegitimate or posthumous. There is no clear authority for the domicile of origin of the children of a putative marriage, or of children legitimated *per subsequens matrimonium*. The domicile of origin of an adopted child is probably that of the adoptive father (when a married couple both adopt the child) or of the sole adoptive parent. The domicile of origin of a foundling is presumably the country where he was found.

2.08   The domicile of origin will be temporarily replaced if the person acquires a domicile of dependence, or a domicile of choice. Where a person abandons a domicile of dependence or of choice

---

[4] The Confirmation of Executors (Scotland) Act 1858 (21 & 22 Vict. c. 56), s. 17, as modified by Sheriff Courts (Scotland) Act 1876 (39 & 40 Vict. c. 70), s. 41, and Finance Act 1975 (c. 7), Sched. 13; Administration of Estates Act 1971 (c. 25), s. 1(1) and (2) and 2(2).

[5] For further commentary, see Anton and Beaumont, *Private International Law* (2nd ed.), pp. 128–129.

[6] *Ibid.* pp. 130–133.

without acquiring a new domicile of dependence or choice, the domicile of origin revives.

Domicile of dependence[7]

Children and young persons

2.09 Under Scots law, until a person has attained the age of 16 years, he cannot acquire an independent domicile[8] and his domicile is deemed to follow that of the person on whom he is dependent—normally his father. However, a child's domicile is deemed to follow that of his mother if either

1. the child was born to an unmarried mother;

2. his father has died;[9] or

3. the parents (whether adoptive or natural[10]) are living apart, and
   (a) the child then has his home with his mother and has no home with his father; or
   (b) the child has at any time had the mother's domicile by virtue of paragraph (a) above and he has not since had a home with his father.[11]

Such a child will retain the mother's domicile after her death, until he has a home with his father.[12] A child may be treated as having a home with his father even if he lives with his father for only a few months in a house belonging to a relative.[13]

2.10 If both parents are dead, the child presumably retains the domicile of the last parent to die, until he is adopted, or acquires a domicile of choice (see paras. 2.13–2.17).

Married women

2.11 Until December 31, 1973, a married woman also took a domicile of dependence, for her domicile followed that of her husband. A woman married before that date retained after January 1, 1974 the domicile of her husband (either as her domicile of origin or of choice, as appropriate), until it was changed by the revival of her domicile of origin or her acquisition of a domicile of choice.[14] After December 31, 1973 the domicile of a married

---

[7] *Ibid.* pp. 133–135.

[8] Age of Legal Capacity (Scotland) Act 1991 (c. 50), s. 7.

[9] Domicile and Matrimonial Proceedings Act 1973 (c. 45), s. 4(4); and *Arnott v. Groom* (1846) 9 D. 142; *Crumpton's J.F. v. Finch-Noyes*, 1918 S.C. 378.

[10] Domicile and Matrimonial Proceedings Act 1973 (c. 45), s. 4(5).

[11] *Ibid.*, s. 4(1) and (2).

[12] *Ibid.* s. 4(3).

[13] See *Williams, Petr.*, 1977 S.L.T. (Notes) 2.

[14] Domicile and Matrimonial Proceedings Act 1973 (c. 45), s. 1(2).

woman is determined by the same factors as any other individual,[14a] though obviously a married woman's domicile will normally be the same as her husband.

2.12   Where a person abandons a domicile of dependence, he either acquires a domicile of choice (see paras. 2.13–2.17) or the domicile of origin revives (see paras. 2.07–2.08).

Domicile of choice[15]

2.13   On attaining the age of 16 years,[16] any person[17] who is *capax*[18] will acquire a domicile of choice if he settles in another country with the intention of making it his permanent home. There must be both residence and intention to settle: residence for even a few days,[19] with an intention to make a permanent home, may be sufficient, but lengthy residence without intention is not.[20]

2.14   For there to be residence, the person need not have a "permanent establishment". Residence for a short period in leased premises,[21] in a room in a hotel or boarding-house,[22] or in a military camp[23] may be sufficient to acquire a domicile of choice, provided that there is adequate evidence of intention.

2.15   The intention to settle in the country must be "unlimited . . . not for any defined period or particular purpose, but general and indefinite in its future duration". The choice of going to the country must be voluntary and "not prescribed by any external necessity, such as the duties of office, the demands of creditors or the relief of illness".[24] Consequently, a person such as a member of the armed forces,[25] a government official,[26] or an

---

[14a] *Ibid.* s. 1(1).

[15] For further commentary, see Anton and Beaumont, *Private International Law* (2nd ed.), pp. 137–143.

[16] Age of Legal Capacity (Scotland) Act 1991 (c. 50), s. 7.

[17] Including a married woman—Domicile and Matrimonial Proceedings Act 1973 (c. 45), s. 1(1).

[18] *Crumpton's J.F.* v. *Finch-Noyes*, 1918 S.C. 378.

[19] *Per* Lord Chelmsford in *Bell* v. *Kennedy* (1868) 6 M. (H.L.) 69 at p. 77.

[20] *Per* Lord Chelmsford in *Udny* v. *Udny* (1869) 7 M. (H.L.) 89 at p. 98; in *Liverpool Royal Infirmary* v. *Ramsay*, 1930 S.C. (H.L.) 83, a Glaswegian who had lived in Liverpool for 45 years before his death, but without the intention of settling there permanently, was held to have died domiciled in Scotland.

[21] In *Macphail* v. *Macphail's Trs.* (1906) 14 S.L.T. 388, a Scot died three months after moving into premises near London which had been leased for two and a half years. It was held that he had acquired a domicile of choice in England.

[22] *Per* Lord Jeffrey (dissenting) in *Arnott* v. *Groom* (1846) 9 D. 142 at p. 150.

[23] *Per* Lord Justice-Clerk Thomson in *Willar* v. *Willar*, 1954 S.C. 144 at p. 149.

[24] *Per* Lord Westbury in *Udny* v. *Udny* (1869) 7 M. (H.L.) 89 at p. 99.

[25] *Wylie* v. *Laye* (1834) 12 S. 927 (soldier); *Sellars* v. *Sellars*, 1942 S.C. 206 (chief stoker in Royal Navy with a shore posting).

[26] *Udny* v. *Udny* (1869) 7 M. (H.L.) 89 (consul).

employee of a company,[27] who is sent abroad in the performance of his duties, does not by his mere presence in that foreign
country acquire a domicile of choice. He may, however, acquire
a domicile of choice there,[28] if there are facts and circumstances—such as "[T]he purchase or permanent occupation of
a house, the transfer to the new area of wife and family, the
succession to a landed estate"[29]—establishing that the person
chose voluntarily to reside there. Acceptance of a permanent
appointment overseas may indicate an intent to settle
permanently.[30]

2.16 Any elements in a person's life history which throw light upon
his intentions may be considered in determining domicile.
These have included his choice of family residence, the purchase of a house, length of residence, marriage in the country
(especially if to a national of the country), the education of his
children, his naturalisation, changing religion, expressions of
intention to friends and colleagues, holding a public office,
making a will in the form of the country and appointing trustees
there, and making declarations in the will as to domicile.[31]

2.17 The onus of proving that a person's domicile has changed lies
on the person asserting it,[32] and the standard of proof is probably now on the balance of probabilities.[33]

2.18 Where a person abandons a domicile of choice—by leaving the
country with the intention of abandoning the domicile—he will
either acquire a new domicile of choice, or his domicile of origin
revives (see paras. 2.07 and 2.08).

SPECIALITIES OF COMMISSARY PRACTICE

Determining domicile is normally not contentious

2.19 In commissary cases, the question of the deceased's last domicile is normally treated as an administrative, and not contentious, matter. Even where domicile could be disputed, the
normal commissary practice is to grant confirmation on the basis
that the deceased was domiciled in the place where he last resided. Only when the averment on domicile is challenged, will
proof require to be lead. As Lord McLaren wrote[34]:

---

[27] *Grant* v. *Grant*, 1931 S.C. 238 (employee with the East India Company).
[28] *e.g. Clarke* v. *Newmarsh* (1836) 14 S. 488; *Willar* v. *Willar*, 1954 S.C. 144.
[29] *Per* Lord Moncrieff in *Sellars* v. *Sellars*, 1942 S.C. 206 at p. 213.
[30] *I.R.C.* v. *Gordon's Exrs.* (1850) 12 D. 657; *Fairbairn* v. *Neville* (1897) 25 R. 192.
[31] See paras. 2.21–2.24.
[32] *Per* Lord Chancellor Cairns in *Bell* v. *Kennedy* (1868) 6 M. (H.L.) 69 at p. 74.
[33] Anton and Beaumont, *Private International Law* (2nd ed.) p. 129; *c.f. Lamb* v.
Lord Advocate, 1976 S.C. 110.
[34] *The Law of Wills and Succession* (3rd ed.), para. 6.

"As residence is the basis of domicile, it follows that the
place where an individual was . . . . . habitually resident,
at the time of his death, shall, in the absence of any conten-
tion to the contrary, be presumed to be his domicile for
purposes connected with the administration of his succession. On this principle, the Commissary Courts grant confirmations to the next of kin of all intestates resident in
Scotland at the time of death, where no competing claim is
made by persons claiming the character of personal representatives under the law of another domicile. But this is only
a rule of administration, and where the fact of domicile is
brought into controversy, there is no presumption in favour
of the last place of residence. The fundamental point is the
ascertainment of the 'origin' of the person whose domicile
is in question, and the onus of proof is on the party seeking
to displace that domicile and to establish a domicile of
choice. The domicile of origin, being admitted or ascertained, becomes the presumed domicile through life, until
it is displaced by proof of an acquired domicile more prox-
imate to the period to which the investigation is directed."

2.20　　Normally, the sheriff or commissary clerk will treat as conclusive an averment as to the domicile of the deceased person on
death.[35] However, the clerk is not bound to accept an averment
as to the domicile, if, from the deceased's description, it would
prima facie appear that he was not so domiciled. Since domicile
involves concepts of both residence, and intention to reside permanently, it is to be expected that an averment as to the deceased's domicile—whether in a petition or inventory—will tie in
with the place of the deceased's last residence. If it does not,
the clerk will seek further evidence in support of the domicile
averred. In practice, if the clerk is not satisfied by the further
evidence, the agent will usually agree to change the averment
as to the deceased's domicile, whether to a different company,
or whether to a "no known domicile, except that the same was
in—[domicile of origin]". However, it is open to the agent to
insist on a hearing before the sheriff, and where the clerk
refuses to confirm executors nominate because of the averment
as to the deceased's domicile, the matter may be resolved in a
petition for special authority to issue confirmation.[36]

[35] See for instance *Hamilton* v. *Hardie* (1888) 16 R. 192, where the affidavit as
to the deceased's Scottish domicile was challenged by the next-of-kin who
alleged that the deceased had been domiciled in England. The other information
contained in the inventory was compatible with a Scottish domicile, and confirmation was granted.
[36] See paras. 19.28–19.33. In a dative case, any discrepancy between the deceased's description and the declared domicile will have been resolved when the
court decerned the executor-dative.

Testamentary declaration on domicile

2.21 Clearly, in commissary cases, the evidence of the deceased cannot be taken. Frequently, in cases of doubt, the deceased may have made a declaration of domicile in his testamentary writing. Generally, the deceased will only have made such a declaration when he is no longer living in the country of the declared domicile. Such a declaration is not conclusive,[37] and if the declared domicile is to be effective, there must be elements in his personal life consistent with it. The court will note whether the deceased had an ulterior motive in making the declaration,[38] for an ulterior motive would reduce the evidential value of the declaration further.

2.22 In one reported case, the court may have treated as of some importance, a statement indicating the testator's domicile, which was inserted by the deceased in his holograph testamentary writing.[39] The deceased had a Scottish domicile of origin but had lived in Liverpool for the 45 years before his death. The evidence on whether he had formed the intention of settling in England permanently was inconclusive, and it was stated that "the description by the deceased of himself as 'a Glasgow man' in his holograph will three months before his death may be accepted as the best evidence of his state of mind".[40] This was not strictly a case of a declaration of domicile. The deceased had merely direced that certain legacies should be anonymous "say a Glasgow man". It is unlikely that a court would place as much significance on a formal declaration of domicile inserted in a professionally prepared testamentary writing, as they did on these few words.

2.23 The deceased may also have made a declaration as to his domicile in other official documents.[41] Such declarations are not conclusive, but will be considered in the light of the other personal factors.

Commissary practice
2.24 When an application for confirmation is presented along with a testamentary writing in which the deceased has made a declara-

---

[37] *Robinson* v. *Robinson's Trs.*, 1934 S.L.T. 183; *Baines's Exr.* v. *Clark*, 1957 S.C. 342.
[38] *McEwan* v. *McEwan*, 1969 S.L.T. 342 (where the motive for a declaration of domicile was to ensure that the appointment of a guardian to the testator's children would not be challenged).
[39] *Liverpool Royal Infirmary* v. *Ramsay*, 1930 S.C. (H.L.) 83, *per* Lord Thankerton at p. 88 and Lord Macmillan at p. 90.
[40] *Per* Lord Macmillan in *Liverpool Royal Infirmary* v. *Ramsay* 1930 S.C. (H.L.) 83 at p. 90.
[41] *Ross* v. *Ross*, 1930 S.C. (H.L.) 1 at p. 6 (declaration in connection with US/ UK taxation); *Woodbury* v. *Sutherland's Trs.*, 1939 S.N. 64 (where the declaration was in a petition to the Lord Lyon for a grant of arms).

tion of domicile which differs from that averred in the application, it is usually necessary to present a petition for special
authority to issue confirmation (see paras. 19.25–19.32), in order
that the question of the deceased's domicile may be judicially
decided.

Domicile—national and local

2.25   In most areas of law, the question of domicile involves identifying a country in which a person was domiciled. In commissary
cases, it is not just a question of determining the country in
which the deceased was domiciled at the time of his death, it
is also necessary to determine, in cases where he died domiciled
in Scotland, his local domicile—within a particular sheriffdom
(and then within a particular court district). National and local
domicile between them determine which court has jurisdiction
in commissary matters (see paras. 2.26, 2.27, 2.32, and 2.42–
2.43).

Scottish domicile—the rules as to which court has jurisdiction?

2.26   Provided that the deceased died domiciled in Scotland, the
Scottish courts will have jurisdiction in commissary matters.
Further, if it can be established that the deceased died domiciled
within a particular sheriffdom, then a court in that sheriffdom
will have jurisdiction in commissary matters.[42] Which court
within the sheriffdom is appropriate will be determined by the
last ordinary residence of the deceased, subject to that court
dealing with commissary matters.[43]

2.27   If the deceased had no fixed or known domicile, except that it
was in Scotland, the commissary court in Edinburgh has
jurisdiction.[44]

Scottish domicile—the practice

Deceased "domiciled in Sheriffdom of — in Scotland"
2.28   It has been seen that the general rule of commissary practice is
that a deceased person cannot have been domiciled in a particular sheriffdom unless, at the time of his death, he had his usual
or principal place of residence there. In most cases, this rule
can easily be applied, and even if the deceased died during a
temporary absence from his usual residence—perhaps during a
holiday or stay in a nursing home—the residence will retain the

---

[42] Confirmation of Executors (Scotland) Act 1858 (21 & 22 Vict. c. 56), s. 3 and
s. 8; *Dowie* v. *Barclay* (1871) 9 M. 726.
[43] See paras. 1.57–1.69.
[44] Confirmation of Executors (Scotland) Act 1858 (21 & 22 Vict. c. 56), s. 3 and
s. 8.

character of being the deceased's usual residence. If however the residence had been given up, and the deceased had become a permanent patient in a hospital or nursing home, then his local domicile would be in the court having jurisdiction over the address of the hospital or nursing home.

2.29 There are recognised exceptions to this general rule. For instance, even when the deceased was not actually residing in the property at the date of his death, he may be treated as being domiciled there if it was a residence (particularly a small estate)—which he had inherited, and continued to keep up.[45]

Deceased "without any fixed or known domicile except the same was in Scotland"

2.30 However, if the deceased, having a Scottish domicile, frequently moved about, from sheriffdom to sheriffdom, within Scotland, and it was unclear whether the moves were temporary or permanent, then the case is held to be one of Scottish domicile, but, as within the limits of Scotland, of floating or uncertain domicile. The same approach is taken in the case of a deceased person with a Scottish domicile of origin, if his Scottish home had been broken up, no local tie remained,[46] he had been living in different places (including places outside Scotland), and there is nothing to indicate where he intended to reside permanently. It is also the appropriate domicile where a Scotsman joined the armed forces and was stationed from time to time, in different countries. It is also the appropriate domicile if an elderly person of Scottish origin, was no longer able to live alone, and had given up his home in Scotland to go to live with relatives, or to live in a nursing home near them, but had retained substantial links with Scotland (*e.g.* maintaining his bank account with a Scottish branch. In all such cases, it is the practice to hold that the national domicile has been retained, though the local domicile has ceased to be "fixed or known":[47] in other words, that "the deceased died without any fixed or known domicile except the same was in Scotland." In such cases, the commissary clerk will require some indication on the face of the inventory to substantiate an averment of no fixed or known domicile. Accordingly, where possible, a former Scottish address of the deceased should be shown, and the deceased should be described as a "native of Scotland."

2.31 See further on Scottish domicile in dative-petitions paragraphs 7.19–7.22.

---

[45] *Hamilton* v. *Hardie* (1888) 16 R. 192; see also *Campbell* v. *Campbell* (1861) 23 D. 256.

[46] *Vincent* v. *Earl of Buchan* (1889) 16 R. 637.

[47] *Meikle*, Aug. 27, 1886, unreported; *Lillie*, Oct. 19, 1869, unreported; *Smith* March 9, 1870, unreported.

Non-Scottish domicile—which court has jurisdiction?

2.32   In the case of persons dying domiciled in a country other than Scotland, the commissary court in Edinburgh has jurisdiction.[48]

2.33   In such a case, confirmation can be obtained only to estate in Scotland—estate in England and Wales, and in Northern Ireland, cannot be included in the confirmation.

Non-Scottish domicile—who is entitled to be confirmed to the Scottish estate?

2.34   In the case of persons dying domiciled in a country other than Scotland, confirmation can be obtained only to estate in Scotland—estate in England and Wales, and in Northern Ireland, cannot be included in the confirmation.

2.35   Where grants of administration—such as confirmation—are made in more than one country, the *lex fori* in each case determines all questions in regard to the administration of assets recovered by virtue of that grant,[49] though the *lex domicilii* determines matters of succession to the deceased's moveable estate. Whether a particular question is to be classified as a matter of administration or of succession is determined by the *lex fori*.[50]

2.36   Where confirmation is to be obtained in Scotland to the Scottish moveable estate of someone who died domiciled outside Scotland, Scots law is the *lex fori*, and Scots law states that the question of who is entitled to the office of executor is determined by the *lex domicilii*.[51] It is irrelevant that such a person would have no claim to office under the internal law of Scotland.[52] In determining the *lex domicilii*, it must be remembered that while domicile is normally on a country basis, in some countries (*e.g.* Australia, Canada and U.S.A.), it is on a state or province basis and it is the law of the state or province in which the deceased died domiciled which must be applied. The question of who is entitled in office under the foreign law is a matter of fact to be proved in a commissary case by the affidavit evidence of an expert in the foreign legal system.

---

[48] Confirmation of Executors (Scotland) Act 1858 (21 & 22 Vict. c. 56, s. 3 and s. 8. Under s. 3, the commissary court in Edinburgh also has jurisdiction when the deceased was "without any fixed or known domicile". In practice, it will be necessary to apply the deceased's domicile of origin, since without any domicile, it is impossible for the clerk to check who is entitled to be confirmed to the Scottish estate (see para. 2.36).

[49] Anton and Beaumont, *Private International Law* (2nd ed.), p. 651; *Preston* v. *Melville* (1841) 2 Rob. 88.

[50] Anton and Beaumont, *Private International Law* (2nd ed.), p. 660.

[51] This is a rule of long standing, which was not altered by the Succession (Scotland) Act 1964 (c. 41) (see s. 37(2)). See also Anton and Beaumont, *Private International Law* (2nd ed.), p. 655; *Stair Memorial Encyclopaedia*, vol 17, para. 349.

[52] *Marchioness of Hastings* v. *Exrs. of Marquess of Hastings* (1852) 14 D. 489.

2.37   Indeed, in any commissary case, a claim to office based on the internal law of Scotland will be refused, unless it has been averred that the deceased died domiciled there.[53] The following cases illustrate the difference between the persons who would have been entitled to office had the deceased died domiciled in Scotland, and the persons who were found to be entitled to office:

    1.   The deceased died domiciled in Costa Rica. His father presented a petition, claiming the office of executor-dative as having right to one-half of the estate under the Intestate Moveable Succession (Scotland) Act 1855. This petition was refused, and a new petition setting forth the petitioner's title according to the law of Costa Rica was granted.[54]

    2.   The deceased died domiciled in Canada, survived by a husband and sons. The sons applied to be decerned *qua* next-of-kin. The husband was not a party to the petition. The commissary held that, the deceased having died domiciled furth of Scotland, the law regulating the succession must be averred, and ordered that the petition be amended. On inquiry, it was ascertained that the next-of-kin was entitled to administer only on the husband renouncing. A renunciation by the husband was produced, and the petitioners were decerned.[55]

    3.   The deceased died domiciled in Paraguay. An English administrator *pendente lite* was appointed in England. He applied to be decerned executor-dative. The petition was refused because first, he had not been appointed by the court of the domicile and secondly, his appointment was for a temporary and limited purpose.[56]

    4.   The deceased died domiciled in New Zealand. The public trustee of New Zealand applied to be decerned executor-dative, producing as his title letters of administration from the court there. His application was opposed, and the office of executor was competed for by the next-of-kin who were resident in Scotland. On inquiry as to the law of New Zealand regulating the appointment of the public trustee as administrator, it appeared that he was not entitled to intervene except in the absence of relatives. The next-of-kin were preferred.[57]

    5.   The deceased died domiciled in Uruguay, leaving a widow and minor children. The widow was decerned on

---

[53] *Whiffen* v. *Lees* (1872) 10 M. 797; *The Public Trustee* (1917) 34 Sh. Ct. Rep. 42.
[54] *Melville*, Sept. 25, 1862, unreported.
[55] *Clark*, Feb. 9, 1874, unreported.
[56] *Whiffin* v. *Lees* (1872) 10 M. 797.
[57] *Cormack*, Nov. 30, 1885, unreported.

evidence that, under the law of Uruguay, she was entitled to one-third of the estate, and retained the sole control of her children and their property during their minority.[58]

2.38   While the law of the domicile determines who is entitled to be confirmed, Scots law (being the law of the country where the property is situated) determines the form of the confirmation, and the procedure to obtain it. Thus, a person seeking to be confirmed as executor-dative to a deceased person domiciled furth of Scotland must produce a bond of caution, although the amount of the caution may be restricted.[59]

2.39   Notes for guidance on the requirements and procedures for obtaining confirmation in cases of foreign domicile are set out at paragraphs 2.51 *et seq.*

Alternative domicile—which court has jurisdiction?

2.40   While no person can have more than one domicile at one time, there are occasions when, on the basis of the evidence available, it cannot be definitely averred whether the deceased died domiciled in one country or another, or perhaps even in one of three different countries. In such cases, an averment of alternative domicile can be made in the application for confirmation.

2.41   Assuming the countries to be France and Scotland, the averment would be to the effect that "The deceased was domiciled in France or alternatively he had no fixed or known domicile except that the same was in Scotland."

2.42   Any such application must be made to the commissary court at Edinburgh, since this is the court which has jurisdiction where either the deceased was domiciled furth of Scotland or the deceased was domiciled in Scotland but without any fixed or known domicile.[60]

2.43   In such cases there is a difficulty if the deceased had settled in Scotland a short time before his death, for then the question would be whether he was domiciled in Scotland within the sheriffdom where he was living, or in, perhaps, the country of his domicile of origin. In such a case, it is impossible to proceed on the basis of an averment of alternative domicile. If the deceased had been domiciled in a sheriffdom in Scotland, the sheriff court of that sheriffdom would have had privative jurisdiction, and

---

[58] *Bowhill*, Nov. 16, 1888, unreported.

[59] See examples 4 and 5 at para. 19.27 for cases where applications to restrict caution were granted on proof of foreign law.

[60] Confirmation of Executors (Scotland) Act 1858 (21 & 22 Vict. c. 56), s. 3 and s. 8.

not the commissary court in Edinburgh. In contrast, if the deceased had been domiciled abroad, the commissary court in Edinburgh would have had jurisdiction, and not the sheriff court. Consequently, in such a case, it is necessary to proceed on the basis of one domicile. Normally, it will be possible to aver that the deceased had acquired a domicile of choice in Scotland, but where there is truly doubt the normal practice is for the commissary or sheriff clerk to refuse to confirm and to require the applicant to apply to the sheriff for special authority to issue confirmation on the basis of a local Scottish domicile. If there is sufficient to aver a Scottish domicile (*e.g.* residence with the intention to settle, even although the residence is short), the petition shall be granted. If the application is refused, a further application should be made to the Commissary Office in Edinburgh, the other domicile being averred.

Procedure in cases of alternative domicile

2.44   In any commissary application, it is necessary to set out the reasons for the alternative averment.

2.45   Since one of the alternative averments is that the deceased died domiciled furth of Scotland, the usual procedure to set up the right of the applicant to confirmation in a case of non-Scottish domicile (see paras. 2.34–2.39) must be followed.

2.46   In all cases where there is an averment of alternative domicile, confirmation may be granted only to estate in Scotland, and not also to that in England and Wales or Northern Ireland. This is true even where the averment is that the deceased was domiciled either in Scotland or in a particular foreign country, for sections 1(1) and (2) and 2(2) of the Administration of Estates Act 1971 only operate "where a person dies domiciled in Scotland", and that can hardly be said in a case where an alternative domicile is averred.

2.47   In testate cases, the general rule is that the deceased's testamentary writing, and right of the applicant to the office of executor, must be in conformity with the laws of both countries.

2.48   If the deceased died intestate, the laws of both countries must again be founded on to determine who is entitled to the office of executor, the application being presented by someone who would be entitled to administer under both systems.

2.49   See further on alternative domiciles in dative-petitions paragraph 7.27.

2.50   Notes for guidance on the requirement and procedure for obtaining confirmation in cases of foreign domicile are set out at the end of this chapter.

NOTES FOR GUIDANCE
ON
THE REQUIREMENTS AND PROCEDURE
IN
OBTAINING CONFIRMATION TO ESTATE IN SCOTLAND
IN
CASES OF FOREIGN DOMICILE

The following notes are of general application:

1. Confirmation dues

2.51   Since confirmation can only be granted to estate in Scotland and a separate title must be obtained in England and Wales and in Northern Ireland to any estate there, the confirmation fee is calculated on the estate in Scotland only.

2. Documents in foreign languages

2.52   Any document in a foreign language (*e.g.* a testamentary writing or court decree) must be accompanied by a certified translation; neither the foreign language document, nor the certified translation are acceptable on their own, and both documents are produced and recorded.[61] The translator must certify the translation in terms of Style 3.07 as a true copy, and must docket the original document as being the document referred to in his translation. The translator must be fluent in the foreign language, but need not be a professional translator.

3. Authentication of foreign decrees, etc.

2.53   A decree from a court in England and Wales, purporting to be sealed or stamped with the seal or stamp of the Supreme Court of any office is received as genuine without further proof or authentication.[62] Similarly, decrees from courts in Commonwealth countries, the Isle of Man, the Channel Islands, the Republic of Ireland and South Africa are apparently accepted as genuine without proof. Before the commissary clerk will recognise a foreign decree, the decree itself must be authenticated (it is not necessary to authenticate the signatory to the decree).

2.54   Grants from countries[63] which are signatories to the 1961 Hague Convention Abolishing the Requirement of Legalisation for

---

[61] *Flahault*, Jan. 12, 1871, unreported; *Chauvin*, April 20, 1881, unreported.
[62] Supreme Court Act 1981 (c. 54), s. 132.
[63] As at the time of writing Andorra, Antigua & Barbuda, Argentina, Armenia, Aruba, Australia, Austria, Bahamas, Barbados, Belarus, Belgium, Belize, Bosnia & Herzegovina, Botswana, Brunei Darussalam, Croatia, Cyprus, Domin-

Foreign Public Documents,[64] must be accompanied by an "apostille", which certifies them as authentic (see Style 3.05). The apostille is signed by the Secretary of State of the issuing state or some other person who is authorised to sign it by the issuing state—*e.g.* an apostille issued by the U.K. is issued by the Foreign and Commonwealth Office.

2.55 Where the grant is from a country which has not signed, ratified or acceded to this convention, at common law, authentication of the grant or extract is normally by a notary public resident in that country and qualified in its laws. [65] A style of authenticating docket is set out in Style 3.06, but other styles are acceptable. It is not necessary for the authentication to state that the persons named in the grant are entitled to the estate.

4. Power of attorney

2.56 Where the executor is resident overseas, it can expedite the issuing of confirmation to the Scottish estate if he is prepared to grant a power of attorney—authorising a person resident in Scotland to present a petition (where necessary); sign a bond of caution (where necessary); give up an inventory of the deceased's Scottish estate, make oath thereto and obtain confirmation etc. This is discussed in greater detail at paragraphs 8.14–8.16 and paragraphs 10.19–10.23.

2.56 Alternatively, it may be possible for the administration to be expedited by the oath to the inventory being made by the consul for the country in which the executor is a national (see further paras. 8.17–8.18 and 10.24–10.25).

5. Capital Taxes Office

2.58 The Inland Revenue A-3 inventory form must be presented; the B-3 and B-4 inventory forms are not acceptable.

2.59 If the question of United Kingdom inheritance tax liability has already been dealt with in England, the Scottish estate should

---

ica, Fiji, Finland, France, Germany, Greece, Grenada, Guyana, Hungary, Israel, Italy, Japan, Kiribati, Lesotho, Liechtenstein, Luxembourg, Macau, Macedonia, Malawi, Malta, Marshall Islands, Mauritius, Mexico, Monaco, Netherlands (& Netherlands, Antilles), Norway, Panama, Portugal (& Madeira), Russia, St Kitts & Nevis, St Lucia, St Vincent & The Grenadines, San Marino, Seychelles, Slovenia, Solomon Islands, South Africa, Spain (& The Canary Islands), Surinam, Swaziland, Switzerland, Tonga, Turkey, Tuvalu, USA (& Puerto Rico), United Kingdom, former Yugoslavia (Serbia & Montenegro), Zimbabwe.

[64] Cmnd 2617 (1965).

[65] *Disbrow* v. *Mackintosh* (1852) 15 D. 123; *Whitehead* v. *Thompson* (1861) 23 D. 772; Anton and Beaumont, *Private International Law* (2nd ed.) p. 758; Dickson on *Evidence* (3rd ed.), 1319–1327; Walker and Walker, *The Law of Evidence in Scotland*, para. 426(b).

be shown in detail, and the English estate in a lump sum, but not extended, and, before confirmation is applied for in Scotland, the inventory must be presented to the Capital Taxes Office in England (P.O. Box 38, Castle Meadow Road, Nottingham, NG2 1BB) to be stamped inheritance tax "paid" or "nil".

2.60   Alternatively, if this is the first time that liability to United Kingdom inheritance tax is being addressed, the total estate in the United Kingdom should be detailed, but only the Scottish estate extended for confirmation. If the estate in the United Kingdom exceeds £5,000, then before confirmation is applied for, the inventory should be submitted for examination and assessment to the Capital Taxes Office at Edinburgh, irrespective of whether or not United Kingdom inheritance tax is payable.

2.61   If the deceased left estate abroad, it need only be referred to in the inventory as "Deceased left estate in — which is being administered there", such foreign estate being excluded from the charge to United Kingdom inheritance tax unless the deceased is treated as domiciled in the United Kingdom for the purposes of inheritance tax.[66]

The following notes are of application to the specific area highlighted:

6. Where a foreign domiciliary died testate and executors-nominate are applying for confirmation

2.62   All testamentary writings must be put up with the inventory for confirmation. Since the validity of a testamentary writing falls to be determined not by Scots law but by the law of the domicile, evidence of its validity under the law of the domicile must be produced before confirmation can be granted. It appears that section 3 of the Executors (Scotland) Act 1900 (which entitles trustees, general disponees, universal legatories and residuary beneficiaries, to be confirmed as executors-nominate) applies only when the testator was domiciled in Scotland at the date of his death,[67] though it has been used where the testator was domiciled in Scotland at the time he executed the will.[68]

[66] See para. 12.02, fn 1.

[67] *Jameson*, Oct. 31, 1902, unreported where a New Zealand will appointed a universal legatory but no executor, the New Zealand grant was of letters of administration with the will annexed (a dative appointment), and the Scottish court gave the equivalent of the court of the domicile—decerniture and confirmation as executor-dative qua universal legatory; *Callander*, April 17, 1903, unreported.

[68] *Bain*, April 1903, unreported, applying what is now s. 4 of the Wills Act 1963 (c. 44).

2.63   The procedures to be adopted to obtain confirmation where the deceased died testate, but domiciled overseas, are set out in this section, but they can usually be simplified where probate has already been obtained in England and Wales to estate there— see paragraphs 2.78–2.85.

7. Two wills

2.63A   On occasion, a deceased may have made two wills, one to dispose of the estate in his country of domicile, and the other to dispose of estate elsewhere. If the commissary clerk is presented with a will dealing exclusively with the Scottish estate in the case of a person who died domiciled outside Scotland, he will require to have produced to him *all* the deceased's testamentary writings (either the originals or certified copies), which should be referred to in the inventory, and docketed and signed as relative thereto) (see paras. 10.59 and 10.66–10.69). He will require to see an opinion from a person (*e.g.* a judge, notary, barrister, solicitor etc.) versant in the laws of the state where the deceased died domiciled as to the validity of the "Scottish will" by the laws of the deceased's domicile, referring to the other will(s) and stating who is entitled by the laws of the deceased's domicile to administer the estate and docketing the will(s) as relative to his opinion. The opinion may take the form of an opinion, judgment, an affidavit or a notarial certificate, according to the forms in use in the country from which it comes.

Foreign probate available

2.64   If the deceased died domiciled in a jurisdiction where it is the practice to issue grants of probate, the original grant (with the will annexed), or an exemplification (that is, an official copy of a document made under the seal of the issuing court or office) must be produced. In either case, the document must be under the hand and seal of the court of issue, and the document itself (not the signatory to it) must be authenticated—see paragraphs 2.53–2.55. An "office copy" of a will[69] is not sufficient.[70]

No Foreign probate but will retained by notary

2.65   If the deceased died domiciled in a jurisdiction where it is not the practice to issue grants of probate and where the will is kept in the custody of a notary, there must be produced

     1.   a notarial copy of the will under the hand and seal of the notary in whose custody it is;

     2.   the notary's signature must be authenticated (see paras. 2.53–2.55); and

---

[69] Issued, for example, in England and Wales under the Supreme Court Act 1981 (c. 54), s. 125.

[70] *Stiven* v. *Myer* (1868) 6 M. 885.

3.   an opinion, given by someone other than the notary
     having custody of the will, stating that the notarial copy
     is entitled to the same faith and credit as the original will,
     which must remain in the custody of the notary, who is
     forbidden to part with the original (see Style 3.04).

No foreign probate but will can be obtained

2.66   If the deceased died domiciled in a jurisdiction where it is not
the practice to issue grants of probate but where the original
will can be obtained, there must be produced

1.   the original will;[71] and

2.   an opinion by a person (*e.g.* a judge, notary, barrister,
     solicitor etc.) versant in the laws of the state where the
     deceased died domiciled as to the validity of the will by
     the laws of the deceased's domicile, and stating who is
     entitled by the laws of the deceased's domicile to adminis-
     ter the estate,[72] and docketing the will as relative to his
     opinion. The opinion may take the form of an opinion, a
     judgment, an affidavit or a notarial certificate, according
     to the forms in use in the country from which it comes
     (Style 3.01).

Letters of administration obtained—deceased left will

2.66A   Under some legal systems, although a deceased person died
intestate, letters of administration are issued where the executors named in the will are, for any reason, not proving the
will. Where letters of administration are issued in such cases
the paperwork necessary is as set out at paragraph 2.64 (the
words "letters of administration" being read for the word
"probate"), and where the grant of administration was not in
favour of the executors nominated by the deceased, a petition
for decerniture must be presented (see Style 6.46) and caution
obtained.

No letters of administration issued—deceased left will

2.66B   The paperwork necessary is as set out at paragraph 2.66 (the
words "letters of administration" being read for the word
"probate"), unless the deceased died domiciled in a juridsdic-
tion where the will is kept in the custody of a notary, where
the necessary paperwork is set out in paragraph 2.65. A petition
for decerniture (see Style 6.47), and caution will be necessary.

---

[71] A notarial copy of the will is acceptable only if the principal has to be kept
in the custody of the notary.

[72] It is understood that under some legal systems, the executor nominated in
the testamentary writing has no right of administration whatsoever and is
merely an advisor or counsellor to the heirs.

Executor declined office

2.67 If any of the executors-nominate decline to act or renounce their rights etc., and the fact of such declinature or renunciation is not specifically referred to in the grant of probate produced, there must be produced either the original declinature or renunciation or a certified copy from the court which granted probate.

Executor assumed

2.68 If an executor has been assumed after the date of the foreign grant of probate, he must prove the foreign law under which he claims to act.[73] There must be produced

1. the original deed of assumption; and

2. an opinion by a person (*e.g.* a judge, notary, barrister, solicitor etc.) versant in the laws of the state where the deceased died domiciled as to the validity of the deed of assumption by the said laws and stating (if such is the case) that the executor assumed is entitled to the administration of the estate, and docketing the deed of assumption as relative to his opinion. The opinion may take the form of an opinion, a judgment, an affidavit or a notarial certificate, according to the forms in use in the country from which it comes (Style 3.01).

No foreign process equivalent to probate, and beneficiaries obtain direct title

2.69 If the deceased died domiciled in a jurisdiction where there is no process equivalent to probate, and the beneficiaries obtain possession to the estate by direct title, there must be produced

1. the will; and

2. an opinion by a person (*e.g.* a judge, notary, barrister, solicitor etc.) versant in the laws of the state where the deceased died domiciled as to the validity of the will by the said laws and stating that the beneficiaries would be entitled to administer the estate without a court grant. The opinion may take the form of an opinion, a judgment, an affidavit or a notarial certificate, according to the forms in use in the country from which it comes (Style 3.01).

8. Where a foreign domiciliary died intestate

2.70 The person who is entitled to be confirmed in Scotland as

---

[73] In *Braund*, Feb. 25, 1891, unreported, a testator died domiciled in England leaving a trust settlement in Scottish form. A new trustee was assumed under the Scottish Trust Acts, and applied for confirmation. The application was objected to, and abandoned.

executor-dative is the person entitled in the country of the deceased's domicile.

Letters of administration issued

2.71　　If a grant of letters of administration has been issued by the courts of the jurisdiction where the deceased died domiciled, the original grant (with, if appropriate, the will annexed), or an exemplification (that is, an official copy of a document made under the seal of the issuing court or office) must be produced. In either case, the document must be under the hand and seal of the court of issue, and the document itself and not the signatory to it must be authenticated—see paragraphs 2.53–2.55. An "office copy" of a will[74] is not sufficient.[75]

2.72　　Where the deceased died intestate a petition for decerniture of the executors must be presented (Style 6.46).

2.73　　Where the deceased died intestate, a bond of caution to the amount of the estate in Scotland must be obtained before confirmation is granted.

No letters of administration issued

2.74　　If the deceased died domiciled in a jurisdiction where it is not the practice to issue grants of letters of administration, there must be produced an opinion by a person (*e.g.* a judge, notary, barrister, solicitor, etc.) versant in the laws of the state where the deceased died domiciled, stating who, by said laws, is entitled to the administration of the estate. The opinion must also set up the validity of any will founded on.

2.75　　If more than one person is entitled to the administration and all the persons so entitled are not applying for confirmation, the opinion should state whether or not consents from the others are required.

2.76　　If no grant has been issued and the persons entitled to the administration are not the executors-nominate of the deceased, a petition for decerniture must be presented (Style 6.47).

2.77　　If confirmation is craved in favour of executors other than executors nominate, caution must be found for the estate in Scotland, although the amount of the caution may be restricted.[76]

---

[74] Issued, for example, in England and Wales under the Supreme Court Act 1981 (c. 54), s. 125, as an alternative to a sealed and certified copy.

[75] *Stiven* v. *Myer* (1868) 6 M. 885.

[76] See examples 4 and 5 at para. 19.27 for cases where applications to restrict caution were granted on proof of foreign law.

9. Procedure where a grant has been obtained in England already

2.78   Frequently, in cases where the deceased had a foreign domicile, he will have left estate in England and Wales as well as in Scotland, and a grant may already have been taken out in the courts there to such estate. The jurisdiction of the English courts, in foreign domicile cases, is restricted to estate in England, and a grant of confirmation must be obtained in Scotland to any estate there.

2.79   In England and Wales, the documents which must be lodged in a foreign domicile case follow the same pattern as those required in Scotland and almost invariably the documents used in the court in England and Wales will satisfy the requirements of the commissary court in Edinburgh. Documents lodged in the probate courts in England are retained by the court and not returned, and so the following procedure is followed:

English grant contains a full copy of the foreign grant of probate

2.80   If a foreign grant of probate has been produced in the English court and the English grant contains a full copy of the foreign grant (including the act of probate and the will etc), the English grant is accepted in Scotland as the equivalent of the foreign grant, and the procedure followed is as narrated in paragraphs 2.62–2.69 as if the foreign grant itself had been produced— the English grant being described in the oath to the Inland Revenue inventory etc as containing a copy of the foreign grant, which is also described. No authentication is required.

English grant does not contain a full copy of the foreign grant of probate

2.81   If a foreign grant has been produced and the English grant contains a copy of the will only but does not contain the act of the foreign probate, then the English grant is acceptable as containing a good copy of the will. However, there must be produced an authenticated extract or certified copy of the foreign act of probate, showing who has actually been appointed to administer the estate in the courts of the place of the deceased's domicile and those persons must also be suitably described in the oath.

English grant, there having been no foreign court probate

2.82   If no grant has been obtained in the foreign court and the original will (or where appropriate a notarial copy) has been produced along with an opinion (or affidavit as it is usually known in England) on the validity of the will, then there must be produced, along with the inventory, the English grant itself (provided it contains a full copy of the testamentary writings) along with an extract or certified copy of the opinion from the probate court in England.

2.83   If, for any reason, the English grant is not available for production here, then an extract or certified copy of the will from the English court should also be obtained.

English grant, no letters of administration issued
2.84   If no grant has been made in the foreign court, and the deceased died intestate, then an extract or certified copy from the English court of the opinion on foreign law should be obtained.

2.85   It should be noted that the persons appointed to administer the estate in England are frequently not entitled to confirmation to the Scottish estate. For instance, the English courts may make a grant in favour of certain executors reserving the rights of the remainder to apply for a grant at a later date, or an executor abroad may appoint someone in England to take out a grant in his own name. Both of those procedures are incompetent in Scotland with this exception, that if the court of the deceased's domicile has issued a grant in favour of one or more executors with a reservation of the rights of others, then that appointment may be recognised by the Scottish court, and confirmation may be issued in favour of the executors to whom the foreign grant was actually made.

NOTE: An English probate registry may issue what is termed "an office copy" (as an alternative to "a sealed and certified copy") of any will,[77] but such an office copy is not sufficient.[78]

10. Additional, *ad omissa* and *ad non executa* inventories

2.86   Where confirmation has been issued and the original executors are still acting, the procedure to obtain an eik to the confirmation follows the same pattern as in the case of a Scottish domicile. Where the application is in respect of *ad omissa* or *ad non executa* estate, while the general procedure follows the normal pattern, particular cases can be very complicated. Because of the great variety of circumstances which can arise it is not possible to give more detailed guidance on this point. The forms etc. used in Scottish domiciles will require to be suitably adapted to suit the particular requirements of a foreign case. It is suggested that practitioners should discuss such cases with the commissary clerk at an early stage.

[77] Supreme Court Act 1981 (c. 54), s. 125.
[78] *Stiven* v. *Myer* (1868) 6 M. 885.

CHAPTER 3

VALIDITY OF TESTAMENTARY WRITINGS: PRE AUGUST 1, 1995 RULES

Introduction

3.01   As discussed in Chapter 1, a decision on the validity of a testamentary writing is outwith the jurisdiction of the court in a commissary case. However, before he will issue confirmation in favour of the executor-nominate, the sheriff or commissary clerk must be satisfied that he has before him a valid and probative (or self-proving) testamentary writing and that, in terms of the documents presented to him, the person applying to be confirmed is the person entitled to the office of executor. Accordingly, the clerk will scrutinise all documents with this in mind. If the clerk has any doubt as to the validity of the documents, or who is entitled to the office of executor, the matter will be referred to the sheriff, in the exercise of his commissary jurisdiction. The sheriff has to determine whether or not confirmation may be issued. If the sheriff does not grant authority to issue confirmation, the beneficiaries may decide to prove the validity of the testamentary writing—a matter which falls within the jurisdiction of the Court of Session.

3.01A   The question of what will or will not satisfy the clerk that there is a valid testamentary writing and who is entitled to the office of executor depends on previous reported decisions and also on the previous decisions of the court concerned. Where there is an unauthenticated alteration to the testamentary writing, the clerk will consider the nature and effect of the alteration. Where a person seeks to be confirmed as executor-nominate, the unauthenticated deletion of a legacy will be ignored, whereas special warrant will be required if the alteration is to a main testamentary provision or the appointment of executors.

3.02   This chapter explores the rules which determine whether a "testamentary writing" is valid. First, there is the question of which legal system determines

> 1.   the formal validity of the testamentary writing (see paras. 3.05–3.11); and
>
> 2.   whether the testator had testamentary capacity (see para. 3.12).

3.03 This chapter then considers the rules affecting the formal validity of a testamentary writing executed before August 1, 1995. Where Scots law is the applicable system, it will be necessary to consider whether, at the time of execution, the testator had testamentary capacity (see paras. 3.13–3.15) and whether the execution met the formal requirements (see para. 3.19 *et seq.*). A distinction will be drawn between those writings which, *ex facie*, are accepted as valid, and those which can only be accepted as valid if fortified by additional evidence. Finally, the rules relating to the revocation (see paras. 3.154–3.176) and alteration (see paras. 3.177–3.189) of testamentary writings are considered.

3.04 There is discussion of how these principles are applied in a variety of unusual circumstances—writings on deposit receipts (see paras. 3.190–3.191), letters to solicitors (see para. 3.192), or friends or relations (see para. 3.193), draft deeds which bear to have been subscribed (see paras. 3.194–3.196) and soldiers wills (see paras. 3.197–3.198).

Which legal system determines the formal validity of a testamentary writing: the rules

3.05 Where a testamentary writing is founded upon in a commissary proceeding, it must be validly executed according to the legal system which regulates its validity.

3.06 In Scotland, at common law, a testamentary writing was treated as validly executed in relation to moveable property if it had been executed in accordance with the requirements of the law of the testator's domicile or the place of execution.[1] The Wills Act 1861[2] provided alternative ways by which a will would be treated as validly executed. The Wills Act 1963 repealed the 1861 Act where the testator died on or after January 1, 1964,[3] but a will executed before that date is still treated as valid if it was treated as valid by the Wills Act 1861.[4] In practice, there are only a few occasions when the provisions of 1861 Act might be relevant: First under the Wills Act 1861, the will of a British subject made out of the United Kingdom is, as regards personal estate, well executed if it was made according to the forms required by the law of the part of the British dominions where he had his domicile of origin.[5] Secondly, it validated wills made by British subjects irrespective of their domicile on death.[5a]

---

[1] A.E. Anton *Private International Law* (1st ed.), pp. 521–522.
[2] (24 & 25 Vict. c. 114).
[3] Wills Act 1963 (c. 44), s. 7(2) and (3).
[4] *Ibid.*, s. 7(4).
[5] Wills Act 1861 (24 & 25 Vict. c. 114), s. 1.
[5a] *Ibid.*, ss. 1 and 2.

3.06A Commissary practice is to apply the Wills Act 1963 only when the deceased died domiciled in Scotland. (As a matter of fact, the Act will also apply when the deceased died domiciled in England and Wales or in Northern Ireland, but the commissary view is that that is strictly a matter for the law of those jurisdictions.) It would appear that the question of whether the Wills Act 1963 would validate the testamentary writing of a person of non-Scottish domicile has not been raised in the courts.

3.07 Under the Wills Act 1963, a testamentary writing is to be treated as properly executed if its execution conforms to:

1. the internal law in force in the territory where the testamentary writing was executed;[6]

2. the internal law in force in the territory where the testator was domiciled, at the time either of the deed's execution or of the testator's death;[7]

3. the internal law in force in the territory where the testator had his habitual residence, at the time either of the deed's execution or of the testator's death;[8]

4. the internal law in force in the state of which the testator was a national, at the time either of the deed's execution or of the testator's death;[9]

5. if executed aboard a vessel or aircraft of any description, the internal law in force in the territory with which, having regard to its registration (if any) and other relevant circumstances, the vessel or aircraft may be taken to have been most closely connected;[10]

6. insofar as it disposes of immoveable property, the internal law in force in the territory where the property was situated;[11] or

7. insofar as it exercises a power of appointment, the law governing the essential validity of the power,[12] but the testamentary writing shall not be treated as improperly executed by reason only that its execution was not in accordance with any formal requirements contained in the instrument creating the power.[13]

---

[6] Wills Act 1963 (c. 44), s. 1.
[7] *Ibid.*
[8] *Ibid.*
[9] *Ibid.*
[10] *Ibid.*, s. 2(1) (a).
[11] *Ibid.*, s. 2(1) (b).
[12] *Ibid.*, s. 2(1) (d).
[13] *Ibid.*, s. 2(2).

3.08   "Internal law", in relation to any territory or state, means the law which would apply in a case where there was no question of the law in force in any other territory or state applying.[14] "State" means a territory or group of territories having its own law of nationality[15]—and where there is in force in a territory or state two or more systems of internal law relating to the formal validity of wills (as is the case in the United Kingdom)— the system to be applied shall be ascertained as follows:

1. if there is in force throughout the territory or state a rule indicating which of those systems can properly be applied in the case in question, that rule shall be followed; or

2. if there is no such rule, the system shall be that with which the testator was most closely connected at the relevant time, and for this purpose the relevant time is the time of the testator's death where the matter is to be determined by reference to circumstances prevailing at his death, and the time of execution of the testamentary writing, in any other case.[16]

3.09   In determining for the purposes of the Wills Act 1963 whether or not the execution of a testamentary writing conforms to a particular law, regard shall be had to the formal requirements at the time of execution, but if there is any alteration in the law of the country affecting testamentary writings, this may be taken into account if it would enable a testamentary writing to be treated as properly executed.[17]

3.10   Where (whether in pursuance of the Wills Act 1963 or not) a law in force outside the United Kingdom falls to be applied in relation to a testamentary writing, any requirement of that law whereby either

1. special formalities are to be observed by a testator answering a particular description; or

2. witnesses to the execution of the deed are to possess a certain qualification,

shall be treated—notwithstanding any rule of that law to the contrary—as a formal requirement only.[18]

---

[14] *Ibid.*, s. 6(1).
[15] *Ibid.*, s. 6(1).
[16] *Ibid.*, s. 6(2).
[17] *Ibid.*, s. 6(3).
[18] *Ibid.*, s. 3.

The international will

3.10A Although the Annex to the Convention providing a Uniform Law on the Form of an International Will (the UNIDROIT Convention), concluded at Washington on October 26, 1973 has yet to be brought into effect in the U.K.[18a] A testator who complies with the provisions of the Annex to the Convention will create a will which will be recognised as formally valid within all the states which are parties to the Convention.[18b] The required formalities are:

1. The [international] will must be made in writing (Article 3(1)).

2. The testator must declare in the presence of two witnesses and of a person authorised to act in connection with international wills[18c] that the document is his will and that he knows the contents thereof. The law under which the authorised person was designated determines who may act as witness (Article 10 and Certificate, para. 10).

3. The testator signs the will or acknowledges his signature in the presence of the two witnesses *and* the authorised person *or* acknowledges his signature (Article 5(1)).[18d]

4. The witness and the authorised person then attest the will by signing it in the presence of the testator.

5. The authorised person then asks the testator to make a declaration about the keeping of the will (Administration of Justice Act 1982, section 28(3)).

6. The authorised person is required to complete a pro forma certificate in relation to the identities of the testator and the witnesses and compliance with the formal requirements. The authorised person keeps one copy of the certificate and passes a copy to the testator.

3.10B In the absence of evidence to the contrary, the certificate of the authorised person will be conclusive as to the formal validity of the international will[18e] but the absence of a certificate, or an irregularity in the certificate, does not affect the formal validity: it merely means that there is not conclusive evidence that the will is formally valid.[18f]

[18a] Administration of Justice Act 1982 (c. 53), ss. 27 and 28 provide for this by the making of a S.I. which has yet to be made.

[18b] Presently; Belgium, certain parts of Canada, Cyprus, Equador, Libya, Niger, Portugal and Yugoslavia.

[18c] In the U.K. solicitors and notaries public, Administration of Justice Act 1982 (c. 53), s. 28.

[18d] Art. 5(2) deals with the situation where the testator is unable to sign.

[18e] Art. 12.

[18f] Art. 13.

Which legal system determines the formal validity of a testamentary writing: commissary practice

3.11   The commissary practice is to apply the Wills Act 1963 only if the deceased died domiciled in Scotland. Where a testamentary writing is founded on as valid under the Wills Act 1963, some courts will require a petition for special authority to issue confirmation, and agents may wish to discuss with the sheriff or commissary clerk, at an early stage, whether this is necessary. The facts necessary to bring the testamentary writing within the relevant statutory provision must be distinctly averred. Where necessary, the court will require evidence in support of the averment. For instance, if it is stated that, in terms of section 1 of the Wills Act 1963, the testamentary writing is properly executed under the laws of the place of execution, but no place of execution is specified in the testamentary writing, there must be produced affidavits by the witnesses to the testamentary writing (Style 2.09), or other evidence, as to the place of execution. Where a legal system other than Scots law determines the validity of a testamentary writing, the opinion of an expert on the laws of that legal system must be obtained and put up with the testamentary writing (see further chapter 2). If the testamentary writing, or the expert's opinion, is in a foreign language it must be accompanied by a certified translation. The translator must certify the translation in terms of Style 3.06. If the testamentary writing has been retained in the hands of an overseas notary and he cannot under the law release it, the procedure set out in "Notes for Guidance" to Chapter 2 under the heading "No foreign probate and will retained by notary" must be adopted.

Testamentary Capacity

Introduction

3.12   The capacity of a person to make a valid testamentary writing in respect of his moveable estate is determined by the *lex domicilii* (presumably at the time of execution rather than at the time of death), and in respect of his immoveable estate, by the *lex situs*.[19] Paragraphs 3.13–3.15 look at the rules of Scots law on capacity.

The youthful testator: the current Scots law rules

3.13   Since September 25, 1991, under Scots law an individual who has attained the age of 12 years[20] has capacity to execute a testamentary writing.[21]

---

[19] Anton and Beaumont, *Private International Law* (2nd ed.), pp. 681–682.
[20] For the date on which an individual attains a particular age see Age of Legal Capacity (Scotland) Act 1991 (c. 50), s. 6.
[21] *Ibid.*, s. 2(2).

The youthful testator: the former Scots law rules

3.14 Prior to September 25, 1991, under Scots law the age at which testamentary capacity was attained depended on the individual's sex—the ages being 12 years in the case of a female and 14 years in the case of a male.[22] At common law, such persons had power to execute a valid testamentary writing in respect of moveable property only,[23] but after September 10, 1964, they were also able to execute one in respect of heritable property.[24]

The *incapax* testator under Scots law

3.15 If a person who is *incapax* executes a testamentary writing, the testamentary writing may, after court action,[25] be reduced.[26] The burden of proof is on the person seeking to have the testamentary writing reduced. It is difficult to show that a testator lacked sufficient capacity to validly execute the testamentary writing. As Viscount Haldane expressed it:

> "The question whether there is such unsoundness of mind as renders it impossible in law to make a testamentary disposition is one of degree. A testator must be able to exercise a rational appreciation of what he is doing. He must understand the nature of his act. But, if he does, he is not required to be highly intelligent. He may be stupid, or he may even be improperly, so far as ethics go, actuated by ill-feeling. He may, again, make his will only in the lucid intervals between two periods of insanity. The question is simply whether he understands what he is about. On the other hand, if his act is the outcome of a delusion so irrational that it is not to be taken as that of one having appreciated what he was doing sufficiently to make his action in the particular case that of a mind sane upon the question, the will cannot stand. But, in that case, if the testator is not generally insane, the will must be shown to have been the outcome of the special delusion. It is not sufficient that the man who disposes of his property should be occasionally subject of a delusion. The delusion must be shown to have been an actual and impelling influence."[27]

Evidence of deteriorating powers is in itself insufficient to establish mental incapacity,[28] but if it can be shown that the testator

---

[22] The ages at which a female or male child became a minor (Erskine, I.vii.1.).

[23] Erskine, I.vii.33.

[24] Succession (Scotland) Act 1964 (c. 41), s. 28.

[25] On actions of reduction see paras. 19.72 *et seq.*

[26] *E.g., Laidlaw* v. *Laidlaw* (1870) 8 M. 882 (where the testator, who was suffering from a painful disease, had been given opiates, and was unable to understand the nature and effect of the deed he signed).

[27] *Sivewright* v. *Sivewright's Trs.*, 1920 S.C. (H.L.) 63 at p. 64.

[28] *West's Trs.* v. *West*, 1980 S.L.T. 6.

had been forced to sign by family or friends on whom he was dependent, the deed is open to reduction on the ground of "incapacity and undue influence"[29] or "facility and circumvention".[30]

The illiterate testator

3.16   The testamentary writing of an illiterate testator should always be notarially executed (see paras. 3.134 *et seq* and Chap. 4).

The blind or partially sighted testator

3.17   It is preferable that a testamentary writing of a blind person should be notarially executed (see paras. 3.134 *et seq* and Chap. 4), for it is then beyond challenge, provided that the formalities are observed. A blind person may also subscribe a deed in ordinary writing himself, but the execution will then be open to challenge on the ground that the testator did not know what he signed.[31] A testamentary writing in Braille, which the testator signed in ordinary writing, his signature being attested, has received effect.[32]

3.18   Section 18(1) of the Conveyancing (Scotland) Act 1924,[33] which provided for notarial executions prior to August 1, 1995, only applied when the granter was "blind or unable to write". Consequently, the provision would not appear to have provided the partially sighted with a safe method of executing deeds.[34]

FORMAL VALIDITY

General outline: the requirements of Scots law

3.19   The rules of Scots law regarding the form of the execution of a

---

[29] *Hamilton* v. *Hardie* (1888) 16 R. 192.

[30] *Gilchrist* v. *Morrison* (1891) 18 R. 599.

[31] For actions of reduction of deeds signed personally by a blind person see *Duff* v. *Earl of Fife's Trs.* (1823) 1 Shaw's App. 498 (the deed was a trust deed relating to a deed of entail) and *Ker* v. *Hotchkis* (1837) 15 S. 983 (the deed was a bond).

[32] *Broadfoot*, Nov. 13, 1905, unreported: the signed Braille testamentary writing, a copy in ordinary writing and the expert's certificate were recorded with the inventory.

[33] (14 & 15 Geo. 5, c. 27).

[34] *C.f. Duff* v. *Earl of Fife's Trs.* (1823) 1 Shaw's App. 498 where it was opined that notarial execution under the Subscription of Deeds (1579 Act c. 80) was restricted to cases where the party could not subscribe, and did not extend to a party who could sign his name but was so blind that he was incapable of reading writing.

testamentary writing executed before August 1, 1995 can briefly be summarised as follows:

1. The deed must be subscribed by the testator at the end (see paras. 3.29–3.47 and paras. 3.72–3.86); and

2. The deed should be either
   (a) subscribed by the testator at the foot of each page (if the deed consists of more than one sheet), his signature being attested by two witnesses, who subscribed at the end of the deed, the designations of the witnesses appearing either in the deed or in the testing clause, or being appended to their subscriptions[35] (see paras. 3.87–3.108);
   (b) holograph of the testator (see paras. 3.112–3.133);
   (c) adopted as holograph by the testator (see paras. 3.50–3.54); or
   (d) otherwise adopted by him in a formal writing (see paras. 3.48–3.49 and paras. 3.55–3.71).

Whether special proof is required before a testamentary writing is accepted as validly executed depends on the method of execution.

3.20 A testamentary writing subscribed by the testator on each page, and attested at the end by two witnesses, who are properly designed, is *ex facie* probative, and may be founded on without further proof. Such a deed may be challenged, but the onus of proving that it was not validly executed falls on the party objecting to it. If the testamentary writing is lacking, in the sense of there being an "informality of execution", then it is necessary for the party seeking to found on it for confirmation to prove in court that it was validly executed (paras.19.38 *et seq.*). But if a solemnity has been omitted (*e.g.* one of the witnesses before whom the testator signed omitted to subscribe), the testamentary writing is fundamentally null and void, and no form of evidence as to its execution can set it up.

3.21 A testamentary writing which was signed prior to August 1, 1995 and which is holograph of the testator, but not witnessed, is improbative and must always be set up by the affidavit evidence of two persons that the writing and signature are in the handwriting of the testator (see paras. 3.120–3.122).

3.22 Where prior to August 1, 1995 the testator had adopted a testamentary writing as holograph it is improbative, and affidavit

---

[35] Conveyancing (Scotland) Act 1874 (37 & 38 Vict. c. 94), s. 38.

evidence of two persons must be obtained as to the handwriting
of the docket and the signature (see para. 3.50).

3.23   Where such an improbative testamentary writing subscribed
prior to August 1, 1995 has been put up with the papers for
confirmation, once confirmation has been granted, the writing
is treated as probative but only insofar as regards entitlement
to any property disposed of in it.[36]

Résumé of statute law on attestation of deeds in Scotland[37]

3.24   The Subscription of Deeds Act 1540[38] provided that "ony obliga-
tioune, band or uther writting" would be valid only if subscribed by the granter "and witnesse"[39] or, if the granter was
unable to write, by a notary. The Subscription of Deeds Act
1579[40] provided that in the case of deeds relating to heritage and
other deeds of great importance sealing was also required, and
if the principal party could not write, it was necessary for two
notaries to subscribe before four witnesses, "designed by their
special dwelling-place or sum other evident tokens". By the Act
of 1584,[41] sealing was dispensed with if a deed was registered.
Accordingly, sealing fell into disuse,[42] and the 1584 Act has since
been repealed.[43] The Act of 1593[44] (since repealed[45]) laid down that
the name and designation of the writer should be mentioned in
the deed at the end, before the insertion of the witnesses. The
Subscription of Deeds Act 1681[46] referred to the custom which
was introduced when writing was less common, that witnesses
to a deed, though not subscribing, were probative witnesses, and
to the possibility that by their forgetfulness they might easily
disown their being witnesses. To remedy this, it was enacted that
a deed would be probative only if the witnesses subscribed; that
the writer and witnesses must be designed in the deed; and that
no witness shall subscribe as witness to any party's subscription
unless he then knew that party and saw him subscribe or heard

---

[36] Succession (Scotland) Act 1964 (c. 41), s. 32(1) and (2) (a).

[37] For a fuller résumé see A.M. Bell, *Lectures on Conveyancing* (2nd ed.), pp.
26–34; A. Menzies, *Lectures on Conveyancing*, Chaps. 4–9; J.P. Wood, *Lectures on
Conveyancing*, pp. 67–72.

[38] Act of 1540 (c. 37 or c. 117).

[39] Presumably witnessed by two or more witnesses although there is doubt as
to whether the witnesses required to subscribe (A.M. Bell, *Lectures on Conveyancing* (3rd ed.) p. 29).

[40] Act of 1579 (c. 18 or c. 80).

[41] Act of 1584 (c. 11 or c. 4).

[42] Erskine, III.ii.7.

[43] Statute Law Revision (Scotland) Act 1964 (c. 80), s. 1 and Sched. 1.

[44] Act of 1593 (c. 25 or c. 179).

[45] Statute Law Revision (Scotland) Act 1964 (c. 80), s. 1 and Sched. 1.

[46] Act of 1681 (c. 5) as amended by Debtors (Scotland) Act 1987 (c. 18), s. 108
and Sched. 8.

him give warrant to a notary or notaries to subscribe for him . . . or that the party did at the time of the witness subscribing acknowledge his subscription. Until 1696 the practice was that deeds consisting of more than one sheet were battered together, sidescribed at the joinings of the sheets and subscribed. The deeds were either folded or rolled up, and if a deed consisted of many sheets, it was very inconvenient to find a particular clause in the deed. With the enactment of the Deeds Act 1696,[47] the writer could choose the former method, or write the deed by way of a book in leaves of paper, but every page had to be numbered and signed by the granter "as the margines were before" and the number of pages had to be mentioned on the last page, on which the witnesses had to sign. However, the courts have held that a deed written on one sheet of paper, no matter how many pages it has been folded to make, is not treated as being written book-wise.[48] Consequently, the Deeds Act 1696 is not applicable, and the deed need only be subscribed. The Form of Deeds (Scotland) Act 1856[49] (since repealed[50]) commented on the fact that the provision in the Deeds Act 1696, as to marking every page by number, had been very generally neglected in practice and that the other safeguards provided by the Act were in themselves amply sufficient. Accordingly, it was enacted that it was no longer necessary to number the pages. Further relaxations in the solemnities for the execution of deeds were provided by section 149 of the Titles to Land Consolidation (Scotland) Act 1868[51] which enacted:

> "All deeds and conveyances, and all documents whatever . . . whether relating or not relating to land, having a testing clause, may be partly written and partly printed or engraved or lithographed: Provided always, that in the testing clause the date, if any, and the name and designations of the witnesses, and the number of the pages of the deed or conveyance or document, if the number be specified, and the name and designation of the writer of the written portions of the body of the deed or conveyance or document shall be expressed at length, and all such deeds, conveyances and documents shall be as valid and effectual as if they had been wholly in writing . . ."

3.25   Sections 38 and 39 (discussed at paras. 19.35 *et seq.*) of the Conveyancing (Scotland) Act 1874[52] made further substantial changes:

> "**38.** It shall be no objection to the probative character of

---

[47] Act of 1696 (c. 15).
[48] *Robertson* v. *Ker* (1742) Mor. 16 App. 955; *Smith* v. *Bank of Scotland* (1824) 2 Shaw's App. 265 at p. 281; *Baird's Trs.* v. *Baird*, 1955 S.C. 286.
[49] 19 & 20 Vict. c. 89.
[50] Statute Law Revision Act 1892 (55 & 56 Vict. c. 19), s. 1 and Sched.
[51] 31 & 32 Vict. c. 101.
[52] 37 & 38 Vict. c. 94.

the deed, instrument, or writing, whether relating to land or not, that the writer or printer is not named or designed, or that the number of pages is not specified, or that the witnesses are not named or designed in the body of such deed, instrument, or writing, or in the testing clause thereof, provided that where the witnesses are not so named and designed their designations shall be appended to or follow their subscriptions; and such designations may be so appended or added at any time before the deed, instrument, or writing shall have been recorded in any register for preservation, or shall have been founded on in any court, and need not be written by the witnesses themselves."

"**39.**[53] No deed, instrument, or writing subscribed by the granter or maker thereof, and bearing to be attested by two witnesses subscribing, and whether relating to land or not, shall be deemed invalid or denied effect according to its legal import because of any informality of execution, but the burden of proving that such deed, instrument, or writing so attested was subscribed by the granter or maker thereof, and by the witnesses by whom such deed, instrument or writing bears to be attested, shall lie upon the party using or upholding the same, and such proof may be led in any action or proceeding in which such deed, instrument, or writing is founded on or objected to, or in a special application to the Court of Session, or to the sheriff within whose jurisdiction the defender in any such application resides, to have it declared that such deed, instrument, or writing was subscribed by such granter or maker and witnesses."

3.26   The Conveyancing (Scotland) Act 1874[54] also brought in a simplified procedure for notarial execution, the former practice of requiring two notaries and four witnesses being superseded by one notary or justice of the peace[55] reading the deed over to the testator and subscribing in his presence and by his authority, all before two witnesses. The Conveyancing (Scotland) Act 1924[56] extended notarial execution to law agents and clarified some aspects of the drafting of the earlier statutory provision which had previously been unclear.

3.27   While the Conveyancing and Feudal Reform (Scotland) Act 1970 provided that, in general, deeds (and any inventory, appendix, schedule, plan or other document annexed thereto) need only be subscribed on the last page,[57] it expressly provided that no change was being made to the law on the subscription of wills and other

[53] As amended by Conveyancing (Scotland) Act 1924 (14 & 15 Geo. 5, c. 27), s. 18 and Succession (Scotland) Act 1964 (c. 41), s. 18.

[54] (37 & 38 Vict. c. 94), s. 41.

[55] A minister was also able to notarise the testamentary writing of a person dwelling in his parish (Erskine, *Institutes* III.ii.23; A.M. Bell, *Lectures on Conveyancing* pp. 45–46).

[56] (14 & 15 Geo. 5. c. 27), s. 18.

[57] Conveyancing and Feudal Reform (Scotland) Act 1970 (c. 35), s. 44(1).

testamentary writings.[58] Consequently, only testamentary writings, dated prior to August 1, 1995, subscribed on every page, and attested by two witness, who are duly designed, are probative.

3.27A The Requirements of Writing (Scotland) Act 1995 comprises a comprehensive code replacing the earlier provisions and the new rules which apply to writings executed on or after August 1, 1995 are considered in the following chapter.

General rules: the writing medium

3.28 A testamentary writing may be written either in ink or in pencil;[59] or it may be typed or printed, or any combination of these, or indeed any method of visible recording in words and figures may be used. For instance, the Braille system of writing for the blind may be used.[60] In England, a testamentary writing in shorthand has been admitted to probate.[61]

SUBSCRIPTION

Subscription: the position of the testator's signature

3.29 It is well established that only Royalty may superscribe, and others must subscribe.[62] As Lord Moncrieff expressed it[63]

"Superscription is confined to royalty, and I know of no case in which superscription by a subject has been sustained as equivalent to subscription except in the case where a postscript or even a codicil (though this is more doubtful) has been sustained though written under a signature. But in these cases the signature was really a proper subscription of the principal letter or will."

3.30 Thus, in a commissary case involving a holograph writing where the appointment of the executor was written after the signature, objection was taken, and the executor who was named was instead confirmed as executor-dative, *qua* next of

---

[58] *Ibid.*, s. 44(2).

[59] *Muir's Trs.* (1869) 8 M. 53; *Simsons* v. *Simsons* (1883) 10 R. 1247; *Tait's Trs.* v. *Chiene*, 1911 S.C. 743; *Russell's Exr.* v. *Duke*, 1946 S.L.T. 242.

[60] *Broadfoot*, Nov. 13, 1905, unreported where the testator signed in ordinary writing and the signature was attested; the signed will, a copy in ordinary writing and the expert's certificate was recorded with the inventory.

[61] *Orrin* v. *Orrin, The Times*, Dec. 20, 1921.

[62] Stair, *Institutions*, IV.xlii.6; *Skinner* v. *Forbes* (1883) 11 R. 88; *Goldie* v. *Shedden* (1885) 13 R. 138; *Foley* v. *Costello* (1904) 6 F. 365; *Taylor's Exxs.* v. *Thom*, 1914 S.C. 79; *McLay* v. *Farrell*, 1950 S.C. 149; *Robbie* v. *Carr*, 1959 S.L.T. (Notes) 16; *Boyd* v. *Buchanan*, 1964 S.L.T. (Notes) 108; *McKillop* v. *Secretary of State for Scotland*, 1951 S.L.C.R. 17.

[63] *Foley* v. *Costello* (1904) 6 F. 365 at p. 370.

kin.[64] Where the testator's signature appears in the middle of the testing clause in the purported testamentary writing, the established commissary practice appears to be to treat the writing as properly subscribed,[65] presumably on the grounds that the law does not require a testing clause.

3.31 By subscribing, the testator shows that the document is the expression of his completed intention, and not merely a draft or memorandum for a testamentary writing. This rule applies to attested and holograph writings alike.[66] Some nineteenth century judgments indicate that the courts might, in appropriate cases, treat an unsigned holograph writing as complete where extrinsic evidence to this effect could be led[67] but this approach was finally discarded by the majority in the full bench decision of *Taylor's Exxs. v. Thom.*[68]

Signature in margin

3.32 In *Robbie v. Carr*,[69] Lord President Clyde, sitting in the Outer House, held that a signature in the margin does not constitute "subscription". Exceptionally, in an unreported case which preceded *Robbie v. Carr*,[70] confirmation was issued to the residuary legatee named in a holograph will which was signed on the last page, not at the foot, but marginally along the left hand side, in the presence of one witness. The testator also wrote there the place and date of signing. There was no room at the foot of the page to sign. In the light of Lord President Clyde's decision in *Robbie v. Carr*, the approach taken to the testamentary writing in the unreported case would appear to be questionable.

Subscription: special problems with holograph writings

3.33 Many of the reported cases, where the question in issue was whether the testator had subscribed, involve holograph writings. Frequently, when a person prepares his own testamentary writing, he omits to sign it, but his name may appear in the opening words, or in the body of the writing. Sometimes one signature appears on a page below (or between) two different testamentary provisions, which it is clear were written at different times.

Signature in body of the deed

3.34 A signature in the body of the deed is not subscription, but

---

[64] *Scott*, Nov. 2, 1887, unreported. Today it is more likely that the residuary beneficiaries would be confirmed as executors-nominate in terms of s.3 of the Executors (Scotland) Act 1900.

[65] *Wood*, Dec. 16, 1921, unreported; *White*, March 15, 1922, unreported; *Cunningham* Feb. 20, 1923, unreported.

[66] In the case of an attested writing, there should be some link between the testator's signature and those of the witnesses. See para. 3.104 below.

[67] *Dunlop v. Dunlop* (1839) 1 D. 912; *Skinner v. Forbes* (1883) 11 R. 88; *Russell's Trs. v. Henderson* (1883) 11 R. 283.

[68] 1914 S.C. 79.

[69] 1959 S.L.T. (Notes) 16.

[70] *Ramsay*, June 12, 1956, unreported.

where the writing above the signature is clearly testamentary in nature, the court may be able to hold that the writing which follows the signature adds nothing to the earlier "will". In one case, a testator wrote:

> "I, the under signed, Leave every thing I possess to Billie & Charlie, to be Divided between them equally.
> The Last Will and Testament of Elizabeth Houston or Gordon or Cairns,
> all my Jewellery, any thing I possess to."

Sheriff Reid considered that the words "Elizabeth Houston or Gordon or Cairns" should not be deprived of the description of "signature" by the words "the Last Will and Testament of" being interposed between them and the words of bequest. The words "the Last Will and Testament of" seemed to him merely explanatory of what she was doing—that is, making her last will and testament. The words "all my Jewellery, any thing I possess to" did not detract from the Sheriff's interpretation:

> "[F]airly read, I consider the last phrase entirely superfluous and otiose in an attempt to clarify the already clear universal character of the previous disposition of her estate to Billie and Charlie; The last word 'to' I consider a misspelling of the word 'too'."

Accordingly, he held that the document was the testator's holograph will subscribed by her.[71-72]

Signature below more than one testamentary writing

3.35   There are a number of cases where the courts have held that one signature can constitute subscription to more than one testamentary writing written above the signature. The approach has been criticised, and it has been doubted whether the approach would now be followed.[73]

3.36   A holograph addition or codicil to a testamentary writing which was not itself signed, but was positioned between the end of the testing clause and the testator's signature to the actual testamentary writing has received effect, on the basis that the signature was validating both deeds.[74] The correctness of this decision has been doubted,[75] but the same approach has been taken in a number of decisions.

3.37   In an unreported commissary case, the testator had inserted the holograph words "Sole executor, J. W. Prestwick" after the testing clause, but before the signature. There was no other appointment of executor or trustee, and the court authorised

---

[71-72] *Cairns* v. *Cairns*, 1949 S.L.T. (Sh. Ct.) 69.
[73] Walker and Walker, *The Law of Evidence in Scotland*, para. 181.
[74] *Gray's Trs.* v. *Dow* (1900) 3 F. 79.
[75] Per Lord Moncrieff in *Foley* v. *Costello* (1904) 6 F. 365 at p. 370.

that the person referred to as "JW" should be confirmed as sole executor.[76]

3.38   In a reported case,[77] the court upheld as a valid appointment of a trustee the following, which was inserted between the end of a holograph will and the testator's subscription:

> "I appoint Hugh Conn Reid, Parkhead, Kilwinning, a trustee, 15/3/51".

Signature above second holograph testamentary writing

3.39   Where below a testamentary writing which was properly subscribed, the deceased had handwritten a testamentary writing which he did not subscribe, the signature above the second testamentary writing cannot, in general, constitute subscription of it. Thus, where the deceased left a signed holograph will, and below her signature she had written "all to Anne McLay", it was held that these words, since they were not subscribed, did not constitute a valid nomination of Anne McLay as the deceased's residuary legatee.[78]

3.40   Exceptionally, the court may find a connecting link between the first writing and the second writing which may justify the second writing being treated as valid.

3.41   In a decision of the Second Division,[79] a holograph but unsubscribed codicil written below the signature to a holograph trust settlement was given effect as part of the settlement. The decision is difficult to justify, apart from the fact that the trust settlement did not expressly revoke an earlier testamentary writing, and the codicil merely expanded on that earlier writing. Lord President Cooper has commented on the decision that "the Second Division found it possible to discover in an unsubscribed addition a connecting link with the main will which, from an examination of the report, it is difficult to rediscover".[80] The decision has been criticised,[81] and it is submitted that it should not be relied on.

3.42   Where a testatrix added to her holograph will, below her subscription the words:-

> "P.S.   James Fraser £1100
>   Alice Fraser Residuary Legatee"

it was held that by virtue of the letters "P.S.", the two additional lines were engrafted on and imported into the writing of which it was a p.s., and were of the nature of a marginal addition or interlineation. Being holograph, the p.s. did not require authen-

---

[76] *Lockhart*, Oct. 24, 1888, unreported.
[77] *Reid's Exrs.* v. *Reid*, 1954 S.L.T. (Notes) 20.
[78] *McLay* v. *Farrell*, 1950 S.C. 149.
[79] *Burnie's Tr.* v. *Lawrie* (1894) 21 R. 1015.
[80] *McLay* v. *Farrell*, 1950 S.C. 149 at p. 154.
[81] Lord Dundas in *Taylor's Exxs.* v. *Thom*, 1914 S.C. 79 at p. 84.

tication. There was the special circumstance that there was no space at the foot of the page for the testatrix to sign her p.s.[82]

Subscription: signature may be separate from testamentary writing

3.43 While the word "subscribed" is normally interpreted as meaning that the signature appears at the end of the writing, a testamentary writing where the signature is separate from the deed may be upheld as validly executed provided that the deed is linked in some way with the signature. Each case turns on the wording of the particular testamentary writing.

3.44 In *Baird's Trs. v. Baird*,[83] the deceased signed a bank order form which was partly written by her daughter and partly printed — the instruction to the bank being to pay out all the money in the account to her daughter on the day of her death. The deceased signed the reverse side again, and two witnesses signed too. The reverse side was otherwise blank, there being no indication of any connection between the two sides. The fact that both sides bore the same date merely showed that they had been filled up within the space of 24 hours. It was held that there was no subscription.

3.45 In *Ferguson, Petr.*[84] a will was written on one sheet of paper, which had been folded to form four pages. At the end of the first page, there was a kind of testing clause, the remainder being carried on to the third page (the second page being blank). The testator signed the first page only, and the witness signed at the end of the testing clause on the second page. It was held that there was a clear distinction between this case and that of *Baird's Trs.*, as in *Ferguson, Petr.*, the docket or testing clause formed a link between the signature of the testator on the first page and the signatures of the witnesses on the second: "the sense, purpose, position, and even the stereotyped form of the connecting sentence lead naturally from page to page to end the document in the accepted way".[85]

3.46 In *Russell's Exr. v. Duke*[86] the deceased had left a formal will dated July 30, 1937 which included a clause directing the payments of legacies "bequeathed by me in any writing under my hand, however informal". On one side of a used envelope, he wrote in pencil bequests of legacies largely to relatives, dated it August 9, 1937 and wrote "over". On the obverse he wrote "Signed Thomas Russell [address] 9th August 1937". Lord Keith held that the use of the word "over" at the foot of one page

---

[82] *Fraser's Exrx. v. Fraser's C.B.*, 1931 S.C. 536.
[83] 1955 S.C. 286.
[84] 1959 S.C. 56.
[85] *Per* Lord Justice-Clerk Thomson at p. 60.
[86] 1946 S.L.T. 242.

formed a clear link between the writing and the signature. The writing on the envelope was accordingly subscribed, and adopted by the clause in the formal will. It received effect as a testamentary writing.

3.47   In *McNeill* v. *McNeill*,[87] the will consisted of a single sheet of paper folded into four pages. The first page ended with a testing clause but was not signed. The second page contained the attested signature of the testator, with the witnesses' designations being appended to their signatures, but the style and language was enough to link the two pages.

Adoption of unsubscribed testamentary writings

3.48   In Scots law, "adoption" is the term used to denote the principle under which an improbative writing is validated by a properly executed deed. Adoption is a question of intention, and has given rise to much litigation. Adoption may be either express (see paras. 3.49–3.70) or implied (see para. 3.71).

Express adoption

3.49   Express adoption may be effected either by an endorsed docket subscribed prior to August 1, 1955 (see paras. 3.50–3.54) or by description (see paras. 3.55–3.70).

Express adoption: endorsed docket

3.50   Express adoption of a deed could be effected prior to August 1, 1995 by a holograph docket, written out on the deed, and duly subscribed by the testator. The handwriting of the holograph docket and signature must be set up by the affidavit evidence of two persons (as required for holograph testamentary writings generally—see paras. 3.120–3.123). The deed, whether wholly or partly in the handwriting of a third party, whether wholly or partly printed or typed, and whether partly holograph of the testator will then receive effect.

3.51   Examples of dockets which, if holograph of, and duly subscribed by the testator, will validate an improbative writing include "I adopt the whole of the above, both printed and written, as holograph, and declare it to be my last will and testament",[88] "I adopt this as holograph",[89] "adopted as holograph"[90] and "accepted as holograph".[91] All that is required is that "by words appended [to the writing], over and above his signature, [the testator] declares expressly or by indubitable

---

[87] 1973 S.L.T. (Sh. Ct.) 16.
[88] *Per* Lord President Inglis in *Macdonald* v. *Cuthbertson* (1890) 18 R. 101 at p. 106.
[89] *Per* Lord Sands in *Cross's Trs.* v. *Cross*, 1921 1 S.L.T. 244 at p. 245.
[90] Lord Guthrie in *Carmichael's Exrs.* v. *Carmichael*, 1909 S.C. 1387 at p. 1389.
[91] *McBeath's Trs.* v. *McBeath*, 1935 S.C. 471.

implication that he adopts the whole writing as his".[92] In an unreported case, the deceased had signed a will which was not in her own handwriting, and had added the words "I adopt the above as holograph" and again had signed her name. On the affidavit evidence by two persons acquainted with her handwriting, that the words were holograph of the testator, warrant was granted to confirm the executors nominated in the will.[93]

3.52 In the case of an offer to purchase heritage, the offer was regarded as holograph where the offeror had written below (rather than above) his signature the words "adopted as holograph".[94]

3.53 It is submitted that one signature only, below the docket, is necessary. Where the writing is on more than one page, either each page should bear a docket to the effect that it is "adopted as holograph", or the docket on the last page should clearly identify all that is adopted (for example, "This and the preceding five pages, adopted as holograph").

3.54 In a rather exceptional decision,[95] typewritten testamentary documents, which contained typewritten statements that they were "typed by, and accepted as holograph by" the deceased, and which were signed by the deceased, were treated as holograph of the deceased, and so were given effect to.

Express adoption: incorporation by description

3.55 Express adoption of an unsubscribed document can be effected by description

"if, in another writing which unmistakably identifies that document, the testator designates and adopts it as containing his will. In that case, the adoptive writing is really the will; and the document containing the directions plays the part of a schedule annexed to and incorporated with it".[96]

Or, put another way,

"a will which is itself either holograph and subscribed or probative may incorporate by reference unsubscribed testamentary directions which are to be found outside of itself— for example, in an unauthenticated writing sufficiently described for identification, or in a model will printed on a

---

[92] *Per* Lord Kinloch in *Maitland's Trs.* v. *Maitland* (1871) 10 M. 79 at p. 84.

[93] *Adam*, May 3, 1890 unreported.

[94] *Gavine's Trs.* v. *Lee* (1883) 10 R. 448.

[95] *McBeath's Trs.* v. *McBeath*, 1935 S.C. 471, discussed further at paras. 3.131–3.133.

[96] *Per* Lord President Clyde in *Stenhouse* v. *Stenhouse*, 1922 S.C. 370 at pp. 372–373.

certain page of a legal style-book, or in the published life of some person, either real or imaginary".[97]

3.56 The adoptive writing must itself be testamentary if it is to validate another writing.[98]

3.57 Further, there must in fact be an adoptive clause in the adoptive writing. In one case, a holograph writing was found inside an unsealed envelope on which was written "My will". The writing began "Sunnybank Alford. My last Will Jessie Taylor". There then followed directions as to the disposal of her whole estate, but no signature. Since there was no subscription, the writing was invalid. It was held that the opening words, which had been signed "Jessie Taylor", could not be a docket of adoption of what followed.[99] The position might have been different if the opening words had been "the unsigned writing which follows is my last will".[1]

3.58 Where the testator's will authorises the executors to give effect to a holograph writing, any subsequent holograph writings must be put up with the other papers for confirmation. Whether or not the commissary or sheriff clerk will require the secondary writing to be set up by affidavit will depend on the terms of the authorisation contained in the principal document, and on the nature of the holograph document produced. Each case will be considered on its merits, and there is no general rule of practice. If the principal document directs that effect is to be given "to any document under my hand", it is likely that no proof will be required if the secondary document is clearly handwritten and signed by the testator. However, if there is any doubt, or substantial assets are disposed of in the secondary writing, the commissary or sheriff clerk is likely to adhere to the strict terms of section 21 of the Succession (Scotland) Act 1964 and require the production of affidavits.

3.59 A testator may in a validly executed testamentary writing adopt by description either a deed which is already in existence, or one which is created subsequently.

Incorporation of an existing document by description
3.60 In each case, it is necessary to consider carefully the terms of the adoptive clause, for it defines the deeds which are adopted.

3.61 A holograph signed codicil was enclosed (along with other testamentary writings) in a sealed envelope which was signed and

---

[97] *Per* Lord Skerrington in *Taylor's Exxs.* v. *Thom*, 1914 S.C. 79 at p. 92.

[98] *Cross's Trs.* v. *Cross*, 1921 1 S.L.T. 244 (where it was held that an improbative codicil signed by the deceased had not been adopted by his holograph subscribed post-script to a letter to his law agent, since the post-script was not testamentary).

[99] *Taylor's Exxs.* v. *Thom*, 1914 S.C. 79.

[1] *Ibid., per* Lord President Strathclyde at p. 83.

dated and bore an endorsement "To my executors". The codicil contained directions to the testator's niece "to distribute gifts in money and kind as shown on the list attached hereto". Also in the same envelope was an unsigned holograph document which was not attached to the codicil, but which contained a list of names and gifts in one part. Although the list was not attached, this portion of the unsigned holograph document was held effectual by adoption, since the testator had placed it with the codicil in an envelope addressed to his executors.[2] Other directions in the unsigned holograph document were declared ineffective, since there was no authority for holding that the testator's holograph endorsement "To my executors" and signature on the envelope could supply the want of signature on the writing.

Incorporation of future writings by description

3.62 A clause is frequently inserted in formal testamentary writings to the effect that the testator directs "that any writing under my hand however informally the same may be expressed" shall receive effect. The wording varies from deed to deed, and in each case, the exact wording is important, for it defines the deeds which can be adopted. Thus where the deceased had directed his trustees to pay such "legacies" as he might leave by any writings under his hand, however informal, provided they were clearly expressive of his intentions, it was held that the clause did not validate a subscribed endorsement on a deposit receipt which bore the words "Pay [AB]: (four thousand, five hundred pounds—1/1/67) £4,500", since the provision made was not a legacy.[3]

3.63 Where the words used are "any writing under my hand", in the absence of a controlling context, the supplementary writings must be signed if they are to receive effect.[4] Subscription means a signature at the end of the supplementary writing, but exceptionally, the courts may be prepared to treat a signature on the reverse side of the supplementary writing as subscription.[5] Where the phrase used is "any writing under my hand" (especially if it is stated that it need not be formal), the adopted writings need not be holograph or attested.[6]

3.64 The leading case on adoption of future writings is *Waterson's*

<hr/>

[2] *Macphail's Trs.* v. *Macphail*, 1940 S.C. 560.

[3] *Gray's Trs.* v. *Murray*, 1970 S.L.T. (Notes) 3.

[4] *Hamilton's Trs.* v. *Hamilton* (1901) 4 F. 266 (where an unsigned holograph memorandum was held not to be validated by a clause in a will enabling payment of all legacies "by any writing under my hand (however informally executed or defective) shewing my wishes and intentions"); *Waterson's Trs.* v. *St. Giles Boys' Club*, 1943 S.C. 369; *Russell's Exr.* v. *Duke* 1946 S.L.T. 242.

[5] *Russell's Exr.* v. *Duke*, 1946 S.L.T. 242 (discussed at para. 3.46).

[6] *Wilsone's Trs.* v. *Stirling* (1861) 24 D. 163; *Young's Trs.* v. *Ross* (1864) 3 M. 10; *Fraser* v. *Forbes' Trs.* (1899) 1 F. 513.

Trs. v. *St. Giles Boys' Club,*[7] where Lord Justice-Clerk Cooper laid down the following rules:

> "the . . . question which must in every such case be answered is a pure question of construction *viz.,* whether the particular writing in question satisfies the description and fulfils the requisites sought to be prescribed by the principal settlement . . .
>
> In this case we are instructed by the testatrix to look for an informal writing 'under my hand'. We are of opinion that the document before us, being unsigned, does not answer to this description.
>
> According to the normal acceptation of the words, a document 'under my hand' means a document signed (*i.e.,* subscribed) by me; and an informal document 'under my hand' means a document signed by me which is defective either in form or expression, or in solemnities of authentication, or in both. For the purpose of determining whether a document is 'under the hand' of the granter, the signature is more than a mere formality or solemnity, and its unique significance as the recognised and indispensable token of deliberate authorisation of a written document, whether formal or informal, has long been accepted by common usage. In this context the word 'hand' is a synonym for 'signature' . . . It is, of course, possible for a testator to make it plain that he is using this, or any other, expression in a special sense, and in such a case the settlement will provide its own vocabulary, and the special sense will prevail. But in the ordinary case the words used must receive their ordinary significance."[8]

3.65 Thus, unsigned holograph writings have been given effect to where the wording was "any writing holograph of myself, whether signed by me or not, or whether found in my repositories, or in the custody of any person to whom I may entrust the same, and which holograph writing shall be as sufficient and effectual as if herein especially engrossed".[9] But where the wording was "any Memorandum or Letter of Instructions addressed to . . . [my trustees] by me, however informally the same may be executed . . .", an unsigned memorandum did not receive effect, since it was considered that although the testator had dispensed with the formalities of execution, he had not dispensed with execution *per se.*[10]

3.66 Depending on the wording of the adoptive clause, there may

[7] 1943 S.C. 369 (overruling *Ronald's Trs.* v. *Lyle,* 1929 S.C. 104; and *Gillespie* v. *Donaldson's Trs.* (1831) 10 S. 174).

[8] Lord Justice-Clerk Cooper, *ibid.,* at p. 374.

[9] *Crosbie* v. *Wilson* (1865) 3 M. 870.

[10] *Snailum's Trs.* v. *Edinburgh Royal Infirmary,*1948 S.L.T. (Notes) 25.

be no dispensation of the formalities. Thus, in one case, the deceased's formal will included a direction to pay out of his estate "any legacies or donations I may choose to leave." He left an envelope on which was written *"To my executors* Miss Margaret Maitland—this Nine hundred Pounds belongs to her. Five hundred to be sunk for her, and the remaining four to be given her *Thomas Maitland"*. Only the words in italics were holograph of the deceased: the words of bequest, the amount bequeathed and the name of the legatee were not holograph. Inside the envelope was a deposit receipt. The court held that the clause in the formal will did not dispense with the ordinary requirements on formalities of execution.[11]

3.67　　As in all cases, it is important that the testator shows testamentary intention in his writings. In one case, the deceased, EF, left a trust disposition and settlement which contained a clause directing his trustees to pay such "legacies" as he might leave by any writings under his hand, however informal, provided they were clearly indicative of his intentions. Two deposit receipts in his own favour were found in his possession. One was endorsed in his own handwriting "Pay [AB] (four thousand five hundred pounds—1/1/67) £4,500" and signed by him. The other was endorsed, in his own handwriting "Pay to [CD], six thousand pounds £6,000, [EF], 26/5/67." The court held that the endorsements possessed no testamentary character in themselves, and that they had not been validated as "legacies" by the deceased's trust disposition and settlement.[12]

3.68　　When, in his will, the deceased reserved power to bequeath legacies "by any writing under my hand however informally the same may be expressed or executed", it has been held that this implied the reservation of a power to revoke a legacy by a similar informal writing.[13]

Envelopes, appropriately docketed and signed, may adopt unsubscribed writings inside

3.69　　The courts have encountered particular difficulty in cases where the deceased left a holograph but unsubscribed testamentary writing in an envelope which is docketed or endorsed by the deceased to the effect that it contains the will of —. An unsubscribed docket cannot adopt a writing inside, but if the docket is subscribed, the question then is whether it is an adoptive docket or a descriptive docket (which will not adopt the

[11] *Maitland's Trs. v. Maitland* (1871) 10 M. 79.
[12] *Gray's Trs. v. Murray,* 1970 S.L.T. (Notes) 3.
[13] *Ronalds' Trs. v. Lyle,* 1929 S.C. 104 (another aspect of this decision was overruled by *Waterston's Trs. v. St. Giles Boys' Club,* 1943 S.C. 369).

contents). The more recent cases indicate that a docket such as "My Will" is merely a descriptive docket. Each case turns on the particular wording on the envelope.

Examples

1. In a decision which has been much criticised,[14] a holograph unsubscribed writing was sustained as a will because:

   (1) it was enclosed in a sealed packet which was addressed to the deceased's nephew, and bore the deceased's signature;

   (2) attached to the packet was an envelope bearing the nephew's name and the testatrix's signature;

   (3) in the envelope was a letter referring to the deceased having made a will, and the letter was signed "Your loving Aunt Margaret";

   (4) the deceased delivered all these to the nephew, saying that the packet contained her will.[15]

   The verbal statement would probably now go for nothing. Reliance on extrinsic circumstances is now disapproved of. This decision was followed in another case,[16] which is equally suspect.

2. In an unreported commissary case, a holograph will which began with the testator's name, but which was not signed, was enclosed in an envelope inscribed "My Will" and this was signed. The will was held to be valid, and warrant to issue confirmation was granted on proof that the will had been found in the envelope in the deceased's repositories.[17] In the light of subsequent reported cases, this decision is questionable.

3. In *Taylor's Exxs.* v. *Thom*,[18] a holograph writing was found inside an unsealed envelope on which was written "My Will". Since the docket on the envelope was unsigned, no attempt was made on it as adopting the holograph writing.

4. An unsigned holograph writing was contained in a sealed envelope on which was written the following docket:-
   "My holograph will, written by me on twenty-fourth

---

[14] *Per* Lord Shand in *Goldie* v. *Shedden* (1885) 13 R. 138 at p. 143; *per* Lord Johnston in *Taylor's Exxs.* v. *Thom*, 1914 S.C. 79 at pp. 87–88; *per* Lord Anderson in *France's J.F.* v. *France's Trs.*, 1916, 1 S.L.T. 126 at p. 127.

[15] *Russell's Trs.* v. *Henderson* (1883) 11 R. 283.

[16] *Murray* v. *Kuffel*, 1910 2 S.L.T. 388.

[17] *Wyld*, Oct. 27, 1887, unreported.

[18] 1914 S.C. 79, discussed further at para. 3.57.

July nineteen hundred and forty at my house [named] and I appoint [A] and [B] to be my executors.

MARGARET FRANCE"

The envelope was also signed across the gummed flap. It was held that there was no will.[19] The parties admitted that the signed docket did not purport to adopt anything.

"(T)he so-called docquet on the envelope was nothing more than a backing of the writ or notification of what was contained in the envelope. This notification was placed on the envelope and her signature written over the flap to prevent unauthorised interference with the contents of the envelope, and the names of her executors were written there to indicate who might authoritatively open the envelope after her death."[20]

5. A holograph document, unsubscribed, beginning with the writer's address and "Will and Testemony of Joseph Stenhouse [date]" was found in a closed envelope on which the following words were handwritten: "Will and Testemony off Joseph Stenhouse for — [name and designation of solicitor]". The writing on the envelope did not adopt the unsubscribed holograph document:

"The writing on the envelope . . . only repeats the heading written at the top of the pretended will, and is incapable, in my opinion, of being construed as anything more than a descriptive docquet. It falls far short of constituting a subscribed adoptive writing".[21]

6. The testator left a sealed envelope which bore the endorsement "To my executors" in his own handwriting and was signed and dated. The envelope contained two codicils and an unsigned holograph document. It was held that the docket on the envelope did not adopt the unsigned holograph document.[22]

Adoption of unsubscribed writings by a docket on the backing

3.70   In much the same way as a docket on an envelope may adopt

---

[19] *France's J.F.* v. *France's Trs.*, 1916 1 S.L.T. 126.
[20] *Per* Lord Anderson in *France's J.F.* v. *France's Trs.*, 1916 1 S.L.T. 126 at p. 127.
[21] *Per* Lord President Clyde in *Stenhouse* v. *Stenhouse*, 1922 S.L.T. 259 at p. 260.
[21] *Macphail's Trs.* v. *Macphail*, 1940 S.C. 560 discussed further at para. 3.61.

a holograph unsubscribed writing found inside the envelope (see para. 3.69), a signed docket on the backing of a holograph but unsubscribed testamentary writing may adopt the testamentary writing. The question is whether the docket is descriptive (in which case it cannot adopt the contents) or adoptive. Each case turns on the particular wording of the docket.

Examples

1. The deceased left a formally executed holograph will dated March 10, 1920, and a holograph writing dated July 21, 1923, which was written on three separate sheets of paper, the first two of which were dated and subscribed, but the last of which was neither dated nor subscribed. On the back of the first page, there was written a holograph and subscribed docket, dated July 21, 1923, which appointed two named individuals to be joint executors "of this my Will" and revoked all former wills and codicils. It was held that this docket, being signed and having sufficiently identified the three separate sheets, adopted them.[23]

2. The deceased left a holograph document dated May 6, 1961, consisting of a sheet of paper normally used as the backing of a printed will form. One side of the sheet contained holograph testamentary provisions, and bore the names of two witnesses, but was not subscribed. On the other side, under the printed words "Will of", the deceased had added her signature and address, and the words "This is my only will, any other is now revoked". The Lord Ordinary held that the docket was only the normal descriptive backing identifying the document as a will, and further that the docket was superscribed (and not subscribed).[24] Accordingly, the writing on the back could not adopt the unsubscribed writing.

Implied adoption

3.71   Lord Sands defined implied adoption as the case "where the [testator], being under the erroneous impression that his deed is validly executed proceeds to validly execute a subsequent writing in terms which shew that he regards the prior deed as valid and means it to be acted upon".[25] Whether the earlier document is impliedly adopted by the subsequent one turns on the wording of the subsequent writing.

---

[23] *Campbell's Exr.* v. *Maudslay*, 1934 S.L.T. 420.
[24] *Boyd* v. *Buchanan*, 1964 S.L.T. (Notes) 108.
[25] *Cross's Trs.* v. *Cross*, 1921 1 S.L.T. 244 at p. 245.

Examples:

1. Under an improbative writing, a testator had appended a holograph subscribed writing which began with the words: "I add to this". It was held that these words impliedly adopted the improbative writing.[26]

2. A woman wrote out to her husband's dictation on one side of a single sheet, a will appointing trustees and disposing of his estate. The husband signed it and intended to have it witnessed the next day. Thereafter, he added on the second side of the same sheet a very short codicil, in his own handwriting, which he subscribed. The codicil only conferred powers and immunities on "my Trustees", and since it was meaningless and ineffectual unless read in relation to the will, it impliedly adopted the will.[27]

3. The testator left two signed documents—an improbative will, partly printed and partly in his own handwriting and a holograph codicil which did not expressly refer to the will, but provided for the abatement of a legacy contained in it. The codicil was held to have impliedly adopted the improbative will and set it up in its entirety.[28]

4. Shortly before her death, Janet Robertson Fraser handed to her sister Alice two holograph writings. The first, dated May 28, 1927, and unsigned, provided for a number of legacies. The second stated "In addition to Will made before my father's death Miss J R Fraser leaves all the money left by her father to Alice Fraser . . . Janet R Fraser Dec 1928 Janet Robertson Fraser January 2nd 1929". In May 1928 Miss Fraser's father had died. Since the parties agreed that the earlier writing was the "will" referred to in the later one, it was held that the earlier writing was adopted by the later one.[29]

5. The deceased left a brown paper parcel on the top of which was an envelope addressed to his niece. The envelope contained a holograph document signed by the deceased. It left some small specific legacies and expressly referred to a document described as "my will", and to

---

[26] *Macintyre* v. *Macfarlane's Trs.*, March 1, 1821, F.C. (the testator's formal trust disposition and settlement included directions to pay "such legacies . . . to such . . . persons as I shall hereafter specify by any codicil hereto, or by any separate writing, memorandum or direction under my hand to my said trust-disponees." This clause would today be treated as validating the improbative but subscribed writing—see paras. 3.62 *et seq.*).

[27] *Cross's Trs.* v. *Cross*, 1921 1 S.L.T. 244.

[28] *Craik's Exx.* v. *Samson*, 1929 S.L.T. 592.

[29] *Fraser's Exx.* v. *Fraser's C.B.*, 1931 S.C. 536.

the fact that the deceased had not had time to have it signed or witnessed. The brown paper parcel contained a printed will form which had been completed in the deceased's handwriting, but which was not signed or witnessed. It was held that the signed holograph writing was a valid testamentary writing, which adopted the unsigned writing in the brown paper parcel.[30]

Subscription to be unaided

3.72 The testator should subscribe unaided. If, due to infirmity or poor literacy skills, the testator has difficulty in signing, it should be considered whether the testamentary writing should be notarially executed (see paras. 3.134 *et seq.* and 4.55 *et seq.*). In no circumstances should the testator's hand be led[31] or controlled, for then the signature will be open to challenge. Supporting the testator's body, or even his arm, will not vitiate the subscription, but holding the testator's wrist in such a way that his writing is thereby controlled will do so.[32] However, merely pointing to the place in the deed where the testator should sign will not give rise to a valid challenge,[33] and in an old decision, which perhaps should not be relied on, it was held that where a testator could sign her name, it was acceptable for her to copy her name, as written out by someone else.[34]

Subscription: method of signature

3.73 The signature must be written by the testator. It may not be impressed by a stamp on to which a specimen signature has been cut,[35] nor by passing an ink roller over a stencil of the signature,[36] nor, it is submitted, may it be typewritten.[37] The testator should not trace or blacken his name written in pencil or with a pin by another.[38]

3.74 The signature need not be legible, provided that it is in the kind of writing which the deceased habitually used to sign his name on deeds.[39] Since legibility is unimportant, and one should

---

[30] *Muir* v. *Muir*, 1950 S.L.T. (Notes) 40.

[31] *Moncrief* v. *Monipenny* (1711) Rob 26; *Clark's Exr.* v. *Cameron*, 1982 S.L.T. 68 (signature to a disposition).

[32] *Noble* v. *Noble* (1875) 3 R. 74.

[33] *Duff* v. *Earl of Fife's Trs.* (1823) 1 Shaw's App. 498.

[34] *Wilson* v. *Raeburn* (1800) Hume 912.

[35] *Stirling Stuart* v. *Stirling Crawfurd's Trs.* (1885) 12 R. 610.

[36] Lord Kinnear in *Whyte* v. *Watt* (1893) 21 R. 165 at p. 166.

[37] See *obiter dicta* in *McBeath's Trs.* v. *McBeath*, 1935 S.C. 471.

[38] *Crosbie* v. *Picken* (1749) Mor. 16814.

[39] *Stirling Stuart* v. *Stirling Crawfurd's Trs.* (1885) 12 R. 610 (see Lord President Inglis at pp. 625–626).

avoid any risk that a testamentary writing may be challenged, it would not be good practice to permit a testator to retouch his signature after execution. However, such retouching may not render the deed invalid, for the burden of proof is on the challenger.[40] If, instead of retouching his signature, the testator altered his signature, the outcome is likely to be different, for then it could be argued that the testator had thereby intended to revoke the testamentary writing. In *Fotheringham's Trs.* v. *Reid*,[41] a married woman signed her trust disposition and settlement with her married name. Subsequently, as she was living apart from her husband, she reverted to using her maiden name. After her death, her trust disposition and settlement was found with her married name deleted from her signature, and her maiden name substituted in her own hand. The alterations had not been witnessed or acknowledged but the parties agreed that the alterations had not been made with the intention of revoking the settlement. In a special case, it was held that the deed was validly authenticated, the deletion of the original signature falling to be ignored in respect that it had not been made with the intention of revoking the trust disposition and settlement.

Subscription: signature on erasure

3.75 While the testator's signature should not, as a matter of practice, be written on an erasure, this need not invalidate the testamentary writing, if it is otherwise *ex facie* validly executed: the burden of proof lies on the objector to prove either that the signature on erasure was not genuine, or that it was not that signature which the witnesses attested to, but the one erased.[42]

Subscription: the form of the signature

3.76 Prior to the Requirements of Writing (Scotland) Act 1995 coming into force, the forms of signature specified in The Lyon King of Arms Act 1672[43] had long been treated as the norm:

> "it is onlie allowed for Noblemen . . . to subscrive by their titles And that all others shall subscrive their Christned names, or the initiall letter therof with there Sirnames and may if they please adject the designations of their Lands prefixing the word Of to the saids designations".

---

[40] *Ibid*.

[41] 1936 S.C. 831.

[42] *Brown* v. *Duncan* (1888) 15 R. 511; *cf.* the *obiter dicta* of Lord Shaw of Dunfermline in *Walker* v. *Whitwell*, 1916 S.C. (H.L.) 75 at p. 87 that a signature on erasure is an informality of execution, which could be rectified under s. 39 of the Conveyancing (Scotland) Act 1874.

[43] Act of 1672 (c. 47 or c. 21).

Consequently, the accepted practice was that a commoner signing his normal signature, used at least some part of his forename, and his complete surname.[44] Subscriptions contrary to
the provisions of the 1672 Act are not invalid—for instance, the
son of a peer, who was not himself a nobleman, might have
subscribed the courtesy title by which he was known, and persons may sign with an abbreviation of their name (*e.g.* "Bill"
for William), which was neither their christian name, nor an
initial letter thereof.[45] Further, the wife of a peer, who was not
a peeress in her own right , would have validly subscribed her
husband's title prefixed by her own christian name, or if she
was a peeress in her own right, her own title prefixed by her
christian name.[46] It is probably also the case that an attested
testamentary writing would be upheld as probative where the
deceased had signed his surname only, for this approach has
been taken in cases involving deeds relating to heritage.[47]

3.77   An incomplete signature (as where the testator signs her forename but only the first few letters of her surname), even
although attested, is ineffective.[48] The case reports indicate that
signature by mark is not sufficient,[49] even if combined with a
partial signature,[50] but more recently, it has been argued that a
mark may constitute a valid subscription where it can be shown
that this was the deceased's normal method of subscription.[51]
Where an executor seeks to be confirmed on the basis of a testamentary writing executed by mark, he must apply to the sheriff
for special warrant to the sheriff clerk to issue confirmation.

3.78   A married woman might use her maiden surname[52] and even
if she signed using her maiden surname as if it were a middle
name (which is not strictly correct), the signature will be
accepted.[53]

---

[44] Bell *Lectures* (3rd ed.) p. 37; Burns *Conveyancing Practice According To the Law
of Scotland* (4th ed.), p. 5; Dickson *Evidence* (3rd ed.) 668, 670–1; Macdonald
Conveyancing Manual 2–19; Walker and Walker, *Evidence*, para. 179(d); Halliday,
Conveyancing Law and Practice in Scotland, Vol I, para. 3–05.

[45] *Per* Lord Dervaird in *American Express Europe Ltd.* v. *Royal Bank of Scotland
plc (No. 2)*, 1989 S.L.T. 650 at p. 654F.

[46] A.M. Bell, *Lectures on Conveyancing* (3rd ed.), p. 37.

[47] *Gordon* v. *Murray* (1765) Mor. 16818; *Earl of Traquair* v. *Gibson* (1724) Mor.
16809 and *American Express Europe Ltd.* v. *Royal Bank of Scotland plc (No. 2)*, 1989
S.L.T. 650.

[48] *Donald* v. *McGregor's Exrs.*, 1926 S.L.T. 103.

[49] *Crosbie* v. *Wilson* (1865) 3 M. 870.

[50] *Donald* v. *McGregor's Exrs.* 1926 S.L.T. 103.

[51] Meston, M.C. and Cusine, D.J., "Execution of Deeds by a Mark". (1993) 38
J.L.S.S. 270.

[52] *Dunlop* v. *Greenlees' Trs.* (1863) 2 M. 1.

[53] *Grieve's Trs.* v. *Japp's Trs.*, 1917 1 S.L.T. 70 (Mrs Joan Colville or Brown
executed a disposition signing "Joan Colville Brown" but a petition under s. 39
of the 1874 Act was dismissed as unnecessary.)

The use of familiar names

3.79　.It has been seen that, under The Lyon King of Arms Act 1672,[54] a commoner's subscription must include his full surname. However, in the case of a holograph testamentary writing which takes the form of a letter, the courts have been prepared to accept, as a valid subscription, a signature without a surname — but the christian name, or the abbreviated or familiar form of it used, must be the normal form adopted by the testator in signing documents of the kind under consideration.[55] Such an approach is unlikely to be adopted in the case of a testamentary writing professionally prepared.[56]

3.80　The courts have also been called upon to determine whether the word "mum" or "mother" can constitute a valid subscription of a testamentary writing, and they will do this by considering all the surrounding facts. In *Pentland* v. *Pentland's Trustees*,[57] a holograph letter which ended with the words "your loving mother" was held not to be validly signed, in respect that the words were descriptive only.

3.81　In contrast, in *Rhodes* v. *Peterson*,[58] a holograph letter beginning "Dearest Dorothy" and ending "lots of love, Mum" was held to have been validly subscribed, when it was proved that this was how the deceased had signed letters to her daughter Dorothy — even although she signed "Evie" in letters to her sons.

3.82　Superficially, these cases appear difficult to reconcile, but it has been observed that the letter in *Pentland's* case was not sent through the post, but was found in the deceased's repositories, after her death.[59] This, combined with the lay-out and the mode of expression of the concluding words, may have influenced the decision.[60]

The use of initials

3.83　Prior to the Requirements of Writing (Scotland) Act 1995 coming into force, there .was doubt as to whether a testator might validly sign using only initials.[61] If the testator was able to sign, and put his initials only on some pages, the testamentary writing will not be probative under the 1696 Act,[62] although the writing could be set up under section 39 of the Conveyancing (Scotland) Act 1874 (see paras. 19.35 *et seq.*). Lord President Inglis stated:

---

[54] Act of 1672 (c. 47 or c. 21).
[55] *Draper* v. *Thomason*, 1954 S.C. 136.
[56] Walker and Walker, *The Law of Evidence in Scotland*, para. 177.
[57] (1908) 46 S.L.R. 291.
[58] 1972 S.L.T. 98.
[59] Lord Hunter in *Rhodes* v. *Peterson*, 1972 S.L.T. 98 at p. 100.
[60] *Per* Lord Ashmore in *Donald* v. *McGregor's Exrs.*, 1926 S.L.T. 103 at p. 104.
[61] See the discussion in Walker and Walker, *Evidence*, para. 179(d), n. 56.
[62] *Gardner* v. *Lucas* (1878) 5 R. (H.L.) 105.

"I think the [1696] Statute requires, as a condition of the writ being valid, that each page shall be signed. . . . I do not think that a marking by initials is signing in the ordinary sense of the term. It may be that a person who does not sign his name in full, and perhaps cannot sign his name in full, but is in use to subscribe deeds by initials, may be held sufficiently to sign a deed if he appends his initials according to his custom".[63]

Indeed, in *Speirs* v. *Home Speirs*,[64] the testator signed by initials only, and the testamentary writing received effect where affidavit evidence was led that this was the testator's normal method of signing.

3.84   The Outer House decision of *Lowrie's Judicial Factor* v. *McMillan's Exx.*[65] may indicate that today the courts will be less restrictive in accepting initials as being a valid signature. In *Lowrie*, the deceased signed by initials a letter which contained testamentary provisions. She had previously signed a formal will with a full signature, and there was no evidence that she normally signed by initials. However, Lord Dunpark observed that the deceased had never previously subscribed a testamentary letter to anyone, and as he considered that there was evidence of concluded testamentary intent, he held that there was a valid execution.

3.85   Where the deceased subscribed a holograph letter, below which she wrote in pencil a post-script which was authenticated only by her initials, Lord Mackintosh expressed the view that as the paper was elsewhere signed, the deceased's initials were sufficient authentication. Accordingly, the post-script was held to be a valid codicil.[66]

Subscription of a mutual will

3.86   The signatures of both (or all) parties to a mutual will should be witnessed. In a case involving a mutual will of two spouses, the husband signed the will in the presence of two witnesses, and the wife signed without witnesses. The will was held as valid *vis a vis* the husband's estate.[67]

---

[63] *Gardner* v. *Lucas* (1878) 5 R. 638 at p. 645, approved in *Gardner* v. *Lucas* (1878) 5 R. (H.L.) 105 per Lord Chancellor Cairns at p.107 and Lord O'Hagan at p. 115.

[64] (1879) 6 R. 1359.

[65] 1972 S.L.T. 159.

[66] *Manson* v. *Edinburgh Royal Institution*, 1948 S.L.T. 196.

[67] *Millar* v. *Birrell* (1876) 4 R. 87.

ATTESTED TESTAMENTARY WRITINGS

Each page to be subscribed

3.87   A testamentary writing executed before August 1, 1995 will be probative if it is subscribed by the testator on each page,[68] in the presence of two subscribing witnesses. If the testator has failed to subscribe all pages, this is an informality of execution which may be remedied by proof under section 39 of the Conveyancing (Scotland) Act 1874 (discussed at para. 19.44).

3.87A   A testamentary writing written on one sheet of paper which is folded to make, say, four pages is not treated as being written "bookwise" within the meaning of The Deeds Act 1696[68a] and will be probative if it is signed on the last page only before two witnesses.[68b] Commissary practice is to grant confirmation to the executors nominated in such a testamentary writing without further proof. It is important to check that when such a testamentary writing has been registered in the Books of Council and Session (or in the sheriff court books) for preservation, the returned extract bears the appropriate docquet. In such cases, the testator's signature and those of the two witnesses[68c] need not be on the same page as the final testamentary provision, provided that there is a link between the two pages.

The number of witnesses

3.88   The Subscription of Deeds Acts 1540[69] and 1681[70] "do not prescribe the number of witnesses necessary in the case of a deed executed by the subscription of the party himself; the rule that two instrumentary witnesses are necessary in such a case flows from the common Law of Scotland, which requires the evidence of two witnesses to prove a fact".[71] Provided that a testamentary writing is subscribed by the testator and by two witnesses, it may be set up as valid in terms of section 39 of the Conveyancing (Scotland) Act 1924 (see paras. 19.35 *et seq.*).

---

[68] The Deeds Act 1696 (c. 15) and Conveyancing and Feudal Reform (Scotland) Act 1970 (c. 35), s. 44(2).

[68a] .Act of 1696 (c. 15); *Robertson* v. *Ker* (1742) Mor. 16,955; *Smith* v. *Bank of Scotland* (1824) 2 Shaw's App. 265; *Baird's Trs.* v. *Baird*, 1955 S.C. 286.

[68b] See *Ferguson, Petr.*, 1959 S.C. 56; and *McNeill* v. *McNeil*, 1973 S.L.T. (Sh. Ct.) 16. discussed at paras. 3.45 and 3.47.

[68c] The requirement of two witnesses has been abolished with effect from August 1, 1995 by the Requirements of Writing (Scotland) Act 1995.

[69] Act of 1540 (c. 37 or c. 117).

[70] The Subscription of Deeds Act 1681 (c. 5), as amended by Debtors (Scotland) Act 1987 (c. 18), s. 108 and Sched. 8.

[71] *Per* Lord Mackintosh in *Ferguson, Petr*, 1959 S.C. 56 at p. 61.

Competent witnesses

Age

3.89 Since September 25, 1991, an individual of or over the age of sixteen years can act as a witness.[72] Prior to September 25, 1991, a child under the age of 14 years (whether male or female) could not act as a witness.[73]

Incapacity

3.90 A blind person[74] or a person who is *non compos mentis* is not a competent witness.

Personal interest

3.91 While it is not good practice for a witness of a deed to be someone with an interest under the deed (such as a named beneficiary,[75] a trustee,[76] or the other testator in the case of a mutual will), it is not a fundamental objection to the validity of the execution that a witness had an interest under the deed. However, since the fact that a witness has an interest may be material if the will is challenged on other grounds (for instance, facility and circumvention) the practice should be avoided. An individual may, but should not, act as a witness to his or her spouse's signature.[77]

Witness must have known the testator

3.92 In the case of a deed executed prior to August 1, 1995, no one may witness a party's signature "unless he then know that party",[78] but a reliable introduction by name is all that was necessary.[79]

Witnesses must have had a mandate from granter

3.93 The testator was required to sign in the presence of his witnesses or acknowledge his signature to them, though the ack-

---

[72] Age of Legal Capacity Act 1991 (c. 50), s. 1(1) (a) and s. 9.

[73] *Davidson* v. *Charteris* (1738) Mor. 16899; Titles to Land Consolidation (Scotland) Act 1868 (31 & 32 Vict. c. 101), s. 139.

[74] *Cuningham* v. *Spence* (1824) 3 S. 205.

[75] *Grahame* v. *Marquis of Montrose* (1685) Mor. 16887; *Ingram* v. *Steinson* (1801) Mor. App. 1 Writ, No. 2; *Simsons* v. *Simsons* (1883) 10 R. 1247.

[76] *Mitchell* v. *Miller* (1742) Mor. 16900; *Ingram* v. *Steinson, supra.*

[77] But see *obiter dicta* by Lord Johnston in *Brownlee* v. *Robb*, 1907 S.C. 1302 at p. 1310 where he opined that where the testator left his estate to his wife, attestation by the wife "would have been more than doubtful".

[78] The Subscription of Deeds Act 1681 (c. 5) as amended by Debtors (Scotland) Act 1987 (c. 18), s. 108 and Sched. 8.

[79] *Brock* v. *Brock*, 1908 S.C. 964.

nowledgment need not have been in words.[80] A party who was a casual, accidental or concealed witness to the execution could not competently act as a witness.[81] The witnesses must have been legitimately present and the testator must have requested—either expressly or impliedly—a party to act as attesting witness.[82]

The function of the witnesses

3.94 The witnesses did not have any concern with the contents of the deed,[83] but they must have seen the testator sign, or alternatively have heard him acknowledge his signature at the time they subscribed.[84] The will might have been subscribed before one witness and acknowledged to the other,[85] or acknowledged to both at different times,[86] although it has been recommended that both witnesses should have been present when the deed was signed or the testator acknowledged his signature.[87] The acknowledgement need not have been in words.[88]

3.95 While a deed which bears to have been executed by the testator prior to August 1, 1995in the presence of two witnesses is probative, it may be challenged, but the burden of proof is on the challenger.[89] Where an action of reduction is raised, the court will hear the evidence of the attesting witnesses as to whether the testator signed in their presence or acknowledged his signature to them. The witnesses—if their overall testimony is to be believed—must be viewed as trustworthy by the court, and their evidence must be corroborated (see para. 19.75).[90]

Must the witness have signed at the time of subscription?

3.96 A witness to a signature cannot subscribe after the testator's

---

[80] *Cumming* v. *Skeoch's Trs.* (1879) 6 R. 963.

[81] *Obiter, per* Lord Justice-Clerk Moncrieff in *Tener's Trs.* v. *Tener's Trs.* (1879) 6 R. 1111 at p. 1115.

[82] *Per* Lord Shaw of Dunfermline in *Walker* v. *Whitwell*, 1916 S.C. (H.L.) 75 at pp. 90 and 91.

[83] *Ormistoun* v. *Hamilton* (1708) Mor. 16890.

[84] The Subscription of Deeds Act 1681 (c. 5) as amended by Debtors (Scotland) Act 1987 (c. 18), s. 108 and Sched. 8.

[85] *e.g., Forrest* v. *Low's Trs.*, 1907 S.C. 1240; *Cumming* v. *Skeoch's Trs.* (1879) 6 R. 540.

[86] *Hogg* v. *Campbell* (1864) 2 M. 848.

[87] Halliday, *Conveyancing Law and Practice in Scotland*, para. 3–14.

[88] *Cumming* v. *Skeoch's Trs.*, *supra.*

[89] *Per* Lord Low in *Young* v. *Paton*, 1910 S.C. 63 at p. 66.

[90] *Per* Lord Moncrieff in *McArthur* v. *McArthur's Trs.*, 1931 S.L.T. 463.

death,[91] for the witness's mandate to act as witness falls with the testator's death.

3.97   In some early decisions, the court sustained deeds as validly executed where the "witnesses" had adhibited their signatures some time after the granters had executed the deeds,[92] but it has been suggested that the *ratio* of these decisions is now questionable.[93]

3.98   The function of the witness to a signature is to connect the signature with the granter but the function of a witness to a notarial execution is to hear and see every step of the formalities: "their signing as witnesses is itself a part of the formalities necessary to constitute notarial execution".[94] Accordingly, the witness to a notarial execution must sign at the time of the notarial execution (see further paras. 3.140 *et seq.*).

The form of a witness's signature

3.99   It is accepted practice that a witness's signature effected prior to August 1, 1995 and which conforms to the requirements of the Lyon King of Arms Act 1672[95] is valid:

> "it is onlie allowed for Noblemen and Bishopes to subscrive by their titles; And that all others shall subscrive their Christned names, or the initiall letter therof with there Sirnames, and may, if they please adject the designations of their Lands prefixing the word Of to the saids designations".

Although a commoner may subscribe a deed by writing his surname, without a christian name or initial, or even his initials alone (see paras. 3.83–3.85), the case reports would suggest that something more was required of a witness. Deeds have been struck down because a witness subscribed using only initials[96]

---

[91] *Brownlee* v. *Robb*, 1907 S.C. 1302; *Walker* v. *Whitwell*, 1916 S.C. (H.L.) 75.

[92] *Frank* v. *Frank* (1795) Mor. 16824 (where the witnesses signed within a quarter of an hour of the granter, the deed having been out of their sight in the interim); *Stewart* v. *Burns* (1877) 4 R. 427 (where parties present when the deed was signed were not then asked to act as witnesses, but signed as witnesses some four months later); *Thomson* v. *Clarkson's Trs.* (1892) 20 R. 59 (granter acknowledged his signature to witnesses, who took deed back to their office and signed three-quarters of an hour later; *Tener's Trs.* v. *Tener's Trs.* (1879) 6 R. 1111 (interval of over two years—overruled by the decision in *Walker* v. *Whitwell*, 1916 S.C. (H.L.) 75, in that the testator in *Tener's Trs.* had died within the two year period).

[93] Halliday, *Conveyancing Law and Practice in Scotland*, para. 3–15.

[94] Per Lord Reid in *Hynd's Tr.* v. *Hynd's Trs.*, 1955 S.C. (H.L.) 1 at p. 19.

[95] Act of 1672 (c. 47 or c. 21); see for example Sheriff-substitute Kermack in *Allan and Crichton, Petrs.*, 1933 S.L.T. (Sh. Ct.) 2.

[96] *Meek* v. *Dunlop* (1707) Mor. 16806.

or surname,[97] but including the designation "Miss" in the signature consisting of a christian name or initial and surname would seem to be an informality of execution, which could be remedied by a petition under section 39 of the Conveyancing (Scotland) Act 1874.[98]

3.100   It is probably the case that a witness's signature need not have been legible.[99]

3.101   A witness could not subscribe by mark.[1]

3.102   A witness who was a married woman might have used her maiden surname and she might even have signed using her maiden surname as if it were a middle name.[2]

3.103   The witness normally added the word "witness" after his signature, although the word might competently have been inserted by someone else. The witness might also have appended his designation to his signature—or it might have been inserted by someone else or the details included in the testing clause.[3]

Position of the witnesses' signatures

3.104   The signatures of the witnesses should normally be below or beside the testator's signature. Exceptionally, a deed may be held to be validly executed if the witnesses signed on a page subsequent to that on which the testator signed, provided that there is a sufficient link between the two. In *Ferguson, Petitioner*,[4] a sheet of paper had been folded in two so as to form four pages. The first page contained the entire testamentary matter in the will and beneath it, the testator's signature, and part of a docket of attestation in English style. The rest of the docket and the signatures of the two witnesses were contained on the third page. The will was held to be validly executed.

---

[97] *Allan and Crichton, Petrs.*, 1933 S.L.T. (Sh. Ct.) 2 (where a witness signed "Mrs Bernard")—a decision criticised by Lord Dervaird in *American Express Europe Ltd.* v. *Royal Bank of Scotland plc. (No. 2)*, 1989 S.L.T. 650 at pp. 652I and 654K; *cf. Ferguson, Petr,*, 1959 S.C. 56 (where no challenge was made where a witness signed "Mme Pion Roux", "Pion Roux" being in all likelihood a double surname).

[98] See para. 19.35 *et seq.*

[99] *Cf. Stirling Stuart* v. *Stirling Crawfurd's Trs.* (1885) 12 R. 610 (where a testator's illegible signature was upheld).

[1] *Meek* v. *Dunlop* (1707) Mor. 16806.

[2] *Nisbet, Petr.* (1897) 24 R. 411 (where a witness, Dorothea Stewart or Kerr signed "Dorothea S. Kerr").

[3] Conveyancing (Scotland) Act 1874 (37 & 38 Vict. c. 94), s. 38.

[4] 1959 S.C. 56.

THE TESTING CLAUSE

The testing clause

3.105 The testing clause might be filled up at any stage—long after the signing, and even after the death of the testator or a witness[5] provided that the testamentary writing has not been recorded in any register for preservation or founded on in judgment,[6] though it may be competently completed while the deed is lodged in a court process:[7] "there is nothing in the law of Scotland requiring the testing clause to be filled up within a specified period".[8]

3.106 The testing clause should specify "whatever is directly connected with the subscription and authentication of the deed".[9] Under Scots law, it has never been essential to specify the place and date of signing[10] or the witnesses' names in a testing clause. In a deed executed prior to August 1, 1995, it is now customary to find the following information inserted:

1. the number of pages;

2. the date of execution: the date of execution can be critical in applying the Wills Act 1963, in determining whether the deceased had testamentary capacity at the time of execution, in determining whether a witness had attained the age at which he was a competent witness, and in determining which, of a number of documents, is the last testamentary writing of the deceased;

3. the place of execution—the place of execution can be critical in applying the Wills Act 1963;

4. any erasures (the correction of errors) in the testamentary writing;

5. any marginal additions or interlineations to the testamentary writing;

6. any blanks in the testamentary writing filled up before subscription;

---

[5] *Per* Lord Dunedin in *Walker* v. *Whitwell*, 1916 S.C. (H.L.) 75 at p. 80.
[6] Conveyancing (Scotland) Act 1874 (37 & 38 Vict. c. 94), s. 38.
[7] *Millar* v. *Birrell* (1876) 4 R. 87.
[8] *Per* Lord Alloway in *Blair* v. *Earl of Galloway* (1827) 6 S. 51 at p. 57, a case where the testing clause was filled up after 32 years.
[9] *Per* Lord Deas in *Smiths* v. *Chambers' Trs.* (1877) 5 R. 97 at pp. 109–110.
[10] Erskine, *Inst.* 3.2.18; *per* Lord Anderson in *Cairney* v. *Macgregor's Trs.*, 1916 1 S.L.T. 357 at p. 359.

7. the names[11] and designations of the witnesses, but this information may instead follow their signatures, and may be inserted by anyone. It is customary to specify the witness's occupation and home (or business) address, but some old reports indicate that it is probably sufficient to design a witness as "AB, doctor of medicine," or "CD, employee of Captain EF" without further description.[12] Merely describing a witness as "indweller in Edinburgh" is insufficient;[13] and

8. any discrepancy between the signature and the full name (as given in the deed or testing clause) of the testator or the witnesses.

3.107 Any mention or assertion made in the testing clause is not conclusive, but the onus of proof is on the challenger.[14]

3.108 In applying the statutes on attestation of deeds, the testing clause is considered to be an integral part of the deed.[15] A testator subscribed a deed, consisting of two loose sheets of paper, only on the second sheet. Apart from his signature, the second sheet contained only the testing clause and the signatures of the witnesses. It was held to be a deed written on two pages, where only the second page was subscribed by the testator, and therefore had to be set up by a petition under section 39 of the Conveyancing (Scotland) Act 1874.[16]

The testing clause should not incorporate testamentary provisions

3.109 It is now clearly established that in a professionally prepared testamentary writing, any part of the testing clause which purports to alter an earlier part of the deed is ineffective.[17] This

---

[11] The full name of a witness need not be inserted provided that when the testing clause is read along with the signature, the witness is sufficiently identified (*McDougall* v. *McDougall* (1875) 2 R. 814, where the surname of a witness in the testing clause was written on erasure).

[12] *Innes* v. *Trs. of Innes* (1800) Hume 911; *cf. Reid* v. *Brown* (1700) noted in *Rule* v. *Craig* (1712) Mor. 16920, *Duncan* v. *Scrimgeour* (1706) Mor. 16914 and *Jamieson* v. *Sheriff* (1708) Mor. 16916 where the designation did not include a place, and the lack was supplied by reference to the place of execution.

[13] *Bailie* v. *Somervel* (1672) Mor. 16913; *Grant* v. *Keir* (1698) Mor. 16913.

[14] *Young* v. *Paton*, 1910 S.C. 63 where the testing clause declared that the execution was at Glasgow, but it was proved to have taken place at Thorntonhall.

[15] *Per* Lord Chancellor Halsbury in *Blair* v. *Assets Co.* (1896) 23 R. (H.L.) 36 at p. 44.

[16] *Bogie's Exr.* v. *Bogie*, 1953 S.L.T. (Sh. Ct.) 32.

[17] *Smiths* v. *Chambers' Trs.* (1877) 5 R. 97, (1878) 5 R. (H.L.) 151; decision of Court of Session approved in *Blair* v. *Assets Co., supra.*

approach is sound since the standard practice is that when the testator signs the deed, there is a large blank between "In Witness Whereof" and where he is asked to sign. Only after he has signed the deed is the testing clause inserted in the blank. Indeed, the testator need never see what is filled up by way of a testing clause after he has executed the deed.

3.110   In *Smiths* v. *Chambers' Trustees*,[18] the testing clause read "In Witness Whereof I have subscribed these presents . . . (but with and under this express provision and declaration, *viz.*, that the whole of the legacies, annuity, and provisions made and provided by this disposition and deed of settlement shall be strictly alimentary, and shall not be arrestable or attachable for the debts or deeds of the persons in whose favour the same are conceived, or any of them, nor be subject or liable to the diligence of their creditors), at St Andrews on . . ." and thereafter continued as normal. The Court of Session held that the portion of the testing clause inserted between the brackets was invalid.

3.111   In *Gibson's Trustees* v. *Lamb*,[19] the testator wrote after the words "In Witness Whereof" in a codicil "This codicil shall not take effect until after the death of my two sisters". The codicil was then signed before two witnesses and a formal testing clause beginning "In Witness Whereof" was inserted. Lord Fleming decided that effect should be given to the holograph clause inserted after the first "In Witness Whereof", on the grounds that the testing clause in fact began with the second "In Witness Whereof" and that what preceded that phrase was not part of the testing clause. It may also be that the court was prepared to take a less strict approach because the addition was holograph of the testator.

HOLOGRAPH TESTAMENTARY WRITINGS

Holograph testamentary writings

Must be subscribed

3.112
"Holograph writs, subscribed, are unquestionably the strongest probation by writ, and least imitable. But if they are not subscribed, they are understood to be incomplete acts from which the party hath resiled".[20]

A testamentary writing is valid by the law of Scotland if it is holograph of the testator and subscribed by him prior to August

---

[18] (1877) 5 R. 97.
[19] 1931 S.L.T. 22.
[20] Stair, IV.xlii.6.

1, 1995: it does not require to be attested by witnesses, and the Subscription of Deeds Act 1681[21] does not apply.[22] Indeed, a subscribed holograph testamentary writing dated prior to August 1, 1995, which bears to have been attested by two witnesses, may still be upheld as valid even where it is admitted that the witnesses did not see the deceased sign, or hear him acknowledge his signature.[23] A holograph testamentary writing which is not subscribed may be validated by a docquet on the backing or on the envelope which contained it (see paras. 3.69 and 3.70).

Essential parts to be holograph

3.113   In order to enjoy the status of being a holograph writing, it is not essential that the whole be written by the testator: if the substantial or essential parts[24] are written by him, the rest may be written by another, or printed, typed or otherwise produced. The essential parts comprise "words indicating an intention to bequeath . . . the beneficiaries must be sufficiently identified, and the subjects of the bequests sufficiently described".[25] The use of the word "to" (preceding a person's name and an item or sum of money) does not, on its own, indicate an intention to bequeath (it may also indicate a gift *inter vivos*), but when combined with the use of the word "residue"[26] or "remainder",[27] it shows testamentary intention. Formal wording is not essential. In the view of Lord President Inglis, "I do not think it matters how inelegant, or how imperfect grammatically a testator's language may be, if it can fairly be construed to mean that he bequeaths certain sums of money to certain individuals, sufficiently designed in the writing itself".[28] A holograph appointment of executors is not an essential: "The nomination of executors is no longer an essential of a testamentary writing. In the absence of such, an executor-dative will be appointed".[29]

Holograph writing improbative

3.114   A holograph testamentary writing executed before August 1,

---

[21] Act of 1681 (c. 5).

[22] McLaren, *Wills and Succession*, (3rd ed.), Vol I, para. 513; *obiter dicta* of Lord McLaren in the dissenting judgment in *Macdonald* v. *Cuthbertson* (1890) 18 R. 101 at p. 107, approved by Lord Hunter in *McBeath's Trs.* v. *McBeath*, 1935 S.C. 471 at pp. 482–483.

[23] *Yeats* v. *Yeats' Trs.* (1833) 11 S. 915; *Harley* v. *Harley's Exr.*, 1957 S.L.T. (Sh. Ct.) 17.

[24] Bell, *Principles*, s. 20; *Laurie* v. *Laurie* (1859) 21 D. 240.

[25] *Per* Lord Guthrie in *Gillies* v. *Glasgow Royal Infirmary*, 1960 S.C. 438 at p. 443.

[26] *Per* Lord President Clyde in *Gillies* v. *Glasgow Royal Infirmary*, *supra*, at p. 442.

[27] *Ayrshire Hospice, Petrs*, 1993 S.L.T. (Sh. Ct.) 75 at p. 76.

[28] *Colvin* v. *Hutchison* (1885) 12 R. 947 at p. 955.

[29] *Per* Lord Jamieson in *Bridgeford's Exr.* v. *Bridgeford*, 1948 S.C. 416 at p. 439.

1995 is not probative, and must be set up before confirmation can be obtained (see paras. 3.120–3.124). However, once confirmation has been obtained, it will be viewed as probative or validly executed for the purposes of determining the ownership of any property passing under it.[30]

Mutual Wills holograph of one party

3.115   A mutual will by two parties, in the handwriting of one, but subscribed by both prior to August 1, 1995, though not attested, is valid as regards the writer's estate.[31] As far as the other person's estate is concerned, the will has no effect, unless he had adopted it as holograph.[32] A mutual will is effective as regards the estate of either party if signed in duplicate prior to August 1, 1995, each copy being in the handwriting of one of the parties and signed by both.[33]

Holograph wills on more than one sheet

3.116   There is no rule of law which requires that a holograph testamentary writing, consisting of more than one sheet, is signed anywhere except at the end of the document, provided that either the sheets are attached together, or it can otherwise be shown that they are part of one writing.

3.117   In *Cranston, Petr.*,[34] the deceased left a holograph writing consisting of nine pages, written bookwise on three sheets of paper, which were not stitched together. The writing was dated, but signed only on the last page. Persons named therein as trustees and executors presented a petition for warrant to issue confirmation in their favour. They averred that the deed had been found in the testator's repositories exactly as it was produced with the petition. It was held that there was no objection on the grounds that the deed had not been signed on all sheets, but only on the last page. It was observed that there might be "cases of detached documents not necessarily shewing themselves to be parts of one writing, and therefore not necessarily authenticated by the signature at the end". In such cases, proof would be required "that they formed one writing, including evidence, it may be, as to when the document or its alleged different parts were formed, as bearing on the question whether the detached parts did form one whole". In *Cranston*, the pages contained "inherent evidence that they form one consecutive deed by their external appearance, and the continuity of the

---

[30] Succession (Scotland) Act 1964 (c. 41), s. 32(1) and (2) (a) as substituted by Requirements of Writing (Scotland) Act 1995 (c. 7), s. (14), Sched 4, para. 40.
[31] *McMillan* v. *McMillan* (1850) 13 D. 187.
[32] *Kirk*, Feb. 21, 1902, unreported.
[33] *Jarvie*, Oct. 6, 1887, unreported.
[34] (1890) 17 R. 410; followed in *Lorimer's Exrs.* v. *Hird* , 1959 S.L.T. (Notes) 8.

sentences at the end of each sheet and the beginning of the next. They are all in the same handwriting".[35]

3.118   Consequently, a holograph testamentary writing, which is subscribed prior to August 1, 1995 on the final page, does not require to be signed on each page or sheet to entitle it to confirmation without proof that it formed one writing, provided that the integrity of the writing can be inferred from the document. When confirmation is sought on the basis of a holograph testamentary writing, written on more than one sheet, but subscribed prior to August 1, 1995 only on the last one, it may be necessary to aver the facts which allow all the sheets to be treated as one document. Whether such an averment is necessary depends on the circumstances. If there is a clear linguistic and stylistic line between the various sheets, it is unlikely that there will be any difficulty. In doubtful cases, the executor will require to petition the sheriff for special warrant to issue confirmation. Then the sheriff would look for averments as to where the separate sheets were found after the deceased's death, such as "the sheets were found stapled together in a desk belonging to the deceased", or that they were "found folded together, in a sealed envelope addressed to XY":

Examples:

1.   After the deceased's death, two holograph writings were found in the same envelope in a locked desk. One commenced with the name of the testator, but was not signed, and the other commenced "also" and bore the deceased's initials in her own hand (which was proved to be her usual method of signing). The use of the word "also" showed that the testator intended the second sheet to be read along with some previous writing, and the circumstances were such as to connect the two pieces of paper, so that they were to be read as together forming the deceased's will.[36]

2.   Two unconnected sheets, on which a holograph will was written, were found together in the private desk of the deceased. One sheet, which commenced with the testator's full name, was not signed, but the other sheet was signed. On the second sheet there followed a holograph signed codicil. Warrant was granted to confirm the executor named therein.[37]

3.   A testatrix, who had executed a formal trust disposition

---

[35] *Per* Lord Shand in *Cranston, Petr.* (1890) 17 R. 410 at pp. 414–415.

[36] *Speirs* v. *Home Speirs* (1879) 6 R. 1359.

[37] *Brown*, May 29, 1884, unreported.

and settlement, left holograph writings of a later date
which consisted of three separate sheets of notepaper
containing testamentary instructions. On one side of the
first sheet, she appointed trustees and made certain specific legacies. On the other side, she signed, inserting the
words "and all other wills I revoke" below her signature
and above that of two witnesses. The second sheet contained the same arrangement of bequest, signature,
revocation clause and witnessing. The third sheet began
with the name of the testatrix's brother, and contained
directions as to her burial. Her signature then followed.
The sheets were placed in an envelope which was itself
placed in a leather case. Thereafter, the testatrix frequently referred to the leather case as containing her will.
It was held that the three sheets could not be regarded
as one document, subscribed by the signature on the third
sheet. As the clauses of revocation occurred after the signatures of the testatrix on the first and second sheets,
they were not subscribed and fell to be read *pro non
scriptis*.[38]

4.   In 1920, the testator formally executed a holograph will.
     He also left a holograph testamentary document con-
     sisting of three separate sheets which were not stitched
     together. The first and second sheets were subscribed by
     him and dated July 21, 1923. The third sheet was not
     signed (or dated). Passing from page to page, the wording
     made continuous sense, but there was clearly no sub-
     scription. A holograph docket, signed by the testator, and
     written on the back of the first page, sufficiently identified
     the three separate sheets as the testator's will, and
     expressly adopted it.[39]

5.   The deceased left five separate sheets of holograph writ-
     ing, which were found folded together. The first sheet
     started like a testamentary writing, and the second and
     third sheets were headed "continued will of Mary A M
     Lorimer". The writing on the third sheet ended half way
     down. The fourth sheet bore what appeared to be an
     incomplete testing clause. The fifth sheet bore the words:
     "My name in full is Mary Anne Murray Lorimer. I never
     use the (Anne) in my signature (sic) as you will perhaps
     notice. Mary Anne Murray Lorimer". As the pages had
     been found folded together, the court treated them as one
     holograph writing, which, by signing her full name on
     the fifth sheet, had been subscribed.[40]

[38] *Harvey's Trs.* v. *Carswell*, 1928 S.N. 45 and 96.
[39] *Campbell's Exr.* v. *Maudslay*, 1934 S.L.T. 420, discussed further at para. 3.70,
example 1.
[40] *Lorimer's Exrs.* v. *Hird*, 1959 S.L.T. (Notes) 8.

The date of a holograph testamentary writing

3.119 A holograph will is deemed to be executed on the date (if any) which it bears.[41]

Commissary practice regarding holograph testamentary writings

3.120 Where a testator bequeaths property in a holograph testamentary writing executed prior to August 1, 1995, confirmation will only be granted to the executors named therein if the court is satisfied by evidence consisting of an affidavit by each of two persons that the writing and signature on the document which is founded on are in the handwriting of the testator.[42] This provision applies whether the holograph testamentary writing comprises

1. The complete testamentary writing of the deceased; or

2. It is dated after (or is believed to be dated after) a probative testamentary writing and the holograph writing either contains a bequest, or alters or qualifies the nomination of executors.

3.121 Even after the enactment of section 21 of the Succession (Scotland) Act 1964, the practice of the courts in commissary cases has been to adopt the procedure set out in the Act of Sederunt of July 19, 1935 relating to affidavit evidence, even although it is expressly stated that the Act of Sederunt is not to apply in proceedings for confirmation of an executor nominate.[43]

3.122 The procedure now applied in relation to affidavit evidence is as follows:

1. Two or more affidavits must be put up to the sheriff from persons who depone that they are well acquainted with the handwriting and signature of the deceased. It is no objection that the deponents have a patrimonial interest in the deceased's estate.

2. Where the sheriff considers that the original affidavits are inadequate, he can require further affidavits to be lodged.

3. The affidavits may either be endorsed on the testament-

---

[41] Conveyancing (Scotland) Act 1874 (37 & 38 Vict. c. 94), s. 40.
[42] Succession (Scotland) Act 1964 (c. 41), s. 21(1) and (2) (inserted by Requirements of Writing (Scotland) Act 1995 (c. 7) 514(1) and Sched. 4, para. 38).
[43] Act of Sederunt (July 19, 1935) s. 2.

ary writing, or on an extract copy thereof, or may be set out in separate documents which must refer *in gremio* to the testamentary writing or extract copy, as applicable.

4. The affidavit must be taken before a magistrate, commissioner of oaths, justice of the peace, notary public or any commissioner whom the sheriff may appoint. The affidavit should not be taken before a notary public who is the pursuer's solicitor, or the partner or employee of such solicitor.

3.123 Section 21 of the Succession (Scotland) Act 1964 introduced a statutory requirement for affidavit evidence to be produced as to the handwriting of the testator in a holograph will, and the practice which existed prior to 1964 as to the form and content of the affidavits continued thereafter.

3.124 A style of affidavit is shown in Style 2.01.

Circumstances in which a defectively executed printed will form may receive effect as a holograph writing

3.125 Many stationers sell printed will forms, which are normally prepared on the assumption that the testator will fill in the blanks (naming legatees, beneficiaries etc) and will sign it in the presence of two witnesses. However, if the testator fails to follow the signing instructions correctly, or, if Scottish, he uses a foreign (*e.g.* English) will form and the execution cannot be validated under the provisions of the Wills Act 1963, the execution may be defective. In such a case, the beneficiaries may seek to argue that the holograph words show the testator's intention, and should receive effect. If such an approach is to be successful, it is essential that:

1. The testator has subscribed the printed will form; and

2. The holograph portion includes the date of execution, which is prior to August 1, 1995 (or it can be proved that it was executed before that date).

3. The testator has written out, in his own hand, the essentials of the will. "In order that a document should receive effect as a will, its testamentary character must be apparent, words indicating an intention to bequeath must be found in it, the beneficiaries must be sufficiently identified, and the subjects of the bequests sufficiently described".[44] The use of the word "to" (preceding a per-

---

[44] *Per* Lord Guthrie in *Gillies v. Glasgow Royal Infirmary*, 1960 S.C. 438 at p. 443.

son's name and an item or sum of money) does not, on its own, indicate an intention to bequeath (it may also indicate a gift *inter vivos*), but when combined with the use of the word "residue"[45] or "remainder",[46] it shows testamentary intention. A holograph appointment of executors is not an essential: "The nomination of executors is no longer an essential of a testamentary writing. In the absence of such, an executor-dative will be appointed":[47] In practice, where the names and designations of the general disponee, universal legatory, or residuary legatee are holograph, section 3 of the Executors (Scotland) Act 1900 may apply, and such persons may be confirmed in a nominate capacity.

3.125A   It is often a difficult question to determine whether the holograph portions in a subscribed (but improbative) printed will form are sufficient to found on for confirmation. Agents may wish to discuss the matter with the sheriff or commissary clerk concerned, but where there is doubt the matter should be resolved by an application to the sheriff for special authority to issue confirmation.

Examples:

1.   The testator had filled in the blanks in a printed will form (drawn in English style), by stating his own name and designation, the name of the executor, the names of beneficiaries, the words "equally and jointly, if one deceased to the survivor only", and the date. He subscribed, but there were no witnesses. The court held that there was no will, since the holograph words were not enough to give the essentials of a will—" words of gift or bequest, and words descriptive of the subject of the gift or bequest" were lacking.[48]

2.   The deceased's signature on a printed will form was not witnessed and consequently was improbative. The holograph portions included the appointment of executors, and a bequest of residue to his children. His wife's name was handwritten, and without actual words of bequest, there followed a holograph list of property. The court rejected all the printed parts, though the holograph parts, amounting to a will, received effect. The bequest to the widow also received effect, Lord President Dunedin

---

[45] *Per* Lord President Clyde in *Gillies* v. *Glasgow Royal Infirmary*, 1960 S.C. 438 at p. 442.

[46] *Ayrshire Hospice, Petrs.*, 1993 S.L.T. (Sh. Ct.) 75 at p. 76.

[47] *Per* Lord Jamieson in *Bridgeford's Exr.* v. *Bridgeford*, 1948 S.C. 416 at p. 439.

[48] *Per* Lord President Inglis in *Macdonald* v. *Cuthbertson* (1890) 18 R. 101 at p. 105.

likening it to a case "where a person leaves a document which is obviously testamentary and leaves a set of names with figures of money opposite them".[49] The expressed *ratio* is not wholly satisfactory, since there were no words of bequest in relation to the widow, but it should be noted that a bequest was reserved from the items listed underneath the widow's name, the list ending with the words "musical instruments, except the piano, which is to become the property of Isabella, my daughter".

3.   A domiciled Scotswoman, who was resident in Scotland, used a printed will form drawn in English style, and signed it before one witness. The holograph portions of the document sufficiently expressed the testamentary intentions of the writer (comprising instructions to pay all debts and for the disposal of what bore to be the whole of the testator's estate). The printed portions, including the appointment of executors (only their names and addresses were in the testator's handwriting) were non-essential and superfluous. The document was held to be a valid holograph will which disposed of the whole estate.[50]

4.   A domiciled Scotsman died leaving a printed will form in which he had filled up the blanks in his own writing. The deceased subscribed the form, but his signature was not attested by witnesses. The printed portions were purely formal, apart from the appointment of a trustee and executor. The holograph passages consisted of a list of names, preceded by the word "To", with sums of money written after the names, and the words "Residue divided into four equal parts, to" followed by another list of names. It was held that the will form was a valid testamentary writing.[51]

5.   The deceased left a will dated May 13, 1942, a codicil dated January 29, 1947, and a printed will form dated "11th August 47". The will form was subscribed by her but attested by only one witness. The deceased had completed the form by filling in her name and address and the words "to my daughter Enid", and "Revoke former will"—she did not specify in her own handwriting what was to go to her daughter. Since an essential part—what was to go to her daughter—was printed, the document was not a valid holograph will, and accordingly the 1942 will and 1947 codicil received effect.[52]

---

[49] *Carmichael's Exrs.* v. *Carmichael*, 1909 S.C. 1387 at p. 1389.
[50] *Bridgeford's Exr.* v. *Bridgeford*, 1948 S.C. 416.
[51] *Gillies* v. *Glasgow Royal Infirmary*, 1960 S.C. 438.
[52] *Tucker* v. *Canch's Tr.*, 1953 S.C. 270 discussed further at para. 3.162.

3.126   In some cases, the deceased may have failed to subscribe the printed will form, or alternatively it may be impossible to show that the words indicating the intention to bequeath (say) the residue—words of bequest, subject matter, and name of beneficiary—are holograph. In two such cases, the printed will form nevertheless received effect where it was shown that the deceased had impliedly adopted it.[53]

Defectively executed printed will form receiving effect as a holograph writing: effect of clauses revoking prior wills and appointing executors

3.127   In some of the earlier reported cases where the will form had not been properly executed by the testator, the issue was whether the holograph sections were sufficient to constitute testamentary bequests. In many printed will forms, there are two standard clauses which are never holograph: the clause revoking prior wills, and the clause appointing executors, where the testator is invited to insert the names and designations of the chosen individuals after the printed words of appointment. Whether these clauses are to be treated as effective turns on the question of whether the whole document is treated as valid if the essentials of a will are holograph or whether only the holograph sections are to receive effect.

3.128   The petitioners, in a petition for warrant to the commissary clerk to issue confirmation in their favour as executors-nominate of the deceased, founded on a will form, partly printed and partly holograph, and signed by the deceased, his signature not being witnessed. The holograph parts of the document effectively disposed of the whole estate, but the names of the petitioners had been inserted in the blank space in the form where the printed words provided for the appointment of executors. The sheriff, after examining the reported cases at some length, held that the appointment of executors was invalid in respect that the words of appointment were printed.[54]

3.129   By the same line of reasoning, a clause printed in a will form which revokes prior wills will not receive effect, if the testator's signature on the will form has not been witnessed. If the holograph portions of the printed will form do not dispose of the deceased's whole estate, then the part of the estate which is not thereby disposed of would pass under any prior testamentary writing (see para. 3.167), or, alternatively, would fall into intestacy.

---

[53] *Craik's Exx.* v. *Samson*, 1929 S.L.T. 592 and *Muir* v. *Muir*, 1950 S.L.T. (Notes) 40 discussed further at para. 3.71, examples 3 and 5.

[54] *Campbell, Petr.*, 1963 S.L.T. (Sh. Ct.) 10. Instead, the general disponee, universal legatory or residuary legatees could be confirmed under s. 3 of the Executors (Scotland) Act 1900 (63 & 64 Vict. c. 55) (see paras. 5.49, and 5.66 *et seq*) or an executor-dative appointed (see Chapter 6).

Can a testamentary writing typewritten by the deceased be treated as holograph?

3.130   The question has arisen as to whether "holograph" of the testator only means "in the testator's handwriting", or whether it can mean "typewritten by the testator".

3.131   The point first came before the court in *McBeath's Trustees* v. *McBeath*,[55] where the deceased signed (in his own handwriting) a typewritten testamentary document, and an addition thereto which was also typewritten, and which altered one of the provisions of the original document. Both the original document and the addition contained a typewritten statement that they were "typed by and accepted as holograph by" the deceased. It was agreed by the parties that for some time prior to his death, because his handwriting had become indecipherable owing to physical disability, the testator had invariably used a typewriter in order to communicate in writing. Further, it was agreed that the testator had typewritten the whole of the documents in question. Because the parties admitted that the document was typewritten by the testator, who had appended his handwritten signature to it, the Inner House (by a simple majority of four to three) held that the document could competently be treated as holograph of the testator, and so was given effect to. Without the admission, proof would have been required.

3.132   In *Chisholm* v. *Chisholm*,[56] the deceased left a signed typewritten testamentary document. Although it was averred that after he had bought a portable typewriter, he had typed all his correspondence, the Lord Ordinary held that the document was not holograph of the deceased. He distinguished the case from that of *McBeath's Trustees* because in *Chisholm* the writing did not contain a statement that it was typed by and accepted as holograph by the deceased.

3.133   In the light of these decisions, it seems unlikely that in the future any court will hold that a signed typewritten document is holograph of the deceased. First, the *ratio* of the majority of the judges in *McBeath's Trustees* was limited to the unusual circumstances of the case. Secondly, even if these or similar unusual circumstances were to re-occur, unless the parties admit that the deceased had typed the document, the problem of proving that the deceased had typed it is likely to be insurmountable.

NOTARIAL EXECUTION

Notarial execution under the 1924 Act

3.134   Prior to the enactment of the Requirements of Writing (Scotland)

---

[55] 1935 S.C. 471.
[56] 1949 S.C. 434.

Act 1995, section 18 of the Conveyancing (Scotland) Act 1924[57] was the most recently enacted statutory provision regulating notarial execution, although the earlier provisions[58] had not been repealed. Since it is unlikely that confirmation will now be sought in respect of an estate where the deceased's testamentary writing was notarially executed in terms of any of the earlier provisions, this part of the text will concentrate on the rules for notarial execution set out in the 1924 Act.

Persons who could, prior to August 1, 1995, notarially execute a testamentary writing under the 1924 Act

3.135   The notarial execution of a testamentary writing could, prior to August 1, 1995, be effected in terms of section 18 of the Conveyancing (Scotland) Act 1924[59] either by

1. a law agent, defined as meaning and including "writers to the signet, solicitors in the supreme courts, procurators in any sheriff court and every person entitled to practise as an agent in a court of law in Scotland";[60] a person may practice as a solicitor and appear in any court in Scotland if he has been admitted as a solicitor, his name is on the role, and he holds a practising certificate issued by the Council of the Law Society of Scotland (although this requirement is dispensed with in the case of solicitors to public departments),[61] but it would appear that a solicitor who did not possess a practising certificate at the time of the notarial execution might nevertheless effect a valid notarial execution.[62]

2. a notary public;

3. a justice of the peace; or

4. a parish minister acting in his own parish. A minister of the Church of Scotland who had been appointed to his charge without limit of time or for a period of years to officiate as

---

[57] (14 & 15 Geo. 5, c. 27), as amended by the Church of Scotland (Property and Endowments) Amendment Act 1933 (23 & 24 Geo. 5, c. 44), s. 13.

[58] The Subscription of Deeds Act 1540 (c. 117); the Subscription of Deeds Act 1579 (c. 80); Subscription of Deeds Act 1681 (c. 5); Conveyancing (Scotland) Act 1874 (37 & 38 Vict. c. 94), s. 41. All these provisions, have, along with s.18 of the Conveyancing (Scotland) Act 1924, been repealed by the Requirements of Writing (Scotland) Act 1995, s. 14(2) and Sched. 5, with effect from August 1, 1995.

[59] (14 & 15 Geo. 5, c. 27).

[60] Conveyancing (Scotland) Act 1924 (14 & 15 Geo. 5, c. 27), s. 2(6).

[61] Solicitors (Scotland) Act 1980 (c. 46), ss. 4 and 25.

[62] *Stephen* v. *Scott*, 1927 S.C. 85.

minister might also notarially execute a testamentary writing anywhere in any parish[63] in which his charge (or any part thereof) was situated.[64] His assistant and successor or his colleague and successor might do likewise.[65] In one unreported case, a notarially executed will had been notarised by "AB, assistant to XY, the parish minister". Since the individual concerned was found to be the minister's assistant only, and not also his successor, it was held that the deed had not been validly executed.

In paragraphs 3.136 *et seq.*, the word "notary" is used to refer to any person who prior to August 1, 1995, was entitled to notarially execute a testamentary writing.

Notary must not have had a personal interest in the testamentary writing

3.136   "Not only in Scotland but in many countries, the notary public has enjoyed from the earliest times a very privileged position as a public functionary, his privilege depending very properly upon his disinterested independence of the transactions which he records or the judicial acts which he performs".[66] Under Scots law, the consequence of a notary having a personal interest in a testamentary writing which he had notarially executed prior to August 1, 1995, is that the writing is null.[67]

Invalid notarial executions
3.137   Prior to August 1, 1995 a notary could not, in any circumstances, make a valid notarial execution of a testamentary writing which named him as a beneficiary; appointed him executor,[68] or trustee,[69] or law agent of the trust entitled to remuneration;[70] or which named one of his partners as a trustee and enabled the trustees to appoint one of their own number to be law agent to

---

[63] A certificate by a principal clerk of the General Assembly, stating the parish in which the charge is situated is conclusive (Church of Scotland (Property and Endowments) Amendment Act 1933 (23 & 24 Geo. 5, c. 44), s. 13(2)).

[64] *Ibid.* s. 13(1). (repealed by the Requirements of Writing (Scotland) Act 1995, s. 14(2) and Sched. 5).

[65] *Ibid.* s. 13(3) and (4). (repealed by the Requirements of Writing (Scotland) Act 1995, s. 14(2) and Sched. 5).

[66] *Per* Lord President Cooper in *Finlay* v. *Finlay's Trs.*, 1948 S.C. 16 at p. 24.

[67] For further discussion see *Stair Memorial Encyclopedia*, vol 6, para. 431.

[68] *Chisholm* v. *Macrae* (1903) 11 S.L.T. 416 (minister was notary and executor-nominate).

[69] *Ferrie* v. *Ferrie's Trs.* (1863) 1 M. 291 (although the trustees had power to appoint one of their own number as factor and law agent, and to allow them reasonable remuneration, the *ratio* of the decision was on the more general ground that the notary would acquire as trustee the management and possession of the estate).

[70] *Newstad* v. *Dansken*, 1918 1 S.L.T. 136.

the estate, able to charge the usual professional remuneration for his services.[71] However, a notarial execution by a partner of the nominated trustee is valid provided that the testamentary writing does not contain the usual clause authorising the remuneration of the trustee for professional services in connection with the estate,[72] or a clause allowing him to be law-agent.[73] It is irrelevant that the appointment of the notary as executor was made conditional on another person predeceasing the testator (as where the testator appoints "A, whom failing B" to be his executor): provided that the notary had a potential and contingent interest at the date of execution, the execution is invalid.[74] Where a testamentary writing appointed a solicitor as a trustee entitled to remuneration, a codicil thereto could not competently have been notarially executed by the solicitor's partner prior to August 1, 1995:[75] "as a person who had a financial interest in the administration of the estate, it appears that he had an interest in the alteration of the destination of the estate, which, at least theoretically, might have affected the amount of the fees ultimately accruing to his firm out of the administration".[76]

Unusual valid notarial executions

3.138 A notarial execution is valid if the notary was a salaried employee of the solicitor who was appointed executor in the testamentary writing.[77] Where the testamentary writing appoints an *ex officio* executor, a person might have validly notarised it if he might possibly (and indeed does) end up as the holder of that office.[78]

International aspects of notarial execution

3.139 A testamentary writing which has been notarially executed will be treated as valid if it is validly executed in terms of the Wills Act 1963, and, unless the law of the domicile is being applied (section 1), it matters not that the notarial execution would have been invalid under the law of the deceased's domicile. In one case, the will of a person domiciled in Scotland was notarially executed in England by the person appointed sole executor,

---

[71] *Wall's Exr's.* (1939) 55 Sh. Ct. Rep. 53 reported as *Trs. of XY*, 1939 S.L.T. (Sh. Ct.) 10; *Finlay* v. *Finlay's Trs.* 1948 S.C. 16; *Gorrie's Tr.* v. *Stiven's Ex.*, 1952 S.C. 1.

[72] *McIldowie* v. *Muller*, 1979 S.C. 271.

[73] Power to employ a law agent implies a power to remunerate him (*Lewis's Trs.* v. *Pirie*, 1912 S.C. 574.

[74] *Paterson's Exrs., Petrs.*, 1956 S.L.T. (Sh. Ct.) 44.

[75] *Crawford's Trs.* v. *Glasgow Royal Infirmary*, 1955 S.C. 367.

[76] *Per* Lord Wheatley in *Crawford's Trs.* v. *Glasgow Royal Infirmary*, 1955 S.C. 367 at p. 370.

[77] *Hynd's Tr.* v. *Hynd's Trs.*, 1955 S.C. (H.L.) 1 *per* Lord Morton of Henryton at pp. 13–14 and Lord Reid at p. 21; followed *Fraser's Exr., Petr.*, 1955 S.L.T. (Sh. Ct.) 35; see also *Aitken, Petr.*, 1965 S.L.T. (Sh. Ct.) 15.

[78] *Aitken, Petr., supra.*

who was entitled to charge professional fees for his services. Under Scots law, the will would have been void, but it was upheld as being validly executed under the laws of the place of execution. In such a case, it is an open question whether a Scottish court would hold that the executor was entitled to charge for his services.[79]

The formalities for a notarial execution under the 1924 Act

3.140   Under section 18(1) of the 1924 Act, as expounded by the Note to Schedule I[80] to that Act, any writing granted after August 1, 1924 but before August 1, 1995 could be notarially executed if the granter "from any cause, permanent or temporary, is blind or unable to write". The notary was required to read the deed over to the testator in the presence of two witnesses.[81] The testator had then to authorise the notary—by word or sign—to subscribe on his behalf. The notary was then required to write out, on the last page of the deed, a holograph docket in the form of Schedule I to the 1924 Act (or in any words to the like effect). He subscribed his own name below the docket[82] and wrote out his designation after his signature. In the case of a testamentary writing, he also signed his own name on any prior pages. The two witnesses, who had been present throughout, subscribed below the notary's signature,[83] in the testator's presence.[84] Finally, a testing clause was normally added giving the usual details without mentioning the fact that the testator did not sign personally. Alternatively, the designations of the witnesses were appended to their respective signatures, and the place and date of signing added to the docket.

3.141   The form of the docket set out in Schedule I is as follows:

> "Read over to, and signed by me for, and by authority of the above-named *A.B.* (*without designation*) who declares

---

[79] *Irving* v. *Snow*, 1956 S.C. 257.

[80] While it is unclear whether the note has statutory force or is merely directory (see Lord Morton of Henryton and Lord Reid in *Hynd's Tr.* v. *Hynd's Trs., supra,* at pp. 11 and 20 respectively), the safest course is to treat the note as having statutory force.

[81] The notary cannot be one of the witnesses to the notarial execution (*Cameron* v. *Holman*, 1951 S.L.C.R. 14).

[82] *Hynd's Tr.* v. *Hynd's Trs., supra.*

[83] It is unclear whether it was essential that the witnesses signed below the notary's signature. The point arose in *Hynd's Tr.* v. *Hynd's Trs.,* 1955 S.C. (H.L.) 1, where the witnesses signed above the notarial docket (compare Lord Morton of Henryton at p. 13 and Lord Reid at pp. 20–21), but the case was decided on other grounds. In *Hardie* v. *Hardie*, Dec. 6, 1810 F.C., a case dating before the 1874 Act, a notarial execution was upheld as valid, where the witnesses signed at the side of the notary's docket.

[84] *Hynd's Tr.* v. *Hynd's Trs., supra.*

that he is blind (*or* is unable to write), all in his presence, and in presence of the witnesses hereto subscribing

> C.D., law agent (*or* notary public), Edinburgh (*or as the case may be*)
>
> *or* E.F., justice of the peace for the county of
>
> *or* G.H.., minister (*or* assistant and successor to the minister) of the parish of
>
> M.N., witness
>
> P.O., witness".

3.142   Section 18 provides that the docket was to be in the form set out in the Schedule "or in any words to the like effect". It was therefore not necessary to adhere slavishly to the wording of the statutory docket, although any deviation had to be made with care. While there is a dearth of reported cases involving a variation on the statutory docket set out in Schedule I to the 1924 Act, there are two reported cases on a notarial execution under section 41 of the Conveyancing (Scotland) Act 1874—the previous statutory provision on notarial execution which also permitted deviation from the wording of the statutory docket. In one case, it was held that it was not necessary for the docket to include the word "authority" (as in the statutory style of docket), and it was sufficient that the docket stated that the testator "approved [of the will] in every respect, and stated that she was unable to subscribe the same from weakness, and having desired [notary] to sign for her".[85] In the other case, the docket bore that the deed had "been previously gone over and explained" to the granter, but not that it had been "read over" to him. An action of reduction of the testamentary writing was raised on the grounds that the solemnities of notarial execution (*viz.*, the notary reading the will to the testator) had not been complied with, but the case was settled before the court determined whether the docket was in "words to the like effect" to those in the statutory docket.[86] However, the omission of the words "who declares that he is unable to write" or anything equivalent is an unacceptable deviation from the statutory docket, though it may be possible to set up the will under section 39 of the Conveyancing (Scotland) Act 1924[87] (see paras. 3.146–3.149).

Notarial execution of mutual wills

3.143   Where a mutual will was notarially executed under the 1924

---

[85] *Atchison's Trs.* v. *Atchison* (1876) 3 R. 388.

[86] *Watson* v. *Beveridge* (1883) 11 R. 40.

[87] *Shiels, Petr.*, 1951 S.L.T. (Sh. Ct.) 36; see also *Cameron* v. *Holman*, 1951 S.L.C.R. 14.

Act, it was undesirable that the agent of one party executed notarially for the other party.[88]

3.144   Where both parties to a mutual will required to have the deed executed for them notarially, it was preferable if two notaries were used,[89] although if the mutual will was revocable by both parties, it is probably unobjectionable for the same notary to have executed for both parties.[90]

3.145   If the mutual will was subscribed notarially for one party and the other party subscribed himself, it is of no objection if the same two individuals witnessed both the subscription by one testator, and the notarial execution for the other.[91]

An informality of execution in a notarially executed deed

3.146   A deed purporting to be notarially executed in terms of section 18(1) of the Conveyancing (Scotland) Act 1924 may receive effect even if there is an informality of execution, if the proof required under section 39 of the Conveyancing (Scotland) Act 1874 can be led.[92]

3.147   Thus, where the law agent had omitted to include in the docket the words "who declares that he is unable to write", it was held that the docket did not comply with section 18(1) of the Conveyancing (Scotland) Act 1924 but that the omission of the words was an "informality of execution" within the meaning of section 39 of the Conveyancing (Scotland) Act 1874, so that the testamentary writing could be set up.[93]

3.148   It matters not that the notary designed himself as "solicitor" (rather than as "law-agent" as in Schedule I),[94] or that there was a clerical error, such as the misspelling of the testator's surname.[95]

3.149   It is a fatal flaw to a notarial execution if the notarial docket and the witnesses' subscriptions are not inserted in the presence of the testator. In *Hynd's Trustee* v. *Hynd's Trustees*,[96] a deed which

---

[88] *Per* Lord Rutherfurd Clark in *Lang* v. *Lang's Trs.* (1889) 16 R. 590 at p. 598.
[89] *Craig* v. *Richartson* (1610) Mor. 16829 and discussion on that case in *Graeme* v. *Graeme's Trs.* (1868) 7 M. 14.
[90] *Graeme* v. *Graeme's Trs., supra.*
[91] *Hardie* v. *Hardie*, Dec. 6, 1810, F.C.
[92] Conveyancing (Scotland) Act 1924 (14 & 15 Geo. 5, c. 27), s. 18(2); on the infelicitous wording of s.18(2) see Sheriff Walker in *Shiels, Petr., supra*, at p. 37; Walker and Walker, *Law of Evidence in Scotland*, para. 186(f).
[93] *Shiels, Petr.*, 1951 S.L.T. (Sh. Ct.) 36.
[94] *Aitken, Petr.*, 1965 S.L.T. (Sh. Ct.) 15.
[95] *Ibid.*
[96] 1955 S.C. (H.L.) 1.

bore to have been notarially executed was held to be invalidly executed where it was shown that the solicitor had signed the will before he had inserted the notarial docket. Because he had required to adjust the statutory docket to acknowledge the fact that the testator had attempted to sign, the solicitor had taken the deed back to the office to insert the docket and the witnesses had inserted their signatures at the office too.

ADDITIONAL SOLEMNITIES FIXED BY TESTATOR

Additional solemnities fixed by the testator

3.150   If in a testamentary writing executed prior to August 1, 1995 a testator fixed additional solemnities of execution beyond those required by law, the testamentary writing may be held to be invalidly executed, if the testator failed to observe these additional solemnities. Thus, where a marriage contract provided that the spouses could change the destination of the fee by any deed sealed by them and delivered in the presence of and attested by two credible witnesses, or by a testamentary writing signed by them and published in the presence of and attested by three credible witnesses, it was held that the destination could only be changed by a testamentary writing which conformed to the specified formalities.[97] In this particular case, the testamentary writing could nevertheless be treated as validly executed for the purpose of the executors named therein obtaining confirmation to any part of the deceased's personal estate (*i.e.* the property not covered by the marriage contract).

3.151   It may be that when the testamentary writing is found, it appears that the additional solemnity had originally been complied with, but the evidence that it had been complied with has since been removed or defaced. The question then is whether the testator thereby revoked the writing. In one case, a testator wrote before signing "In testimony of this being my last will and testament, I hereto set my hand and seal, and declare it to be written upon three pages, and signed in my own handwriting". When the deed was found in his repositories after his death, the seal had been cut off, and therefore it was held that the deed had been revoked.[98]

3.152   The courts seem to take a more benign approach where the testamentary writing is holograph and the testator declares that the deed is subscribed before two witnesses, but it is not in

---

[97] *Campbell's Trs.* v. *Campbell* (1903) 5 F. 366.
[98] *Nasmyth* v. *Hare* (1821) 1 Shaw's App. 65.

fact witnessed. In an early reported decision,[99] the testator of a holograph testamentary writing declared in the deed that he had subscribed before two named witnesses. Where it was shown that one of the witnesses did not see him sign, or acknowledge his signature, the deed nevertheless received effect as a holograph writing. In other words, the court did not consider that he had prescribed an additional solemnity (*viz.* that there must be two witnesses to his subscription of a holograph writing).

3.153   There seems to be no obvious reason why the courts should take one approach to a testator prescribing additional formalities in a holograph testamentary writing and another approach if he were to do the same in a testamentary writing formally executed.

REVOCATION OF TESTAMENTARY WRITINGS

Revocation

3.154   Provided that he has not entered into an onerous undertaking not to revoke a testamentary writing,[1] as where he was a party to a mutual will, and provided that he is of sound mind, a testator may at any time revoke a testamentary writing either expressly (paras. 3.158–3.162) or impliedly (paras. 3.166–3.169). Sometimes subsequent events may raise the legal presumption that the earlier testamentary writing has been revoked (paras. 3.170–3.176).

3.155   The onus of proving that an *ex facie* valid testamentary writing has been revoked is on the party who claims that it has been revoked.[2]

3.156   Where the testator's domicile has changed between the time of revocation and death, the question of whether he did revoke a testamentary writing is determined by the law of his domicile at the time of the revocation (rather than at the time of death).[3]

---

[99] *Yeats* v. *Yeats' Trs.* (1833) 11 S. 915; see also *Jones* v. *Pursey* (1886) 23 S.L.R. 628 where the Court of Session instructed the sheriff to issue confirmation in favour of persons who had been nominated as executor in, *inter alia*, a holograph deed bearing to be signed before two witnesses, but which was not in fact witnessed, without prejudice to any question as to the validity of the deed. See also *Harley* v. *Harley's Exr.*, 1957 S.L.T. (Sh. Ct.) 17.

[1] *Curdy* v. *Boyd* (1775) Mor. 15946; *Paterson* v. *Paterson* (1893) 20 R. 484.

[2] *Per* Lord Truro in *Stoddart* v. *Grant* (1851) 1 Macq. 163 at p. 175; *per* Lord Avonside in *Macrorie's Exrs.* v. *McLaren*, 1984 S.L.T. 271 at p. 272.

[3] Anton & Beaumont, *Private International Law* (2nd ed.), pp. 694–696.

Formal validity of a testamentary writing purporting to revoke a prior testamentary writing

3.157   Sometimes it is necessary to determine whether a testamentary writing which revokes either the whole of, or a clause in, a prior testamentary writing has been validly executed. In this event, section 2(1)(c) of the Wills Act 1963 provides that the later testamentary writing will be treated as properly executed if its execution conformed to any law by reference to which the prior testamentary writing would be so treated.[4] This is in addition to the rules for formal validity of testamentary writings detailed at paragraphs 3.07–3.10.

Express revocation

3.158   It is preferable that a testamentary writing is expressly revoked. Accordingly, it is customary for all professionally prepared testamentary writings to include a clause to the effect; "And I revoke all prior testamentary writings". If the clause revoking the prior testamentary writing does not clearly identify a particular prior writing, that prior writing shall receive effect, insofar as it is not inconsistent with any subsequent one.[5]

3.159   It will also be sufficient if the testator destroys the testamentary writing himself, or sends a signed letter to his solicitor, instructing him to destroy the testamentary writing. If the letter is not delivered to the solicitor during the testator's lifetime, the mandate falls on his death, and the testamentary writing will receive effect.[6] If a testamentary writing is destroyed without the testator's authorisation, it is not revoked, and an action to prove the tenor of the writing may then be brought.[6a]

Revocation of a mutual will

3.160   Where two parties have entered into a mutual will, unless there are contractual provisions that the deed is irrevocable, each may alter their will in relation to their own property.[7] The question of whether a mutual will is irrevocable (as being contractual) or revocable (as being testamentary) depends on the interpretation of the particular mutual will, but there are certain presumptions. Liferent provisions in favour of the other party to the mutual will and fee provisions in favour of the issue of the marriage of the parties to the mutual will are contractual (and so irrevocable).[8] Provisions in favour of other parties are testament-

---

[4] Wills Act 1963 (c. 44), s. 2(1) (c).

[5] *Gordon's Exr.* v. *Macqueen*, 1907 S.C. 373.

[6] *France's J.F.* v. *France's Trs.*, 1916 1 S.L.T. 126.

[6a] *Cullen's Exr.* v. *Elphinstone*, 1948 S.C. 662.

[7] *Saxby's Exrs.* v. *Saxby's Exrs.*, 1952 S.C. 352; *obiter dicta per* Lord McLaren in *Martin* v. *Ferguson's Trs.* (1892) 19 R. 474 at p. 480 and Lord President Dunedin in *Lawrie's Exr.* v. *Haig*, 1913 S.C. 1159 at p. 1161.

[8] *Robertson's Trs.* v. *Bond's Trs.* (1900) 2 F. 1097.

ary.[9] Where power was reserved to the survivor to dispose of estate acquired after the first deed, there is a presumption that the mutual settlement is contractual.[10] It is possible for the parties to a mutual will, which contains contractual provisions, to reserve powers of revocation.[11]

Revocation clause in a printed will form

3.161   It has been seen at paragraph 3.125 that where a printed will form is improbative, it may still receive effect if it is subscribed prior to August 1, 1995, and the essential parts are holograph. In such a case, it is unlikely that the clause revoking prior testamentary writings will receive effect, since the standard modern printed will form includes this clause in the printed portion. In this event, it is thought that the prior testamentary writing would receive effect to the extent that the printed will form does not dispose of the deceased's whole estate.

3.162   If, however, the essential parts of the improbative printed will form are not holograph, it will not receive effect, even if subscribed (unless it had been subscribed on or after August 1, 1995). Where the will form was subscribed, and the holograph portion included the words "revoke former will", but not other essential parts, the revocation clause did not receive effect, and the deceased's prior trust disposition and settlement received effect.[12]

Revival of revoked testamentary writing

3.163   It should be noted that where a testamentary writing has been expressly revoked by a subsequent testamentary writing, and that subsequent testamentary writing is itself subsequently revoked, the first writing is then by implication revived, unless the testator had given express instructions for the first will to be destroyed[13]: "authority to destroy a probative deed should not readily be implied".[14]

3.164   If the deceased's solicitor destroys an earlier testamentary writing without his client's express instructions, and the subsequent testamentary writing is thereafter reduced — whether because the testator was of unsound mind at the time of execution or because it was void *ab initio* having been notarially executed by a solicitor who had an interest under it — the destruction is unauthorised. Once decree has been obtained in an action to

---

[9] *United Free Church of Scotland* v. *Black*, 1909 S.C. 25.
[10] *Lawrie's Exr.* v. *Haig*, 1913 S.C. 1159.
[11] *Dewar's Trs.* v. *Dewar's Trs.*, 1950 S.L.T. 191.
[12] *Tucker* v. *Canch's Tr.*, 1953 S.C. 270.
[13] *Scott's J.F.* v. *Johnston*, 1971 S.L.T. (Notes) 41.
[14] *Per* Lord Birnam in *Cullen's Exr.* v. *Elphinstone*, 1948 S.C. 662.

prove the tenor of the destroyed testamentary writing, it will receive effect.[15]

3.165   If, having been handed to the testator, the second testamentary writing has disappeared by the time of the testator's death, it is presumed that the deceased destroyed it *animo revocandi* and the first testamentary writing will receive effect, unless it can be shown that the testator had given express instructions for its destruction.[16] It may also be possible to ensure that the first will is not revived if it can be shown that there was some other reason for it being kept.

Implied revocation

3.166   A testamentary writing dealing with the whole of the testator's estate is held to revoke all prior testamentary writings by implication, even if there is no clause of express revocation.[17] If a prior testamentary writing, which included a clause adopting informal writings, is revoked by implication by a subsequent universal settlement, any informal writings will be treated as unauthenticated.[18]

3.167   Where the subsequent testamentary writing does not contain a residue clause, it is not a universal settlement, and it will receive effect along with the prior universal will.[19] If all the testamentary writings are capable of standing together, all will be sustained.[20]

3.168   A testator left two trust dispositions and settlements, the later one expressly revoking the earlier one. Some years later, he executed a codicil in the following terms: "I . . . having considered the [original] Trust Disposition and Settlement, have resolved to make the following alterations and additions thereon . . . [list] . . . and with these alterations and additions, I hereby homologate and approve of the said Trust Disposition and Settlement in all other respects". In such circumstances, the later trust disposition and settlement was revoked by implication and the earlier one was revived.[21]

3.169   A testatrix executed a trust disposition and settlement, which expressly revoked all former testamentary writings, and

---

[15] *Cullen's Exr.* v. *Elphinstone*, 1948 S.C. 662.

[16] *Bruce's J.F.* v. *Lord Advocate*, 1969 S.L.T. 337.

[17] *Moncrieff*, March 19, 1883, unreported; *Sibbald's Trs.* v. *Greig* (1871) 9 M. 399; *Dick's Trs.* v. *Dick*, 1907 S.C. 953; *Rutherford's Trs.* v. *Dickie*, 1907 S.C. 1280; *Macrorie's Exrs.* v. *McLaren*, 1984 S.L.T. 271.

[18] *Macrorie's Exrs.* v. *McLaren, supra.*

[19] *Stoddart* v. *Grant* (1851) 1 Macq. 163; *Duthie Exrs.* v. *Taylor*, 1986 S.L.T. 142.

[20] *Cox*, July 19, 1893, unreported; *Tronsons* v. *Tronsons* (1884) 12 R. 155.

[21] *Mellis* v. *Mellis's Tr.* (1898) 25 R. 720.

reserved a power of alteration or revocation by any writing however informally executed. Thereafter, on a separate sheet, she
executed a codicil modifying this settlement. A year later, she
executed a second codicil, which was written on the settlement,
and bore to be a codicil to the foregoing trust disposition and
settlement, and concluded "except in so far as hereby altered,
I confirm my said trust-disposition and settlement in all
respects, and provide that it and this codicil shall be read and
construed together as forming one document". It was held that
the second codicil did not revoke the first codicil, the court considering that the first codicil was part of the trust disposition
and settlement.[22]

Presumptive revocation—by birth of child

3.170   The *conditio si testator sine liberis decesserit* gives rise to a presumption that where a testamentary writing makes no provision for
a child born subsequent to the writing, the writing is thereby
revoked if a child is subsequently born to the testator, whether
that child is legitimate or illegitimate.[23] The rule applies whether
the testator had no children at the time of executing the testamentary writing—or whether he already had a child.[24] The right
to challenge the testamentary writing is personal to the child
born subsequent to the writing[25] and the presumption will be
revoked if it can be established that the testator intended the
writing to stand notwithstanding the birth.[26] The revocation is
total—of the administrative as well as of the beneficial
provisions.[27]

3.170A   When confirmation is sought on the basis of a testamentary
writing, and the commissary or sheriff clerk is aware that a
child was born to the testator after he executed the testamentary
writing and that child is still under the age of 18 years, an
application must be made to the sheriff for special authority to
issue confirmation. It is a matter for the sheriff to decide
whether confirmation should be granted to the executor nominated in the testamentary writing.

3.170B   It may be appropriate to include in the petition an averment as

---

[22] *Scott's Trs.* v. *Duke*, 1916 S.C. 732.

[23] Law Reform (Miscellaneous Provisions) (Scotland) Act 1968 (c. 70), s. 6(2).

[24] *Elder's Trs.* v. *Elder* (1894) 21 R. 704; *Nicolson* v. *Nicolson's Tutrix*, 1922 S.C. 649.

[25] *Watt* v. *Jervie* (1760) Mor. 6401; *Smith's Trs.* v. *Grant*, 35 S.L.R. 129; *Stevenson's Trs.* v. *Stevenson*, 1932 S.C. 657.

[26] *Yule* v. *Yule* (1758) Mor. 6400; *Millar's Trs.* v. *Millar* (1893) 20 R. 1040; *Elder's Trs.* v. *Elder* (1895) 21 R. 704; *Stuart-Gordon* v. *Stuart-Gordon* (1899) 1 F. 1005; *Knox's Trs.* v. *Knox*, 1907 S.C. 1123; *Stevenson's Trs.* v. *Stevenson*, 1932 S.C. 657.

[27] *Knox's Trs.* v. *Knox, supra.*

to the amount of the posthumous child's claim (by way of legitim) if the testamentary writing receives effect, and contrast that with the amount he would receive if the testamentary writing were to be challenged under the *conditio* and subsequently held to be revoked. For example, where the deceased left only one testamentary writing, which is revoked as a result of the *conditio*, his estate falls to be distributed under the rules of intestate succession. Where the deceased was survived by a spouse and children, the spouse will, except in the case of a large estate, receive the whole estate in satisfaction of her prior rights. In contrast, if the testamentary writing is not challenged, the children will share the legitim fund of one-third of the net moveable estate.

3.170C It is also appropriate to include in the petition averments as to the facts rebutting the presumption. This occurred where children were born to the testator after the date of the testamentary writing, but a marriage settlement was produced which provided for the children of the marriage, and declared that the provision in favour of the children should be accepted by them in full satisfaction and discharge of legitim and every other claim competent to them.[27a] More recently, the sheriff, in considering a petition for the appointment of an executor-dative to be decerned where a child had been born to the deceased after the testamentary writing was executed, was not prepared to consider whether the presumption raised by the *conditio* had been rebutted by the deceased setting up an *inter vivos* trust for the child.[27b]

3.171 Where the testator's final testamentary writing is revoked as a result of the *conditio*, the question is then whether an earlier testamentary writing may thereby be revived.

3.172 In *Elder's Trustees* v. *Elder*[28] (a decision of the First Division) the deceased had left two testamentary writings. The prior one included a provision for *nascituri*. The later one expressly revoked the prior one, but made no provision for *nascituri*. A further child was born and, after the deceased's death, a court action established that the later will had been impliedly revoked under the *conditio*.[29] The question was then raised of whether the earlier will had thereby been revived. The court held that there was no presumption that the earlier will, having been expressly revoked by the later will, was revived. Lord McLaren stated:

[27a] *Johnston*, March 24, 1947, unreported; but see Succession (Scotland) Act 1964 (c. 41), s 12 with regard to marriage contracts executed after September 10, 1964.

[27b] *Myers, Petr.*, Aug. 2, 1974, unreported.

[28] (1895) 22 R. 505.

[29] *Elder's Trs.* v. *Elder* (1894) 21 R. 704.

> "I think that the equitable rule in question [the *conditio*] must be confined to testamentary gifts, and that a clause of revocation must receive effect according to its tenor".[30]

3.173   In *Nicolson* v. *Nicolson's Tutrix*[31] (a decision of the Second Division), the deceased left two testamentary writings. The later one was a universal settlement which accordingly revoked the prior will by implication, but it did not contain provisions for *nascituri*. A child having been subsequently born, the later testamentary writing was held to have been reduced under the *conditio* and the prior will was held to have revived, the court distinguishing *Nicolson* from *Elder* on the ground that only in *Elder* was there a clause in the later testamentary writing expressly revoking prior writings. Reliance was placed on the distinction drawn between express and implied revocation by Lord Justice-Clerk Inglis:

> "Where a revocation of a previous settlement is merely implied in a new conveyance, it is impossible to set aside the conveyance without sweeping away also the effect of the implication; and where a revocation is made conditional, by express words, on the new conveyance receiving effect, there also it is impossible to defeat the new conveyance without setting aside the conditional revocation. But . . . [where] there is a substantive and independent revocation expressed in words, and not conditional but absolute . . . I am disposed to think that [the heir] could not have set aside the revocation *ex capite lecti* even if he had been inclined to attempt it."[32]

3.174   It may be that the two decisions stem from different approaches to the *conditio*: on the one hand, it may be viewed as a condition implied by law in the testamentary writing, but on the other hand, it may be viewed as a rule of equity—ascertaining the testator's presumed intention in the changed circumstances. The latter approach was taken in *Elder*. In contrast, in *Nicolson*, the implied revocation of the first will by the execution of the second one was swept away when the second will itself was revoked under the *conditio*.

Implied revocation under other legal systems

3.175   Under other legal systems, a testamentary writing can be revoked by implication for other reasons—such as the subsequent marriage of the testator, or the subsequent divorce of

---

[30] (1895) 22 R. 505 at p. 512.
[31] 1922 S.C. 649.
[32] *Leith* v. *Leith* (1863) 1 M. 949 at p. 955.

the testator.[33] The sheriff or commissary clerk will not consider whether a testamentary writing has been revoked under the laws of some previous domicile, even if it is clear from the papers placed before him that the testator had been domiciled somewhere other than Scotland for part of his life. The clerk will, if presented with a valid and probative testamentary writing, issue confirmation on the basis of it and he will not look further. A party who seeks to argue that the writing has been impliedly revoked under another legal system must raise an action (quite separate from the commissary process) to have it declared that the writing was revoked by implication.

3.176 It is to be noted that where there is a question whether a testamentary writing has been revoked under the laws of another legal system by the testator's subsequent marriage, Scots law provides that it is the law of the testator's domicile at the time of the marriage which determines the effect of the marriage on the testamentary writing.[34]

ALTERATIONS AND DELETIONS

Alterations to a probative testamentary writing

3.177 The definitive judgment on the effect to be given to additions or deletions made before August 1, 1995 to a probative testamentary writing after execution is provided by Lord McLaren in *Pattison's Trustees* v. *University of Edinburgh*[35]:

> "(1) If a will or codicil is found with the signature cancelled, or with lines drawn through the dispositive or other essential clause of the instrument, then, on proof that the cancellation was done by the testator himself, or by his order, with the intention of revoking the will, the will is to be held revoked; otherwise it is treated as a subsisting will. . . .

> "(2) If a will or codicil is found with one or more of the legacies or particular provisions scored out, I should hold that this raises no case for inquiry as to the testator's intention to revoke the instrument in whole, but that a question is raised as to the intention to revoke the particular provision; and I should not hold the provision revoked unless upon evidence that the scoring was done by the testator himself or by his direction with the intention of revoking

---

[33] Though, in the case of divorce, it is normally only that portion of the testamentary writing which benefits the former spouse which is revoked.

[34] *Westerman's Exr.* v. *Schwab* (1905) 8 F. 132; Anton, *Private International Law* (1st ed.), pp. 536–537; also Anton & Beaumont (2nd ed.), p. 695.

[35] (1888) 16 R. 73 at pp. 76–77.

the clause. If the deletion were authenticated by the testator's initials, recognisable as his handwriting, I should hold this to be sufficient proof that the deletion was the act of the testator, the full signature being only necessary to an act of positive disposition or bequest . . .

"(3) If a will or codicil is found with marginal or interlineal additions, apparently in the testator's handwriting, I should not hold these to be part of the instrument, except in so far as they are authenticated by the signature or initials of the testator. My reason is that our law does not give any effect to unsigned writings even when holograph . . . I think that in the case of marginal additions or interlineations, the authentication may be by initials; on the ground that the subscription at the end of the writing covers everything, and that the initial letters of the granter's name suffice to authenticate the new matter as part of the instrument.

"(4) When the will or codicil contains words scored out and others inserted in their place, I think that the cancellation of the words in the original writing is conditional on the substituted words taking effect. Accordingly, if the substituted words are rejected on the ground that they are unsigned, the deletion is also to be rejected, and the will ought to be read in its original form".

Lord Murray[36] has expressed the view that Lord McLaren's comments apply to deletions and additions inserted before the testamentary writing was executed as well as to those effected afterwards.

3.178   The fallacy of this approach has been pointed out[37]—the question of what has been executed is a different one from the question of whether a deed or clause has been revoked.[38] Indeed, the validity of a pre-execution alteration or deletion is more accurately categorised as a matter relating to the law of execution of deeds.

Pre-execution alterations made prior to August 1, 1995 which are authenticated: probative testamentary writings

3.179   A properly authenticated alteration—whether an erasure, writing on erasure, writing on a correcting fluid, interlineation or interpolation—forms part of the probative writing in which it is found, and does not deprive it of its probative quality.[39] An

---

[36] *Syme's Exrs.* v. *Cherrie*, 1986 S.L.T. 161.
[37] K.G.C. Reid, "Execution or Revocation", 1986 S.L.T. (News) 129.
[38] Walker and Walker, *The Law of Evidence in Scotland*, para. 181.
[39] Dickson, *Evidence* (3rd ed.), para. 729; Walker and Walker, *The Law of Evidence in Scotland*, para. 180(b).

alteration made prior to August 1, 1995 will be treated as properly authenticated if it is referred to in the testing clause (all the words being quoted and the exact position, by line and page, being specified), and the alteration appears from the body of the deed and from the language of the testing clause to have been inserted before subscription.[40] In the case of a marginal addition, as well as being specified in the testing clause, the testing clause should state that the addition was signed by the granter in the presence of the witnesses and the addition should be authenticated by the testator signing his first name or initial on one side, and his surname or initial on the other.[41] Unless the alteration is declared in the testing clause, the law presumes that any such alteration was made after the deed had been executed[42] and where the alteration was made before August 1, 1995, the presumption is irrebutable save where section 39 of the Conveyancing (Scotland) Act 1874 is applicable.[43]

Post-execution alterations which are authenticated: probative testamentary writings

3.180 Unless it is declared in the testing clause, the law presumes that any alteration—whether an erasure, writing an erasure, writing on a correcting fluid, interlineation or interpolation—is made after the deed has been executed[44] and in the case of deeds and alterations made prior to August 1, 1995, the presumption is irrebutable save where section 39 of the Conveyancing (Scotland) Act 1874 is applicable.[45]

3.181 A post-execution alteration made prior to August 1, 1995 will receive effect where it has been authenticated—by the testator initialling it or signing at each side of it[46-47]—or it is proved that the alteration has been made by him. Where a holograph marginal addition has been inserted in place of part of a deed which bears to have been deleted, and only the deletion has been authenticated, it is likely that the marginal addition will

---

[40] Dickson *Evidence* (3rd ed.), para. 728; Walker and Walker, *The Law of Evidence in Scotland*, para. 180(b).

[41] Walker and Walker, *supra*, para. 180(b).

[42] Stair, *Inst.*, IV.xlii.19; Erskine, *Principles*, 3,2,20; *per* the Lord Chancellor in *Gollan* v. *Gollan*, (1863) 4 Macq. 585 at p. 587; *Shepherd* v. *Grant's Trs.* (1844) 6 D. 464, affirmed by *Grant's Trs.* v. *Shepherd* (1847) 6 Bell's App. 153.

[43] Walker and Walker, *supra*, para. 186(e).

[44] Stair *Inst.*, IV.xlii.19; Erskine, *Principles* 3,2,20; *per* the Lord Chancellor in *Gollan* v. *Gollan*, 4 Macq. 587 at p. 587; *Shepherd* v. *Grant's Trs.* (1844) 6 D. 464 affirmed by *Grant's Trs* v. *Shepherd* (1847) 6 Bell's App. 153.

[45] Walker and Walker, *supra*, para. 186(e).

[46-47] *Caledonian Banking Co.* v. *Fraser* (1874) 11 S.L.R. 345; *Gray's Trs.* v. *Dow* (1900) 3 F. 79.

not receive effect.[48] Any unauthenticated alteration is treated *pro non scripto*,[49] and effect will be given to the deed, ignoring such alteration. When the unauthenticated alteration is a deletion or writing on erasure, the question then is whether the words treated *pro non scriptis* are *in substantialibus*, for then the deed will be treated as revoked.

Testator's signature deleted or written on erasure

3.182   If a testamentary writing is found with the signature deleted lying in, say, a locked drawer in the testator's desk, then, in the absence of other factors it will be assumed that the writing had been revoked by the testator.

3.183   In *Fotheringham's Trustees* v. *Reid*,[50] a married woman signed her trust disposition and settlement with her married name. Subsequently, as she was living apart from her husband, she reverted to using her maiden name. After her death, her trust disposition and settlement was found with her married name deleted from her signature and her maiden name substituted in her own hand. The alterations had not been witnessed or acknowledged but the parties agreed that the alterations had not been made with the intention of revoking the settlement. In a special case, it was held that the deed was validly authenticated, the deletion of the original signature falling to be ignored in respect that it had not been made with the intention of revoking the trust disposition and settlement.

Appointment of trustee or executor deleted or written on erasure

3.184   Where the name of a trustee or executor is deleted[51] or written on erasure,[52] this is not an alteration *in substantialibus*, and the rest of the deed will receive effect: others may have been nominated, or constructively appointed under section 3 of the Executors (Scotland) Act 1900[53] or may be decerned by the court.

Nomination of beneficiary in a universal settlement deleted or written on erasure

3.185   In the case of a universal settlement, the name of the sole executor and universal legatee is *in substantialibus*.[54]

---

[48] *Per* Lord Curriehill in *Royal Infirmary of Edinburgh* v. *Lord Advocate* (1861) 23 D. 1213.

[49] *Kemps* v. *Ferguson* (1802) Mor. 16949; *Kedder* v. *Reid* (1840) 1 Rob. App. 183; *Boswell* v. *Boswell* (1852) 14 D. 378; *Munro* v. *Butler Johnstone* (1868) 7 M. 250.

[50] 1936 S.C. 831.

[51] *Earl of Traquair* v. *Henderson* (1822) 1 S. 527.

[52] *Robertson* v. *Ogilvie's Trs.* (1844) 7 D. 236.

[53] (63 & 64 Vict. c. 55)—see paras. 5.49 *et seq.*

[54] *Cf. Kedder* v. *Reid* (1840) 1 Rob. App. 183 (where a *mortis causa* disposition of land showed the name of the disponee as "John", the letters "OHN" being clearly written on erasure).

Words showing testamentary intent deleted or written on erasure

3.186 If words showing testamentary intent have been deleted or written on erasure, then it will not be clear whether the deceased intended the writing to be testamentary or to be an *inter vivos* deed of gift. If all that is left is the word "to" (preceding a person's name and an item or sum of money), this does not, on its own, indicate an intention to bequeath (it may also indicate a gift *inter vivos*), and must be combined with the use of a word like "residue"[55] or "remainder"[56] to show testamentary intention.

3.187 Where the alteration is holograph of the testator, there have been cases where the alterations have received effect even although the full formalities of authentication have not been complied with.[57] Such an approach does not comply with Lord McLaren's third tenet in *Pattison's Trustees* v. *University of Edinburgh* (quoted at para. 3.177), and it is doubtful if that approach would now be followed.[58] Certainly, holograph marginal additions, which have not been signed or initialled, will be treated as deliberative, and will not receive testamentary effect,[59] especially if the addition is in pencil.[60]

Alterations to a copy of a probative testamentary writing

3.188 Where the testator has made deletions or alterations not to the principal but to a copy of his testamentary writing, they will be given effect to only if it can be shown that the testator intended to alter the principal will, and authenticated the deletions or alterations. In one case, the testator had cut out the residue clause in a typewritten copy of her trust disposition and settlement, and she had adhibited her signature twice to the margin of the hole, and had written below:

> "As I don't have money to cover any more I thought it better to cut out what had been written."

It was held that the testatrix had effectually revoked the residue clause in her trust disposition and settlement.[61]

---

[55] *Per* Lord President Clyde in *Gillies* v. *Glasgow Royal Infirmary*, 1960 S.C. 438 at p. 442.

[56] *Ayrshire Hospice, Petrs.*, 1993 S.L.T. (Sh. Ct.) 76.

[57] *Royal Infirmary of Edinburgh* v. *Lord Advocate* (1861) 23 D. 1213; *Caledonian Banking Co.* v. *Fraser* (1874) 44 S.L.R. 345; *Lawson* v. *Lawson*, 1954 S.L.T. (Notes) 60.

[58] Walker and Walker, *The Law of Evidence in Scotland*, para. 181; *Brown* v. *Maxwell's Exrs.* (1884) 11 R. 821.

[59] *Brown* v. *Maxwell's Exrs.* (1884) 11 R. 821.

[60] *Pettigrew's Trs.* v. *Pettigrew* (1884) 12 R. 249; *Manson* v. *Edinburgh Royal Institution*, 1948 S.L.T. 196.

[61] *Thomson's Trs.* v. *Bowhill Baptist Church*, 1956 S.C. 217.

Alterations to a holograph testamentary writing

3.189   Alterations made prior to August 1, 1995 to a holograph testamentary writing will receive effect if it can be shown that they
were made by the deceased and with the intention of altering
the deed. It will be clear that this is the case if the deceased
had authenticated his holograph alterations by his signature or
initials. If the alterations are in the testator's own hand, this
will prove that they were made by him,[62] but the question is
then whether he made them with the intention of altering the
deed. Where such a deed is found undisturbed in the deceased's
repositories after his death, there is a presumption that he made
the alterations with testamentary intent, and in such cases deletions which have not otherwise been authenticated have
received effect, where there was no doubt as to the genuineness
of the deletion.[63] If a holograph testamentary writing written in
ink bears to have been altered by a holograph writing in pencil,
it is presumed to be deliberative.[64] Any unauthenticated alteration will be of no effect and will be treated *pro non scriptis*, unless
the deceased's signature of the holograph writing has been witnessed and the alteration referred to in the testing clause (see
paras. 3.87 and 3.106).

MISCELLANEOUS MATTERS

Bequests written on deposit receipts, etc.[65]

3.190   Individuals have frequently been tempted to bequeath bank
deposit receipts and other similar simple documents of debt
by docketing or endorsing them. The practice is fraught with
difficulties. A court will not give effect to the docket if the
deceased had not subscribed it, or if he did not use clear testamentary language in the docket. For instance, if the deceased
used the word "to" (followed by a person's name and an item
or sum of money), it will be viewed as a donation, which the
deceased had not completed, rather than as a testamentary
bequest. If the docket is not endorsed on the actual document
of debt, it can be difficult to identify what the individual intended to bequeath.

3.191   The following cases illustrate the problems in this area. Each
case turns on the wording of the particular docket, and it is
difficult to reconcile one decision with another.

---

[62] *Per* Lord Mackenzie in *Robertson* v. *Ogilvie's Trs.* (1844) 7 D. 236 at p. 242.
[63] *Nasmyth* v. *Hare* (1821) 1 Shaw's App. 65; *Milne's Exr.* v. *Waugh*, 1913 S.C.
203; *Allan's Exrx.* v. *Allan*, 1920 S.C. 732.
[64] *Lamont* v. *Mags. of Glasgow* (1887) 14 R. 603; *Munro's Exrs.* v. *Munro* (1890)
18 R. 122; *Currie's Trs.* v. *Currie* (1904) 7 F. 364.
[65] See also donations *inter vivos* and *mortis causa* at paras. 12.12 *et seq.*

Examples:

1. A bank deposit receipt in the name of the deceased was found pinned to a holograph signed writing which read "The bill within this paper you will give . ." followed by names of people with sums after each, adding up to the exact amount in the deposit receipt. The use of the words "you will give" indicated testamentary intent, and the legacies were sustained.[66]

2. On the back of a bank deposit receipt, the depositor, Lewis Shedden, had written "Mr Lewis Shedden I leave this to my sister Janet Shedden". This failed since there was no subscription.[67]

3. A bank deposit receipt in the deceased's name was enclosed in a sealed envelope on which was the holograph writing "Beatrice Burn Roberts from her father John Burn". The Lord Ordinary was of the view that the wording did not distinguish between a gift and a legacy, but in the Inner House it was sustained as a legacy.[68]

4. Four I.O.U.s were found lying pinned together, enclosed in a letter from the borrower, which served as a wrapper. On the back of that letter, the creditor had written in her own hand "I don't want this money paid up" and had signed it. This was sustained as a legacy releasing the borrowers. It should be noted that in this case the deceased had left a trust disposition and settlement in which she reserved power to alter, innovate or revoke it in whole or in part by any writing under her hand clearly expressing her wishes, however informally the same might be executed.[69]

5. Two acknowledgements of debt were enclosed in an envelope on which was a signed holograph writing which read: "To my trustees. This not to be opened but burnt". It was recognised that this might have received effect as a legacy of release, but special circumstances—pencil scoring across the writing on the envelope and the fact that the envelope which had been sealed had been opened by the testator—led to an inference that the direction had been cancelled.[70]

6. A bank deposit receipt for £450 in the name of the

---

[66] *Panton* v. *Gillies* (1824) 2 S. 536.
[67] *Goldie* v. *Shedden* (1885) 13 R. 138.
[68] *Roberts* v. *Burn's Exr.*, 1914 1 S.L.T. 509.
[69] *Mitchell's Trs.* v. *Pride*, 1912 S.C. 600.
[70] *Lennie* v. *Lennie's Trs.*, 1914 1 S.L.T. 258.

deceased was found endorsed by her, and with a holograph signed writing pinned to it: "£150 to AB (*designed*), £150 to CD (*designed*), £150 to EF (*designed*)". The court held that there were no bequests. One difficulty was that there was nothing to show that the deceased had intended to make a legacy, rather than an uncompleted donation *inter vivos*.[71]

7.   There was found in the deceased's repositories a sealed envelope on which he had written and signed the words "Only to be opened at my death". The envelope contained a sheet of paper on which he had written and signed the words "I, JG, am holding in trust for [named individual]" two deposit receipts for specified amounts. It was discovered that his bankers had in their custody two deposit receipts which acknowledged that the bank had "received from JG in trust for [the named individual]" the specified amounts. The writing on the sheet found in the envelope bore to have been signed on the day following the deposit of the two amounts with the bank. The proceeds of the deposit receipts were claimed by the individual named in them, on the view that the deceased had either made a donation *mortis causa*, or a testamentary bequest. On the latter count it was held that she had failed to establish a testamentary bequest, in respect that the holograph writing on the sealed envelope had no testamentary effect.[72]

8.   Two deposit receipts in the deceased's favour were found in his possession. On one, in his own writing, there was endorsed: "Pay CD (four thousand, five hundred pounds—1/1/67) £4,500" and signed by him. The other was endorsed, also in his handwriting: "Pay to EF six thousand pounds, £6,000", and was signed and dated. The court held that, in themselves, the endorsements possessed no testamentary character. Further, since the endorsements were not "legacies", they were not validated by the clause in the deceased's trust disposition and settlement, which directed his trustees to pay such "legacies as he might leave by any writings under his hand, however informal, provided they were clearly expressive of his intentions".[73]

Letter of instructions to lawyer—or testamentary writing?

3.192   It is sometimes difficult to determine whether a letter sent by a

---

[71] *Cameron's Trs.* v. *Mackenzie*, 1915 S.C. 313.

[72] *Graham's Trs.* v. *Gillies*, 1956 S.C. 437, *sub nom. Graham's Trs.* v. *Graham*, 1957 S.L.T. 43.

[73] *Gray's Trs.* v. *Murray*, 1970 S.L.T. (Notes) 3.

deceased person to his or her solicitor is entitled to receive effect as a completed testamentary writing or whether it is merely deliberative, a letter of instructions to draft a formal testamentary writing. The decisions indicate that the court will first consider the terms of the letter. Only if it is unclear whether the letter was intended as a testamentary writing will the court turn to consider extrinsic circumstances to help determine the issue.

Held testamentary

1. A lady was found drowned in circumstances which suggested suicide. She left a formal trust disposition and settlement and codicil in the hands of her solicitor. A letter in an envelope stamped and addressed to her solicitor was found in her handbag, which she had left at the boarding house where she was staying. The letter commenced: "I wish to make an alteration to my will". The terms of the letter made material alterations to her trust disposition and settlement and codicil. The Lord Ordinary held that, in the circumstances, the handbag in the boarding house was a "repository" in which the testatrix might naturally keep a testamentary document and that the letter fell to be treated as a holograph subscribed writing found in her repositories which should receive testamentary effect.[74] The Lord Ordinary's reasoning is not given in the report, and as has been observed "it is impossible to know how far the question of suicide affected his decision".[75]

2. A testatrix left a trust disposition and settlement in which she provided for the disposal of jewellery and personal effects as she might direct by informal writings. After her death, a holograph document addressed to her solicitor (who was also her testamentary trustee) was found which had been subscribed by her and witnessed by two witnesses. It began: "To Mr R—, W.S., I want to add some additional clauses to my Will [followed by list]". It was in a sealed envelope also addressed to her solicitor and found in a drawer in her dressing table. It was held that there was sufficient doubt as to the testamentary character of the document to require reference to extrinsic circumstances, but having regard to these, the document constituted a valid testamentary writing, rather than a letter of instructions to her solicitor with a view to his preparing a formal testamentary document.[76]

---

[74] *Eadie's Trs.* v. *Lauder*, 1952 S.L.T. (Notes) 15.

[75] Per Lord Guest in *McLaren's Trs.* v. *Mitchell and Brattan*, 1959 S.C. 183 at p. 187.

[76] *MacLaren's Trs.* v. *Mitchell & Brattan, supra.*

3.   The deceased left a formal trust disposition and settle-
     ment, with her papers at death. Beside it there were
     found four papers, on separate sheets of letter paper,
     each signed and dated and holograph of the deceased.
     One writing which began with the words: "To be handed
     to [name of law agent], a codicil to my deed; should I be
     taken away suddenly, my trustees would act upon it the
     same as if it were written as a codicil to my settlement",
     was held to be a valid testamentary writing.[77]

Held not to be testamentary

1.   A deceased person signed a will on October 30, 1798. He
     sent to his law agent a signed paper which was dated
     October 21, 1805 and which began: "I wish a codicil to be
     made to my last will and testament in the following
     manner" and continued with detailed testamentary provi-
     sions. The covering letter included the statement: "I send
     you the codicil I wish to be made to my last will and
     testament". The writing of October 21, 1805 was held to
     be merely a paper of instructions.[78] Lord Chancellor Eldon
     expressed the view that although much of the language
     used was of a testamentary nature, the words "I wish a
     codicil to be made to my last will and testament in the
     following manner" denoted that a will should be made
     at a future time. The words were also capable of being
     understood in a present sense, consistent with the pur-
     pose of then framing an actual codicil and this would
     have been the outcome had the deceased kept the papers.
     However, as he had sent the papers with the covering
     letter to his law agent, they could be viewed only as a
     paper of instructions.[79]

2.   The deceased left a formal trust disposition and settle-
     ment, with her papers at death. Beside it there were
     found four papers, on separate sheets of letter paper,
     each signed and dated and holograph of the deceased.
     One writing was headed "codicil" and ended with the
     words: "This is to be handed to [name of law agent] to
     add to my settlement". Accordingly, despite the heading,
     this writing was held to be merely an instruction to her
     law agent.[80]

3.   "Memo to let [name of law agent] know that I wish (the
     bequest and) name of [blank] Cunningham to be erased

[77] *Lowson* v. *Ford* (1866) 4 M. 631.
[78] *Munro* v. *Coutts* (1813) 1 Dow (H.L.) 437.
[79] *Ibid.* at pp. 452–453.
[80] *Lowson* v. *Ford* (1866) 4 M. 631.

from my settlement; and I do hereby desire it to be done". This was signed and found in the deceased's repositories. The deceased's settlement named more than one beneficiary with the surname Cunningham. It was held that the letter was not of the nature of a testamentary writing, but was really a memorandum to her lawyers which was not carried into effect.[81]

4. A testatrix made a holograph will in the form of a letter addressed to a person whom she appointed as executor. In it she disposed of the residue of her estate. When the will was found in her repositories after her death, the residue clause had been deleted in ink without authentication. A codicil was also found which extrinsic facts showed had been signed at the same time as the deletion but was ineffectual as it was neither holograph nor tested. It was held that the codicil and deletion were interdependent and since the codicil was merely deliberative, the deletion must be taken *pro non scripto*.[82]

5. A lady sent to her law agent a holograph *ex facie* validwill dated October 1912. With it she sent a covering letter, dated November 26, 1916, which stated: "What I enclose along with this note is the substance of what I have twice written out on notepaper, once two years before Oct./12 and again about that date, and I wish the date Oct./12 to be retained . . . I don't wish this will lengthened or stretched out in any way further than is absolutely necessary to make it legal. I give my reason for what I have done. I wish that retained in the Will." The law agent, treating the enclosed document as notes for the preparation of a formal will which he already had requested, drafted a trust disposition and settlement which he submitted to his client. She retained the draft and died in 1921 without having taken any further steps in the matter. It was held that the terms of the covering letter, in conjunction with the extrinsic evidence, negatived the view that the document was intended by the deceased to be a completed testament, but rather that it was a memorandum of instructions to draft a will.[83]

6. A medical man sent to his law agent a signed holograph document beginning with the words: "This is my last will and testament." With it he sent a covering letter which stated: "I am sending you a rough draft of what I would like my will to be . . . kindly put it into legal form". The

[81] *Cunningham* v. *Murray's Trs.* (1871) 9 M. 713.
[82] *Gemmell's Exr.* v. *Stirling*, 1923 S.L.T. 384.
[83] *Wilson* v. *Hovell*, 1924 S.C. 1.

agent, treating the document as a memorandum of instructions, prepared the draft of a formal will which he submitted to his client, but before the formal will was completed the client died suddenly. It was held that although the document was *ex facie* valid, the covering letter raised a question as to its true character which could be proved by extrinsic evidence—the correspondence between the deceased and his lawyer. It was further held that it had been proved by extrinsic evidence that the document was intended as a memorandum or note of instructions only.[84]

7.   A testatrix left a formal will, which authorised payment of legacies "contained in any codicil or writing under (her) hand whether formally executed or not". She also left an informally executed writing which was in the form of a letter addressed to her solicitors, dated three years after the will, containing the words: "I wish this to be paid out after my death, although it may not be strictly legal, if I have no opportunity to get it in proper (legal) form . . .". The following year she executed a formal codicil which contained no reference to the bequests in the informal writing. The informal writing was accordingly held to be invalid, as the testatrix had had the opportunity referred to, but had not made use of it.[85]

Letter to a relative or friend—or testamentary writing?

3.193   A letter to a relative or friend, provided that it is holograph and subscribed (see para. 3.76–3.85), and dated prior to August 1, 1995 may be held to be a testamentary writing, where the words are clearly testamentary[86]—that is, the wording is in contemplation of the writer's death, and is apropriate to present testamentary provision. The fact that part of the letter deals with trivial matters is irrelevant.[87]

Subscribed "draft" deeds

3.194   Since the courts must be satisfied that a writing embodies a testator's concluded testamentary intent, there are difficulties where a testator bears to have executed a writing, admittedly testamentary in nature, which bears the word "draft". In one case, a testator left a holograph writing which bore to be sub-

---

[84] *Young's Trs.* v. *Henderson*, 1925 S.C. 749.
[85] *Butler's Exrs.* v. *Walker*, 1935 S.N. 85.
[86] *Ritchie* v. *Whish* (1880) 8 R. 101.
[87] *Per* Lord Patrick in *Draper* v. *Thomason*, 1954 S.L.T. 222 at p. 224.

scribed by him, but was headed "draft of codicil", and contained a blank in the ultimate destination of the estate. The writing had been left in an unlocked drawer, which did not contain the deceased's important papers. Law agents had drawn up a settlement and two codicils which the testator had earlier signed. In these circumstances, the court held that the writing was a draft and not an operative testamentary writing.[88]

3.195 However, the fact that a deed is headed "draft" does not automatically mean that it can never receive effect:

> "when these words were written it is difficult to suppose that he meant it to be anything but a draft. The question comes to be, whether, and at what time, it came to be changed from a draft to a perfect testamentary document? It is signed and if it could be proved that the original was unsigned, and that it was signed *post intervallum*, that would intelligibly fix the point of time when the change took place".[89]

Examples:

1. A signed holograph document headed "Heads by AB for his last will and testament" was upheld as a testamentary writing.[90]

2. A signed holograph document, which was in form a proper testamentary writing, but was headed "Notes of intended settlement" was upheld as a testamentary writing.[91] Lord Chancellor Selbourne stated that "The word 'notes' . . . by no means necessarily implies that something more is afterwards to be done . . . It is not equivalent to 'instructions'"[92] and that the use of "intended" in "intended settlement" did not imply that something had to be done later, but rather that the whole phrase meant "This is the settlement which I intend to make of my estate after my death".

3. A trust disposition and settlement bore on the backing the letters "Dft". It was signed and attested about five years after it was received from law agents and retained until death a year or two later. The deceased had stated verbally that he had made a will and had indicated what its terms were—which were those set out in the draft

---

[88] *Forsyth's Trs.* v. *Forsyth* (1872) 10 M. 616.
[89] *Per* Lord President Inglis, *ibid.*, at p. 618.
[90] *Tod*, Jan. 17, 1859, unreported.
[91] *Hamilton* v. *White* (1881) 8 R. 940 affirmed (1882) 9 R. (H.L.) 53.
[92] *Ibid.*, at pp. 57–58.

deed. A petition under section 39 of the Conveyancing (Scotland) Act 1874 was granted.[93]

4. A document headed "Instructions to make a Will" was proved in England and resealed in Scotland.[94]

5. A holograph will by a testatrix appointing trustees contained *inter alia* the following provision: "As this is merely a preliminary, not a finished, will and testament, I have not particularised as to the personalty as I may do later. That can go to the Indigent Gentlewomen's of Scotland Fund or the Society of Antiquaries". There was no further will or testamentary instructions, and the Society of Antiquaries declined any right to the bequest. It was held that the provision relating to personalty had testamentary force and was not void from uncertainty.[95]

6. Where the deceased had previously signed a formal testament and two codicils prepared by his lawyers, a signed holograph document headed "Draft of Codicil" which contained a new disposition of his estate to his children, and a blank for the ultimate destination, failing children and their issue, was found in a chest with ordinary clothing (not papers), whereas his proper will was in a locked drawer. The holograph document was held not to be a testamentary writing.[96]

7. A holograph codicil, signed and dated, and marked "rough" (a word used by the testator for "draft") was found in a locked safe in a sealed envelope, addressed to the deceased's law agent. It was tied up with a copy of his formal trust disposition and settlement. The testator made drafts of many documents, often signed them, and usually preserved them after the principals were dispatched. The testator had not told anyone about the holograph codicil. Indeed, subsequent to signing it, he had signed various codicils to his trust disposition and settlement, all prepared by his law agent, including one signed a month after the date of the holograph one. The holograph codicil did not receive effect.[97]

Holograph deeds which are *ex facie* valid but are drafts

3.196   Sometimes it can be shown that a signed document, which is

---

[93] *Inglis' Trs.* v. *Inglis* (1901) 4 F. 365.

[94] *Tennant*, July 3, 1867, unreported.

[95] *Flockhart's Trs.* v. *Bourlet*, 1934 S.N. 23 (the report does not contain the *ratio* of the decision).

[96] *Forsyth's Trs.* v. *Forsyth* (1872) 10 M. 616.

[97] *Sprot's Trs.* v. *Sprot*, 1909 S.C. 272.

not marked draft, has wording within it which means that it is merely a memorandum for consideration. In one case, a testator died in May 1922 leaving (1) a formal trust disposition and settlement dated July 5, 1918; (2) a holograph codicil thereto dated August 14, 1919; and (3) a signed pencil document concluding: "This my last will and testament has been written in my own handwriting (here insert date)". This pencil document was written by the testator about a fortnight before his death. On a consideration of the circumstances the Lord Ordinary held that it was not a valid and completed document. The real difficulty was that the words "(here insert date)" pointed to the execution of another document at some future date: in other words, it was merely a memorandum for further consideration.[98]

Soldiers' wills

3.197　While it has long been the case in England that a soldier on active service had certain privileges in making a will, and the normal rules of formal execution are relaxed,[99] it would appear that a Scottish soldier enjoys no such privileges or relaxations.

3.198　The concept of a "Soldier's Testament" originated in Roman law.[1] While Stair, before dealing with the law of succession in Scotland, gives a summary of the Roman law of testation, including a paragraph on "Military Testaments",[2] it does not appear that the Roman law concept of *testamentum militare* has been adopted into Scots law. In one case the point was raised,[3] but the case was instead decided on the ground that the writing failed to show completed testamentary act. Doubt was expressed as to whether a Scottish soldier enjoyed any special privileges in making a will. The original wills of soldiers (and airman) are deposited with the Commissary Court in Edinburgh (see further para. 18.08).

---

[98] *Walker's Trs.* v. *Walker*, 1923 S.L.T. 387.

[99] The rules seem to apply where the deceased was domiciled in England and Wales either at the date of the will or at the time of death (*Halsbury's Laws of England*, vol. 17, para. 829, ff. 3—see generally on soldiers' wills, vol. 17, paras. 825–829 and vol. 50 paras. 270–272).

[1] Justinian, *Inst.*, II.11.

[2] Stair, *Institutions*, III.viii.5.

[3] *Stuart* v. *Stuart*, 1942 S.C. 510.

CHAPTER 4

VALIDITY OF TESTAMENTARY WRITINGS EXECUTED ON OR AFTER AUGUST 1, 1995

Introduction

4.01 Before a Scottish court will confirm a person as executor-nominate—or decern a person as executor-dative *qua* disponee or legatee—a valid testamentary writing must be produced. The Requirements of Writing (Scotland) Act 1995[1] amends the law relating to the formal validity of testamentary writings executed in Scotland on or after August 1, 1995, and while the preceding chapter explores the "old" rules which determine whether a "testamentary writing" is validly executed, this chapter explores the "new" ones. Where relevant, reference is made to the appropriate paragraphs of the preceding chapter, but readers should at all times bear in mind that they should treat with caution the report of a case under the "old" rules which turns on a testamentary writing being holograph of the testator, or adopted as holograph by him: no special privilege attaches to such a writing if it was executed on or after August 1, 1995 (see paras. 4.13, 4.21 and 4.54). The procedures involved in setting up a testamentary writing, alteration etc. which is not self-proving will be dealt with in the separate Supplement.

When do the new rules apply?

4.02 Where a question arises as to whether a testamentary writing can be set up under the "old" rules, or whether its validity can be determined only in the light of the Requirements of Writing (Scotland) Act 1995, then:

    1. If a date of subscription is specified in the deed or testing clause or equivalent, and there is nothing in the document or testing clause or equivalent which indicates that the statement as to the date is incorrect, then the statement as to the date is presumed to be correct.[2] If the date is prior to August 1, 1995, the "old" rules set out in Chapter 3 will apply, but if the date is on or after that day, the rules set out in this Chapter will apply.

---

[1] (c. 7).

[2] Requirements of Writing (Scotland) Act 1995 (c. 7), s. 3(10).

2. If the presumption at 1 above is not applicable, then evidence may be led before the court as to the date of execution (for full procedure see paras. 4.96–4.97) and if the court is satisfied, this will give rise to a presumption as to the date of execution.[3] If the presumed date of execution is prior to August 1, 1995, the "old" rules set out in Chapter 3 will apply, but if the presumed date is on or after that day, the rules set out in this Chapter will apply.

3. If it cannot be ascertained whether a testamentary writing was executed before August 1, 1995, or on or after that date, it is presumed to have been executed after that date[4] and the rules set out in this Chapter will apply.

4.02A   These rules can have unexpected consequences. For example, it may be discovered after a person's death that he left two testamentary writings, one of which he had prepared himself and signed (but didn't date), and the other of which was professionally prepared, containing a clause revoking prior wills, bearing a date prior to August 1, 1995 and is validly executed. Unless evidence can be led as to the date of signing of the "D.I.Y." will, it is presumed to be executed after August 1, 1995, and if it is not self-proving (see paras. 4.08–4.09), it may be set up in an action in terms of section 4(1) of the 1995 Act (see paras. 4.92–4.94). Then, it will receive effect as being the testator's last testamentary writing, for being presumed to have been executed on or after August 1, 1995, it impliedly revokes the professionally prepared will. Obviously the presumption as to the date of signing may be rebutted but the burden of proof will be on the challenger. In contrast, under the "old" rules, there was no presumption which would have favoured the undated will, as being the last testamentary writing.

Which legal system determines the formal validity of a testamentary writing: the rules

4.03   See paragraphs 3.05–3.10 for the rules and paragraph 3.11 for the commissary practice.

TESTAMENTARY CAPACITY

4.04   See paragraphs 3.12–3.15.

---

[3] Requirements of Writing (Scotland) Act 1995 (c. 7), s. 4(2) and (5) (b).
[4] *Ibid.*, s. 14(6).

INABILITY TO SUBSCRIBE

The illiterate testator

4.05   The testamentary writing of an illiterate testator should always be notarially executed (see paras. 4.55 *et seq*).

The blind or partially sighted testator

4.06   It is preferable that the testamentary writing of a blind person should be notarially executed (see para. 4.55 *et seq*), for it is then beyond challenge, provided that the formalities are observed. A blind person may also subscribe a deed in ordinary writing himself,[5] but the execution will then be open to challenge on the ground that the testator did not know what he signed (see para. 3.17). A testamentary writing in Braille, which the testator signed in ordinary writing, his signature being attested, has received effect.[6]

4.07   Section 9(1) of the Requirements of Writing (Scotland) Act 1995, which provides for notarial execution, only applies when the testator declares that he is "blind or unable to write". Consequently, the provision may not provide the partially sighted with a safe method of executing deeds.[7] If a partially sighted person personally subscribes a testamentary writing, but his sight is so poor that he cannot read the whole document himself, it would be prudent for it to be read over to him before he subscribes, for the onus of proof lies on the person who subsequently seeks to have the deed reduced, to show that the partially sighted person was not aware of the contents of the deed.

FORMAL VALIDITY

General outline: the requirements of Scots law

4.08   The rules of Scots law regarding the form of the execution of a

---

[5] Requirements of Writing (Scotland) Act 1995 (c. 7), s. 9(7).

[6] *Broadfoot*, Nov. 13, 1905, unreported: the signed Braille testamentary writing, a copy in ordinary writing and the expert's certificate were recorded with the inventory.

[7] *Cf. Duff* v. *Earl of Fife's Trs.* (1823) 1 Shaw's App. 498 where it was opined that notarial execution under the Act 1579 (c. 80) was restricted to cases where the party could not subscribe, and did not extend to a party who could sign his name but was so blind that he was incapable of reading writing.

testamentary writing executed on or after August 1, 1995[8] can briefly be summarised as follows:

1. The testamentary writing must be subscribed by the test-ator[9]—that is, signed at the end of the last page[10] (see paras. 4.15 and 4.27–4.33).

2. If it consists of more than one sheet, the testamentary writing must be "signed by him on every sheet".[11] By the use of the word "signed", the 1995 Act makes it clear that the signature need not be at the foot of the sheet, though it would clearly be good practice for the testator to do this.

    and

3. The testator's signature should be attested by one com-petent[12] witness,[13] who must sign the deed immediately after the testator signs or acknowledges his signature, the whole process being continuous.[14] The witness's name and address should appear either in the deed or in the testing clause or its equivalent (see paras. 4.50–4.52).[15] The witness's name and address may appear in his own hand or in the hand of someone else, or in typewritten or printed form,[16] and they may be added at any time before the writing is founded on in legal proceedings or registered for preservation in the Books of Council and Session or in the sheriff court books.[17]

4.09   If it appears from the face of a testamentary writing that the above mentioned formalities have been complied with, the writing is said to be self proving and is presumed in law to have been subscribed by the testator, unless there is something in the writing itself or in the testing clause or its equivalent which indicates either

1. that the testamentary writing was not subscribed by the testator as it bears to have been subscribed;[18] or

2. that the writing was not validly witnessed by virtue of any of the following

[8] Requirements of Writing (Scotland) Act 1995 (c. 7), s. 15(2).
[9] *Ibid.*, s. 1(2) (c), s. 2(1) and s. 3(1) (a).
[10] *Ibid.*, s. 7(1).
[11] *Ibid.*, s. 3(2).
[12] See paras. 4.36–4.42.
[13] Requirements of Writing (Scotland) Act 1995 (c. 7), s. 3(1)(b).
[14] *Ibid.*, s. 3(4) (e).
[15] *Ibid.*, s. 3(1) (b).
[16] *Ibid.*, s. 3(3) (b).
[17] *Ibid.*, s. 3(3) (a).
[18] *Ibid.*, s. 3(1) (c) (i).

(a) the signature which bears to be the witness's signature not being such a signature (whether by reason of forgery or otherwise);[19] or

(b) in the case of a mutual will, the person who signed as the witness to the subscription of one testator being the other testator;[20] or

(c) the person who signed as witness not knowing the testator at the time of signing;[21] or

(d) the person who signed as witness being under the age of 16 years at the time of signing;[22] or

(e) the person who signed as witness being mentally incapable of acting as a witness at the time of signing;[23] or

(f) the person who signed as witness not witnessing the testator's subscription;[24] or

(g) the person who signed as witness not signing the writing after the testator, or the testator's subscription or, as the case may be, acknowledgement of his subscription and the witness's subscription not being one continuous process.[25]

4.10 If the testamentary writing is presumed in law to have been subscribed by the testator, it may be founded on without further proof. Such a deed may be challenged, but the onus of proving that it was not validly executed falls on the party objecting to it (see para. 4.90).

4.11 Where the testamentary writing bears to have been subscribed by the testator, but he had failed to sign all sheets, or no person subscribed as witness, or there is something in the writing or in the testing clause or its equivalent which means that it is not *ex facie* valid, it may be set up by a court action if it can be proved in court that it had been subscribed by the testator[26] (see paras. 4.92–4.94). If the court is so satisfied, either the writing will be endorsed with a certificate to that effect, or if it has already been registered in the Books of Council and Session or in the sheriff court books, the court will grant decree to that effect.[27] Such a certificate or decree will give rise to a presumption that the writing has been subscribed by the testator.[28]

---

[19] Requirements of Writing (Scotland) Act 1995 (c. 7), s. 3(1) (c) (ii) and (4) (a).
[20] *Ibid.*, s. 3(1) (c) (ii) and (4) (b).
[21] *Ibid.*, s. 3(1) (c) (ii) and (4) (c) (i).
[22] *Ibid.*, s. 3(1) (c) (ii) and (4) (c) (ii).
[23] *Ibid.*, s. 3(1) (c) (ii) and (4) (c) (iii).
[24] *Ibid.*, s. 3(1) (c) (ii) and (4) (d).
[25] *Ibid.*, s. 3(1) (c) (ii) and (4) (e).
[26] *Ibid.*, s. 4(1).
[27] *Ibid.*
[28] *Ibid.*, s. 4(5) (a).

Annexations to a testamentary writing

4.12   It would seem that the effect of section 8 of the Requirements of Writing (Scotland) Act 1995 is that where there is a schedule or annexation to a testamentary writing, the schedule or annexation (even if it contains dispositive provisions[29]) will receive effect without being subscribed by the testator, provided that it is referred to in the writing and annexed to it, and is identified on its face as being the annexation referred to in the writing.[30] The only exception is where the testamentary writing bequeaths land, and the annexation describes or shows all or any part of the land: then, if the annexation consists of plan(s), drawing(s), photograph(s) or other representation(s) of the land, the testator must, in addition, sign each page, and if it is an inventory, appendix, schedule or other writing, the last page.[31] However, notwithstanding the terms of section 8, it is good practice for a testator to sign *every* page of the Schedule or other annexation to his testamentary writing, for the annexation may then be set up (see paras. 4.92–4.93).

Holograph writings and writings adopted as holograph

4.13   No special privileges attach to holograph writings or writings adopted as holograph, which are subscribed or presumed to have been subscribed on or after August 1, 1995.[32] Consequently, any holograph writing executed on or after August 1, 1995, will require to be set up in the same manner as any other testamentary writing which is not self proving (see paras. 4.92–4.94.).

General rules: the writing medium

4.14   See paragraph 3.28.

SUBSCRIPTION

Subscription: the position of the testator's signature

4.15   A testamentary writing executed on or after August 1, 1995 must be subscribed, that is, it must be signed by the testator at

---

[29] For instance, where a testator directs in his testamentary writing that effect shall be given to the bequests specified in the schedule annexed to it, and the schedule lists a number of pecuniary legacies.

[30] Requirements of Writing (Scotland) Act 1995 (c. 7), s. 7(1) and s. 8(1).

[31] *Ibid.*, s. 8(2) and (3).

[32] *Ibid.*, s. 11(3) (b) (i).

the end of the last page (excluding any annexation).[33] It is submitted that the requirement of signing "at the end of the last
page" means that a testamentary writing which a testator signed
at the end of the writing (i.e. in a formal will, after the words
"In Witness Whereof") is formally subscribed by him and it is
not essential that the testator signed at the foot of the page on
which those words appear.

4.16   Her Majesty may still superscribe.[34]

Subscription: special problems with writings prepared by the testator

4.17   Many of the cases on the "old law", where the question in
issue was whether the testator had subscribed, involve writings
prepared by the testator himself. These cases are discussed fully
at paragraphs 3.33–3.47, and are illustrative of the approach
which it is thought that a court might take in deciding whether
a testamentary writing is subscribed by the testator for the purposes of an application under section 4 of the Requirements of
Writing (Scotland) Act 1995 (see paras. 4.92–4.94). However,
cases which turn on the special status previously given to holograph writings would not now be followed.[35]

Unsubscribed testamentary writings may have been adopted by the testator

4.18   In Scots law, "adoption" is the term used to denote the principle
under which a writing executed prior to August 1, 1995, which
is not probative (and indeed may not have been subscribed by
the testator) may be validated by a properly executed deed.
Under the old law, adoption is a question of intention, and
might be either express (see paras. 3.49–3.70) or implied (see
para. 3.70); express adoption may be effected either by an
endorsed docket (see paras. 3.50–3.54) or by description (see
paras. 3.55–3.70). It has been suggested that, following the
Requirements of Writing (Scotland) Act 1995 coming into effect,
adoption may no longer be recognised as a way of validating
an informal writing. Thus, in his annotations to the 1995 Act,
Professor Kenneth G. C. Reid comments in relation to section
1(2) (c) of the Act:

---

[33] Requirements of Writing (Scotland) Act 1995 (c. 7), s. 7(1).

[34] *Ibid.*, s. 13(1) (a); on the Crown executing a testamentary writing
bequeathing his or her private estates in Scotland, see Crown Private Estates
Act 1862 (25 & 26 Vict., c. 37), s. 6.

[35] Requirements of Writing (Scotland) Act 1995 (c. 7), s. 11(3) (b) (i).

"The previous law allowed a testator to provide in his will for the validity of future informal testamentary writings. It is unclear whether such 'enfranchising' clauses are now effective. This is because a future informal writing may be classified either as a will or as a codicil, and so would itself require to be in formal writing by para. (c)."

Professor Reid's comment raises a question as to whether a court will recognise any "adoption" (whether express or implied) as in itself a valid way of a testator ensuring that testamentary effect will be given to an "informal" writing which is not self proving. One must then question whether a distinction falls to be drawn between a testamentary writing which adopts another writing which is already in existence (the "adopted" writing being viewed as a schedule or annexation to the testamentary writing and receiving effect as such an annexation— see paragraph 4.12) and a testamentary writing which adopts future writings (the future writings being viewed as codicils and thus requiring to be subscribed).

4.19   It is, however, submitted that the doctrine of adoption is not strictly part of the law of evidence relating to the execution of a testamentary writing and therefore section 1(2) (c) of the 1995 Act would have no application. It is also to be noted that, except in section 1(2) (c) of the 1995 Act, the words "testamentary document" are used throughout the 1995 Act—a phrase which, it is submitted, is more likely to encompass an informal writing of a testamentary nature than the words in section 1(2) (c). It will, however, fall to the courts to determine whether section 1(2) (c) of the 1995 Act applies to all (or any) informal writings which would, under the previous law, have been adopted. Given that the objective of the 1995 Act would appear to have been to liberalise the rules on executing deeds, it would indeed be bizarre if the effect of the Act is to make invalid a writing which would have been validly adopted under the old rules.

4.20   Until the matter is judicially determined, it is likely that commissary practice will, in general, be to accept as valid an informal writing which bears to have been adopted by a validly executed testamentary writing—which is either probative, or otherwise validly executed under the "old" rules, or, in terms of section 3(1) of the Requirements of Writing (Scotland) Act 1995, is presumed to have been subscribed by the deceased, or, in terms of section 4(1), is held to have been subscribed by the deceased. The position is likely to be different where the informal writing bears to appoint an executor or to substantially alter the distribution of the deceased's estate and, in such a case, it is likely that the practice will be that the informal writing must be set up under the procedure provided by section 4(1) of the 1995 Act (see paras. 4.92–4.93).

Express adoption: endorsed docket on unsubscribed writings

4.21 Under the law applying to deeds executed before August 1, 1995, a testator could expressly adopt a deed by writing a docket such as "Adopted as holograph" in his own hand at the end of the deed, and then subscribing the docket (see paras. 3.50–3.54). Where the docket was subscribed or is presumed to have been subscribed on or after August 1, 1995, no special privilege attaches to the docket[36] and it will effectively be treated as *pro non scripto*.

4.22 However, the deed may still receive effect if, in terms of section 3(1) of the Requirements of Writing (Scotland) Act 1995, the deceased is presumed to have subscribed the docket (*i.e.* he subscribed the docket and his signature was witnessed, with the witness's name and address being inserted), or, following an application under section 4(1), the court holds that the docket was subscribed by the deceased (see paras. 4.92–4.94). There will certainly be no difficulty if such a docket were inserted at the end of the testamentary writing. If the docket is inserted elsewhere, the courts may take a different view, for, if the former doctrine of "adoption" no longer has effect, then the writing, not being subscribed, cannot receive effect.

Express adoption: incorporation of future unsubscribed writings by description

4.23 Under the law prior to August 1, 1995, express adoption of an unsubscribed document could be effected by description "if, in another writing which unmistakably identifies that document, the testator designates and adopts it as containing his will"[37]— indeed, the adopted writing might be a future writing (see paras. 3.62–3.68). There is some doubt as to whether, since August 1, 1995, such a writing may be adopted (see paras. 4.18–4.20). If an informal writing dealing, perhaps, with the disposal of jewellery or personal effects, falls to be considered—in the language of section 1(2) (c) of the 1995 Act—as "any will, testamentary trust disposition and settlement or codicil"[38], then the informal writing must be set up under section 4 of the 1995 Act (see para. 4.92–4.94) if it is to receive effect. This should not prove an insurmountable difficulty, provided that the informal writing was, as is generally the case, subscribed. In addition,

---

[36] Requirements of Writing (Scotland) Act 1995 (c. 7), s. 11(3) (b) (i).

[37] *Per* Lord President Clyde in *Stenhouse* v. *Stenhouse*, 1922 S.C. 370 at pp. 372–373.

[38] See the note to s. 1(2) (c) of the Annotations to the Requirements of Writing (Scotland) Act 1995 referred to at para. 4.18.

in some cases, it may be possible to validate the informal writing as an annexation to the will under section 8 of the 1995 Act (see para. 4.12).

Express adoption: endorsed dockets on envelopes containing unsubscribed writings or on backings to unsubscribed writings

4.24 Prior to August 1, 1995, the law gave effect to an informal writing which was validated by an adoptive docket on the envelope which contained it, or on the backing to the writing (see paras. 3.69–3.70). Where such a docket was subscribed or is presumed to have been subscribed on or after August 1, 1995, it is unclear whether effect will be given to it (see para. 4.18–4.20). If the docket contains a testamentary provision, refers to the informal writing and is signed, and the informal writing refers to the docket, it may be possible to set up the docket as a testamentary writing, with the informal writing being an annexation thereto.[39]

Implied adoption of unsubscribed writings

4.25 Lord Sands defined implied adoption as the case "where the [testator], being under the erroneous impression that his deed is validly executed proceeds to validly execute a subsequent writing in terms which shew that he regards the prior deed as valid and means it to be acted upon",[40] the exact wording of the subsequent writing determining whether the earlier document is impliedly adopted by the subsequent one (for cases see para. 3.71). It is arguable that where the earlier writing dates from after August 1, 1995, it cannot be impliedly adopted by a later testamentary writing.[41]

Subscription to be unaided

4.26 See paragraph 3.72. If, due to infirmity or poor literacy skills, the testator has difficulty in signing, it should be considered whether the testamentary writing should be notarially executed (see para. 4.55 *et seq*).

Subscription: method of signature

4.27 The signature must be written by the testator.[42] The testator

---

[39] Requirements of Writing (Scotland) Act 1995 (c. 7). ss. 4(1) and 8(1) and (3).
[40] *Cross's Trs.* v. *Cross*, 1921, 1 S.L.T. 244 at p. 245.
[41] Requirements of Writing (Scotland) Act 1995 (c. 7), s. 1(2) (c).
[42] *Ibid.*, s. 3(1) (a) and (c) (i).

should not trace or blacken his name written in pencil or with a pin by another.[43]

4.28   Since legibility is unimportant, it is not good practice to permit a testator to retouch his signature after execution. Where a testamentary writing bears the deceased's signature which is clearly retouched, it is possible that the sheriff or commissary clerk may require special authority from the sheriff to confirm the executor-nominate. In this event, it is thought that the sheriff will normally view the testamentary writing as being a deed subscribed by the testator for the purposes of the 1995 Act, but it will be open to anyone to challenge it (see para. 4.29).

Subscription: signature on erasure

4.29   If the testator's signature is written on an erasure, or on correcting fluid, it is likely that the sheriff or commissary clerk will require special authority from the sheriff to confirm the executor-nominated in that testamentary writing. It is thought that in most cases, the sheriff will view the testamentary writing as being subscribed by the testator for the purposes of the 1995 Act, but it will be open to anyone to prove that the writing was not signed by the testator, or that the witness witnessed the earlier subscription (which had been erased) and not the one on the writing, when found (see para. 4.90).[44]

Subscription: the form of the signature

4.30   The Requirements of Writing (Scotland) Act 1995 has considerably extended what constitutes an acceptable signature. The old rules still apply to the nobility and members of the Royal Family:[45] a peer may still sign by his title; his son (if not himself a nobleman), the courtesy title by which he is known; and a peer's wife (who is not a peeress in her own right), her husband's title prefixed by her own christian name, or (if she is a peeress in her own right), her own title prefixed by her christian name.[46] For others, a signature may either be

1.   the full name by which the testator is identified in the testamentary writing or in any testing clause or the equivalent;[47] a territorial designation may be added;[48] or

---

[43] *Crosbie* v. *Picken* (1749) Mor. 16814.
[44] *Cf. Brown* v. *Duncan* (1888) 15 R. 511.
[45] Requirements of Writing (Scotland) Act 1995 (c. 7), s. 7(6).
[46] Bell, *Lectures on Conveyancing* (3rd ed), p. 37.
[47] Requirements of Writing (Scotland) Act 1995.
[48] Requirements of Writing (Scotland) Act 1995 (c. 7), s. 14(5).

2. the testator's surname, preceded by at least one forename (or an initial or abbreviation or familiar form of a forename);[49] a territorial designation may be added;[50] or

3. any other "name or description or an initial or mark if it is established that the name, description, initial or mark

    (a) was the testator's usual method of signing, or his usual method of signing documents of the type in question; or

    (b) was intended by the testator as his signature of the document".[51]

4.31 If the form of the testator's signature satisfies either category 1 or category 2 above, it will automatically be treated as a valid subscription by the testator for the purposes of section 3(1) (a), but if it satisfies category 3, this is not the case,[52] and it will be necessary to go to court to prove that it had been subscribed by the testator[53] (see para. 4.103). If the court is satisfied that the particular "signature" was the testator's usual method of signing, or was intended by him as his signature of the document, the writing will be endorsed with a certificate to the effect that it was subscribed by the testator, or, if it has already been registered in the Books of Council and Session or in the sheriff court books, the court will grant decree to the same effect.[54] Such a certificate or decree will give rise to a presumption that the testamentary writing had been subscribed by the testator.[55]

4.32 An incomplete signature (as where the testator signs his forename but only the first few letters of his surname), even although attested, will be ineffective, unless it can be shown that this was his normal method of signing or intended by him as his signature of the writing. Thus, if the witness could give evidence that after writing the incomplete signature, the testator had remarked "That's the best I can do. That will have to pass for my signature", the writing is, likely to receive effect. In contrast if he had said "I can't finish in it. I haven't the strength in the hand to sign," it is unlikely to receive effect.

4.33 At the time of writing it is unclear what approach will be taken if different pages of a testamentary writing bear different "signatures". It is submitted that no special notice will be taken if the signatures all fall within the categories numbered 1 and 2 at paragraph 4.30, but if one falls within category 3, then proof must be led.

---

[49] Requirements of Writing (Scotland) Act 1995 (c. 7), s. 7(2) (b).
[50] *Ibid.*, s. 14(5).
[51] *Ibid.*, s. 7(2) (c).
[52] *Ibid.*, s. 7(2) (c), read with s. 3(1).
[53] *Ibid.*, s. 4(1).
[54] *Ibid.*
[55] *Ibid.*, s. 4(5) (a).

Subscription of a mutual will

4.34   The signature of each party to a mutual will must be witnessed. One party to the mutual will may not witness the signature of the other.[56] If one person witnesses the signature of both parties, it is necessary for the witness to sign only once.[57]

4.35   If one party to a mutual will signed in the presence of a witness, but the other did not, it will be presumed that the mutual will was subscribed by the former,[58] and will be held to be valid *vis a vis* his estate.[59] The mutual will will not be presumed to have been subscribed by the latter, though it can be set up under section 4 of the 1995 Act (see paras 4.92–4.93).

Incompetent witnesses

4.36   The following notes provide guidance as to who may competently witness a testator's signature. However, it should be remembered that even if a testamentary writing is not properly witnessed, it may still be set up by a court action provided that it was subscribed by the testator (see paras. 4.92–4.93), and thus receive effect.

Age

4.37   Since September 25, 1991, an individual of or over the age of 16 years can act as a witness.[60] If it appears from the face of the testamentary writing or the testing clause or its equivalent that the person who signed as witness was under the age of 16 years at the time of signing,[61] or, if in a subsequent proceeding relating to the testamentary writing, it is so established,[62] the presumption that the writing was subscribed by the testator is lost.

Blindness

4.38   A blind person cannot see a testator subscribing his testamentary writing, nor can he identify what the testator may acknowledge as his signature. A blind person is therefore not a competent witness. If it appears from the face of the testamentary writing or the testing clause or its equivalent that the person who signed as witness did not witness the testator's subscription because he was blind,[63] or, in a subsequent proceeding

---

[56] Requirements of Writing (Scotland) Act 1995 (c. 7), s. 3(1) (c) (ii) and (4) (b).
[57] *Ibid.*, s. 7(5).
[58] *Ibid.*, s. 3(1).
[59] Cf. *Millar* v. *Birrell* (1876) 4 R. 87.
[60] Age of Legal Capacity (Scotland) Act 1991 (c. 50), s. 1(1) (a) and s. 9.
[61] Requirements of Writing (Scotland) Act 1995 (c. 7), s. 3(1) (c) (ii) and (4) (c) (ii).
[62] *Ibid.*, s. 3(4) (c)(ii).
[63] *Ibid.*, s. 3(1) (c) (ii) and (4) (d).

relating to the testamentary writing, it is so established,[64] the presumption that the writing was subscribed by the testator is lost.

Mental incapacity

4.39 A person mentally incapable of acting as a witness is not a competent witness. If it appears from the face of the testamentary writing or the testing clause or its equivalent that the person who signed as witness was mentally incapable of acting as witness at the time of signing,[65] or, in a subsequent proceeding relating to the testamentary writing, it is so established,[66] the presumption that the writing was subscribed by the testator is lost.

Personal interest

4.40 While it is not good practice for the witness of a deed to be someone with an interest under the deed (such as a named beneficiary,[67] a trustee,[68] or the other testator in the case of a mutual will), it is not a fundamental objection to the validity of the execution that the witness had an interest under the deed. However, since the fact that the witness had an interest may be material if the will is challenged on other grounds (for instance, facility and circumvention) the practice should be avoided. An individual may, but should not, act as a witness to his or her spouse's signature.[69]

Witness must know testator and must have mandate from him

4.41 The witness should, at the time of signing, know the testator,[70] but it is sufficient if he had credible information at that time of the testator's identity,[71] such as a reliable introduction by name. If it appears from the face of the testamentary writing or the testing clause or its equivalent, that the person who signed as witness did not, at the time of signing, know the testator,[72] or, in a subsequent proceeding relating to the testamentary writing, it is so established,[73] the presumption that the writing was sub-

---

[64] Requirements of Writing (Scotland) Act 1995 (c. 7), s. 3(4) (d).

[65] *Ibid.*, s. 3(1) (c) (ii) and (4) (c) (iii).

[66] *Ibid.*, s. 3(4) (c)(iii).

[67] *Graham* v. *Marquis of Montrose* (1685) Mor. 16887; *Ingram* v. *Steinson* (1801) Mor. App. 1 Writ No. 2; *Simsons* v. *Simsons* (1883) 10 R. 1247.

[68] *Mitchell* v. *Miller* (1742) Mor. 16900; *Ingram* v. *Steinson, supra.*

[69] But see *obiter dicta* by Lord Johnston in *Brownlee* v. *Robb*, 1907 S.C. 1302 at p. 1310 where he opined that where the testator left his estate to his wife, attestation by the wife "would have been more than doubtful".

[70] Requirements of Writing (Scotland) Act 1995 (c. 7), s. 3(4) (c) (i).

[71] *Ibid.*, s. 3(5).

[72] *Ibid.*, s. 3(1) (c) (ii) and (4) (c) (i).

[73] *Ibid.*, s. 3(4) (c)(i).

scribed by the testator is lost, but it may still be set up by court action (see paras. 4.92–4.93).

4.42   In a case under the "old" law, the view was expressed that a party who was a casual, accidental or concealed witness to the execution could not competently act as a witness,[74] and this would still seem to be good law.

The function of the witness

4.43   The witness to a testamentary writing does not have any concern with the contents of the deed,[75] but to be a witness, he must either

   1.   see the testator subscribe the document; or

   2.   have the testator acknowledge his subscription to him:[76] it is probably still the case that the acknowledgement need not be in words,[77] but a verbal acknowledgement is more normal.

4.44   If it appears from the face of the testamentary writing or the testing clause or its equivalent, that the person who signed as witness did not witness the subscription,[78] or, in a subsequent proceeding relating to the testamentary writing, it is so established,[79] the presumption that the writing was subscribed by the testator is lost, though it may still be set up by court action (see paras. 4.92–4.93).

Must the witness sign at the time of subscription?

4.45   The witness to a testator's signature must sign immediately after the testator has signed or acknowledged his signature to the witness. If it appears from the face of the testamentary writing or its testing clause or its equivalent that the person who signed as witness did not sign after the testator, or "that the (testator's) subscription or, as the case may be, acknowledgement of his subscription and the person's signature as witness of that subscription were not one continuous process",[80] or, in a sub-

---

[74] *Obiter, per* Lord Justice Clerk Moncrieff in *Tener's Trs.* v. *Tener's Trs.* (1879) 6 R. 1111 at p. 1115.
[75] *Ormistoun* v. *Hamilton* (1708) Mor. 16890.
[76] Requirements of Writing (Scotland) Act 1995 (c. 7), s. 3(7).
[77] *Cumming* v. *Skeoch's Trs.* (1879) 6 R. 540, 963.
[78] Requirements of Writing (Scotland) Act 1995 (c. 7), s. 3(1) (c) (ii) and (4) (d).
[79] *Ibid.,* s. 3(4) (d).
[80] *Ibid.,* s. 3(1) (c) (ii) and (4) (e). Section 3(6) contains special rules to cover the situation where one person witnesses the signature of two or more parties to a deed.

sequent proceeding relating to the testamentary writing, it is so established,[81] the presumption that the writing was subscribed by the testator is lost, though it may still be set up by court action (see paras. 4.92–4.93).

The form of the witness's signature

4.46   The 1995 Act specifies what constitutes the signature of a witness. A witness may use either

1. the full name by which he is identified in the document or in any testing clause or its equivalent; or

2. his surname, preceded by at least one forename, or an initial or abbreviation or familiar form of a forename.[82]

The witness may also add a territorial designation to his signature.[83]

4.47   If the person purporting to act as a witness to a deed signs any other name or description or writes his initials only, or makes a mark, the deed is not witnessed, and will not receive effect. It is probably the case that the witness's signature need not be legible,[84] though if it is truly illegible, it may be impossible to show that it meets the statutory requirements, as set out in paragraph 4.46.

4.48   The old rules as to what constitutes a valid signature by the nobility and members of the Royal Family still apply[85]: a peer may still sign by his title; his son (if not himself a nobleman), the courtesy title by which he is known; a peer's wife (who is not a peeress in her own right), her husband's title prefixed by her own christian name, or (if she is a peeress in her own right), her own title prefixed by her christian name.[86]

Position of the signature of the witness

4.49   The Requirements of Writing (Scotland) Act 1995 does not specifically deal with the question of where in a deed the witness

---

[81] Requirements of Writing (Scotland) Act 1995 (c. 7), s. 3(4) (e). Section 3(6) contains special rules to cover the situation where one person witnesses the signature of two or more parties to a deed.
[82] *Ibid.*, s. 7(5) (a) and (b).
[83] *Ibid.*, s. 14(5).
[84] *Cf. Stirling Stuart* v. *Stirling Crawfurd's Trs.* (1885) 12 R. 610 (where a testator's illegible signature was upheld).
[85] Requirements of Writing (Scotland) Act 1995 (c. 7), s. 7(6).
[86] Bell, *Lectures on Conveyancing* (3rd ed), p. 37.

should sign, for it merely states that "the document (should bear) to have been signed by a person as a witness of that granter's subscription".[87] The signature of the witness is normally below or beside the testator's signature, but if, in a deed subscribed or presumed to have been subscribed on or after August 1, 1995, the witness signs on a subsequent page it may be set up by an application to the court under section 4 of the 1995 Act (see paras. 4.92–4.93).

THE TESTING CLAUSE

The testing clause

4.50   A testing clause is customary, though not essential. It may be filled up at any stage—long after the signing, and even after the death of the testator or witness.[88] However, once the testamentary writing has been founded on in legal proceedings or registered for preservation in the Books of Council and Session or in the sheriff court books, the name and address of the witness may not be added.[89]

4.51   The Secretary of State has power to prescribe, by statutory instrument, the form of a testing clause, although it will still be competent to set out the necessary information in the traditional form of testing clause.[90] At the time of writing, no such statutory instrument has been made.

4.52   The testing clause should specify "whatever is directly connected with the subscription and authentication of the deed".[91] Under Scots law, it has never been essential to specify the place and date of signing[92] or the witness's name in a testing clause, and even under the Requirements of Writing (Scotland) Act 1995, this is still the case. However, it is now customary to insert the following information:

1.   The number of pages;

2.   The date of execution: the date of execution determines whether the Requirements of Writing (Scotland) Act 1995 applies, whether the deceased had testamentary capacity at the time of execution, and which, of a number of docu-

---

[87] Requirements of Writing (Scotland) Act 1995 (c. 7), s. 3(1) (b).
[88] *Per* Lord Dunedin in *Walker* v. *Whitwell*, 1916 S.C. (H.L.) 75 at p. 80.
[89] Requirements of Writing (Scotland) Act 1995 (c. 7), s. 3(3) (a).
[90] *Ibid.*, s. 10(1) and (2).
[91] *Per* Lord Deas in *Smiths* v. *Chambers' Trs.* (1877) 5 R. 97 at pp. 109–110.
[92] Erskine, *Inst.* III.ii.18; *Per* Lord Anderson in *Cairney* v. *Macgregor's Trs.*, 1916, 1 S.L.T. 357 at p. 359.

ments, constitutes the deceased's last testamentary writing; it can also be critical in applying the Wills Act 1963, to determine whether the writing is formally valid;

3. The place of execution: the place of execution can be critical in applying the Wills Act 1963;

4. Any erasures (the correction of errors) made in the testamentary writing before subscription;

5. Any marginal additions or interlineations made to the testamentary writing before subscription;

6. Any blanks in the testamentary writing filled up before subscription;

7. The name and address of the witness; and

8. Any discrepancy between the signature and the full name (as given in the deed or testing clause) of either the testator or the witness.

The testing clause should not incorporate testamentary provisions

4.53 See paragraph 3.109.

HOLOGRAPH TESTAMENTARY WRITINGS

Holograph testamentary writings

4.54 The law does not attribute any special privilege to a testamentary writing which is holograph of the testator and executed on or after August 1, 1995.[93] If such a writing is to receive effect, it must be either self proving (that is, signed on each page by the testator and subscribed by him on the final page in the presence of one witness, the witness's name and address being inserted), or set up in a court action (see paras. 4.92–4.94).

NOTARIAL EXECUTION

Persons who may notarially execute a testamentary writing

4.55 The notarial execution of a testamentary writing may be effected

---

[93] Requirements of Writing (Scotland) Act 1995 (c. 7), s. 11(3) (b) (i).

in terms of section 9 of the Requirements of Writing (Scotland) Act 1995 either by

1. a solicitor who has in force a practising certificate as defined in section 4(c) of the Solicitors (Scotland) Act 1980;

2. an advocate;

3. a justice of the peace;

4. a sheriff clerk; and

5. in relation to documents executed outwith Scotland, a notary public or any other person with official authority under the law of the place of execution to execute documents on behalf of persons who are blind or unable to write.[94]

From August 1, 1995, a testamentary writing cannot be notarially executed by a parish minister.[95]

4.56   In this chapter, the word "notary" is used to refer to any person who is statutorily entitled to execute a testamentary writing notarially.

Notary should not have a personal interest in the testamentary writing

4.57   If, prior to August 1, 1995, a notary had executed a testamentary writing in which he had a personal interest, the writing was null.[96] In contrast, where on or after August 1, 1995, a notary executes notarially a writing

"which confers on [the notary] or his spouse, son or daughter a benefit in money or money's worth (whether directly or indirectly), [the document] shall be invalid to the extent, but only to the extent, that it confers such benefit."[97]

Thus, if a notarially executed testamentary writing appointed the notary himself, or his partner, to be trustee or executor, the writing and the notary's appointment as trustee or executor would be valid and he would be entitled to be confirmed as such, but the clause in the testamentary writing permitting the trustee or executor to charge remuneration for his services

[94] Requirements of Writing (Scotland) Act 1995 (c. 7), s. 9(6).
[95] The Church of Scotland (Property and Endowments) (Amendment) Act 1933 (23 & 24 Geo. 5, c. 44), s. 13 was repealed by Requirements of Writing (Scotland) Act 1995 (c. 7), s. 14(2) Sched. 5.
[96] See paras. 3.136–3.137.
[97] Requirements of Writing (Scotland) Act 1995 (c. 7), s. 9(4).

would be treated as invalid *vis a vis* the notary or his partner.

4.58   Again, if a deceased person had made a will bequeathing a legacy to a charity and the residue to a person who was the son of a solicitor, and subsequently that solicitor notarially executed a codicil to that will, which, revoked the legacy to the charity, since this revocation would indirectly benefit the notary's son, the clause in the codicil revoking the legacy would be treated as invalid.

4.59   It is unclear what the consequences would be if a codicil was notarially executed by a solicitor whose partner had been appointed trustee, entitled to remuneration, in the original testamentary writing—would he only be able to charge a fee on the basis of the original testamentary instructions? or would he not be able to charge a fee at all?[98]

The formalities of a notarial execution

4.60   When a testamentary writing falls to be notarially executed on or after August 1, 1995, the formalities are as follows:

1.   The testator must declare to the notary "that he is blind or unable to write".[99]

2.   The notary may either read the testamentary writing over to the testator,[1] or the testator may make a declaration that he does not wish him to do so.[2]

3.   The testator must authorise the notary to subscribe for him,[3] and this must be evident from the testamentary writing.[4]

4.   The notary, on behalf of the testator, subscribes the testamentary writing,[5] signing his own name.'[6]

5.   If the testamentary writing consists of more than one

[98] *Irving v. Snow*, 1956 S.C. 257.
[99] Requirements of Writing (Scotland) Act 1995 (c. 7), s. 9(1).
[1] *Ibid.*, s. 9(1) (a).
[2] *Ibid.*, s. 9(1) (b).
[3] *Ibid.*, s. 9(1).
[4] *Ibid.*, s. 3(1) (a) as applied to notarial executions by s. 9(3) and modified by Sched. 3, para. 2.
[5] *Ibid.*, s. 9(1).
[6] *Ibid.*, s. 3(1) (a) as applied to notarial executions by s. 9(3) and modified by Sched. 3, para. 1. As to the form of the notary's signature, see paras. 4.30–4.31.

sheet, the notary signs his own name[7] on each prior sheet.[8]

6.   The whole process takes place in the presence of the test-ator,[9] and of one competent[10] witness. The witness must sign[11] as witness to the notary's subscription,[12] and of the whole process outlined at 2 and 3 above.[13] The witness should sign immediately after the notary subscribes, the whole process being continuous.[14] The witness's name and address must appear either in the deed, the testing clause or its equivalent[15] and may be inserted in his own hand or in the hand of someone else or in typewritten or printed form,[16] and they may be added at any time before the writing is founded on in legal proceedings or regis-tered for preservation in the Books of Council and Session or in the sheriff court books.[17]

Normally, there will be a notarial docket, for the testa-mentary writing or testing clause or its equivalent must state that the writing was read to the testator by the notary before subscription (or that it was not so read because the testator did not wish the notary to do so).

4.61   If it appears from the face of the testamentary writing that the above formalities have been complied with, the testamentary writing is presumed in law to have been subscribed by the notary and the statement as to the writing having been read over or the declaration made is presumed to be correct,[18] unless there is something in the writing itself or in the testing clause or its equivalent which indicates either

1.   that the testamentary writing was not subscribed by the notary as it bears to have been subscribed;[19] or

2.   that the statement as to the writing having been read over

---

[7] Requirements of Writing (Scotland) Act 1995 (c. 7).

[8] *Ibid.*, ss. 9(1) and 3(2).

[9] *Ibid.*, s. 9(2).

[10] See paras. 4.36–4.42, the statutory references to s. 3(4) of the Requirements of Writing (Scotland) Act 1995 being modified by s. 9(3) and Sched. 3, para. 4. and the provision set out in s. 3(7) being deleted by Sched. 3, para. 6.

[11] For the form of a witness's signature, see paras. 4.46–4.48.

[12] Requirements of Writing (Scotland) Act 1995 (c. 7), s. 3(4) (d) as modified by s. 9(3) and Sched. 3, para. 4.

[13] *Ibid.*, s. 3(4) (dd) as modified by s. 9(3) and Sched. 3, para. 4.

[14] *Ibid.*, s. 3(4) (e) as modified by s. 9(3) and Sched. 3, para. 4.

[15] *Ibid.*, s. 3(1) (c) as modified by s. 9(3) and Sched. 3, para. 2.

[16] *Ibid.*, s. 3(3) (c) as applied to notarial executions by s. 9(3) and modified by Sched. 3, para. 3.

[17] *Ibid.*, s. 3(3) (a) as applied to notarial executions by s. 9(3).

[18] *Ibid.*, s. 3(1) (d) as modified by s. 9(3) and Sched. 3, para. 2.

[19] *Ibid.*, s. 3(1) (d) (i) as modified by s. 9(3) and Sched. 3, para. 2.

to the testator by the notary before subscription, or as to the testator declaring that he did not wish this done, is incorrect;[20] or

3.   that the writing was not validly witnessed by virtue of any of the following:

      (a)   the signature which bears to be the witness's signature not being such a signature (whether by reason of forgery or otherwise);[21] or

      (b)   in the case of a mutual will, the person who signed as the witness to the notary's subscription being the other testator;[22] or

      (c)   the person who signed as witness not knowing the testator at the time of signing;[23] or

      (d)   the person who signed as witness being under the age of 16 years at the time of signing;[24] or

      (e)   the person who signed as witness being mentally incapable of acting as a witness at the time of signing;[25] or

      (f)   the person who signed as witness not seeing the notary's subscriber;[26] or

      (g)   the person who signed as witness not witnessing the testator granting authority to the notary to subscribe the writing on his behalf, or not witnessing the notary reading the writing to the testator (or the testator declaring that he did not wish the notary to do so);[27] or

      (h)   the person who signed as witness not signing the writing after the notary, or the notary's subscription and the witness's signature not being one continuous process.[28]

4.62   If the testamentary writing is presumed in law to have been

---

[20] Requirements of Writing (Scotland) Act 1995 (c. 7), s. 3(1) (d) (ii) as modified by s. 9(3) and Sched. 3, para. 2.

[21] *Ibid.*, s. 3(1) (d) (iii) and s. 3(4) (a) as modified by s. 9(3) and Sched. 3, paras. 2 and 4.

[22] *Ibid.*, s. 3(1) (d) (iii) and s. 3(4) (b) as modified by s. 9(3) and Sched. 3, paras. 2 and 4.

[23] *Ibid.*, s. 3(1) (d) (iii) and s. 3(4) (c) (i) as modified by s. 9(3) and Sched. 3, paras. 2 and 4.

[24] *Ibid.*, s. 3(1) (d) (iii) and s. 3(4) (c) (ii) as modified by s. 9(3) and Sched. 3, paras. 2 and 4.

[25] *Ibid.*, s. 3(1) (d) (iii) and s. 3(4) (c) (iii) as modified by s. 9(3) and Sched. 3, paras. 2 and 4.

[26] *Ibid.*, s. 3(1) (d) (iii) and (4) (d) as modified by s. 9(3) and Sched. 3, paras. 2 and 4.

[27] *Ibid.*, s. 3(1) (d) (iii) and (4) (dd) as modified by s. 9(3) and Sched. 3, paras. 2 and 4.

[28] *Ibid.*, s. 3(1) (d) (iii) and (4) (e) as modified by s. 9(3) and Sched. 3, paras. 2 and 4.

subscribed by the testator, it may be founded on without further proof. Such a deed may be challenged, but the onus of proving that it was not validly executed falls on the party objecting to it (see para. 4.91).

4.63 Where the testamentary writing bears to have been subscribed by the notary under section 9 of the Requirements of Writing (Scotland) Act 1995 on behalf of the testator, but he has failed to sign all sheets, or no person subscribed as witness, or the procedure of reading over the deed (or the testator declaring that he did not wish this done) was not followed or there is something in the writing or in the testing clause or its equivalent which means that it is not *ex facie* valid, it may still be set up by a court action if it can be proved in court that it had been subscribed by the notary with the authority of the testator and that the notary read the writing to the testator before subscription or did not read it because the testator did not wish him to do so[29] (see para. 4.95). If the court is so satisfied, either the writing will be endorsed with a certificate to that effect, or if it has already been registered in the Books of Council and Session or in the sheriff court books, the court will grant decree to that effect.[30] Such a decree or certificate will give rise to a presumption that the writing has been subscribed by the notary and the procedure of reading over the deed (or the testator declaring that he did not wish this done) duly complied with.[31]

Notarial execution of mutual wills

4.64 Where a mutual will has to be notarially executed, it is undesirable that the agent of one party executes notarially for the other party.[32]

4.65 Where both parties to a mutual will require to have the deed executed for them notarially, it is preferable if two notaries are used,[33] although if the mutual will is revocable by both parties, it is probably unobjectionable for the same notary to execute for both parties.[34]

4.66 If the mutual will is subscribed notarially for one party and the other party subscribes himself, it is of no objection if the same

[29] Requirements of Writing (Scotland) Act 1995 (c. 7), s. 4(1) as modified by s. 9(3) and Sched. 3, para. 7.
[30] *Ibid.*, s. 4(1) as modified by s. 9(3) and Sched. 3, para. 7.
[31] *Ibid.*, s. 4(5) (a), (as modified by s. 9(3) and Sched. 3, para. 8), and s. 9(2).
[32] *Per* Lord Rutherfurd Clark in *Lang* v. *Lang's Trs.* (1889) 16 R. 590 at p. 598.
[33] *Craig* v. *Richartson* (1610) Mor. 16,829 and discussion on that case in *Graeme* v. *Graeme's Trs.* (1868) 7 M. 14.
[34] *Graeme* v. *Graeme's Trs.* (1868) 7 M. 14.

person witnesses both the subscription by one testator, and the notarial execution for the other.[35]

International aspects of notarial execution

4.67   A testamentary writing, which has been notarially executed, is treated as valid if it is validly executed in terms of the Wills Act 1963 (see paras. 3.07 *et seq.*). Where Scots law is to be applied, the notarial execution will be treated as valid if it was executed in terms of section 9 of the Requirements of Writing (Scotland) Act 1995 by "a notary public or any other person with official authority under the law of the place of execution to execute documents on behalf of persons who are blind or unable to write".[36]

ADDITIONAL SOLEMNITIES FIXED BY TESTATOR

May a testator fix additional formalities beyond those prescribed by the Requirements of Writing (Scotland) Act 1995

4.68   While there have been cases where it was recognised that a testator could self impose additional formalities beyond those required by law for the execution of a testamentary writing (see paras. 3.150 *et seq.*), this is no longer the case. Section 2(1) of the Requirements of Writing (Scotland) Act 1995 provides that

> "No document required by section 1(2) of this Act [which includes the making of any will, testamentary trust disposition and settlement or codicil] shall be valid in respect of the formalities of execution unless it is subscribed by the granter of it . . . but nothing apart from such subscription shall be required for the document to be valid as aforesaid."

Accordingly, in the case of a testamentary writing executed or presumed to be executed on or after August 1, 1995, no additional formalities imposed by the testator will be required for the writing to be treated as formally valid: it is sufficient if the writing complies with the requirements of the 1995 Act.

REVOCATION OF TESTAMENTARY WRITINGS

Revocation

4.69   Provided that he has not entered into an onerous undertaking

---

[35] Requirements of Writing (Scotland) Act 1995 (c. 7), s. 7(5) as applied to notarial executions by s. 9(3).

[36] *Ibid,,* s. 9(6).

not to revoke a testamentary writing,[37] as where he was a party to a mutual will, and provided that he is of sound mind, a testator may at any time revoke a testamentary writing either expressly or impliedly. Sometimes subsequent events may raise the legal presumption that the earlier testamentary writing has been revoked. As the Requirements of Writing (Scotland) Act 1995 made no change to this aspect of the law on the formal validity of testamentary writings,[37] readers are referred to the appropriate paragraphs in Chapter 3.

ALTERATIONS AND DELETIONS

Alterations

4.70   The following rules apply to any interlineation, marginal addition, deletion, substitution, erasure or anything written on erasure.[38] Except where specific rules apply to a particular kind of alteration, the word "alteration" will be used throughout this chapter to cover lineations, marginal additions, deletions, substitutions, erasures and anything written on erasure.

When do the rules under the 1995 Act apply?

4.71   The Requirements of Writing (Scotland) Act 1995 clearly applies to pre-execution alterations made to a testamentary entry after the commencement of the Act on August 1, 1995.[39].

4.72   It is less clear whether the 1995 Act applies to any post-execution alteration made on or after August 1, 1995, or only to a post-execution alteration where the testamentary writing was itself executed on or after August 1, 1995. It is arguable that section 14(3) (a) of the Requirements of Writing (Scotland) Act 1995 ensures that a testamentary writing executed under the "old" rules, does not require to be altered by an alteration under the 1995 Act. However, section 14(6) of the 1995 Act raises a presumption that the Act is to apply when it cannot be ascertained "whether a document was executed before or after the commencement of the Act". Is a post execution alteration caught by s. 14(6)? It is submitted that the word "document" is not appropriate to describe an interlineation, marginal addition, substitution, or writing on erasure, and therefore the presumption under section 14(6) would seem to be inapplicable. It would therefore seem that where a testamentary writing executed

---

[37] *Curdy* v. *Boyd* (1775) Mor. 15,946; *Paterson* v. *Paterson* (1893) 20 R. 484.
[38] Requirements of Writing (Scotland) Act 1995 (c. 7), s. 12(1).
[39] *Ibid.*, ss. 1(2) (c), 5 and 15(2).

before August 1, 1995[40] bears an interlineation, marginal addition, substitution, or writing on erasure which is undated, the pre-1995 rules will be applicable. Even if the 1995 rules apply, the absence of a witness (or the use of initials by the testator) is not fatal (see para. 4.100–4.102). Where a question arises as to the date of post-execution alteration, then.

1. if the alteration bears to have been signed and a date of subscription is specified in the alteration or testing clause or its equivalent, and there is nothing in the document or alteration or testing clause or its equivalent which indicates that the statement as to the date is incorrect, then the statement as to the date is presumed to be correct;[41]

2. if the presumption at 1 above is not applicable, but the alteration is signed by the granter, then evidence may be led before the court as to the date of signing (for full procedure see para. 4.98 and if the court is satisfied, this will give rise to a presumption as to the date of signing.[42]

The general rules under the 1995 Act

4.73 If a testamentary writing contains an alteration, it will be treated as formally valid if either

1. the alteration was made before the document was subscribed by the testator;[43] or

2. the alteration, having been made after the document was subscribed, was signed by the testator.[44]

Alterations made before the testator subscribed

4.74 It will be presumed that an alteration was made before the testator subscribed and, as such, forms part of the writing as subscribed[45] if

1. the testamentary writing is formally valid (see paras. 4.08–4.09);

---

[40] Clearly, if the testamentary writing bears to have been executed on or after August 1, 1995, any alteration made to it after execution must have been made after the 1995 Act came into force.

[41] Requirements of Writing (Scotland) Act 1995 (c. 7), Sched. 1, para. 1(10).

[42] *Ibid.*, Sched. 1, para. 2(2).

[43] *Ibid.*, s. 5(1) (a).

[44] *Ibid.*, s. 5(1) (b).

[45] *Ibid.*, s. 5(4).

2. it is stated in the writing or in the testing clause or its equivalent, that the alteration was made before the document was subscribed; and

3. nothing in the document or in the testing clause or its equivalent indicates that the alteration was made after the writing was subscribed by the testator.[46]

4.75 Alternatively, application may be made to the court (see para. 4.99), and if the court is satisfied that the alteration was made before the writing was subscribed by the granter and, as such, forms part of the writing, a certificate to this effect shall be endorsed on the writing, or, if the writing has already been registered in the Books of Council and Session or in the sheriff court books, decree to this effect shall be granted.[47]

Alterations made after the testator subscribed

4.76 The rules which apply where a testamentary writing was altered under the 1995 Act depend on whether the alteration is simply a deletion or erasure, or whether the alteration is an interlineation, marginal addition, substitution, or writing on erasure.

Deletions and erasures: old rules may still apply

4.77 The old rules which enabled any provision in a testamentary writing to be revoked by deletion or erasure without being authenticated by the testator still stand[48] (see para. 3.57).

Alterations generally: the new rules

4.78 While prior to August 1, 1995, an alteration (such as an interlineation, marginal addition, substitution or writing on erasure) could be made to a testamentary writing merely by the testator initialling it, such an alteration made under the 1995 Act should be signed by the testator and witnessed. The formal requirements are as follows:

1. The alteration must be signed by the testator (see paras. 4.30–4.31 for what constitutes an acceptable signature by a testator).[49] By the use of the word "signed" in the 1995 Act, it is intended that interlineation, marginal addition,

[46] Requirements of Writing (Scotland) Act 1995 (c. 7), s. 5(5).
[47] *Ibid.*, s. 5(6).
[48] *Ibid.*, s. 5(2) (a).
[49] *Ibid.*, s. 5(8) and Sched. 1, para. 1(1) (a).

substitution or writing on erasure need not be *subscribed*. While it is acceptable for a signature at the side of an interlineation which is signed at the side—although not technically a *sub*scribed—to receive effect, it is unclear why an alteration consisting of, say, a full page should receive effect provided only that the testator has signed somewhere on the page. This is clearly at variance with the long-standing principle that a testamentary writing must be *sub*scribed if it is to receive effect, and would seem to open the way to fraud. Accordingly, it would be good practice (though not strictly essential) for the testator to sign at the foot of the alteration.

2. If the alteration consists of more than one sheet, it must be signed by the testator "on every sheet".[50] Again, it would be good practice (though not strictly essential) for the testator to sign at the foot of each sheet of the alteration.

3. The testator's sigtnature should be attested by one witness (see paras. 4.46–4.48 for what constitutes an acceptable signature of a witness) immediately after the testator signs or acknowledges his signature the whole process being continuous.[51] The witness's name and address should appear either in the alteration, or in the testing clause or its equivalent,[52] written in his own hand or in the hand of someone else or typewritten or printed,[53] and they may be added at any time before the writing is founded on in legal proceedings or registered for preservation in the Books of Council and Session or in the sheriff court books.[54]

4.79   If it appears from the face of the alteration that the above mentioned formalities have been complied with, the alteration is presumed in law to have been subscribed by the testator.[55] Unless there is something in the writing itself or the alteration, or in the testing clause or its equivalent which indicates either

1. that the alteration was not signed by the testator as it bears to have been signed;[56] or

2. that the alteration was not validly witnessed by virtue of any of the following:

---

[50] Requirements of Writing (Scotland) Act 1995 (c. 7), s. 5(8) and Sched. 1, para. 1(2).
[51] *Ibid.*, s. 5(8) and Sched. 1, para. 1(4) (e).
[52] *Ibid.*, s. 5(8) and Sched. 1, para. 1(1) (b).
[53] *Ibid.*, s. 5(8) and Sched. 1, para. 1(3) (b).
[54] *Ibid.*, s. 5(8) and Sched. 1, para. 1(3) (a).
[55] *Ibid.*, s. 5(8) and Sched. 1, para. 1(1).
[56] *Ibid.*, s. 5(8) and Sched. 1, para. 1(1) (c)(i).

    (a)   the signature which bears to be the witness's signature not being such a signature (whether by reason of forgery or otherwise);[57] or

    (b)   in the case of a mutual will, the person who signed the alteration as the witness to the signature of one testator being the other testator;[58] or

    (c)   the person who signed the alteration as witness did not know the testator at the time of his signature;[59] or

    (d)   the person who signed the alteration as witness being under the age of 16 years at the time of his signature;[60] or

    (e)   the person who signed the alteration as witness being mentally incapable of acting as a witness at the time of his signature;[61] or

    (f)   the person who signed the alteration as witness not witnessing the testator's signature;[62] or

    (g)   the person who signed the alteration as witness not signing the alteration after the testator, or the testator's signature or, as the case may be, acknowledgement of his signature and the witness's signature not being one continuous process.[63]

4.80   If the alteration is presumed in law to have been signed by the testator, it is said to be "self-proving" and may be founded on without further proof. The alteration may be challenged, but the onus of proving that it was not validly signed falls on the party objecting to it (see para. 4.90A).

4.81   Where the alteration bears to have been signed by the testator, but he has failed to sign all sheets, or no person signed as witness, or there is something in the testamentary writing or alteration or in the testing clause or its equivalent which means that it is not *ex facie* valid, the alteration may still be set up by a court action if it can be proved in court that it had been signed by the testator[64] (see paras. 4.100 and 14.102). If the court is satisfied that the alteration was subscribed by the deceased, either the testamentary writing will be endorsed with a certific-

---

[57] Requirements of Writing (Scotland) Act 1995 (c. 7), s. 5(8) and Sched. 1, para. 1(1) (c) (ii) and (4) (a).

[58] *Ibid.*, s. 5(8) and Sched. 1, para. 1(1) (c) (ii) and (4) (b).

[59] *Ibid.*, Sched. 1, para. 1(1) (c) (ii) and (4) (c) (i). It is sufficient if at the time of witnessing, the witness had credible information as to the testator's identity (see para. 1(5)).

[60] *Ibid,*, s. 5(8) and Sched. 1, para. 1(1) (c) (ii) and (4) (c) (ii).

[61] *Ibid.*, s. 5(8) and Sched. 1, para. 1(1) (c) (ii) and (4) (c) (iii).

[62] *Ibid.*, s. 5(8) and Sched. 1, para. 1(1) (c) (ii) and (4) (d).

[63] *Ibid.*, s. 5(8) and Sched. 1, para. 1(1) (c) (ii) and (4) (e).

[64] *Ibid.*, s. 5(8) and Sched. 1, para. 2(1).

ate to that effect, or if it has already been registered in the Books of Council and Session or in the sheriff court books, the court will grant decree to that effect.[65] Such a certificate or decree will give rise to a presumption that the alteration has been subscribed by the testator.[66]

4.82 If the alteration is not self proving, and has not been set up by court action under Schedule 1, paragraph 2(1), it will be treated *pro non scripto*, and effect will be given to the testamentary writing, the alteration being ignored. If the unauthenticated alteration is an erasure or a writing on erasure, and the erased words are *in substantialibus*, the deed will be treated as revoked (for examples, see paras 3.181, 3.185–3.186).

Alterations to a copy of a probative testamentary writing

4.83 Where the testator has made deletions or alterations not to the principal but to a copy of his testamentary writing, they will be given effect to only if it can be shown that the testator intended to alter the principal testamentary writing, and authenticated the deletions or alterations. In one case, the testator had cut out the residue clause in a typewritten copy of her trust disposition and settlement, and she had adhibited her signature twice to the margin of the hole, and written below:

> "As I don't have money to cover any more I thought it better to cut out what had been written."

It was held that the testatrix had effectually revoked the residue clause in her trust disposition and settlement.[67] Unless the testator had also inserted a date prior to August 1, 1995, such an alteration must be set up by an application to the court in terms of paragraph 2(1) of Schedule 1 to the Requirements of Writing (Scotland) Act 1995.

Holograph alterations to a testamentary writing

4.84 Under the old law, holograph but unauthenticated alterations to a testamentary writing have received effect. Under the Requirements of Writing (Scotland) Act 1995, no special status is given to holograph writings.[68] It is submitted that if a holograph alteration which is presumed to have been made on or after August 1, 1995 is to receive effect, it must, if made before execu-

---

[65] Requirements of Writing (Scotland) Act 1995 (c. 7), s. 5(8) and Sched. 1, para. 2(1).

[66] *Ibid.*, s. 5(8) and Sched. 1, para. 2(5) (a).

[67] *Thomson's Trs. v. Bowhill Baptist Church*, 1956 S.C. 217.

[68] Requirements of Writing (Scotland) Act 1995 (c. 7), s. 11(3) (b) (i).

tion, be declared in the testing clause, and if made after execution, be signed and preferably witnessed.

MISCELLANEOUS MATTERS

Bequests written on deposit receipts etc.[69]

4.85   Individuals have frequently attempted to bequeath bank deposit receipts and other similar simple documents of debt by docketing or endorsing them. The practice is fraught with difficulties. A court will not give effect to the docket if the deceased had not subscribed it, or if he did not use clear testamentary language of bequest in the docket. If the docket is not endorsed on the actual document of debt, it can be difficult to identify what the individual intended to bequeath. (For cases see paras. 3.190–3.191.) However, if the document of debt contains clear testamentary language and is subscribed, only informality or execution may be remedied by an action in terms of section 4 of the 1995 Act (see paras. 4.92–4.93).

Letter of instructions to lawyer—or testamentary writing?

4.86   See paragraph 3.192. Further, if either the deceased does not sign each page of the letter, or his subscription on the final page is not witnessed, the writing must be set up by court action in terms of section 4(1) of the 1995 Act (see para. 4.92).

Letter to a relative or friend—or testamentary writing?

4.87   See paragraph 3.193. Further, if either the deceased does not sign each page of the letter, or his subscription on the final page is not witnessed by one witness, the writing must be set up by court action in terms of section 4 of the 1995 Act (see para. 4.92).

Subscribed "draft" deeds

4.88   See paragraphs 3.194–3.196.

Soldiers' wills

4.89   See paragraphs 3.197–3.198.

---

[69] See also donations *inter vivos* and *mortis causa* at para. 12.12 *et seq.*

COURT PROCEDURES UNDER THE 1995 ACT CHALLENGING THE
TESTAMENTARY WRITING

Challenging a self proving testamentary writing under the Requirements of Writing (Scotland) Act 1995

4.90   The validity of the subscription of a testamentary writing which is self proving (see paras. 4.08–4.09) may be challenged, but the burden of proof is on the challenger to rebut the presumption under section 3(1) of the Requirements of Writing (Scotland) Act 1995 that the writing was subscribed by the granter. The question of the validity of the subscription of a testamentary writing may be raised in any proceedings relating to the writing,[70] and the burden will be discharged if it is established either that:

1. The signature which bears to be the witness's signature is not such a signature (whether by reason of forgery or otherwise).[71] For what constitutes the signature of a witness see paragraphs 4.46–4.48.

2. In the case of a mutual will, the person who signed as the witness to the subscription of one testator is the other testator.[72]

3. The person who signed as witness did not know the testator at the time of his signature.[73]

4. The person who signed as witness was under the age of 16 years at the time of signing.[74]

5. The person who signed as witness was mentally incapable of acting as a witness at the time of signing.[75]

6. The person who signed as witness did not witness the testator's subscription[76] — either by seeing the testator subscribe, or by the testator acknowledging his subscription to him.[77]

7. The person who signed as witness did not sign the writ-

---

[70] Requirements of Writing (Scotland) Act 1995 (c. 7), s. 3(4).
[71] *Ibid.*, s. 3(4) (a).
[72] *Ibid.*, s. 3(4) (b).
[73] *Ibid.*, s. 3(4) (c) (i). The witness must also have had credible information at the time of witnessing as to the testator's identity (see s.3(5)).
[74] *Ibid.*, s. 3(4) (c) (ii).
[75] *Ibid.*, s. 3(4) (c) (iii).
[76] *Ibid.*, s. 3(4) (d).
[77] *Ibid.*, s. 3(7).

ing after the testator, or the testator's subscription or, as the case may be, acknowledgement of his subscription and the witness's subscription were not one continuous process.[78]

8. The name or address of the witness was added after the document was founded on in legal proceedings or registered for preservation in the Books of Council and Session or in the sheriff court books, or is erroneous in any material respect;[79]

9. If the testamentary writing consists of more than one sheet, a signature on any sheet bearing to be the signature of the testator is not such a signature (whether by reason of forgery or otherwise).[80] For what constitutes the signature of the testator, see paragraphs 4.30–4.31.

Challenging alterations which are *ex facie* valid under the 1995 Act

4.90A   The question of the validity of post-execution alterations to a testamentary writing which appears to be *ex facie* valid (see paras. 4.76–4.80) may be raised in any proceedings relating to the alteration of the writing,[81] and the burden of proof that the alteration was not signed by the testator will be discharged if it can be established either that:

1. The signature which bears to be the witness's signature is not such a signature (whether by reason of forgery or otherwise);[82] or

2. In the case of a mutual will, the person who signed the alteration as the witness to the subscription of one testator is the other testator;[83] or

3. The person who signed the alteration as witness did not know the testator at the time of his signature;[84] or

4. The person who signed the alteration as witness was

---

[78] Requirements of Writing (Scotland) Act 1995 (c. 7), s. 3(4) (e).
[79] *Ibid.*, s. 3(4) (f).
[80] *Ibid.*, s. 3(4) (g).
[81] *Ibid.*, s. 5(8) and Sched. 1, para. 1(4).
[82] *Ibid.*, s. 5(8) and Sched. 1, para. 1(4) (a).
[83] *Ibid.*, s. 5(8) and Sched. 1, para. 1(4) (b).
[84] *Ibid.*, s. 5(8) and Sched. 1, para. 1(4) (c) (i). It is sufficient if at the time of witnessing, the witness had credible information as to the testator's identity (see para. 1(5)).

under the age of 16 years at the time of his signature;[85] or

5. The person who signed the alteration as witness was mentally incapable of acting as a witness at the time of his signature;[86] or

6. The person who signed the alteration as witness did not witness the testator's subscription;[87] or

7. The person who signed the alteration as witness did not sign the alteration after the testator, or the testator's subscription or, as the case may be, acknowledgement of his subscription and the witness's subscription were not one continuous process;[88] or

8. The name or address of the witness of the testator's signature was added after the alteration was founded on in legal proceedings or registered for preservation in the Books of Council and Session or in the sheriff court books or is erroneous in any material respect;[89] or

9. In the case of an alteration consisting of more than one sheet, a signature on any sheet of the alteration bearing to be the signature of the testator is not such a signature (whether by reason of forgery or otherwise).[90]

Challenging an *ex facie* valid notarial execution

4.91 The validity of the subscription of a notarially executed testamentary writing which is self proving (see paras. 4.60–4.61) may be challenged, but the burden of proof is on the challenger to rebut the presumption under section 3(1) of the Requirements of Writing (Scotland) Act 1995 that it was subscribed by the notary and that the statement as to it being read over (or the testator asking that this doesn't happen) is correct.[91] The question of the validity of the notary's subscription of a testamentary writing may be raised in any proceedings relating to the writing,[92] and the burden will be discharged if it is established that:

---

[85] Requirements of Writing (Scotland) Act 1995 (c. 7), s. 5(8) and Sched. 1, para. 1(4) (c) (ii).

[86] *Ibid.*, s. 5(8) and Sched. 1, para. 1(4) (c) (iii).

[87] *Ibid.*, s. 5(8) and Sched. 1, para. 1(4) (d).

[88] *Ibid.*, s. 5(8) and Sched. 1, para. 1(4) (e).

[89] *Ibid.*, s. 5(8) and Sched. 1, para. 1(4) (f).

[90] *Ibid.*, Sched. 1, para. 1(4) (g).

[91] As applied to notarial executions by Requirements of Writing (Scotland) Act 1995 (c, 7), s. 9(3) and Sched. 3, para. 2.

[92] Requirements of Writing (Scotland) Act 1995 (c. 7), s. 3(4) as applied to notarial executions by s. 9(3) and Sched. 3, para. 4.

1. The signature which bears to be the witness's signature is not such a signature (whether by reason of forgery or otherwise);[93] or

2. In the case of a mutual will, the person who signed as the witness to the notary's subscription is the other testator;[94] or

3. The person who signed as witness did not know the testator at the time of signing;[95] or

4. The person who signed as witness was under the age of 16 years at the time of signing;[96] or

5. The person who signed as witness was mentally incapable of acting as a witness at the time of signing;[97] or

6. The person who signed as witness did not see the notary's subscription;[98] or

7. The person who signed as witness did not witness the testator granting authority to the notary to subscribe the writing on his behalf, or did not witness the notary reading the writing to the testator (or the declaration that the testator did not wish him to do so);[99] or

8. The person who signed as witness did not sign the writing after the notary, or the notary's subscription and the witness's subscription were not one continuous process;[1] or

9. The name or address of the witness was added after the document was founded on in legal proceedings or registered for preservation in the Books of Council and Session

---

[93] Requirements of Writing (Scotland) Act 1995 (c. 7), s. 3(4) (a) inserted for notarial execution by s. 9(3) and Sched. 3, para. 4.

[94] *Ibid.*, s. 3(4) (b) and inserted for notarial executions by s. 9(3) and Sched. 3, para. 4.

[95] *Ibid.*, s. 3(4) (c) (i) inserted for notarial executions by s. 9(3) and Sched. 3, para. 4.

[96] *Ibid.*, s. 3(4) (c) (ii) inserted for notarial executions by s. 9(3) and Sched. 3, para. 4.

[97] *Ibid,*, s. 3(4) (c) (iii) inserted for notarial executions by s. 9(3) and Sched. 3, para. 4.

[98] *Ibid.*, s. 3(4) (d) inserted for notarial executions by s. 9(3) and Sched. 3, para. 4.

[99] *Ibid.*, s. 3(4) (dd) inserted for notarial executions by s. 9(3) and Sched. 3, para. 4.

[1] *Ibid.*, s. 3(4) (e) inserted for notarial executions by s. 9(3) and Sched. 3, para. 4.

or in the sheriff court books, or is erroneous in any material respect;[2] or

10. If the testamentary writing consists of more than one sheet, a signature on any sheet bearing to be the signature of the notary is not such a signature (whether by reason of forgery or otherwise).[3] For what constitutes the signature of the notary, see paragraphs 4.30–4.31.

SETTING UP A DEFECTIVELY EXECUTED WRITING

Setting up informal writings under the Requirements of Writing (Scotland) Act 1995

4.92 The Requirements of Writing (Scotland) Act 1995, *inter alia*, repealed the Conveyancing (Scotland) Act 1874, section 39 insofar as affects testamentary writings executed or presumed to be executed in Scotland after the commencement of the Act on August 1, 1995.[4]

4.93 Where a testamentary writing executed on or after August 1, 1995 is not self proving—perhaps because the testator had failed to sign all the sheets, or no person subscribed as witness, or there is something in the writing or in the testing clause or its equivalent which means that it is not *ex facie* valid—the testamentary writing may still be set up if it bears to have been subscribed by the testator.[5] A person with an interest in the writing may make an application to the court, either as a summary application (to the sheriff in whose sheriffdom the applicant resides, or if he does not reside in Scotland, the sheriff at Edinburgh) or as incidental to and in the course of other proceedings.[6] Normally, a testamentary writing will be set up in the course of the confirmation process, in the sheriff court of the deceased's last domicile.[7] Evidence will normally be taken by affidavit.[8] If the court is satisfied that the writing was subscribed by the deceased, either the writing will be endorsed with a certificate to that effect, or if it has already been registered in the Books of Council and Session or in the sheriff court books,

---

[2] Requirements of Writing (Scotland) Act 1995 (c. 7), s. 3(4) (f) inserted for notarial executions by s. 9(3) and Sched. 3, para. 4.

[3] *Ibid.,* s. 3(4) (g) inserted for notarial executions by s. 9(3) and Sched. 3, para. 4.

[4] *Ibid.,* ss. 14(2), and (3) (a), and 15(2) and Sched. 5.

[5] *Ibid.,* s. 4(1).

[6] *Ibid.,* s. 4(4) & (6).

[7] *Cf.* the jurisdiction under s. 4(6) (a) which is determined on the basis of the applicant's residence.

[8] *Ibid.,* s. 4(3).

the court will grant decree to that effect.[9] Such certificate or decree will give rise to a presumption that the writing has been subscribed by the testator.[10]

4.94 This procedure can be used to set up a testamentary writing which is holograph of the testator or was "adopted as holograph" by him, or even a defectively executed printed Will Form—provided that the writing is not dated prior to (or can be shown to be signed prior to) August 1, 1995.

Setting up a notarial execution which lacks a formality

4.95 Where the testamentary writing bears to have been subscribed by a notary under section 9 of the Requirements of Writing (Scotland) Act 1995 on behalf of the testator, but he had failed to sign all sheets, or no person subscribed as witness, or there is something in the writing or in the testing clause or its equivalent which means that it is not *ex facie* valid, it may still be set up by a court action if it can be proved in court that it had been subscribed by the notary with the authority of the testator and that the notary read the writing to the testator before subscription (or did not read it because the testator did not wish him to do so).[11] A person with an interest in the writing may make an application to the court, either as a summary application (to the sheriff in whose sheriffdom the applicant resides, or if he does not reside in Scotland, the sheriff at Edinburgh) or as incidental to and in the course of other proceedings.[12] Normally, the notarial execution of a testamentary writing will be set up in the course of the confirmation process, in the sheriff court of the deceased's last domicile.[13] Evidence will normally be taken by affidavit.[14] If the court is satisfied that the writing was subscribed by the notary with the authority of the testator and that the notary read the writing to the testator before subscription (or that the testator declared that he did not want him to do so), either the writing will be endorsed with a certificate to that effect, or if it has already been registered in the Books of Council and Session or in the sheriff court books, the court will grant decree to that effect.[15] Such certificate or decree will give rise to a presumption that the writing has been subscribed notarially.[16]

---

[9] Requirements of Writing (Scotland) Act 1995 (c. 7), s. 4(1).

[10] *Ibid.*, s. 4(5) (a).

[11] *Ibid.*, s. 4(1) as inserted for notarial executions by s. 9(3) and Sched, 3, para. 7.

[12] *Ibid.*, s. 4(4) and (6).

[13] *Cf.* the jurisdiction under s. 4(6) (a) which is determined on the basis of the applicant's residence.

[14] *Ibid.*, s. 4(3).

[15] *Ibid.*, s. 4(1) as inserted for notarial executions by s. 9(3) and Sched. 3, para. 7.

[16] *Ibid.*, s. 4(5) (a) as modified by s. 9(3) and Sched. 3, para. 8.

Proving the date or place of subscription of testamentary writings under the Requirements of Writing (Scotland) Act 1995

4.96   Where a testamentary writing bears to have been subscribed by the testator, and the deed or testing clause or its equivalent bears to state the date or place of subscription which appears *ex facie* of the deed and testing clause etc to be correct, then it is presumed under section 3(10) of the Requirements of Writing (Scotland) Act 1995 that the deed was subscribed by the testator on the date or at the place specified. The presumption as to the date of subscription will be of significance in determining which of a number of deeds is the testator's last testamentary writing, and in applying the Wills Act 1963. The presumption as to the place of execution can be of significance when it is necessary to apply the Wills Act 1963.

4.97   Where no date or place of subscription is stated in the deed, testing clause, or its equivalent, or such statement appeared *ex facie* of the deed to be incorrect, the presumption does not apply. Instead, any person who has an interest in the document may apply to the court for a determination as to either the date or place of execution, provided that the writing bears to have been subscribed by the testator.[17] The court application may be either a summary application (to the sheriff in whose sheriffdom the applicant resides, or if he does not reside in Scotland, the sheriff at Edinburgh) or as incidental to and in the course of other proceedings.[18] Normally, the date or place of execution will be established in the course of the confirmation process in the sheriff court of the deceased's last domicile.[19] Evidence will normally be taken by affidavit.[20] If the court is satisfied as to the date or place of subscription, either the writing will be endorsed with a certificate to that effect, or if it has already been registered in the Books of Council and Session or in the sheriff court books, the court will grant decree to that effect.[21] Such certificate or decree will give rise to a presumption that the writing has been subscribed by the testator.[22]

Proving the date *or* place of signing of post-execution alterations under the 1995 Act

4.98   Where a question arises as to the place *or* date of signing of an alteration to a testamentary writing under the 1995 Act, then

---

[17] Requirements of Writing (Scotland) Act 1995 (c. 7), s. 4(2).
[18] *Ibid.*, s. 4(4) and (6).
[19] *Cf.* the jurisdiction under s. 4(6) (a) which is determined on the basis of the applicant's residence.
[20] *Ibid.*, s. 4(3).
[21] *Ibid.*, s. 4(2).
[22] *Ibid.* s. 4(5).

provided that the alteration was signed by the granter, evidence may be led before the court as to the place or date of signing. If the court is satisfied, this will give rise to a presumption as to the place or date of signing.[23] The procedures stated at para. 4.97 apply here *mutatis mutandis*.

Court finding that alteration made prior to subscription

4.99   Application may be made to the court, for a finding that an alteration was made *before* the document was subscribed by the granter. The court application may be either a summary application (to the sheriff in whose sheriffdom the applicant resides, or if he does not reside in Scotland, the sheriff at Edinburgh) or as incidental to and in the course of other proceedings.[24] Normally, the finding as to the timing of the alteration will be made in the course of the confirmation process, in the sheriff court of the deceased's last domicile.[25] Evidence will normally be taken by affidavit,[26] though any evidence written or oral is competent.[27] If the court is satisfied, either the writing will be endorsed with a certificate to that effect, or if it has already been registered in the Books of Council and Session or in the sheriff court books, the court will grant decree to that effect.[28] Such certificate or decree will give rise to a presumption that the alteration was made before the writing was subscribed by the testator and as such the alteration forms part of the writing as subscribed.[29]

Alterations made after the testator subscribed

4.100   Where the alteration bears to have been signed by the testator, but he had failed to sign all sheets, or no person signed as witness, or there is something in the testamentary writing or alteration or in the testing clause or its equivalent which means that it is not *ex facie* valid, the alteration may nevertheless be set up by a court action if it can be proved in court that it had been signed by the testator[30]:

4.101   Normally, evidence will be taken by affidavit.[31] If the court is

---

[23] Requirements of Writing (Scotland) Act 1995 (c. 7), Sched. 1, para. 2(2).
[24] *Ibid.*, s. 4(4) and (6) as applied by s. 5(7).
[25] *Cf.* the jurisdiction under Requirements of Writing (Scotland) Act 1995 (c. 7), s. 4(6) (a) which is determined on the basis of the applicant's residence.
[26] *Ibid.*, s. 4(3), as applied by s. 5(7).
[27] *Ibid.* s. 5(3).
[28] *Ibid.*, s. 5(6).
[29] *Ibid.*, s. 5(4).
[30] *Ibid.*, s. 5(8) and Sched. 1, para. 2(1).
[31] *Ibid.*, s. 5(8) and Sched. 1, para. 2(3).

satisfied that the alteration was subscribed by the deceased, either the testamentary writing will be endorsed with a certificate to that effect, or if it has already been registered in the Books of Council and Session or in the sheriff court books, the court will grant decree to that effect.[32] Such a decree will give rise to a presumption that the alteration has been subscribed by the testator.[33]

4.102   If the alteration is not self proving, and has not been set up by court action under Schedule 1, paragraph 2(1), it will be treated *pro non scripto*, and effect will be given to the testamentary writing, the alteration being ignored. If the unauthenticated alteration is an erasure or a writing on erasure, and the erased words are *in substantialibus*, the deed will be treated as revoked (for examples, see paras. 3.181 and 3.184–3.185).

Validating Unusual "signatures"

4.103   Under section 7(2) (c) of the Requirements of Writing (Scotland) Act 1995, it is possible to establish that a testator signed a testamentary writing where he used a name (other than his full name as stated in the document or testing clause or equivalent, or his surname, preceded by at least one forename or an initial or abbreviation or familiar form of a forename), description, initial or mark if it is established that the name, description, initial or mark—

1.   was his usual method of signing, or his usual method of signing documents of the type in question; or

2.   was intended by him as his signature of the document.[34]

Proof that the document was subscribed by the testator must be led under section 4(1) of the Requirements of Writing (Scotland) Act 1995 (see paras. 4.92–4.93).

---

[32] Requirements of Writing (Scotland) Act 1995 (c. 7), s. 5(8) and Sched. 1, para. 2(1).
[33] *Ibid.*, s. 5(8) and Sched, 1, para. 2(5).
[34] *Ibid.*, s. 7(2) (c).

CHAPTER 5

CONFIRMATION OF EXECUTORS-NOMINATE

Introduction

5.01 Where a deceased person has nominated—either expressly or by implication—a person to be his or her executor, confirmation will be granted in favour of the named person, rather than in favour of anyone else. Such a person is referred to as the deceased's "executor-nominate." The term is also used to describe a person who has been assumed as an executor by the executor-nominate of the deceased. In such cases the person's position as an executor can be traced back to the deceased's nomination. Finally, the term is used where, in the absence of the testator naming an executor, the court treats the testamentary trustee, general disponee, universal legatory or residuary legatee named by the testator as the executor-nominate.

5.02 The nomination or appointment of an executor-nominate may be categorised either as

1. express, in a testamentary writing of the deceased (see paras. 5.05–5.44);

2. implied from a testamentary writing of the deceased (see paras. 5.45–5.48);

3. constructive—in terms of section 3 of the Executors (Scotland) Act 1900 (see paras. 5.49–5.96); or

4. through assumption by an executor-nominate (see paras. 5.97–5.103).

The nomination of an executor will lapse if it is subsequently revoked by the testator (see paras. 5.104–5.116). On the death of the testator, the executor nominated by the testator is entitled to confirmation, unless he declines the office (see paras. 5.117–5.123) or resigns (see paras. 5.124—5.127). In exceptional circumstances, an executor-nominate can be removed by the court (see paras. 5.128–5.132).

Interpreting the words of the testator

5.03 In determining who is executor-nominate, the court may be called upon to construe the meaning of the testator's testamentary writing. Normally, the words used must be given their ordinary meaning but the testator's intention may be discovered from within the testamentary writing itself:

> "It is trite to say that the duty of the Court is to discover the intention of the testator. It is equally trite, but not so frequently remembered, that that intention must be discovered within the four corners of the Will by a construction of the words used by him. 'It is not what the testator meant but what is the meaning of his words.' There are cases where the courts have been able to depart from the ordinary grammatical meaning of the words used, but this is permissible only if the testator has shown in the Will that he meant the words to be used in a secondary sense."[1]

If the testamentary writing is holograph, the court may be more lax in interpreting it, than in interpreting a formal settlement prepared by a solicitor.[2]

5.04   In commissary practice, a particular difficulty arises in interpreting the testator's testamentary writing where no one conforms exactly with the person named as executor in the testamentary writing. This can occur when the testator misnamed his executor, or omitted a portion of the name, or wrongly or insufficiently designed him, or did not design him at all. Where the person intended to be appointed is otherwise sufficiently identified, any misdescription may be rectified by an averment in the oath or affirmation; but where this is not the case, a special application must be made to the court,[3] explaining the discrepancy or supplying the deficiency, and setting out the applicant's connection with the deceased, and the grounds upon which he avers that he is the person entitled to be confirmed (Styles 4.04 and 4.05). Affidavits setting up the identity of the executor may be required (Style 2.03).

1. Express Appointment

Standard form

5.05   In a simple will, an express appointment of an executor could take the form: "I appoint AB and CD to be my executors." A more complicated deed may provide

---

[1] *Per* Lord Justice-Clerk Thomson in *Ross's J. F.* v. *Martin*, 1954 S.C. 18 at p. 24.
[2] See, for instance, Lord Medwyn in *Scott* v. *Scott* (1852) 14 O. 1057 at p. 1061; Lord Gifford in *Dunsmure* v. *Dunsmure* (1879) 7 R. 261 at p. 264; Lord Justice-Clerk Alness in *Elrick's Trs.* v. *Robinson*, 1932 S.C. 448 at p. 452; Lord Mackintosh in *Ross's J.F.* v. *Martin*, 1954 S.C. 18 at p. 29; Lord Kinnear in *Allan's Exr.* v. *Allan*, 1908 S.C. 807 at p. 812; Lord Hill Watson in *Reid's Exs.* v. *Reid*, 1954 S.L.T. (Notes) 20.
[3] See paras. 28 *et seq.*

"I nominate and appoint AB and CD as my Trustees, and assign, dispone, convey and make over to them and to such other person or persons as I may hereafter appoint or who may be assumed to act hereunder and to the acceptor or acceptors, survivor and survivors of them as Trustees and Trustee for the purposes aftermentioned . . . And I appoint my Trustees to be my Executors."

5.06   An equally valid express appointment will be made if the testator, without naming his executors, designates persons sufficiently, so that they can be identified.[4] In such a case, before confirmation can be granted, it will be necessary to prepare an initial writ for special authority to issue confirmation, in which the condescendence will name and design those identified in the testamentary writing as the nominated executors.[5]

Appointment or a direction to assume?

5.07   Before confirmation will be granted in favour of an executor expressly nominated by the deceased, the words of appointment in the testamentary writing must be clear and unequivocal. In *Lawson*,[6] a testator stated in a codicil that he "wished and desired A to be made a trustee." It was held that this was not an appointment of A as a trustee, but a direction to assume—and that A must be assumed as a trustee unless he declined office.[7] A direction to assume is to be distinguished from a mere recommendation to assume. In *Roy*,[8] the deceased merely recommended that her trustees assume A. They did not, and were confirmed alone.

Testator delegating the appointment of his executors

5.08   A string of unreported commissary cases are authority for confirmation-nominate being granted in favour of a person nominated as executor, not by the deceased himself, but by a person whom the deceased so empowered. In such cases, the deed of appointment will require to be put up with the testamentary writings and inventory for confirmation, referred to in the oath or affirmation, and docketed as relative thereto.[9]

    1.   Where the testator, in his will, had given power to a bene-

---

[4] *Per* Lord Robertson in *Martin* v. *Ferguson's Trs.* (1892) 19 R. 474 at p. 478, where the testator had written "the same trustees as my brother John."

[5] See paras. 19–28 *et seq.* and Styles 4.02 and 4.03.

[6] April 1, 1878, unreported.

[7] See paras. 5.97–5.102A on the assumption of an executor by the nominated executors.

[8] Feb. 4, 1863, unreported.

[9] See Style 8.05.

ficiary to nominate an executor, confirmation was issued in favour of the executors appointed in a deed of nomination executed by the beneficiary.[10]

2. A testator of Scottish domicile gave power to two sons who were abroad to appoint "whomsoever they may appoint in this country" to administer the estate. Confirmation was granted in favour of the person whom the sons, by a letter of appointment, appointed to administer the estate in Scotland.[11]

3. A testator by a will made and proved in Victoria, Australia, appointed executors of his Australian estate and empowered them to appoint executors of his estate elsewhere. The Australian executors appointed three Scotsmen to be executors of the United Kingdom estate, and confirmation was issued to the Scotsmen, as executors-nominate.[12]

4. A testator of Canadian domicile appointed two executors to administer his Canadian estate and empowered them to appoint one named individual and "any one of my sisters" to be special executors and trustees to administer estate in Great Britain. Confirmation was granted in favour of the named individual and a sister of the deceased, on production of the Canadian grant of probate in favour of the Canadian executors along with a deed of appointment by them in favour of the named individual and the sister.[13]

5. The deceased had appointed A as executor "with power to name another if she thinks fit." A appointed B by a deed, and both were confirmed.[14]

5.09   It is submitted that it would be more appropriate nowadays to view the last three of these cases as examples of a testator granting powers to named executors to assume additional executors.[15]

Appointment of a class as executors

5.10   Normally, the persons whom the deceased intended to be executors are named and designed in the testamentary writing, but

---

[10] *Hinds*, March 11, 1859, unreported.
[11] *Ewing*, Feb. 15, 1915, unreported.
[12] *MacGregor*, Sept. 6, 1900, unreported.
[13] *Zimmerman*, July 7, 1964, unreported.
[14] *Parker*, Nov. 10, 1881, unreported.
[15] See paras. 5.97 *et seq*.

occasionally they are merely described as members of a class, such as "heirs," "children," "family," etc. In these cases, there must be specification and, if necessary, proof of the individuals who fit the description, and all of them must be accounted for. Where proof is necessary, a petition is raised which sets forth the facts, and craves confirmation.[16]

5.11   The following are examples of the approach taken in such cases:

1.   Where "the children who shall succeed" at the testator's death were appointed executors, warrant was granted to confirm those to whom the description applied.[17]

2.   Where the deceased had written to her sister: "I request that you and your family may be executors of my Will," warrant was granted to confirm the sister's eldest son, on the production of a declinature from the sister and all her other children.[18]

3.   A nomination was of "A and heirs." A had died leaving three children, one of whom was abroad, but his address was unknown, and another declined to act. The third child was confirmed.[19]

4.   A husband and wife, in a mutual will, appointed on the death of the survivor, "their respective next-of-kin" as executors. The next-of-kin were very numerous, and some of them were abroad. One of them, with the consent of the majority of the others, was confirmed alone on his finding caution.[20]

See paragraphs 5.71–5.78 for some of the common terms used in class appointments.

Appointment of members of a class in succession

5.12   It is not uncommon for the testator to appoint parties in succession. Thus, in one case, a testator appointed his wife, whom failing, his "children in succession, if need be, from the eldest downwards." Where the wife predeceased the testator, warrant was granted to confirm the eldest surviving child.[21]
    As to the meaning of "failing," see paragraphs 5.28–5.32 and 5.51–5.53.

---

[16] See paras. 19.35 *et seq.*
[17] *Carrick*, Dec. 10, 1873, unreported.
[18] *White*, June 24, 1871, unreported.
[19] *Reid*, May 20, 1873, unreported. See para. 8.10 and 8.20–8.21 regarding an executor abroad whose address is unknown.
[20] *Robertson*, Oct. 25, 1862, unreported.
[21] *Bremner*, March 17, 1881, unreported.

Appointment of executor *ex officio*

5.13   Occasionally, the testator will appoint as an executor the holder of a certain specified office. In such cases it is only the person in office at the time confirmation is craved who is confirmed, and not also his successors in office, for the right of a successor to act emerges only when his predecessor dies in office or retires. If eik is required, the then office holder will be confirmed *ad omissa*.

5.14   Examples of *ex officio* appointments include "A, B, C, and the president of the college of surgeons and rector of the High School *ex officio*"[22]; "A, B and C and the present minister of North Esk Church and the present town clerk and their successors in office"[23]; and "JM, general treasurer of the Free Church, or his successors in office."[24] A very common *ex officio* appointment is "the senior partner for the time being of the firm of Messrs [firm of solicitors]." Some courts require affidavit evidence as to who is, at the time, the specified officer of the specified body, or the senior partner of the specified firm, and agents should discuss with the sheriff clerk's staff, at an early stage, whether affidavit evidence is required.

5.15   Where the office and body have ceased to exist before confirmation is sought, depending on the terms of the documents whereby the functions of the old body are transferred to any successor body, the *ex officio* appointment may have lapsed.[25] If the office has ceased, the appointment of an *ex officio* trustee will have lapsed.

Appointment of a company as an executor

5.16   Where a company or body is nominated as executor, the company or body itself is confirmed. The oath or affirmation to the inventory will be taken by an authorised officer of the company or body, and a certified copy of the resolution, minute of meeting or other authority in his favour must be produced with the inventory, referred to in the oath or affirmation and docketed as relative thereto.[26] Thus, confirmation has been issued in

---

[22] *Sibbald*, Jan. 6, 1869, unreported.

[23] *Hall*, Jan. 3, 1889, unreported.

[24] *Tharp*, Sept. 27, 1878, unreported.

[25] *Parish Council of Kilmarnock* v. *Ossington's Trs.* (1896) 23 R. 833 (where the appointment of "the chairman of the Parochial Board of the Parish of Kilmarnock and his successors in office for the time being, so long as such Board shall exist" was held not to pass to the Chairman of the Parish Council although s. 21 of the Local Government (Scotland) Act 1894 had provided that "every reference in any . . . deed or instrument to a parochial board . . . shall be read and construed as referring to a parish council constituted under this Act").

[26] *Cf.* Styles 8.06 and 8.09.

favour of "the governors of the hospital founded by the crafts of Edinburgh and Mary Erskine, and known by the name of the Trades Maiden Hospital," the inventory being given up and oath or affirmation made by the treasurer to the governors, as specially authorised by them.[27]

Appointment of a NHS hospital as executor

5.17   While it is very unusual for a hospital to be appointed executor or trustee, it occasionally is treated as executor-nominate *qua* general disponee, universal legatory or residuary legatee in terms of section 3 of the Executors (Scotland) Act 1900.[28] If the bequest is to a NHS trust hospital, since a NHS Trust "has power to accept, hold and administer any property on trust for purposes relating to any service which it is their function to make arrangements for, administer or provide,"[29] confirmation may be issued in favour of the trustees, but a petition for special authority requires to be presented first. If the bequest is to a hospital which is not run by a NHS Trust, the health board has similar powers[30] but the board must appoint some person to sign the necessary documents on its behalf, before the petition for special authority may be made, and a copy of the resolution must be lodged with the inventory for confirmation, referred to in the oath or affirmation, and docketed as relative thereto.

5.18   A local health council also has power to hold property in trust for purposes relating to any statutory function[31] but the council must appoint someone to sign documents on its behalf, before the petition for special authority may be made, and a copy of the resolution must be lodged with the inventory for confirmation, referred to in the oath or affirmation, and docketed as relative thereto.

Solicitors' nominee companies

5.19   It is now fairly common practice for law firms to set up a limited liability company to handle the firm's trust and executry business and for the clients of that firm to appoint the nominee

---

[27] *Scott*, Sept. 12, 1854, unreported.

[28] 63 & 64 Vict. c. 55, discussed at para. 5.49 *et seq.*

[29] National Health Service (Scotland) Act 1978 (c. 29), s. 12G(1), inserted by National Health Service and Community Care Act 1990 (c. 19), s. 33.

[30] National Health Service (Scotland) Act 1978 (c. 29), s. 83(1).

[31] National Health Service (Scotland) Act 1978 (c. 29), s. 83(2).

company[32] as executor. When the inventory to the deceased's estate is deponed to before a notary public he should have no connection with the nominee company or the legal firm.

Alteration in the name of the executor

5.20   Where there has been a change in the name of the executor since the date of the appointment in the testamentary writing, the alteration must be referred to in the oath or affirmation to the inventory.[33] If the alteration has been made by statute, the Act of Parliament should be referred to. The normal commissary practice is to accept the declaration in the oath or affirmation as conclusive, although in the case, for instance of a company whose name has been changed, documentary evidence (in the form of a certificate of change of name) will be required.

A firm as executor

5.21   Where a firm such as "Smith and Jones" are appointed executors, and it is desired to have the individual partners of the firm confirmed by name, it will be necessary to have a special warrant petition in which the applicant partners are identified.

Acceptors and survivors

5.22   Normally, where the testator has appointed more than one executor, the office enures to the acceptors and survivors, so that the appointment does not fall so long as one of the named executors survives and acts. The exceptions are where the testator expressed the contrary, where the appointment is joint,[34] where a *sine qua non* executor was appointed who is not acting,[35] or where a quorum of executors was specified and less than the quorum have accepted and survived.[36]

---

[32] There are undoubted benefits of choosing such an executor (it will not become *incapax* or be allowed to die) but it may not always be an appropriate choice. In a trust case (*Ommanney, Petr.*, 1966 S.L.T. (Notes) 13), the view was expressed that a company is "not a suitable party to exercise . . . a discretion involving personal and family considerations for its proper exercise." Only solicitors should be directors of such a company (Recommendation of the Professional Practice Committee of the Law Society of Scotland [1986] J.L.S. 322).

[33] See Style 8.07.

[34] See paras. 5.23–5.24.

[35] See paras. 5.26–5.27.

[36] *Per* Lord Justice-Clerk Hope in *Gordon's Trs.* v. *Eglinton* (1851) 13 D. 1381 at p. 1383; *Findlay and Others* (1855) 17 D. 1014; *Oswald's Trs.* v. *City of Glasgow Bank* (1879) 6 R. 461; Stair, I.xii.13; McLaren, *Wills and Succession* (3rd ed.), pp. 898–900, paras. 1660–1664.

Joint appointment

5.23   In cases of a joint nomination, the executors are confirmed in the same terms as those in which they are appointed.[37]

5.24   Where the testator appoints executors jointly, the nomination falls if all do not act.[38] Where A, B and C were appointed joint executors, and C declined, the nomination was held to have lapsed.[39] A testatrix by her will appointed A and B "individually and jointly" to be her executors, and by a codicil appointed C to act "in conjunction" with them or the survivor. When A and B both predeceased the testator, it was held that the nomination of C had fallen, and confirmation in his favour was refused.[40]

Sine qua non executor

5.25   Where one of a number of executors is appointed *sine qua non*, during his survivance, he must be a party to every act of executorship. In such cases, he should be the party deponing to the inventory or, alternatively, must consent to another of the executors so deponing[41] and written evidence of such consent should be put up with the inventory when confirmation is applied for. Confirmation will be granted subject to the condition that the particular executor is *sine qua non*, as a limitation on the right of the other executors to act.

5.26   When an executor who has been appointed *sine qua non* declines to act, the consequences turn on the interpretation of the precise words of his appointment.

> "The result of the failure of a *sine qua non* upon the existence of the trust is doubtful. The one view is that his acceptance is essential unless it clearly appears from the deed that his acceptance was not intended by the truster to be a condition of the constitution of the trust. The other view is that 'the right of veto is a personal privilege conferred on the trustee in the case of his acceptance; whence it follows that, if he declines, the trust may be administered by a *quorum* of the other trustees in the ordinary way'."[42]

5.27   On the view that the acceptance of the *sine qua non* executor is essential, in one case where the *sine qua non* executor declined to act, the court refused the petition for warrant to issue con-

---

[37] *Innes*, Nov. 25, 1887, unreported.
[38] Stair, I.xii.13; McLaren, *Wills and Succession* (3rd ed.), p. 896, para. 1657.
[39] *Fiddes*, March 24, 1874, unreported.
[40] *Kirby*, June 13, 1892, unreported.
[41] *Maconochie*, Oct. 2, 1885, unreported.
[42] *Stair Memorial Encyclopedia*, Vol. 15, p. 207, referring to McLaren, *Wills and Succession*, Vol. 2, para. 1656.

firmation in favour of the other executor-nominate, and the next-of-kin was preferred.[43] Where the terms and conception of the testamentary writing are such that it does appear that the testator's intention was that the "trust" would continue even if the *sine qua non* executor did not accept office, confirmation will be granted in favour of the accepting executor where the *sine qua non* executor refuses office.[44]

Substitutes as executor

5.28   Frequently, a testator will nominate one person to be his executor but then go on to provide an alternative, or substitute, executor in the event of the first appointment failing. The substitute executor may be nominated in a different deed to that in which the original appointment was made.[45]

5.29   Where the testator provides that a named person is to take office as executor only if he survives the testator for a certain period, whom failing another is to be executor, the first chosen executor has no title to act until the stated period has elapsed. Equally, the nomination of a substitute executor is held not to take effect until his right to act emerges. Only once the stated period has expired can confirmation be applied for—whether by the first chosen executor, or by the substitute executor, as appropriate.

5.30   Each such nomination of a substitute executor falls to be interpreted on its own terms.[46]

5.31   If the nomination takes the form "A, whom failing B," with no specification as to what is to constitute "failure," the substitution will take effect whether the "failure" of A arises from his death,[47] declinature[48] or inability to act,[49] whether that failure happens before A is confirmed or after.[50] Thus, where the testator and A die simultaneously, or in circumstances rendering it uncertain which, if either of them, survived the other, B will be confirmed.

---

[43] *Thomson* (July 23, 1881); *cf. Drummore* v. *Somervil* (1742) Mor. 14703, where the truster had provided for trustees to act on the death or incapacity of the *sine qua non* trustee, and the court inferred that he had intended also to cover the situation of the *sine qua non* trustee refusing to accept office.

[44] (Unnamed) 1935 S.L.R. 178, following *Forbes* v. *Earl of Galloway's Trs.* (1808) 5 Pat. 226.

[45] *Smith & Others, Petrs.*, 1927 S.L.T. (Sh. Ct.) 18.

[46] See *obiter* comments in *Glasgow Western Infirmary* v. *Cairns*, 1944 S.C. 488.

[47] *Brown* v. *Hastie*, 1911 S.C. 304.

[48] *Hunter's Exrs., Petrs.*, 1992 S.L.T. 1141.

[49] *Morson*, Feb. 18, 1864, unreported.

[50] In which case B would be confirmed *ad omissa* or *ad non executa, ad omissa vel male appretiata* (*e.g. Smith & Others, Petrs.*, 1927 S.L.T. (Sh. Ct.) 18). See paras. 17.17–17.30.

5.32 If, however, the testator nominated "A, whom failing by his predecease, B" and both survived, B could not be confirmed though A had declined, for the testamentary writing had limited "failure" to death.[51]

Conditional appointment of executor

5.33 Where the executor's right to act is made contingent upon some event or circumstances, such as marriage, attaining a particular age or residence in Scotland, the facts showing whether the contingency has or has not occurred must be set out, and a special application for confirmation may be necessary if a legal issue has to be established before it can be shown that the contingency has or has not occurred[51a]. Unless the condition has been fulfilled, the nomination will not receive effect. Thus, where three executors were named, but two of them had the sole right to act in the first place, and the third only on the death of one of the others, the two who were entitled to act at the time were alone confirmed.[52]

5.34 Sometimes the terms of a conditional appointment are such that, in the events which happen, there will be no nominated executor who can be confirmed. For instance, where a testator appointed his wife as executor but, if she should not be living at the time of his death, his children, and the wife survived him but died without confirming, the nomination was held to have fallen, and one of the children was appointed executor-dative.[53] The same result occurred where the testator had appointed executors in the event of his death before reaching New Zealand, and he died after landing at Dunedin.[54]

5.35 An executor's right to act is frequently made conditional on his being resident in this country. Thus, where the nomination was in favour of three executors "or any one or more of them who may be in Great Britain at my death" and one was abroad, the two others alone were confirmed.[55] In contrast, if the testamentary writing gives a majority of the executors in this country power to act without an executor who is resident abroad, confirmation will be granted in favour of all of the executors (including any resident abroad), though the grant of confirmation will be qualified with the declaration that an executor's

---

[51] *Steele*, April 15, 1861, unreported. The problem could today be avoided by A assuming B as an executor, and then himself resigning.

[51a] At an early stage in proceedings, the agent should discuss the case informally with a member of the sheriff clerk's staff.

[52] *Robb*, March 13, 1878, unreported.

[53] *Cormack*, Jan. 12, 1883, unreported.

[54] *Lamont*, July, 1883, unreported.

[55] *Innes*, Feb. 9, 1882, unreported.

right to act is conditional on his being resident in this country. Thus, where the deceased had named A and B as executors, but declared that either of them should be entitled to act alone when only one of them was in Great Britain, both were confirmed subject to that declaration which was repeated in the confirmation.[56] And where a majority of executors in this country were declared a quorum, and three were in this country and three abroad, all six were confirmed subject to the declaration.[57]

Limited appointment of executor

5.36   Very occasionally, a condition limits the period during which the executor is entitled to act, for instance, a widow until she remarries or a person until a child reaches a particular age. In such cases, the confirmation is granted subject to the limitation. Thus, where a testator appointed his wife and A to be his trustees and executors, under declaration that if his wife remarried, her right to act should cease, and that certain parties named should then be assumed as trustees, the confirmation was limited accordingly.[58]

5.37   Confirmation in favour of an executor *ex officio* is always limited to the time he holds office.

5.38   Where a testatrix directed her trustees, whom she had appointed her executors, to assume such a number of trustees as would make up their number to four immediately their number was diminished to less than four by non-acceptance, resignation or death, such a direction was quoted in the confirmation, and the executors confirmed subject to the condition attached to their appointment as trustees.[59]

Partial appointment

5.39   Separate executors are sometimes appointed to manage different portions of the estate. This may happen where the testator makes two wills, each dealing with a specified portion of his estate, and appointing a special set of executors to manage it; or it may be done in one instrument, by defining the estate to be administered by each body of executors. However, the appointment of two sets of executors to attend to different parts of the estate must be unequivocal. Where the testator had nominated three executors and subsequently wrote to one of them—

---

[56] *Key*, Feb. 11, 1880, unreported; *Allan*, April 10, 1884, unreported.
[57] *Menzies*, Dec. 18, 1868, unreported.
[58] *Mason*, April 23, 1889, unreported.
[59] *Clark*, Dec. 1, 1885, unreported.

"As soon as possible take out confirmation. You will of course consider it prudent to sell the library as soon as possible"—it was held that the testator had not placed the recipient in the position of sole executor *quoad* the sale of the library.[60]

5.40 Where the testator has estate in different countries, the expedient is sometimes used of appointing different sets of executors to administer the estate in each country. Where a Scottish domiciled person appointed different sets of executors for his United Kingdom estate and for his overseas estate, the Scottish courts will confirm the United Kingdom executors to the United Kingdom estate,[61] though the overseas estate will have to be reported for inheritance tax purposes.

5.41 Where different sets of executors are appointed for different portions of United Kingdom estate, each portion must be distinguished in the inventory, and the executors appointed to administer a particular portion will crave and be granted confirmation to it.[62-63] In such cases, unless one of the executors happens to be common to both (or all) sets of executors, the inventory must be deponed to by a representative of each set of executors. Where there are two deponents, they may concur in the same deposition; or each may depone separately to the same inventory.[64] The following examples illustrate what happens:

1. Where a special executor had been named to deal with one item of estate, confirmation was granted accordingly.[65]

2. Where two wills dealt each with separate branches of the same estate, and contained a distinct nomination of executors, who, with one exception, were the same in both wills, the whole estate was given up in one inventory under different heads, and the confirmation limited the executors' right to act to the estate specified in the inventory falling within the terms of their respective appointments.[66]

3. Where one will appointed separate executors for Scotland and England, the estate in both countries was included in the confirmation, and the whole executors were con-

[60] *Mackenzie* v. *Mackenzie* (1886) 13 R. 507.
[61] Sheriff-substitute Scott in *Kennion's Exrs.*, 1939 S.L.T. (Sh. Ct.) 5 at p. 7, para. 6.
[62-63] As there can be no partial confirmation, the whole estate must be included in one confirmation.
[64] *Brown*, June 7, 1886, unreported.
[65] *Torrance*, Feb. 19, 1886, unreported; *Moore* April 10, 1879, unreported.
[66] *Muir*, May 26, 1886, unreported; *Collins*, July 9, 1924, unreported.

firmed, their right to act being limited in terms of their nomination.[67]

5.42 Following the enactment of the Administration of Estates Act 1971 it is now unusual (except where the deceased was domiciled outside the United Kingdom) for probate to be obtained in England and Wales and confirmation to be obtained separately in Scotland in the same executry.[68] However, where a testator died domiciled in England leaving separate wills for his Scottish and English estate, with a different set of executors in the two countries, the Scottish executors were confirmed to the estate in Scotland alone, on exhibiting a copy of the English will along with the inventory.[69] In a similar case, where the executors under both wills were the same persons, the whole documents were proved in England, but since the Scottish estate was not included in the probate, an inventory thereof was given up in Scotland, and the probate was recorded there.[70]

5.43 In certain cases, the separate appointment of executors may fail:

1. A testator left two wills. Under the first will, the testator conveyed a specific sum "in whatever way invested" and appointed executors to deal with it. On the testator's death, the item was so mixed up with other investments that it could not be distinguished. With the consent of the executors under the first will, the executors appointed under the second will (to whom the rest of the estate had been conveyed) applied for confirmation in their favour, and this was granted.[71]

2. A testator bequeathed a specific legacy to X and appointed him executor of the item in question. The legacy lapsed on X's predecease. It was held competent for the general executor to include the specific article in his confirmation, though it had been specially excepted from his appointment.[72]

3. Special executors were appointed to deal with a certain portion of the estate but they declined to apply for confirmation. With the consent of the special executors, the general executors petitioned and were confirmed to the whole estate.[73]

---

[67] *Leslie*, Dec. 2, 1861, unreported.
[68] See paras. 14.12–14.13, 14.36 and 14.40 *et seq.*
[69] *Simpson*, Sept. 20, 1887, unreported.
[70] *Scarlett*, Oct. 23, 1888, unreported.
[71] *Horsburgh*, Jan. 13, 1868, unreported.
[72] *Cunningham*, March 12, 1877, unreported.
[73] *Miller*, March 2, 1888, unreported.

Order of executors

5.44   Confirmation will be granted in favour of the executors in the
order in which they are named in the testamentary writings. On
occasion, it may be desirable for the executors to be confirmed in
a different order.[74] In such a case, all the acting executors must
sign a letter of request stating specifically the order of executors
in which they wish the confirmation to be issued, and the letter
must be lodged with the inventory. After the crave for confirmation in the oath or affirmation, there should be added: "in
favour of the said executors and it is requested that the deponent [*or other person to be first named*] be the first named executor
in said confirmation."

2. IMPLIED APPOINTMENT

General

5.45   While it is clearly preferable for a testator to expressly appoint
executors, the court will confirm as executor-nominate any
person upon whom the testator has conferred executorial
powers, whether he has done so expressly or by implication.[75]
Thus, where the testator had, in a holograph will, provided "I
leave and bequeath to AB £200, with power to see this Will
executed," it was held that this was an implied appointment of
AB as executor.[76] Where the will stated that CD was "to see this
my Will carried into effect,"[77] this was also held to be an implied
appointment. In all cases where the appointment of an executor
is implied, a special warrant to issue confirmation is normally
required.

5.46   An implied appointment may be made by conferring executorial
powers, without using any special terms. Examples include:

"Judicial factor to carry out the purposes of this Trust"[78];
"I wish my estate to be managed by X" along with W,

---

[74] For instance, a company registrar will, in normal course, dispatch dividends
and other mail to the person named first in the confirmation. If it is preferable
that another executor receives such mail, one solution is to reorder the names
in the confirmation.

[75] The practice can be traced back to the unreported decision of *Ross* (March
9, 1833), where the testator had nominated trustees "for seeing this my will
carried into effect," but not executors. Such a provision would now be covered
by s. 3 of the Executors (Scotland) Act 1900 (63 & 64 Vict., c.55) ; see paras. 5.49
and 5.54–5.56.

[76] *Dundas* v. *Dundas* (1837) 15 S. 427.

[77] *Ross*, March 9, 1833, unreported.

[78] *Tod, Petr.* (1890) 18 R. 152.

whom the testator had previously nominated as his trustee and executor[79]; and

"my dear brother if alive and dear Robert will see to it."[80]

5.47 Although no authorities were cited, previous editions of this book have given the following as examples of implied appointments:

"to use for the benefit of my family";
"to pay all claims";
"to administer";
"to carry these matters through";
"to manage anything I may leave";
"to dispose of my estate";
"to see our Will faithfully and honestly carried out";
"to see to the due fulfilment of my wishes";
"to take possession and divide";
"to carry out the instructions of this Will";
"to have the entire management of my estate in every way"; and
"to see all my business done."

5.48 In determining whether the office of executor has been conferred by implication, the sheriff must consider the whole scope and purport of the testamentary writing. This approach is seen in *Denman* v. *Torry*.[81] The testator had made two holograph wills, neither of which contained an express appointment of an executor. In the first, a legacy was left in the following terms: "my executor, Mr T, to get £100." In the second, it was provided that "my executor [unnamed] to have £100." The First Division held that this was an insufficient nomination, and confirmation was granted, not in favour of Mr T, but in favour of the next-of-kin. Lord President Robertson[82] indicated that a reference to a man as executor may not have the same effect as an appointment of him as executor. This approach does not appear to have been followed by the courts in the following unreported decisions:

1. In *McKay* (November 3, 1959, unreported), the deceased's holograph will contained a bequest "£100 to Mr M as Trustee." The deceased's solicitors held the will which was in a sealed envelope addressed to the trustee. Confirmation was granted in favour of Mr M.

2. In *Murray* (February 29, 1968, unreported) a will contained a bequest "To Mrs AB (Niece) executor £200." Confirmation was granted in favour of Mrs AB.

---

[79] *Martin* v. *Ferguson's Trs.* (1892) 19 R. 474 (where the critical factor was the link with W, who had previously been nominated executrix).

[80] *Blanche*, Dec. 11, 1911, unreported.

[81] (1899) 1 F. 881.

[82] (1899) 1 F. 812 at p. 883.

3. Constructive Appointment

Section 3 of the Executors (Scotland) Act 1900[83]

5.49   Section 3, as amended, provides that:

> "Where a testator has not appointed any person to act as his executor or failing any person so appointed, the testamentary trustees of such testator, original or assumed, or appointed by the supreme court or [the sheriff court[84]] (if any) failing whom any general disponee or universal legatory or residuary legatee appointed by such testator, shall be held to be his executor-nominate and entitled to confirmation in that character."

This section provides a remedy for most situations where the testamentary writings of the deceased fail to provide for the appointment of an executor. It would seem to apply only where the deceased was domiciled in Scotland.

The order of priority

5.50   Section 3 gives a strict order of priority for those to be confirmed as executors-nominate. First, those whom the testator appointed as executors. Secondly, the testamentary trustees of the testator, whether the original ones appointed by the testator, or ones assumed by earlier trustees, or ones appointed by the court. Thirdly, any general disponee, universal legatory or residuary legatee appointed by the testator.

"Failure" of an executor or testamentary trustee

5.51   The remedy provided by section 3 of the 1900 Act is only relevant if there has been either no appointment, or the "failure" of an appointment. Such a "failure" can arise as a result of the executor or testamentary trustee predeceasing the testator, dying with the testator in a common calamity, declining to act, becoming *incapax*,[85] or even dying after confirmation has been issued, in which last event, confirmation *ad non executa* will be granted.[86]

5.52   An example of the incapacity of an executor is the unreported case of *Forman*.[87] A testator appointed her three daughters and

---

[83] 63 & 64 Vict. c. 55.

[84] Inserted by Law Reform (Miscellaneous Provisions) (Scotland) Act 1980 (c. 55), s. 28(1) and Sched. 2, para. 2.

[85] See, for instance, *Martin* v. *Ferguson's Trs.* (1892) 19 R. 474.

[86] Where the failure is due to the death of the executor or testamentary trustee after confirmation has been issued, s. 3 will enable an executor to be confirmed *ad non executa*, *Forrest* March 9, 1904, unreported.

[87] March 28, 1904, unreported.

son to be her universal legatees and the son to be sole executor. By the time confirmation had to be obtained the son was incapacitated by physical and mental weakness from acting as executor. Two of the daughters declined to act as executors. The third daughter was confirmed as sole executor-nominate. Current commissary practice is to view any ill-health, which in the opinion of a doctor makes the nominated executor incapable of fulfilling his role, as being failure: it is not necessary that the executor is *incapax*, in the legal sense.

5.53   Where the last surviving trustee or executor is *incapax* at the time when confirmation is to be applied for, it may be possible for his *curator bonis* to be confirmed as executor-dative but there are other possible solutions.[88]

Constructive appointment: trustees

5.54   Where the testator has not appointed executors, or such appointment has failed, the testamentary trustees, whether original, assumed, or appointed by the court, will be confirmed as executors-nominate.

5.55   Where section 3 is invoked by testamentary trustees, a separate petition is not required and the inventory will be completed with the modifications outlined in Style 8.08.

5.56   Professor Meston has commented that: "Provided that it is clear from the whole tenor of the deceased's will, or from the terms of an appointment of trustees by the court, that there is not intended to be any bar to the persons in question taking up office as executors, they will be entitled to this office in preference to all others whose claim is merely through relationship."[89] There seems to be no authority for such a proviso to the express provisions of the 1900 Act—merely a continuation of pre-1900 commissary practice,[90] which was to regard testamentary trustees as constructively being executors-nominate if the contrary intention did not appear on the face of the testamentary writing.

Substitute trustees

5.57   As for substitute executors see paragraphs 5.28–5.32.

[88] See para. 8.53.
[89] M.C. Meston, *The Succession (Scotland) Act 1964* (4th ed.), p. 97.
[90] See, for example, *Ross*, March 9, 1833, unreported, discussed at para. 5.45.

Assumed trustees

5.58   Trustees may have the power of assumption specifically given
to them in the testamentary writing, in which case the power
must be exercised in the terms granted. In *Lawson*,[91] the testator,
in a codicil, "wished and desired A to be made a trustee," and
it was held that this was not an appointment, but a direction to
assume, and that A must be assumed unless he declined.

5.59   In all other cases, statute imputes to the trustees an unfettered
power of assumption, unless the contrary be expressed in the
testamentary writing.[92] In *Allan's Trustees* v. *Hairstens*,[93] where
a truster gave her trustees power to assume new trustees "in
place of such of their number as shall die or resign or become
incapacitated," it was held that this was not a direction contrary
to the statutory power of assumption.

5.60   Where the trustees originally named in the testamentary writing
would have been entitled to confirmation as executors-
nominate, any trustees whom they may have assumed are also
entitled to confirmation as executors-nominate: the deed of
assumption must be put up to the clerk along with the original
testamentary writing, referred to in the oath or affirmation and
docketed and signed as relative to the inventory.

5.61   It is no bar to the application of section 3 of the 1900 Act if,
having assumed a new trustee or trustees,[93a] the original
trustees resign.[94] See also paragraphs 5.97–5.102 on assump-
tions generally.

English trusts

5.62   The provisions of the Trusts (Scotland) Acts do not apply to
English and other foreign trusts.[95] Accordingly, when the
deceased dies domiciled abroad his testamentary trustees
cannot assume a new trustee under section 3(*b*) of the Trusts
(Scotland) Act 1921.

Appointed by the court

5.63   Where trustees cannot be assumed under a trust deed, or the

[91] April 1, 1878, unreported.
[92] Trusts (Scotland) Act 1921 (11 & 12 Geo. 5, c. 58), s. 3(*b*). For an example
of a case where the contrary is expressed, see *Munro's Trs.* v. *Young* (1887) 14
R. 574.
[93] (1878) 5 R. 576.
[93a] Cf. *Kennedy, Petr.*, 1983 S.L.T. (Sh.Ct) 10.
[94] *Thomson*, Jan. 9, 1900, unreported.
[95] In *Brockie* (1875) 2 R. 923 and *Carruther's Trs.* v. *Allan's Trs.* (1896) 24 R. 238
the Scottish courts refused jurisdiction in petitions relating to English trusts
whose property included heritage in Scotland.

sole trustee is insane or has become incapable of acting by reason of physical or mental disability, or by being absent continuously from the United Kingdom for a period of six months, or having disappeared for a like period, a beneficiary may apply to the Court of Session or sheriff court for the appointment of a trustee or trustees. On the court making the appointment any previous trustee who has become insane or *incapax* shall cease to be a trustee.[96] In one case, the court limited the number of trustees which it appointed to the first three names proposed.[97]

5.64   Trustees may petition the court for authority to assume new trustees, where this is at variance with the purposes of the trust.[98]

Examples of court-appointed trustees where the appointment of executors failed

5.65   Where a testator left a holograph will which required trustees, but contained no appointment of trustees, the beneficiaries presented a petition for the appointment of trustees under section 22 of the Trusts (Scotland) Act 1921. The prayer was granted on the ground that this was a trust deed under which trustees could not be assumed.[99] Where the deceased, by a holograph will, directed that trustees be appointed "to see my Will executed free from responsibility," but failed to make any appointment either of trustees or executors, the beneficiaries applied to the Court of Session and two trustees were appointed. Thereupon, the sheriff granted warrant to issue confirmation in favour of the trustees so appointed as executors-nominate.[1] In a holograph will, a testator made no express appointment of trustees but nominated A, B and C to be his joint executors. One declined, so the nomination fell, and an application was made for the appointment of trustees. The application was granted, and the trustees were confirmed as executors-nominate.[2]

Constructive appointment: general disponee, universal legatory and residuary legatee

5.66   Where the remedy afforded by section 3 of the 1900 Act is invoked by a general disponee, universal legatory or residuary legatee, it is not necessary for one of these terms to be used in the testamentary writing: it is sufficient that the applicant

---

[96] Trusts (Scotland) Act 1921 (11 & 12 Geo. 5, c. 58), s. 22, as amended by Law Reform (Miscellaneous Provisions) (Scotland) Act 1980 (c. 55), s. 13(*a*).

[97] *The Glasgow Lock Hospital, Petr.*, 1949 S.L.T. (Notes) 26.

[98] Trusts (Scotland) Act 1921 (11 & 12 Geo. 5, c. 58), s. 5.

[99] *Auld and Another, Petrs.*, 1925 S.L.T. 83.

[1] *Lee*, Dec. 7, 1889, unreported.

[2] *Fiddes*, Mar. 24, 1874, unreported.

possesses such character. The term "general disponee" is used where the estate includes both heritage and moveables, and the term "universal legatory" where it comprises only moveable items.

Special warrant

5.67   Where it is clear from the whole tenor of the testamentary writing that the applicant for confirmation as executor-nominate (under section 3) has in fact the character of general disponee, universal legatory or residuary legatee which he claims, it is not necessary for him to petition the sheriff for special warrant to the sheriff or commissary clerk to issue confirmation in his favour. If there is doubt as to whether the applicant has the character he claims, commissary practice requires that a special warrant to issue confirmation (see Styles 4.09 and 4.10) must be applied for and obtained before confirmation will be granted. If the applicant is unable to show that, according to the whole tenor of the will, he is entitled to the office claimed, the heirs on intestacy may be preferred.[3-4]

Residuary legatee, etc., wrongly named

5.68   On occasion, there may be a difficulty in identifying the residuary beneficiary, and in the event of dispute an action of multiple poinding may be necessary to determine who is the beneficiary. In *Keiller* v. *Thomson's Trustees*,[5] the deceased had left a bequest to "Janet Keiller or Williamson, confectioner in Dundee." The court upheld the claim of Agnes Keiller or Wedderspoon, confectioner in Dundee, whose sister Janet Keiller (married in Broughty Ferry) did not lodge a claim, after evidence of Agnes's connection with the deceased, including the fact that she had been named in his previous testamentary writings. In *Keiller* v. *Thomson's Trustees*,[6] a legacy to "William Keillor, confectioner in Dundee" was claimed by William Keiller, confectioner in Montrose, and by James Keiller, confectioner in Dundee. James's claim was sustained after it had been established that there was no such person as "William Keillor, confectioner in Dundee," that James was a friend and relation of Thomson and that he was the only confectioner of that name in Dundee, William having worked for him until a few months before Thomson's death, when he had set himself up as a confectioner in Montrose. In a petition for special directions to the

---

[3-4] *Per* Lord Mackenzie in *McGown* v. *McKinlay* (1835) 14 S. 105 at p. 106; *Jerdon* v. *Forrest* (1897) 24 R. 395 (both pre-1900 cases involving dative appointments).
[5] (1824) 3 S. 279.
[6] (1826) 4 S. 730.

sheriff clerk to issue confirmation in favour of a person claiming to be, for example, the residuary legatee, where there is doubt as to the beneficiary's identity, the facts favouring the claimant as being the mis-named beneficiary should be set out.

Identifying the residuary legatees, etc., where they are a class

5.69 Where a testamentary writing makes provision for a class of individuals to benefit, and it is the individual members of this class who fall to be decerned as executors-nominate *qua* general disponees, universal legatories or residuary beneficiaries, the petition to the court setting out the facts and craving confirmation will have the effect of determining who the members of the class are. Sometimes the court requires the petitioners to produce affidavits corroborating the facts set out in the petition, as where the testamentary beneficiaries are the testator's "children" and whether such affidavits are necessary should be discussed with the sheriff clerk at an early stage.

5.70 A testamentary provision benefiting a class may, for instance, be "to my children," or "to my only sister's children," and the following notes provide some guidance as to how such phrases will be interpreted where the testator died domiciled in Scotland and the will is to be interpreted according to Scots law.[7]

5.71 Statute and case law provide some guidance as to the meaning of some of the terms commonly used to define a class. The general rule is that the members of the class fall to be identified at the time that the succession opens or takes effect.[8]

Children
5.72 See "illegitimate persons" and "adopted persons" below.

Family
5.73 The term "family" is normally limited to sons and daughters only,[9] though it has been held to include grandchildren.[10] See also "illegitimate persons" and "adopted persons" below.

Issue
5.74 The term "issue" has no technical meaning in the law of Scotland:

---

[7] In cases involving other systems of law, the matter is much more complex, and readers are directed to Anton and Beaumont, *Private International Law* (2nd ed., 1990) pp. 692–694.

[8] *Maxwell* v. *Maxwell* (1864) 3 M. 318.

[9] *Low's Trs.* v. *Whitworth* (1892) 19 R. 431; *Macdonald's Trs.* v. *Macdonald* (1900) 8 S.L.T. 226; *Searcy's Trs.* v. *Allbary*, 1907 S.C. 823; *Greig's Trs.* v. *Simpson*, 1918 S.C. 321.

[10] *Irvine* v. *Irvine* (1873) 11 M. 892; 45 Scot. Jur. 546.

"It may mean children and it may mean descendants generally, according to the way in which it is used, and the terms
of the clause in which the word or words occur, and the
mind of the testator in so far as it can be gathered either
from the particular clause or from the whole scope or purpose of his settlement."[11]

Its primary meaning is to include not only children but also
direct descendants, no matter how remote.[12] The context may,
however, show that the testator used "issue" in a more limited
sense, as comprising immediate children only.[13]

See also "illegitimate persons" and "adopted persons" below.

Illegitimate persons

5.75
1. When construing a testamentary writing which comes
into operation after June 8, 1968, the fact that a person
has been legitimated shall generally be ignored.[14]

2. In interpreting a testamentary writing executed on or after
December 8, 1986, "the fact that a person's parents are
not or have not been married to one another shall be
left out of account in establishing the legal relationship
between the person and any other person; and accordingly any such relationship shall have effect as if the parents were or had been married to one another,"[15] unless
the writing expressly makes a distinction between legitimate and illegitimate persons[16]—as by using the phrase
"the lawful issue of X." For deeds executed on or after
November 25, 1968, a similar effect was achieved by section 5(1) of the Law Reform (Miscellaneous Provisions)
(Scotland) Act 1968 which enacted that a provision in
favour of a class determined by a blood relationship was
to include persons who were illegitimate, unless the contrary intention was apparent.[17] In older wills, there is a
very strong presumption that phrases such as "issue" and
"children" do not include illegitimate persons[18]: but "the
interpretation of the word 'children,' as used by any given
testator, may be varied according to the state of the facts
and the testator's knowledge of the facts."[19]

[11] Lord President Inglis in *Young's Trs.* v. *McNab* (1883) 10 R. 1165 at p. 1168.
[12] *Murray's Trs.* v. *Mackie and Others*, 1959 S.L.T. 129 and the cases referred to
therein by Lord Guest.
[13] *Cattanach's Trs.* v. *Cattanach* (1902) 4 F. 205.
[14] Legitimation (Scotland) Act 1968 (c. 22), s. 2(3) and (4).
[15] Law Reform (Parent and Child) (Scotland) Act 1986 (c. 9), s. 1(1) and (2).
[16] *Ibid.* s. 1(4).
[17] Applied in *Russell* v. *Wood's Trs.*, 1987 S.L.T. 503.
[18] *Mitchell's Trs.* v. *Cables* (1893) 1 S.L.T. 156 (*per* Lord Kincairney); *Scott's Trs.*
v. *Smart*, 1954 S.C. 12; *Allan, Petr.*, 1991 S.L.T. 203; McLaren, *Wills and Succession*, Vol. 1, para. 642.
[19] *Scott's Trs.* v. *Smart*, 1953 S.C. 12 at pp. 16–17.

Adopted persons

5.76

1. In a testamentary writing executed after September 10, 1964, a provision referring to a child of the testator includes his or her adopted children, unless the contrary intention is apparent.[20] If the testamentary writing had been executed before that date, a reference to "child" is presumed not to include adopted children.[21]

2. In a testamentary writing executed after September 10, 1964 and after the adoption order was made unless the contrary intention is apparent
   (a) a provision referring to an adopter's child includes his or her adopted children[22];
   (b) a provision referring to the child of the adopted person's natural parent or parents does not include the adopted person[22a];
   (c) in a reference to persons related to the adopted person in a particular degree, an adopted child is treated as falling into the same category as the natural child of the adopter.[23]

If the testamentary writing had been executed before September 10, 1994, the above presumptions do not apply.[24]

3. Where a child was adopted by married parents jointly, a reference in a testamentary writing executed after September 10, 1964 to, say, a sister of the natural son of the adoptive parents will include the adopted daughter, whereas if there was only one adopting parent, or the adopters were not married, the relationship is brother or sister of the half blood.[25]

Relation

5.77 A bequest to the testator's "nearest relations then alive" was held, in the context of the particular testamentary writing, to include the children of the testator's half sister, as well as the testator's brother of the full blood.[26]

Next-of-kin

5.78 Unless the context indicates to the contrary, a bequest to the testator's "nearest in kin" is to the relative nearest in blood to

---

[20] Succession (Scotland) Act 1964 (c. 41), s. 23(1), but where the adopter died before September 10, 1964, see also Law Reform (Miscellaneous Provisions) (Scotland) Act 1966 (c. 19), s. 5.

[21] Succession (Scotland) Act 1964 (c. 41), s. 23(4).

[22] *Ibid.*, s. 23(2) (*a*).

[22a] *Ibid.*, s. 23(2) (*b*).

[23] *Ibid.*, s. 23(2) (*c*).

[24] *Ibid.*, s. 23(4). See *Spencer's Trs* v. *Ruggles*, 1982 S.L.T. 165.

[25] *Ibid.*, s. 24(1).

[26] *Scott* v. *Scott* (1852) 14 D. 1057, decided at a time when the law gave relations of the full blood a preferential claim to those of the half blood.

the testator on his father's side at the date of his death (see para. 6.21), rather than to the heirs on intestacy under the statutory rules.[27]

More than one general disponee, universal legatory or residuary legatee

5.79   Where there is more than one general disponee, universal legatory or residuary legatee, all are held to be executors-nominate, and will be entitled to be confirmed. If only some of those eligible are to be confirmed in a nominate capacity, the others must either be incapacitated or decline to act. For instance, where the bequest was "all to my daughters" and the testator left five daughters, four of whom declined to act, the fifth was confirmed as executrix-nominate *qua* general disponee.[28] In another case, a testatrix appointed her three daughters and son to be universal legatories, and the son to be sole executor. The son was incapacitated by physical and mental weakness, and two daughters declined the executorship. The third daughter was confirmed as sole executrix-nominate.[29]

General disponee, universal legatory or residuary legatee must have a vested right

5.80   It is of the essence of the statutory provision that the bequest must have vested in the general disponee, universal legatory or residuary legatee. Where the provision is in favour of a class of beneficiaries, some may have a vested right and others not. Previous editions of this work have suggested that those with vested rights will be entitled to confirmation under section 3. However, it is submitted that, since some of the beneficiaries who will share in the estate cannot, at the time, be decerned as executors-nominate (since they do not have a vested right) the preferable course is for those with a vested right to be confirmed as executors-dative. It is unknown what approach the court might take if the right has vested subject to defeasance.

Conditional bequest

5.80A   The testator may have made the bequest to the general disponee, universal legatory or residuary legatee subject to a condition. In this event, the petition for special directions will include averments showing that the condition has been fulfilled. Where the bequest to the general disponees was subject to the proviso

---

[27] *Young's Trs.* v. *Janes* (1880) 8 R. 242. See also *Gregory's Trs.* v. *Alison* (1889) 16 R. (H.L.) 10.

[28] *Cowan*, Jan. 10, 1910, unreported.

[29] *Forman*, March 28, 1904, unreported.

that they "shall have always provided a home for me," it was held that the condition was fulfilled where the disponees had made their home available to the testator even although she had not lived with them.[29a]

Executor-nominate or executor-dative?

5.81   As discussed at paragraphs 6.14–6.20, it is possible for the universal or residuary beneficiaries of a deceased person to apply to be decerned either as executor-dative or as executor-nominate *qua* universal or residuary beneficiary. Although a nominate appointment is preferable to a dative appointment, since caution is not normally required, in some cases a dative appointment may be necessary, if using the remedy under section 3 of the 1900 Act is inappropriate:

1. Section 3 of the 1900 Act has been interpreted as providing that *all* universal or residuary beneficiaries—not simply one of their number—will become executors-nominate. Thus, it may prove an impossible remedy where all the residuary beneficiaries do not concur in asking to be confirmed as executors-nominate.[30] And it may prove a cumbersome remedy where there are many beneficiaries to trace and to take instructions from. Again, if a child *in utero* at the time of the testator's death stood to share in the estate if born alive,[31] no progress can be made in obtaining confirmation until the child is born. In such cases, it will be more expedient for one or more of the residuary beneficiaries to apply to be decerned executor-dative: in this event, there will be no need to intimate the application to the other residuary beneficiaries.[32]

2. If one or more of the general disponees, universal legatories or residuary legatees has predeceased the testator, and their share has fallen into intestacy,[33] section 3 of the 1900 Act is not applicable, and the surviving beneficiaries can only be confirmed as executors-dative.[34]

3. If one of the general disponees, universal legatories or

[29a] *Miller, Petrs.*, 1977 S.L.T. (Sh. Ct.) 67.

[30] *Millar*, Dec. 28, 1921, unreported.

[31] *Qui in utero est pro jam nato habetur*; Digest, I.v.7.; Erskine, III.viii.76); Bankton, I.lxxii.1.); Bell, *Prin.*, § 1642.

[32] *Millar, deceased*, Sheriff Principal, Dec. 28, 1921, unreported.

[33] As where the will does not provide for the bequests to accresce to the survivors (*Paxton's Trs.* v. *Cowie, etc.* (1886) 13 R. 1191; *Fraser's Trs.* v. *Fraser*, 1980 S.L.T. 211), or the *conditio si institutus sine liberis decesserit* is not applicable.

[34] *Landells*, Feb. 10, 1960, unreported; *Paxton's Trs.* v. *Cowie, etc.* (1886) 13 R. 1191; *Fraser's Trs.* v. *Fraser*, 1980 S.L.T. 211.

residuary legatees has unlawfully killed the testator, it is a rule of public policy that he cannot receive any part of the testator's estate though he may apply to the court for an order modifying the rule.[35] Since the testator is unlikely to have made testamentary provision for the eventuality of being killed by the nominated beneficiary (even although provision may have been made for the situation of the beneficiary failing to survive the testator), it is likely that the beneficiary's share will fall into intestacy.[36] In such circumstances, section 3 of the 1900 Act is not applicable, and the surviving beneficiaries can only be confirmed as executors-dative.

4. Where a general disponee, universal legatory or residuary legatee has died after the testator, his heir cannot avail himself of the 1900 Act, and he must be decerned executor-dative, either *qua* representative of the general disponee, universal legatory or residuary legatee, or *qua* general disponee, etc., by succession, having first been confirmed as executor to the estate of the dead general disponee, universal legatory or residuary beneficiary.[37]

General disponee, universal legatory or residuary legatee—or merely a specific legatee?

5.82   The interpretation of holograph testamentary writings is frequently difficult, a particular problem being whether the words used are sufficiently all-embracing to include heritage. Prior to the enactment of section 20 of the Titles to Land Consolidation (Scotland) Act 1868, heritage could be only conveyed in a testamentary writing if it was in the form of a *de praesenti* conveyance. While thereafter land could be bequeathed by simpler words (being sufficient to transfer moveables), it is frequently unclear whether the testator intended to include heritage in his bequest, although the courts will normally endeavour to avoid a result whereby the testator dies partly intestate. The following examples illustrate the problems. In each case (unless the contrary is stated) the court held that the bequest was of the whole of the estate, or the whole of the residue of the estate, so entitling the beneficiary or beneficiaries to confirmation as executor-nominate under section 3 of the 1900 Act:

1. Testamentary gift to A of "house with contents—and also all moneys which I may possess."[38]

---

[35] See, further, paras. 8.30–8.32.
[36] *Hunter's Exrs., Petrs.,* 1992 S.L.T. 1141.
[37] See para. 5.93.
[38] *Wilson,* Oct. 20, 1900, unreported.

2. "I leave to A all that belongs to me in money and other things."[39]

3. "All my monies and belongings" was held to include heritage.[40]

4. "All to my daughters."[41]

5. "All my worldly goods."[42]

6. "Sole heir and legatee without reserve and qualification."[43]

7. "Anything, either money or property, left at my wife's death."[44]

8. "Belongings" have been held to be equivalent to "possessions," and as such have carried the whole estate.[45]

9. "Any other capital."[46]

10. "All the property, goods, money, gear, stock, shares, boats, scrip, etc."[47]

11. A bequest of "the whole of property ether in money, bonds, debets, bussness, and other afficts whotsoever [sic]" was held not to include a lease of an inn, in respect that the general bequest of "the whole property" (which would have included the lease), was derogated by the enumeration of specifics, which did not encompass heritage.[48]

12. "In order to prevent any dispute after my death regarding the disposal of my property . . . the whole of the means and effects in my possession or belonging to me at the time of my decease."[49]

---

[39] *Ferguson*, Sept. 28, 1900, unreported.
[40] *Simson's Trs.* v. *Simson*, 1921 S.C. 14.
[41] *Cowan*, Jan. 10, 1910, unreported.
[42] *Cadger* v. *Ronald's Trs.*, 1946 S.L.T. (Notes) 24.
[43] *Herman*, Sept. 17, 1902, unreported.
[44] *Forsyth*, Sept. 10, 1900, unreported.
[45] *Macintyre* v. *Miller* (1900) 7 S.L.T. 435.
[46] *Auld's Trs.* v. *Auld's Trs.*, 1933 S.C. 176.
[47] *Oag's Curator* v. *Corner, etc.* (1885) 12 R. 1162.
[48] *Edmond* v. *Edmond* (1873) 11 M. 348 *per* Lord President Inglis at p. 350.
[49] *Forsyth* v. *Turnbull* (1887) 15 R. 172 (*cf.* the earlier approach noted by Lord Justice-Clerk Moncreiff at p. 176 that where a will was prepared by a man of business, the words "means and effects" had been restricted to personal property. The earlier approach is illustrated in *Pitcairn* v. *Pitcairn* (1870) 8 M. 604, where a bequest of "my effects" was held not to include lands but to be limited to moveables, especially corporeal moveables; *per* Lord President Inglis at p. 609).

13. "Means and substance."[50]

14. "All means and moveables."[51]

15. "Money" or "moneys," where the will, prepared without professional assistance, had provided for a specific legacy of the heritage.[52] "Money" is normally interpreted as meaning the whole moveable estate not otherwise disposed of,[53] and only in exceptional circumstances has it been held to include heritage.[54]

General disponee, universal legatory or residuary legatee? Full fee or liferent?

5.83   Another problem area occurs where the residue of the estate bears to be left in liferent and fee. Generally, provided that the fee has vested, the fiar will be entitled to be confirmed as executor-nominate *qua* universal legatory or residuary legatee under section 3 of the 1900 Act.

5.84   The practice is against a liferenter being so confirmed—though exceptionally it may be possible to show that the liferenter is in fact the general disponee. Examples include cases where, at the time the trust commenced, the fee was to be held for beneficiaries who were unknown or incapable of being ascertained,[55-56] cases where the fee was not disposed of in the testamentary writing, and cases where the fiar predeceased the testator, without there being a destination over in favour of someone else. Occasionally, the testator bears to have absolutely disposed of his estate to one person, and then provides for its ultimate disposal on that person's death. If this is held to be a provision by way of liferent and fee, the first beneficiary will not be able to be confirmed as executor-nominate under section 3 of the 1900 Act.

5.85   The following examples illustrate the type of problems incurred in "liferent and fee" cases:

1. The liferenter of the deceased's estate, even when he has

---

[50] *Maclagan's Trs.* v. *Lord Advocate* (1903) 11 S.L.T. 227.

[51] *Hardy Trs. & Others, Petrs.* (1871) 9 M. 736.

[52] *Easson* v. *Thomson's Trs.* (1879) 7 R. 251.

[53] Including, in the case of a holograph will, the fee arising under a trust deed in which the testator had a vested interest: *Dunsmure* v. *Dunsmure* (1879) 7 R. 261 (although the interpretation of the will was, perhaps, rather more generous than would be expected today).

[54] *Keith* v. *Fraser* (1883) 20 S.L.R. 785; *Ord* v. *Ord*, 1927 S.C. 77; *Fraser's Exrx.* v. *Fraser's C.B.*, 1931 S.C. 536.

[55-56] Trusts (Scotland) Act 1921 (11 & 12 Geo. 5, c. 58), s. 8.

power to test on it, is not the deceased's universal legatory.[57]

If, however, the liferenter has an unqualified power to dispose of the whole trust fund, he is entitled to the fee.[58]

2. Where the testator bequeathed her personal estate to A "to be used by him for the term of his natural life," since there was no trust and no other disposal of capital, A was held to be the fiar,[59] and as such would have been entitled to be decerned as executor-nominate *qua* general disponee. This decision is not of general application, for it is more common for the court to determine, when interpreting a testamentary writing in which the fee is undisposed of, that the fee passes under the rules of intestate succession.[60]

3. Where the testator provided that "all I possess I leave to my husband and after him to my sister and her heirs," the husband was held to be the fiar, and so confirmed as executor-nominate *qua* general disponee.[61] Similarly, where the testator had bequeathed the residue of his estate to his wife, and provided that "if my wife would remarry or die, I wish all my . . . estate to be equally divided between my surviving sisters and brother" the wife was held to have an absolute bequest of the fee.[62]

4. Where the testator provided "anything A may desire to dispose of or realise after my decease such as Library and Stamp Collection may be done. On her decease everything of mine to be sold and the proceeds divided as follows," A was held to take the fee.[63]

5. A direction to trustees "to pay, convey and make over" the residue of the testator's estate "to [his] wife for her free use and enjoyment during her life so long as she shall remain my widow" with provision for the disposal

---

[57] *McGown* v. *McKinlay* (1835) 14 S. 105; *Alves* v. *Alves* (1861) 23 D. 712; *Pursell* v. *Elder* (1865) 3 M. (H.L.) 59; *Morris* v. *Tennant* (1858) 30 Scot. Jur. 943; *Forrest's Trs.* v. *Reid* (1904) 7 F. 142.

[58] *Per* Lord Justice-Clerk Westbury in *Pursell* v. *Elder* (1865) 3 M. (H.L.) 59 at p. 68; *Rattray's Trs.* v. *Rattray* (1899) 1 F. 510 (the direction was to pay to the liferenter's "heirs and assignees," and the word "assignees" was held to be equivalent to an unqualified power of disposal).

[59] *Lethem* v. *Evans*, 1918 1 S.L.T. 27.

[60] *Spink's Exrs.* v. *Simpson* (1894) 21 R. 551; *Sim* v. *Duncan* (1900) 2 F. 434; *Innes's Trs.* v. *Innes*, 1948 S.C. 406.

[61] *Reid* v. *Dobie*, 1921 S.C. 662.

[62] *Smart* v. *Smart's Trs*, 1926 S.C. 392.

[63] *Cochrane's Exx.* v. *Cochrane*, 1947 S.C. 134.

of the fee on her death was held to constitute a liferent for the widow.[63a]

6. Where a beneficiary of full age has a vested, unqualified and indefeasible right of fee, he is entitled to have the property transferred to him, even although the testator has directed that his trustees retain the property for a given period.[64]

A conditional bequest? The legacy to the "spouse," etc.

5.86   Where the testator makes a bequest to "my spouse, AB," from whom the testator is subsequently divorced, the question must then be asked whether the bequest to AB has lapsed. Each case turns on the interpretation of the terms of the particular testamentary writing, and it is up to the challenger to prove that the bequest was conditional on the beneficiary being the testator's spouse on death.[65] In one case, the testator left an alimentary liferent of the residue of his estate to his wife, whom he described as such and also named, and whom he later divorced. Since the liferent was stated to be for the wife's own maintenance and support, and for the maintenance and support of the testator's children, it was held that the bequest was a gift to the woman in her capacity as the testator's wife and, following the divorce, she was not qualified to receive the liferent.[66] But if the testamentary writing does not contain an indication that the provision for the wife was in the nature of family provision, the bequest will receive effect even after divorce, the words "my wife" being a mere term of description.[67]

5.87   A bequest to the testator's "fiancée, Mrs M" was similarly held to be valid, the words "my fiancée" being descriptive only, and not a condition of the bequest.[68]

Common calamity or simultaneous deaths involving testator and beneficiary

5.88   Where the testator and the general disponee, universal legatory

---

[63a] *Innes's Trs. v. Innes,* 1948 S.C. 406.

[64] *Miller's Trs. v. Miller* (1890) 18 R. 301; *Yuill's Trs. v. Thomson* (1902) 4 F. 815; *Donaldson's Trs. v. Donaldson,* 1916 S.C. (H.L.) 55; *Smith's Trs. v. Michael,* 1972 S.L.T. 89.

[65] *Henderson's J. F. v. Henderson,* 1930 S.L.T. 743.

[66] *Pirie's Trs. v. Pirie,* 1962 S.C. 43; see also *Towse's Tr. v. Towse,* 1924 S.L.T. 465.

[67] *Henderson' J. F. v. Henderson,* 1930 S.L.T. 743; *Couper's J. F. v. Valentine,* 1976 S.L.T. 83.

[68] *Ormiston's Exrx. v. Laws,* 1966 S.C. 47.

or residuary beneficiary have died in circumstances indicating that they died simultaneously, or rendering it uncertain which, if either, survived the other, then section 31 of the Succession (Scotland) Act 1964 sets out certain presumptions for the purposes of succession to their estates:

1. Where the *commorientes* were spouses, it is presumed that neither survived the other. Consequently, if there is no destination over, the residuary estate will be distributed under the rules of intestate succession, and the heirs on intestacy may be confirmed as executors-dative. If there is a destination over which applies "in the event of the spouse predeceasing" the testator, then on a common calamity the estate will pass into intestacy too.[69-70] But if the destination over is conditional on the spouse not surviving the testator for a period of (say) 30 days, the circumstances of the deaths are normally such that it is clear that the destinee succeeds.

2. Where the *commorientes* were not spouses, it is normally presumed that the younger survived the elder, and their respective testamentary writings are interpreted on this basis. Thus, if the elder left his whole estate to the younger, the executors of the younger (whether nominate or dative) will, on the failure of the executor-nominate and trustees, be entitled to be confirmed as executors-dative *qua* nominate as trustee, universal legatory by succession in terms of section 3 of the 1900 Act. And if the younger left his whole estate to the elder, if there was a destination over, it will pass to the destinee who may be confirmed as executor-nominate. If there is no destinee, the younger's estate will pass into intestacy, and his heirs on intestacy may be decerned as executors-dative.

5.88A The exception to the general rules outlined above is where the elder left money to the younger, whom failing another person (X), but the younger died intestate. In such a case, it is presumed that the elder survived the younger, so that X is entitled to be confirmed as the elder's executor-nominate in terms of section 3 of the 1900 Act.[71]

5.88B The presumptions set out in section 31 of the Succession (Scotland) Act 1964 do not apply if it can be proved that one of the parties survived the other. The standard of proof is on the balance of probabilities.[71a]

[69-70] *Ross's J. F.* v. *Martin*, 1954 S.C. 18.
[71] The heirs on intestacy of the younger will be entitled to be decerned his executor-dative, but will not confirm to any part of the elder's estate.
[71a] *Lamb* v. *Lord Advocate*, 1976 S.C. 110.

5.88C For the purpose of calculating the inheritance tax due on their respective estates a different assumption applies.[71b]

Beneficiary has unlawfully killed the testator

5.89 If a beneficiary has unlawfully killed the testator, it is a rule of public policy that he cannot receive any part of the testator's estate,[71c] though he may apply to the court for an order modifying the rule.[72] In determining to whom the estate will pass, the terms of the deceased's testamentary writing will be considered. In *Hunter's Executors, Petitioners*,[73] a husband murdered his wife. The wife's testamentary writing had provided that her estate should pass to her husband "whom failing should he predecease me or should we die simultaneously to" X. The Inner House held that, while public policy required that the husband's right be forfeited, it did not require that the wife's estate be distributed as if the husband had predeceased her and in the context of the particular testamentary writing, the estate fell into intestacy.[74] The position is different if the beneficiary has been convicted of murdering his or her parent or grandparent, for then the succession of the estate is dealt with as if the murderer had predeceased the parent or grandparent.[74a]

Derivative titles, etc.

5.90 The person (A) claiming to be confirmed as executor-nominate to X's estate under section 3 of the 1900 Act may not be the original legatee under X's testamentary writing. For instance, the original legatee, B, may have predeceased X, and there may be a destination over to A in X's will. Or A may come in as B's child to take B's share under the *conditio si institutus sine liberis decesserit*, where B was X's child or his nephew or niece and X had made provision for B of the sort which a parent might make for his child. Or again, B may have taken a vested right and sold or assigned that right before A died.

5.91 Where A is the first person in whom the right under the testamentary writing vests, he clearly falls with section 3. Thus, where the bequest was "to B and B's heirs," and B predeceased the testator, confirmation was issued in favour of A, B's heir, as substitute general disponee.[75] In such a case, an application for special warrant to issue confirmation may be required.

[71b] Inheritance Act 1984 (c. 51), s.4(2).

[71c] *Smith, Petr.*, 1979 S.L.T. (Sh. Ct.) 35.

[72] See, further, para. 8.30.

[73] 1992 S.L.T. 1141.

[74] *Cf.* approach discussed in *Re H (Deceased)* [1990] 1 F.L.R. 441.

[74a] Parricide Act 1594 (c. 30): rule may apply to heritage only; Bankton, II ccci 30.

[75] *Muir*, Mar. 23, 1906, unreported; *Anderson*, Oct. 16, 1911, unreported.

5.92 Where B took a vested right, and then sold that right to A, there is nothing to prevent B, if still alive, from confirming under section 3, and the confirmation will then accresce to the assignee, A. If B had died before X (but after assigning), A is entitled to confirmation, but the case does not fall under section 3 of the 1900 Act, and the practice is that he must apply as executor-dative to X.

5.93 The situation is very different if B took a vested right and then died, without winding up X's estate. Double confirmation is then required:

1. Confirmation of A, as B's executor (nominate or dative, as appropriate) to B's estate, including therein B's right to the residue of X's estate.

2. Confirmation of A as executor-dative to the estate of X as his residuary legatee by succession.

The meaning of terms commonly used in testamentary writings for substitutions

5.94 The terms of each testamentary writing must be considered carefully, for the testator may have given a particular word a special meaning. For the meaning of some terms commonly used in denoting blood relationship see paragraphs 5.70–5.78 above. Case law provides further guidance as to the following terms:

Representatives

5.95 The interpretation to be given to the word "representatives" (as in the phrase "to A, whom failing to A's representatives") turns on the particular terms of the deed in which it is used.[76] Generally, in a testamentary writing, where the representatives are conditional institutes, the term means heirs on intestacy rather than executors or testamentary heirs.[77] But where the context was the bequest of a legacy to A, whom failing by his predecease of the testator "to A's executors and representatives whomsoever," the term was held to mean A's executors-nominate.[78]

---

[76] *Per* Lord President Inglis in *Manson* v. *Hutcheon* (1874) 1 R. 371, where the term was held to mean the executors-nominate.

[77] *Stewart* v. *Stewart*, May 21, 1802, F.C., where, under the pre-1964 succession rules, the bequest fell to the brother's next-of-kin.

[78] *Scott's Exrs.* v. *Methven's Exrs.* (1890) 17 R. 389.

Nearest heirs or heirs

5.96   A testamentary gift left to A, whom failing to A's "heirs, executors and successors whomsoever" passes to A's heirs on intestacy, and not to his testamentary representatives.[79] A's "heirs"
fall to be ascertained at the time of A's death,[80] even if the
distribution may be postponed, and even although this may
have the effect of giving a fee to a child dying in minority, when
other clauses have declared that nothing shall vest in the child
until majority.[81] Where A died domiciled in Scotland after September 10, 1964, the heirs on intestacy are those listed in section
2(1) of the Succession (Scotland) Act 1964,[82] but ignoring any
claim of the surviving spouse to *jus relictae* or *relicti*.[83]

4. ASSUMPTION BY AN EXECUTOR-NOMINATE

Powers to assumption contained in the testamentary writing

5.97   The testamentary writing may give the executors express
powers to assume new executors, and the powers of assumption must then be exercised in accordance with the testamentary
directions. Thus, where the testator had nominated A to be her
executor, and directed him to assume B as a trustee, A was
confirmed alone only on production of B's declinature.[84] Something less than a formal direction may have the same result.
Where the testator stated that he "wished and desired A to be
made a trustee," it was held that A must be assumed as a
trustee, unless he declined office.[85] But where the testator had
"recommended" that her trustees assume A, the trustees were
confirmed alone, without requiring A to decline office.[86]

Statutory powers of assumption

5.98   Under statute, all executors-nominate have an unfettered power

---

[79] *Lady Kinnaird's Trs.* v. *Ogilvy*, 1911 S.C. 1136; and *Mackenzie's Trs.* v. *George-
son*, 1923 S.C. 517 (where the destination was "to their respective heirs and
executors").

[80] See *MacMillan, Petr.*, 1987 S.L.T. (Sh. Ct.) 50 where the issue was who was
the heir of a trustee for the purpose of establishing right to act as trustee for
the purposes of section 6 of the Law Reform (Miscellaneous Provisions)
(Scotland) Act 1980. Sheriff O'Brien stated at p. 51L that "there should be no
difference in determining who is 'heir' for the purposes of succession and for
the purposes of administering the estate."

[81] *Anderson's Trs.* v. *Forrest*, 1917 S.C. 321.

[82] *Allan, Petrs.*, 1991 S.L.T. 202.

[83] *Per* Lord Sands in *Smith's Trs.* v. *Macpherson's Trs.*, 1926 S.L.T. 669 at p. 674.

[84] *Miller*, April 17, 1862, unreported.

[85] *Lawson*, April 1, 1878, unreported.

[86] *Roy*, Feb. 4, 1863, unreported.

to assume new executors, unless the contrary is expressed in the testamentary writing.[87] Where the testator provided that his wife "and any other whom she may select to act along with her should be trustees and executors," it was held that this was a clear case where the testator had limited the executors' power of assumption—the wife alone could assume new executors or trustees.[88] If the testator had appointed someone as "sole executor", the use of the word "sole" is normally taken as meaning that the executor cannot assume a new executor. An executor-dative does not have power to assume new executors.[89]

The form of a deed of assumption

5.99   A deed of assumption should be in accordance with the style contained in Appendix B to the Trusts (Scotland) Act 1921. The deed if executed prior to August 1, 1995 should be probative, or if executed on or after that date self-proving. It does not require to be stamped, provided that it contains a certificate certifying that it falls within category A of The Stamp Duty (Exempt Instruments) Regulations 1987.[90] Generally all the old executors will sign the deed of assumption, but, unless the testamentary writing provides otherwise, signature by a *quorum* will generally be sufficient.[91–92]

5.100   Where the testamentary writing nominates persons to be "trustees and executors," the deed of assumption should be of "trustees and executors." If the deed of assumption were of "trustees" only, it could be argued that, since trustees are entitled to the office of executors-nominate only on the failure of the executors,[93] confirmation should be granted in favour of the original executors only.

The effect of the deed of assumption

5.101   Where new executors have been assumed, the deed of assumption must be put up with the inventory for confirmation, along with the testamentary writing, referred to in the oath or

---

[87] Trusts (Scotland) Act 1921 (11 & 12 Geo. 5, c. 58), ss. 2, 3(*b*) and 21 and Sched. B, as applied to executors-nominate by virtue of Executors (Scotland) Act 1900 (63 & 64 Vict. c. 55), s. 2.

[88] *Thomson's Tr., Petr.*, 1984 S.L.T. (Notes) 27. See also the trust cases of *Allan's Trs.* v. *Hairstens* (1878) 5 R. 576 and *Munro's Trs.* v. *Young* (1887) 14 R. 574 discussed at n. 86.

[89] Succession (Scotland) Act 1964 (c.41), s.20.

[90] S.I. 1987 No. 516.

[91–92] Trusts (Scotland) Act 1921 (11 & 12 Geo. 5, c. 58), s. 3(*b*).

[93] Executors (Scotland) Act 1900 (63 & 64 Vict. c. 55), s. 3; see para. 5.54.

affirmation and docketed as relative thereto. Confirmation will then be granted in favour of the original and the assumed executors. Thus, where in a mutual will by Mr and Mrs A, the testators nominated the survivor, and on the death of the survivor, their four sons to be the executors, on Mr A's death, Mrs A assumed her four sons to act along with her, and all five were confirmed.[94]

5.102   It is competent for a sole executor-nominate to execute a deed of assumption of a new executor, and then to resign,[95] the assumed executor alone being confirmed.

5.102A   If there is thought to be doubt as to whether the assumption is contrary to the terms of the testamentary writing, it will be necessary to apply to the sheriff for special warrant to issue confirmation.

Assumption by executors nominate *qua* general disponees, universal legatories and residuary beneficiaries

5.103   Since section 3 of the Executors (Scotland) Act 1900 merely provides that in the absence of executors or trustees, the general disponee, universal legatory and residuary legatee "shall be held to be the [testator's] executor-nominate," it is only once the petition for special directions and the confirmation have been granted that they are confirmed as executors and, consequently, only thereafter can they assume new executors under the statutory powers.

5. Revocation of the Appointment of an Executor

Revocation

5.104   A testator may revoke the appointment of an executor, either expressly (paras. 5.105–5.108) or impliedly (paras. 5.109–112). Sometimes subsequent events may raise the legal presumption that the whole of a testamentary writing has been revoked (paras. 5.113–5.115).

Express revocation

5.105   The testator may at any time expressly revoke—in writing— either the appointment of a particular executor, or the whole of

---

[94] *Rutherford*, April 9, 1878, unreported.
[95] *Kennedy, Petr.*, 1983 S.L.T. (Sh. Ct.) 10.

a testamentary writing,[96] so that any appointment of executors made therein will fall. Even where the original appointment of trustees or executors was contained in a mutual will which contained contractual provisions which were irrevocable, the appointment of trustees or executors is always revocable.[97]

5.106   Frequently, the testator will revoke the appointment of an executor by deleting his name from the clause of appointment in the testamentary writing, and such a deletion should be properly authenticated.[98]

5.107   Where the executor's name has been deleted, but the deletion has not been authenticated, the difficulty can be circumvented by producing a declinature from the person whose appointment is in doubt.[99] Thus, where the names of three executors had been deleted, and three others interlined, confirmation was granted in favour of those whose names had been interlined only on production of renunciations by the three whose names had been deleted.[1]

5.108   In another case, the testator had appointed A and B to be his trustees and executors. The names of A and B as trustees were deleted, but not their designations, nor their appointment as executors. On the will, the testator had written (undated) "trustees now C, D and E." The commissary held that the nomination of A and B had not been effectively revoked, and granted authority to confirm A along with C, D and E, B being dead.[2]

Implied revocation

5.109   A trust deed dealing with the whole of the testator's estate is held to revoke all prior testamentary writings, even if there is no clause of express revocation,[3] and consequently, the appointment of executors in the earlier writings will thereby be revoked. However, it is only to the extent that the two deeds are inconsistent that the provisions of the earlier one are

---

[96] For fuller discussion see paras. 3.158–3.159. The writing revoking the testamentary provision or the whole testamentarywriting should either be probative of, holograph, or adopted as holograph if executed prior to August 1, 1995; or self-proving if executed on or after that date.

[97] Per Lord McLaren in *Martin* v. *Ferguson's Trs.* (1892) 19 R. 474 at p. 480.

[98] If deletion made before August 1, 1995 see paras. 3.180–3.181, and if made on or after August 1, 1995 see para. 4.08.

[99] *Conquer*, June 16, 1905, unreported.

[1] *Cockburn*, Jan. 5, 1872, unreported.

[2] *Miller*, June 14, 1872, unreported.

[3] *Sibbald's Trs.* v. *Greig* (1871) 9 M. 399; *Moncrieff*, March 19, 1883, unreported.

revoked,[4] so that where the earlier one contained, *inter alia*, the appointment of an executor, and the later one only bequests of pecuniary legacies, the appointment of the executor was sustained.[5]

5.110   The appointment of a "sole executor" in the later writing has been held to supersede all previous appointments.[6] Again, the appointment of "A to be my executor" has been held to supersede the appointment of three executors in an earlier testamentary writing, so that A alone was confirmed.[7]

5.111   The fact that the testator may, in a subsequent writing, revoke a bequest to persons whom he also appointed to be his executors, does not imply that he has also revoked their appointment as executors. Thus, where the testator had appointed certain persons to be executors and universal legatories, but, by subsequent writings, withdrew the beneficial interest from all but one of them while expressly confirming the will in all other respects, it was held that they were all entitled to the office of executor.[8]

5.112   Where a testator's earlier trust disposition and settlement had been expressly revoked by one executed some months later it was held that it was revived by a codicil executed some years later, which modified it in the following terms:

> "I . . . having considered the (original) Trust Disposition and Settlement, have resolved to make the following alterations and additions thereon . . . (list) . . . and with these alterations and additions, I hereby homologate and approve of the said Trust Disposition and Settlement in all other respects."

In such circumstances, the later trust disposition and settlement and, in particular, its appointment of executors, was revoked by implication.[9]

Presumptive revocation—by birth of child

5.113   For a fuller discussion of the *conditio si testator sine liberis decesserit* and the question of whether a prior testamentary writing may thereby be revived see paragraphs 3.170–3.174

5.114   Where a testamentary writing is revoked as a result of invoking

---

[4] If all the testamentary writings are capable of standing together, all will be sustained: *Tronsons v. Tronsons* (1884) 12 R. 155; *Cox*, July 19, 1893, unreported.
[5] *Walker*, Oct. 5, 1979, unreported.
[6] *Horsburgh*, Jan. 13, 1868, unreported; *Wilson*, May 16, 1884, unreported.
[7] *Alexander*, March 19, 1860, unreported.
[8] *Scott v. Peebles* (1870) 8 M. 959.
[9] *Mellis v. Mellis's Tr.* (1898) 25 R. 720.

the *conditio*, the administrative provisions as well as the disposit-
·ive ones are revoked.[10]

5.115   If it appears from the papers that a child born after the date of
the testamentary writing has not yet reached the age of 18 years
at the date of the application for confirmation, it is the practice
of the court to refuse to issue confirmation on such a testamentary writing and for an application to be made to the sheriff for
special authority to issue confirmation. In a pre-1964 decision
the sheriff principal refused to grant such authority, and the
deceased's widow was subsequently confirmed as executrix-
dative *qua* relict, the will being produced and recorded along
with the Inland Revenue inventory of the estate.[11]

5.116   If the presumption raised by the *conditio* can be rebutted, confirmation will be granted in favour of the executor appointed in
the testamentary writing.

6. DECLINATURE OR RESIGNATION OF AN EXECUTOR

**Circumstances where an executor should decline or resign
office**

5.117   A person who has been nominated executor may choose to
decline or resign office because of his ill-health or other personal
considerations.

5.118   He should also decline or resign office if he foresees a conflict
between himself as an individual and the trustees, unless the
testator had known of the cause of the conflict when he made
the appointment.[12-13] An executor who has taken action in a
personal capacity which is incompatible with the performance
of his duties as executor must resign,[14] unless the adverse interest had been known to the testator.[15] It is, however, no bar to
his continuing in office that he is planning to claim legal rights,
rather than accept the testamentary provision in his favour,[16]
for if, having accepted office and claimed legal rights, there is
a conflict between his role as executor and his position as claimant, the appropriate course of action would be for a judicial
factor to be appointed to take over the administration of the

---

[10] *Knox's Trs.* v. *Knox*, 1907 S.C. 1123, but see below on the revocation of the
clause revoking prior testamentary writings.
[11] *Smith*, May 9, 1935, unreported; followed in Inverness, *Myers, Petr.* August
2, 1974, unreported.
[12-13] *Anderson* v. *Hare*, 1952 S.L.T. (Sh. Ct.) 40.
[14] *Cherry* v. *Patrick*, 1910 S.C. 32.
[15] See, for instance, *Anderson* v. *Hare*, 1952 S.L.T. (Sh. Ct.) 40.
[16] *Smart* v. *Smart*, 1926 S.C. 392; *Anderson* v. *Hare*, 1952 S.L.T. (Sh. Ct.) 40.

estate.[17] He may, however, have to decline or resign office in order to protect his own position as a beneficiary. For instance, if the deceased had been the tenant of an agricultural holding, and did not bequeath it, the executor may require to appoint the lease to a near-relative successor in terms of section 16 of the Succession (Scotland) Act 1964, but due to the operation of the doctrine of *auctor in rem suam* he is effectively debarred from transferring the holding to himself.[17a]

Declinature by executor

5.119   Confirmation will always be issued in favour of the whole surviving executors-nominate unless they have declined to act. Thus, where the deceased's widow had obtained decerniture as executrix-dative and, in giving up the inventory, had produced a will naming three executors, two of whom had declined, the commissary refused to authorise confirmation without intimation to the third executor and obtaining his declinature.[18]

5.120   It will be necessary to produce evidence that an executor has declined to act before confirmation will be issued in favour of the remaining executors, and the declinature must be produced along with the testamentary writing, referred to in the oath or affirmation, and docketed as relative thereto. The declinature may be in the form of a minute of declinature, or of a statement written on the will or in a letter, or of an excerpt from the minutes of the meeting at which the declining executor was present and recorded his declinature. Exceptionally, where the declining executor was unable to write, a declaration made personally to the clerk of court has been accepted. A declinature by a *curator bonis* for his ward has been accepted,[19] but there is doubt whether a declinature which has not been authorised by the Accountant of Court is legally effective.

5.121   While the declinature should be drawn in terms which are clear and unequivocal, the courts have on occasion been quite liberal in their interpretation. Thus, where four executors had been nominated and two applied for confirmation, deponing that the other two had declined, the court accepted as evidence of the declinature a minute of a meeting attended by all four, at which the two applicants had been authorised to obtain confirmation in their own favour.[20]

5.122   Where three individuals were nominated as executors and two

---

[17] *Per* Lord President Clyde in *Smart* v. *Smart's Trs*, 1926 S.C. 392 at p. 400
[17a] See *Inglis* v. *Inglis*, 1983 S.L.T. 437.
[18] *Wright*, Jan. 28, 1867, unreported.
[19] *Macara*, Dec. 17, 1885, unreported.
[20] *Menzies*, Jan. 3, 1861, unreported.

declined to accept office "in the meantime," confirmation was granted in favour of the third individual. Nothing was decided as to what would happen if the others subsequently sought confirmation.[21]

5.123 It would seem that the declinature of an executor may subsequently be revoked. Where one of three executors-nominate declined, but withdrew his declinature before anything had been done, he was confirmed with the others.[22]

Resignation of executor

5.124 Where an executor-nominate has accepted office, he has an unfettered power to resign as executor,[23] subject to three exceptions:

1. The testamentary writing states that the executor is not able to resign office.[24] In such a case, the executor may apply to the court for authority to resign.[25]

2. He is a sole executor and has not assumed another executor,[26] nor has the court appointed new executors or a judicial factor.[27]

3. He has accepted a legacy or bequest conditional on accepting the office or was entitled to receive remuneration for his services as executor, and the testator did not expressly authorise him to resign in such circumstances.[28]

5.125 If an executor-nominate resigns before confirmation is obtained, the deed of resignation must be produced along with the testamentary writing, referred to in the oath or affirmation, and docketed as relative thereto. Where it has been provided that

---

[21] *Mathison*, April 2, 1867, unreported.

[22] *McQueen*, April 22, 1890, unreported.

[23] Trusts (Scotland) Act 1921 (11 & 12 Geo. 5, c. 58), ss. 2, 3(*a*), as applied to executors by virtue of Executors (Scotland) Act 1900 (63 & 64 Vict. c. 55), s. 2.

[24] Trusts (Scotland) Act 1921 (11 & 12 Geo. 5, c. 58), ss. 2, 3(*b*) and 21 and Sched. B, as applied to executors by virtue of Executors (Scotland) Act 1900 (63 & 64 Vict., c. 55), s. 2.

[25] Trusts (Scotland) Act 1921 (11 & 12 Geo. 5, c. 58), s. 5, as applied to executors by virtue of Executors (Scotland) Act 1900 (63 & 64 Vict. c. 55), s. 2.

[26] One executor would, in fact, be sufficient: *Kennedy, Petr.*, 1983 S.L.T. (Sh. Ct.) 10.

[27] Trusts (Scotland) Act 1921 (11 & 12 Geo. 5, c. 58), ss. 2, 3(*a*) proviso (1), as applied to executors by virtue of Executors (Scotland) Act 1900 (63 & 64 Vict. c. 55), s. 2.

[28] Trusts (Scotland) Act 1921 (11 & 12 Geo. 5, c. 58), ss. 2, 3(*a*) proviso (2), as applied to executors by virtue of Executors (Scotland) Act 1900 (63 & 64 Vict. c. 55), s. 2.

the resignation will take effect from the expiry of a particular period, confirmation can be issued in favour of the accepting and continuing executors, even prior to the expiry of the period, for such a resignation cannot be revoked.[29]

5.126 Where an individual has been appointed as both trustee and executor, his resignation as a trustee implies resignation as an executor unless otherwise expressly declared.[30] Thus, where an individual appointed as a trustee and executor accepted office as trustee, but declined to act as executor, the declinature was treated as sufficient.[31]

The form of the resignation

5.127 An executor resigning office will normally do so by signing a minute of resignation in accordance with the style contained in Appendix A of the Trusts (Scotland) Act 1921.[32-33] If executed prior to August 1, 1995 it should be probative and if executed on or after that date, it should be self-proving.[34] No Stamp duty is payable on it provided that it contains a certificate certifying that it falls within category A of The Stamp Duty (Exempt Instruments) Regulations 1987.[35] Such a deed may be registered in the Books of Council and Session, and is effective from the date it is intimated to the last co-executor to receive notice.

7. REMOVAL OF AN EXECUTOR BY THE COURT

Removal of executor by court

5.128 A co-executor or beneficiary may apply to the Court of Session or the appropriate sheriff court for the removal of an executor who is insane, or incapable of acting because of physical or mental disability, or who is absent from the United Kingdom continuously for a period of at least six months, or who has disappeared for a similar period.[36]

5.129 The Court of Session also has a common-law jurisdiction to

---

[29] *Fullarton's Trs.* v. *James* (1895) 23 R. 105.

[30] Trusts (Scotland) Act 1921 (11 & 12 Geo. 5, c. 58), s. 28.

[31] *Baird*, Oct. 30, 1883, unreported.

[32-33] Trusts (Scotland) Act 1921 (11 & 12 Geo. 5, c. 58), s. 19(1), as extended to executors by Executors (Scotland) Act 1900 (63 & 64 Vict. c. 55), s. 2.

[34] See para. 3.27, if subscribed prior to August, 1995; See para. 4.08 if subscribed on or after August 1, 1995; though not being a testamentary writing it need only be subscribed on the final page.

[35] S.I. 1987 No. 516.

[36] Trusts (Scotland) Act 1921 (11 & 12 Geo. 5, c. 58), s. 23, as amended by Law Reform (Miscellaneous Provisions) (Scotland) Act 1980 (c. 55), s. 13(*b*) and as applied to executors by Executors (Scotland) Act (63 & 64 Vict. c. 55), s. 2.

remove an executor who, as an individual, has an interest which is clearly incompatible with his duties as executor,[37] but the mere fact of an adverse interest would not of itself justify removal in every circumstance,[38] particularly where the interest was known to the testator.[39] The fact that an executor is bankrupt is on its own no ground for removing him from office,[40] but if the bankrupt is alleged to owe money to the estate, removal may be appropriate.[41]

5.130   Where an executor has been removed from office by the court, the oath or affirmation must refer to the decree.

5.131   Where one of a number of confirmed executors became insane, and was removed by a decree of the Court of Session in terms of section 23 of the Trusts (Scotland) Act 1921, additional estate was thereafter discovered, and an eik to the confirmation was issued in favour of the remaining executors, the fact that one of the confirmed executors had been removed being referred to in the eik.[42]

5.132   Where it is a sole executor-nominate who has been removed due to insanity or physical or mental disability, the Court of Session or the appropriate sheriff court may appoint a new executor or executors on the application of the beneficiaries.[43] It is submitted that confirmation or an eik to the confirmation would then be granted in favour of the court-appointed executor, with appropriate reference to the court decree.

Confirmation nominate and challenge to the testamentary writing

5.133   A judicial factor may be appointed where there is an application for confirmation-nominate, and the testamentary writing is challenged. The authority for this proposition is *Henderson* v. *Henderson*,[44] where a Scotsman, who had been divorced by his wife, left a holograph will dated before the date of the divorce decree, under which he bequeathed to her by name his whole residuary estate. She applied for confirmation as executrix *qua* universal legatory. His next-of-kin opposed this application, and them-

[37] *Cherry* v. *Patrick*, 1910 S.C. 32.
[38] MacKenzie Stuart on *Trusts*, pp. 317–318; Menzies on *Trusts*, pp. 902 *et seq.*
[39] *Per* Lord Neaves in *Neilson, Petr.* (1865) 3 M. 559 at pp. 561.
[40] *Ibid.* (case involved a trustee).
[41] *Whittle* v. *Carruthers* (1896) 23 R. 775.
[42] *Stewart*, Nov. 8, 1945, unreported.
[43] Trusts (Scotland) Act 1921 (11 & 12 Geo. 5, c. 58), s. 22, as amended by Law Reform (Miscellaneous Provisions) (Scotland) Act 1980 (c. 55), s. 13(*a*) and as applied to executors by Executors (Scotland) Act 1900 (63 & 64 Vict. c. 55), s. 2.
[44] 1930 S.L.T. 23.

selves presented a petition for the appointment of a judicial factor, on the ground that the divorce rendered the will inoperative, and that they intended to challenge it. The Lord Ordinary appointed the judicial factor for three reasons: the delay in getting confirmation if the will were challenged, the fact that all competing parties were resident in England, and that if the ex-wife were confirmed as executrix *qua* general disponee she would take the estate under no trust condition, but for her own behoof only.

Executors-nominate and caution

5.134   The few circumstances in which executors-nominate require to find caution are discussed at paragraph 9.03.

CHAPTER 6

CONFIRMATION OF EXECUTORS-DATIVE

Introduction

6.01 An executor-dative is the person appointed, not by the deceased, but by the court, to administer an estate. The great majority of dative petitions arise because the deceased died intestate but there are a number of circumstances (see paras. 5.81 and 6.14–6.15) where a dative appointment may be necessary, even although the deceased left a testamentary writing.

The order of preference for executors-dative

6.02 As Lord President Robertson stated:

> "The duty of the Sheriff as Commissary is to determine who is entitled to the office of executor on the face either of the deeds which are put before the Court, or of the relation to the deceased which is set out as the title of the applicant."[1]

6.03 In doing this, the practice[2] is to follow the order of preference set out in the "Orders to be Observed in the Confirmation of all Testaments" (forming part of the instructions to the commissaries) which were issued in 1666 by the archbishops and bishops, with the authority of the supreme court[3]:

1. general disponee, universal legatory or residuary legatee;

2. the next-of-kin;

3. the creditors;

4. special legatees—*i.e.* legatees other than general disponees, universal legatories or residuary legatees;

5. the procurator fiscal.

6.04 Though in early times, the order of preference does not always

---

[1] *Martin* v. *Ferguson's Trs.* (1892) 19 R. 474 at p. 487.

[2] Ersk., III.ix.32; Bell, *Comm.*, II.xiv.3 (6th ed.).

[3] Reproduced in the Acts of Sederunt of the Lords of Council and Session from 1553 to 1790, pp. 98–100.

appear to have been adhered to, this ended with the decision in *Crawfurd* v. *Ure*[4] where the testator's general disponee was confirmed in preference to the next-of-kin, the justification being that the former had right to the whole estate, and the latter did not.

6.05 Over the centuries, statutory legislation has modified the 1666 list. Thus, section 3 of the Executors (Scotland) Act 1900 enables general disponees, universal legatories and residuary legatees to be confirmed as executors-nominate, and although the dative procedure has not been abolished, it is largely superseded in such cases. The Succession (Scotland) Act 1964 introduced completely new categories of heirs entitled to claim on an intestate estate, and enacted that the surviving spouse has the right— treated in practice as the exclusive right—to the office of executor-dative where he or she takes the whole intestate estate in satisfaction of prior rights. Nevertheless, the order of preference laid out in 1666 is still substantially followed in commissary cases.

6.06 In general, contemporary commissary practice is that the person with the beneficial interest in the deceased's estate will be found entitled to the office of executor-dative.

Next-of-kin and the reforms of the Succession (Scotland) Act 1964

6.07 The term "next-of-kin" refers to the nearest collateral relation of the deceased of the father's side (see para. 6.21), who was, as such, the heir to the deceased's intestate moveable estate at common law. Where the deceased died intestate, the 1666 Order enabled the next-of-kin to be decerned as executors-dative, so that the right to the office of executor then coalesced with the beneficial interest in the estate. In the light of the reforms of the Succession (Scotland) Act 1964, it is appropriate to pose the question whether the concept of "next-of-kin" has any significance in contemporary commissary practice.

6.08 While the term "next-of-kin" does not appear in the Succession (Scotland) Act 1964, or in any subsequent statute amending it, the concept of "next-of-kin"—in so far as rights of succession were concerned—was abolished by implication.[5] There were, however, no comparable changes to the rules regulating the administration of executry estates, and indeed Schedules 1 and 2 of the Act of Sederunt (Confirmation of Executors) 1964[6]

---

[4] (1755) Mor. 3818.
[5] Succession (Scotland) Act 1964 (c. 41).
[6] S.I. 1964 No. 1143.

expressly provided for the appointment of executors-dative *qua* next-of-kin even after the Succession (Scotland) Act 1964 came into operation. It is therefore submitted that an intestate's "next-of-kin" is still entitled to be decerned as executor-dative.[6a]

6.09   It might be argued that the meaning of "next-of-kin" has been modified by the changes to intestate succession effected by the Succession (Scotland) Act 1964. However, after a previous statutory modification to the rules on intestate succession, the term "next-of-kin," occurring in a testamentary writing, was held to have retained its common law meaning.[7] Further, the pre-1964 statutory modifications of the intestate succession rules had little effect on commissary practice. While it was accepted that, in the absence of the next-of-kin, the person with a right to succeed to part of the estate should be entitled to be confirmed,[8] the Inner House decision of *Stewart* v. *Kerr*[9] established that where the next-of-kin sought appointment as executor, he was entitled to the office, to the exclusion of a person with a statutory right to share in the estate.[10] Thus, it came about that it was no longer the invariable rule that the person with the beneficial interest in the estate was the person entitled to the office of executor.[11] Indeed, while a widow might receive the whole of her late husband's estate under the Intestate Husband's Estate (Scotland) Act 1911, she was originally not entitled to the office of executrix, and it took express enactment for her to be able to be confirmed as executrix-dative *qua* relict.[12]

6.10   It should, however, be noted that there are a number of reported decisions dating from the mid-nineteenth century, in which, in a competition for the office of executor-dative, a party with the beneficial interest in the estate was preferred to the next-of-kin. In *Webster* v. *Shiress*,[13] a person who was entitled to share in the intestate estate was conjoined in the office along with the next-of-kin, Lord Justice-Clerk Moncrieff opining:

> "As the father succeeded to half the moveable estate, he has half the interest in the succession, and, according to the universal rule in intestate moveable succession is entitled to a share of the administration."[14]

[6a] See also M. C. Meston, *The Succession (Scotland) Act 1964* (4th ed.), pp. 98–100.

[7] *Young's Trs.* v. *Janes* (1880) 8 R. 242.

[8] *Per* Lord President Inglis in *Muir* (1876) 4 R. 74 at p. 75.

[9] (1890) 17 R. 707; followed in *Campbell* v. *Falconer* (1892) 19 R.563.

[10] The deceased's husband, having the *jus relicti* in terms of the Married Women's Property (Scotland) Act 1881 (44 & 45 Vict. c. 21), s. 6, was not confirmed.

[11] *Bones* v. *Morrison* (1866) 5 M. 240; see also *McGown* v.*McKinlay* (1835) 14 S. 105.

[12] Intestate Husband's Estate (Scotland) Act 1919 (9 Geo. 5, c. 9), s. 3 (1).

[13] (1878) 6 R. 102.

[14] *Ibid.* at p. 105.

6.11   However, the approach in *Webster* v. *Shiress* was not followed in later cases, although it was referred to in the argument (though not in the judgment as reported) in *Stewart* v. *Kerr*.[15] In *Macpherson* v. *Macpherson*,[16] a niece of the half blood of the deceased was preferred to a nephew of the full blood, who was the next-of-kin, but the reason for this was that the nephew had assigned to her his interest in the deceased's succession and as such she was the only party interested in the estate. The decision should perhaps be viewed as an instance of the court protecting the equitable interests of the niece, against the person who assigned the right to her, rather than as establishing any broader principle.

6.12   It is therefore submitted that the term "next-of-kin" in the context of the administration of an executry estate does not encompass the heirs on intestacy under the Succession (Scotland) Act 1964.

6.13   Generally, there is no competition in dative petitions. Usually the petitioner is the heir to the intestate estate in terms of the Succession (Scotland) Act 1964 and he will consequently be decerned. But where there is competition between the heir under the Succession (Scotland) Act 1964 and the next-of-kin, it is submitted that, in the light of the decision of *Stewart* v. *Kerr*,[17] the "next-of-kin" will have priority to be decerned executor-dative. It would seem that the sole exception to this general rule is provided by the situation where the surviving spouse's prior rights exhaust the whole intestate estate.[18]

ORDER OF PREFERENCE FOR EXECUTORS-DATIVE

I. General disponees, universal legatory or residuary legatee

A dative or a nominate appointment?

6.14   Where the deceased died testate, it may nevertheless be necessary to have an executor-dative appointed, as where there is no executor-nominate, express or implied, and the remedy under section 3 of the Executors (Scotland) Act 1900 is not available.[19] This can occur where:

1.   all the residuary beneficiaries do not concur in asking for confirmation as executors-nominate[20];

---

[15] (1890) 17 R. 707.
[16] (1855) 17 D. 358.
[17] (1890) 17 R. 707.
[18] *Doonan*, Feb. 22, 1979, unreported; discussed at para. 6.38.
[19] See para. 5.49 *et seq.*
[20] *Millar*, Dec. 28, 1921, unreported.

2. there are so many beneficiaries that it is impracticable to trace them and to take instructions from them;

3. a child *in utero* at the time of the testator's death stands to share in the estate if born alive,[21] and no progress can be made in obtaining confirmation under section 3 until the child is born;

4. one or more of the general disponees, universal legatories or residuary legatees has predeceased the testator and, because the will does not provide for the bequests to accresce to the survivors, his share falls into intestacy[22];

5. one or more of the general disponees, universal legatories or residuary legatees died after the testator;

6. one or more of the general disponees, universal legatories or residuary legatees survived the testator, sold his right in the estate to another and then died[23];

7. one of the general disponees, universal legatories or residuary legatees unlawfully killed the testator, and his share falls into intestacy.[24]

6.15 In such cases, it will be necessary for one or more of the residuary beneficiaries to apply for decerniture as executor(s)-dative: in this event, there will be no need to intimate the application to the other residuary beneficiaries.[25] However, it is preferable if the remedy provided by section 3 of the Executors (Scotland) Act 1900 can be used,[26] since this will avoid the expense of obtaining caution which is required before confirmation can be granted in dative cases.

Who can be confirmed qua *general disponee, etc.*

6.16 A general disponee, universal legatory or residuary legatee may be decerned executor-dative *qua* general disponee, universal legatory or residuary legatee. A company may be confirmed as executor-dative *qua* general disponee, universal legatory or residuary legatee.[27]

---

[21] *Qui in utero est pro jam nato habetur*; Digest (I.v.7.); Bankton, Vol. 1, p. 72, para. 1; Bell, *Prin.* § 1642.

[22] *Landells* Feb. 10, 1960, unreported; *Paxton's Trs.* v. *Cowie* (1886) 13 R. 1191; *Fraser's Trs.* v. *Fraser*, 1980 S.L.T. 211.

[23] While the assignee may not be decerned as executor-nominate, he may be decerned as executor-dative.

[24] *Hunter's Exrs., Petrs.*, 1992 S.L.T. 1141.

[25] *Millar*, Dec. 28, 1921, unreported.

[26] See para. 5.49 *et seq.*

[27] *Grierson*, Jan. 14, 1890, unreported, where the Edinburgh Royal Infirmary was decerned *qua* universal legatory.

6.17   Where decerniture as executor-dative *qua* general disponee, universal legatory or residuary legatee is sought, the petitioner will require to put up with the petition the deceased's testamentary writing in which he is named as a beneficiary.

6.18   If there is doubt as to whether the applicant has the character he claims, *e.g.* that he is residuary legatee, the court will not grant confirmation until it has been determined by court process that he indeed has the character claimed.[28] This may involve the affidavit evidence of two witnesses that the applicant is the "issue" (or other relative) of a particular person, or a legal debate as to the meaning of the testamentary writing.

6.19   On the question of whether a person is the deceased's general disponee, universal legatory or residuary beneficiary, see paras. 5.66–5.96.

6.20   Where the legatee dies after the legacy has vested, but before expeding confirmation, his representatives, if they are to administer the testator's estate, require first to confirm to the legatee's estate and thereafter will be decerned as executors-dative to the testator *qua* legatee by succession,[29] or *qua* representative to the general disponee or universal legatory.[30]

II. The next-of-kin

6.21   In Scots law, the term "next-of-kin" applies to the surviving members of the class of relatives nearest in degree to the intestate who would formerly have inherited the deceased's intestate moveable estate. The order is children, grandchildren, great-grandchildren, etc., full brothers and sisters, half brothers and sisters related through the father, the father, collaterals of the father, the father's parents, etc. It will be noted that the intestate's spouse, mother[31] and maternal relations are completely excluded.

6.22   Where one of the next-of-kin survives the deceased, but dies before confirmation is granted, the right to confirmation trans-

---

[28] See *dicta* of Lord Justice-Clerk MacDonald and Lord Young in *Jerdon* v. *Forrest* (1897) 24 R. 395 where the holograph will had stated that the petitioner "to be my heir," and after provision of some pecuniary legacies "the rest to X, if she will have it, and if not, to the Bible Society." See also Lord Mackenzie in *McGown* v. *McKinlay* (1835) 14 S. 105 at p. 106.

[29] Bell, *Prin.* § 1896.

[30] *Goskirk*, March 19, 1912, unreported.

[31] *Muir* (1876) 4 R. 74.

mits to the representatives of the deceased next-of-kin,[32] though the representative must first confirm to the estate of the deceased next-of-kin. The term "representatives" includes the heirs of the deceased next-of-kin, his assignees[33] and the issue of a person who, had he survived, would have been one of the next-of-kin.[34]

6.23   Where the deceased was not domiciled in Scotland at the time of his death, the next-of-kin according to the law of the deceased's domicile will be preferred.[35]

III. The heirs on intestacy

Intestate succession under the Succession (Scotland) Act 1964

6.24   **Introduction** Where a person dies intestate on or after September 10, 1964, and Scots law regulates the succession to the whole or part of his estate,[36] the rules set out in Parts I and II of the Succession (Scotland) Act 1964 apply.

6.25   The rules of intestate succession which applied before September 10, 1964 are not discussed in this edition, and readers who are faced with administering an estate of someone who died before that date are directed to the seventh edition of this work.

6.26   **Intestate estate?** For the purposes of the Succession (Scotland) Act 1964, "intestate estate" means so much of a person's estate as is undisposed of by testamentary disposition—be that the whole or part of the estate.[37] Thus, the rules regarding succession to intestate estate set out in the 1964 Act will apply when the deceased died without making a testamentary writing or when, in the events which happened, part of his estate was undisposed of by testamentary writing[38]:

---

[32] Confirmation of Executors (Scotland) Act 1823 (4 Geo. 4, c. 98), s. 1, as amended by Statute Law Revision (No. 2) Act 1890 (53 & 54 Vict., c. 51), Sched., Pt. II; *Webster* v. *Shiress* (1878) 6 R. 102; *Chrystal* v. *Chrystal*, 1923 S.L.T. (Sh. Ct.) 69.

[33] *Mann* v. *Thomas* (1830) 8 S. 468.

[34] *Dowie* v. *Barclay* (1871) 9 M. 726.

[35] *Marchioness of Hastings* v. *Exrs. of Marquess of Hastings* (1852) 14 D. 489.

[36] Under Scots law, the succession to an intestate's heritable estate is determined by the *lex situs* (so that Scots law will regulate the succession to heritage in Scotland) whereas the *lex domicilii* determines the succession to the intestate's moveable estate (so that Scots law will regulate the succession to the worldwide moveable estate of a person who died domiciled in Scotland): Anton and Beaumont, *Private International Law* (2nd ed.), pp. 675–680.

[37] Succession (Scotland) Act 1964 (c. 41), s. 36(1).

[38] *Kerr, Petr.*, 1968 S.L.T. (Sh. Ct.) 61; *Munro's Trs., Petrs.*, 1971 S.L.T. 313.

"It makes no difference whether the estate is undisposed of because of events that have happened before the death of the deceased, such as the earlier deaths of beneficiaries named in her testamentary disposition, or of events that happen after her death, such as a claim to legal rights."[39]

6.27   **The first charge: Prior rights of surviving spouse** Where the deceased died intestate, and was survived by a spouse, the spouse is entitled to certain prior rights on the estate.

1.   *Succession (Scotland) Act 1964, section 8(1), (2), (4)–(6)* Irrespective of the domicile of the deceased,[39a] the surviving spouse is entitled to the deceased's interest in a dwelling-house[40] situated in Scotland[41] in which the surviving spouse was ordinarily resident at the date of the deceased's death,[42] but where the house is worth more than a specified value,[43] or forms part of subjects leased by the deceased, or was used by the deceased for carrying on a trade, profession or occupation, where there would be a substantial loss to the estate if the house was disposed of separately from the assets of the trade, profession or occupation, the surviving spouse is not entitled to the house itself. Instead, he or she will receive a cash sum, equal to the value of the house, up to a maximum of the specified value.[44] The value of the deceased's interest in the property is calculated after deducting any secured debts.[45] The 1964 Act contains no guidance as to how a debt which is secured over the house and over a life policy

---

[39] Lord Fraser in *Munro's Trs., Petrs.*, 1971 S.L.T. 313 at p. 317.

[39a] Anton and Beaumont, *Private International Law* (2nd ed.) p. 674.

[40] Whether as heritable proprietor or as tenant.

[41] Anton and Beaumont, *Private International Law* (2nd ed.), pp. 674–675; R.D. Leslie, "Prior rights in succession: the international dimension," 1988 S.L.T. (News) 105; M.C. Meston, *The Succession (Scotland) Act 1964* (4th ed.), pp. 117–118; Scottish Law Commission Memo. No. 71, para. 6 (2) (a).

[42] Where there was more than one residence in which the surviving spouse was ordinarily resident, he or she has six months from the deceased's death to elect which residence he or she wishes to inherit (Succession (Scotland) Act 1964 (c. 41), s. 8(1)).

[43] For deaths between June 10, 1964 and May 22, 1973, £15,000 (Succession (Scotland) Act 1964 (c. 41), s. 8(1) (*b*)).
For deaths between May 23, 1973 and July 31, 1981, £30,000 (Succession (Scotland) Act 1973 (c. 25), s. 1(1) (*a*)).
For deaths between August 1, 1981 and April 30, 1988, £50,000 (S.I. 1981 No. 806).
For deaths between May 1, 1988 and November 25, 1993, £65,000 (S.I. 1988 No. 633).
For deaths on or after November 26, 1993, £110,000 (S.I. 1993 No. 2690).

[44] *Ibid.*

[45] Succession (Scotland) Act 1964 (c. 41), s. 8(6) (*d*).

should be allocated, but it is suggested that it should be allocated *pro rata*.[46]

2. *Succession (Scotland) Act 1964, section 8(3)–(6)* Provided that the deceased died domiciled in Scotland, the surviving spouse is entitled to the furniture and plenishings in the dwelling-house[47] in which the surviving spouse was ordinarily resident[48] at the date of the deceased's death, up to a specified value.[49] Under this head are included garden effects, domestic animals, plate, plated articles, linen, china, glass, books, pictures, articles of household use and consumable stores. Any article or animal used for business purposes, or any money or securities for money is excluded. Heirlooms—that is, articles with such associations with the intestate's family that they ought to pass to a member of the intestate's family rather than the surviving spouse—are also excluded.

3. *Succession (Scotland) Act 1964, section 9* The surviving spouse is entitled to a cash right, the amount of which depends on whether the deceased was survived by issue[50] or not,[51] and which is to be met rateably from the

[46] See *Graham* v. *Graham* (1898) 5 S.L.T. 319; Gretton "Endowment Mortgages and the Law of Succession" (1987) 32 J.L.S. 303.

[47] Probably restricted to a dwelling-house in Scotland: see R.D. Leslie, "Prior rights in succession: the international dimension," 1988 S.L.T. (News) 105; Meston, *The Succession (Scotland) Act 1964* (4th ed.), p. 117; *cf.* Scottish Law Commission Consultative Memorandum No. 71, para. 6 (2) (b) and (3).

[48] Where there was more than one residence in which the surviving spouse was ordinarily resident, he or she has six months from the deceased's death to elect which set of contents he or she wishes to inherit (Succession (Scotland) Act 1964 (c. 41), s. 8 (3)).

[49] For deaths between June 10, 1964 and May 22, 1973, £5,000 (Succession (Scotland) Act 1964 (c. 41), s. 8 (3)).
For deaths between May 23, 1973 and July 31, 1981, £8,000 (Succession (Scotland) Act 1973 (c. 25), s. 1 (1) (*a*)).
For deaths between August 1, 1981 and April 30, 1988, £10,000 (S.I. 1981 No. 806).
For deaths between May 1, 1988 and November 25, 1993, £12,000 (S.I. 1988 No. 633).
For deaths on or after November 26, 1993, £20,000 (S.I. 1993 No. 2690).

[50] After December 8, 1986, defined as "issue however remote" (Succession (Scotland) Act 1964 (c. 41), s. 36 (1), as amended by Law Reform (Parent and Child) (Scotland) Act 1986 (c. 9), Sched. 2).

[51] For deaths between June 10, 1964 and May 22, 1973, £2,500 if issue and £5,000 if no issue (Succession (Scotland) Act 1964 (c. 41), s. 9).
For deaths between May 23, 1973 and July 31, 1981, £4,000 if issue and £8,000 if no issue (Succession (Scotland) Act 1973 (c. 25), s. 1 (1) (*a*)).
For deaths between August 1, 1981 and April 30, 1988, £15,000 if issue and £25,000 if no issue (S.I. 1981 No. 806).
For deaths between May 1, 1988 and November 25, 1993, £21,000 if issue and £35,000 if no issue (S.I. 1988 No. 633).

deceased's heritable estate in Scotland and his worldwide moveable estate.[52] Where the deceased is survived by a widow who is carrying a child *in utero* at the time of the death, and there were no other issue, the widow's prior rights will be cut down only if the child is born alive.[53]

6.28   **Surviving spouse's prior rights exhaust the whole intestate estate** Section 9(4) of the Succession (Scotland) Act 1964, provides that "where . . . a surviving spouse has right to the whole intestate estate,[54] he or she shall have the right to be appointed executor."[55] In such a case, the surviving spouse is not required to find caution before being confirmed as executor-dative.[56]

6.29   As is evident from the cases discussed at paragraphs 6.38–6.41, the current commissary practice is to treat the surviving spouse whose prior rights exhaust the whole intestate estate as the *sole* person with the right to be appointed executor, so that if the deceased was survived by a spouse, an application by someone other than the surviving spouse will be refused, unless it is averred that the estate is, or is believed to be, more than the amount of the surviving spouse's prior rights under section 9(1) of the Succession (Scotland) Act 1964.

6.30   **Critique of commissary practice** It is submitted that the current approach—of treating a surviving spouse whose prior rights exhaust the whole intestate estate as having the *exclusive* right to be appointed executor-dative—goes further than the 1964 Act prescribed. Indeed, the current practice is as if section 9(4) had been amended by inserting the word "exclusive," so

For deaths on or after November 26, 1993, £30,000 if issue and £50,000 if no issue (S.I. 1993 No. 2690).

[52] Where the deceased was not domiciled in Scotland at the time of his death, it has been suggested that the cash right will be exigible only from his heritable estate in Scotland: M.C. Meston, "Prior Rights in Scottish Heritage" (1967) 12 J.L.S. 401; R.D. Leslie, "Prior rights in succession: the international dimension," 1988 S.L.T. 105.

[53] *Qui in utero est pro jam nato habetur*; Digest, I.v.7.; Bankton, Vol. 1, p. 72, para. 1; and Bell, *Prin.* § 1642.

[54] Defined as so much of the deceased's intestate estate as is undisposed of by testamentary disposition, including, for instance, a deed containing a destination under which property passes on the deceased's death (Succession (Scotland) Act 1964 (c. 41), s. 36 (1)).

[55] Succession (Scotland) Act 1964 (c. 41), s. 9 (4); *Kerr, Petr.*, 1968 S.L.T. (Sh. Ct.) 61; *Doonan*, Feb. 22, 1979, unreported. Section 9(4) applies where "the whole of the intestate estate" is exhausted in meeting the surviving spouse's prior rights to financial provision under s. 9(1), but s. 9(6) (a) defines "intestate estate" as "so much of the net intestate estate as remains after the satisfaction of any claims under" s. 8 (prior rights in a dwelling-house and furniture).

[56] Confirmation of Executors (Scotland) Act 1823 (4 Geo. 4, c. 98), s. 2, as amended by Statute Law Revision Act 1888 (51 Vict. c. 3), Sched., Pt. I, Statute Law Revision (No. 2) Act 1890 (53 & 54 Vict. c. 51), Sched., Pt. II and Law Reform (Miscellaneous Provisions) (Scotland) Act 1980 (c. 55), s. 5.

that the subsection read: "where . . . a surviving spouse has right to the whole of the intestate estate, he or she shall have the *exclusive* right to be appointed executor."

6.31 Although the approach has been endorsed in the unreported shrieval decisions discussed at paragraphs 6.38–6.41, the matter has not yet been tested in the Court of Session.

6.32 It is submitted that without statutory justification, the current commissary practice follows the former practice under the Intestate Husband's Estate (Scotland) Act 1919,[57] whereby a surviving spouse, whose rights under the Intestate Husband's Estate (Scotland) Act 1911[58] exhausted the deceased's whole estate, was treated as having "an exclusive claim to the office of executrix-dative."[59] However, this former practice was an inevitable consequence of the statutory provisions then applying. The 1919 Act, as amended, enabled the surviving spouse, who was entitled in terms of the 1911 Act (as amended) to the whole of the deceased spouse's intestate estate, to apply to the sheriff for decree "that the estate belonged absolutely and exclusively to him/her," and the surviving spouse had to produce in court an inventory of the estate.[60] Once granted, the decree was warrant for the surviving spouse being granted confirmation as executrix-dative *qua* relict, or *qua* surviving spouse.[61]

6.33 In contrast, the 1964 Act merely provides that the surviving spouse whose prior rights exhaust the intestate estate "has the right to be appointed executor", and this without any proof. Only in the case of an estate proceeding under the Small Estates Acts,[62] where the petition is put up with the inventory of the deceased's estate, is evidence led as to the amount of the estate at the time when the surviving spouse petitions for appointment as executor-dative.

6.34 The current commissary practice may, in part, be attributable to the way in which the Act of Sederunt (Confirmation of Executors) 1964 is framed.[63] The Act of Sederunt directs[64] that

---

[57] 9 Geo. 5, c. 9, as amended by Law Reform (Miscellaneous Provisions) (Scotland) Act 1940 (3 & 4 Geo. 6, c. 42), s. 5.

[58] 1 & 2 Geo. 5, c. 10, as amended by Law Reform (Miscellaneous Provisions) (Scotland) Act 1940 (3 & 4 Geo. 6, c. 42), s. 5.

[59] Currie (4th ed.), pp. 72–73.

[60] Intestate Husband's Estate (Scotland) Act 1919 (9 Geo. 5, c. 9), ss. 1 and 3 (1), as amended by Law Reform (Miscellaneous Provisions) (Scotland) Act 1940 (3 & 4 Geo. 6, c. 42), s. 5.

[61] Intestate Husband's Estate (Scotland) Act 1919 (9 Geo. 5, c. 9), s. 3 (1).

[62] *i.e.* where the whole estate is less than £17,000: see Chap. 11.

[63] S.I. 1964 No. 1143.

[64] *Ibid.*, s. 6 (1).

"the form of petition for the appointment of an executor to a deceased person shall be as nearly as may be in the form set forth in Schedule 2" thereto. Condescendence 2 of the Form indicates that where "the deceased was survived by a spouse who is not the pursuer, the reason must be given why the application is not made by the surviving spouse unless . . . it is averred that the estate of the deceased exceeds the prior rights of the surviving spouse." This implies that where the surviving spouse is pursuer, he or she has merely to *aver* that he or she is the widow or surviving husband of the deceased,[65] although it would appear from section 9(4) of the Succession (Scotland) Act 1964, that the surviving spouse must aver that he or she is the widow or surviving husband of the deceased and has right to the whole intestate estate. Condesendence 2 of the Form also implies that reason must be given if someone other than the surviving spouse is the pursuer. It is a bizarre consequence of Condescendence 2 of the Form that any surviving spouse would be entitled to be decerned as executor-dative, even if the bulk of the estate is to be distributed in terms of section 2 of the 1964 Act.

6.35 For the reasons set out above, it is submitted that there is no reason for treating the surviving spouse whose prior rights exhaust the deceased spouse's intestate estate as the *sole* person with the right to be appointed executor. It is further submitted that where the surviving spouse has not sought office as executor, the next-of-kin may be so decerned, even if it is clear that the intestate estate will be fully exhausted in meeting the surviving spouse's prior rights.

6.36 The rationale for the current approach may be based on the assumption that the person with the beneficial interest in the estate is entitled to the office of executor-dative to the exclusion of all others.[66] However, it should be remembered that the surviving spouse whose prior rights to financial provision exhaust the whole intestate estate may not be the only person with a beneficial interest in the estate: the deceased may have made a testamentary writing disposing of part of the estate only, and the surviving spouse's prior rights would then apply only to part of the deceased's estate.[67]

6.37 Further, the view has been expressed by Lord Justice-Clerk Inglis that, where there was no competition, the next-of-kin would, without beneficial interest, be entitled to the office of executor-dative.[68] On this approach, and on a literal interpretation of section 9(4), even if the estate is exhausted in meeting

---

[65] See, for instance, Form 45, p. 463, in the 7th edition of this work.

[66] Meston, *The Succession (Scotland) Act 1964* (4th ed.), p. 97.

[67] See definition of "intestate estate" contained in ss. 36 (1) and 9 (6) (*a*) of the Succession (Scotland) Act 1964 (c. 41).

[68] *Bones* v. *Morrison* (1866) 5 M. 240 at p. 243.

the surviving spouse's prior rights, the next-of-kin would be entitled to the office of executor, if the surviving spouse has not sought office.

6.38   **Cases illustrating current commissary practice** In *Doonan*,[69] the deceased had separated from his wife, almost 30 years before he died. His wife had emigrated to Australia, but no trace of her could be found there. Since the value of the deceased's estate was less than the widow's prior rights under section 9(1), the sheriff refused to appoint the deceased's sister as executrix-dative *qua* next-of-kin.

6.39   In *Forrest*,[70] a widow did not wish to act, and it was averred that it was not yet known whether the estate exceeded the amount of the widow's prior rights. In these circumstances, a son of the deceased was confirmed *qua* next-of-kin on production of a declinature and consent from the widow.

6.40   In *Jack*,[71] the widow was *incapax*, and although the son had produced a medical certificate to this effect, the court refused to confirm him as executor-dative *qua* next-of-kin and insisted that a *curator bonis* be appointed to the widow. Thereafter, the *curator bonis* could decline office on her behalf, or be decerned *qua curator bonis* to the relict of the deceased.

6.41   It should be noted that the approach taken in *Jack* does not accord with that taken in the case of an executor-nominate who has become *incapax* where, if a *curator-bonis* has not been appointed, a medical certificate will suffice to exclude the *incapax* from the office of executor (see, further, paras. 8.42–8.44). Prima facie, a statement as to the deceased's incapacity, coupled with a medical certificate, would appear—in the language of Condescendence 2 of the Form of Petition for the appointment of an executor set out in the Act of Sederunt (Confirmation of Executors) 1964—to be sufficient "reason why the application is not made by the surviving spouse." The decision in *Jack* can only be explained in light of the current commissary practice that if there was no averment that the estate exceeded (or was believed to exceed) the amount of the widow's prior rights, the surviving spouse has the exclusive right to be decerned executor.

6.42   **Difficulties where surviving spouse has disappeared** If the deceased's family has lost contact with the surviving spouse, but the surviving spouse would have received the whole of the deceased's intestate estate had he or she survived, current commissary practice will not permit the next-of-kin[72] to be con-

---

[69] Feb. 22, 1979, unreported.
[70] Feb. 28, 1966, unreported.
[71] March 2 1967, unreported.
[72] *Doonan*, Dec. 22, 1979, unreported.

firmed as executor-dative. It would therefore seem that unless the spouse can be traced, or an action to prove that he or she is dead brought in an appropriate court,[73] then nothing can be done to wind up the deceased's estate. The only way in which the deceased's family and friends can get title to assets to pay the deceased's debts and funeral expenses and, indeed, to aliment any children of the deceased,[74] is to seek the appointment of an executor-dative *qua* funerator or *qua* creditor. In such a case, the executor will receive only sufficient funds to pay the funeral account or debts, as appropriate, and the residue of the estate will fall into limbo until the missing spouse is traced.

6.43   It is to be regretted that current commissary practice ensures that there is no easy solution for a case where the deceased died intestate leaving a modest estate but his or her spouse has disappeared. After all, the costs of searching for a missing spouse, or having such spouse declared dead in a foreign jurisdiction, will be a large burden on a small estate—but yet, if the estate had been such that it exceeded the amount of the surviving spouse's claim, a relative of the deceased could have been appointed executor-dative as next-of-kin or as a relation entitled to share in the intestate estate, and could have taken out missing beneficiary indemnity against the risk of the missing spouse appearing to claim his or her legal rights. For the reasons set out at paragraphs 6.30–6.37, the current approach in such cases may be open to challenge, and indeed, it is understood that some courts in the West of Scotland will, in such circumstances decern the deceased's child as executor on the basis of an averment that "It is believed that the deceased's widow does not wish to be decerned executrix-dative."

6.44   **Surviving spouse's prior rights under section 9(1) do not exhaust the whole estate** Where the surviving spouse's prior rights to financial provision do not exhaust the whole intestate estate, section 9(4) does not enable the surviving spouse to be decerned as executor. Nevertheless, the current commissary practice is that, since the surviving spouse has a beneficial interest in the deceased's estate, the surviving spouse will, on application, be decerned. Alternatively, the deceased's heirs (or possibly the next-of-kin) may be decerned in that capacity,[75] provided that it is averred that the estate of the deceased exceeds the prior rights of the surviving spouse,[76] and, indeed, both the surviving spouse and the heirs may be decerned jointly.

---

[73] See para. 7.13, fn 22 for circumstances when such an action may be brought in Scotland.

[74] Family Law (Scotland) Act 1985 (c. 37), s. 1 (1), (4) and (5); but decree must have been obtained against the deceased parent before his or her death.

[75] *Forrest*, Feb. 28, 1966, unreported.

[76] Act of Sederunt (Confirmation of Executors) 1964, Sched. 2, Cond. 2, note thereto.

6.45 If the deceased left a testamentary writing which failed to appoint a trustee or executor, and bequeathed part only of his estate, the surviving spouse would be entitled to prior rights to be satisfied out of the intestate estate. In such a case, the surviving spouse would be treated as entitled to the office of executor, in preference to the specific or pecuniary legatee.

6.46 **Deceased is a separated wife** It should be noted that the rights of the surviving spouse described in paragraphs 6.27 *et seq.* fall to be modified where the deceased was a married woman who had been granted decree of separation *a mensa et thoro* and who did not thereafter resume cohabitation with her husband:

> "on her decease [all property which she may acquire or which may come to or devolve upon her after decree] shall, in case she die intestate, pass to her heirs and representatives, in like manner as if her husband had been then dead."[77]

6.47 In such a case, provided that the wife acquired additional property after the date of the decree of separation, the husband, while he will be entitled to be appointed executor-dative *qua* surviving husband, cannot exclude others from being appointed executor, since his prior rights under section 9 of the Succession (Scotland) Act 1964 can never exhaust the whole intestate estate.

6.48 **Who is the surviving spouse?** Apart from the case of the married woman who has been granted decree of separation *a mensa et thoro* and does not thereafter resume cohabitation with her husband (see paras. 6.46–6.47), a man and woman who have gone through a regular ceremony of marriage and who have not been divorced are spouses, and the succession to their intestate estates and the administration thereof will be dealt with as indicated at paragraphs 6.27 *et seq.* The spouses may, however, contract out of the intestate succession rules applying, by each, renouncing all succession rights in the other's estate, whether in a marriage contract or in a separation agreement (which would, of course, be no longer effective if the spouses had thereafter had a reconciliation).[77a]

6.49 If, however, either the man or woman had completely lacked the capacity to give consent to the marriage, or either of the parties was already married or was under the age of 16 years, or the parties were within the prohibited degrees of relation-

---

[77] Conjugal Right (Scotland) Amendment Act 1861 (24 & 25 Vict. c. 86), s. 6, as amended by Family Law (Scotland) Act 1985 (c. 37), s. 28 (2) and Sched. 2. For fuller discussion see *The Law of Husband and Wife in Scotland* (3rd ed.) by Eric M. Clive, pp. 657–658.

[77a] *Bennett* v. *Rennie*, 1988 S.C.L.R. 307.

ship, or the formalities had not been complied with, anyone with a legitimate interest may raise an action of declarator of nullity of marriage at any time (even after the death of the parties). Such a marriage is void *ab initio,* and the surviving party will have no rights in the deceased's estate. If one of the parties was impotent, the marriage is merely voidable, and only the parties to the marriage can seek to have it set aside, and this while they are both alive.[78] Consequently, a disaffected relative, who would otherwise have inherited the deceased's estate, cannot have a voidable marriage annulled.

6.50   Where a man and woman have been living together without going through a regular ceremony of marriage, and one dies, the survivor is not the deceased's surviving spouse. It will be necessary for the survivor to raise an action of declarator of marriage by cohabitation with habit and repute, and prove that both parties were free to marry, and that they were generally known as husband and wife.[79] Only if decree is granted can the survivor claim legal and prior rights, *jus relicti/ae* and rights under section 2(1) (*e*) of the Succession (Scotland) Act 1964 in the deceased's estate.

6.51   **Legal rights** Unless legally excluded, discharged or satisfied, a widow has by law her *jus relictae,* the widower his *jus relicti,*[80] and the surviving children, both legitimate and illegitimate,[81] have their right to legitim[82] in the estate of a person who died domiciled in Scotland. The issue (both legitimate and illegitimate) of predeceasing children share what their parents would have inherited.[83]

6.52   A widow or widower may already have discharged his or her legal rights—for instance, under a marriage contract. Children may also have separately discharged their legitim right—for instance, in exchange for an *inter vivos* gift. Where the parents had executed a marriage contract prior to September 10, 1964,

---

[78] On void and voidable marriages, see Eric M. Clive *op. cit.,* Chaps. 7 and 8.
[79] Eric M. Clive, *op. cit.,* pp. 48–67 and 107–111.
[80] Married Women's Property (Scotland) Act 1881 (44 & 45 Vict. c. 21), s. 6, as amended by Statute Law Revision Act 1894 (57 & 58 Vict. c. 56), Sched. 1.
[81] Law Reform (Parent and Child) (Scotland) Act 1986 (c. 9), ss. 1 and 9(1) (*d*) (for deaths after December 8, 1986).
[82] In the case of a claim on the mother's estate, Married Women's Property (Scotland) Act 1881 (44 & 45 Vict. c. 21), s. 7, as amended by Statute Law Revision Act 1894 (57 & 58 Vict. c. 56), Sched. 1.
[83] Succession (Scotland) Act 1964 (c. 41), s. 11 (as amended by Law Reform (Miscellaneous Provisions) (Scotland) Act 1968 (c. 70), s. 3, Sched. 1, paras. 3–6 and Law Reform (Parent and Child) (Scotland) Act 1986 (c. 9), s. 10 (2), Sched. 2), s. 36 (1) (as amended by Law Reform (Parent and Child) (Scotland) Act 1986 (c. 9), s. 10 (2), Sched. 2) and s. 36 (5) (inserted by Law Reform (Parent and Child) (Scotland) Act 1986 (c. 9), s. 10 (1), Sched. 1, para. 7 (2)).

the parents may have included a provision discharging the right to legitim of any children born of the marriage, but in a marriage contract executed after that date, such a provision will be treated *pro non scripto*.[84]

6.53   Where the deceased is survived by a widow or widower, and by issue, the surviving spouse receives one-third of the net moveable estate, and the issue share a further one-third of the net moveable estate. Where the deceased is survived by a widow or widower, but no issue, the surviving spouse will receive one-half of the net moveable estate. And where the deceased was survived by issue only, the issue will share one-half of the net moveable estate.

6.54   For the purposes of computing the amount of a legal rights claim, the net moveable estate is computed by ensuring that any debts secured over heritage are deducted from the heritable estate,[85] and the funeral expenses, any debts secured over the moveable estate,[86] any unsecured debts, the expenses of confirmation, and the relict's mournings[87] are deducted from the gross moveable estate. The prior rights of the surviving spouse are then applied, the financial provision under section 9 of the Succession (Scotland) Act 1964 being apportioned *pro rata* between the heritable and moveable property,[87a] and a deduction of the appropriate amounts made in arriving at the net moveable estate.[88] There is a fuller discussion of the classification of heritage and moveable estate at paragraphs 10.84–10.85.

6.55   A person seeking to be confirmed as executor on the basis of a claim to legal rights on the deceased's estate may do so only as an executor-creditor[89] (see, further, paras. 6.77 *et seq.*) Where the deceased died intestate, such a person will generally be entitled to be decerned *qua* surviving spouse or *qua* child of the deceased, and decerniture in that capacity, being to the whole estate (and not just to the value of the legal rights claim) is preferable.

---

[84] Succession (Scotland) Act 1964 (c. 41), s. 12.

[85] Stair, III.v.17; *Muir's Trs.* v. *Muir*, 1916 1 S.L.T. 372; *Douglas's Trs.* v. *Douglas* (1868) 6 M. 223; *Bain* v. *Reeves* (1861) 23 D. 416; *Brand* v. *Scott's Trs.* (1892) 19 R. 768; Succession (Scotland) Act 1964 (c. 41), s. 14 (3). This rule will be modified if the deceased had left an express direction to different effect, though a general direction to pay debts is insufficient (*MacLeod's Trs.* (1871) 9 M. 903 at p. 906). A debt secured over heritable and moveable estate will be apportioned *pro rata*: *Graham* v. *Graham* (1898) 5 S.L.T. 319; Gretton, "Endowment mortgages and the law of succession" (1987) 32 J.L.S. 303.

[86] *Grant* v. *Hill's Exrs.*, 1922 S.L.T. 124; *Stewart* v. *Stewart* (1891) 19 R. 310.

[87] *Moncrief* v. *Monipenny* (1713) Mor. 3945.

[87a] Succession (Scotland) Act 1964 (c. 41) s. 9(3).

[88] *Ibid.*, s. 10 (2).

[89] *Stevin* v. *Govan* (1622) Mor. 3843.

6.56   **Section 2: heirs on intestacy** The Succession (Scotland) Act 1964 lists in order the categories of persons to whom the succession to the intestate estate[90] of a deceased person opens up. The heirs of an intestate are to be determined at the time of his death.[91] When considering each category (other than those of the parents or spouse of the deceased), it should be remembered that the issue of any predeceasing member of that category comes into their parent's place, and if the heirs are of different degrees to the deceased, they will share *per stirpes* what their predeceasing ancestor would have inherited had he survived.[92] Where all of the heirs are of the same degree to the deceased, they will share the estate *per capita*. Brothers, sisters, uncles and aunts of the half blood stand to inherit,[93] though those of the whole blood succeed in preference to those of the half blood.[94] There is no distinction made between relationships through the deceased's father, and those through the deceased's mother,[95] and no account taken of the fact that a person was illegitimate.[96]. Any person sharing in the deceased's estate under the intestate succession rules may be decerned as executor-dative. Where there is competition for the office of executor-dative, between a person who inherits by virtue of representing a deceased parent, and someone who inherits in their own right, the latter will be preferred to the office.[96a] Professor Meston has suggested that where the petitioner is, in addition to being an heir under the Succession (Scotland) Act 1964, the deceased's next-of-kin, he he should be decerned as executor-dative *qua* next-of-kin.[96b]

6.57   The statutory order of intestate succession is as follows:

1. Any surviving children of the deceased shall share the whole intestate estate.[97]

If there are no surviving children (or issue of predeceasing children):

---

[90] *i.e.* the intestate estate in so far as it has not been used to meet the prior rights, *jus relictae* or *jus relicti* of the surviving spouse or legitim rights of the issue (Succession (Scotland) Act 1964 (c. 41) s. 1 (2)), and extending to heritable estate in Scotland and worldwide moveable estate (where the deceased died domiciled in Scotland) or extending only to heritable estate in Scotland (where the deceased died domiciled elsewhere).

[91] *Per* Lord Weir in *MacLean* v. *MacLean*, 1988 S.L.T. 626 at p. 627.

[92] Succession (Scotland) Act 1964 (c. 41), ss. 5 (1) and 6.

[93] *Ibid.*, s. 2 (2).

[94] *Ibid.*, s. 3.

[95] See, for instance, Succession (Scotland) Act 1964 (c. 41), ss. 2 (1) (*f*), (*g*) and (*h*) and 3.

[96] Where the deceased died on or after December 8, 1986, Succession (Scotland) Act 1964 (c. 41), s. 36 (5), inserted by Law Reform (Parent and Child) (Scotland) Act 1986 (c. 9), s. 10 (1) and Sched. 1, para. 7 (2).

[96a] Succession (Scotland) Act 1964 (c. 41) s. 5(2) See further para. 7.39

[96b] Meston, *The Succession (Scotland) Act* 1964 (4th. ed.) pp. 98–99.

[97] Succession (Scotland) Act 1964 (c. 41), s. 2 (1) (*a*).

2. If the deceased is survived by either or both parents, and by a brother or sister, the surviving parent or parents shall share one-half of the intestate estate, and the brother(s) and sister(s) the other half.[98]

3. If the deceased is survived by neither parent, but by a brother or sister, the brother(s) and sister(s) shall share the whole intestate estate.[99]

4. If the deceased was survived by either or both parents, but not by brothers or sisters, the surviving parent or parents shall share the whole intestate estate.[1]

If there are no surviving children, parents, brothers or sisters (or issue of predeceasing children, brothers or sisters):

5. The deceased's surviving spouse shall inherit the whole intestate estate.[2] It should be noted that, on the death of a married woman who had obtained a decree of separation *a mensa et thoro* against her husband, and had not thereafter cohabited with him, the succession to any property acquired by her after the separation shall pass to her heirs as if her husband had predeceased her.[3]

If there are no surviving children, parents, brothers, sisters or spouse (or issue of predeceasing children, brothers or sisters):

6. The deceased's surviving uncle(s) and aunt(s) (being brothers or sisters of either parent) shall share the whole intestate estate.[4]

If there are no surviving children, parents, brothers, sisters, spouse, uncles or aunts (or issue of predeceasing children, brothers, sisters, uncles or aunts):

7. The deceased's surviving grandparent or grandparents shall share the whole intestate estate.[5]

If there are no surviving children, parents, brothers, sisters, spouse, uncles, aunts or grandparents (or issue of predeceasing children, brothers, sisters, uncles, aunts or grandparents):

8. The brothers or sisters of any grandparent of the deceased shall share the whole intestate estate.[6]

---

[98] Succession (Scotland) Act 1964, (c. 41), s. 2 (1) (*b*).

[99] *Ibid.*, s. 2 (1) (*c*).

[1] *Ibid.*, s. 2 (1) (*d*).

[2] *Ibid.*, s. 2 (1) (*e*).

[3] Conjugal Rights (Scotland) Amendment Act 1861 (24 & 25 Vict. c. 86), s. 6, as amended by Family Law (Scotland) Act 1985 (c. 37), s. 28 (2) and Sched. 2.

[4] Succession (Scotland) Act 1964 (c. 41), s. 2 (1) (*f*).

[5] *Ibid.*, s. 2 (1) (*g*).

[6] *Ibid.*, s. 2 (1) (*h*).

If there are no surviving children, parents, brothers, sisters, spouse, uncles, aunts, grandparents, great-uncles or great-aunts (or issue thereof):

9. The succession opens up to the prior ancestors of the deceased, generation by generation successively, though it should be noted that failing ancestors of any generation, the brothers and sisters of any of those ancestors shall share the intestate estate, before the succession opens up to ancestors of a more remote generation.

If there are no descendants or ancestors:

10. The Crown inherits as *ultimus haeres*.[7] This is a caduciary right,[8] and not a right of succession.

In Scotland, the Queen's and Lord Treasurer's Remembrancer acts on behalf of the Treasury, and is responsible for the administration of such estates. Anyone holding the estate of a deceased person who cannot find heirs, must hand over the estate to the Queen's and Lord Treasurer's Remembrancer rather than seek the appointment of a judicial factor,[9] though an exception may be made where there are "reasonable grounds to believe that further and more expensive investigation (perhaps in a distant part of the world) would disclose the existence of heirs, who were known to be alive within a few years of the deceased intestate's death."[10] However, it would appear that the right of a creditor of the deceased to be decerned as executor-dative *qua* creditor will prevail over the Crown's rights, as *ultimus haeres*.[10a]

Where a solicitor advises the Queen's and Lord Treasurer's Remembrancer that an estate appears to have fallen to the Crown, the Queen's and Lord Treasurer's Remembrancer will require the solicitor to complete:
(1) a statement of particulars, setting out all the information which the solicitor has on the family circumstances of the deceased;
(2) a statement of the deceased's assets and liabilities.

---

[7] Stair, III.iii.47; A.R.G. McMillan, *The Law of Bona Vacantia in Scotland* (1936), p. 17 *et seq.*, pp. 34–35; Succession (Scotland) Act 1964 (c. 41), s. 7.

[8] Stair, III.iii.47; W. Galbraith Miller (1902) 124 Jur. Rev. 152; A.R.G. McMillan, *The Law of Bona Vacantia in Scotland* (1936) pp. 9–10; *cf.* McLaren, *Wills and Succession* (3rd ed.), Vol. I, Chap. IV, s. I, paras. 136–143 and see also Supplementary Volume by D. Oswald Dykes (1936), pp. 15–17.

[9] *Rutherford* v. *Lord Advocate*, 1932 S.C. 674.

[10] *Per* Lord President Clyde in *Rutherford* v. *Lord Advocate*, 1932 S.C. 674 at p. 680.

[10a] *Irvine* v. *King's and Lord Treasurer's Remembrancer* (1949) 65 Sh. Ct. Rep. 53.

Only if the deceased's assets exceed the liabilities will the Queen's and Lord Treasurer's Remembrancer intervene. He will then require the solicitor to advertise for heirs in *The Scotsman* or *The Herald*, and in a local newspaper[11] on one occasion, in the case of smaller estates, and on two occasions, in the case of larger estates. If there is no response to the adverts, the solicitor will send all the executry papers which he has and his own business account[12] to the Queen's and Lord Treasurer's Remembrancer. Without obtaining confirmation, the Queen's and Lord Treasurer's Remembrancer will take possession of the estate, both heritable and moveable, real and personal, situated in Scotland, and, where the intestate died domiciled in Scotland, in England and Wales.[13]

Once the estate has been ingathered and the debts paid, the Queen's and Lord Treasurer's Remembrancer will consider any Petitions for Gifts, which should be submitted with affidavits of supporting witnesses. The three main grounds for making a gift of the whole or part of the deceased's estate are:
(1) the claimant had a relationship with the deceased;
(2) the claimant had rendered services to the deceased; and
(3) the deceased had expressed an intention to dispose of his estate (or part of his estate) to the claimant.

A memorandum explaining the procedure for a Petition for Gifts can be obtained from the Queen's and Lord Treasurer's Remembrancer.

6.58   **An heir—but there is an illegitimate birth?** Although, under Scots law, illegitimate children originally had very limited rights to inherit on intestacy, recent legislation has largely equated their position with that of legitimate children.

6.59   *(a) Deceased died on or after December 8, 1986* Where the intestate died on or after December 8, 1986, the fact that a relationship is illegitimate is completely ignored in determining how the estate is to be divided.

"The fact that a person's parents are not or have not been married to one another shall be left out of account in establishing the legal relationship between the person and another person; and accordingly any such relationship shall

---

[11] The solicitor will not require to advertise in the *Edinburgh Gazette*.
[12] Where the solicitor had been the deceased's curator, the Accountant of Court must first audit the solicitor's account.
[13] Law Reform (Miscellaneous Provisions) (Scotland) Act 1940 (c. 42), s. 6 (1), as amended by Administration of Estates Act 1971 (c. 25), s. 7, Sched. 1, para. 4.

have effect as if the parents were or had been married to one another."[14]

6.60   *(b) Deceased died on or after November 25, 1968 but before December 8, 1986* Where the intestate died on or after November 25, 1968, but before December 8, 1986:

1.   Even if the deceased had been born illegitimate, both parents were able to claim on the estate.[15]

2.   The deceased's legitimate and illegitimate children would share the estate on an equal basis.[16] However, grandchildren could not represent their parents, where there was an illegitimate link,[17] save with the exception of the legitimate issue of an illegitimate child of the deceased, who could represent his or her deceased parent.[18]
     Examples:
     A, a widow, died intestate in 1970. She was predeceased by her only two children, B and C. B left one legitimate child, D. C left one illegitimate child, E. D would take all A's estate, and was entitled to office as executor-dative.
     A, a widow, died intestate in 1970. She was predeceased by her only two children, B and C. B was legitimate, but C was illegitimate. Both B and C had one legitimate child, D and E respectively. D and E would each be entitled to an equal share of A's estate (as representing their deceased parents) and would have an equal right to the office of executor-dative to A.[19]

3.   The deceased's natural brothers and sisters (born of the same parents) could not claim on the intestate estate.[20]

6.61   **Commissary practice where there is an illegitimate link between the deceased and the petitioner** Formerly, where the relationship between the pursuer and the deceased involved an illegitimate birth, commissary practice required the production of a birth certificate or a decree of paternity. Such productions

---

[14] Law Reform (Parent and Child) (Scotland) Act 1986 (c. 9), s. 1 (1), inserted in Succession (Scotland) Act 1964 (c. 41), s. 36 (5) by s. 10 and Sched. 1, para. 7 (2) of the 1986 Act.

[15] Succession (Scotland) Act 1964 (c. 41), s. 4 (2), inserted by Law Reform (Miscellaneous Provisions) (Scotland) Act 1968 (c. 70), s. 1.

[16] *Ibid.*, s. 4 (1), inserted by Law Reform (Miscellaneous Provisions) (Scotland) Act 1968 (c. 70), s. 1.

[17] *Ibid.*, s. 4 (4), inserted by Law Reform (Miscellaneous Provisions) (Scotland) Act 1968 (c. 70), s. 1.

[18] *Ibid.*, s. 5 (1).

[19] *Spittal*, July 14, 1969, unreported.

[20] Succession (Scotland) Act 1964 (c. 41), s. 4 (4), inserted by Law Reform (Miscellaneous Provisions) (Scotland) Act 1968 (c. 70), s. 1.

are no longer required,[21] and it is sufficient if the relationship is correctly averred. In this connection, the following presumptions should be born in mind: under Scots law, since December 8, 1986

1. a man is the father of a child if he was married to the child's mother at any time between the child's conception and birth[22]; and

2. a man is the father of a child if he and the child's mother both acknowledged that he was the father, and he is shown as such in the Register of Births.[23]

In such cases, it is competent to challenge the appointment of the executor-dative by seeking to lead parole evidence to show, on the balance of probabilities,[24] that a particular man was not the father of a particular child, but this would only be for the purposes of the commissary proceedings.[25] The presumption will also be displaced by the production of a declarator of parentage, non-parentage, legitimacy, legitimation or illegitimacy.

6.62 The unreported decision of *Meehan*[26] has been doubted,[27] but since the Law Reform (Parent and Child) (Scotland) Act 1986 came into force, the decision illustrates the approach which should now be adopted. A married woman had left her husband (A), and commenced an association with another man (B), with whom she cohabited. As a result of her relationship with B, a child was conceived. Subsequently, the husband died. Thereafter, B died and the child sought to be decerned executrix-dative *qua* illegitimate child to B. Notwithstanding the presumption *pater est quem nuptiae demonstrant*, an extract birth certificate showing B as the father and bearing his signature was produced in process (though this would no longer be necessary),[28] and decree was granted without further proof.

6.63 **Adopted children** The following rules apply whether the adoption order was made in Scotland, England and Wales, Northern Ireland, Isle of Man, or the Channel Islands, was an overseas adoption of a description (being an adoption of a child)

---

[21] *McLaughlin, Petr.*, 1987 S.L.T. (Sh. Ct.) 87.

[22] Law Reform (Parent and Child) (Scotland) Act 1986 (c. 9), s. 5 (1).

[23] *Ibid.*, s. 5 (2).

[24] *Ibid.*, s. 5 (4).

[25] *Ibid.*, s. 7 (5).

[26] Edinburgh, Feb. 16, 1970.

[27] *Per* Sheriff Kelbie in *McLaughlin, Petr.*, 1987 S.L.T. (Sh. Ct.) 87 at p. 90 J–K.

[28] An averment of the relationship would be sufficient: *McLaughlin, Petr.*, 1987 S.L.T. (Sh. Ct.) 87.

specified by order of the Secretary of State, or was any other adoption otherwise recognised by the law of Scotland.[29]

6.64   For the purposes of intestate succession to the estate of a person dying domiciled in Scotland, an adopted child is to be treated as the child of the adopter, and not as the child of any other person.[30] This rule is subject to one exception, namely that an adopted person whose adopter (or if adopted by a married couple, both adopters) died before September 10, 1964 is treated as the child of his or her natural parents.[31]

6.65   Where the child has been adopted by two spouses jointly, and the couple have another child (whether adopted or not), both children are treated as brother(s) or sister(s) of the whole blood.[32] If, however, the child had been adopted by one person only, and that person has another child (whether adopted or not), the children will be treated as brother(s) or sister(s) of the half blood.[33] And if the child was adopted by two spouses jointly, and one spouse independently has a child (whether adopted or not), the children will also be treated as brother(s) or sister(s) of the half blood.[34]

6.66   It is technically possible for a court order to revoke a Scottish adoption order granted before June 8, 1968, under which the adopters adopted their natural child, if section 4 of the Legitimation (Scotland) Act 1968 legitimated the child. On an intestacy occurring before the adoption order is revoked, the succession will be dealt with as if the child were the adopted child of the adopters. On an intestacy occurring after the adoption order is revoked, the succession will be dealt with as if the child were the legitimate child of the parents.[35]

6.67   **Common calamity or simultaneous deaths** Section 31(1) of the Succession (Scotland) Act 1964 makes special provision for the succession to the estate of persons who have died "in circumstances indicating that they died simultaneously or rendering it uncertain which, if either, of them survived the other." However, if it is proved which person survived the other, section 31(1) is not applicable. The standard of proof required to establish which of two persons survived the other is on the balance of probabilities.[36] Thus, if the pursuer can prove that,

---

[29] Succession (Scotland) Act 1964 (c. 41), s. 23 (5), as amended by Adoption (Scotland) Act 1978 (c. 28), s. 66 and Sched. 3, para. 4.
[30] Succession (Scotland) Act 1964 (c. 41), s. 23 (1).
[31] Law Reform (Miscellaneous Provisions) (Scotland) Act 1966 (c. 19), s. 5.
[32] Succession (Scotland) Act 1964 (c. 41), s. 24 (1) (*a*).
[33] *Ibid.*, s. 24 (1) (*b*).
[34] *Ibid.*
[35] Legitimation (Scotland) Act 1968 (c. 22), s. 6 (1) and (2).
[36] *Lamb* v. *Lord Advocate*, 1976 S.C. 110.

on the balance of probabilities, A died before B and that he is in these circumstances B's heir under the Succession (Scotland) Act 1964, then he will be entitled, *inter alia*, to decerniture as executor-dative of B. If he cannot so prove then the presumptions set out in section 31(1) will apply.

6.68 Where spouses die intestate[37] in a common calamity to which section 31(1) applies, it is presumed that neither survived the other and, consequently, neither has a claim for prior or legal rights on the other's estate. Their estates will separately pass to their respective heirs in terms of section 2 of the Succession (Scotland) Act 1964, and such heirs may petition to be decerned executors-dative. See Style 6.29.

6.69 Where persons who are not married die in a common calamity to which section 31(1) applies, the younger is presumed to survive the elder and:

    1. in administering the estate of the younger, if he dies intestate,[38] his heirs on intestacy (excluding the elder) are entitled to be decerned his executors-dative and should confirm, *inter alia*, to his inheritance (if any) from the elder's estate.

    2. in administering the estate of the elder, if he dies intestate,[39] his heirs will be confirmed as executors-dative. If the younger is, by virtue of legitim claims and/or rights under section 2 of the Succession (Scotland) Act 1964, the sole heir of the elder on intestacy, it will be necessary to have an executor (whether dative or nominate) confirmed on the younger's estate, and he will then be decerned to the elder's estate as executor-dative *qua* representative of the deceased heir.

6.70 Where persons who are not married die in a common calamity to which section 31(1) applies and, while the younger is intestate,[40] the elder leaves a testamentary writing making provision for the younger, whom failing a third party, it is presumed that the elder survived the younger. While the younger's estate is wound up as set out at 1. above, the elder's estate is wound up in terms of the testamentary writing with the legacy in question passing to the third party.

---

[37] Either because they did not leave a testamentary writing, or because the testamentary writing which they left has resulted in an intestacy (*Lamb* v. *Lord Advocate*, 1976 S.C. 110).

[38] *Ibid.*

[39] *Ibid.*

[40] *Ibid.*

6.71   For the purposes of calculating the Inheritance Tax due on their respective estates, a different assumption applies.[40a]

6.72   **Intestate heir has unlawfully killed the deceased** A person who has unlawfully killed another cannot normally inherit any part of the deceased's estate.

6.73   *(a) Killing of a parent or grandparent* The Parricide Act 1594 provides:

> "quhatsumeuir he be that hes slayne and sall heireftir slay his father or mother guidschir or guddame and hes bene alreddie or salbe heireftir convict be ane assyise The committaris of the said cryme and his posteritie in linea recta salbe disheresit in all tyme heireftir fra thair landis heretages takis possessionis And the samyn sall apertene to the nixt collaterall and narrest of blude quha vtherwayes micht succeid falyeing of the richt lyne."

Accordingly, where a person is convicted of killing his or her parent or grandparent, the succession to the estate is dealt with as if the murderer had predeceased the parent or grandparent, without having issue.[40b]

6.74   *(b) Other unlawful killings* It is a rule of public policy that where a person has unlawfully killed the deceased, he cannot receive any part of the deceased's estate,[41] though, provided he has not been convicted of the murder of the deceased,[42] he may apply to the court[42a] for an order modifying the rule.[43] Such an order will be granted if the court is satisfied that "having regard to the conduct of the offender and of the deceased and to such other circumstances as appear to the court to be material, the justice of the case" requires it.[44] In such a case, the offender may receive part, but not the whole,[45] of the deceased's estate on intestacy.

6.75   It is unclear who is to inherit the part of the deceased's estate which the heir has forfeited through the unlawful killing. It has been suggested that the estate will be distributed as if the heir

---

[40a] Inheritance Tax Act, 1984 (c. 51), s. 4(2).

[40b] The rule may apply only to succession to heritage, Bankton, II, ccci, 30.

[41] *Smith, Petr.*, 1979 S.L.T. (Sh. Ct.) 3; see *Burns* v. *Secretary of State for Social Services*, 1985 S.L.T. 351.

[42] Forfeiture Act 1982 (c. 34), s. 5.

[42a] By petition to the Inner House, or probably also by an action of declarator (*Paterson, Petr.*, 1986 S.L.T. 121).

[43] Forfeiture Act 1982 (c. 34), s. 2 (1).

[44] *Ibid.*, s. 2 (2); for likely factors see Lord Cameron in *Paterson, Petr.*, 1986 S.L.T. 121 at p. 123 C-E; and *Gilchrist, Petr.*, 1990 S.L.T. 494.

[45] *Cross, Petr.*, 1987 S.L.T. 384; *cf.* the contrary approach in England, Vinelott J. *Re K. decd* [1985] Ch. 85 at p. 100 A-E.

had died before the deceased.[46] However, in *Hunter's Executors, Petitioners,*[47] (a testate case), the Inner House held that, while public policy required that the beneficiary's right be forfeited, it did not require that the deceased's estate be distributed as if the beneficiary had predeceased the deceased. On the basis of the *ratio* in *Hunter's Executors,* if the deceased had been killed by his or her spouse, the surviving spouse's prior and legal rights would be forfeited, and would fall into intestacy. But if the deceased had been killed by an heir whose rights stem from section 2 of the Succession (Scotland) Act 1964 then, if the heir's right is forfeited (but not on the basis of having predeceased the intestate), there is no one else who is entitled to inherit in place of the heir, and the estate would presumably fall to the Crown. Since a Scottish court can apparently only order that the heir will receive part of the estate on intestacy,[48] part will always fall to the Crown.

6.76   A person who is debarred from inheriting on intestacy will not be able to be appointed as executor-dative as heir under the Succession (Scotland) Act 1964, though it may be competent for such a person, if he or she is the next-of-kin, to be decerned in that capacity. It is submitted that a person who unlawfully killed the deceased but who has successfully applied to the court for an order under section 2 of the Forfeiture Act 1982 is entitled to be decerned executor-dative as heir under the Succession (Scotland) Act 1964.

IV. Executor-dative *qua* creditor

Difference between an executor-creditor and other executors

6.77   Confirmation as an executor-creditor is quite different from confirmation in any other capacity.

6.78   First, it is, in substance, not a mere completion of title (as in the case of other categories of confirmation), but a diligence by which estate in Scotland which belongs to a deceased person is attached in security and for payment of debts due by him or by his next-of-kin (see para. 6.88). As Lord Curriehill expressed it, the fallacy

> "consists in overlooking the true nature and legal character of a confirmation as executor-creditor. The parties are led into that fallacy by the diligence being called a confirmation. It is, no doubt, of the nature[49] of a confirmation, but its

---

[46] *Stair Memorial Encyclopedia*, Vol. 24, para. 672; Scottish Law Commission Report No. 124, para. 7.15.

[47] 1992 S.L.T. 1141.

[48] *Cross, Petr.*, 1987 S.L.T. 384.

[49] By "nature" Lord Curriehill must mean "form."

true legal character is, that it is legal diligence or execution. Confirmation by an executor of any other character is the proper *aditio haereditatis in mobilibus*, a mode of making up a title to the defunct by a representative. But the confirmation of an executor-creditor is a species of legal execution and diligence for the payment of debt, and the true effect of it is to create a *nexus* on the fund, and that *nexus* is subject to two limitations. One is the amount of the debt itself. If the party attaches a fund which is worth £10,000, while his debt is only £5,000, he creates a *nexus* upon that fund to the extent of £5,000, and the rest does not belong to him in his own right at all. And then in the second place, there is a limitation put upon it by the valuation that he is bound by law to put on it. I think that both of these things limit the extent of the right he acquires by the diligence; but that right, in its nature and legal character, is a security for the debt."[50]

6.79   Secondly, whereas other confirmations apply to the whole assets of the deceased, confirmation as an executor-creditor may be, and indeed usually is, partial only; in other words it is limited to particular assets or parts of assets.

6.80   And finally, if the deceased was domiciled furth of Scotland, the laws of the domicile can exceptionally be ignored, both as far as administrative and beneficial right is concerned and, provided that the asset is situated in Scotland, the Scottish procedures will be applied, irrespective of the law of the deceased's domicile or the domicile of his executors or administrators.[51] Consequently, an executor-creditor is not required to aver that, under the law of the domicile of the deceased, he is entitled to administer.[52]

Why a creditor may become an executor-creditor

6.81   Where a person dies leaving a debt, the creditor will normally recover the debt from the deceased's executor, but if no executor has taken up office, the creditor has two options:

1. Whether the deceased died solvent or insolvent, if he "left no settlement appointing trustees or other parties having power to manage his estate or part thereof or in the event of such persons not accepting or acting," the deceased's creditor may apply to have a judicial factor appointed.[53]

---

[50] *Smith's Trs.* v. *Grant* (1862) 24 D. 1142 at p. 1169.
[51] *Per* Lord Deas in *Smith's Trs.* v. *Grant*, above at p. 1173, Anton and Beaumont, *Private International Law* (2nd ed.) pp. 657–8.
[52] *Tod*, Jan. 21, 1869; *Malcolm*, Oct. 11, 1878, unreported, a case of alternative domicile.
[53] Judicial Factors (Scotland) Act 1889 (52 and 53 Vict. c. 39), s. 11A (1), inserted by the Bankruptcy (Scotland) Act 1985 (c. 66), s. 75 (1) and Sched. 7, para. 4. For further discussion see paras. 8.82–8.97.

Once appointed, the judicial factor will administer the estate, *including* paying the deceased's debts.

2. The deceased's creditor may apply to be appointed executor-creditor, and confirmed as such. In this way, once confirmation is granted, estate which had belonged to the deceased is attached in security and for payment of debts due by the deceased.

6.82 The executor-creditor option avoids the expenditure attendant on the appointment of a judicial factor (professional charges, accountant of court's fees, etc.). As will be seen, it does not guarantee the creditor any preferential rights in the deceased's estate.

The petitioner must be a creditor

6.83 In all cases where a petitioner seeks appointment as an executor-creditor, it is essential that the legal relationship is one of creditor and debtor. Thus, where the purchaser of a flat had taken entry and paid the price, but had not received a disposition from the seller before she died, the sheriff refused to decern the purchaser as executor-creditor to the seller: the purchaser "cannot in my opinion be described as a creditor of the deceased, either by a liquid or illiquid ground of debt. His remedy may include procedure by an action for adjudication in implement."[54]

Circumstances where confirmation as executor-creditor is excluded

6.84 There are a number of circumstances where a creditor cannot execute diligence by being confirmed executor-creditor.

1. An executor of any kind has confirmed to the same asset or assets at the same value. For instance, a number of executors-creditors may have been confirmed, each taking up different assets, or different shares in the same asset, or excess value in the same asset.

2. A grant of representation or probate from England and Wales or Northern Ireland which contains a statement that the deceased was domiciled there, or a grant which has been resealed in Scotland under the Colonial Probates Act 1892 is equivalent to a Scottish confirmation, and so bars the creditor's diligence in this form. Other non-Scottish grants of representation or probate do not similarly bar the creditor's diligence.[55]

3. Possession by the deceased's successors, *e.g.* his testa-

---

[54] *Stokes*, Jan. 18, 1990, unreported.
[55] *Smith's Trs.* v. *Grant* (1862) 24 D. 1142.

mentary trustees, executors-nominate or the beneficial successor of his estate, of such kind and character as to exclude confirmation by an executor-creditor[56]:

"There can be no doubt that, by the law of Scotland, the person in right of the moveable succession, whether testate or intestate, may by possession so vest it in himself as to exclude the necessity of confirmation, and enable him to maintain a preferable claim to it, in the same way as if actually confirmed. The most frequent exhibition of this principle is either in the case of those moveables which are capable of actual apprehension, such as furniture or pictures, or in that of debts due to the deceased, in regard to which a constructive possession has been held admissible, as by receiving payment of interest or a bond of corroboration, or the like."[57]

Until such executors are confirmed, they are vitious intromitters, and liable to pay the deceased's debts (see, further, para. 1.49 *et seq.*).

4. The deceased's successors have a completed right to the asset. Instances are a special assignation by the deceased, *e.g.* a specific legacy intimated to the holder of the asset or debtor,[58] or a bond of corroboration granted by the debtor in favour of the deceased's successors.

5. Once the deceased's estate has been sequestrated, it is not possible to be confirmed as executor-creditor.[59]

6.85 Doubt has been expressed as to the competency of appointing an executor-creditor where executors are nominated and acting (and have not renounced), although they have not yet confirmed,[60] but in *Smith's Trustees* v. *Grant*,[61] the confirmation of executors-creditors was upheld even although the deceased had appointed testamentary trustees in whose favour probate had been granted in India (the country of the deceased's domicile) though confirmation had not been granted in Scotland. Further decree-dative does not exclude an executor-creditor being confirmed.[62]

Who may be confirmed as executor-creditor?
6.86 The 1695 Act anent Executry and Moveables enables two distinct

---

[56] *Smith's Trs.* v. *Grant* (1862) 24 D. 1142.
[57] *Per* Lord Kinloch in *Smith's Trs.* v. *Grant* (1862) 24 D. 1142 at p. 1153.
[58] Act Anent the Confirmation of Testaments 1690 (c. 56).
[59] Bankruptcy (Scotland) Act 1985 (c. 66), s. 37 (8).
[60] *Obiter per* Lord Avonside in *Emslie* v. *Tognarelli's Exrs.*, 1967 S.L.T. (Notes) 66 at p. 67.
[61] (1862) 24 D. 1142.
[62] Bell, *Comm.*, ii, 79 *et seq.*

categories of persons to be confirmed as executors-dative *qua* creditors:

1. Where the deceased owed money to a creditor, the creditor may be decerned (Style 6.30). A person seeking to be confirmed as executor on the basis of a claim to legal rights on the estate of the deceased must do so as an executor-creditor.[63]

2. Where the next-of-kin (see para. 6.88) of the deceased owed money to a creditor, and has not confirmed to the deceased's estate, the creditor may have himself decerned as executor-dative to the deceased. Thus, the trustee on the sequestrated estate of the deceased's next-of-kin has been confirmed to the estate of the deceased.[64]

6.87   There is a practical difference between an executor-creditor who was owed money by the deceased, and one who was owed money by the deceased's next-of-kin, and that is in relation to the ranking of their diligence. At common law, the personal estate of a deceased person is preferentially available for payment of his own debts, before being taken to meet the debts of his next-of-kin or testate successors. This preference was unlimited in time, so long as the assets could be identified, and that is still the position when there has been confirmation.[65] The Act anent Executry and Moveables 1695 cut down the preference of the deceased's creditors over the creditors of the next-of-kin, to those of the deceased's creditors who confirmed within a year and a day of the death. However, the creditors of the deceased's next-of-kin may competently confirm within this period.

6.88   **Next-of-kin** The 1695 Act, by enabling the creditor of the "next-of-kin" to be confirmed as executor-creditor, gave such a creditor a remedy where the next-of-kin refused or delayed to confirm to the estate of someone who had left him money. It can be argued that the word "next-of-kin" in this context can be interpreted as including the deceased's intestate heirs in terms of section 2 of the Succession (Scotland) Act 1964.[65a] The point has yet to be determined by the courts.

6.89   If the creditor of an heir (whether testate or intestate) of the deceased holds an assignation of the debtor's interest in the estate, he may confirm as derivative successor, but this will not give him any preference on the estate. Alternatively, such a

---

[63] *Stevin* v. *Govan* (1622) Mor. 3843.
[64] *Macdonald*, July 9, 1857, unreported.
[65] Bell, *Comm.*, ii, 79 *et seq.*
[65a] Succession (Scotland) Act 1964 (c. 41), s. 34(1) and Sched. 2, para. 2(a).

creditor can only recover his debt out of the estate by an arrest-
ment in the hands of the executors.

Different persons who may be confirmed as executors-creditors

6.90   There is no restriction on the legal personae which may be confirmed as executors-creditors. An incorporated company has
been decerned, the oath to the inventory being taken by the
secretary.[66] In the case of a debt owed to a partnership, either
the firm "along with A and B, the individual partners thereof"[67] may be decerned, or the individual partners by name.[68]
Where the deceased had granted a bill to two trustees, one was
decerned *qua* creditor, the other being abroad.[69] The liquidators
of a bank have been decerned executors-dative *qua* creditors on
the estate of a deceased shareholder.[70] And under the Companies Act 1862,[71] the liquidators of the City of Glasgow Bank were
entitled to be decerned and confirmed "*qua* liquidators of the
City of Glasgow Bank, of which the deceased was a
contributor."[72]

6.91   A creditor may not be confirmed as executor-creditor on his
debtor's estate after the debtor's sequestration.[73]

Liquid debt

6.92   Before he can be confirmed as executor-creditor, the creditor
must have a liquid debt:

1.   The amount of the debt must be clear — except in the cases
      of the price of goods fixed by oral contract, of rent, and
      the exact amount must be fixed by an obligatory writing
      or by the judgment of a competent court.[74]

2.   The sum must be due.

3.   The debt must be proved or admitted.

6.93   Thus, a bond or bill granted by the deceased, or a decree of a

---

[66] *Whitson* Jan. 15, 1874, unreported.
[67] *Fortune*, Nov. 16, 1855, unreported.
[68] *Sibbald*, April 17, 1862, unreported.
[69] *Hitchcock*, June 2, 1870, unreported.
[70] *Bishop*, Oct. 31, 1861, unreported.
[71] 25 & 26 Vict. c. 89, s. 74 which provided that the liability of a person to
contribute to the assets of the company on being wound up "shall be deemed
to create a debt accruing at the time when his liability commenced."
[72] *Mackenzie*, Feb. 14, 1879, unreported.
[73] Bankruptcy (Scotland) Act 1985 (c. 66), s. 37 (8).
[74] *Per* Lord Kinnear in *Robertson & Co.* v. *Bird & Co.* (1897) 24 R. 1076 at
p. 1078; a judgment from a foreign court will be recognised, *Stiven* v. *Myer*
(1868) 6 M. 370.

competent court granted against the deceased during his life-time, is sufficient. The creditor under a heritable bond has been decerned executor-creditor in virtue of the personal obligation in the bond,[75] as presumably may the creditor under a standard security (Style 6.30).

6.94 The position of the holder of an IOU is far from clear. The previous edition of this work stated that "a holograph IOU might now be accepted"[76] but, since the genuineness of the handwriting must be proved,[77] and there are various defences open to the debtor,[78] it is submitted that, at least for these purposes, the holder of an IOU should not be treated as having a liquid debt.[79]

6.95 In one case the trustees under a contract of marriage, by which the deceased wife had assigned to them the whole estate then belonging to her, or which she might acquire during the marriage, were decerned and confirmed *qua* creditors to certain company shares which fell under the assignation, but which had not been transferred to the trustees.[80] In the seventh edition of this work, at p. 145, it was therefore concluded that the obligation need not be pecuniary and might be *ad factum praestandum* but this would appear to be contrary to the general principle set out at paragraph 6.83 above.

6.96 Where the obligation was created under the laws of another country, the court will require the opinion of an expert on the foreign law as to its validity. Thus, decerniture was granted to a creditor under a bill drawn and accepted in India and endorsed by the creditor in London, there being produced the opinion of an English barrister, skilled in Indian law, that the bill was in order, both as regards form and stamp, under Indian law.[81]

Illiquid debt
6.97 If the creditor has not a liquid ground of debt, his debt must first be constituted.

6.98 The 1695 Act anent Executry and Moveables enables the creditor

---

[75] *Trent*, Jan. 28, 1887, unreported.
[76] 7th ed., p. 145.
[77] Per Lord President Inglis in *Haldane* v. *Speirs* (1872) 10 M. 537 at p. 541.
[78] *The Scottish Law of Debt*, by W.A. Wilson (2nd ed.), para. 6.14.
[79] Cf. *Irvine* v. *K. & L.T.R.* (1949) 65 Sh. Ct. Rep. 53 where the holder of two IOUs was decerned executor-dative *qua* creditor.
[80] *Brash*, Oct. 7, 1887 unreported; *Jazdowski*, March 19, 1889, unreported.
[81] *Tod*, Nov. 20, 1885, unreported.

to constitute his claim by charging[82] all[83] of the deceased's next-of-kin[84] to confirm as executor to the deceased within 20 days. The next-of-kin must either confirm or renounce.[85] Unless the next-of-kin renounce, they will be treated as vitious intromitters.[86] The creditor may then proceed to have his debt constituted, and the *haereditas jacens* of moveables declared liable by a decree of *cognitionis causa*, and thereafter he may be decerned executor-dative to the deceased.

6.99   Under modern practice, the charge and subsequent renunciation of the next-of-kin may be dispensed with where the creditor restricts his claim to a decree *cognitionis causa tantum*[87] against all known next-of-kin.[88] In this context, "next-of-kin" must be taken to mean the heirs on intestacy under the laws of the deceased's domicile on death,[89] or the deceased's universal legatees.[90] Once decree *cognitionis causa tantum* has been granted, the debt, being now liquid, can be the basis of an application for confirmation as executor-creditor.

6.100   Where the deceased's widow was abroad, arrestments were used by the assignee of the creditor to found jurisdiction before the action of cognition could be brought.[91]

Full inventory

6.101   Every inventory given up by an executor-creditor must be a full and complete inventory of the estate, though the confirmation may be limited.

Partial confirmation

6.102   Section 4 of the Confirmation of Executors (Scotland) Act 1823[92] provides that, in the case of confirmation by an executor-

---

[82] The charge proceeds on letters passing under the signet. See *The Practice of the Sheriff Courts of Scotland in Civil Causes*, by John Dove Wilson (3rd ed.), p. 393, fn2.

[83] *Smith* v. *Tasker*, 1955 S.L.T. 347; *Stevens* v. *Thomson*, 1971 S.L.T. 135 (including those not subject to the jurisdiction of the Scottish courts); *cf.* Inner House decision of *Davidson, Pirie & Co.* v. *Dihle's Reps.* (1900) 2 F. 640 (where the creditors called *all* the known representatives of the deceased).

[84] *i.e.* the heirs on intestacy under the laws of the deceased's domicile on death (*per* Lord Kinloch in *Smith's Trs.* v. *Grant* (1862) 24 D. 1142 at p. 1156).

[85] *Davidson* v. *Clark* (1867) 6 M. 151.

[86] But only to the extent of the succession devolving on them (Lord Ordinary in *Davidson* v. *Clark*, above.

[87] *Per* Lord Guthrie in *Smith* v. *Tasker*, 1955 S.L.T. 347 at p. 348; *Forrest* v. *Forrest* (1863) 1 M. 806; *Ferrier* v. *Crockart*, 1937 S.L.T. 205.

[88] *Smith* v. *Tasker*, above; *Stevens* v. *Thomson*, 1971 S.L.T. 136.

[89] *Per* Lord Kinloch in *Smith's Trs.* v. *Grant* (1862) 24 D. 1142 at p. 1156.

[90] *Rodney*, June 3, 1887, unreported, where the only defenders called were the universal legatories.

[91] *Clarkson*, Feb. 1, 1889, unreported.

[92] 4 Geo. 4, c. 98.

creditor, such confirmation may be limited to the amount of the debt and the sum confirmed to which such creditor shall make oath, provided that notice of the petition for appointment as executor-creditor be inserted at least once in the *Edinburgh Gazette*. The first deliverance on the petition will order publication. The practice is to publish in the next *Gazette*. The advertisement must include the deliverance. There is no specified time thereafter for the case to call. A copy of the *Gazette* must be produced in court.

6.103 In the instructions issued by the Commissaries of Edinburgh, dated January 1, 1824, they directed that confirmation by an executor-creditor might comprehend no more of the inventory recorded than a sum equal in amount to the debt due and the expense of confirmation; in other words, it might be a confirmation to any extent the executor desired and the sheriff considered reasonable. Accordingly, although the inventory must disclose the whole of the deceased's estate, it is possible to confirm only to certain items in the inventory,[93] or to a portion of one item sufficient to meet the creditor's claim, as may be specified in the oath to the inventory.[94] The creditor need not depone to the verity of his debt, only to the inventory given up.[95]

6.104 While formerly an executor-creditor could confirm to moveable estate only, it now seems competent for the confirmation to include the deceased's heritable estate.[96]

6.105 Only the items of estate to which confirmation is craved in whole or in part are quoted in the grant of confirmation. An executor-creditor, like other executors-dative, is bound to recover the whole estate confirmed by him, and if he recovers more than sufficient to satisfy his claim, he is liable to account for the excess as an ordinary executor would.

6.106 A partial confirmation does not carry more than the sum confirmed. Where a creditor estimates the value of the item, and it subsequently transpires that the item is worth more and the debt was greater than the sum confirmed to, all that the creditor attaches is the value of the original estimate.[97]

6.107 A creditor confirming *ad omissa vel male appretiata* may call a creditor partially confirmed to account for what he has drawn beyond the sum confirmed.[98]

---

[93] *Macdonald*, Dec. 17, 1888, unreported; *Jazdowski*, March 19, 1889, unreported.
[94] *Bradley*, Feb. 10, 1880 and June 12, 1883, unreported.
[95] *Greig* v. *Christie* (1837) 15 S. 697.
[96] Succession (Scotland) Act 1964 (c. 41), s. 14; W.A. Wilson, *The Scottish Law of Debt* (2nd ed.), p. 301.
[97] *Smith's Trs.* v. *Grant* (1862) 24 D. 1142.
[98] *Lee* v. *Jones*, May 17, 1816, F.C.

6.108   A confirmation *ad male appretiata* was issued in favour of an executor-creditor, containing the same item of estate as had been confirmed in favour of another executor-creditor, but valued at £100 more. The additional value only was confirmed, and the first executor neither objected nor asked to be conjoined in the second confirmation.[99]

Bond of caution

6.109   Notwithstanding the terms of section 2 of the Confirmation of Executors (Scotland) Act 1823,[1] it is commissary practice that where the executor-creditor confirms to part of the deceased's estate, he must find caution to the extent of the total estate, even although he confirms to part only.

Ranking of diligence

6.110   Generally, a creditor of the deceased who is decerned *and* confirmed[2] as executor within six months of the death will have a preferential claim on the estate as against creditors who come along after the six month period has expired.[3] The preference covers not just the debt but also the expenses of the first executor-creditor's diligence.[4] The preference is, however, postponed to privileged debts.[5]

6.111   Other creditors with liquid debts can obtain an equality of ranking with the executor-creditor by—within the six month period—citing the executor-creditor[6] or being decerned and confirmed executor-creditor,[7] but they must bear a proportion of the expenses of the first executor-creditor's confirmation. The easiest method of another creditor securing this equality is for him to appear before the executor-creditor is confirmed, and to be conjoined in the confirmation as executor-creditor within the six months.[8] Even if the executor-creditor has realised the asset to which he confirmed, he has to distribute its proceeds rateably among all the creditors entitled to rank with him.[9]

---

[99] *Malcolm*, Nov. 30, 1878, unreported.

[1] Confirmation of Executors (Scotland) Act 1823 (4 Geo. 4, c. 98), s. 2, as amended by Statute Law Revision Act 1888 (57 Vict. c. 3) Sched., Part I and Law Reform (Miscellaneous Provisions) (Scotland) Act 1980 (c. 55), s. 5.

[2] Decerniture without confirmation gives no preference: Bell, *Comm.*, ii, 81, *Willison* v. *Dewar* (1840) 3D. 273.

[3] Act of Sederunt of February 28, 1662; see *Sanderson* v. *Lockhart-Mure*, 1946 S.C. 298.

[4] *Wilson and Ross* v. *Taylor and Fraser* (1809) Hume 172.

[5] Stair, III.viii.64; *Crawford* v. *Hutton* (1680) Mor. 11832.

[6] Act of Sederunt, of February 28, 1662; *Ramsay* v. *Nairn* (1708) Mor. 3934.

[7] Act of Sederunt of February 28, 1662; see *Sanderson* v. *Lockhart-Mure*, 1946 S.C. 298; but if the executor has not confirmed, citing within the six month period will have no effect: *McDowal* v. *Creditors of McDowal* (1742, Feb. 19) Mor. 3936.

[8] *Lee* v. *Jones*, May 17, 1816, F.C.

[9] *Ramsay* v. *Nairn* (1708) Mor. 3934.

6.112   If no executor-creditor confirms within the six month period, the first to do so thereafter obtains a preference. Once the six month period has expired, confirmation in favour of an executor-nominate or an ordinary executor-dative who is himself a creditor, is as good as confirmation *qua* executor-creditor—so giving him a prior right to any funds in his hands before a judicial claim or diligence by other creditors.[10] Creditors who cite the executor-creditor after the six months are ranked *pari passu inter se* if the one has not obtained decree before citation by the other.[11]

6.113   Neither the dependence of an action of multiplepoinding nor the consignation of the funds prevents the funds being subsequently attached by an executor-creditor confirming to it.[12]

6.114   Where a creditor of the deceased confirms within a year and a day of the death, he has priority to a creditor of the deceased's next-of-kin who confirms thereafter.[13]

6.115   If, within 12 months of the death, the deceased's estate has been sequestrated, or a judicial factor has been appointed under section 11A of the Judicial Factors (Scotland) Act 1889 to administer an estate which is absolutely insolvent, an executor-creditor has no preference on the funds confirmed to, as against the permanent trustee or judicial factor, but he is entitled to the expenses incurred in obtaining confirmation.[14]

V. Executor-dative *qua* funerator

6.116   Confirmation as executor-dative *qua* funerator is held to be competent only in small estates where the next-of-kin are unknown or unable to act, or, after due intimation, do not claim the office of executor. See Style 6.31.

6.117   The applicant must aver all he has been able to ascertain about the relatives of the deceased, and whether they decline to act. If there are no known next-of-kin, intimation requires to be made to the Queen's and Lord Treasurer's Remembrancer.

6.118   In order to establish his right, the applicant must produce:

1.   where the applicant is the undertaker, his own account;

---

[10] *Macleod* v. *Wilson* (1837) 15 S. 1043; Bell, *Comm.*, II.v.3.3(2).1; *McDowall* v. *Creditors of McDowall* (1744, Dec. 21) Mor. 3936.
[11] *Graeme* v. *Murray* (1738) Mor. 3141.
[12] *Smith's Trs.* v. *Grant* (1862) 24 D. 1142.
[13] 1695 Act anent Executry and Moveables (c. 41).
[14] Bankruptcy (Scotland) Act 1985 (c. 66), s. 37 (9). See also Judicial Factors (Scotland) Act 1889 (c. 39), s. 11A (2), inserted by Bankruptcy (Scotland) Act 1985 (c. 66), s. 51 and Sched. 1.

2. where the applicant has paid the undertaker's account, the receipted account.

Where the applicant has already been reimbursed for the funeral account, decerniture *qua* funerator is incompetent.

6.119   Intimation is made in the *Edinburgh Gazette* and in such other papers as the sheriff may consider necessary. See Style 6.31.

6.120   Where a funerator had been decerned but not confirmed, a next-of-kin who appeared was preferred, and the funerator's appointment was recalled, without expenses, on the ground that he had not communicated the death to the next-of-kin.[15]

VI. Executor-dative *qua* special legatee

6.121   Under this heading all legatees other than general disponees, universal legatories or residuary legatees can be appointed as executors-dative.[16] This category includes a person to whom the deceased has bequeathed a specific article, investment or debt, or upon whom he has conferred any limited interest, such as of liferent[17] or of fee.

VII. The procurator fiscal as executor-dative

6.122   A procurator fiscal is entitled to be confirmed as executor-dative, if no one else comes forward[18] but this process has probably fallen into desuetude, having been superseded by the heirs applying for the appointment of a judicial factor.[19] Since most of the cases in which it might be appropriate for a procurator fiscal to be confirmed are those where it would appear that the estate has fallen to the Crown as *ultimus haeres*, the procurator fiscal would, in such a case, pass the papers to the Queen's and Lord Treasurer's Remembrancer.

6.123   The 1695 Act anent Executry and Moveables enabled the creditors of the next-of-kin, where the next-of-kin did not confirm to the deceased's moveables to require the procurator fiscal to

---

[15] *Pyper*, March 4, 1869, unreported.

[16] Ersk., III.ix.32; Bell, *Comm.*, ii, 78 (5th ed.); *for* Lord Rutherford Clark in *Stewart* v. *Kerr* (1890) 17 R. 707 at p. 708.

[17] Even if the liferenter has power to dispose of part of it: *McGown* v. *McKinlay* (1835) 14 S. 105.

[18] "Orders to be Observed in the Confirmation of all Testaments" forming part of the instructions to the commissaries, issued in 1666 by the archbishops and bishops with the authority of the supreme court (Acts of Sederunt, Vol. 1, 1553 to 1790, p. 99).

[19] Ersk., III.ix.32; McLaren, *Wills and Succession*, Vol. II, para. 1587.

confirm and assign to them, under the peril and pain of his being liable for the debt, if he refused.

6.124 Every petition for the appointment of a procurator fiscal of court as executor-dative should set out the parties at whose request, and the circumstances under which, it is presented. If it appears that the deceased died without any known legal representatives, and that the Crown may have an interest as *ultimus haeres*, special intimation must be made to the Queen's and Lord Treasurer's Remembrancer.[20] In a case where the deceased person had left considerable personal estate, and no executor-nominate or heir on intestacy applied for confirmation, the procurator fiscal was, at the instance of persons having claims against the deceased, decerned and confirmed as executor. He thereafter realised the estate, and, since the deceased was illegitimate and had never married, it was handed over to the Crown.[21]

Procurator fiscal as executor where intestate's spouse has disappeared

6.125 It has been seen (paras. 6.27–6.43) that the current practice of treating the deceased's surviving spouse, whose prior rights would exhaust the whole intestate estate, as the person having the exclusive right to be appointed executor-dative produces difficulties where the surviving spouse has disappeared. Traders who seek to recover the deceased's funeral account and debts may be decerned as executors-creditor, but if the deceased's family have paid these accounts, they may not be decerned as executors-creditors. It is suggested that if the procurator fiscal were decerned, he would be able to reimburse the family for such outlays.

[20] Order by Commissary dated May 28, 1872.
[21] *Grant*, Dec. 29, 1870, unreported.

CHAPTER 7

THE FORM AND PROCEDURE IN DATIVE PETITIONS

Introduction

7.01   This chapter contains a discussion of the procedure to be adopted when an executor-dative is to be decerned. It should be remembered that, in all cases where it is clear that the estate is absolutely insolvent (*i.e.* the deceased's liabilities are greater than his assets[1]), it is inappropriate to proceed with a dative petition, for section 8(4) of the Bankruptcy (Scotland) Act 1985 denies any protection to an executor decerned in such circumstances (see, further, paras. 1.49–1.56).

How many executors-dative can be appointed?

7.02   While the normal practice is for one individual to seek appointment as executor-dative, it is competent for the sheriff to appoint more than one executor-dative, provided that each can prove that he or she is entitled to be decerned.[2] They may be decerned in different capacities.[3]

7.03   Confirmation in favour of two or more executors-dative enures to the survivors, on the death of one.[4] Hence, the appointment of more than one executor-dative saves the inconvenience and expense of having an executor *ad non executa* appointed where the sole executor-dative dies before the administration of the estate is concluded. For this reason, the appointment of more than one executor-dative should be sought where it is anticipated that the administration of the estate will take a number of years. However if one of two or more executors dies after being decerned but before being confirmed, it will be necessary to have the appointment recalled, and the surviving executor and executors decerned of new.

---

[1] Bankruptcy (Scotland) Act 1985 (c. 66), s. 73 (2).
[2] *Per* Lord President Inglis in *Muir, Petr.* (1876) 4 R. 74 at p. 75.
[3] *Muir, Petr.* (1876) 4 R. 74.
[4] Executors (Scotland) Act 1900 (63 & 64 Vict. c. 55), s. 4.

No limited appointment of an executor-dative

7.04 While in England it is possible for an executor to be appointed for a limited period only (*e.g.* pending the outcome of litigation), in Scotland, there is no such thing as a limited appointment of an executor-dative.[5] Once decerned and confirmed, an executor-dative will go on to complete the entire administration of the estate,[6] and may not resign office.[7]

Problem categories of executors-dative

7.05 Certain executries present particular problems in identifying the appropriate person to be appointed executor-dative—some relating to the lack of legal capacity of the eligible parties (such as those who are *incapax*, or who are under the age of 16 years) and others relating to the fact that the eligible parties run the risk of becoming *auctor in rem suam* if they take up office (such as where the deceased was a tenant farmer and the potential executor may wish the lease transferred to himself). These and similar issues are explored more fully in Chapter 8.

Which court?

7.06 A petition for the appointment of an executor-dative shall be presented to the sheriff clerk of the sheriffdom in which the deceased died domiciled or, where the deceased died domiciled furth of Scotland, or though domiciled in Scotland, died without any fixed or known domicile there, to the commissary clerk in Edinburgh.[8]

7.07 Each sheriffdom is divided into districts for ordinary sheriff court purposes. Where the deceased died domiciled in a particular sheriffdom, the petition should be presented to the sheriff clerk of the sheriff court district[9] in which the deceased died domiciled. But where there is doubt as to the sheriff court district in which the deceased was domiciled on death, the petition may be presented to the sheriff clerk of any district within the sheriffdom.[10]

---

[5] *Johnston's Exr.* v. *Dobie*, 1907 S.C. 31.
[6] *Whiffin* v. *Lees* (1872) 10 M. 797, *per* Lord Ardmillan at p. 802 and Lord Kinloch at p. 803.
[7] Succession (Scotland) Act 1964 (c. 41), s. 20.
[8] Confirmation of Executors (Scotland) Act 1858 (21 & 22 Vict. c. 56), s. 3; Act of Sederunt (Confirmation of Executors) 1964 (S.I. 1964 No. 1143).
[9] See paras. 1.58–1.69 for list of courts attending to commissary business.
[10] Act of Sederunt (Commissary Business) 1975 (S.I. 1975 No. 539), s. 3 (2).

Who may raise the petition?

7.08   See generally Chapter 6. The petition must be subscribed by the petitioner or his agent.[11] There may be more than one petitioner.

Preparation of petition: Petition to be in proper form

7.09   The form of the petition for the appointment of an executor-dative should be in the form set out in Schedule 2 to the Act of Sederunt (Confirmation of Executors) 1964.[12] It is therefore necessary for the pursuer to show

1. the place where the deceased died (see, below, paras. 7.10—7.15);

2. the date of the deceased's death (see, below, paras. 7.10–7.16);

3. whether the deceased died intestate (and if not, details of his testamentary writings with the pursuer's right to be decerned executor-dative being related to the terms of the testamentary writings[13]) (see, below, para. 7.17);

4. the deceased's domicile at death (see, below, paras. 7.18–7.29);

5. the relationship, character or title of the pursuer which gives him right to apply to be appointed executor (see paras. 7.15 and 7.30–7.39).

Averment as to place and date of death

7.10   It is necessary to aver that the person died at a specified place and on a specified date.[14] No proof will be required unless the averment is challenged.

7.11   Normally, the place of death is clear and will be revealed on

---

[11] Confirmation of Executors (Scotland) Act 1858 (21 & 22 Vict. c. 56), s. 2, as amended by Statute Law Revision Act 1892 (55 & 56 Vict. c. 19), Sched. In due course, the petition may also be subscribed by an executry practitioner or a recognised financial institution providing executry services within the meaning of s. 23 of the Law Reform (Miscellaneous Provisions) (Scotland) Act 1990 (c. 40), s. 74 (1) Sched. 8, para. 22 (1).

[12] S.I. 1984 No. 1143.

[13] In *Jerdon* v. *Forrest* (1897) 24 R. 395 the court confirmed the deceased's sister as executor-dative *qua* next-of-kin, although there existed a holograph will which could be interpreted as meaning that someone else was appointed as general disponee and universal legatory (and as such, entitled to confirmation).

[14] *Knox*, Dec. 23, 1873, unreported.

the death certificate. If the deceased died in a road accident, it would be sufficient to aver that the deceased died "on the A123 public road between the towns of x and y" or "on the A123 public road near the village of x." If he died aboard a vessel at sea, or on an offshore installation, then the averment should be to the effect that the deceased "died aboard [ship], latitude x, longitude y" or should otherwise show the position of the ship or rig. And if in an aeroplane, the averment should specify the actual position (if known) or an approximate position, such as "40 miles west of Lisbon," "over Dieppe" or "over northern France."

7.12   Normally, too, the date of death is clear, the most frequently occurring case where there is doubt being where the deceased's body was not found for days or even weeks after the death. In such cases, the wording of the death certificate should be followed.

Missing person

7.13   A further case of difficulty is where no body is found. In this case, the requirement to state the place and date of death is dispensed with, provided that the pursuer avers that to the best of his or her knowledge and belief the person is dead, and further avers that there is produced

1.   A duly certified copy of a decree or judgment issued by a court in any country furth of Scotland in which the person was domiciled or habitually resident on the date on which he was last known to be alive, declaring that the person has died or is presumed to have died, or has died or is presumed to have died on a specified date or within a specified period[15]; or

2.   A certificate or intimation issued by or on behalf of a competent authority within the United Kingdom that the person has died, is presumed to have died, or is lost or missing in circumstances affording reasonable ground for the belief that he has died as a result of an incident in or in connection with a ship, aircraft, hovercraft or offshore installation.[16]
     This provision enables the estate of a person who has been lost in a ship, aircraft, hovercraft or offshore installation to be wound up without a formal action of declarator of death, provided that there has been a formal and exhaustive investigation. The competent authorities are

---

[15] Presumption of Death (Scotland) Act 1977 (c. 27), ss. 10 and 11.
[16] *Ibid.*, s. 11.

the Registrar General for Shipping and Seamen,[17] where the deceased died on board ship or was an employee on a United Kingdom registered or owned ship[18] or died on or near an offshore installation, or an emergency survival craft belonging to an offshore installation[19]; the Civil Aviation Authority, where the deceased died in any part of the world in an aircraft registered in the United Kingdom, or the deceased was a passenger in a United Kingdom registered aircraft who died outside the United Kingdom as a result of an accident[20]; and the Department of Trade and Industry, where the deceased died aboard a United Kingdom registered hovercraft or in its lifeboat or liferaft.[21]

An action of declarator

7.14   Alternatively, where an action of declarator of the death of a person who was missing and was thought to have died, or was not known to be alive for a period of at least seven years, has been brought in a Scottish court,[22] the decree (if granted) will either state the time and place of death, or that the missing person died at the end of the day occurring seven years after the date on which he was last known to be alive.[23] The petition for the appointment of an executor-dative to the person declared dead will disclose the date of death as being in accordance with the decree, and an extract of the decree must be produced.

7.15   As part of the action of declarator, the court may also determine the domicile of the missing person at his death,[24] and any question relating to any interest in property arising as a consequence of the death of the missing person.[25] Unless the court determines otherwise, insurance cover must be taken out against the risk of any person having an interest seeking to have the decree

---

[17] St Agnes Road, Gabalfa, Cardiff CF4 4UX.

[18] S.I. 1979 No. 1577.

[19] S.I. 1972 No. 1542.

[20] S.I. 1948 No. 1411 ("aircraft" includes balloons, gliders, airships etc.).

[21] S.I. 1972 No. 1513 (also of U.K. citizens on hovercraft which is carrying passengers to or from the U.K. and which is not registered in the U.K.).

[22] Presumption of Death (Scotland) Act 1977 (c. 27), s. 1 (3) (Court of Session) and 1 (4) (Sheriff Court); under s. 1 (3) such an action may be brought where either

   (a)   the missing person was domiciled in Scotland on the date on which he was last known to be alive, or had been habitually resident there throughout the period of one year ending with that date; or

   (b)   the action was raised by the spouse of the missing person, who was domiciled in Scotland at the date of raising the action, or was habitually resident there throughout the period of one year ending with that date.

[23] Presumption of Death (Scotland) Act 1977 (c. 27), s. 2 (1).

[24] *Ibid.*, s. 2 (2).

[25] *Ibid.*

varied or recalled[26]—in this way, heirs who receive the deceased's estate from the executor are protected against their inheritance subsequently being reclaimed if the person declared dead were subsequently to reappear.

Common calamities

7.16   Where two or more people die in a common calamity, the exact times when the deaths occurred may be critical for they will often determine, in the case of an intestacy, whether one of the deceased persons will inherit the other's estate (see, further, paras. 6.67 *et seq.*), and who is entitled to be decerned as executor-dative. If it is impossible to show either from the death certificates or by proving on the balance of probabilities that one survived the other, the presumptions set out in section 31 of the Succession (Scotland) Act 1964 applies and must be set out in the petition (see Style 6.29).

Averment that the deceased died intestate (and if not, details of his testamentary writings with the pursuer's right to be decerned executor-dative being related to the terms of the testamentary writings)

7.17   See Styles 6.01, 6.02 and 6.32 for avernments where deceased left a testamentary writing.

Averment as to the deceased's domicile at death

7.18   The domicile of the deceased must be averred in order to determine the jurisdiction.[27] In all cases, the designation of the deceased in the crave of the petition should bear out the averment on domicile, otherwise the reasons for averring the domicile should be set out in the petition, and further evidence on the question of domicile may be required. Frequently, an accommodation address such as "care of" a bank or firm of solicitors is given in the deceased's designation, and while these addresses may be required in the confirmation for the purpose of identifying the deceased as the owner of certain investments, they are not sufficient to set up a domicile for the deceased.

Scottish domicile, in particular sheriffdom
7.19   Normally, the averment will be that "the deceased was domi-

---

[26] Presumption of Death (Scotland) Act 1977 (c. 27), s. 6.
[27] Confirmation of Executors (Scotland) Act 1858 (21 & 22 Vict. c. 56), s. 3, as amended by Act of Sederunt (Confirmation of Executors) 1964 (S.I. 1964 No. 1143) and as read with the Sheriff Courts (Scotland) Act 1876 (39 & 40 Vict. c. 70), s. 35 and the Sheriff Courts (Scotland) Act 1971 (c. 58), s. 46 (1), Sched. 1, para. 1.

ciled in the Sheriffdom of x in Scotland." Where the place of residence given for the deceased is within the sheriffdom in which it is averred that he died domiciled, then no difficulty arises. However, if it is stated that he resided in a sheriffdom other than that averred for the domicile, then the reasons for making the averment of domicile must be given.

Scottish domicile but uncertainty as to sheriffdom

7.20   If the deceased died domiciled in Scotland, but it is unclear in which particular sheriffdom the deceased died domiciled, it is usual to aver that the deceased died "without any fixed or known domicile except that the same was in Scotland"; such an averment not only brings the case within the jurisdiction of the Commissary Court in Edinburgh, but also shows that the title of the applicant must be determined by the law of Scotland, so that no statement as to the law of the domicile is required.

7.21   The deceased's designation should bring out the averment of uncertain domicile. For instance, if the deceased had been a long term patient in a mental hospital, there might be doubt about the sheriffdom in which he was domiciled[28] and the deceased's last residential address in Scotland should be given, followed by the last address as "latterly temporarily residing at [mental hospital]" or "latterly a patient at [mental hospital]." If a previous Scottish address is not known, then, if appropriate, the deceased should be described as "a native of Scotland."

Scottish domicile though resident abroad

7.22   Where the deceased retained his Scottish domicile, but died while resident abroad, the court in Edinburgh has exclusive jurisdiction. In such cases, it must be averred that the deceased had no fixed or known domicile except that the same was in Scotland, and that he died resident abroad. In order to bear out the averment on domicile, in addition to stating his last residential address abroad, either his previous residential address in Scotland should be stated or, if appropriate, he should be described as "a native of Scotland."

Domicile not in Scotland

7.23   Where it is averred that "the deceased was domiciled in [country other than Scotland]," the court in Edinburgh has exclusive jurisdiction.

7.24   The documents which require to be put up with the petition depend on whether or not a grant of probate (or representation) has been issued in the country of the deceased's domicile (see paras. 2.62 *et seq.* for details).

---

[28] *e.g. Crumpton's J.F.* v. *Finch-Noyes*, 1918 S.C. 378, where the court, faced with determining the deceased's domicile on death, considered only his activities prior to being detained.

7.25   It should be noted that when confirmation is obtained to the estate of a person who died domiciled abroad, only Scottish estate may be confirmed to.

Country of domicile uncertain

7.26   Where there is uncertainty as to the country of the deceased's domicile, the court in Edinburgh has exclusive jurisdiction. The averment will be that the deceased "was without any fixed or known domicile." This is understood to mean that the domicile has not been ascertained. In all such cases, the cause of the uncertainty should be succinctly stated in the initial writ.

7.27   Where the domicile is uncertain, it generally arises in an alternative form, for example, where it is averred that the deceased was domiciled either in Scotland or in another country (where he was residing at the time of his death). In such cases, it is necessary to state the law as to who would be entitled to act as executor under each legal system which might be appropriate. The opinion of an expert on the foreign legal system must be produced. If it should appear that, under one foreign legal system, someone other than the applicant might possibly fall to be preferred, the consent of that other person should be produced.

7.28   If the deceased had only settled in Scotland a short time before his death, it may be unclear whether he was domiciled in Scotland (in the sheriffdom where he was living) or in the country where he was domiciled before he arrived in Scotland. This is a thoroughly awkward case, for if he had been domiciled in a particular sheriffdom, the sheriff court in that sheriffdom would have privative jurisdiction in commissary matters, whereas if he had been domiciled abroad, the court in Edinburgh would have had jurisdiction. Consequently, proceeding on the basis of an alternative domicile in such circumstances is impossible, and it will be necessary to proceed on the basis of a domicile in one or other place.

7.29   In all cases where the country of the deceased's domicile is uncertain (even if one of the countries is Scotland), when confirmation is obtained, it will be noted that only Scottish estate may be confirmed to.

Averment as to the relationship, character or title of the pursuer which gives him right to apply to be appointed executor

7.30   The pursuer must aver what relationship, character or title he has which gives him the right to apply for confirmation as executor.

7.31   Under the regulations issued by the Commissaries of Edinburgh in 1817 in relation to edicts, but now applied to initial writs, it is necessary to specify "the degree of propinquity of the (petitioner) to the deceased, and by whom related" and, if the petitioner is a creditor, "the ground of debt shall be specially narrated in it; if at the instance of a disponee or legatee the deed under which he claims to be confirmed shall also be specially mentioned." Further, it was ordered that the documents founded on had to be produced before decerniture. The application of these regulations has occasionally revealed the fact that the applicant has no right or title to the office or to share in the succession to the deceased's estate.

7.32   The averments must show that there is no individual who has a subsisting prior claim to the office of executor.[29] While in a case where heirs under the Succession (Scotland) Act 1964, who are of different degrees of propinquity to the deceased compete for the office of executor-dative, the heir of the closest degree will be preferred,[30] any heir sharing in the estate may be decerned, if there is no competition. Indeed, with the consent of the heir who has a preferential claim to the office, two persons may be decerned as executors-dative, in different capacities (see further paras. 7.38–7.39).

7.32A   Where the pursuer is seeking appointment by virtue of his right to share in the intestate estate of the deceased, the averments must eliminate all categories of persons who, if they had survived the deceased, would have had a prior claim to the office of executor, and must detail all surviving relatives of the deceased, though neither their names nor addresses need be given.[31] The court will determine who is entitled to the office on the basis of these averments,[32] without hearing parole evidence,[33] and that whether the relationship involves an illegitimate link[34] or not. As Sheriff Lees stated:

> "If the pursuer claims to be one of the next-of-kin of the deceased, and furnishes the few particulars which the statute desiderates, and if on publication there is no challenge made, then I am afraid there is no alternative but to decern in the executry as craved. Others of equal degree of kinship may apply to be conjoined, or, where the applicant is subject to some special disqualification, persons with an interest to object to the appointment may come forward and object if confirmation has not issued. But where the petition does not disclose that there is someone with a prior title,

---

[29] Act of Sederunt (Confirmation of Executors) 1964 (S.I. 1964 No. 1143), Sched. 2, Cond. 2, note thereto.
[30] Succession (Scotland) Act 1964 (c. 41), s. 5 (2).
[31] *Henderson, Petr.* (1906) 22 Sh. Ct. Rep. 186.
[32] *McLaughlin, Petr.*, 1987 S.L.T. (Sh. Ct.) 87; *Henderson, Petr.* (1906) 22 Sh. Ct. Rep. 186.
[33] *Smith, Petr.*, 1979 S.L.T. (Sh. Ct.) 35.
[34] *McLaughlin, Petr.*, 1987 S.L.T. (Sh. Ct.) 87. See, further, at paras. 6.58–6.62.

or that the applicant himself is subject to some disqualification, then I think the Court has no option but to decern."[35]

7.33 Thus, the court has refused to decern the deceased's uncle as executor-dative where the averments disclosed that there was in existence a child whose birth certificate showed the deceased as being her father.[36]

7.34 Where the petitioner and the deceased are related through an illegitimate birth or an adoption, current commissary practice does not require any specific averment — except to the extent necessary to explain differences in the parties's surnames (see para. 7.36). Thus, an illegitimate child can petition to be executor of his or her father, and only if they had different surnames will it be necessary to aver that the petitioner is the illegitimate child of the deceased.

The averments

7.35 In satisfying the court that the petitioner is entitled to be decerned as executor-dative, it is necessary to eliminate all possible categories of persons who would have had a prior claim to the office of executor. For instance, if the petitioner is the deceased's son, it would be sufficient to aver that the deceased was a widow (or widower); or, if the petitioner is the deceased's sister, that the deceased died unmarried and without issue. If a person — such as the deceased's spouse — who has a prima facie prior claim to the office of executor, has or may have survived the deceased, his right must be eliminated. One of the following averments may be appropriate in the case of eliminating the rights of the spouse:

1. The deceased was married. Having died in circumstances rendering it uncertain which survived the other, the surviving spouse is, in terms of section 31 of the Succession (Scotland) Act 1964, presumed not to have survived the deceased (see, further, paras. 6.67–6.71);

2. The deceased was married. The surviving spouse has forfeited his right to inherit by virtue of killing the deceased,[37] and has not obtained an order under the Forfeiture Act 1982 (see, further, paras. 6.74–6.76);

3. The deceased was married. The surviving spouse has declined office and has consented to the pursuer acting[38] — or his *curator bonis* has so done on his behalf.

---

[35] *Henderson, Petr.* (1906) 22 Sh. Ct. Rep. 186 at p. 187.
[36] *Smith, Petr.*, 1979 S.L.T. (Sh. Ct.) 35.
[37] *Ibid.*
[38] See *Forrest* (Feb. 28, 1966), unreported, noted at para. 6.39. The declinature and consent would require to be put up as productions.

7.35A   More usually, the petitioner will be one of many parties who is entitled to the office of executor, and then an averment in the form of the second variation to condescencence 3 of Style 6.06 would be expected.

Practical tips

7.36   **(a) Family relationship** Though not essential, it is good practice when a petitioner is seeking appointment on the basis either of rights of succession to the deceased's intestate estate, or of being the next-of-kin of the deceased, to show a linkage between the petitioner's surname and the deceased's surname: for instance, where a married sister seeks to be decerned executor-dative *qua* sister to her brother, John Smith, she should be designed as "Mrs Jean Smith or Brown." A copy of the family tree may also be helpful.

7.37   **(b) Is the deceased survived by a spouse?** In petitioning for the appointment of an executor to a person who has been married, it is necessary to bear in mind the current commissary practice of treating certain surviving spouses as having the exclusive right to be decerned as executor-dative.[39] Consequently, if the petitioner is not the deceased's surviving spouse, it is necessary to aver either:

1.   that "the deceased died unmarried"; or

2.   that "the deceased was divorced from his wife/her husband on [date] conform to certificate of divorce dated [date] from [court]" and the extract decree of divorce should be produced[40]; or

3.   that "the deceased was survived by his wife/her husband, but that the estate of the deceased exceeds the prior rights of the surviving spouse"; or

4.   the reason why the application is not being made by the surviving spouse.

7.38   **(c) Two petitioners** It has been established that two persons, each of whom might have been separately decerned as executors-dative, though in different characters, may be jointly decerned,[41] though if one (such as the surviving spouse) has a prior claim, he or she must consent to the joint appointment.

---

[39] Succession (Scotland) Act 1964 (c. 41), s. 9 (2) and (4); *Kerr, Petr.*, 1968 S.L.T. (Sh. Ct.) 61; see fuller discussion at paras. 6.28 *et seq.*

[40] The requirement to produce an extract decree of divorce sits oddly with the practice, described at paras. 6.61, 7.30 and 7.32A that only averments as to the relatives of the deceased are required.

[41] *Per* Lord President Inglis in *Muir, Petr.* (1876) 4 R. 74 at p. 75.

7.39   **(d) Claimant by representation** Where the issue of a deceased person are entitled to represent their parent in the succession to the intestate estate in terms of section 5(1) Succession (Scotland) Act 1964, if there is competition, their right to be appointed executor-dative is postponed to anyone inheriting directly.[42] Thus, if an intestate estate fell to be shared equally by the deceased's father (as sole surviving parent) and the deceased's nephew (as the only child of the deceased's only brother who had predeceased him, the deceased having no sisters) the deceased's father would be preferred to the office of executor in preference to the nephew, if there was competition. If there was no competition, that nephew would be decerned—the consent of the deceased's father not being required.

Judicial discretion to select an executor?

7.40   The question of whether the court has any limited jurisdiction to select an executor-dative, not from within those of the first degree of preference, but from "persons in the neighbouring orders of preference upon discretional grounds" is probably still open.[43]

Productions with the petition

7.41   Where the pursuer is seeking to be decerned as executor-dative in a capacity other than as a relative of the deceased, he must produce with the petition prima facie evidence of his title to the office[44]—such as the testamentary writing appointing him general disponee, universal legatory or residuary legatee or, if he is the deceased's creditor, the documents vouching the debts.[45] If the deceased's body was never found, the appropriate certified copy decree or judgment or certificate or intimation must be produced (see paras. 7–13–7.14).

7.42   Where productions are to be lodged, an inventory of productions should be prepared.

Court dues for petition

7.43   The petition should be presented with the appropriate dues,[46] currently £9.00.

---

[42] Succession (Scotland) Act 1964 (c. 41), s. 5 (2).
[43] *Per* Lord Mackay in *Crolla, Petr.*, 1942 S.C. 21 at pp. 24–25.
[44] See *dicta* of Lord President Robertson in *Martin* v. *Ferguson's Trs.* (1892) 19 R. 474 at p. 478 reproduced at para. 6.02.
[45] Dobie, *Sheriff Court Practice*, p. 437.
[46] S.I. 1992 No. 413.

Intimation of petition

General

7.44 Every petition for the appointment of an executor must be intimated, and for this purpose it is necessary to put up two plain
copies of the petition when lodging it. The petition shall be
intimated by the sheriff clerk affixing a full copy of it on the
door of the sheriff court house, or in some conspicuous place
of the court or of the office of the sheriff clerk, in such manner
as the sheriff shall direct.[47] Thereafter, the sheriff clerk will certify this fact on the petition by docketing it: "Intimated and
published in terms of the statute," dating it and signing it, and
this will be sufficient evidence of such intimation.[48]

Special

7.45 Statute requires all executors already decerned or confirmed to
the deceased person to be given special intimation of any subsequent petition presented for the appointment of an executor
with reference to the estate of the same deceased person.[49] In
practice, intimation will also be made even if decree or confirmation has not been granted. A person who has lodged a
caveat will also receive intimation of the petition and, occasionally, the sheriff may require the petition to be intimated to
specified persons. In all cases, intimation will be effected by
first class recorded delivery,[50-51] with a notice to the following
effect printed on the envelope:

> "This letter contains an intimation from [specify court]. If
> delivery of the letter cannot be made at the address shown
> it is to be returned immediately to [give the official name
> and office or place of business of the clerk of court]."[52]

7.46 Except where the sheriff so directs, there is no need to intimate
the petition to all persons who would have an equal right along
with the pursuer to seek appointment as executor-dative—such

---

[47] Act of Sederunt (Edictal Citations, Commissary Petitions and Petitions of
Service) 1971, s. 2 (2) (S.I. 1971 No. 1165). Thus, by order dated August 12, 1971,
the sheriff principal of Lothians and Peebles directed that petitions presented in
the commissariot of Edinburgh shall be intimated by full copies being affixed
to the notice boards of the sheriff court house, Edinburgh, and of the commissary office, Edinburgh.

[48] Sheriff Courts (Scotland) Act 1876 (39 & 40 Vict. c. 70), s. 44, as amended
by Act of Sederunt (Confirmation of Executors Amendment No. 2) 1971, s. 2
(S.I. 1971 No. 1655).

[49] Sheriff Courts (Scotland) Act 1876 (39 & 40 Vict. c. 70), s. 44, as amended
by Act of Sederunt (Confirmation of Executors Amendment No. 2) 1971, s. 2
(S.I. 1971 No. 1655).

[50-51] Sheriff Courts (Scotland) Act 1907 (7 Edw. 7 c. 51), Sched. 5.3(1) (as substituted by S.I. 1993 No. 1956).

[52] Sheriff Courts (Scotland) Act 1907 (7 Edw. 7, c. 51), Sched. r. 5.3(3) (as
substituted by S.I. 1993 No. 1956).

as all others sharing the deceased's estate along with the petitioner.

Procedure where the executry petition is unopposed

7.47 In normal course, the executor-dative will be decerned nine days after the sheriff or commissary clerk has certified intimation and publication of the petition for the appointment of the executor-dative.[53] The procedure in unopposed commissary cases is that set out in the Act of Sederunt (Unopposed Executory Petitions) 1948[54]:

> "that in all petitions for the appointment of an executor or executors to a deceased person where intimation and publication have been duly made and a certificate of intimation and publication has been duly endorsed upon the petition by the Sheriff Clerk or Commissary Clerk, and nine clear days have expired from the date of such certification without any answers to the petition, and no competing petition or caveat has been lodged . . . it shall not be necessary for the petition or application to be called in Court or for the petitioner or applicant or his solicitor to attend . . ., but the petition . . . may be laid by the Sheriff Clerk or Commissary Clerk before the Sheriff in Chambers, who, if satisfied that the petition . . . is in proper form and that the proceedings have been regular, may, without hearing any party, decern the Petitioner or Petitioners, executor or executors . . . as craved, or may, in his discretion direct the petition or application to be called and heard in Court *quam primum*."

The procedure where the executry petition is opposed

7.48 Anyone who wishes to be conjoined in or to compete for the appointment should lodge a notice of appearance within the *induciae*, and should at the same time present a petition for his own appointment as executor-dative. The procedure is more fully discussed at paras. 19.10–19.14.

7.49 The Edinburgh practice where intimation is ordered is to include in the first deliverance an order for objections within, normally, 14 days, and in this event, there is no need for a notice of appearance.

[53] Confirmation of Executors (Scotland) Act 1858 (21 & 22 Vict. c. 56), s. 6.
[54] S.I. 1948 No. 621.

Possible grounds of challenge

7.50   The pursuer's competence or age (provided he or she is over 16 years) is not a relevant ground of challenge:

> "I do not think that . . . we have anything to do with the comparative capacity of the respective claimants to administer an estate. That is not a relevant consideration. Lady Denman is the next of kin, and is entitled to be confirmed as executor, unless anyone having a prior title comes forward to defeat her claim. Whether she is incapacitated by age or infirmity for the permanent administration of an estate is a different question."[55]

7.51   Likewise, the fact that the pursuer is resident overseas will not be a bar on the pursuer being decerned executor-dative:

> "The only objection stated to X being appointed is that she is resident in Canada. We are told that she is not settled there permanently, and that she intends to return to this country. In any case, she cannot be decerned executor-dative without finding caution, and the actual management of the estate is a matter of business which will be carried on by business men in the ordinary way."[56]

7.52   There are undoubted problems if a challenger seeks to establish that the relationship between the pursuer and the deceased is not as craved. In practice, such a challenge will usually only occur if it is alleged that the one is not the father of the other. It is to be remembered that since December 8, 1986, the law presumes that:

1.   a man is the father of a child if he was married to the child's mother at any time between the child's conception and birth[57]; and

2.   a man is the father of a child if he and the child's mother both acknowledged that he was the father, and he is shown as such in the Register of Births.[58]

7.53   In such cases, it is competent to challenge the appointment of the executor-dative by seeking to lead parole evidence to show, on the balance of probabilities,[59] that the applicant was not the child (or parent) of the deceased, but such proof would only be for the purposes of the commissary proceedings.[60] The pre-

---

[55] *Per* Lord Kinnear in *Lady Denman* v. *Torry* (1899) 1 F. 881 at p. 883.
[56] *Per* Lord Justice-Clerk MacDonald in *Jerdon* v. *Forrest* (1897) 24 R. 395 at p. 398.
[57] Law Reform (Parent and Child) (Scotland) Act 1986 (c. 9), s. 5 (1) (*a*).
[58] *Ibid.*, s. 5 (1) (*b*).
[59] *Ibid.*, s. 5 (4).
[60] *Ibid.*, s. 7 (5).

sumption will also be displaced by the production of a declarator of parentage, non-parentage, legitimacy, legitimation or illegitimacy. The unreported decision of *Meehan*[61] has been doubted,[62] but since the Law Reform (Parent and Child) (Scotland) Act 1986 came into operation, the decision illustrates the approach which should now be adopted. In *Meehan*, a married woman had left her husband and had commenced an association with another man, with whom she cohabited. As a result of the adulterous association, a child was conceived. Subsequently, the husband died. Thereafter, the wife's cohabitee died and the child sought to be decerned executrix-dative *qua* illegitimate child to him. An extract birth certificate signed by the deceased was produced in process,[63] and decree was granted.

Extracting the decree

7.54 A decree dative may generally be extracted on the expiration of three lawful days after it has been pronounced[64] and will be issued in terms of the following style[65]:

> SHERIFFDOM OF . . ., AT . . .
> At . . ., the . . . day of . . . Nineteen hundred and . . ., SITTING IN JUDGMENT, . . ., Sheriff of the Sheriffdom of . . ., in a Petition before the Sheriff Court of the said Sheriffdom at . . ., at the instance of AB [*design*], Pursuer, [*state relationship, character or title the pursuer has, giving him right to apply for the appointment of executor*] of the deceased CD [*design*], who died at . . . on the . . . day of . . . Nineteen hundred and . . . and had at the time of his death his ordinary or principal domicile in the Sheriffdom of . . . [*or as the case may be*], for his decerniture as Executor-dative to the said deceased; the said Sheriff DECERNED and hereby DECERNS, the said AB Executor-dative *qua* [*capacity*] to the said deceased CD. Extracted at . . . this . . . day of . . . Nineteen hundred and . . . by me, Sheriff/Commissary Clerk of . . .
>
> [*Signed*]
> Sheriff/Commissary Clerk

7.55 However, where there has been competition for the office, an extract will not be issued without an order from the sheriff until

---

[61] Edinburgh, Feb. 16, 1970, unreported.
[62] *Per* Sheriff Kelbie in *McLaughlin, Petr.*, 1987 S.L.T. (Sh. Ct.) 87 at p. 90 J–K.
[63] Production of a birth certificate is not now necessary: it is sufficient to aver that the pursuer was the deceased's illegitimate daughter (*McLaughlin, Petr.*, 1987 S.L.T. (Sh. Ct.) 87).
[64] Confirmation of Executors (Scotland) Act 1858 (21 & 22 Vict. c. 56), s. 6.
[65] S.I. 1964 No. 1143, Sched. 1 (Act of Sederunt (Confirmation of Executors) 1964).

the period has elapsed within which it would be competent to appeal—that is, 14 days after decree.[66] In one case, where confirmation was issued two days after decree-dative had been granted, the confirmation was reduced on the ground that the decree-dative was not final.[67]

Recall of decree-dative

7.56   At any time before confirmation is issued,[68] a decree-dative may be recalled, either by way of a minute on the original initial writ by the party decerned as executor (see Styles 6.40–6.43), or by a separate initial writ by someone else (see para. 19.15), with a new executor being conjoined or substituted (Style 6.39). This can happen, even although the decree has been extracted, if confirmation has not been issued,[69] in which case there may be reserved from the new decree-dative any competent proceedings which may have been taken under the old extract.[70] The procedure of the decerned executor minuting for the recall of the decree may be used to correct errors. Thus, when the date of death had been wrongly stated in the initial writ, the decree was recalled in order to clear the way for a new initial writ.[71] The procedure may also be used where it has transpired that an executor-dative is unnecessary, because a will has been found or where two or more exceutors have been decerned and one has either died or wishes to withdraw.

No additional executor once confirmation granted

7.57   Except where the earlier confirmation was in favour of an executor-creditor, once confirmation has been granted, no other executor may be decerned without the first confirmation being reduced.[72]

Next step: Confirmation

7.58   The person decerned as executor-dative is entitled to sue debtors to the estate, but he cannot uplift or grant discharges

---

[66] Sheriff Courts (Scotland) Act 1907 (7 Edw. 7, c. 51), s. 39, Sched. 1, r. 30.4, as inserted by S.I. 1993 No. 1956.

[67] *Collings* v. *Bell*, Dec. 6, 1889, unreported.

[68] In *Nisbet*, Haddington, Dec. 1882, unreported it was held that it was competent to apply for the recall of a decree-dative even when the confirmation had been prepared and signed by the clerk, but was lying in his hands undelivered.

[69] *Webster* v. *Shiress* (1878) 6 R. 102; *Macpherson* v. *Macpherson* (1855) 17 D. 358.

[70] *Cochrane*, Jan. 15, 1853, unreported; *Forbes*, June 11, 1889, unreported.

[71] *McBride*, May 23–30, 1913, unreported.

[72] *Todd* v. *Todd* (1886) 2 Sh. Ct. Rep. 83.

until he has given up the inventory, found caution and expeded confirmation, and consequently he should proceed to do this without delay.

7.59 Where more than one executor-dative has been appointed, all must concur in giving up the inventory and expeding confirmation—although, as a matter of practice, the sheriff or commissary clerk does not require evidence of the concurrence of the executor or executors-dative who do not depone. If one of the executors-dative dies or wishes to withdraw before confirmation is issued, the others are required to obtain either

1. a recall of the decerniture in terms of a minute on the petition (See Styles 6.42 and 6.43) and a new decerniture in their own favour[73]; or

2. special authority (equivalent to a judicial restriction of the decree-dative in their favour) of the sheriff to confirm them as "survivors."[74]

7.60 Once the executors-dative have been confirmed, the appointment enures to the survivor on the death of one.[75]

The position of the executor-dative

7.61 An executor-dative has all the powers, privileges and immunities which gratuitous trustees have under statute or common law, with these exceptions[76]:

1. an executor-dative cannot resign office;

2. an executor-dative cannot assume new executors;

3. with the exception of the deceased's surviving spouse who has right to the whole estate by virtue of sections 8 and 9(2) of the Succession (Scotland) Act 1964,[77] an executor-dative must find caution for his intromissions.

7.62 Where more than two executors-dative survive, a majority shall be a quorum, and each is liable only for his own acts and intromissions.[78]

---

[73] *Stewart*, June 24, 1875, unreported.
[74] *Lamond*, Dec. 16, 1859, unreported; *Paul*, Oct. 23, 1882, unreported.
[75] Executors (Scotland) Act 1900 (63 & 64 Vict. c. 55), s. 4.
[76] Succession (Scotland) Act 1964 (c. 41), s. 20.
[77] Confirmation of Executors (Scotland) Act 1823 (4 Geo. 4, c. 98), s. 2, as amended by Statute Law Revision Act 1888 (51 Vict. c. 3), Sched., Pt. 1, Statute Law Revision (No. 2) Act 1890 (53 & 54 Vict. c. 51), Sched., Pt. II and Law Reform (Miscellaneous Provisions) (Scotland) Act 1980 (c. 55), s. 5.
[78] Executors (Scotland) Act 1900 (63 & 64 Vict. c. 55), s. 4.

CHAPTER 8

PROBLEM GROUPS OF EXECUTORS

Introduction

8.01   There are various categories of individuals whose appointment
as executor complicates the administration of an executry estate.
In this chapter, the practical and legal complications of the following situations are explored, and the solutions to each problem are discussed:

A.   Deceased was a tenant farmer or crofter (8.02–8.03A)
B.   Person to be executor has disappeared (8.04–8.07)
C.   Person to be executor is abroad (8.08–8.21)
D.   Person to be executor is blind (8.22–8.24)
E.   Person to be executor is under detention, enemy alien, etc.
     (8.25–8.27)
F.   Person to be executor is financially embarrassed (8.28)
G.   Person to be executor killed the deceased (8.29–8.32)
H.   Person to be executor suffers from ill-health (8.33–8.40)
I.   Person to be executor is *incapax* (8.41–8.55)
J.   Person to be executor is under age (8.56–8.67)

The final section of the chapter (8.68–8.97) explores the possibility of a judicial factor being appointed to wind up an executry
estate.

A. Deceased Was A Tenant Farmer or Crofter

8.02   If the deceased was a tenant farmer, a close family member who
accepts office as executor may find that his rights of succession
are affected. For instance, if an executor-dative appoints the
deceased's interest in a tenancy[1] to himself, as an individual,
the transfer can be reduced, in that the executor has been *auctor
in rem suam*.[2] There will, however, be no problem if the deceased
left a testamentary writing bequeathing his interest in the lease
to the executor.[3]

---

[1] In terms of Succession (Scotland) Act 1964 (c.41), s. 16, as amended by Law
Reform (Miscellaneous Provisions) (Scotland) Act 1968 (c.70), Sched. 2, paras.
22–26 and Agricultural Holdings (Scotland) Act 1991 (c.55), Sched. 11, para. 24.
[2] *Inglis* v. *Inglis*, 1983 S.L.T. 437.
[3] In terms of Agricultural Holdings (Scotland) Act 1991 (c.55), s. 11.

8.03   The problem is particularly acute if the deceased died intestate, survived by a spouse and infant children, for in such a case the surviving spouse is the obvious executor-dative, but yet the only heir on intestacy whom the landlord is likely to accept as tenant.

8.03A   Similar problems to those described at paragraphs 8.02–8.03 exist where the deceased was the tenant of a croft, and had failed to bequeath it.

B. DISAPPEARANCE OF POSSIBLE EXECUTOR

Appointment of an executor-nominate who has disappeared

8.04   Where it is a sole executor-nominate who has disappeared for a period of at least six months, a beneficiary may petition the Court of Session or the sheriff court for the appointment of a new executor or executors,[4] who may then be confirmed as executor(s)-nominate in place of the original executor-nominate, with appropriate reference to the court decree in the oath.

8.05   Where it is known before confirmation is obtained that one of the executors-nominate has disappeared for a period of at least six months, a co-executor or a beneficiary may make application to the Court of Session or to the sheriff court to have him removed from office.[5] The remaining executors may then be confirmed as executors-nominate, with appropriate reference being made to the court decree in the oath.

8.06   Alternatively, where one of the executors-nominate has changed his address, and his current address cannot be ascertained, the other executors-nominate may petition for authority for confirmation to be issued in their own favour. Where the executor who has disappeared has a beneficial interest in the estate, the court would probably insist on caution being obtained to the extent of his interest, before issuing confirmation in favour of the other executors.[6]

Possible executor-dative has disappeared

8.07   Where a person who is eligible to be appointed executor-dative has disappeared, it is usually possible to find someone who has an equal right in the succession to the deceased's estate who will be decerned in normal course. Alternatively, the deceased's next-of-kin may be decerned. There is an exception where the missing person is the deceased's spouse, whose prior rights

---

[4] Trusts (Scotland) Act 1921 (11 & 12 Geo. 5, c.58), s. 22, as amended by Law Reform (Miscellaneous Provisions) (Scotland) Act 1980 (c.55), s. 13(*a*).

[5] Trusts (Scotland) Act 1921 (11 & 12 Geo. 5, c.58), s. 23, as amended by the Law Reform (Miscellaneous Provisions) (Scotland) Act 1980 (c.55), s. 13(*b*).

[6] *Purvis*, July 9, 1863, unreported; *Templeton*, March 10, 1866, unreported.

exhaust the whole intestate estate, for in such a case, current commissary practice is that the surviving spouse has the exclusive right to be decerned executor-dative,[7] and no progress can be made in administering the estate until the surviving spouse has been located (see, further, paras. 6.28–6.43).

C. POSSIBLE EXECUTOR IS ABROAD

Appointment of an executor resident abroad

8.08   It is no objection either to a person being decerned as executor or to the confirmation of a person as executor (whether nominate or dative) that he is resident abroad.[8]

8.09   Where a person overseas has been nominated executor, it will often reduce the delay in administering the estate if he were to decline office or, if he is sole executor, assume another executor, and himself resign (see para. 5.124, fn. 25). In an urgent case, a cabled declinature has been accepted, and it is submitted that one sent by fax would be equally acceptable.[9]

8.10   If the administration of the estate will be unduly complicated by an overseas executor acting, and it is impractical to obtain his declinature or resignation, the following court procedures may be used:

1.   Where a sole executor-nominate is appointed, and he has been absent from the United Kingdom for at least six months, a beneficiary may petition the Court of Session or the sheriff court for the appointment of a new executor or executors,[10] who may then be confirmed as executor(s)-nominate in place of the original executor-nominate, with appropriate reference to the court decree in the oath.

2.   Where it is known before confirmation is obtained that one of the executors-nominate has been overseas for a period of at least six months, a co-executor or a beneficiary may make application to the Court of Session or to the sheriff court to have him removed from office.[11] The

[7] Succession (Scotland) Act 1964 (c.41), s. 9(4).
[8] *Jerdon* v. *Forrest* (1897) 24 R. 395, where in a case of competition between persons applying to be decerned executor-dative, an individual resident in Canada was appointed, it being noted (see Lord Justice-Clerk Macdonald at p. 398) that she intended to return to Scotland, that she would require to find caution, and the management of the estate would be dealt with by a Scottish lawyer.
[9] At the time of writing, the sheriff court rules do not permit business to be conducted by fax.
[10] Trusts (Scotland) Act 1921 (11 & 12 Geo. 5, c.58), s. 22, as amended by Law Reform (Miscellaneous Provisions) (Scotland) Act 1980 (c.55), s. 13(a).
[11] Trusts (Scotland) Act 1921 (11 & 12 Geo. 5, c.58), s. 23, as amended by the Law Reform (Miscellaneous Provisions) (Scotland) Act 1980 (c.55), s. 13(b).

remaining executors may then be confirmed as executors-nominate, with appropriate reference being made to the court decree in the oath.

8.11 Where the person overseas wishes to act or, in a dative case, there is no other person eligible to be decerned, the practical solutions to the inaccessibility of the overseas executor are those set out at paragraphs 8.14 to 8.18.

Overseas executor: executor physically present in United Kingdom

8.12 If a sole executor is resident overseas but is physically within the United Kingdom when confirmation is applied for, he must personally make oath to the inventory and the procedures described in paragraphs 8.14–8.19 will be inapplicable.

8.13 Where there are two or more executors, and only one of them is resident abroad, it will be normal practice for a UK based executor to sign the inventory.

Overseas executor abroad

Power of attorney

8.14 Where there is no executor in the United Kingdom, while it is possible for the inventory to be sent overseas for signature, it is more normal for the executor or executors to grant a factory or power of attorney in favour of someone in Scotland, authorising him to give up an inventory, make oath thereto, and expede confirmation in his, her or their names. It should be noted that in such cases it is the executors who are confirmed, not the factor or attorney. If an executor-dative has to be appointed, and the appropriate person is abroad, the power of attorney will include power to present the petition, which will run in the name of the person resident abroad, who will be decerned and confirmed.[12] If it is desired that the factor or attorney should also proceed to realise the estate, powers to that effect are added.

8.15 Acceptable styles for the appointment of an attorney are set out in Styles 7.01–7.03 and a style for the consequent variation in the inventory is set out in Style 8.12. If executed in Scotland, the power of attorney should be subscribed on the last page only, in the presence of one witness, with the usual testing clause added[13]. If the power of attorney was executed outwith Scotland, the current commissary practice is that, unless the

---

[12] *Millar*, July 23, 1943 unreported.
[13] See para. 4.08, though the Power of Attorney need only be signed on the last page.

execution conforms to Scottish formalities, evidence must be produced that the execution meets the formalities of the place of execution.

8.16   Styles 7.01–7.03 should only be varied with care and in particular, it should be noted that it is not sufficient for the Power of Attorney to authorise an application for probate or letters of administration or resealing. Where a power of attorney appointed the attorneys "for the purpose of obtaining Letters of Administration (with the said Will annexed) of the estate of the said deceased to be granted to them or him . . . for my use and benefit until I shall duly apply for and obtain Probate of the said Will to be granted to me," confirmation was refused on the grounds that a person cannot delegate his right to the office of executor. A petition was presented for special authority to accept the power of attorney solely for the purpose of craving confirmation in favour of the executor, but this was refused and another power of attorney in the proper form had to be obtained.[14]

Consular official may sign
8.17   If the person who could be appointed executor-dative is a national of one of certain states,[15] is not resident in Scotland, and has not granted a power of attorney, a consular official of the state may apply on behalf of the overseas person to be appointed executor, as if he had been authorised by a power of attorney.[16]

8.18   The consular official may also apply on behalf of the overseas executor to be confirmed as executor-nominate or executor-dative, and may then ingather the estate, all as if authorised by a power of attorney.[17] In so doing, the consular official is not protected by diplomatic community.[17a]

Court may appoint factor
8.19   Finally, where the overseas person has not granted a power of attorney (or the power is inadequate), the court may, under the Act of Sederunt of February 13, 1730, appoint a factor *loco*

---

[14] *Millar*, July 23, 1943 unreported.

[15] Austria (S.I. 1963 No. 1927), Belgium (S.I. 1964 No. 1399), Bulgaria (S.I. 1968 No. 1861), Czechoslovakia (S.I. 1976 No. 1216), Denmark (S.I. 1963 No. 370), Egypt (S.I. 1986 No. 216), France (S.I. 1953 No. 1455), Germany (S.I. 1957 No. 2052), Greece (S.I. 1953 No. 1454), Hungary (S.I. 1971 No. 1845), Italy (S.I. 1957 No. 2053), Japan (S.I. 1965 No. 1714), Mexico (S.I. 1955 No. 425), Mongolia (S.I. 1976 No. 1150), Norway (S.I. 1951 No. 1165), Poland (S.I. 1971 No. 1238), Spain (S.I. 1963 No. 614), Sweden (S.I. 1952 No. 1218), USSR (S.I. 1968 No. 1378), Yugoslavia (S.I. 1966 No. 443). Further, if the deceased was the subject of Finland (S.I. 1939 No. 1452), Thailand (S.I. 1939 No. 1457) or Turkey (S.I. 1939 No. 1458).

[16] Consular Conventions Act 1949 (c.29) s. 2(1).

[17] *Ibid.*, s. 2(1) and (2).

[17a] *Ibid.*, s. 3.

absentis to ingather the estate (see, further, paras. 8.68–8.71). However, in an era of speedy worldwide communications, this solution will rarely be adopted, for normally there will be little difficulty or delay if the overseas executor is asked to sign a fresh power of attorney.

Overseas executor-nominate may be omitted from confirmation

8.20 Where an executor-nominate has gone abroad, and his current address is unknown, the sheriff may grant confirmation to the remaining executors without requiring his declinature, or a decree obtained for his removal from office under section 23 of the Trusts (Scotland) Act 1921.[18] A style initial writ for special authority to issue confirmation is set out at Style 4.06. However, if the missing executor has a beneficial interest in the estate, the court would probably insist on caution being obtained to the extent of his interest, before issuing confirmation in favour of the other executors.[19]

8.21 Where an executor-nominate has gone abroad, and his current address is known, it is unclear whether the sheriff would exclude him from confirmation. Last century, the sheriff could be persuaded to grant confirmation omitting an overseas executor-nominate whose address was known if it could be shown that the delay necessary to communicate with him, in order to obtain his acceptance or declinature of office, would be injurious to the estate, and it was considered probable that he would decline.[20] A style initial writ for special authority to issue confirmation is set out at Style 4.07. It is submitted that, with modern developments in communications, the sheriff is unlikely to take this approach today, unless the executor-nominate lived in a place which was particularly difficult to contact. In an urgent case, a cabled declinature has been accepted, and it is submitted that one sent by fax would be equally acceptable.

D. POSSIBLE EXECUTOR IS BLIND

Appointment of a blind executor

8.22 Where a blind person has been appointed executor-nominate, there are obvious practical problems if he accepts office, and he

---

[18] (11 & 12 Geo. 5, c.58), s. 23, as amended by Law Reform (Miscellaneous Provisions (Scotland) Act 1980 (c.55), s. 13(*b*). See para. 8.10.

[19] *Purvis*, July 9, 1863 unreported; *Templeton*, March 10, 1866, unreported.

[20] Additional factors which influenced the decision of the sheriff have included the fact that the overseas executor had no beneficial interest, and the fact that a majority of the executors-nominate would be confirmed.

may instead decide to decline office or, if he is sole executor, assume another executor, and himself resign (see para. 5.124). Such a deed should be executed by notarial execution (see, further, para. 4.55 *et seq.*). It would not be competent for the blind person to grant a power of attorney to another to confirm on his behalf, where he is resident in the United Kingdom.[21]

8.23 For similar practical reasons, the appointment of a blind executor-dative should be avoided if there is an alternative person qualified and able to act. In appropriate cases, this may involve a consent by the blind person, which should be executed notarially.

8.24 If a *curator bonis* is appointed to a blind person,[22] the procedures set out at paragraphs 8.50–8.53 may then be adopted.

E. POSSIBLE EXECUTOR UNDER DETENTION, ENEMY ALIEN, ETC.

Persons under detention

8.25 A British subject who is, during wartime, under detention at a place outwith the jurisdiction of the Scottish courts, may be decerned as executor-dative,[23] and confirmed as executor, since internment does not deprive him of his civil rights, but merely restricts his movements.

Enemy aliens

8.26 An enemy alien, who is resident in the United Kingdom, may be decerned as executor-dative,[24] and may also be confirmed as executor-nominate or executor-dative.

8.27 Where the enemy alien is only one of a number of persons entitled to be appointed executor-dative, and the others are British subjects, the court might, in the exercise of its discretion, prefer one of the British subjects to the office.[25]

---

[21] *Leishman,* Dec. 17, 1980, unreported, discussed below at para. 8.39.

[22] A *curator bonis* has been appointed to a person who was blind and deaf and unable to manage his own affairs (*Duncan,* 1915 2 S.L.T. 50).

[23] *Crolla,* 1942 S.C. 21.

[24] *Schulze, Petr.,* 1917 1 S.L.T. 176.

[25] *Per* Lord Guthrie in *Schulze, Petr.,* 1917 1 S.L.T. 176 at p. 178.

F. Possible Executor Financially Embarrassed

Persons who are insolvent or bankrupt

8.28   A person who is insolvent and *vergens ad inopiam* is not thereby disqualified from office as executor-dative,[26] nor is an undischarged bankrupt,[27] and confirmation cannot be refused to such a person.

G. Possible Executor Killed Deceased

Persons convicted of unlawfully killing the deceased

8.29   If a person who has been convicted of killing the deceased has been appointed executor-nominate, he will be entitled to act, though it will often be more appropriate for him to resign office.[28] Apart from this, it will be unusual for the convicted person to be the deceased's executor.

8.30   It is a rule of public policy that a person who has unlawfully killed the deceased cannot receive any part of the deceased's estate.[29] In particular, where a person is convicted of killing his or her parent or grandparent, the succession to the estate is dealt with as if the murderer had predeceased the parent or grandparent.[30] If the convicted person and the victim are of a different relationship, the convicted person, provided that he has not been convicted of murder,[31] may apply to the court[31a] for an order modifying the rule.[32] Such an order will be granted if the court is satisfied that "having regard to the conduct of the offender and of the deceased and to such other circumstances as appear to the court to be material, the justice of the case" requires it.[33] In such a case, the offender may receive part, but not the whole,[34] of his inheritance.

---

[26] *Per* sheriff-substitute Menzies in *Chrystal*, v. *Chrystal*, 1923 S.L.T. (Sh. Ct.) 69 at p. 71.

[27] *Wilson*, Nov. 24, 1886, unreported.

[28] See *Hunter's Exrs., Petrs.*, 1992 S.LT. 1141 where the person convicted of murdering the deceased declined the office of trustee and executor-nominate.

[29] *Burns* v. *Secretary of State for Social Services*, 1985 S.L.T. 351.

[30] Parricide Act 1594 (c.30); rule may apply to heritage only: Bankton II, ccci, 30.

[31] Forfeiture Act 1982 (c.34), s. 5.

[31a] By petition to the Inner House, or probably also by action of declarator. (*Paterson, Petr.*, 1986 S.L.T. 121).

[32] Forfeiture Act 1982, (c. 34) s. 2(1).

[33] Forfeiture Act 1982 (c.34), s. 2(2); for likely factors see Lord Cameron in *Paterson, Petr.*, 1986 S.L.T. 121 at p. 123 C–E; see also *obiter*, *Re H. Decd.* [1990] 1 F.L.R. 441 and *Gilchrist, Petr*, 1990 S.L.T. 494.

[34] *Cross, Petr.*, 1987 S.L.T. 384; *cf.* the contrary approach in England *per* Vinelott J., *Re K. Decd.* [1985] Ch. 85 at p. 100 A–E.

8.31   Since a person who has been convicted of unlawfully killing the deceased can never receive the whole of his entitlement under the deceased's testamentary writing, and part will pass on intestacy he cannot be confirmed as executor-nominate *qua* general disponee, universal legatee or residuary legatee under section 3 of the 1900 Act, nor as an executor-dative *qua* general disponee or universal legatory. However, provided that the court established that the convicted person might receive part of his entitlement, it is submitted that it would be competent for him to be confirmed as executor-dative *qua* residuary legatee.

8.32   Where the person killed died intestate, the person convicted of the unlawful killing may only be decerned executor-dative *qua* relative entitled to succeed under the Succession (Scotland) Act 1964,[35] if he has successfully applied to the court for an order under section 2 of the Forfeiture Act 1982. Where there is competition for the office of executor-dative between a relative who has not been convicted of the deceased's unlawful killing and one who has, there is no logical reason why the former should be preferred: the court has established that both should share in the estate.

H. Possible Executor Suffers from Ill-health

Executor-nominate suffers from ill-health

8.33   It occasionally happens that, because of old age and infirmity or mental or bodily incapacity, an executor-nominate is unable to act, to grant a declinature, or to assume a new executor and then resign. What then should be done depends on the terms of the testamentary writing. On no account should the executor grant a power of attorney, since he cannot delegate his duties as executor by granting a power of attorney (see para. 8.39).

8.34   If there are other executors-nominate, a medical certificate should be obtained, and the other executors-nominate may then be confirmed, on the medical certificate being put up with the inventory, referred to in the deposition, and docketed as relative thereto.

8.35   If a person suffering from ill-health is the sole executor-nominate, the incapacity, as evidenced by the medical certificate, will be viewed as "failure" of the original appointment, and the remedies provided by section 3 of the Executors (Scotland) Act 1900 may be invoked.[36] If, therefore, testament-

---

[35] *Smith, Petr.*, 1979 S.L.T. (Sh. Ct.) 35.
[36] See para. 5.51 *et seq.*

ary trustees are to be confirmed, the medical certificate must be put up with the inventory, referred to in the deposition, and docketed as relative thereto. If an application has to be made for special warrant to issue confirmation-nominate to a general disponee, universal legatory or residuary legatee, the medical certificate must be produced, and narrated in the condescendence. Alternatively, but more expensively, either

1. a beneficiary may petition the Court of Session or the appropriate sheriff court for the appointment of a new executor or executors[37]: the court appointed executor or executors would then be confirmed as executors-nominate, with appropriate reference in the deposition to the court decree;

2. a *curator bonis* may be appointed to a person who is physically infirm,[38] such as a person incapacitated by paralysis,[39] a person incapacitated by a stroke of apoplexy,[40] a person who has been deaf and dumb since birth[41] and a person who is blind and deaf and unable to manage his own affairs[42]: the procedures set out at paragraphs 8.50–8.52 may then be adopted.

Executor-dative suffers from ill-health

8.36   Where two or more executors-dative have been decerned, and one has fallen ill, before they are confirmed, the appointment should be recalled (see paras. 19.15–19.17) on production of the medical certificate as to condition of the ill executor and the other executor(s) decerned of new.

8.37   Where a sole executor-dative, after being decerned, is struck down by illness, either

1. "any person having interest in the trust estate" may petition the Court of Session or the appropriate sheriff court for appointment of a new executor or executors[43]: the court appointed executor or executors would then be confirmed as executor(s)-dative, with appropriate reference to the court decree;

[37] Trusts (Scotland) Act 1921 (11 & 12 Geo. 5, c.58), s. 22, as amended by Law Reform (Miscellaneous Provisions) (Scotland) Act 1980 (c.55), s. 13(*a*).
[38] Walker, *Principles of Scottish Private Law* (4th ed.), Vol. I, p. 326.
[39] *Eadie* v. *MacBean's C.B.* (1885) 12 R. 660; *Howie, Petr.* (1826) 5 S. 77.
[40] *Forster, Petr.*, (1848) 11 D. 1031.
[41] *Blaikie, Petr.*, (1827) 5 S. 268.
[42] *Duncan & Others, Petrs.*, 1915 2 S.L.T. 50.
[43] Trusts (Scotland) Act 1921 (11 & 12 Geo. 5, c.58), s. 22, as amended by Law Reform (Miscellaneous Provisions) (Scotland) Act 1980 (c.55), s. 13(*a*).

2. the appointment may be recalled[44]; or

3. a *curator bonis* may be appointed to a person who is physically infirm,[45] such as a person incapacitated by paralysis,[46] a person incapacitated by a stroke of apoplexy,[47] a person who has been deaf and dumb since birth[48] and a person who is blind and deaf and unable to manage his own affairs[49]: the procedures set out at paragraph 8.53 may then be adopted.

8.38   An executor-dative cannot assume another executor, nor can he resign office.[50]

Ill-health: a Power of Attorney?

8.39   An executor who is suffering from ill-health cannot competently delegate to an attorney power to give up an inventory to the deceased's estate, make oath thereto, record the same in the court books, or crave confirmation in favour of the sick person, as executor. In *Leishman*,[51] Mr Leishman had suffered a cerebral haemorrhage as a result of which he was partially paralysed and could not speak. He was decerned as executor dative *qua* husband to his late wife, but three days earlier he had granted a power of attorney in favour of his solicitor which included the standard clause used by an executor living overseas enabling a United Kingdom resident person to apply for confirmation in his name. However, Sheriff Macvicar refused to grant warrant to the clerk to issue confirmation on the basis of an inventory signed by the attorney for the husband.

> "The 'foreign executor' exception appears to me to entrench upon the basic principle of non-delegation, and upon the various statutory requirements[52] . . . to such an extent that it ought not to be extended except by express statutory provision. The exception has so far been strictly limited in its scope and is justified by reasons of practical convenience, which are easily ascertainable and admit of no dubiety. To extend it would lead to the undesirable necessity of examining the circumstances of each case, in order to meas-

---

[44] See para. 19.15–19.17A.

[45] Walker, *Principles of Scottish Private Law* (4th ed.), Vol. I, p. 326.

[46] *Eadie* v. *MacBean's C.B.* (1885) 12 R. 660; *Howie, Petr.* (1826) 5 S. 77.

[47] *Forster, Petr.* (1848) 11 D. 1031.

[48] *Blaikie, Petr.* (1827) 5 S. 268.

[49] *Duncan & Others, Petrs.*, 1915 2 S.L.T. 50.

[50] Succession (Scotland) Act 1964 (c.41), s. 20.

[51] Dec. 17, 1980, unreported.

[52] *e.g.* Probate and Legacy Duties Act 1808 (48 Geo. 3, c.149), s. 38, as amended; False Oaths (Scotland) Act 1933 (23 & 24 Geo. 5, c.20), s. 1; and Inheritance Tax Act 1984 (c.51), ss. 216 and 261.

ure the degree of inconvenience which would be caused if the executor were required to carry out his duties in person. In my opinion, the proper principle to be applied is that, if a person entitled to be confirmed as executor does not feel able to accept the fiduciary responsibilities of the office and to carry out his duties in person, his proper course is to decline the office."

8.40   While the principled stand of Sheriff Macvicar is to be applauded, it does present practical problems where the surviving spouse's prior rights exhaust the whole of the deceased's intestate estate since, in such cases, it is unclear whether a child of the marriage could be decerned as executor-dative *qua* next-of-kin (see paras. 6.28–6.41). On the one hand, in *Forrest*[53] (where it was averred that it was not known whether the estate would exceed the surviving spouse's prior rights), the deceased's son was decerned on production of a declinature from the surviving spouse. On the other hand, in *Jack*,[54] a medical certificate as to the surviving spouse's incapacity did not enable the son to be confirmed as executor-dative. It is difficult to see how the administration of such an executry estate can proceed where the surviving spouse is fully *capax*, but is so ill as to be unable to perform the duties of office,[55] unless the court is prepared to by-pass the surviving spouse on production of a declinature in all cases—even in those where it is clear that the surviving spouse will receive the whole estate in satisfaction of prior rights.

I. Possible Executor Is *Incapax*

Appointment of an *incapax* as executor

8.41   A person who is entitled to be decerned as executor, or confirmed as such, cannot be decerned or confirmed personally if he is *incapax*, whether in the sense of imbecility or insane delusions. Generally, a *curator bonis* will be appointed to look after the property of an *incapax*[56] and, as will be seen, may often act for the *incapax* in connection with executry matters.

Incapax executor-nominate does not have a *curator bonis*

8.42   If there is no *curator bonis* acting for a person who is *incapax*

---

[53] Feb. 28, 1966, unreported.

[54] March 2, 1967, unreported.

[55] In general, a surviving spouse who is in ill-health will appoint an attorney to look after his own financial affairs, rather than entering into the more complicated and expensive procedure of having a *curator bonis* appointed.

[56] Including persons suffering from a physical affliction which affects their intellectual capacity.

and who has been appointed an executor-nominate, a medical certificate as to the *incapax's* health must be obtained.

8.43   If there are other executors-nominate, they may then be confirmed, the medical certificate being put up with the inventory, referred to in the deposition, and docketed as relative thereto.

8.44   If the *incapax* was the sole executor-nominate, the incapacity, as evidenced by the medical certificate, is viewed as "failure" of the original appointment, and the remedies provided by section 3 of the Executors (Scotland) Act 1900 may be invoked.[57] If, therefore, testamentary trustees are to be confirmed, the medical certificate must be put up with the inventory, referred to in the deposition, and docketed as relative thereto. If an application has to be made for special warrant to issue confirmation-nominate to a general disponee, universal legatory or residuary legatee, the medical certificate which discloses the executor-nominate's ill-health must be produced, and narrated in the condescendence.

Incapax is the person entitled to be decerned executor-dative but does not have *curator bonis*

8.45   Where a person eligible to be decerned as executor-dative is *incapax*, the procedure to be adopted depends on the rights of the *incapax* in the estate.

8.46   Where, for instance, the deceased's heirs are her two sisters, one of whom is *incapax*, the other would simply be decerned executrix-dative, without even producing a medical certificate.

8.47   Where the *incapax* is the sole heir on intestacy (but is not the surviving spouse), it is submitted that the deceased's next-of-kin might be decerned as executors-dative in that capacity, on production of the medical certificate, and with the circumstances narrated in the condescendence. Alternatively, under the Act of Sederunt of February 13, 1730, a factor *curator bonis* may be decerned (see, further, paras. 8.68–8.71).

8.48   But where the deceased's heir is the surviving spouse whose prior rights exhaust the whole intestate estate, the only solution may be to have a *curator bonis* appointed. In *Jack*,[58] where the *incapax* was the deceased's surviving spouse, the court held that the son of the marriage could not be decerned as executor-dative *qua* next-of-kin, simply on production of a medical certificate, but that a *curator bonis* must be appointed to the *incapax*, who

---

[57] See paras. 5.50 *et seq.*
[58] March 2, 1967, unreported, see paras. 6.40 and 8.40.

could then act as appropriate. The explanation for this decision may lie in the fact that there was no averment that the deceased's estate exceeded the prior rights of his widow: had the deceased's estate been completely exhausted in meeting the surviving spouse's prior rights, the commissary practice is that the son would not have had a title to be appointed as executor.

8.49 It is submitted that the approach in *Jack* is not of universal application, since under the Act of Sederunt of February 13, 1730, a factor *curator bonis* may only be decerned as executor if no one else having a title offers to confirm to the estate.[59]

Incapax executor-nominate has *curator bonis*

8.50 Paragraphs 8.51–8.52 set out the current commissary practice where an *incapax* executor-nominate has a *curator bonis*. It is submitted that the practice described is not in accordance with the only provision regulating the right of a *curator bonis* to be appointed executor on behalf of the ward—the Act of Sederunt of February 13, 1730. The Act of Sederunt provides that a factor *curator bonis* may only be decerned as executor if no one else having a title offers to confirm to the estate[60]; accordingly, where others
eligible offer to confirm, the *curator bonis* can have no title to object. As will be seen, the current practice is to require a declinature (in the form of a letter) from the *curator bonis* (on behalf of his ward) before anyone else may be confirmed, although there is some doubt as to whether such a letter of declinature is legally effective if the *curator* has not obtained the authority of the court to decline.

Current commissary practice
8.51 Where a number of executors are nominated and, before confirmation is applied for, one has become *incapax*, the *curator bonis* can decline office, on behalf of his ward.[61] The other executors-nominate may then be confirmed, the declinature (in the form of a letter) being put up with the confirmation, referred to in the deposition, and docketed as relative thereto.

8.52 The position is more difficult if it is the sole executor, or the last surviving executor, who has become *incapax*.

   1. If someone other than the *incapax* is the universal legatory, general disponee or residuary legatee, it would be

---

[59] *Martin* v. *Ferguson's Trs.* (1892) 19 R. 474.

[60] *Ibid.*

[61] *Macara*, Dec. 17, 1885, unreported *cf. Laidlaw, Petr.* (1882) 10 R. 130 where a ward who had no beneficial interest in the estate had been appointed a testamentary trustee, and the ward's *curator bonis* petitioned for authority to resign the trust.

appropriate for the *curator bonis* to decline office, on behalf of his ward,[62] leaving the universal legatory, general disponee or residuary legatee to become executor-nominate or executor-dative in that capacity,[63] in terms of section 3 of the Executors (Scotland) Act 1900. The declinature (in the form of a letter stating that the *curator* does not intend applying for appointment as executor *qua curator*, supported by a medical certificate as to the incapacity) must be produced, and narrated in the condescendence in the application for special warrant to issue confirmation to the general disponee, universal legatory or residuary legatee or, if special warrant is unnecessary, put up with the inventory, referred to in the deposition and docketed as relative thereto.

2. If the *incapax* is also the universal legatory, or sole general disponee or residuary legatee, confirmation in his favour can be granted on an inventory given up by his *curator bonis*.[64] However, this procedure should be used with caution, particularly if there is estate abroad, since although the confirmation may be resealed, it is possible that the curator's right to sign on behalf of the executor may not be accepted outwith Scotland.

3. Where the *incapax* is the universal legatory, general disponee or residuary legatee, the *curator bonis* may present a petition to be decerned as executor-dative *qua curator bonis* to the universal legatory, general disponee or residuary legatee of the deceased,[65] in terms of section 7 of the Act of Sederunt of February 13, 1730 (discussed at paras. 8.68–8.71). Being a dative appointment, the executor must find caution but, since the confirmation goes out in the name of the *curator bonis*, there will be no difficulty in ingathering estate abroad. The style of the dative petition is set out in Style 6.34.

4. Where a sole executor-nominate has become *incapax*, an alternative if expensive solution would be for a beneficiary to petition the Court of Session or the appropriate sheriff court for the appointment of a new executor or executors.[66] The court appointed executor or executors

---

[62] He must obtain authority to do so: *Laidlaw; Petr.* (1882) 10 R. 130.

[63] See paras. 5.66 *et seq.* and 6.16 *et seq.*

[64] Confirmation was granted in favour on an insane person who had been named sole executor and had a liferent interest in the estate in the unreported cases of *Lumsdaine*, April 21, 1868, unreported and *Pattison*, Nov. 17, 1871, unreported. Likewise, where she was universal legatory in the unreported case of *Peterson* (Oct. 3, 1884, unreported).

[65] *Dickson*, May 2, 1963, unreported.

[66] Trusts (Scotland) Act 1921 (11 & 12 Geo. 5, c.58), s. 22, as amended by Law Reform (Miscellaneous Provisions) (Scotland) Act 1980 (c.55), s. 13(*a*).

would then be confirmed as executors-nominate, with appropriate reference in the oath to the court decree.

Incapax is a person entitled to be decerned executor-dative but has a *curator bonis*

8.53   Where the *incapax* has a *curator bonis*, then either

1. if someone other than the *incapax* is available to be decerned as executor, it would be appropriate for the *curator bonis* to decline office, on behalf of his ward,[67] leaving the other person to be decerned as executor-dative, the declinature (in the form of a letter stating that the *curator* does not intend applying for appointment as executor *qua curator*, supported by a medical certificate as to the incapacity) being produced, and narrated in the condescendence in the initial writ;[67a]

2. the *incapax* may be decerned and confirmed on an initial writ and inventory given up by his *curator bonis*: however, this procedure should be used with caution, particularly if there is estate abroad, since although the confirmation may be resealed, it is possible that the curator's right to sign on behalf of the executor may not be accepted outwith Scotland;

3. the *curator bonis* may present a petition to be decerned as executor-dative *qua curator bonis* to the (mother or other relation) of the deceased,[68] in terms of section 7 of the Act of Sederunt of February 13, 1730 (discussed at paras. 8.68–8.71), and he will thereafter be confirmed in like capacity.

Executor becomes *incapax* after confirmation is granted: eik

8.54   If, after confirmation has been issued, a sole or last surviving executor becomes *incapax*, an eik to the confirmation may be expede in the executor's name on the application of the *curator bonis*.[69] Alternatively (but more expensively), a beneficiary may petition the Court of Session or the appropriate sheriff court for the appointment of a new executor or executors,[70] and an eik to the confirmation may be expede in name of such executor(s), with appropriate reference in the oath to the court decree.

---

[67] He must obtain authority to do so: *Laidlaw* (1882) 10 R. 130.
[67a] See *Jack*, March 2, 1967, unreported; discussed at para. 6.40.
[68] *Dickson*, May 2, 1963, unreported.
[69] *Mailer*, Nov. 1, 1888, unreported.
[70] Trusts (Scotland) Act 1921 (11 & 12 Geo. 5, c.58), s. 22, as amended by Law Reform (Miscellaneous Provisions) (Scotland) Act 1980 (c.55), s. 13(*a*).

8.55   If one of a number of confirmed executors becomes *incapax*, an eik to the confirmation will be granted in favour of the other executors only once a petition for removal of the *incapax* executor is granted,[71] appropriate reference to the decree being made in the oath.

J. POSSIBLE EXECUTOR UNDER AGE

Appointment of person under the age of 18 years as executor

8.56   Prior to September 25, 1991 it was recognised[72] that a minor or pupil could competently be confirmed in his or her own name, or with the consent or concurrence of the child's tutor or curator. Alternatively, the child's tutor or curator could be decerned and confirmed on behalf of the child.[73]

8.57   Since September 25, 1991, a person under the age of 16 years does not have the capacity to bring civil proceedings (such as seek appointment as executor-dative), to act as a trustee (which presumably in this context includes "executor"), or to decline the appointment.[74] After that age, he does have capacity,[75] subject to the fact that a prejudicial transaction entered into before he is aged 18 may be set aside by the court.[76] Consequently, it is desirable that all the named executors are over the age of 18 at the time when the testamentary writing is executed or, alternatively, that the appointment ·of a younger person as executor is made conditional on his (or her) having attained the age of 18 years at the time of the testator's death.

8.58   Where a person under the age of 16 years has a guardian, the guardian has the powers which a tutor formerly had in relation to his pupil.[77] Since such a child cannot bring, or take any step in, civil proceedings,[78] the former practices which involved the guardian being decerned and confirmed *along with* the child are no longer competent. However, the guardian may be decerned and confirmed *on behalf of* the child[79] and may also decline the appointment on his or her behalf.

---

[71] Under Trusts (Scotland) Act 1921 (11 & 12 Geo. 5, c.58), s. 23, as amended by Law Reform (Miscellaneous Provisions) (Scotland) Act 1980 (c.55), s. 13(*b*).

[72] See 7th ed. of this work at pp. 90–91 and 120–121.

[73] *Swayne, Petr.* (1822) 1 S. 479, where deceased left an infant daughter. His brother was served tutor-at-law and was confirmed, for the daughter's behoof, as executor. See also *Kirktouns* (1662) Mor. 16268 and *Watherstone* (1665) Mor. 16275.

[74] Age of Legal Capacity (Scotland) Act 1991 (c.50), ss. 1(1)(*a*) and 9.

[75] *Ibid.*, ss. 1(1)(*b*) and 9.

[76] *Ibid.*, s. 3.

[77] *Ibid.*, s. 5(1).

[78] *Ibid.*, s. 9.

[79] *Swayne, Petr.* (1822) 1 S. 479, where deceased left an infant daughter. His brother was served tutor-at-law and was confirmed, for the daughter's behoof, as executor.

8.59 Although the child, had he or she been over the age of 16 years, would have been entitled to a nominate appointment, there is a divergence of practice between different sheriff courts as to whether the guardian should be confirmed in a nominate or dative capacity. In the Aberdeen case of *Leslie and Ritchie*,[80-81] the deceased left a holograph testamentary writing which failed to appoint trustees and executors, but named two very young children as the residuary beneficiaries. The court granted a petition brought by the mothers of the two children *qua* guardians of their children to be decerned executrices-nominate *qua* residuary beneficiaries in terms of section 3 of the Executors (Scotland) Act 1900. In contrast, the practice of the Edinburgh court is to decern all guardians in a dative capacity, the rationale being that the guardians were not individually named by the deceased and, accordingly, cannot be decerned as executors-nominate; and that the child beneficiary should have the benefit of the protection afforded by caution—even although there is no legal requirement for a guardian to obtain caution before intromitting with other funds of the child.

8.60 For the style of petition for the appointment of an executor-dative *qua* guardian for a person who is under the age of 16 years see Style 6.28.

8.61 Where a person under the age of 16 years does not have a guardian, a commissary factor may be appointed and decerned as executor (see paras. 8.72–8.76).

Guardians to persons under the age of 16 years

8.62 A child's mother, unless she has been deprived of her parental rights, has guardianship rights over her child, whether or not she has been married to the child's father.[82]

8.63 A child's father has parental rights including guardianship rights over the child only if he is married to the child's mother, or was married to her at the time of the child's conception or subsequently (or was a party to a purported marriage to the child's mother[83]), and has not been deprived

---

[80-81] Aberdeen, April 1, 1993, unreported.

[82] Law Reform (Parent and Child) (Scotland) Act 1986 (c.9), ss. 2(1)(*a*) and 8, as amended by the Age of Legal Capacity (Scotland) Act 1991 (c.50), Scheds. 1 and 2.

[83] The marriage either being voidable or being void but believed by the father in good faith at the time to be valid (Law Reform (Parent and Child) (Scotland) Act 1986 (c.9), s. 2(2)).

of his parental rights.[84] He may also be appointed guardian by the court.[85]

8.64   An adoption order transfers to the adoptive parents parental rights relating to the adopted child, so that the adoptive parents have guardianship rights over the child to the exclusion of any person who was the child's guardian or had guardianship rights over the child prior to the adoption order.[86]

8.65   Parental rights with respect to a child (including the right of guardianship) may be vested in a local authority or voluntary organisation by virtue of a resolution of a local authority.[87] Where the local authority or voluntary organisation is to be appointed executor *qua* guardian for the child, a copy of the resolution must (in dative cases) be put up with the petition. Thus, in 1966, the Corporation of the City of Edinburgh, having assumed parental rights over an illegitimate pupil child under the then applicable statutory provision,[88–89] was decerned and confirmed along with the child on the estate of the mother.[90]

8.66   A guardian may be appointed to a person under the age of 16 in one of two ways[91]:

1.   a parent who has guardianship rights over his or her child may appoint a person to be the child's guardian after his or her death—the appointment must be in writing and signed by the parent[92]; or

2.   the court may appoint a guardian.[93]

[84] Law Reform (Parent and Child) (Scotland) Act 1986 (c.9), ss. 2(1)(*b*) and 8, as amended by the Age of Legal Capacity (Scotland) Act 1991 (c.50), Sched. 1, para. 43 and Sched. 2).

[85] Law Reform (Parent and Child) (Scotland) Act 1986 (c.9), ss. 3 and 8, as amended by Age of Legal Capacity (Scotland) Act 1991 (c.50), Sched. 1, para. 43 and Sched. 2.

[86] Adoption (Scotland) Act 1978 (c.28), s. 12(1) and (3), as amended by Age of Legal Capacity (Scotland) Act 1991 (c.50), Sched. 2.

[87] Social Work (Scotland) Act 1968 (c.49), ss. 16(1) and (3) and 16A(1) (as inserted by Children Act 1975 (c.72), ss. 74 and 75).

[88–89] Children Act 1948 (11 & 12 Geo. 6, c.43), s. 2.

[90] *McKenzie, Decd.*, May 20, 1966, unreported. The child himself would now not be included in the decerniture and confirmation (see para. 8.58).

[91] Age of Legal Capacity (Scotland) Act 1991 (c.50), s. 5(2).

[92] Law Reform (Parent and Child) (Scotland) Act 1986 (c.9), s. 4, as amended by Age of Legal Capacity (Scotland) Act 1991 (c.50), Sched. 1, para. 41.

[93] Law Reform (Parent and Child) (Scotland) Act 1986 (c.9), ss. 3 and 8, as amended by Age of Legal Capacity (Scotland) Act 1991 (c.50), Sched. 1, para. 43 and Sched. 2; prior to December 8, 1986, the Guardianship Act 1973 (c.29), s. 10.

8.67 Where two persons are guardians to a child, either may act without the consent of the other unless the deed or decree of appointment provides otherwise.[94]

COURT APPOINTEES TO ADMINISTER AN EXECUTRY ESTATE

Judicial Factors: the 1730 Act of Sederunt

8.68 Since 1707, the Court of Session, acting under the *nobile officium*, has appointed factors to manage the affairs of others. Eventually, the Act of Sederunt of February 13, 1730 regulated the duties of factors looking after the estates of the following wards:

1. pupils not having tutors (factor *loco tutoris*);

2. persons absent that have not sufficiently empowered persons to act for them (factor *loco absentis*); and

3. persons who are under some incapacity for the time to manage their own estates (factor *curator bonis*).

8.69 Section 7 of the Act of Sederunt empowers the factor, where the ward has right to the whole or part of an executry estate, but no one else having a title offers to confirm to the estate, to confirm to any "money or effects or moveables" in his own name as executor-dative, and as factor appointed by the Lords of Council and Session or by the sheriff[95] on the estate of the ward. The factor is now enabled to confirm to heritable estate too.[96] If someone who has title offers to confirm, they will be preferred to the factor.[97] Since, even if the deceased left a testamentary writing, the factor will be decerned as executor-dative, he must find caution in relation to the executry estate, prior to being confirmed. Having been confirmed, he will administer the estate for the benefit of all having an interest in the estate, including the ward. The appointment of a factor as executor continues until the administration of the estate is complete, and is not terminated by the end of the factory.[98]

---

[94] Law Reform (Parent and Child) (Scotland) Act 1986 (c.9), s. 2(4).

[95] Judicial Factors (Scotland) Act 1880 (43 & 44 Vict. c.4), ss. 3 and 4, as amended by Law Reform (Miscellaneous Provisions) (Scotland) Act 1980 (c.55), s. 14.

[96] Succession (Scotland)Act 1964 (c.41), s. 14(1).

[97] *e.g. Martin* v. *Ferguson's Trs.* (1892) 19 R. 474.

[98] *Johnston's Exr.* v. *Dobie*, 1907 S.C. 31 (where the appointment of an executor-dative *qua* factor to pupil and minor children was not terminated by the wards attaining majority).

Contemporary use of Act of Sederunt of 1730

8.70 Section 7 of the Act of Sederunt appears still to be in force,[99] although since September 25, 1991, it has been incompetent to appoint a factor *loco tutoris*.[1]

8.71 A factor *loco absentis* or *curator bonis* may still be decerned as an executor-dative, although the appointment by the court of a factor *loco absentis* must now seldom occur, in view of the speed of international communications (which normally enable a power of attorney to be signed anywhere in the world and returned to Scotland within a few days), and the provisions of the Presumption of Life (Scotland) Act 1977 (under which a person can be declared dead if he has not been known to have been alive within the previous seven years).

The commissary factor on an intestate estate

8.72 In former times, when the person entitled to be decerned or confirmed as executor was a pupil or minor child who did not have a guardian, the commissaries used to appoint a curator or factor with power to act for or with the child as executor. In 1837, this practice was sanctioned by the Court of Session,[2] and since the commissary factor is a form of judicial factor, it would appear not to have been abolished by section 5(4) of the Age of Legal Capacity (Scotland) Act 1991, although the practice is now discouraged.[3]

8.73 Where a person, who is under the age of 16 and has no guardian or parent with parental rights, would, if over that age, be entitled to be decerned and confirmed as executor-dative, the sheriff may appoint a commissary factor and decern him executor-dative. On finding caution, the factor is confirmed as executor-dative *qua* factor for the child.[4] Two former practices which involved the child being decerned[5] are no longer compet-

---

[99] N.M.L. Walker, *Judicial Factors* (1974), p. 7.

[1] Age of Legal Capacity (Scotland) Act 1991 (c.50), s. 5(4).

[2] *Johnstone* v. *Lowden* (1838) 16 S. 541.

[3] With a view to minimising the cost of two petitions and two bonds of caution, and the risks associated with an appointment of this nature, see Accountant of Court's Note of June 1, 1938.

[4] *Johnstone* v. *Lowden* (1838) 16 S. 541, where the practice of appointing commissary factors was approved by the First Division; see, for example, *Matheson's C.B.* v. *Mathesons* (1889) 16 R. 701.

[5] (1) The person under age was decerned as executor-dative. The sheriff appointed a factor. On finding caution, the factor was confirmed as executor-dative *qua* factor for the young person (*Johnstone* v. *Lowden* (1838) 16 S. 541); and (2) the sheriff appointed the factor and then decerned both the factor and the young person. On finding caution, they would both be confirmed.

ent, since a person under the age of 16 years does not have capacity to bring civil proceedings.[6]

8.74 The application should be made to the sheriff or commissary clerk within whose jurisdiction the deceased was domiciled when he died, and should be by initial writ, at the instance of the person (normally the relative with whom the child resides) wishing to act as commissary factor and, normally, the child's nearest lawful relatives (both maternal and paternal). Productions will include a draft inventory of the deceased's estate, and the consents of any of the child's relatives who are not pursuers. The initial writ must be intimated to the Accountant of Court, and any relatives who are neither pursuers nor consenters. If there is more than one child affected, all should be dealt with in the one application.

8.75 Where a person is appointed factor, and as such is appointed executor-dative, he is to be viewed as a factor, and as such is under the administration of the Accountant of Court.[7] Since he may obtain a judicial discharge as factor, the effect is to discharge his actings as executor[8]: no other executor can obtain a judicial discharge.

8.76 The factor administers the executry estate as executor, and not as factor, and so cannot set losses incurred in his capacity as executor against the factory estate,[9] though if there was a credit balance on the executry account, the factor could properly pay it over to himself in his capacity as *curator bonis*.[10]

8.77 Where the child under the age of 16 years has a guardian the appropriate procedure is that described at paragraphs 8.57 *et seq.*

Judicial factors on an intestate estate at common law

Intestate estates

8.78 At common law, the court may appoint a judicial factor on an estate where this is seen to be expedient, as where there is no one eligible and willing to be confirmed as executor, or where the executors have been removed from office.[11] Thus, an

---

[6] Age of Legal Capacity (Scotland) Act 1991 (c.50), ss. 1(1)(*a*) and 9.

[7] *Accountant of Court*, 1907 S.C. 909.

[8] *Haston, Petr.* (1930) 46 S.L.R. 141.

[9] *Matheson's C.B.* v. *Mathesons* (1889) 16 R. 701 (where M. was decerned executor-dative *qua* factor for the three pupil children of his deceased brother, and was subsequently appointed *curator bonis* to them).

[10] *Per* Lord President Inglis in *Matheson's C.B.* v. *Mathesons* (1889) 16 R. 701 at p. 703; Lord Shand at p. 704.

[11] For grounds for superseding executors, see further N.M.L. Walker, *Judicial Factors*, pp. 34–37.

application for the appointment of a judicial factor was granted where executors-dative had left part of the estate unadminis-tered,[12] but was refused where the deceased's heir could not be found, but was presumed still to be alive, and had appointed factors to act for him.[13]

8.79   At common law, judicial factors have been appointed on intest-ate estates at the instance of the next-of-kin,[14] a remote relative,[15] the *curator bonis* of the deceased,[16] the deceased's solicitors,[17] a residuary legatee[18] and a creditor of the deceased.[19] Where it appears that the deceased died intestate and left no heirs on intestacy, the appropriate course of action is for the Queen's and Lord Treasurer's Remembrancer to uplift.[20]

8.80   On the appearance of someone eligible and willing to be con-firmed executor-dative, the factory may be recalled.[21] However, this rarely happens nowadays, since a judicial factor has full powers to protect, ingather and realiee the deceased's estate and pay it to the parties entitled thereto, and petitioning for the appointment of an executor-dative at a later stage, would merely add to the expenses of administration.

Testate estates
8.81   Judicial factors have been appointed at common law at the instance of the beneficiaries of the estate,[22] either because of the failure[23] of the appointment of the executors-nominate, or the

---

[12] *McDougall, Petr.* (1853) 15 D. 776.

[13] *Steel and Ors., Petr.* (1874) 11 S.L.R. 160.

[14] *Macdonald, Petr.* (1849) 11 D. 1028.

[15] *Young, Petr.* (1851) 13 D. 950.

[16] *Macdonald, Petr.* (1849) 11 D. 1028 (where petition presented by deceased's *curator bonis* and one of the nearest-of-kin).

[17] *Hope, Oliphant and Mackay, Petrs.* (1851) 13 D. 951 (where there was doubt as to whether the deceased had testamentary capacity, and in addition he had written and signed an informal writing); *Wood, Petr.* (1855) 17 D. 580 (where there was uncertainty as to who was the next-of-kin, and no one had sought office as executor); *Turnbull* v. *Ross's Judicial Factor*, 1916 2 S.L.T. 249 (where, pending the appearance of the next-of-kin, a judicial factor was appointed on the estate of a deceased person whose heirs on intestacy were proving difficult to trace); but *cf. Handyside* v. *Lord Advocate*, 1909 1 S.L.T. 268, where next-of-kin was unknown.

[18] *Patrick, Petr.* (1850) 12 D. 911.

[19] *Hope, Petr.* (1850) 12 D. 912, where a judicial factor and factor *loco absentis* was appointed on the estate of the deceased on the application of a creditor of the deceased, with the concurrence of his representatives and the nearest-of-kin in Scotland (but not the eldest son who resided in Sidney).

[20] See para. 6.57(10).

[21] *Turnball* v. *Ross's J.F.*, 1916 2 S.L.T. 249.

[22] *Leslie's J.F.*, 1925 S.C. 464.

[23] *e.g.* death of the executor (*Leslie's J.F.*, 1925 S.C. 464), but not merely the executor being abroad (*Duncan, Petr.* (1850) 12 D. 913).

executors-nominate could not continue in office due to a conflict of interest.[24]

Section 11A of the Judicial Factors (Scotland) Act 1889[25]

8.82   This provision was inserted by the Bankruptcy (Scotland) Act 1985, Schedule 7, paragraph 4, and replaces the earlier and almost identical provisions in the Bankruptcy (Scotland) Acts 1856 and 1913.

1. Circumstances where remedy may be available

8.83   Section 11A[26] provides for the appointment of a judicial factor where a person dies "having left no settlement appointing trustees or other parties having power to manage his estate or part thereof, or in the event of such parties not accepting or acting." Thus, a judicial factor may be appointed under this section where the deceased died either intestate or testate, but without making an effective appointment of trustees or executors.

2. Who may seek the appointment

8.84   The application under section 11A may be made only by the creditor(s) of a deceased person, or persons having an interest in the succession to the deceased's estate. This contrasts with the common law appointment, which may be instigated by a remote relative, a *curator bonis* of the deceased, or the deceased's solicitors.[27]

3. Which court?

8.85   The application must be to either

1.   the Court of Session;

2.   the sheriff of the sheriffdom within which the deceased resided;

3.   the sheriff of the sheriffdom within which the deceased carried on business during the year immediately preceding the date of the petition; or

4.   the sheriff of the sheriffdom within which is situated heritage which belonged to the deceased at the time of his death.

---

[24] *Birnie* v. *Christie* (1891) 19 R. 334; *Thomson & Other, Petrs.* (1871) 8 S.L.R. 623.

[25] 52 & 53 Vict. c.39.

[26] Inserted by the Bankruptcy (Scotland) Act 1985 (c.66), Sched. 7, para. 4.

[27] See para. 8.79.

4. The form and procedure of the petition or application

8.86　The Acts of Sederunt prescribe the form of the petition (in the case of the Court of Session) or summary application (in the case of the sheriff court) for the appointment of a judicial factor on the estate of a deceased person. Provision is made for the intimation of the petition

1.　on the walls of court (certificate to be produced with petition);

2.　in the minute book (certificate to be produced with petition);

3.　in the *Edinburgh Gazette* (copy *Gazette* to be produced with petition); and

4.　by service of a full copy of the petition on the representatives of the deceased named in the petition who are not parties thereto (execution of service to be produced with petition).

5. The court's role

8.87　The court will order intimation of the petition to the deceased's creditors and to such other interested parties as is considered necessary. After hearing the parties, the court may appoint a judicial factor, who will administer the estate subject to the supervision of the Accountant of Court in accordance with the Judicial Factors (Scotland) Acts 1880 and 1889, and relative Acts of Sederunt.[28] The appointment can normally only take place after the elapse of 14 days from the insert in the *Edinburgh Gazette* and service of the petition—although the court may make an interim appointment of a factor at an earlier date.

8.88　The court has a discretion whether to appoint a judicial factor or not: "it is not a ground for displacing executors that they have personal interests conflicting with their duty as executors. The law supposes that they are able to reconcile their interest and their duty until the contrary is proved."[29] Under the almost identical provisions in the Bankruptcy (Scotland) Acts 1856 and 1913, the court has refused to make the appointment where

---

[28] In the Court of Session, Rules of Court 1965, r. 201 (S.I. 1965 No. 321, as amended by S.I. 1967 No. 487 and S.I. 1986 No. 514) and in the sheriff court, Judicial Factors Rules 1992 (S.I. 1992 No. 272).

[29] *Per* Lord McLaren in *Birnie* v. *Christie* (1891) 19 R. 334 at p. 338 (probably common law application) quoted with approval by Lord Pearson in *Lamb* (1902) 9 S.L.T. 438 (statutory application).

1. executors-nominate had obtained confirmation after the petition was presented[30];

2. the deceased's widow had been decerned executrix-dative[31];

3. steps had been taken to have all the deceased's children decerned executors-dative, but two of the children then sought the apointment of a judicial factor, averring that one of the children was too young (being aged 20) and, having been in business with the deceased, was an interested party[32]; and

4. the estate was being administered by a person who had right to the liferent under a marriage contract and who was the father of the fiars.[33]

8.89   The court has made the appointment

1. where the potential executor-dative, having a claim on the estate in respect of an unconstituted debt, could not reconcile his personal interest with his duty as executor[34];

2. where the petitioners were creditors of the deceased, who had supported the deceased's executrix-dative for three years in continuing the deceased's farming operations, but the executrix had, before repaying the debt, breached the terms of their agreement[35];

3. where the next-of-kin had returned to this country in order to be decerned executor-dative but had then immediately returned abroad and there was then no one in this country willing to administer the estate, rents, etc., had to be uplifted otherwise the estate would suffer a loss, and it was doubtful whether the heritable creditors would be paid off in full[36]: the court preferred the factor[37];

4. where there was an application for a residuary legatee to be confirmed *qua* residuary legatee, and the deceased's

---

[30] *London & Brazilian Bank Ltd.* v. *Lumsden's Trs.*, 1913 1 S.L.T. 262; *Curle's Trs.* (1893) 1 S.L.T. 340.

[31] *Begg & Co.* (1893) 1 S.L.T. 274.

[32] *Bathgate* v. *Kelly*, 1926 S.L.T. 155.

[33] *Marshall* v. *Graham* (1859) 21 D. 203.

[34] *Lamb* (1902) 9 S.L.T. 438.

[35] *Macdonald, Fraser & Co.* v. *Cairns's Exrx.*, 1932 S.C. 699.

[36] It should be remembered that where an estate is absolutely insolvent, an executor should not act, but the special procedures set out in the Bankruptcy (Scotland) Act 1985 should be adopted. See paras. 1.54–1.56.

[37] *Masterton* v. *Erskine's Trs.* (1887) 14 R. 712.

next-of-kin challenged the interpretation of the deceased's testamentary writing on which the residuary legatee relied, a judicial factor was appointed so that the
administration of the estate could proceed.[38]

6. Caution

8.90   The judicial factor normally has to find caution within one
month of his being appointed, though the court may extend
this period. The bond of caution must be delivered to the
Accountant of Court, and only once he has indicated that he is
satisfied as to the caution will the certified copy interlocutor
appointing the factor be issued.[39]

7. Outline of the procedure which a judicial factor must follow

8.91   All judicial factors are under the supervision of the Accountant
of Court.[40]

8.92   The Acts of Sederunt prescribe the procedure for the factor
advertising for claims; examining and satisfying himself as to
the claims submitted; preparing, within six months of his first
appointment, a full inventory of the deceased's estate which is
to be lodged with supporting vouchers with the Accountant of
Court; and preparing a statement of funds and scheme of division amongst the creditors.

8.93   The judicial factor has a first charge on the funds realised for
payment of the costs of his appointment and his administration.
Thereafter the funds can be used within six months of the deceased's death to pay the deathbed and funeral expenses of the
deceased, and the preferential claims on a bankruptcy. After
the expiry of the six months, other debts can be paid (special
provision is made for the situation where the debts exceed the
funds).

8.94   Where there are surplus funds, the factor must prepare for the
Accountant of Court a statement of the amount of the residue,
the parties claiming the same and their respective grounds of
claim. The Accountant will then report back to the court, which
will determine to whom the factor will pay out the estate,
though the court can require the factor to continue to administer
the surplus estate. The factor has to advise the parties claiming
the estate of the date on which the court will consider his report
and that of the Accountant of Court.

8.95   The factor may be discharged if he petitions the court. The peti-

---

[38] *Henderson* v. *Henderson*, 1930 S.L.T. 23.
[39] In Court of Session, Rules of Court 1965, r. 200 (S.I. 1965 No. 321, as
amended by S.I. 1967 No. 487 and S.I. 1985 No. 1600), and in sheriff court,
Judicial Factors Rules 1992, rr. 9 and 10 (S.I. 1992 No. 272).
[40] Judicial Factors (Scotland) Act 1889 (52 & 53 Vict. c.39), s. 6.

tion must be served on the representatives of the deceased and on the judicial factor's cautioner; and a notice must be inserted in the *Edinburgh Gazette*. There must be lodged in process a copy of the *Edinburgh Gazette* containing the notice, an execution or acceptance of service of the petition and a certificate of intimation on the walls and in the minute book. The petition shall not be disposed of until 14 days after such service and notice.

Judicial factor's title to uplift the executry estate

8.96 By virtue of the official certified copy of his appointment, a judicial factor has title to uplift the deceased's estate in Scotland or in the British Commonwealth,[41] and need not apply for confirmation,[42] though he may do so.[43] Indeed, if the deceased had held estate in a foreign country outside the Commonwealth, it may be necessary for the judicial factor to confirm to the estate, in order to satisfy the officials of the foreign court that he has right to administer the foreign estate but the Accountant of Court will only approve the expenses of confirmation if it is shown that it was necessary to obtain confirmation. Confirmation will, for example, be necessary to transfer the deceased's interest as a tenant of an agricultural holding or of a croft under section 16 of the Succession (Scotland) Act 1964.[43a] If he does not apply for confirmation, the title of administration ends with the factory, whereas it does not if he is confirmed.[44]

8.97 In order that the judicial factor may be confirmed, he must

1. present a petition for his decerniture as executor-dative (see Style 6.33): thereafter, on production of the Act and Warrant of his appointment, the judicial factor will be decerned as executor-dative; and

2. find caution: while the bond of caution relative to the judicial factor's main title (as factor) is given back, the bond relative to his ancillary title (as executor) is not.

---

[41] *Ibid.*, s. 13, as amended by S.I. 1967 No. 487.

[42] *Ibid.*, s. 11A, inserted by Bankruptcy (Scotland) Act 1985 (c.66), Sched. 7, para. 4.

[43] *Dodd*, Oct. 7, 1910, unreported where the *curator bonis* of one of the next-of-kin was decerned and confirmed as such.

[43a] c. 41, as amended by Law Reform (Miscellaneous Provisions) (Scotland) Act 1968, (c. 70), Sched. 2.

[44] *Cf. Johnston's Exr.* v. *Dobie*, 1907 S.C. 31 (a case involving a factor *loco tutoris*).

CHAPTER 9

CAUTION

Introduction

9.01 Caution—a fidelity guarantee—is intended to protect the inheritance of beneficiaries on an executry estate from the defalcations of the executors. Originally, caution had to be obtained before confirmation would be granted in any executry estate, but statute has restricted the categories of executors who will be confirmed only once caution is found. This chapter describes the circumstances where caution is presently required, and the rules regulating it.

WHEN CAUTION IS REQUIRED

Executor-dative confirmations

9.02 Caution is required before confirmation will be granted in favour of any executor-dative—the only exception being an executor-dative or executrix-dative *qua* surviving spouse or relict of the deceased, where the whole estate will be absorbed in meeting the prior rights of the surviving spouse.[1]

Executor-nominate confirmations

9.03 While the Confirmation of Executors (Scotland) Act 1823[2] dispensed with the need for executors-nominate to obtain caution, there are exceptional cases where caution has been required before confirmation will be issued in favour of executors-nominate.

1. Where the testator had been a party to a mutual will which appointed executors, but had also signed subsequently a further testamentary writing which did not revoke the mutual will, the appointment of executors under the second deed failed and confirmation was

---

[1] Law Reform (Miscellaneous Provisions) (Scotland) Act 1980 (c.55), s. 5, amending Confirmation of Executors (Scotland) Act 1823 (4 Geo. 4, c. 98), s. 2.
[2] *Ibid.*

granted to one of the executors under the mutual will on his finding substantial caution.[3]

2. In a mutual will, a husband and wife appointed, as their executors, on the death of the survivor "their respective next-of-kin." The next-of-kin were very numerous, and some were abroad, and one of them, with the consent of the majority, was confirmed alone on his finding caution.[4]

3. Where the deceased nominated as an executor an individual whose current address could not be ascertained, and the executor had a beneficial interest under the testamentary writing, caution to the extent of the interest of the absent executor had to be obtained before confirmation was granted in favour of the other named executors.[5]

9.04 Apart from such exceptions, the sheriff or commissary clerk does not require caution before executors-nominate will be confirmed.

Resealing of grants under the Colonial Probates Act 1892

9.05 Where letters of administration are to be resealed in Scotland, caution must be obtained in respect of the estate in Scotland.[6] Caution may also be required for the payment of debts due to creditors residing in the United Kingdom, where either a grant of probate or letters of administration is to be resealed in Scotland.[7]

WHO MAY BE CAUTIONER

9.06 Commissary practice is to accept as a cautioner any company which has been accepted as cautioner in the Court of Session[8] or a private individual, though the latter is seldom, if ever, encountered nowadays.[9] However, as Lord Walker observed in

---

[3] *Trotter*, July 28, 1888, unreported.

[4] *Robertson*, Oct. 25, 1862, unreported.

[5] *Purvis*, July 9, 1863, unreported; *Templeton*, March 10, 1866, unreported.

[6] Colonial Probates Act 1892 (55 & 56 Vict. c.6), s. 2(2)(*b*), which provides that caution must be obtained for the estate in the *United Kingdom*, but see Administration of Estates Act 1971 (c.25), s. 11.

[7] Colonial Probates Act 1892 (55 & 56 Vict. c.6), s. 2(3), but see Administration of Estates Act 1971 (c.25), s. 11.

[8] Judicial Factors Act 1849 (12 & 13 Vict. c.51), s. 27 and Act of Sederunt (Rules of Court, consolidation and amendment) 1965, Rule 200(*e*)(iv) (S.I. 1965 No. 321).

[9] When a private individual is encountered as cautioner it is usually in connection with small estates.

Harrison v. *Butters & Anor.*,[10] the practice of using an insurance company as cautioner introduces a risk to the security of the estate, as where a bond of caution is void *ab initio* owing to essential error as to the identity of the person to whom it was issued. It would seem that, although a private individual may act as cautioner, he may not charge a premium, unless authorised to carry out insurance business.[11]

9.07   The qualifications for cautioner are as follows.

1.   The cautioner must be resident in Scotland, or otherwise subject to the jurisdiction of the Scottish courts—a member of a Scottish firm has been accepted, though resident in England.[12]

2.   The cautioner must not be beneficially interested in the succession. This rule is intended to provide against two or more beneficiaries colluding to appropriate the estate to themselves, without intimating to all interested parties. It is thought that a cautioner who has no interest, except to see that all possible claims are satisfied, affords the best guarantee that the executor will perform his duties properly.

3.   With a view to ensuring the independence of the cautioner, a cautioner should not be the solicitor, or a partner in the firm of solicitors, acting in the case.[13]

4.   Where a private individual is acting as cautioner, the court must be satisfied as to his ability to guarantee the amount of estate in the bond. In the past, a certificate from a justice of the peace that the individual has sufficient means has been accepted.[14] In other cases, the sheriff clerk has required actual evidence, such as a bank book showing a sufficient deposit, or a statement from a bank manager certifying that the individual is worth the amount of the bond required.

THE BOND OF CAUTION

9.08   In each executry where caution is required, there must be

---

[10] *Harrison* v. *Butters & Anor.*, 1969 S.L.T. 183 at p. 184.

[11] Insurance Companies Act 1982 (c.50); see definition of insurance business in s. 95(*a*).

[12] *Dudgeon*, April 23, 1862, unreported.

[13] In the past, some courts took the view that such persons could act as cautioners. See 7th ed. of this work, p. 232, para. 4.

[14] *e.g. French and Anor., Petrs.* (1871) 9 M. 741.

lodged along with the inventory a separate bond of caution (see Styles 9.01 and 9.02) which must be self-proving as regards the signature of the cautioner and all the executor(s) to be confirmed. Further, except in the case of a bond to be put up with an application under the Small Estates Acts (which will refer to the applicant as the person who "is to be decerned and confirmed"), the bond must be executed by the cautioner and by the executor(s) *after* the sheriff has granted the decree of decerniture. Each executor must be designed (name, address and capacity of appointment) in the bond of caution to tie in exactly with the designation in the testamentary writing or decree dative, and in the inventory. Unless the court has restricted the amount of the caution (see paras. 19.18–19.27), the amount of the caution must not be less than the amount of the estate to be confirmed to (see, further, paras. 9.11–9.15).

Executors and cautioner prorogate jurisdiction

9.09 The terms of the bond are such that both the executor(s) and the cautioner subject themselves to the jurisdiction of the court in which confirmation is to be granted, and appoint the sheriff clerk's office as a domicile where they may be cited at the instance of all interested.[15] Thus, a cautioner, who resided in another sheriffdom, but who had subjected himself to the jurisdiction of the Sheriff Court of Renfrewshire in the bond of caution, was held bound to answer in that court when sued by one of the next-of-kin interested in the estate.[16]

9.10 The decision of *Halliday's Executor* v. *Halliday's Executors*[17] has been cited as authority for the parties to a bond of caution not being subject to the jurisdiction of the sheriff court in which the bond was lodged. The claim in *Halliday* did not arise from the bond of caution but was brought by one of the deceased's creditors against the executors. Further, it has been suggested[18] that the particular commissary court involved did not then adopt the now universal practice of requiring the executors to sign the bond of caution, along with the cautioner. In this event, it could hardly be argued that the executors had prorogated the jurisdiction of the particular sheriff court.

[15] "And both parties subject themselves, their heirs and successors, to the jurisdiction of the Sheriff Principal of . . . in the premises and appoint the Sheriff-Clerk's Office, in . . . , as a domicile whereat they may be cited to all diets of Court, at the instance of all and sundry having interests as law will, — holding any Citation legally affixed and left for them, or their foresaids, upon the walls of the said Office as sufficient as if they were personally summoned."

[16] *Kirkwood* v. *Kirkwood* (1890) 6 Sh. Ct. Rep. 43.

[17] (1886) 14 R. 251.

[18] Sheriff Cowan in *Kirkwood* v. *Kirkwood* , above at p. 45.

The amount of the caution

9.11 Unless the court has restricted the amount of the caution (see paras. 19.18–19.27), the amount of the caution is the gross amount of the estate, both heritable and moveable, real and personal, situated in Scotland, England and Wales, and Northern Ireland, without any deduction for debts or funeral expenses. This is the case in all dative appointments, including the case of an executor-creditor who may confirm to only part of the estate.

9.12 If one of the deceased's debts has been secured over one of the deceased's assets,[19] it is competent to show the debt in the inventory, by deducting it from the particular asset. For instance, where a debt is secured over heritage, the heritage (and debt) may be shown in the inventory as follows:

 1. Dwellinghouse No. 52 Brown Street, Aberdeen, being the subjects described in the disposition by New Homes Limited in favour of the John Smith recorded GRS (Aberdeen) June 1, 1990   £80,000

  Less: Secured loan from Scotland's Building Society   <u>60,000</u>

                  20,000

9.13 A similar presentation may be used in the following cases:

 a corporeal moveable which has been pledged in security of a debt;

 an incorporeal moveable which has been assigned[20] in security of a debt;

 a registered ship which has been mortgaged in security of a debt, and the mortgage registered by the registrar of the ship's port registry[21];

 a registered fishing vessel (or a share therein) which has been mortgaged in security of a debt, and the mortgage registered by the Secretary of State[22];

 an aircraft and its spare parts,[23] which have been mortgaged in security of a debt, and the mortgage entered in the register of aircraft mortgages kept by the Civil Aviation Authority.

---

[19] See, further, W. A. Wilson, *The Scottish Law of Debt* (2nd ed. 1991), Chaps. 7 and 8.

[20] An assignation will be binding on the deceased's executors, even if it has not been intimated—see *Brownlee v. Robb*, 1907 S.C. 1302; *Strawbridge's Trs. v. Bank of Scotland*, 1935 S.L.T. 568.

[21] Merchant Shipping Act 1894 (57 & 58 Vict. c.60), s. 31, as substituted by Merchant Shipping Act 1988 (c.12), s. 10, Sched. 1, para. 21.

[22] Merchant Shipping Act 1988 (c.12), s. 21 and Sched. 3.

[23] S.I. 1972 No. 1268, arts. 3 and 4.

9.14 While it is equally competent for the asset to be included in the inventory and the debt to be separately disclosed in the inventory of debts, deducting the debt from the asset in this way has the benefit of reducing the cost of the bond of caution.

9.15 It is not necessary to obtain caution for estate overseas.

9.16 It is possible for the executor to apply to the court to have the amount of the caution restricted,[24] but it cannot be completely dispensed with.[25] The application for restriction of caution should not be included in the petition for appointment of an executor-dative.[26]

9.17 Where it is necessary to obtain an eik to the confirmation, caution will be required for any increase in the gross value of the estate: if there is no new estate, or the new estate is of no value, no further caution is required.[27]

9.18 Where confirmation *ad non executa* is required, caution must be obtained for the full value of the estate to be confirmed *ad non executa*.

9.19 There is no machinery for substituting one cautioner for another, or for requiring a new cautioner when the original cautioner has become bankrupt, left the country, or died. In these circumstances, if additional estate is discovered necessitating an eik to the confirmation, a bond of caution must be obtained from a different cautioner for the additional estate.

Legal charges for bond of caution

9.20 A solicitor may charge £21.80 for preparing a bond of caution—whether obtained through the medium of a guarantee company, or through a private individual. In the latter event, the charge covers not just getting the bond signed and lodging it with the clerk of court, but also procuring attestation of the cautioner's sufficiency.[28]

Bond is non-returnable

9.21 According to settled practice, the bond of caution will be retained by the sheriff clerk, and is never given up.

---

[24] See, further, paras. 19.18–19.27.
[25] *Preston*, March 11, 1874, unreported.
[26] *Girdwood* (1930) 46 Sh. Ct. Rep. 115.
[27] *Wilson*, Sept. 22, 1905, unreported.
[28] Act of Sederunt (Fees of Solicitors in the Sheriff Court) (Amendment and Further Provisions) 1993 (S.I. 1993 No. 3080) Chap. VI, as amended by S.I. 1994 No. 1142.

CAUTIONER'S LIABILITY

9.22		The cautioner's obligation under a bond of caution only extends to the estate which the executor has confirmed to, and will not cover other estate which has been paid to the executor[29] — such as discretionary payments from pension trustees.[30]

9.23		It should be remembered that the cautioner can only be pursued once all attempts to recover the moneys from the deceased's executor have failed.[31]

9.24		The cautioner will be relieved from his obligations by the actings of the beneficiaries, as where the beneficiaries have not done diligence against the executor's own estate,[32] or by the actings of the executor, as where there had been non-disclosure or material error in the completion of the application for the bond.[33]

9.25		Further, the cautioner's obligation under a bond of caution, being properly a cautionary obligation, prescribes after five years.[34] While it has been held that the previous rules for septennial prescription for cautionary obligations — the Act anent Principals and Cautioners 1695 (c.5) — did not apply to judicial cautioners, such as cautioners in a confirmation,[35] the reason for this was "because the act [of 1695] is confined to persons engaged for others in bonds or contracts for sums of money,"[36] rather than that the obligation of a judicial cautioner was not a cautionary obligation. There would therefore seem to be no reason why the Prescription and Limitation (Scotland) Act 1973 does not apply to a cautioner's obligation under a bond of caution.

More than one cautioner

9.26		Where two or more cautioners are conjoined in the bond, they are bound jointly and severally, and each is good for the whole

---

[29] *Napier* v. *Menzies* (1740) Mor. 3849; *Murdoch* v. *McKirdy* (1826) 4 S. 479.
[30] (1967) 12 J.L.S. 258.
[31] *Arnot* v. *Abernethy* (1623) Mor. 3587; *Stewart* v. *Fisher* (1623) Mor. 3588; *Birsbane* v. *Monteith* (1662) Mor. 3588; see also *Douglas* v. *Lindsay* (1662) Mor. 8125 where decree was granted against the cautioner but decree was suspended until the executor had been pursued.
[32] *Per* Lord Ormidale in *Macfarlane* v. *Anstruther and Others* (1870) 9 M. 117 at pp. 119–120.
[33] *Harrison* v. *Butters & Anor.*, 1969 S.L.T. 183 where a lady who was divorced from the deceased purported to be his widow in applying for a bond of caution.
[34] Prescription and Limitation (Scotland) Act 1973 (c.52), s. 6 and Sched. 1, paras. 1(g) and 2(c).
[35] *Gallie* v. *Ross* (1836) 14 S. 647.
[36] Ersk. III. vii. 23.

obligation. In the past, when the norm was for private indi-viduals to act as cautioners, it might not be possible for the executors to find one cautioner for the whole estate. Instead, the court might accept two cautioners, each of whom was liable only for one-half of the estate confirmed.

CHECK LIST FOR BONDS OF CAUTION

9.27   In preparing a bond of caution, it is essential to ensure

1. that the bond of caution is executed after the sheriff has granted decree of decerniture of the executor(s)-dative;

2. that all executors to be confirmed sign the bond of caution;

3. that the designation of each executor (name, address and capacity of his appointment) in the bond of caution ties in exactly with that in the testamentary writing or decree dative, and in the inventory; and

4. that the amount of caution provided for in the bond is not less than the amount of the gross estate to be con-firmed to.

CHAPTER 10

PREPARATION OF THE INVENTORY

Introduction

10.01 Since confirmation vests the deceased's estate in the executor for the purposes of administration,[1] confirmation is normally an essential step in winding up an executry estate. In order to obtain confirmation, an executor must exhibit[2] to the proper sheriff court,[3] *inter alia*, a full and true inventory of the deceased's estate and effects (both heritable[4] and moveable) in Scotland and, provided that the deceased died domiciled in Scotland, the real and personal estate in England and Wales and Northern Ireland[5] and elsewhere, distinguishing what is in Scotland from what is elsewhere. This chapter explores a variety of matters pertinent to the completion and the submission of an inventory with particular reference to the completion of the CAP Form A-3. Readers are also referred, for general guidance, to the Inland Revenue's CAP Form A-5 (1986) "Instructions for the completion of Inland Revenue Inventory Form CAP A-3 (1986)" and CAP Form A-5 (1986) Supplement, instructions for completing the Forms B-3 and B-4.

Partial Confirmation

10.02 While originally it was perfectly competent for an executor to confirm to only part of the estate, such "partial confirmation" was abolished by the Confirmation of Executors (Scotland) Act 1823. Section 3 of this Act provided that all persons requiring

---

[1] Succession (Scotland) Act 1964 (c. 41), s. 14(1).
[2] Unless otherwise indicated, the requirements are prescribed by the Probate and Legacy Duties Act 1808 (48 Geo. 3, c. 14), s. 38 as amended by Finance Act 1949 (12 & 13 Geo. 6, c. 47), s. 52(10) and Sched. 11, Pt. V; Finance Act 1975 (c. 7), s. 52(2) and Sched. 13, Pt. I and *prosp.* Law Reform (Miscellaneous Provisions) (Scotland) Act 1990 (c. 40), s. 74 and Sched. 8, para. 19 and Sched. 9.
[3] Sheriff Courts (Scotland) Act 1876 (39 & 40 Vict. c. 70), s. 35 gave the sheriffs jurisdiction in commissary matters, and this was confirmed by Sheriff Courts (Scotland) Act 1907 (7 Edw. 7, c. 51), s. 5.
[4] Succession (Scotland) Act 1964 (c. 41), s. 14(1).
[5] Confirmation of Executors (Scotland) Act 1858 (21 & 22 Vict. c. 56), s. 9 as amended by Statute Law Revision Act 1892 (55 & 56 Vict. c. 19), s. 1 and Sched., Administration of Estates Act 1971 (c. 25), s. 6(1) and Sched. 2, Pt. 1 and Finance Act 1975 (c. 7), s. 52(2) and Sched. 13.

confirmation—with the exception of executors-creditor, who might limit their confirmation to the amount of their debt[6]—were bound to confirm to the whole moveable estate known at the time, to which they should make oath.[7] Section 14(1) of the Succession (Scotland) Act 1964 had the effect of requiring heritable estate in Scotland also to be included in the confirmation. However, it is submitted that confirmation to Scottish estate alone is not partial confirmation[8] and that there is technically no objection to confirming only to the Scottish estate of a person who died domiciled in Scotland—although it must be remembered that the rest of his estate must be included in the account for inheritance tax purposes.

The Forms

10.03 The inventory must be completed either on an official Inland Revenue form[9]—either the CAP Form A-3, B-3 or B-4—or on an approved substitute form generated by computer.[10] Copies of the official forms can be obtained from the Capital Taxes Office, 16 Picardy Place, Edinburgh, or from head post offices.

Preliminary check-list

10.04 Before the inventory can be completed, it is necessary to have an executor available to act. Ideally, the deceased will have named an executor or executors (or even trustees) in a properly executed testamentary writing.

10.05 Some defects in the formalities of execution of a testamentary writing, may be resolved simply. For instance if a witness is not named or designed in the testing clause, after due inquiry, the missing details may be inserted before the deed is recorded for

---

[6] Confirmation of Executors (Scotland) Act 1823 (4 Geo. 4, c. 98), s. 4 *prosp.* amended by Law Reform (Miscellaneous Provisions) (Scotland) Act 1990 (c. 40), s. 74(1) and Sched. 8, para. 20.

[7] Confirmation of Executors (Scotland) Act 1823 (4 Geo. 4, c. 98), s. 3 *prosp.* amended by Law Reform (Miscellaneous Provisions) (Scotland) Act 1990 (c. 40), s. 74(1) and Sched. 8, para. 20, enabling a declaration to be made.

[8] *Kennion's Exrs.*, 1939 S.L.T. (Sh. Ct.) 5 where it was opined that the Confirmation and Probate Act 1858 merely provided a convenient method of an executor obtaining title to English estate, and did not replace the older more cumbersome process of obtaining confirmation to Scottish estate, and probate or letters of administration to the estate in England and Wales. It is submitted that just like the 1858 Act, the Administration of Estates Act 1971 did not replace the older process.

[9] IHTA 1984 (c. 51), ss. 257, 261.

[10] SP 2/93; see also Press Release of January 13, 1993.

preservation or founded on in court action.[10a] Where such action is not possible, and there is doubt as to whether the writing was properly executed, and it was executed prior to August, 1995 it will be necessary for the executor either

1. to raise a separate action of due execution under section 39 of the Conveyancing (Scotland) Act 1874, in either the Court of Session or in the sheriff court (see paras. 19.35 *et seq*); or

2. to apply to the sheriff court by initial writ for (a) proof that the testamentary writing was duly executed and (b) special authority for appointment as executor-nominate or dative, as appropriate (see, further, paragraph 19.14).

10.06 If the testamentary writing was executed on or after August 1, 1995, any doubt as to the validity of the execution will be resolved by a successful application to the court under section 4 of the Requirements of Writing (Scotland) Act 1995 (see paras. 4.93 *et seq.*) If the deceased died domiciled in Scotland, but had executed his final testamentary writing abroad, it will be necessary to obtain

1. if the executor avers that the testamentary writing is validly executed in terms of the Wills Act 1963 in accordance with the law of a country other than Scotland, the opinion of someone expert in the law of that country, to the effect that the testamentary writing is validly executed under that law;

2. where the testamentary writing or the opinion on foreign law is not written in English, a certified translation thereof (see para. 2.52).

10.07 If the deceased, instead of naming an executor, merely identified him, it will be necessary for the person identified to apply to the sheriff for special authority for his appointment as executor-nominate, submitting two affidavits that he is in fact the person referred to (see, further, paras. 5.06 and 19.28).

10.08 If the deceased did not appoint an executor or trustee, it will be necessary either for the general disponee, universal legatory or residuary legatee to be confirmed as executor-nominate in terms of section 3 of the Executors (Scotland) Act 1900 (see paras. 5.66 *et seq.*) or for the appointment of an executor-dative (see paras. 6.14 *et seq*, Chapter 7 and paras. 19.07–19.14).

[10a] If testamentary writing executed prior to August 1, 1995, Conveyancing (Scotland) Act 1874, (37 & 38 Vict. c.94), s.38; otherwise Requirements of Writing (Scotland) Act 1995 (c.7), s.3(3).

10.09   If the deceased did not die domiciled in Scotland, the points discussed in Chapter 2 (especially the Notes for Guidance) must be considered.

Oath or Affirmation?

10.10   "Every person . . . who as executor . . . nearest in kin, creditor . . . or otherwise shall intromit with. . . . any estate or effects . . . of any person . . . shall . . . before (he) shall be confirmed executor . . . testamentary or dative, exhibit upon Oath or affirmation in the proper Commissary Court in Scotland . . . a full and true inventory . . . of all the estate."[11]

10.11   A person who objects to being sworn is entitled to make a solemn affirmation, which is of the same force and effect as an oath.[12]

10.12   A falsehood contained in an oath required for revenue matters, or a false inventory of property given up for confirmation, may result in a charge of perjury at common law.[13] There is also a statutory offence: where a person makes a statement on oath, or an affirmation, which "he knows to be false or does not believe to be true," he is guilty of an offence and shall be liable on conviction to imprisonment for a term not exceeding five years or a fine or both.[14]

10.13   Legislation[15] has been passed which will enable an executor signing an inventory to make a declaration (rather than an oath or affirmation). At the time of writing the statutory instrument to bring this provision into effect has not been made.

Persons before whom an affirmation or oath may be taken

10.14   An oath or affirmation to an inventory may be taken before a sheriff principal, a sheriff, any commissioner appointed by a sheriff principal or sheriff, any sheriff clerk or sheriff clerk depute, any notary public, magistrate or justice of the peace in

---

[11] Probate and Legacy Duties Act 1808 (48 Geo. 3, c. 149), s. 38, as amended by Finance Act 1949 (12 & 13 Geo. 6, c. 47), s. 52(10), Sched. 11, Pt. V, Finance Act 1975 (c. 7), s. 52(2), Sched. 13, Pt. 1 and *prosp.* Law Reform (Miscellaneous Provisions) (Scotland) Act 1990 (c. 40), s. 74, Sched. 8, para. 19 and Sched. 9 (permitting a declaration to be made, rather than an oath or affirmation).

[12] Oaths Act 1978 (c. 19), s. 5.

[13] Alison, *Criminal Law in Scotland*, p. 472.

[14] False Oaths (Scotland) Act 1933 (23 and 24 Geo. 5, c. 20), ss. 1 and 7(1) as amended by Administration of Justice Act 1977 (c. 38), s. 32(4), Sched. 5, Pt. III.

[15] Law Reform (Miscellaneous Provisions) (Scotland) Act 1990 (c. 40), s. 74(1), Sched. 8, paras. 19–20, 22(2), 24, 25 and Sched. 9.

the United Kingdom; or (if taken in England and Wales or Northern Ireland) before any commissioner for oaths appointed by the courts of these countries[16]; or (if taken in England and Wales) by a solicitor holding a current practising certificate, provided that he is not the deponent's solicitor and does not have an interest in the estate[17]; or (if taken at a place outside the United Kingdom) before any British consul, local magistrate, or notary public practising in the foreign country, or admitted and practising in Great Britain or Northern Ireland,[18] or before certain United Kingdom consular officials posted to that country,[19] or, if the deponent is a member of the armed forces, or a civilian attached thereto, before officers of certain higher ranks of the armed forces.[19a]

10.15   The person before whom the oath or affirmation is made should be completely impartial, and should not have an interest in the estate. For instance, he should not be a beneficiary of the estate, or the partner or co-executor of the deponing executor, and it is preferable if he is not a solicitor in the legal firm hired by the executors to administer the estate.[19b]

Who may depone

10.16   If confirmation is required, the oath or affirmation must be taken by someone who is entitled to confirmation either as executor-nominate or as executor-dative. Where there is more than one executor, only one need depone. If there is a *sine qua non* executor, he must depone. In other cases, the practice is for the executor first named in the testamentary writing to depone, but there is in fact no rule to this effect.

10.17   Where the deponent is unable to sign, the practice is that there

---

[16] Confirmation of Executors (Scotland) Act 1858 (21 & 22 Vict. c. 56), s. 11; Executors (Scotland) Act 1900 (63 & 64 Vict. c. 55), s. 8.

[17] Solicitors Act 1974 (c. 47), s. 81(1) and (2).

[18] Confirmation of Executors (Scotland) Act 1858 (21 & 22 Vict. c. 56), s. 11 and Executors (Scotland) Act 1900 (63 & 64 Vict. c. 55), s. 8.

[19] *e.g.* ambassador, envoy, minister, charge d'affairs, secretary of embassy or legation, consul, vice-consul, acting consul, pro-consul, consular agent, acting consular general, acting vice-consul, and acting consular agent, or counsellor, (Commissioners for Oaths Act 1889 (52 & 53 Vict. c. 10), s. 6 as amended by Commissioners for Oaths Act 1891 (54 & 55 Vict. c. 50), s. 2, and Oaths and Evidence (Overseas Authorities and Countries) Act 1963 (c. 27), s. 3). Consular officials of a state which represents United Kingdom interests in a particular foreign country may also notarise there (Evidence and Powers of Attorney Act 1943 (6 & 7 Geo. 6, c. 18), s. 4).

[19a] Emergency Laws (Miscellaneous Provisions) Act 1953 (c.47), s.10; Army Act 1955 (c.18), s.204; Air Force Act 1955 (c.19), s.204, all as amended by Armed Forces Act 1971 (c.33), s.70 and by Armed Forces Act 1981 (c.55), s.19.

[19b] *Cf. Barr, Petr.*, 1960 S.L.T. (Sh. Ct.) 7.

is added to the deposition a statement to that effect, setting out the cause of the inability, and the person before whom the deposition is made signs alone.[19c]

10.18   If the inventory is being given up purely for Inland Revenue purposes, and confirmation is not required, anyone who has a vested interest in the executry estate as heir on intestacy, legatee or otherwise, may lodge the account.[20]

SPECIAL DEPONENTS

Executor overseas

Oath or affirmation made by attorney

10.19   Where an executor is abroad, he may, with a view to simplifying the administration of the estate, appoint someone in Scotland as his attorney—to take the oath or make affirmation, give up the necessary inventory, obtain confirmation, and perhaps also to take possession of, make up title to, and uplift the estate and grant discharges, etc. This practice has received judicial approval:

> "There may be many cases . . . in which it is absolutely necessary for the realisation of the trust estate, that the trustees should employ some one to act for them. They could not all go to Shanghai; and it was quite within the course of their duty to appoint X as their agent and attorney to perform their duty of realisation."[21]

10.20   The style of the power of attorney should conform to Style 7.01. The power of attorney will normally be executed in accordance with the formalities of the place of execution, and if it was not executed in Scotland, it should be accompanied by a notarial certificate relating to its attestation, or some form of statutory declaration verifying its authenticity.[22]

10.21   A power of attorney does not require to be stamped.[23]

10.22   The appointment of the attorney must be exhibited and signed as relative to the oath, and if not already registered in the Sheriff

---

[19c] The reason for this practice is unclear but it is to be observed that the relevant statutory provisions all refer to the executor making oath or affirmation — but do not refer to him signing before the relevant official.

[20] IHTA 1984 (c. 51), s. 216(2).

[21] *Per* Lord Kinloch in *Lamond's Trs.* v. *Croom* (1871) 9 M. 662.

[22] Anton and Beaumont, *Private International Law* (2nd ed.), p. 308.

[23] Finance Act 1985 (c. 54), s. 85(1) and Sched. 24.

Court Books[24] will be recorded along with the inventory. If the document is in a foreign language, an authenticated translation must be submitted (see para. 2.52), and will be recorded too.

10.23   The confirmation is always issued in favour of the executor and not in favour of the attorney.[25]

Oath or affirmation made by consul

10.24   If the person who is to be confirmed as executor-nominate or dative is a national of one of certain states,[26] or is the subject of certain other states[27] but is not resident in Scotland, and has not granted a power of attorney, a consular officer of the state may apply on behalf of the overseas person for confirmation as executor, as if he had been authorised by a power of attorney.[28]

10.25   Thereafter the officer or his successors in office shall be entitled to receive and administer the estate as if authorised by a power of attorney.[29]

Company (including a nominee company) deponing

10.26   When the executor is a company, an officer of the company is normally appointed to take the oath or make affirmation on behalf of the company. A certified copy of the resolution, nomination, minute of meeting or other authority in favour of the officer must be produced with the inventory and referred to in the oath or affirmation, and docketed as relative thereto. The confirmation is always issued in favour of the company.

10.27   A foreign company may appoint an attorney in the usual way.[30]

---

[24] Act of Sederunt to Simplify Registration in Commissary Court Books of July 18, 1944.

[25] *Millar* July 23, 1943, unreported, discussed, further, at paras. 8.14 and 8.16.

[26] Austria (S.I. 1963 No. 1927), Belgium (S.I. 1964 No. 1399), Bulgaria (S.I. 1968 No. 1861), Czechoslovakia (S.I. 1976 No. 1216), Denmark (S.I. 1963 No. 370), Egypt (S.I. 1986 No. 216), France (S.I. 1953 No. 1455), Germany (S.I. 1957 No. 2052), Greece (S.I. 1953 No. 1454), Hungary (S.I. 1971 No. 1845), Italy (S.I. 1957 No. 2053), Japan (S.I. 1965 No. 1714), Mexico (S.I. 1955 No. 425), Mongolia (S.I. 1976 No. 1150), Norway (S.I. 1951 No. 1165), Poland (S.I. 1971 No. 1238), Spain (S.I. 1963 No. 614), Sweden (S.I. 1952 No. 1218), USSR (S.I. 1968 No. 1378) and Yugoslavia (S.I. 1966 No. 443), all S.I.s made under the Consular Conventions Act 1949 (12 & 13 Geo. 6, c.29).

[27] Finland (S.I. 1939 No. 1452), Thailand (S.I. 1939 No. 1457), or Turkey (S.I. 1939 No. 1458), all S.I.s made under the Domicile Act 1961 (24 & 25 Vict. c.21), s.4, and still effective following the enactment of the Consular Conventions Act 1949 (12 & 13 Geo. 6, c.29), s.8.

[28] Consular Conventions Act 1949 (12 and 13 Geo. 6, c. 29), s. 2(1).

[29] *Ibid.*, s. 2(2).

[30] See paras. 10.19–10.23.

Partnership deponing

10.28 Where a partnership is executor, a partner will sign, using either his own name or the firm name.[30a]

Persons suffering from ill health

10.29 A *curator bonis* of an *incapax* may depone instead of the *incapax* (see paras. 8.41 and 8.50–8.53). A person who is merely suffering from a disability or ill health which makes it difficult (though not impossible) for him to sign, must either act or (if an executor-nominate) may resign office (see paras. 5.124–5.125), or (if an executor-dative) a petition may be made for the recall of his appointment (see paras. 19.15–19.17). Such a person cannot delegate his duties by executing a power of attorney.[31]

Persons under the age of 16 years

10.30 A person under the age of 16 years lacks the capacity to depone, but his guardian may depone instead (see paras. 8.56–8.67).

COMPLETION OF PAGE 1

10.31 The basic details of the deceased must be inserted: the title and full names of the deceased, the dates of birth and death,[32] the place of last residence, the place of death and the deceased's occupation or other designation (*e.g.* widow, spinster, retired).

10.32 If the deceased used more than one name (or some of the investments or any testamentary writings disclose another address, these should be indicated thus:

SURNAME	SMITH (formerly BROWN)
FORENAMES	ANNIE (otherwise ANNABEL)
ADDRESS	11 UNION ROW, ABERDEEN (formerly 12 PRINCES STREET, EDINBURGH)

10.33 The place of last residence should bear out the averment of

---

[30a] Requirements of Writing (Scotland) Act 1995 (c.7), s.7(7), Sched. 2, para. 2(1) and (2).

[31] *Leishman*, Dec. 17, 1980, unreported, discussed further at para. 8.39.

[32] Shown by number (*e.g.* [01|01|95] for January 1, 1995).

domicile set out at paragraph 1 on page 2: if it does not, a detailed explanation as to the domicile averred should be set out at paragraph 1 on page 2.

10.34 Where there is difficulty as to either the place of death or the date of death (as where the deceased died in an accident, or where the body was not found for some time after the death, or where no body has been found) the guidelines set out at paragraphs 7.10–7.15 should be followed.

10.35 The appropriate deletion must be made so that it is clear whether the executors are "nominate" or "dative".

10.36 The *full* names and the *current* addresses of the executors to be confirmed should be listed, following the order in which they are set out in the testamentary writing or decree-dative. A person who was appointed executor, but who is not to be confirmed (as where he declined office) should not be listed here. If an executor was shown in the testamentary writing as residing at a previous address, the linking between the old and the current addresses must be specified at paragraph 2 on page 2 of the inventory.

10.37 In dative cases, all details must correspond with those contained in the initial writ.

10.38 The "Total Estate for Confirmation" (*i.e.* before deducting debts) is brought forward from the "Summary for Confirmation" (see para. 10.198).

COMPLETION OF PAGE 2

Preamble

10.39 It is necessary to insert the place and date where the oath or affirmation was administered and the full name, address and designation (*e.g.* "notary public") of the person administering the oath or affirmation (see paras. 10.14–10.15).

10.40 Confirmation will not be granted upon an executor's oath which is more than six months old. In such cases, the crave is held to be abandoned, and the oath should be re-sworn. Where the inventory has originally merely been recorded, if it is desired to obtain confirmation more than six months thereafter, a special oath may be required (Form 98 in the 7th edition).

Executor named in testamentary writing, etc., to be identified with the deponent

10.41 The name, designation and address of the deponing executor should be set out in such a way as to correspond with the signature to the inventory, and also to tie in his current name, designation and address, as set out on page 1 of the inventory, with those specified in the testamentary writing or decree-dative. Any error in the spelling of an executor's name should be corrected. If the deponing executor had been an unmarried woman when the deceased appointed her as his executor, and she thereafter married and took her husband's surname, her surname before and after marriage should be given.

> *Example:* If the testamentary writing nominated "my cousin, James Smith, 1 New Street, Dundee to be executor," but by the time confirmation is being applied for, this cousin resided at "3 Fair View, Dundee" and signed the inventory "James F Smith", the preamble might run as follows:
> "appeared James Smith, cousin of the said deceased, residing sometime at 1 New Street, Dundee and now at 3 Fair View, there, and otherwise known as James Frank Smith."
> Alternatively, the preamble might run as follows
> "appeared James Frank Smith, cousin of the said deceased, residing at 3 Fair View, Dundee"
> and the deposition at paragraph 2 might read:
> "The said deponent is named in the said Will as James Smith and is designed in the said Will as residing at 1 New Street, Dundee and now resides at 3 Fair View, there."

10.42   Occasionally, the testator may name a person as executor, without specifying the person's address.

> *Example:* If the testamentary writing nominated "my cousin, Jean Smith, to be executrix," the preamble might run "appeared Jean Smith, cousin of the said deceased, residing at 3 Fair View, Dundee, referred to in the Will after-specified as 'my cousin, Jean Smith'."

Paragraph 1

10.43   The deceased's full name (and any alternative names) as shown on page 1 should be stated. It is not necessary to repeat the deceased's address (whether his last address or a previous one which must be specified as a link), provided that all such addresses have been set out on page 1.

10.44   The deceased's domicile must be stated. See further paragraphs 7.18–7.29. The sheriff clerk is not bound to accept an averment as to domicile if, from the deceased's description in the inventory, it would prima facie appear that he was not so domiciled. Thus, if the domicile stated does not correspond with the place of last residence disclosed on page 1 of the inventory, appropriate explanation must be given.

10.45   If the deceased died domiciled in Scotland, it should, as appropriate, be stated either that he died domiciled "in the Sheriffdom of . . . in Scotland", or that "He had, at the time of his death, no fixed or known domicile save that the same was in Scotland" (the words "Domiciled in" being deleted). The executor's oath or affirmation that the deceased died domiciled in Scotland is sufficient warrant to authorise the sheriff clerk to note this in the confirmation[33] and also to include in the confirmation any items of estate in England and Wales and Northern Ireland, provided that they are separately valued.[34] Since the sheriff clerk noting a Scottish domicile in this way "shall be evidence and have effect for the purposes of [the 1858] Act only,"[35] it does not preclude further inquiry if a question arises on an issue such as the validity of a testamentary writing, liability for inheritance tax or entitlement to legal rights on the deceased's estate.

10.46 If the deceased died domiciled somewhere other than Scotland, confirmation may only be given to his Scottish estate, but if the inventory is the first account for inheritance tax purposes, it will be necessary to list all other United Kingdom estate after the summary for confirmation.

Paragraph 2 (general)

10.47 The current and previous names and addresses of all the executors to be confirmed (apart from the deponing executor) should be narrated, in order that the description of each executor contained in the testamentary writing or decree-dative is linked to his or her current description, as set out on page 1 of the inventory. See paragraphs 10.41–10.42.

10.48 In all cases, the capacity of the executor (whether nominate or dative) must be stated.

10.49 Where the deceased's name, designation and address, as disclosed on page 1 of the inventory, differs from that shown in a testamentary writing, the practice is to add at the end of paragraph 2, an explanation such as "In the said Will, the deceased is described as . . ."

---

[33] Sheriff Courts (Scotland) Act 1876 (39 & 40 Vict. c. 70), s. 41 as amended by Statute Law Revision Act 1883 (46 & 47 Vict. c. 39), Sched.

[34] Confirmation of Executors (Scotland) Act 1858 (21 & 22 Vict. c. 56), s. 9, as amended by Statute Law Revision Act 1892 (55 & 56 Vict. c. 19), s. 1 and Sched., Administration of Estates Act 1971 (c. 25), ss. 6 and 12(1) and Sched. 2, and Finance Act 1975 (c. 7), s. 52(2), Sched. 13.

[35] Sheriff Courts (Scotland) Act 1876 (39 & 40 Vict. c. 70), s. 41 as amended by Statute Law Revision Act 1883 (46 & 47 Vict. c. 39), Sched.; Confirmation of Executors (Scotland) Act 1858 (21 & 22 Vict. c. 56), s. 17 as amended by Finance Act 1975 (c. 7), s. 52(2), Sched. 13 (commented on by Lord Chancellor Selborne in *Orr Ewing's Trs.* v. *Orr Ewing* (1885) 13 R. (H.L.) 1 at pp. 11–12).

Paragraph 2 (the rules: dative appointments)

10.50   Where the deponent is an executor-dative, the full capacity of the appointment as specified in the decree should be stated, the decree described, and the date of the decree narrated: *e.g.* "executor-dative *qua* brother of the full blood conform to decree granted by the Sheriff of Grampian, Highland and Islands at Aberdeen on [*date*]".

10.51   If an executor-dative died after decerniture, it should be stated that "X [*design*] was also decerned executor-dative *qua* . . . as aforesaid, but died without being confirmed." If the deponent is acting under a mandate, power of attorney, etc., the mandate should be referred to, and produced, docketed and signed as relative to the inventory.

10.52   In the case of a dative appointment where the deceased left a valid testamentary writing, as well as describing the decree and its date, the testamentary writing must be referred to, and produced, docketed and signed as relative to the inventory.

Paragraph 2 (the rules: nominate appointments)

10.53   Where the deponent is an executor-nominate, it is necessary to specify those of the following documents which are relevant to the particular case:

    1.   The document(s) containing his nomination, with the names and designations of the whole executors (if any) nominated along with him, specifying all those who have died by stating that X "predeceased the said deceased," or "died after the said deceased but without being confirmed"; the date of death of a predeceasing executor need not be specified;

    2.   Where the deceased recalled or superseded the nomination of an executor, the document containing that recall;

    3.   Where a nominated executor has declined to accept office, the letter of declinature;

    4.   Where an executor has been assumed, the deed of assumption;

    5.   Where a trustee has been appointed by the court, the decree of appointment;

    6.   Where an executor is *incapax*, but does not have a *curator bonis*, a medical certificate as to the executor's incapacity;

    7.   Where the deponent is acting under an appointment,

such as a judicial factor or *curator bonis*, the decree of appointment;

8.   Where the deponent is acting under a mandate, a power of attorney or other authority, the mandate, power of attorney, etc.

10.54   In each case, the documents should be described in full, specifying the date of signing and (where appropriate) the recording details. All such documents must be *ex facie* valid.

10.55   Where a change of circumstance has occurred after the oath or affirmation was taken but before the inventory is recorded or confirmation granted—such as the death of an executor[36] or the discovery of a testamentary writing[37]—an additional oath may be given up by the same or another executor (see Form 97(7) in the 7th edition).

A. Specialities where testamentary writing was executed prior to August 1, 1995

Holograph testamentary writings
10.56   If the testamentary writing was signed prior to August 1, 1995 and is holograph, it must be so described, and the affidavit evidence of two persons that the writing and signature are in the handwriting of the deceased must be put up with it[37a] (see paras. 3.120–3.124).

Foreign testamentary writings
10.56A   If it is desired to found on the Wills Act 1963, and the testamentary writing has not been executed in accordance with Scottish formalities, the grounds for founding on the Wills Act must be specified. For instance,

"The said Will was executed at . . . ., ... (State)" or "The deceased was habitually resident in . . . . at the time of the execution of said Will".

Further affidavits in support may be required — in the first example, as to the place of execution (if this is not set out in the Will) (see Style 2.09), and in the second example, as to the deceased's habitual residence at the given time. Expert evidence as to the attestation of deeds under the foreign law is required. Any documents in a foreign language must be accompanied[37b] by a certified translation (see para. 2.52).

---

[36] *Ramsay*, Sept. 19, 1882, unreported.
[37] *Collins*, Oct. 28, 1882, unreported.
[37a] Succession (Scotland) Act 1964 (c. 41), s.21.
[37b] Confirmation cannot be granted on the basis of the translation alone.

B. Specialities where testamentary writing was executed on or after August 1, 1995

10.57   Section 21A of the Succession (Scotland) Act 1964, introduced by paragraph 39 of Schedule 4 to the Requirements of Writing (Scotland) Act 1995, provides that:

> Confirmation of an executor to property disposed of in a testamentary writing executed after the commencement of the Requirements of Writing (Scotland) Act 1995 shall not be granted unless the formal validity of the document is governed —
> (a) by Scots law and the document is presumed under section 3 or 4 of that Act to have been subscribed by the granter so disposing of that property; or
> (b) by a law other than Scots law and the court is satisfied that the document is formally valid according to the law governing such validity.

Scots law applicable

10.57A   Where Scots law applies, the testamentary writing must either be self-proving (in terms of section 3 of the Requirements of Writing (Scotland) Act 1995) or set up after court action in terms of section 4 thereof (see paras. 4.92–4.94).

Foreign law applicable

If it is desired to found on the Wills Act 1963, and the testamentary writing has not been executed in accordance with Scottish formalities, the grounds for founding on the Wills Act must be specified. For instance,

> "The said Will was executed at . . . ., ... (State)" or
> "The deceased was habitually resident in . . . .. at the time of the execution of said Will".

Further affidavits in support may be required — in the first example, as to the place of execution (if this is not set out in the will) (see Style 2.09), and in the second example, as to the deceased's habitual residence at the given time. Expert evidence as to the attestation of deeds under the foreign law is required. Any documents in a foreign language must be accompanied[37c] by a certified translation (see paras. 2.52–2.54).

Associated documents

10.59   All documents referred to in the deposition (with the exception of a decree of decerniture of an executor granted in the same court) must be lodged with the inventory, having been docketed as follows:[38]

[37c] Confirmation cannot be granted on the basis of the translation alone.

[38] Walker and Walker, *The Law of Evidence in Scotland* (1964), p. 205.

[Place of signing inventory, date when inventory signed]
Referred to in my deposition of this date to the Inventory
of the estate of the late *[full name of the deceased]*

. . . .
(signature of deponent)   (signature and designation
                               of person administering the
                               oath)

NOTE: It is essential that the place and date shown in such
       dockets are identical to those stated in the preamble on
       page 2 of the CAP Form A-3 (see para. 10.39).

10.60   Only the following documents will be acceptable evidence: an
         interlocutor authenticated by the judge or clerk of court, an
         extract interlocutor,[39] the original of a document, a properly
         authenticated copy from a register of probative writs (*e.g.* an
         extract of a deed registered in the Books of Council and Session),
         or a copy (known either as an exemplification or an apostille[40])
         from a notary from a country where such a copy is entitled to
         the same credit and effects as the original or from a court of
         probate. Where confirmation is required to the Scottish estate
         of a person who died domiciled abroad, and probate has already
         been granted in England and Wales, see paragraphs 2.80–2.81
         for a way around producing the actual testamentary writings.

10.61   Where an unrecorded document has been lost or mislaid,[41] or
         where nothing better can be obtained,[42] a plain copy may be
         exhibited and recorded, but unauthenticated copies are accept-
         able for recording purposes only.

10.62   All such documents are recorded along with the inventory in
         the commissary court books, either in full (by being put on
         microfilm[43]) or if the document has already been registered in
         the Register of Deeds and Probative Writs in the sheriff court,
         by reference to the folio or volume in which it was reproduced
         or engrossed.[44]

Paragraph 3

10.63   "Execut" must be completed to read "executor," "executors,"
         "executrix" or "executrices," as appropriate.

10.64   Where only one executor is applying for confirmation, "along

[39] Walker and Walker, *The Law of Evidence in Scotland* (1964), p. 227.
[40] An apostille is not strictly a copy, but a précise annexed to a copy.
[41] *Craigie*, July 6, 1875, unreported.
[42] *Dryburgh*, June 4, 1878, unreported.
[43] Act of Sederunt of December 17, 1992 (S.I. 1992 No. 3256).
[44] Act of Sederunt of July 18, 1944 (S.I. 1944 No. 860).

.with the said" should be deleted. In other cases, the full names (but not the designations) of the other executors should be inserted.

Paragraph 4 (Statutory duty to record all dispositive writings)

10.65   Where the deceased died intestate, the words "other than that before mentioned" should be deleted.

10.66   If there are in fact other "testamentary settlements or writings relative to the disposal of the deceased's estate or any part thereof," the sentence should continue "apart from [*specify deed or deeds*] which are produced herewith," for it is provided that:

> "any testament or other writing relating to the disposal of (the) estate and effects, or any part thereof, which the person or persons exhibiting such inventory shall have in his, her, or their custody or power . . . (if any such there be) shall be recorded in the books of . . . court."[45]

10.67   It is therefore incumbent on the executors to produce all writings "in . . . their custody or power" which relate to the disposal of the deceased's estate, whether or not the writings appoint executors. A writing is within the "power" of the executors if an extract or official copy can be obtained.

10.68   Writings "relating to the disposal of the estate" include all valid and effectual documents of a testamentary character relating to any portion of the deceased's estate executed by him,[46] or by another under powers conferred by him to alter the destination.[47] An onerous deed such as an antenuptial marriage contract will not require to be produced unless it contains testamentary provisions which have become operative.

10.69   Writings "relating to the disposal of the estate" do not include any writings which have been revoked or which are inoperative. This can be seen from considering the cases relating to mutual wills. Where two sisters executed a mutual will leaving their whole estates to the survivor, and by another mutual will they disposed of the estate after the death of the survivor (who had power to revoke the second will), the second will, not being a final and effective writing relating to the disposal of the estate of the first sister to die, was not recorded with her inventory.[48]

---

[45] Probate and Legacy Duties Act 1808 (48 Geo. 3, c. 149), s. 38, as amended by Finance Act 1949 (12 & 13 Geo. 6, c. 47), s. 52(10), Sched. 11, Pt. V, Finance Act 1975 (c. 7), s. 52(2), Sched. 13, Pt. 1 and *prosp.* Law Reform (Miscellaneous Provisions) (Scotland) Act 1990 (c. 40), Sched. 8, para. 19 and Sched. 19.

[46] *Muir*, July 31, 1880, unreported.

[47] *Gibb*, Oct. 23, 1866, unreported.

[48] *Dunlop*, March 14, 1887, unreported.

Where a mutual will had a codicil appended, to take effect only in the event of both parties dying at the same time, and one survived, the codicil was not recorded.[49] Where two sisters made a mutual will, reserving power to alter or cancel it at pleasure on the first death, it was held that it was sufficient to record such parts of the will as were operative on the first death.[50] It is submitted that where the deceased's testamentary writing provided that on his death, in specified circumstances (such as the testator's spouse predeceasing him), certain bequests specified in a supplementary writing should receive effect, there is no requirement to put the supplementary writing up for recording unless the specified event has occurred.

10.70 Generally, with the exceptions discussed in the previous paragraph, applications to omit from the record a portion of a testamentary writing will be refused.[51] A petition for special authority to omit certain words, which were of a libellous nature and did not affect the appointment of the executor or the disposal of the estate, has been granted,[52] but it has been doubted whether there is power to do this.[53]

10.71 Where additional writings are discovered after the inventory has been given up, but before confirmation is issued, they may be exhibited and recorded with an additional oath[54]; if the confirmation has been issued, and an additional inventory requires to be given up, they are then exhibited and recorded.[55]

10.72 A mutual will must be exhibited with the inventory of the second testator to die even although it has already been recorded in full in the same commissary court books with the inventory of the first testator to die. Normally, it will be recorded again for ease of reference, and the document will be docketed as having been again recorded.

Paragraph 5

10.73 Where the inventory extends beyond page five, the number of the final page of the inventory should be inserted.

Paragraph 6

10.74 Deletions should be made as necessary to show only those juris-

---

[49] *Dalzell*, Dec. 8, 1886, unreported.
[50] *Maxwell, Petr.*, 1925 S.L.T. (Sh. Ct.) 47.
[51] *Brown*, Dec. 19, 1865, unreported.
[52] See 7th ed. of this work at p. 194.
[53] *Per* Sheriff-Substitute Fyfe in *Maxwell, Petr.*, 1925 S.L.T. (Sh. Ct.) 47 at p. 49.
[54] *McFarlane*, Dec. 27, 1876, unreported.
[55] *Seymour*, Jan. 7, 1868, unreported.

dictions in the United Kingdom in which is located estate to be included in the confirmation.

10.75 The total for confirmation should be inserted.

10.76 In the rare case where confirmation is not required, and the inventory is simply to be recorded,[56] the word "not" should be inserted to read between "is" and "required." Merely recording the inventory has the merit of being cheaper than obtaining confirmation, but does not afford the executors protection from a charge of vitious intromission.[57]

COMPLETION OF PAGES 3–4

10.77 Since the CAP Form A-3 doubles as the inventory of the deceased's estate and as the Inland Revenue account, the executor is required to disclose all property on which inheritance tax is payable in consequence of the death. Pages 3 and 4 raise questions pertinent to the calculation of inheritance tax, and readers are referred to paragraphs 12.10–12.35.

10.77A The answers to question 7 on page 4 have a significance for commissary purposes, since they may be used, in conjunction with the details of the estate disclosed in the inventory, to determine the accuracy of an averment that the deceased's widow is entitled to the whole intestate estate in satisfaction of her prior rights. Similarly the answers may reveal whether *conditio si testator sine liberis decesserit* may be argued by a child of the testator.

THE INVENTORY: INTRODUCTION

General

10.78 Where the deceased died domiciled in Scotland, the inventory must contain all the moveable and heritable[58] estate in Scotland, and the real and personal estate in England and Wales and in Northern Ireland,[59] and confirmation will be granted thereon. Estate situated elsewhere (including the Channel Islands and the Isle of Man[60]) cannot be confirmed to, but a note of such

---

[56] Confirmation of Executors (Scotland) Act 1858 (21 & 22 Vict. c. 56), s. 8 as amended by S.I. 1964 No. 1143.

[57] See paras. 1.49–1.53.

[58] Succession (Scotland) Act 1964 (c. 41), s. 14(1).

[59] Administration of Estates Act 1971 (c. 25), ss. 1(1) and 6(1).

[60] In the Interpretation Act 1978 (c. 30), s. 5 and Sched. 1, "England" and "Wales" are defined in terms of the Local Government Act 1972 (c. 70), s. 269.

estate should be appended to the total for confirmation. Inheritance tax is payable on the worldwide estate.

10.79   Where the deceased died domiciled outside of Scotland, only the moveable and heritable[61] estate in Scotland may be confirmed to. If the Scottish confirmation is the first "grant" from a United Kingdom court, a note of the estate in England and Wales and in Northern Ireland must be appended below the total for confirmation. Inheritance tax should be paid on the whole United Kingdom estate. See further paragraphs 2.60, 12.02 and 15.11.

Determining the jurisdiction where an asset is situated

10.80   As has been seen at paragraphs 10.78–10.79, the jurisdiction in which an item of estate is situated will determine whether confirmation can be obtained to the item and may determine whether United Kingdom inheritance tax is payable on it.

10.81   The deceased's estate must be listed in the inventory under separate headings for:

    1.   "Estate in Scotland" (heritable property first—see paras. 10.84–10.85);

    2.   "Estate in England and Wales";

    3.   "Estate in Northern Ireland"[62];

    4.   After the "Summary for Confirmation," "Estate abroad."

10.82   The following notes are merely illustrative[62a]:

Interests in land: These are situated where the land is itself situated.

Tangible moveable property (including currency): Tangible moveable property is normally situated where it is physically located at the time of the death.

Business assets (interest in a partnership and sole trader): The deceased's interest in such assets is situated where the business is

---

[61] Succession (Scotland) Act 1964 (c. 41), s. 14(1).

[62] Confirmation of Executors (Scotland) Act 1858 (21 & 22 Vict. c. 56), s. 9 as amended by Statute Law Revision Act 1892 (55 & 56 Vict. c. 19), Administration of Estates Act 1971 (c. 25), s. 6(1), Sched. 2, Pt. 1 and Finance Act 1975 (c. 7), s. 52(2), Sched. 13.

[62a] *Cf.* Civil Jurisdiction and Judgments Act 1982 (c.27) and Taxation of Capital Gains Act 1992 (c.43), s.275.

carried on,[62b] and if it is carried on in more than one country, it will be treated as situated at its head office.

Bank account: A bank account is situated where the branch holding the account is situated.[63]

Debts: A debt situated in the country where it can be enforced, which is normally where the debtor resides,[64] or in the place where the document of debt states that the obligation to repay is to be performed.[65]

Government Stock, National Savings Certificates, National Savings Income Bonds, Premium Bonds and other savings products of the U.K. Government: These may be treated as estate in Scotland, or in England and Wales,[65a] and on being included in the confirmation under either heading will be paid out.[65b]

Insurance policy moneys: These are situated where the issuer resides, and if the issuer has a residence in more than one country, at the office where the policy proceeds are primarily payable.[66]

Interests in trusts and executry estates: Where the deceased had an absolute right to an item as against the trustees/executors, the interest is situated where the asset is itself situated. But if the deceased only had a right to bring an action of accounting against the trustees/executors in respect of his inheritance, the interest is situated where the right could be enforced: *e.g.* where the trust was domiciled.

Shares and securities—Registered: These are situated where the shares may be registered, that is, where the company's register is kept.[67] If the company has a dual register, the shares are situated where the shares may be transferred,[68] and if they may be transferred on more than one register, where the deceased was most likely to have dealt with them.[69] Under the Companies Act 1985, the register of a company registered in England and

---

[62b] *Laidlay's Trs.* v. *Lord Advocate* (1890) 17 R. (H.L.) 67.

[63] *R.* v. *Lovitt* [1912] A.C. 212.

[64] *English, Scottish and Australian Bank Ltd.* v. *I.R.C.* [1932] A.C. 238.

[65] *Kwok* v. *Commissioners of Estate Duty* [1988] S.T.C. 728.

[65a] See Lord Gillies in *Milligan* v. *Milligan* (1826) 4 S. 432 at p. 434; *cf. Brooks Associates Inc.* v. *Basu* [1893] Q.B. 220.

[65b] In the case of Government Stock, see Finance (No. 2) Act 1915 (5 & 6 Geo. 5, c. 89), s.48 as amended.

[66] *New York Life Ins. Co.* v. *Public Trustee* [1924] 2 Ch. 101.

[67] *Att. Gen.* v. *Higgins,* 2 H. & N. 339.

[68] *Standard Chartered Bank Ltd.* v. *I.R.C.* [1978] 3 All E.R. 644.

[69] *R.* v. *Williams* [1942] A.C. 541; *Standard Chartered Bank Ltd.* v. *I.R.C.* [1978] 3 All E.R. 644.

Wales must be kept in England and Wales, and likewise, the register of a company registered in Scotland must be kept in Scotland.[70] In certain circumstances, a branch register for a United Kingdom company may be set up in certain overseas countries and the holdings of members resident there will be registered on that branch register and their shares may be transferred on that register.[71]

Securities—Bearer: These are situated where the share certificate is at the time of the death.

Ships and aircraft: These are situated where registered or where located.

10.83   For inheritance tax purposes, different rules to those outlined above may be applied if a Double Taxation Agreement (between the United Kingdom and another country which seeks to charge a tax similar to inheritance tax on the death) provides differently: this is of significance in determining when the deceased died domiciled outside the United Kingdom, which items of estate will be assessed to United Kingdom inheritance tax.

Is an asset heritable or moveable?

10.84   While originally the distinction made in Scots law between heritable and moveable estate was crucial in executry practice in that there were different heirs and different systems of administration for the two categories of estate, the Succession (Scotland) Act 1964 all but abolished the distinction. The only practical consequences of the distinction are now limited to calculations of legitim, *jus relicti* and *jus relictae*,[72] the odd occasion where the deceased made a specific bequest of "all my heritable estate" or "all my moveable estate,"[73] and the requirement to list in the inventory, the deceased's heritable estate in Scotland before his moveable estate there.

10.85   In the text below, the main categories of estate are discussed under the appropriate general head of "Heritable Estate" or "Moveable Estate." It must be remembered that the contracts[74] or actings[75] of the deceased may have converted what is prima facie heritable property to moveable, or vice versa, and that

---

[70] Companies Act 1985 (c. 6), s. 353(1).

[71] *Ibid.*, s. 362 and Sched. 14.

[72] *Stair Memorial Encyclopaedia*, vol. 25, paras. 693, 703 and 773; Meston, *The Succession (Scotland) Act 1964* (4th ed.), pp. 18–19.

[73] *e.g. Hughes Trs.* v. *Corsane* (1890) 18 R. 299.

[74] *e.g.* selling land, and then dying before the conveyancing is effected.

[75] *e.g.* having building materials delivered to a house plot he owned and then dying before the building work commenced.

the doctrine of constructive conversion may convert an inheritance under a will or trust from heritable to moveable estate or vice versa. Where the distinction between heritable and moveable estate will affect the rights of beneficiaries, reference should be made to the appropriate texts,[76] and the estate listed in the inventory under the two heads accordingly.

Valuation

10.86 The CAP Form A-3 doubles as the Inland Revenue account, in which, on page 9, the executor must declare that "to the best of (his) knowledge and belief pages 5 to 9 of this account specify all appropriate property and its value."[77] Where the value of property included in the account has been estimated, the declaration should be amended to read:

> "after making the fullest inquiries that are reasonably practicable in the circumstances, the executor is unable to ascertain the exact value of [*specify*] item of estate. The executor undertakes to deliver a further account of this item as soon as its value is ascertained."[78]

10.87 In practice, the CTO in Scotland do not insist on such a statement being included, and it is normally sufficient if the estimated value is clearly marked as such. Once confirmation has been granted, the inventory is forwarded to the CTO for examination, and at this stage the CTO may itself, or through the District Valuer's Office (in the case of land in the United Kingdom), query specific valuations.

10.88 Even before confirmation is granted, the sheriff clerk will examine the inventory to ensure that it appears to be "a full and true inventory of the deceased's estate,"[79] and that all items of estate appear to have been properly valued. In this regard, the following general comments should be borne in mind.

Estimated values

10.89 While normally professional valuations will be obtained for such

---

[76] Gloag and Henderson, *An Introduction to the Laws of Scotland* (9th ed., 1987, paras. 36.3–12; 42.9 and 44.11; *Stair Memorial Encyclopaedia*, vol. 18, paras. 11.15 and vol. 25, paras. 778, 783; McLaren, *Wills and Succession* (3rd ed., 1894), pp. 194–245; Meston, *The Succession (Scotland) Act 1964* (4th ed.), pp. 31–32 and 57–60.

[77] IHTA 1984 (c. 51), s. 216(1).

[78] *Ibid.*, s. 216(3) as amended by Finance Act 1986 (c. 41), s. 101(3), Sched. 19, para. 29(2).

[79] Probate and Legacy Duties Act 1808 (48 Geo. 3, c. 149), s. 38 as amended by Finance Act 1949 (12 & 13 Geo. 6, c. 47), s. 52, Sched. 11, Pt. V, Finance Act 1975 (c. 7), s. 52, Sched. 13, Pt. I and *prosp.* Law Reform (Miscellaneous Provisions) (Scotland) Act 1990 (c. 40), s. 74, Sched. 8, para. 19 and Sched. 9.

items as heritage and corporeal moveables (including furniture and personal effects), there is no requirement to obtain a professional valuation for such items, and an estimated value will be accepted, provided that it appears to be genuine, and is clearly shown as "estimated by executors."

10.90   Estimated values will not be accepted for items which can be readily valued, such as bank accounts.

10.91   Frequently an income tax repayment is shown in the inventory as "estimated at £x." This will be accepted, because it is impossible to quantify a person's income tax liability until his whole finances are ascertained.

10.92   Where the deceased was entitled to money from a trust fund, an estimated value for the balance due to him will be accepted.

Nil values

10.93   Where an explanation is given why a "nil" value has been shown, the nil value will be accepted. "Nil" values will be accepted where adequate explanation is given:

1.   The deceased had sold an item of heritage before he died but had not conveyed it to the purchaser and the proceeds are shown as a separate item of estate (see paras. 10.117 *et seq.*).

2.   An item of heritage where the title was held by the deceased as an individual, but the property is partnership property, and the deceased's share of its value is included in his interest in the partnership (see para. 10.127).

3.   The title to an item of heritage where the title was held by the deceased as an individual as an individual but he subsequently signed a deed of trust in terms of which he held the property for a third party and a note of the property is appended to the inventory in terms of section 6 of the Executors (Scotland) Act 1900 (see, further, para. 16.04). (The Capital Taxes Office may wish to make further inquiries in this connection).

4.   A share holding in a company which is in receivership or in a creditors' voluntary liquidation at the time of the deceased's death.

10.94   A dash ("—") will not be accepted by the commissary or sheriff clerk as indicating a "nil" value. The nil value should always be shown as follows:

		£
Able Airways Ltd		
200 Ord 25p shares	Nil	0.00
(Company in creditors' voluntary liquidation)		

A "nil" value will not be accepted for a bank account, building society account, arrears of pension, or insurance policy.

Nominal Values

10.95 It is not acceptable to disclose a nominal value such as "say £1.00," since such is clearly not an estimate of the value of the item of estate.

Accrued Income

10.96 At common law, only interest on money accrues from day to day.[80] Under statute, all rents, annuities, salaries, pensions, dividends, bonuses and other periodical payment in the nature of income (excluding annual sums payable on a policy of assurance[81]) must also be apportioned on a day-by-day basis.[82] The statute does not apply to partnership profits, even if they are termed a dividend.[83]

10.97 Accordingly, apportionments of interest, rents, annuities, etc. are necessary whether the deceased had been entitled to receive the interest, etc., or had been liable to pay it.[84] Thus, if the deceased had been a landlord who collected rent in arrears, the inventory must include the rent which has accrued between the last date the rent fell due and the date of death.[85] Conversely, if the rent was payable in advance, the rent apportioned for the period from the date of death to the next payment date will fall to be treated as a debt on his estate. Further, if the deceased had been a tenant who paid rent in arrears, the rent apportioned for the period from the last payment date to the date of death would be a debt on his estate.

10.98 If the deceased had owned shares, no such apportionment need be made since the market value of the shares already reflects in part the anticipated dividend.

Pounds?—or Pounds and Pence?

10.99 While formerly every item in the inventory had to be valued to a penny, it is now competent to value each item to the nearest pound:[86] it is safer to round the value up (rather than down),

[80] Ersk., *Inst.*, II.ix.64–66; Bell, *Comm.*, ii.8.
[81] Apportionment Act 1870 (33 & 34 Vict. c. 35), s. 6.
[82] *Ibid.*, ss. 2 and 5.
[83] *Jones* v. *Ogle* (1872) L.R. 8 Ch. 192; *Re Cox's Trusts.* (1878) 9 Ch. D. 159.
[84] *Learmonth* v. *Sinclair's Trs.* (1878) 5 R. 548.
[85] *Balfour's Exrs.* v. *I.R.C.*, 1909 S.C. 619; *Lord Herries* v. *Maxwell's Curator* (1873) 11 M. 396.
[86] 1990 J.L.S. 215.

since there is then no risk of it being alleged that part of the estate to be ingathered has not been included in the confirmation. Standard practice is still to use pence, since this simplifies the final accounting with the executry beneficiaries.

I ESTATE IN SCOTLAND

NOTE: Irrespective of where the deceased was domiciled at the time of his death, all his estate in Scotland must be disclosed in the inventory.

10.100   The estate in Scotland falls to be divided between heritable estate (which should be reported first) and moveable estate (see paras. 10.84–10.85).

A. Heritage in Scotland

General: description of heritable property

10.101   In listing an item of heritage it will be sufficient if the inventory contains "such a description as will be sufficient to identify the property or interest therein as a separate item in the deceased person's estate."[87]

10.102   Normally, a conveyancing "common-law description" will be adequate, but if the title is made up of a number of separate conveyances (as is often the case with a rural property), it will be preferable to set out a short conveyancing description by reference, in terms of section 8 of the Conveyancing (Scotland) Act 1924. In each case, it is necessary to examine the title and search thoroughly, to ensure that all relevant deeds are specified. Where a number of split-off deeds have been granted since the recording of that last disposition containing a full conveyancing description, one way of avoiding a lengthy entry in the inventory is as follows:

> 1.   *Ground at Cloverywood, Crathie*
>   ALL and WHOLE the subjects in the Parish of [   ] and County of Aberdeen described in the Disposition by AB in favour of CD dated [   ] and recorded GRS (Aberdeen) on [   ] under the exceptions (One) to (Four) in the Disposition by the Trustees of EF in favour of GH dated [   ] and recorded said GRS on [   ] and under the exception of the following deeds all granted by IJ and recorded in the said Register.

---

[87] Act of Sederunt (Confirmation of Executors) 1964 (S.I. 1964 No. 1143) as amended by Act of Sederunt (Confirmation of Executors Amendment) 1966 (S.I. 1966 No. 593).

Deed	*Grantee*	*Recording date*
———	———	———————

If the title is in the Land Register, it is good practice to state the registration number. The description of each heritable property should be able to stand on its own: for instance, the description of a piece of ground by reference to a disposition recorded in the "said" Division of the General Register of Sasines is inept.

10.103 If the property is licensed, this should be stated, and an indication given of the type of business carried on.

Heritable property burdened with a debt

10.104 For succession purposes, unless there is an express direction to pay the heritable debt out of the general (or moveable) estate, a debt secured over heritage falls to be paid *primo loco* out of the heritage on which it is a burden.[88]

10.105 Where a debt has been secured over heritage, in completing the inventory, the amount of the loan outstanding at the date of the deceased's death may be deducted either as a debt (at page 8 of the CAP Form A-3) or from the value of the heritable item over which it is secured.[89] The former approach is the one normally used and is preferred by the Capital Taxes Office. However, there are circumstances where the latter approach aids the administration process: it may reduce the dues of confirmation and, if caution is required, the amount of the caution (see para. 19.11). The only disadvantage is that it puts into the public domain some details of the deceased's finances. When the agent deducts a secured debt from the value of the heritage, as a courtesy to the Capital Taxes Office, he should annotate the list of debts at page 8 of the CAP FORM A-3, by stating that in addition to the debts listed, a debt of £X has been deducted from the value of Item 1 (or whatever) of the inventory. The amount of this debt should not be brought into the "total column" on page 8.

10.106 When the heritage and the debt are to be shown in the inventory, they would appear as follows:

1. *Dwelling-house, 2 Ann Street, Anytown*
   being the subjects described in the Disposition by New Homes Limited in favour of John Smith recorded GRS (Aberdeen) 1st June 1990   £80,000
   Less: Secured loan from Scotland's Building Society   £60,000   £20,000

---

[88] *Fraser* v. *Spalding & Fraser* (1804) 5 Pat. 642; *Douglas's Trs.* v. *Douglas* (1868) 6 M. 223; *MacLeod's Trs.* (1871) 9 M. 903; *Muir's Trs.* v. *Muir*, 1916 1 S.L.T. 372; Succession (Scotland) Act 1964 (c.41), s.14(3).

[89] IHTA (c. 51), s. 162(4).

10.107   Where a life policy has been assigned to the lender as additional security, the debt should be apportioned *pro rata* between (a) the value of the heritage less any preferably secured debts and (b) the value of the life policy less expenses.[90] The claim on the life policy should be shown as follows:

> 10. *Scotland's Building Society*
>   Proceeds of Alba Insurance Co. plc
>   Policy No. . . .   £
>   *Less:* Share of debt secured to Building
>   Society   £   £

or alternatively[91]

> 10. *Alba Insurance Co. plc*
>   Policy No. . . .   £
>   *Less:* Share of debt secured to Scot-
>   land's Building Society   £   £

Heritable property: registered in the names of the deceased and others in pro indiviso *shares*

10.108   Where title to the property is taken in *pro indiviso* shares, without a special destination over, the deceased's *pro indiviso* share of the property must be disclosed in the inventory of his estate, for confirmation in favour of the deceased's executors is a necessary link in title. For the valuation of the deceased's interest in the property see paragraph 12.57.

Heritable property: subject to a special destination[91a]

10.109   Proviso (*a*) to section 36(2) of the Succession (Scotland) Act 1964 provides that if the deceased left a testamentary writing executed after September 10, 1964:

> "where any heritable property belonging to a deceased person at the date of his death is subject to a special destination in favour of any person, the property shall not be treated for the purposes of this Act as part of the estate of the deceased unless the destination is one which could competently be, and has in fact been, evacuated by the deceased by testamentary disposition or otherwise; and in that case the property shall be treated for the purposes of this Act as if it were part of the deceased's estate on which he has tested."

Accordingly, where the title to property owned by the deceased

---

[90] *Graham* v. *Graham* (1898) 5 S.L.T. 319; Meston, *The Succession (Scotland) Act 1964* (4th ed.), p. 32.

[91] *Heath* v. *Grant's Trs.*, 1913 S.C. 78; G.L. Gretton, "Endowment Mortgages and the Law of Succession," 1987 J.L.S. 303 at p. 304.

[91a] See generally Gretton and Reid, *Conveyancing*, Chap. 24.

is subject to a special destination, the special destination will transfer the title to the destinee, unless the deceased had revoked the destination in his testamentary writings.[92] It has been opined that the term "special destination," as used in the proviso to section 36(2), refers to a destination "in which the particular property in the deed is disponed to the particular person (or persons) specifically nominated by the granter, without regard to the normal operation of the law of succession on intestacy."[93]

10.110 If a special destination has not been revoked, and the destination has a survivorship provision (*e.g.* "to A and B and to the survivor of them), the deceased's interest in the heritage should not be shown in the inventory to his estate,[94] but must be shown on page 3 at Part 4, and on page 9 at Section 3 under the heading "other property." The entry on page 9 should be annotated: "this property is subject to a special destination in favour of the survivor which could not be/has not been [*as appropriate*] evacuated by the deceased." If a special destination to named individuals (*e.g.* "to A and B and to the survivor to them") has been revoked, the deceased's interest in the property should be shown in the inventory to his estate, and confirmation obtained.

10.111 If a destination is to person who was not named (*e.g.* "to A and on the death of A to A's eldest son alive at the time of A's death"), it is necessary for the executor to confirm to the item of estate, in order to pass good title to the person entitled thereto under the destination.[95]

10.112 Where property does pass under a destination, the destinee is liable for inheritance tax on the value passing[96] and, even although the executor makes up title to the heritage in order to pass it on to the destinee, the executor is not liable.[97]

Revocation of a contractual destination to heritable property[97a]
10.113 Where the disponee provided the whole purchase price, the

---

[92] *Bisset* v. *Walker* (1799) Mor. 7; See, further, paras. 10.113–10.115.

[93] Lord Justice-Clerk Wheatley in *Cormack* v. *McIldowie's Exrs.*, 1975 S.L.T. 214 at p. 218. Professor Halliday criticised this view as being too restrictive, and suggested that the term should also apply to destinations to a class of persons who are not specifically named (1977) J.L.S. 16).

[94] Succession (Scotland) Act 1964 (c.41), s. 36(2), proviso (*a*); A. J. McDonald, (1965) 10 J.L.S. 73; M. C. Meston, *The Succession (Scotland) Act 1964* (4th ed.), p. 105.

[95] Succession (Scotland) Act 1964 (c. 41), s. 18(2); Halliday, *Conveyancing Law and Practice in Scotland*, vol. 2, para. 21–16.

[96] IHTA 1984 (c. 51), s. 200(1)(*c*).

[97] *Ibid.*, s. 209(1).

[97a] See generally 1984 S.L.T. (News) 133.

destination can be revoked by him—either by *inter vivos* or testamentary deed.[98] Where the disponee was given his interest in the property, he can never revoke the destination.[99] Where the disponee had contributed only part of the purchase price, he cannot evacuate the destination by a testamentary writing, though he could have evacuated it by an *inter vivos* deed.[1]

10.114   In establishing whether the disponees have all contributed to the purchase price, and if so, in what proportions, the narrative of the disposition is conclusive[2]; and extrinsic evidence which contradicts the narrative will only exceptionally be admitted when all parties are agreed that the price was funded in a different way from that stated in the narrative.[3]

10.115   Where the special destination can be revoked by testamentary writing (*i.e.* only where the disponee had provided the whole of the purchase price), the question is whether the testamentary writing has in fact revoked the destination. A testamentary writing executed before September 10, 1964 may revoke a special destination by implication.[4] If the testamentary writing is executed on or after September 10, 1964, it must expressly refer to the destination and state that the testator intends to evacuate it.[5] Accordingly, it is now unusual for a contractual destination to be revoked, for the drafter of the testamentary writing must be aware both of the law and of the existence of the contractual

---

[98] *Hay's Trs.* v. *Hay's Trs.*, 1951 S.C. 329; *Brown's Trs.* v. *Brown*, 1943 S.C. 488.

[99] *Brown's Trs.* v. *Brown*, 1943 S.C. 488 (purchase by A and conveyance to "A and B and C and the survivors and survivor of them") and *Renouf's Trs.* v. *Haining*, 1951 S.C. 497 (purchase by A and conveyance to "B and C jointly and the survivor of them").

[1] *Perrett's Trs.* v. *Perrett*, 1909 S.C. 522; *Chalmers' Trs.* v. *Thomson's Exx.*, 1923 S.C. 271; *Shand's Trs.* v. *Shand's Trs.*, 1966 S.C. 178; *Steele* v. *Caldwell and Ors.*, 1979 S.L.T. 228; *Marshall* v. *Marshall's Exr.*, 1987 S.L.T. 49; *Gordon-Rogers* v. *Thomson's Exrs.*, 1988 S.L.T. 618; *Smith* v. *Mackintosh*, 1989 S.L.T. 148.

[2] *Gordon-Rogers* v. *Thomson's Exrs.*, 1988 S.L.T. 618 (Lord Morison at p. 620I appears to have been fortified in this approach by the extrinsic evidence being parole); *Smith* v. *Mackintosh*, 1989 S.L.T. 148.

[3] *Hay's Tr.* v. *Hay's Trs.*, 1951 S.C. 329 where the narrative of the disposition stated that the purchase price had been paid by A and Mrs A, but the parties agreed that the whole price had been paid by Mrs A. Lord Sutherland, in *Smith* v. *Mackintosh*, 1989 S.L.T. 148 at p. 149F, commented that the fact that, in *Hay's Trs.*, the court was prepared to proceed on the basis of the facts agreed by the parties, did not necessarily mean that the court would have investigated the accuracy of the narrative of the disposition, had it been disputed. It seems unlikely that the error could be rectified under s. 8 of the Law Reform (Miscellaneous Provisions) (Scotland) Act 1985 (c. 73).

[4] *Campbell* v. *Campbell* (1878) 7 R. (H.L.) 100.

[5] Succession (Scotland) Act 1964 (c. 41), s. 30 as applied in (1) *Stirling's Trs.* v. *Stirling*, 1977 S.C. 139 where Lord President Emslie at p. 232 expressed the view that "the plain intention (in enacting s. 30) was to bring to an end the difficulties and uncertainties involved in a search for a testator's implied intention to evacuate a special destination"; and (2) *Marshall* v. *Marshall's Exr.*, 1987 S.L.T. 49.

destination. In particular, a contractual destination is unlikely to
be revoked by a testamentary writing, prepared by the testator
himself, for he is unlikely to appreciate the legal niceties even
although the testamentary provisions are clearly incompatible
with the operation of the destination.[6]

The hidden destination to heritable property

10.116 Even where the title to a property was originally taken in the
names of A and B, with a survivorship destination, and A has
conveyed his interest in the property to B, on B's death his
original one-half interest in the property will pass to A under
the destination. Only the one-half interest which B acquired
from A will require to be confirmed to, and will pass under B's
testamentary writing or under the rules of intestate succession.[7]

Heritable property sold at time of death

10.117 When the deceased has contracted to buy or sell heritage, and
the conveyance has not been effected at his death, the doctrine
of constructive conversion will apply.

10.118 Where the deceased died after concluding a bargain for the sale
of heritage in Scotland owned by him, but prior to delivering
the disposition of the property to the purchaser, he has not
divested himself of any part of his right of property in the heritage,[8] and his executors must confirm to it, in order to pass
on good title to the purchaser. However, the conclusion of the
bargain—whether voluntary or as the result of a compulsory[9] or
judicial sale[10]—converts the value of the heritage into moveable
estate, and so the value will be moveable in the deceased's
succession.[11]

10.119 In such circumstances, if the whole price has been paid, the
heritage should be shown in the inventory as follows:

1. *Dwelling-house, 2 Ann Street, Anytown*
   Property sold for £x, the purchase price
   being included in Item 10 below   NIL

10.120 If none or only part of the price has been paid, the heritage
should be shown in the inventory as follows:

---

[6] *e.g. Marshall* v. *Marshall's Exr.*, 1987 S.L.T. 49 where, in a holograph will,
the deceased bequeathed heritage to his daughter, but did not expressly mention the destination.

[7] See *Johnstone*, 1985 S.L.T. (News) 18; Meston, "Completion of Title," in *A
Scots Conveyancing Miscellany*, 57 at p. 62, "Special Destinations."

[8] *Sharp* v. *Thomson*, 1995 S.L.T. 837.

[9] *Heron* v. *Espie* (1856) 18 D. 917 (compulsory purchase under statutory
powers).

[10] *Macfarlane* v. *Greig* (1895) 22 R. 405 (sale following an action of division and
sale); *Howden Petr.*, 1910 2 S.L.T. 250 (sale by bondholder).

[11] *Chiesley* v. *His Sisters* (1704) Mor. 5531; *c.f. Polloks' Trs.* v. *Anderson* (1902) 4
F. 455.

1. *Dwelling-house, 2 Ann Street, Anytown*
    Property sold for £x, partly paid (included
    in Item 10 below) balance outstanding £y
    (see Item 12 below)   NIL

but the balance of the price outstanding (£y), should be shown as an asset of the moveable estate as follows:

12. *Mr [name and address of purchaser]*
    Claim under missives for the sale of Item 1
    above   £y

10.121   This approach would be modified if only part of the heritage had been sold. Then the heritage should be shown as follows:

2. *Anyluck Farm, by Anytown*
    [Short conveyancing description] comprising
    (1) 220 acres, including farmhouse and steading
         valued at   £x
    (2) 10 acre field sold for [*and continue as at 10.119
        or 10.120 above*]   £x

10.122   In such circumstances, the option to pay inheritance tax due on a transfer of land by instalments cannot be claimed,[12] and the deceased's estate is not eligible for business relief,[13] or agricultural relief.[14]

10.123   Where the deceased had entered into a bargain for the sale of heritage in Scotland owned by him, but the bargain was subject to a suspensive condition (*e.g.* the sale of a public house conditional on the transfer of the license) which had not been purified at the date of death, then it could be argued that the property remains heritable.[15]

10.124   Where the deceased died before concluding a bargain for the sale of heritage in Scotland owned by him, the property remains heritable,[16] and should be shown in the inventory in the normal way. The only significance which can be attached to the abortive sale is that it may give some indication of the "market value" of the property at the time of the death.

Heritable property purchased at the time of death
10.125   When the deceased has contracted to buy heritage, and the conveyance has not been effected at his death, the doctrine of constructive conversion will apply.

---

[12] IHTA 1984 (c. 51), s. 227(4).

[13] *Ibid.*, s. 113.

[14] *Ibid.*, s. 124.

[15] *Cf. McArthur's Exrs.* v. *Guild*, 1908 S.C. 743 (a case involving the ademption of a legacy).

[16] *Ramsay* v. *Ramsay* (1887) 15 R. 25.

10.126 Where at the time of the deceased's death, he had entered into a contract to purchase heritable property, but the disposition in his favour has not been recorded, the right of property remains with the seller,[17] even although the purchaser may have paid for the property and be in occupation. The right to claim the conveyance is heritable, and valued at the purchase price,[18] and if part of the price has not been paid, this is an unsecured debt, set primarily against moveable estate.

Heritable property in fact a partnership asset

10.127 Where the title to heritage is in the name of the deceased as an individual, but, although this is not evident from the title deeds, the heritage was, in fact, owned by a partnership in which the deceased was a partner, the deceased's executors must confirm to the heritage, in order to pass on good title to the partnership. In such circumstances, the heritage should be shown in the inventory as follows:

2.   *Anyluck Farm, by Anytown*
     [*Description*]
     Property transferred by the deceased into
     the Partnership of "Messrs A & B" and the
     computation of the deceased's interest in
     the partnership capital (see Item 12 below)
     is based on, *inter alia*, the capital value of
     the land.   value   NIL

and the interest in the partnership as follows:

12. *Messrs A & B*
     Deceased's interest in partnership property
     (including value of item 2 above)   £103,450.00

10.127A The position is different if the title is in the name of the deceased, as the sole or last surviving trustee for the partnership, for then the procedure provided by section 6 of the Excutors (Scotland) Act 1900 (see paras. 16.04–16.09) may be adapted.[18a]

Leases of land in Scotland held by the deceased

10.128 Where the deceased held a "liferent lease"—*i.e.* a tenancy expressed to expire on the deceased's death—confirmation should not be obtained.[19] A lease "to A" which does not expressly exclude heirs will be presumed to be a lease "to A and A's heirs," and confirmation should be obtained,[20] since

---

[17] *Sharp* v. *Thomson*, 1995 S.L.T. 837.

[18] *Kerr* v. *Shaw and Home* (1714) Mor. 5532; *Ramsay* v. *Ramsay* (1887) 15 R. 25.

[18a] Halliday, *Conveyancing Law and Practice in Scotland*, vol. 2, para. 22–28(i); Gretton and Reid, *Conveyancing*, p. 423.

[19] Succession (Scotland) Act 1964 (c. 41), s. 36(2).

[20] *Reid's Trs.* v. *Macpherson & Ors.*, 1975 S.L.T. 101; *Cormack* v. *McIldowie's Exr.*, 1975 S.L.T. 214.

thereafter, if there is a condition (expressly or by implication) prohibiting assignation, the executor may—if the lease is not the subject of a valid bequest—transfer the lease to "any of the persons entitled to succeed to the deceased's intestate estate, or to claim legal rights or the prior rights of a surviving spouse out of the estate."[21] Accordingly, confirmation should be obtained to any lease of an agricultural holding (including a lease held on tacit relocation[22]) or a crofting tenancy. For valuation see paragraphs 12.67–12.70.

Leasehold property in Scotland—special destination

10.129 Where leasehold property is held by two or more individuals under a destination, the destination cannot normally be altered either by *inter vivos* or testamentary deed, and the property will always pass under the destination.[23] A distinction falls to be drawn between:

1. a lease to two lessees and the survivor and his heirs;

2. a lease to two lessees and their heirs.

10.130 It will not be necessary for the lease to be disclosed in the inventory of the deceased's estate, though it should feature in the CAP Form A-3, at Part 4 on page 3, and in Section 3 under the heading "other property" on page 9. A lease such as one "to A and his heirs excluding assignees and subtenants" is not subject to a special destination.[24]

10.131 It has been suggested that there will not be an automatic destination of a lease to the survivor of two tenants where the tenants hold under an assignation, rather than under the original lease.[25]

Succession to a tenancy

10.132 Where the deceased held a tenancy under the Rent Acts, the tenancy does not require to be included in the confirmation.[26]

---

[21] Succession (Scotland) Act 1964 (c. 41), s. 16(1).

[22] *Rotherwick's Trs.* v. *Hope & Ors.*, 1975 S.L.T. 187.

[23] *Macalister* v. *Macalister* (1859) 21 D. 560; *Johnstone* v. *Kennedy*, 1956 S.L.T. 73; *Robertson's Tr.* v. *Roberts*, 1982 S.L.T. 22. For fuller discussion see Halliday, *Conveyancing Law and Practice in Scotland*, vol. 4, para. 49.16.; Rankine, *Leases* (3rd ed.) at p. 85; Bell, *Leases* (1825) pp. 147–148; Paton and Cameron, *Landlord and Tenant* (1967), at p. 62; and Halliday, (1977) 22 J.L.S. 16.

[24] *Reid's Trs.* v. *MacPherson & Ors.*, 1975 S.L.T. 101; *Cormack* v. *McIldowie's Exrs.*, 1975 S.L.T. 214.

[25] Gretton, "Destinations and Leases," 1982 S.L.T. (News) 213. See *Walker* v. *Galbraith* (1895) 23 R. 347.

[26] A public sector tenancy passes by operation of law (Tenants' Rights, etc. (Scotland) Act 1980 (c. 52), s. 13) as does a statutory tenancy (Rent (Scotland) Act 1971 (c. 28), s. 3(1)(*b*) and Sched. 1 as amended).

Superiorities

10.133 A superiority, like any other right in land should be confirmed to. The value of a superiority will normally be based on a capitalisation of any unredeemed feuduties. Arrears of feuduty are moveable.[27]

Loans made by deceased secured by ex facie *absolute disposition*

10.134 A security constituted by an *ex facie* absolute disposition qualified by back bond or letter[28] is heritable in the succession of the creditor.

10.135 Where there is believed to be little prospect of recovering the full amount lent, see paragraphs 10.144–10.146 for how the item might be shown in the inventory. Arrears of interest are moveable.[29]

Annuities

10.136 Rights having a tract over future time and not having a relation to any capital sum or stock are heritable.[30] Accordingly, a right to an annuity is heritable,[31] although a payment due at the time of the deceased's death is moveable.[32]

Rights of succession: as person entitled to prior rights

10.137 On her death, the deceased (Mrs A) may have been entitled to unrealised prior rights on the estate of Mr A, Mrs A's predeceasing spouse. If Mrs A had been entitled to Mr A's interest in a dwelling-house, the right is presumably heritable in Mrs A's succession, whereas if Mrs A had been given a cash sum in lieu of interest, the right to the cash sum is presumably moveable in the succession to Mrs A's estate.[33] The prior rights should be disclosed in the inventory to Mrs A's estate as follows:

> *Mr Angus Astor's Executors*
> Prior rights under s. 8 of the Succession
> (Scotland) Act 1964   (estimated)   £x

---

[27] *Martin* v. *Agnew* (1755) Mor. 5457.

[28] Titles to Land Consolidation (Scotland) Act 1868 (31 & 32 Vict. c. 101), s. 117 (as amended by Succession (Scotland) Act 1964 (c. 41), s. 34(1) and (2), Sched. 2, para. 4 and Sched. 3) and definition of "heritable security" contained in s. 3.

[29] Ersk., II.ii.6.

[30] *Ibid.*

[31] *Reid* v. *McWalter* (1878) 5 R. 630.

[32] Ersk., II.ii.7.

[33] It is thought that the following texts, which appear to contain statements to the effect that the right to the cash sum is heritable, are in fact dealing with the question of whether the claim on the deceased spouse's estate is to heritage or moveables: Anton and Beaumont, *Private International Law* (2nd ed.), p. 513; Meston, *The Succession (Scotland) Act 1964* (4th ed.), p. 37; Scot. Law Comm. Consultative Memorandum No. 71, para. 6(2)(*a*).

B. Moveable estate in Scotland

Household goods

10.138   While normally professional valuations will be obtained for household goods, personal effects and other items of tangible moveable property, there is no requirement to obtain a professional valuation for such items, and an estimated value will be accepted, provided that it appears to be genuine, and is clearly shown as "estimated by executors." A solicitor cannot (although a private individual may) sell upholstered furniture made on or after January 1, 1950 which does not meet the 1988 safety standards,[34] and such items manufactured after January 1, 1950 must be valued subject to such a restricted market place.[35]

10.139   Where the deceased was a married person, the presumption is that the spouses owned equal shares in any household goods (other than those gifted by or inherited from a third party). Household goods means

> "any goods (including decorative or ornamental goods) kept or used at any time during the marriage in any matrimonial home for the joint domestic purposes of the parties to the marriage, other than

(a)   money or securities;

(b)   any motor car, caravan or other road vehicle;

(c)   any domestic animal."[36]

10.140   It follows that the household effects belonging to a spouse should normally be shown in the inventory as follows:

> *Contents of 2 Ann Street, Anytown*
> Owned in common by deceased
> and spouse.
> As valued by Messrs . . ., Licensed
> Valuers, Anytown   £500.00
> Whereof one half is   £250.00

Loans made by deceased secured by heritable bonds, bonds and dispositions in security, standard securities, etc.

10.141   All heritable bonds, bonds and dispositions in security, bonds of annual rent, bonds of annuity and standard securities[36a] (but not *ex facie* absolute dispositions[37]) are moveable in the succes-

---

[34] Furniture & Furnishings (Fire) (Safety) Regulations 1988 (S.I. 1988 No. 1324).
[35] Law Society Gazette, April 29, 1993, p. 14.
[36] Family Law (Scotland) Act 1985 (c. 37), s. 25.
[36a] Conveyancing and Feudal Reform (Scotland) Act 1970 (c.35), s.32.
[37] See paras. 10.134–10.135.

sion to the creditor's estate, though for the purposes of claiming legitim and legal rights of husband and wife such bonds are heritable.[38]

10.142   The amount of the bond should be confirmed to, together with any interest due to the deceased but unpaid at the time of his death, and any accrued interest.[39]

Example:

> James Smith, 2 South Street, Anytown
> Loan p. £3,000 secured by Bond and Disposition in Security over 2 South Street, Anytown   £3,000.00
> *Add:* Interest due Whitsunday 1994   61.00
> Interest from Whitsunday 1994 to date of death
>   35.50   £3,096.50

10.143   Where there is believed to be little prospect of recovering the full amount lent, see paragraphs 10.144–10.146 for how the item might be shown in the inventory.

Sums lent under Personal Bonds and Debts due to the deceased

10.144   Personal bonds are moveable in the creditor's succession, unless they purport to expressly exclude the creditor's executors.[40] In the case of a bond, the amount of the bond should be confirmed to, together with any interest due to the deceased but unpaid at the time of his death, and any accrued interest.[41] In the case of a debt, the amount of the debt should be confirmed to.

Loan or debt not fully recoverable?

10.145   With the exception of an executor-creditor,[42] the executor must confirm to the loan or debt at its full value as at the date of death, if he wishes to recover the full amount, since a debtor can insist on the full amount being confirmed to before he pays: if the debtor pays over more than the sum confirmed to, he

---

[38] Titles to Land Consolidation (Scotland) Act 1868 (31 & 32 Vict. c. 101), s. 117 (as amended by Succession (Scotland) Act 1964 (c. 41), s. 34(1) and (2), Sched. 2, para. 4 and Sched. 3), and definition of "heritable security" contained in s. 3.

[39] See paras. 10.96–10.97.

[40] Bonds Act 1661 (c. 244 (or c. 32)), as amended by Statute Law Revision (Scotland) Act 1964 (c. 80), Sched. 1; Meston, *The Succession (Scotland) Act 1964* (4th ed.), pp. 59–60.

[41] See paras. 10.96–10.97.

[42] See paras. 6.101–6.103.

renders himself liable to pay over again the unconfirmed part of the debt to anyone who might confirm to it.[43]

10.146 If after full consideration of the facts, the executor believes that he is unlikely to recover the full amount of the loan or debt (say £3,000), he confirms to the full amount of the loan, but values it only at the figure which he considers is recoverable (say £1,200), as follows:

1. *Loan to J. Smith, 3 Reid Street,*
    Anytown
    Per personal bond   £3,000.00
    Valued per executor at   £1,200.00

10.146A If it transpires that more of the loan than the value shown may be recovered an eik must be obtained in respect of the excess.[43a]

Arrears of rent, interest, etc.
10.147 Any rents due to the deceased but unpaid at the time of his death, and any accrued rent[44] must be confirmed to. Similarly, arrears of interest are moveable (even when the loan from which it is derived is heritable).[45]

Deceased was in business on own account
10.148 Where the deceased carried on business on his own, the various assets of the business (including the goodwill,[46] if any) must be entered in detail in the inventory. The debts should be listed in the schedule for debts and funeral expenses in Schedule 1 on page 8, and a deduction made in respect of any bad or doubtful debts.

Partnership interest
10.149 Where the deceased was a partner in a partnership carrying on business in Scotland, his interest in the partnership (irrespective of whether the partnership owns heritable property) is moveable in the succession of the deceased partner.[47] The net value of the deceased's interest in the partnership should be shown as a single item of estate.

10.150 Where a partner dies, his interest in the partnership will be ascertained from the terms of the partnership agreement (or any

---

[43] *Buchanan* v. *Royal Bank* (1842) 5 D. 211; Ersk., III.ix.30–36.
[43a] *Cf. Brown* v. *Millar* (1853) 16 D.225.
[44] See paras. 10.96–10.97.
[45] Ersk., II.ii.7.
[46] See para. 10.156.
[47] Partnership Act 1890 (53 & 54 Vict. c. 39), s. 22.

variation thereof), or may be inferred from a course of dealing,[48] or may as be set out in the Partnership Act 1890.[49]

10.151   On a dissolution on death, the Partnership Act 1890 provides that after meeting the firm's debts, the advances made by the partners are repaid, then the partners capital and finally the balance remaining will be shared in the proportion in which the profits are divisible[50] — that is equally, unless the partners have by agreement, express or implied, agreed on different proportions.[51]

10.152   In the absence of agreement to the contrary,[52] a deceased partner's interest in the partnership capital is calculated by revaluing the partnership assets (including the goodwill (if any) of the business,[53] the heritage, and the value of any lease held by the firm) at their current values calculated at the date of death[54] (rather than adopting their historic or nominal values as used in recent partnership accounts).[55] Partnership debts and loans are deducted. If the agreement provides that the deceased's capital will be paid out by instalments over a period of years, but no interest is payable on the outstanding capital, the deceased's share of the capital value of the partnership may be discounted to take account of the late payment. Similarly, if the partnership assets are difficult to realise a discount on the values may be negotiated.

10.153   Accordingly, it is normal practice to have the partnership assets — lock, stock and barrel — revalued by a professional valuer at the time of death (or such other time as may be specified in the partnership agreement).

10.154   It is often a nice question whether a particular item — be it land, a lease of land,[55a] an insurance policy,[56] a boat,[57] a patent or whatever — is partnership property, or is the personal property

---

[48] If the matter had been dealt with in a formal probative deed (partnership agreement), it would seem that it may not be varied by an oral agreement (*Starrett & Anor.* v. *Pia*, 1968 S.L.T. (Notes) 28).

[49] Partnership Act 1890 (53 & 54 Vict. c. 39), s. 19.

[50] *Ibid.*, s. 44.

[51] *Ibid.*, s. 24.

[52] *e.g.*, *Thom's Exx.* v. *Russel & Aitken*, 1983 S.L.T. 335; the partners agreeing that "proper books be kept" is not treated as an agreement to the contrary (*Noble* v. *Noble*, 1983 S.L.T. 339).

[53] See para. 10.156.

[54] *Clark* v. *Watson*, 1982 S.L.T. 450.

[55] *Noble* v. *Noble*, 1983 S.L.T. 339; *Shaw* v. *Shaw*, 1968 S.L.T. (Notes) 94; *Clark* v. *Watson*, 1982 S.L.T. 450; *Stair Memorial Encyclopaedia*, vol. 16, paras. 1104 and 1140.

[55a] *McNiven* v. *Peffers* (1868) 7 M. 181.

[56] *e.g.* *Forrester* v. *Robson's Trs.* (1875) 2 R. 755.

[57] *Davie* v. *Buchanan* (1880) 8 R. 319.

of an individual partner.[57a] The way in which the title is held is, in itself, irrelevant,[58] and the mere use of property for partnership purposes is not enough to stamp it with the character of partnership property.[59] Property will be partnership property:

1. if the partners have clearly agreed so[59a]—for instance, the partnership agreement may expressly state that the property is owned by the partnership;

2. if the property was bought with partnership money—unless the contrary intention appears[60];

3. if it is brought into the partnership accounts as an asset of the partnership, and its value credited to the capital of one of the partners[61]; or

4. if the partners otherwise treat it as partnership property.[62]

It is against the property being partnership property if one of the partners withdrew part of his capital to help finance the purchase.[63]

Joint venture

10.155   The deceased's interest in a joint venture (which may indeed be a joint venture to sell land for development[64]) is moveable in his succession.[65]

Goodwill

10.156   "Goodwill" will be an asset of many, but not of all businesses: currently, there is no goodwill in most professional partnerships. Generally, the goodwill of a business will be moveable (and an asset of the business) but in the case of a business carried on in licensed premises, the goodwill may be either heritable or moveable, or partly both. In the case of a public house in a large town or city, goodwill is generally heritable,[66] whereas with a country inn, the goodwill may be largely moveable.[67] This distinction will be significant when the licensed premises are owned by one individual, but the business is carried on by a partnership, for the heritable goodwill belongs exclusively to

---

[57a] *Stair Memorial Encyclopedia*, vol. 16, para. 1072; Miller, *Partnership*, (2nd ed.), Chap. 9, p. 389.

[58] *Waterer* v. *Waterer* (1873) L.R. 15 Eq. 402.

[59] *Wilson* v. *Threshie* (1825) 4 S. 361.

[59a] Partnership Act 1890 (53 & 54 Vict. c.39), ss. 20 and 21.

[60] Partnership Act 1890 (53 & 54 Vict. c. 39), s. 21; *e.g. Forrester* v. *Robson's Trs.* (1875) 2 R. 755.

[61] *Robinson* v. *Ashton* (1875) L.R. 20 Eq. 25.

[62] *Waterer* v. *Waterer* (1873) L.R. 15 Eq. 402.

[63] *Smith* v. *Smith* (1890) 5 Ves. 189.

[64] Cf. *Keith* v. *Penn & Johnston* (1840) 2 D. 633.

[65] *Lord Advocate* v. *Macfarlane's Trs.* (1893) 31 S.L.R. 357.

[66] *Philp's Exr.* v. *Philp's Exr.* (1894) 21 R. 482 at p. 489; *Graham's Trs.* v. *Graham* (1904) 6 F. 1015; *Muirhead's Trs.* v. *Muirhead* (1905) 7 F. 496.

[67] Per Lord McLaren in *Graham's Trs.* v. *Graham* (1904) 6 F. 1015 at p. 1019.

the heritable proprietor, and only the value of the moveable goodwill is partnership property. Where the goodwill is heritable, the premises and goodwill fall to be valued as one single item of estate.[68]

Life Policies

10.157   **In name of deceased on his own life** Where the deceased has taken out a life policy on his own life, with the proceeds payable, for example, to his "executors, administrators and assignees," the policy forms part of the deceased's estate,[69] and must be included in the confirmation.

10.158   **In name of deceased on another's life** Where the proceeds of a life policy taken out on someone else's life are payable to the deceased, the policy forms part of the deceased's estate.[70] The policy must be valued at its actuarial "open market" (and not surrender) value.[71]

10.159   **In name of another on deceased's life** Where a wife takes out a life policy on her husband's life, with the proceeds payable to the wife, the policy does not form part of the deceased's husband's estate, but is payable to the wife without confirmation.[72]

10.160   **On joint lives of deceased and another** Where the deceased and another person took out a life policy on their joint lives, the treatment of the policy on death depends on the terms of the policy:

1. If the sum assured is payable on the first death to the survivor, the policy need not be included in the inventory to the deceased's estate, although it will require to be disclosed on page 3 of the CAP Form A-3. In such a case, any premiums paid by the deceased will be treated as *inter vivos* transfers of value for inheritance tax purposes.

2. If the sum assured is payable on the first death to the executors of the deceased, the policy must be included in the inventory to the deceased's estate, and confirmed to.

3. If the sum assured is payable on the second death to the executors of the second deceased, on the first death, the policy need not be included in the inventory to the deceased's estate, although it will require to be disclosed on page 3 of the CAP Form A-3, and any premiums paid by the first deceased will be treated as *inter vivos* transfers of

[68] *Coles' Exrs.* v. *I.R.C.*, 1973 S.L.T. (Lands Tr.) 24.
[69] *Muirhead* v. *Muirhead's Factor* (1867) 6 M. 95.
[70] *Ibid.*
[71] *Pringle's Trs.* v. *Hamilton* (1872) 10 M. 621; *Chalmer's Trs.* (1882) 9 R. 743.
[72] *Grant,* May 2, 1872, unreported.

value for inheritance tax purposes. On the second death, the policy must be included in the inventory to the deceased's estate, and confirmed to.

4.   There may in fact be two policies in one document — one for each life assured. Under each policy, the sum assured will be payable to the assured's executors on the assured's death, but with each policy becoming void as soon as the other policy has matured on death. In such a case, on the first death, the policy must be included in the inventory to the first deceased's estate, and confirmed to.

10.161   **Written under the Married Women's Policies of Assurance (Scotland) Act 1880[73] and 1980[74]** The 1880 Act, as amended by the 1980 Act, enables a man or woman to put a life policy effected on his or her own life in trust for his or her spouse, or for his or her children, or for his or her spouse *and* children (or any of them). "Children" can include those not yet born, adopted children, and illegitimate children, but cannot include children of the assured's spouse unless adopted by the assured. "Spouse" includes someone who becomes the assured's spouse after the policy is taken out.

10.162   A policy written only for such beneficiaries (even where it does not mention the Acts) vests in the trustees immediately it is written and is irrevocable. Such a policy should not be confirmed to but will require to be reported on page 3 of the CAP Form A-3. If the deceased had been the last surviving trustee, in order to make up title to the policy, the procedure discussed at paragraphs 16.04–16.09 should be adopted.

10.163   **Non-statutory trusts** It is possible that the deceased may have put a policy payable to him into a trust. As with any trust, there must be delivery to the trustees. Where the truster appoints himself sole trustee, constructive[75] delivery of the trust property after the trust policy has come into existence[76] is adequate.

10.164   If there has been delivery (whether actual or constructive), and the deceased was the last surviving trustee, the procedure discussed at paragraphs 16.04–16.09 should be adopted in order to make up title to the policy. If there has not been delivery, the policy proceeds remain part of the deceased's estate and should be confirmed to.

---

[73] 43 & 44 Vict. c. 26.

[74] Married Women's Property of Assurance (Scotland) (Amendment) Act 1980 (c. 56).

[75] *Allan's Trs.* v. *I.R.C.*, 1971 S.L.T. 62; 1971 S.C. (H.L.) 45; *Clark's Trs.* v. *I.R.C.*, 1972 S.L.T. 190.

[76] *Kerr's Trs.* v. *I.R.C.*, 1974 S.L.T. 193; (*sub nom. Kerr's Trs.* v. *Lord Advocate*) 1974 S.C. 115.

10.165   **Assigned** A life policy can be assigned in security of a debt, or as an *inter vivos* gift. In both cases, consideration must be given as to how the policy should be reported in the answers to question 1 on page 3 and in Section 3 on page 9 of the CAP Form A-3.

10.166   The Policies of Assurance Act 1867[77] prescribes the form of the assignation of a life policy. The assignation may either be endorsed on the policy, or set out separately:

> "I, AB of . . . in consideration of . . . do hereby assign unto CD of . . . his executors, administrators and assigns the [*within*] policy of assurance granted . . . [*here describe the policy*] IN WITNESS[78]"

10.167   Once the assurance company has received written notice of the date and purport of the assignment, the assignee is entitled to payment, and the date on which such notice is received regulates the priority of claims.[79] Failure to intimate at all means that the assignee has no rights in the policy as against the deceased's executors or creditors.[80] The intimation can competently be made after the death of the assignor, and thereafter the assignee will, on production of the death certificate, be entitled to the proceeds of the policy in preference to the executors of the assignor.[81] However, prior to such intimation, the life company will pay out the proceeds of the life policy to the executors of the assignor on production of the death certificate and confirmation to the policy.[82]

10.168   Where the proceeds of the life policy exceed the debt in security for which it was assigned, confirmation should be obtained for the reversion of the policy.

10.169   **International dimension** Where the deceased had taken out a life policy with a company operating in a country different to that of the deceased's domicile, the "proper law" applicable to the creation of the assurance policy[83] will be applied in deter-

---

[77] 30 & 31 Vict. c. 144.

[78] Policies of Assurance Act 1867 (30 & 31 Vict. c. 136), s. 5 and Sched.

[79] Policies of Assurance Act 1867 (30 & 31 Vict. c. 136), s. 3.

[80] *Strachan* v. *McDougle* (1835) 13 S. 954; *Caledonian Insurance Co.* v. *Beattie* (1898) 5 S.L.T. 349.

[81] *Brownlee* v. *Robb*, 1907 S.C. 1302.

[82] *McDowal* v. *Fullertun* (1714) Mor. 840; *McGill* v. *Laurestoun* (1558) Mor. 843.

[83] Anton and Beaumont, *Private International Law* (2nd ed.), pp. 621–623. See *Pender* v. *Commercial Bank of Scotland*, 1940 S.L.T. 306, where the question of whether a domiciled Scotsman could assign a life policy taken out with the Edinburgh office of an English insurance company fell to be determined under Scots law, which was the legal system which both purchaser and insurer intended should govern the policy when it was taken out. *Cf. Schumann* v. *Scottish Widows' Fund* (1886) 13 R. 678 where, according to Anton at p. 622, n. 67, it was

mining whether the policy has been validly assigned. Only if the assignment is effective under the proper law will the company pay out the proceeds to the assignee: otherwise the assignor's executors must confirm to the policy, and the company will pay out to them.

10.170   However, as between the assignee and the assignor's executors, the validity of the assignation (in particular the capacity of the parties, and the formal or essential validity of the assignation itself) is determined according to the proper law of the assignation.[84] It is not thought that where the insurance company concerned operates in another EC country, the Contracts (Applicable Law) Act 1990 will alter the principles set out above.[85]

10.171   *Jus quaesitum tertio* Exceptionally, it may be possible to show that where the deceased took out a policy on a third party's life, intending it to be ultimately for the benefit of the third party, the third party has a *jus quaesitum tertio*[86] in the policy proceeds, even although the policy has not been delivered to him.

10.171A   In such a case, the policy should be confirmed to — but if the facts giving rise to the *ius quaesitum tertio* are referred to, a "nil" value may be extended. Such a policy should also be disclosed at page 3 of the CAP Form A-3.

Other Policies: Personal accident or contingency policies
10.172   Such policies (that is, excluding life policies) are worth nothing until the death, accident or contingency occurs. If the policy continues after the deceased's death, it should be included in the confirmation, but valued at "nil."

A time-share
10.173   The ownership of a time-share is not heritable: depending on how the time-share is constituted, it is either a share holding in a company, or a membership of a club. Nevertheless, the practice of the Capital Taxes Office is to refer the question of the value of a timeshare in Scotland to the District Valuer's Office.

Income Tax or Capital Gains Tax repayments
10.174   Where a tax repayment is due to the deceased's estate, the figure given should be the accurate figure, or a genuine estimate.

---

assumed that Scots law would determine the assignability of a policy taken out by a domiciled German with a Scottish insurance company.
[84] Anton and Beaumont, *Private International Law* (2nd ed.), pp. 623–624; *Strachan* v. *McDougle* (1835) 13 S. 954; *Scottish Provident Institution* v. *Cohen & Co.* (1888) 16 R. 112; *Tayler* v. *Scott* (1847) 9 D. 1504.
[85] Anton and Beaumont, *Private International Law* (2nd ed.), p. 626.
[86] *Carmichael* v. *Carmichael's Exx.*, 1920 S.C. (H.L.) 195.

Bank and Building Society Accounts

10.175 If these are to be treated as estate in Scotland, they must be specified as being at a Scottish branch, for instance:

> 2. *Bank of Scotland, Head Office, Aberdeen*
> Current account Number . . .

Any interest accrued to the date of death should be shown (see paras. 10.96–10.97). With the exception of a TESSA (Tax Exempt Special Savings Account) where the interest accrued to the date of death is tax free, all interest should be shown net of basic rate income tax.

Government Stock

10.175A The deceased's total holding of British Government Stocks can be shown as one item of estate, entitled "British Government Stocks", with the individual stocks being specified and valued thereunder.

Premium Bonds

10.175B Where a prize was drawn prior to the holder's death, the prize must be confirmed to.

Personal Equity Plan

10.175C A PEP (Personal Equity Plan) should be listed under the head of the Plan Manager or Nominee Company. Each shareholding and bank account in the PEP portfolio should be listed and separately valued.

Moveable property registered in the names of persons including the deceased

10.176 Moveable property such as stock or share certificates, bonds and other documents of debt are frequently registered in the names of two or more parties. Sometimes, though not always, the registration includes a survivorship destination. Where one of the registered holders dies, such investments are frequently transferred into the name of the survivor or survivors, simply on the production of the death certificate.[87] Such a transfer should be viewed primarily as an administrative arrangement of the particular investment body, and does not affect the proprietary interests of the various registered holders and their executors *inter se*. The inventory must disclose the proprietary interest of the deceased holder.

10.177 The following principles can be gleaned from the case reports:

---

[87] For example, if the operating instruction on a bank account in Scotland permits signatures by "A or B or survivor," on the death of A, B can still withdraw all the funds. (*Cf.* the position where both holders must sign on a withdrawal: on A's death, the account becomes inoperable until confirmation to A's estate is exhibited.)

1. **The law applicable to the debt** In the absence of evidence
    to the contrary, a special destination in a stock or share
    certificate, bond or other document of debt, may be
    deemed to be contractual, and as such will be interpreted
    according to the applicable law of the debt.[88]
    In the case of an investment in a bank, building society
    or a new issue of shares, the application form or pro-
    spectus will determine the proper law as between the
    investors and the investment body.

2. **Scots law the applicable law: ownership in common**
    Where Scots law is the applicable law, a moveable asset
    which was purchased by A and B and registered in their
    names without a survivorship destination, will, on A's
    death, be owned as to one-half by B and the other half
    will pass to A's executors who must confirm to it.[89–90]
    If the asset had been purchased by A alone, though title
    is taken in the names of A and B, ownership remains with
    A, unless donation to B can be proved,[91] and, on A's
    death, the whole asset must be confirmed to; however,
    in the opinion of Lord President Clyde, the registration by
    A of the asset in the names of A and B (without delivery to
    B) constitutes a valid nomination of B as successor to A
    to one-half of the investment.[92]
    It should be noted that where, after October 30, 1985, a
    married person makes an investment from the joint
    house-keeping money, each spouse is treated as owning
    one-half each, irrespective of how the title is taken.[93]

3. **Scots law the applicable law: destination (general)**
    Where Scots law is the applicable law, an asset purchased
    by A and B and registered in the names of "A and B and
    the survivor of them" will, on A's death, pass automatic-
    ally to B,[94] unless the destination had been revoked by
    A's testamentary writings.[95] In such a case, A's executors
    do not require to confirm to the asset, although it should
    be disclosed in the CAP Form A-3, at Part 4 on page 3,
    and in Section 3 under the heading "other property" on
    page 9.
    If the asset had been purchased by A alone, even

---

[88] Anton and Beaumont, *Private International Law* (2nd ed.), p. 694; *Connell's Trs.* v. *Connell's Trs.* (1886) 13 R. 1175.

[89–90] *Connell's Trs.* v. *Connells's Trs.* (1886) 13 R. 1175.

[91] For there to be donation, there must be delivery of the document of title to the donee or his agent: *Hill* v. *Hill* (1755) Mor. 11580; *Walker's Trs.* v. *Walker* (1878) 5 R. 965.

[92] *Dennis* v. *Aitchison*, 1923 S.C. 819 at p. 825.

[93] Family Law (Scotland) Act 1985 (c. 37), s. 26.

[94] *Cunningham* v. *Cunningham*, 1924 S.C. 581.

[95] *Brydon's C. B.* v. *Brydon's Trs.* (1898) 25 R. 708.

although B has no proprietary interest in the asset while A is alive,[96] the whole of the asset will transmit to B on A's death in terms of the destination,[97] unless the destination has been revoked by A's testamentary writings.[98] The whole of the asset must be included in the inventory to A's estate.

Where the asset was purchased by A but registered in the names of "B and C and the survivor of them," neither B nor C can revoke the destination by testamentary provision.[99]

4. **Scots law the applicable law: destination (bank accounts, and deposit receipts and building society accounts)**
Although most of the cases discussed in this section involve deposit receipts, the legal principles apply equally to bank[1] and building society accounts, where Scots law is the proper law. The term "money investment" will be used to denote all such accounts and receipts.

A money investment is not a document of title, and accordingly, it is not possible to infer who owns the money from the terms in which the money is deposited.[2] Further, a money investment cannot operate as a testamentary writing.[3]

While a money investment which is taken in the names of "A and B or the survivor of them" may be paid out to B on A's death, B will have to account to A's executors for B's share of the investment: ownership of the money deposited is in proportion to the original investments made by A and B,[4] and should be disclosed in the inventory to A's estate accordingly.

There is, in general, a presumption for equality.[5] Where

---

[96] B would have a proprietary interest in the asset if donation to him can be proved. For there to be donation, there must normally be delivery of the document of title to B or his agent: *Hill* v. *Hill* (1755) Mor. 11580; *Walker's Trs.* v. *Walker* (1878) 5 R. 965.

[97] *Walker's Trs.* v. *Walker* (1878) 5 R. 965; *per* Lord President Clyde in *Dennis* v. *Aitchison*, 1923 S.C. 819 at p. 825; see also *Buchan* v. *Porteous* (1879) 7 R. 211, where the court took a liberal approach in interpreting the wording of a destination.

[98] *Dennis* v. *Aitchison*, 1924 S.C. (H.L.) 122.

[99] *Taylor's Exrs.* v. *Brunton*, 1939 S.C. 444 following *Renouf's Trs.* v. *Haining*, 1919 S.C. 497 (destination in title to heritage).

[1] *Forrest-Hamilton's Tr.* v. *Forrest-Hamilton*, 1970 S.L.T. 338.

[2] *Per* Lord Low in *Allan's Exr.* v. *Union Bank of Scotland Ltd.*, 1909 S.C. 206 at p. 211.

[3] *Dinwoodie's Exx.* v. *Carruther's Exr.* (1895) 23 R. 234.

[4] *Dinwoodie's Exx.* v. *Carruther's Exr.* (1895) 23 R. 234 where in a dispute over rights to a deposit receipt in an English bank between two investors who were domiciled and resident in Scotland, the issue between the depositors was held to be governed by Scots law.

[5] *Trotter* v. *Spence* (1885) 22 S.L.R. 353.

A and B are husband and wife, if the monthly investment is derived from an allowance made for the couple's "joint household expenses or for similar purposes," the money investment is treated as belonging to them equally.[6]

Bank of Scotland, Anytown Branch		
Sum of £10,000 invested . . . in name of deceased and B [design] expressed to be payable to them or either or the survivor, investment funds provided equally	£10,000.00	
Add: Interest accrued thereon to date of death	51.00	
		Whereof one-half
	£10,051.00	£5,025.50

If A alone had provided that money to purchase the money investment, it will remain in his estate and pass to his heirs (and not to B).[7] It should be disclosed in the inventory as follows:

Bank of Scotland, Anytown Branch		
Sum of £10,000 invested . . . in name of deceased and B [design] expressed to be payable to them or either or the survivor, which sum of £10,000 was wholly the deceased's money and remained his property	£10,000.00	
Add: Interest accrued thereon to date of death	102.00	£10,102.00

While the survivorship provision will not operate as a testamentary bequest of the funds,[8] it may be possible for B to prove that A made a donation to him, whether *inter vivos*[9] or *mortis causa*.[10]

---

[6] Family Law (Scotland) Act 1985 (c. 37), s. 26 (see for instance the "housekeeping" account discussed in *Forrest-Hamilton's Tr.* v. *Forrest-Hamilton*, 1970 S.L.T. 338, under the previous provision, Married Women's Property Act 1964 (c. 19), s. 1).

[7] *Cuthill* v. *Burns* (1862) 24 D. 849.

[8] *Watt's Trs.* v. *Mackenzie* (1869) 7 M. 930; *Jamieson* v. *McLeod* (1880) 7 R. 1131; *Miller* v. *Miller* (1874) 1 R. 1107; *Connell's Trs.* v. *Connell's Trs.* (1886) 13 R. 1175.

[9] *e.g. McCubbin's Exrs.* v. *Tait* (1868) 6 M. 310 (the rubric refers to *donatio mortis causa* but the brief report bears that the case involved an *inter vivos* donation); see further, para. 12.12–12.13.

[10] *Crosbie* v. *Wright* (1880) 7 R. 823; *Macfarlane's Trs.* v. *Miller* (1898) 25 R. 1201 and *Macpherson's Exxr.* v. *Mackay*, 1932 S.C. 505; bank account cases: *Blyth* v.

5. **Scots law the proper law: revocation of destination by testamentary writing** Where the moveable property subject to the special destination was purchased after the testamentary writing was executed, the destination is the last expression of the deceased's will, and so will not be revoked.[11]

If the testator purchased the moveable property before the testamentary writing was executed, the presumption is that the testamentary writing will not normally revoke the special destination.[12] This presumption will be rebutted if the testamentary writing contains a clause which is sufficiently widely drafted as to be construed as a revocation of the destination[13] as opposed to a general clause revoking all prior testamentary writings made by the testator[14]; or it can be displaced by extraneous circumstances—such as where it would be impossible to fulfil the trust purposes in the subsequent testamentary writing unless it operated as a revocation of the special destination,[15] or the testator's knowledge of the state of health of the destinee.[16]

It has been held that the subsequent signing of a codicil does not have the effect of post-dating the original testamentary writing to the date of the codicil.[17]

6. **Scots law to be applied? Or another legal system?** Where the applicable law of the debt is not Scots law, the court will presume that the principles applicable are the same as those under Scots law.[18–19] This presumption can however be rebutted—by admission; by proof of the foreign law as a matter of fact; by a remit (of consent) to a foreign

---

Curle (1885) 12 R. 674; *Boucher's Trs.* v. *Boucher's Trs.* (1907) 15 S.L.T. 157; see further, para. 12.07.

[11] *Per* Lord President Dunedin in *Perrett's Trs.* v. *Perrett*, 1909 S.C. 522 at p. 527; *Dennis* v. *Aitchison*, 1923 S.C. 819 (this aspect of the special case was not appealed to the House of Lords: 1924 S.C. (H.L.) 122); *Cunningham* v. *Cunningham*, 1924 S.C. 581.

[12] *Per* Lord President Inglis in *Walker's Exr.* v. *Walker* (1878) 5 R. 965 at p. 969; *per* Lord President Dunedin in *Perrett's Trs.* v. *Perrett*, 1909 S.C. 522 at p. 527; *Cunningham* v. *Cunningham*, 1924 S.C. 581; *Murray's Exrs.* v. *Geekie*, 1929 S.C. 633.

[13] *Brydon's C. B.* v. *Brydon's Trs.* (1898) 25 R. 708; *Turnbull's Trs.* v. *Robertson*, 1911 S.C. 1288.

[14] *Connell's Trs.* v. *Connell's Trs.* (1886) 13 R. 1175; *Paterson's J. F.* v. *Paterson's Trs.* (1897) 24 R. 499.

[15] *Per* Lord President Dunedin in *Perrett's Trs.* v. *Perrett*, 1909 S.C. 522 at p. 527; *Brydon's C. B.* v. *Brydon's Trs.* (1898) 25 R. 708; *Dennis* v. *Aitchison*, 1923 S.C. 819, *affd.* 1924 S.C. (H.L.) 122.

[16] *Brydon's C. B.* v. *Brydon's Trs.* (1898) 25 R. 708.

[17] *Per* Lord Ormdale in *Cunningham* v. *Cunningham*, 1924 S.C. 581, following *Scott's Trs.* v. *Duke*, 1916 S.C. 732.

[18–19] *e.g. Macfarlane's Trs.* v. *Miller* (1898) 25 R. 1201.

lawyer; or by a case stated under the British Law Ascertainment Act 1859 (*re* the law of former British dominions). While a person domiciled in Scotland may hold estate jointly with another in any part of the world, the following paragraph outlines only the relevant English rules—which would, in any particular case, require to be proved as a matter of fact.

7. **English law the applicable law: joint tenancy** If a question of English law is raised in a Scottish court, the English law must be proved as a matter of fact.

    Under English law, where an asset is registered in the names of A and B (joint tenancy), survivorship is always presumed, and on A's death, the asset passes automatically to B, for a joint tenancy cannot be severed by A's testamentary writings. In such cases, it is technically not necessary to include the asset in the inventory to A's estate, though confirmation is commonly requested before the asset will be paid out. If the asset does not feature in the inventory, it must of course feature in the CAP Form A-3, at Part 4 on page 3, and in Section 3 under the heading "other property" on page 9.

8. **Government stock** Although government stock is administered in England, provided that the investors were domiciled in Scotland, the destination to the stock will be construed according to Scots law.[20] The rationale of this approach seems to be that the investors would have distinguished making an investment in the United Kingdom government from making an investment in a purely English body.

    A similar approach has been taken in the case of an investment in an English local authority,[21] but, in the light of *Connell's Trs.* v. *Connell's Trs.*,[22] the correctness of this decision should be doubted, for it appears to have been based on a presumption that Scots law governed the destination.

Property subject to a valid nomination

10.178   Where an inventory is prepared of the deceased's estate, property passing under a valid nomination must be included, even although the nominee will be able to ingather the asset nominated without exhibiting confirmation.

Rights of succession: as residuary legatee

10.179   On his death, the deceased (A) may have had a vested

---

[20] *Cunningham* v. *Cunningham*, 1924 S.C. 581.
[21] *Colenso's Exr.* v. *Davidson*, 1930 S.L.T. 357.
[22] (1886) 13 R. 1175.

right, as universal legatee or as a residuary beneficiary, to an estate, or part of an estate of a testator, (B). In completing the inventory to A's estate, it will be necessary to show the right as an asset.

Miss Barbara Beatrice Brown's Executry
Administered by Messrs A & B, Anytown.
CTO ref ST . . .
Share of residue   £x

10.180   Normally a succession right is moveable, but whether it is heritable or moveable turns on the particular estate and if the question is significant, reference should be made to the appropriate texts discussed at paragraphs 10.84–10.85.

10.181   It should be remembered that if inheritance tax had been paid on Miss Brown's estate, and the two deaths were within five years of each other, Quick Succession Relief may be claimed.[23]

Rights of succession: as legatee
10.182   On his death, the deceased (A) may have had, as a specific or pecuniary legatee, a vested right to a legacy left to him by B but which had not been transferred to him before he died. In completing the inventory to A's estate, it will be necessary to show the legacy as an asset.

Miss Barbara Beatrice Brown's Executors
Administered by Messrs A & B, Anytown.
CTO ref ST . . .
Legacy   £x

10.183   The right to the legacy will be disclosed as heritable estate or moveable estate, depending on the character of the specific bequest. A specific legacy of a house will be heritable. A pecuniary legacy will be moveable, even if all the assets in B's estate were heritable.

10.184   It should be remembered that if inheritance tax had been paid on B's estate, and the two deaths were within five years of each other, Quick Succession Relief may be claimed.[24]

Rights of succession: as person entitled to prior rights
10.185   On her death, the deceased (Mrs A) may have been entitled to unrealised prior rights on the estate of Mr A, Mrs A's predeceasing spouse. With the exception of the prior right (to the dwelling-house) under section 8 of the Succession (Scotland) Act 1964 (see para. 10.137), all prior rights are moveable in Mrs A's succession. The prior rights should be disclosed in the inventory to Mrs A's estate as follows:

[23] See para. 12.06.
[24] See para. 12.106.

Mr Angus Astor's Executors
Prior rights under s. 8 of the Succession (Scotland)
Act 1964
(as valued by Messrs . . . .)   £x

or

Prior rights under s. 9 of the Succession (Scotland)
Act 1964   (estimated)   £x

or as appropriate.

Rights of succession: as person entitled to legal rights

10.186   On his death, the deceased (A) may have been entitled to
unrealised legal rights on B's estate, whether of *jus relictae, jus
relicti* or legitim. All are moveable estate and should be disclosed
in the inventory to A's estate as follows:

Mr Bruce Brown's Executors
Administered by Messrs A & B, Anytown.
CTO ref ST . . .
Entitlement to legitim   (estimated)   £x

Trust property

10.187   Where the deceased was a beneficiary of a trust, his interest in
the trust must be disclosed in the inventory, and confirmation
may be granted thereto:

Mrs Jane Smith's 1963 Trust
Administered by Messrs A and B, Anytown
Balance of revenue due to deceased   £x

10.188   If the deceased was the sole or last surviving trustee or executor,
title can be made up to the trust or executry property as
described at paragraph 16.04.

Resulting trusts

10.189   A resulting trust can occur in a wide variety of circumstances.
Where the contractual purposes of any *inter vivos* trust are fulfilled[25] or have failed,[26] there is a resulting trust for the truster.
Similarly, if the trust funds are more than sufficient to meet the
trust purposes, the surplus is executry estate, and should be
confirmed to.[27]

10.190   If the fulfilment or failure of the trust purposes occurs before
the truster's death, then the right to the trust fund must be
confirmed to. If the fulfilment or failure occurs after the truster's

---

[25] *Anderson* v. *Smoke* (1898) 25 R. 493.
[26] *Cf.* testamentary trust cases: *Robbie's J.F.* v. *Macrae* (1893) 20 R. 358.
[27] *Clerk*, March 10, 1868, unreported; *Mathison* May 26, 1879, unreported.

death, an eik to the original confirmation must then be obtained in respect of the truster's right to the trust fund, even if the reversionary interest was valueless at the time of the deceased's death.[28] In all cases, the value placed on the resulting trust will be the value of the property at the date of death.

10.191 Since the deceased's right is a right to call the trustees to account, even if the trust funds are invested in heritage, the right is moveable in the deceased's succession.[29]

Court actions: Right of reduction

10.192 Where the deceased was entitled to bring an action of reduction, this need not be confirmed to:

> "the right of raising necessary actions is part of the office of executor. It accrues to the office—because the executorship is a general title of administration, and needs no special confirmation."[30]

Court actions: Right to Damages for Personal Injuries

10.193 A claim to damages for personal injuries to the deceased which relates to patrimonial loss attributable to a period prior to the deceased's death transmits to his executors and should be confirmed to—but a right to damages by way of solatium, or of compensation for patrimonial loss attributable to a period after the deceased's death does not transmit.[31]

10.194 Where a deceased person (A) had on death a right to claim damages in respect of the death of another person, a claim for loss of support up to the date of A's death does transmit to A's executors, and should be confirmed to, but a right to damages by way of solatium or a loss of society award does not.[32]

Rights of intellectual property such as copyright[33]

10.195 Such rights must be confirmed to. Copyright and design right are moveable property.[34]

Motor vehicles

10.195A The make, model, engine size and registration number should be supplied. Where the vehicle has a "cherished" number plate, the plate should be valued separately from the vehicle itself.

---

[28] *Per* Lord Justice-Clerk Inglis in *Lord Advocate* v. *Meiklam* (1860) 23 D. 57 at p. 63.

[29] *Meiklam's Trs.* v. *Meiklam's Trs.* (1852) 15 D. 159 at p. 163.

[30] *Per* Lord McLaren in *Johnston's Exr.* v. *Dobie*, 1907 S.C. 31 at p. 35.

[31] Damages (Scotland) Act 1976 (c. 13), s. 27.

[32] Damages (Scotland) Act 1976 (c. 13), s. 3.

[33] *Mackay* v. *Mackay*, 1914 S.C. 200.

[34] Copyright, Designs and Patents Act 1988 (c. 48), ss. 90(1) and 222(1).

ESTATE IN ENGLAND AND WALES

NOTE: An executor can only confirm to estate in England and Wales if the deceased had been domiciled in Scotland when he died. Even if the deceased had not been domiciled in Scotland, it may still be necessary for the estate in England and Wales to be disclosed in the inventory for inheritance tax purposes (see para. 2.60) and appended below the "Summary for Confirmation."

10.196 Where confirmation can be obtained, the inventory should disclose separately all interests in land in England and Wales held by the deceased, and all personal estate there, and the value of the estate in England and Wales should be shown separately.[35] In identifying the personal estate in England and Wales, the rules discussed at paragraphs 10.80–10.81 should be borne in mind in conjunction with the various categories of Scottish estate discussed at paragraphs 10.138–10.195.

ESTATE IN NORTHERN IRELAND

NOTE: An executor can only confirm to estate in Northern Ireland if the deceased had been domiciled in Scotland when he died. Even if the deceased had not been domiciled in Scotland, it may still be necessary for the estate in Northern Ireland to be disclosed in the inventory for inheritance tax purposes (see para. 2.60) and appended below the "Summary for Confirmation."

10.197 Where confirmation can be obtained, the inventory should disclose separately all interests in land in Northern Ireland held by the deceased and all personal estate there, and the value of the estate in Northern Ireland should be shown separately.[36] In identifying the personal estate in Northern Ireland, the rules discussed at paragraphs 10.80–10.81 should be borne in mind in conjunction with the various categories of Scottish estate discussed at paragraphs 10.138–10.195.

SUMMARY FOR CONFIRMATION

10.198 After the inventory of the Estate in Scotland, the Estate in Eng-

---

[35] Confirmation of Executors (Scotland) Act 1858 (21 & 22 Vict. c. 56), s. 9 as amended by Statute Law Revision Act 1892 (55 & 56 Vict. c. 19), Administration of Estates Act 1971 (c. 25), ss. 6, 12(1) and Sched. 2, Pt. 1 and Finance Act 1975 (c. 7), ss. 52(2) and 59 and Sched. 13.
[36] *Ibid.*

land and Wales (if appropriate) and the Estate in Northern Ireland (if appropriate), comes the Summary for Confirmation, which is set out as follows:

SUMMARY FOR CONFIRMATION
I   ESTATE IN SCOTLAND   £
II   ESTATE IN ENGLAND AND WALES £
III ESTATE IN NORTHERN IRELAND   £ _____

TOTAL FOR CONFIRMATION   £ _____

Overseas Estate

10.199   If the deceased died domiciled in Scotland but held estate abroad, an account of the foreign estate must be given for inheritance tax purposes, although confirmation cannot be obtained to such estate. A list of such estate should be appended to the "Total for Confirmation," listed under the headings of each country in which estate is situated. Estate in the Channel Islands or the Isle of Man is estate abroad. The items should each be described fully, but their value should not be extended into the right-hand column.

10.199A   Sometimes it may prove impossible to place a value on an item of "Estate Abroad" before confirmation is obtained — *e.g.* a Swiss bank will not reveal to an executor the amount invested by the deceased until confirmation is exhibited. In such circumstances, a nominal value may be placed on the item, provided that an explanation is given as to why a nominal value has been inserted and the inventory is submitted to the Capital Taxes Office for tax assessment before confirmation is sought. Indeed, the Capital Taxes Office requires sight of such an inventory even if the estate is otherwise "excepted estate" (see para. 12.118) or is fully relieved from tax exemptions or reliefs shown on page 10 of the inventory.

Estate held by deceased as last surviving trustee

10.200   If the deceased had been the sole or last surviivng trustee, details of the trust property should be annexed to the "Total for Confirmation"—see, further, paragraphs 16.04 *et seq.*

Discretionary payments including superannuation death benefits

10.201   A payment made in terms of a discretionary scheme to the deceased's surviving spouse or family need not be confirmed to, and no inheritance tax is payable thereon. Such payments include:

1.   death benefits payable under discretionary trusts from tax

approved occupational pension and retirement annuity schemes[37];

2.   lump sums paid under the Principal Civil Service Pension Scheme or the Judicial Pensions Act 1981;

3.   grant paid from the Scottish Solicitors' Guarantee Fund after the death of the claimant;

4.   compensation paid by the Criminal Injuries Compensation Board after the death of the claimant;

5.   damages, compensation money or other benefits payable in respect of the deceased under the Carriage by Air Act 1961, National Insurance (Industrial Injuries) Acts, etc.;

6.   damages payable to the deceased's family for loss of society under the Damages (Scotland) Act 1976.

10.202 Such discretionary payments fall to be distinguished from those payments to which executors have a contractual right. In the pension field, the following payments must be confirmed to and inheritance tax is payable thereon:

1.   any repayment of pension contributions made in consequence of the deceased having died before retirement;

2.   pension payments made to the executors as part of a fixed term entitlement under the policy;

3.   pension payments due up to the date of death[38]; and

4.   if the deceased had a general power to nominate a benefit under the pension scheme, but he had not made a nomination, the benefit forms part of his estate on death.[39]

---

[37] 1986 S.L.T. (News) 206; SP 10/86.
[38] See paras. 10.96–10.98.
[39] IHTA 1984 (c. 51), s. 151(4).

CHAPTER 11

SMALL ESTATES

Introduction

11.01   It was formerly necessary to employ an agent to obtain confirmation to all executry estates and the costs of so doing, and of meeting the court fees, were particularly burdensome on smaller estates. Since 1875, various statutes have simplified the procedure for obtaining confirmation to small estates and have reduced the costs. Instead of requiring to employ a solicitor, the deceased's family or friends can go to the clerk of court, who is obliged to prepare the inventory and oath on the Form B-3, take the oath of the applicant, and do all that is necessary in order that confirmation may be delivered to the applicant. The only charge is the official fee for recording the inventory and any testamentary writings and for issuing confirmation. A solicitor may also use the small estates procedure to obtain confirmation on behalf of a client.

Optional procedure

11.02   Where an estate falls within the limits set for the small estates procedure, it is not compulsory to adopt the procedure, but there are certain advantages in so doing:

1.   Where the deceased did not provide for executors-nominate, it is not necessary to petition separately for the appointment of an executor-dative.

2.   The executor is relieved of the task of preparing the inventory, etc., himself, or of paying a solicitor to do it for him.

If the applicant does not wish to avail himself of the small estates procedure, he must use either the Form B-4 or the Form A-3 and, where the deceased died intestate, petition for his appointment as executor.

History of the Small Estates Acts

11.03   The Small Estates Acts comprise the Intestates' Widows and Children (Scotland) Act 1875 (as amended) and the Small Testate Estates (Scotland) Act 1876 (as amended). The 1875 Act originally applied only where the person seeking confirmation was the widow or child (or children) of an intestate or the child (or children) of an intestate widow, and the deceased died domiciled in a particular sheriffdom in Scotland, leaving personal estate not exceeding £150. The 1876 Act applied only to executors-nominate, where the deceased died domiciled in a particular sheriffdom in Scotland leaving real and personal estate not exceeding £150.

11.04   Subsequently, section 34(1) of the Customs and Inland Revenue Act 1881[1] extended both Acts to *all* applicants for confirmation, wherever the deceased may have died domiciled, provided that the whole personal estate (without deducting debts and funeral expenses) did not exceed £300. In 1894, the financial limit was again raised, and was applied to the whole heritable and moveable estate subject to estate duty, excluding property settled otherwise than by the will of the deceased.[2] The financial limit was raised again in 1961, for deaths occurring on or after April 10, 1946.[3]

Present requirements

11.05   The Intestates' Widows and Children (Scotland) Act 1875 (38 & 39 Vict. c. 41) (as amended) now applies where any deceased died intestate, domiciled in Scotland, leaving estate within the present limits, and may be used by "an applicant for confirmation." Accordingly, the procedure would not appear to be limited to the deceased's near relatives but now extends to *anyone* who could have sought decerniture as an executor-dative (see further Chapter 6), including creditors with a liquid debt and funerators, with the oath[4] and inventory[5] being modified accordingly.

11.06   The Small Testate Estates (Scotland) Act 1876 (39 & 40 Vict. c. 24) (as amended) now applies where a deceased died leaving a will or other testamentary writing, domiciled in Scotland, leaving estate within the present limits.

11.07   In both cases, no distinction is made between a deceased leaving heritable estate and one leaving only moveable estate.[6]

[1] Repealed by the Confirmation of Small Estates (Scotland) Act 1979 (c.22), s. 2 and Sched. with effect from July 1, 1980 (S.I. 1980 No. 734).
[2] Finance Act 1894 (57 & 58 Vict. c.30), ss. 16 and 23(7).
[3] Small Estates (Representation) Act 1961 (c.37).
[4] Sched. A to the 1875 and 1876 Acts.
[5] Sched. B to the 1875 and 1876 Acts.
[6] Succession (Scotland) Act 1964 (c.41), s. 14(1).

Present financial limits

11.08   The Confirmation to Small Estates (Scotland) Act 1979 c.22 came into force on July 1, 1980[7] and provided that the small estates procedure was to apply on or after that date where the whole estate did not exceed £10,000.[7a] Section 1(3) of the 1979 Act made provision for the limit to be altered by statutory instrument, and thus the limit was raised to £13,000, with effect from December 27, 1984,[8] and again to £17,000, with effect from April 1, 1989.[9] These limits are applied where the deceased died on or after the specified date.

11.09   There is no statutory definition of "whole estate" but it is submitted that it covers

1. the heritable and moveable, and real and personal estate of the deceased, wherever situated;

2. the deceased's share of property held jointly with another (excluding property held under special destinations)[9a]; and

3. property nominated by the deceased during his lifetime but still *in bonis* at the time of the deceased's death.

11.10   Debts and funeral expenses cannot be deducted in computing "whole estate." Other matters relevant to the inheritance tax charge on the deceased's death (such as gifts made within seven years of the death) are to be ignored. Thus, in exceptional cases, the small estates procedure may apply (because the estate to be confirmed to is below the financial limit) but inheritance tax may be payable as where heritage of a significant value is passing under a special destination or where the chargeable lifetime transfers exhaust the nil rate band.

Circumstances where the small estates procedure is inappropriate

11.11   The small estates procedure is not appropriate in contentious cases and no application can be received under the Small Estates Acts in any of the following cases:

---

[7] S.I. 1980 No. 734.
[7a] Confirmation to Small Estates (Scotland) Act 1979 (c. 22), s 1(1) and (2).
[8] S.I. 1984 No. 1848.
[9] S.I. 1989 No. 289.
[9a] *Sandford, Petr.*, 1993 S.L.T. (Sh. Ct.) 48.

1. Where there is competition for the office of executor. In that case, a petition must be presented to the sheriff, and a record made up in common form.[10]

2. Where there is an attack on the validity of the testamentary writing.

3. Where proof of execution is required.

4. Where special warrant for confirmation is required.

5. Where the deceased died domiciled somewhere other than Scotland.[11]

6. Where the deceased had no fixed or known domicile (whether in Scotland or elsewhere).

7. Where a creditor with an illiquid debt seeks appointment.

8. Where an executor-dative has already been decerned.

Procedure

11.12   The application can be made to any sheriff clerk's office. If prepared in a different sheriff court district to that in which the deceased died domiciled, the sheriff clerk will forward the application to the appropriate court on request.

11.13   In intestate estates, the need for a petition for the appointment of an executor-dative is dispensed with. There is no separate decerniture. Instead, the decerniture is included in the grant of confirmation.

11.14   The Form B-3 will be completed, either by the applicant himself or by the sheriff clerk, on the basis of information which the applicant provides. If the clerk has reason to believe that the value of the estate exceeds the statutory limit, he will refuse to proceed until he is satisfied that the estate does not exceed the statutory limit.[12] He may require such proof as he may think necessary to establish the applicant's identity and relationship (*i.e.* the applicant's title to the office of executor, whether arising under a will, by relationship or otherwise).[13] For instance:

---

[10] *Duncan,* Oct. 31, 1889, unreported.
[11] Intestates' Widows and Children (Scotland) Act 1875 (38 & 39 Vict. c.41), s. 3 and Small Testate Estates (Scotland) Act 1876 (39 & 40 Vict. c.24), s. 3.
[12] Intestates' Widows and Children (Scotland) Act 1875 (38 & 39 Vict. c.41), s. 5 and Small Testate Estates (Scotland) Act 1876 (39 & 40 Vict. c.24), s. 5.
[13] Intestates' Widows and Children (Scotland) Act 1875 (38 & 39 Vict. c.41) s. 4 and Small Testate Estates (Scotland) Act 1876 (39 & 40 Vict. c.24), s. 4.

1. If the applicant is applying by virtue of relationship, then the full information regarding his relationship must be given in the oath—just as in a petition for the appointment of an executor. The proof required in practice is the evidence of two witnesses who attend with the applicant, and whose depositions are taken by the clerk, and recorded with the inventory and oath. In many cases, the sheriff clerk will dispense with such proof of identity, but the practice here varies in different courts.

2. If the applicant is applying by virtue of being the deceased's creditor or funerator, a properly vouched invoice or value added tax invoice (as appropriate) or a receipted funeral account must be produced. The statutory notice is inserted in the *Edinburgh Gazette* and a copy is produced before confirmation is issued (see further paras. 6.108 and 6.116–6.119).

3. Where the applicant claims under a will, the document itself, if *ex facie* validly executed, proves his title on his identity being established.

4. If a holograph will executed before August 1, 1995 is founded on, the evidence of the witnesses setting up the handwriting and signature may be included in the proof.

5. Some courts (*e.g.* Glasgow) require production of the death certificate unless the application is made through a solicitor.

11.15 The normal rules relating to the production of caution apply (see Chapter 9) with this difference, that the bond of caution refers to the applicant as a person who "is to be decerned and confirmed."

11.16 While the Law Reform (Miscellaneous Provisions) (Scotland) Act 1990[14] contains enabling legislation for an executor simply to make a declaration as to the accuracy of the information contained in the inventory, this procedure is not at the time of writing in force. It is still necessary for an executor to make an oath or affirmation, since the statutory instrument which will bring into force the provisions of the 1990 Act has not yet been made.

11.17 The oath or affirmation of the executor may be taken by the sheriff, by the sheriff or commissary clerk, before any commissioner appointed by the sheriff principal, before any magistrate within the United Kingdom, before any justice of the peace

---

[14] (c.40), Sched. 8, Pt. II and Sched. 9.

within the United Kingdom, or by any British consul[15]; by a notary public[16]; by a Commissioner for Oaths appointed by a court in England and Wales or Northern Ireland[17]; or by a solicitor empowered to administer oaths in England and Wales;[18] or if taken at a place outside the United Kingdom, before any British consul, local magistrate, or notary public practising in such foreign country, or admitted and practising in Great Britain or Northern Ireland[19]; before certain consular officials[20]; or, if made by a member of the armed services, or certain civilians attached to the armed services, before officers of certain higher ranks of the armed forces.[21]

11.18 Normally, where the Form B-3 procedure is adopted, the executor will make the oath or affirmation before the sheriff or commissary clerk who has prepared the Form B-3.

11.19 Where the applicant resides in England, he need not make a personal visit to the appropriate court, and may instead apply by post. Once the sheriff or commissary clerk has prepared the Form B-3 it will be forwarded to the applicant, who will then appear before any of the other authorised parties.

11.20 The inventory, having been deponed to, is recorded along with any testamentary writings, and confirmation is expede and delivered to the applicant on payment of the fees.

Additional estates: confirmation *ad omissa*

11.21 Where confirmation has been issued under the Small Estates Acts, it may subsequently be discovered that there is additional estate, or the need for amended valuations or other corrections. If the amount of these, when added to the sum already given

---

[15] Small Testate Estates (Scotland) Act 1876 (39 & 40 Vict. c.24), s. 6 invoking Confirmation of Executors (Scotland) Act 1858 (21 & 22 Vict. c.56), s. 11; Executors (Scotland) Act 1900 (63 & 64 Vict. c.55), s. 8.

[16] Executors (Scotland) Act 1900 (63 & 64 Vict. c.55), s. 8.

[17] Executors (Scotland) Act 1900 (63 & 64 Vict. c.55), s. 8.

[18] That is, a solicitor holding a practising certificate which is in force, provided that he is not solicitor to the deponent or has an interest in the estate (Solicitors Act 1974 (c.47), s. 81(1) and (2)).

[19] Executors (Scotland) Act 1900 (63 & 64 Vict. c.55), s. 8.

[20] *e.g.* ambassador, envoy, Minister, *chargé d'affaires*, secretary of embassy or legation, consul, vice-consul, acting consul, pro-consul, or consular agent (Commissioner for Oaths Act 1889 (52 & 53 Vict. c.10), s. 6); or acting consul-general, acting vice-consul and acting consular agent (Commissioners for Oaths Act 1891 (54 & 55 Vict. c. 50), s. 2 or counsellor (Oaths and Evidence (Overseas Authorities and Countries) Act 1963 (c. 27), s. 3).

[21] Emergency Laws (Miscellaneous Provisions) Act 1953 (c.47), s. 10; Army Act 1955 (c.18), s. 204; Air Force Act 1955 (c.19), s. 204; all as amended by Armed Forces Act 1971 (c.33), s. 70 and by Armed Forces Act 1981 (c. 55), s. 19.

up, does not exceed the limit within which confirmation under the Small Estates Acts is competent, application may be made to the clerk of court to prepare an additional inventory and to issue an eik under the same conditions as an original confirmation. But if the total exceeds the limit for confirmation under the Small Estates Acts, the practice has been adopted of granting a title to the new estate in the form of a confirmation *ad omissa*, which confers a distinct title to the estate contained in it, in no way affecting or depending upon the validity of the previous confirmation, though granted in favour of the same person. Only the newly discovered estate is confirmed to, the original confirmation still remaining a sufficient title to the estate contained in it.

11.22 Where the original confirmation was granted in favour of an executor-nominate, he may apply for confirmation-nominate *ad omissa* by preparing and giving up an inventory and oath setting forth the circumstances under which it has become necessary (see Style 8.16).

11.23 Where the original confirmation was in favour of an executor-dative, he must apply by petition for decerniture as executor-dative *ad omissa* before giving up the new inventory (see Style 6.38). An additional bond of caution (to cover the additional estate) will normally also be required.

Original executor dead: confirmation *ad omissa* or *ad non executa*

11.24 Where the executor originally confirmed has died, and additional estate is discovered, or part of the estate originally confirmed to has not been fully administered, it is competent to issue an *ad omissa* or *ad non executa* confirmation under the small estates procedure. Again, in dative cases, no petition is necessary.

CHAPTER 12

THE INVENTORY AND THE CAPITAL TAXES
OFFICE

Introduction

12.01 This chapter explores the circumstances in which United Kingdom inheritance tax is payable on an executry estate (para. 12.02); the role of the inventory as an account for inheritance tax purposes (paras. 12.03–12.06); the completion of the tax part of the inventory (paras. 12.07–12.35, 12.90 and 12.96–12.113); the inheritance tax valuation rules (paras. 12.36–12.89 and 12.91–98) and the role of the sheriff clerk in ensuring that an executry estate can only be ingathered once the inheritance tax due on it has been paid (paras. 12.114–12.117).

Liability to United Kingdom Inheritance Tax

12.02 United Kingdom inheritance tax is payable on a death as follows:

    1. where the deceased died domiciled (either within the general legal meaning of that term, or within the extended meaning of that term for inheritance tax purposes[1]) in Scotland, England and Wales, or Northern Ireland, on his world-wide estate,[2] with the exception of certain pensions payable in respect of overseas service[3];

    2. where the deceased died domiciled in the Channel Islands or the Isle of Man, on his United Kingdom estate with the exception of
      (a) war savings certificates;
      (b) national savings certificates;
      (c) premium savings bonds;

---

[1] A person not domiciled in the U.K. is treated for the purposes of IHT as domiciled in the U.K. if:
(a) he was domiciled in the U.K. within the three years immediately preceding the transfer; or
(b) he was resident in the U.K. for income tax purposes in not less than 17 of the 20 years of assessment ending with the year of assessment in which the transfer occurred (IHTA 1984 (c. 51), s. 267).
[2] IHTA 1984 (c. 51), ss. 5(1) and 6(1).
[3] *Ibid.*, s. 153.

366

      (d)   deposits with the national savings bank;

      (e)   certified contractual savings schemes within the meaning of section 326 of the Income and Corporation Taxes Act 1988; and

      (f)   certain pensions payable in respect of overseas service[4];

3. where the deceased died domiciled outside the United Kingdom, on his estate in the United Kingdom; in addition, the following items situated in the United Kingdom are excluded from the inheritance tax charge in the circumstances indicated:

      (a)   a foreign currency bank account in the United Kingdom, where the deceased was neither resident nor ordinarily resident in the United Kingdom at the time of his death[5];

      (b)   exempt gilts where the deceased was not ordinarily resident in the United Kingdom[6];

      (c)   any tangible moveable property and emoluments due, where the deceased was a member of a visiting armed force[7];

      (d)   any tangible moveable property where the deceased was a diplomatic agent who was neither a United Kingdom national nor permanently resident in the United Kingdom, or where the deceased was a member of the family of such a diplomatic agent[8]; and

      (e)   certain pensions payable in respect of overseas service.[9]

Delivery of Accounts

12.03   Executors are under a statutory duty to deliver to the Board of the Inland Revenue an account specifying all property which formed part of the deceased's estate immediately before his death.[10] The account must be completed on an official Inland

---

[4] IHTA 1984 (c. 51), s. 153; s. 6(3) as amended by ICTA 1988 (c. 1), s. 844, Sched. 29, para. 32..

[5] *Ibid.*, s. 157 as amended.

[6] IHTA 1984 (c. 51), s. 6(2); see Foster's, *Inheritance Tax*, para. J3.21 for current list of exempt gilts.

[7] IHTA 1984 (c. 51), s. 6(4) and s. 155 as amended by S.I. 1986 No. 948.

[8] Art. 39, para. 4 of Vienna Convention on Diplomatic Relations signed in 1961, brought into effect by Diplomatic Privileges Act 1964 (c. 81), s. 2, applied to IHT by IHTA (c. 51), s. 273, Sched. 6, para. 1.

[9] IHTA 1984 (c. 51), s. 153.

[10] The duty to report does not extend to property treated as part of the deceased's estate for IHT purposes by virtue of the "gift with reservation" rules (IHTA 1984 (c. 51), s. 216(3) as amended by Finance Act 1986 (c. 41), Sched. 19, para. 29(2)).

Revenue form,[11] or on an approved substitute form generated by computer.[12] Where, in Scotland, executors exhibit an inventory (or additional inventory) of the deceased's estate to the appropriate sheriff court as required under section 38 of the Probate and Legacy Duties Act 1808,[13] the inventory CAP Form B-3 (in the case of small estates, see Chap. 11), CAP Form B-4 (in the case of excepted estates — see paras. 12.118–12.119) and CAP Form A-3 (in all other cases), constitutes the account for inheritance tax purposes.[14] Thus, in most estates, when executors apply for confirmation, they fulfil their statutory duty to deliver an account for inheritance tax purposes.

12.04 Once confirmation has been granted thereon, the sheriff (or commissary) clerk transmits the inventories to the Capital Taxes Office in Edinburgh.

Time-limit for delivery of the account
12.05 Executors are required to deliver the account to the Capital Taxes Office not later than the end of the twelfth month after the end of the month in which the death occurred (or, if later, within three months of their accepting office).[15–16]

12.06 Certain limited sanctions can be used against executors who do not comply with the time-limit for delivery — a penalty of up to £50, and if the non-compliance continues after it has been declared by a court or by the special commissioners, an additional penalty of up to £10 per day.[17]

Completion of the inheritance tax part of the inventory

12.07 Practitioners faced with calculating the inheritance tax due on the estate of a dead person are referred to the specialist literature on the subject, including the Inland Revenue's booklet IHT 1, and encyclopedias such as Dymond's *Capital Taxes*, Foster's *Inheritance Tax* and CCH Edition's *Inheritance Tax Reporter*. Paragraphs 12.10–12.35 contain general comments on aspects of substantive and tax law which may be of assistance in completing pages 3 and 4 of the inventory. Paragraphs 12.36–12.89 contain notes on the valuation of items of taxable estate. Paragraphs 12.90–12.113 outline the tax considerations relevant to completing pages 8–12 of the inventory.

---

[11] IHTA 1984 (c. 51), s. 257.
[12] SP 2/93; see also Press Release of January 13, 1993.
[13] 48 Geo. 3, c. 149, as amended by Finance Act 1949 (12 & 13 Geo. 6, c. 47), s. 52(10), and Sched. 11, Pt. V; Finance Act 1975 (c. 7), s. 59(5), Sched. 13, Pt. 1; and Law Reform (Miscellaneous Provisions) (Scotland) Act 1990 (c. 40), s. 74(1), Sched. 8, para. 19.
[14] IHTA 1984 (c. 51), s. 261.
[15–16] IHTA 1984 (c. 51), s. 216(6)(a).
[17] *Ibid.*, s. 245.

12.08 The staff of the CTO in Scotland are always willing to assist practitioners who are faced with a specific problem, but it should be remembered that while such advice will be in accordance with the Revenue's current practice, it should not be viewed as definitive on either general law or tax law.

QUESTIONS ON PAGES 3 AND 4 OF CAP FORM A-3

12.09 The questions on pages 3 and 4 are designed to elicit information pertinent to the inheritance tax charge.

Question 1: Gifts by the deceased

12.10 Inheritance tax is payable on the following gifts:

1. Any gift made by the deceased within the seven years before his death,[18] and

2. Any gift made by the deceased on or after March 18, 1986 where the deceased reserved a benefit, which he continued to enjoy during the seven years leading up to his death.[19]

12.11 The law of Scotland recognises donations *inter vivos* and *mortis causa*. Such a donation may take the form of A making an outright gift of property which he owned to B, or of A transferring the title to his property into the names of himself and B, as where a share certificate is registered in the names of husband and wife, or of parent and child.

Donations inter vivos[20]

12.12 A donation *inter vivos* by A to B may be proved where

1. there has been delivery to B: A must have divested himself of and have invested B with the subject of the gift[21]; where the gift is a transfer into a trust, and A declares himself to be sole trustee, the trust must, if constituted on or after August 1, 1995, be constituted by a document complying with section 2 of the Requirements of Writing (Scotland) Act 1995; and

2. *animus donandi de praesenti* can be shown.[22]

---

[18] IHTA 1984 (c. 51), s. 3A(4) (inserted by Finance Act 1986 (c. 41), s. 101(1), Sched. 19, para. 1).
[19] Finance Act 1986 (c. 41), s. 102 (amended by Finance Act 1989 (c. 26), s. 171(5), (6)) and Sched. 20 as amended.
[20] For fuller discussion see *Stair Memorial Encyclopaedia*, vol. 8, paras. 601–700.
[21] *McNicol* v. *McDougall* (1889) 17 R. 25; *Boucher's Trs.* v. *Boucher's Trs.* (1907) 15 S.L.T. 157.
[22] *McCubbin's Exrs.* v. *Tait* (1868) 6 M. 310.

12.13   It is a fact against donation *inter vivos* if the transfer is of the whole of A's estate.[23] The date of the gift is the date of delivery.[24]

Donation mortis causa[25]

12.14   The classic definition of a *donatio mortis causa* is that of Lord President Inglis in *Morris* v. *Riddick*[26]:

> "*donatio mortis causa* in the law of Scotland may, I think, be defined as a conveyance of an immoveable or incorporeal right, or a transference of moveables or money by delivery, so that the property is immediately transferred to the grantee, upon the condition that he shall hold for the granter so long as he lives, subject to his power of revocation, and, failing such revocation, then for the grantee on the death of the granter."

12.15   A donation *mortis causa* by A to B may be proved where:

1.   The gift was made in contemplation of death, but not necessarily in immediate apprehension of death[27];

2.   There has been actual[28] or constructive[29] delivery to B: establishing mere intention to deliver is not enough[30]; and

3.   *Animus donandi de praesenti* can be shown.[31] It is a factor against donation if the alleged donation would leave too little estate to carry out the deceased's testamentary instructions.[32] There is no presumption that a later will revokes a donation *mortis causa*.[33] Motive (as well as

---

[23] See, for example, *Swan's Exrs.* v. *McDougall* (1868) 5 S.L.R. 675; *Dawson* v. *McKenzie* (1891) 19 R. 261; *Lord Advocate* v. *McCourt* (1893) 20 R. 488.

[24] *Thomas* v. *Lord Advocate*, 1953 S.C. 151; *Lombardi's Tr.* v. *Lombardi*, 1982 S.L.T. 81. For fuller discussion see *Stair Memorial Encyclopaedia*, vol. 19, para. 1604 (gift of corporeal moveable property), para. 1605 (gift of incorporeal moveable property) and para. 1606 (gifts by cheques and cash).

[25] For fuller discussion see *Stair Memorial Encyclopaedia*, vol. 8, para. 607.

[26] (1867) 5 M. 1036 at p. 1041.

[27] *Crosbie's Trs.* v. *Wright* (1880) 7 R. 823; *Blyth* v. *Curle* (1885) 12 R. 674; *Macpherson's Exx.* v. *Mackay*, 1932 S.C. 505; Lord Moncrieff in *Aiken's Exrs.* v. *Aiken*, 1937 S.C. 678 at p. 690; Lord President Clyde in *Graham's Trs.* v. *Gillies*, 1956 S.C. 437 at p. 447.

[28] *Macpherson's Exx.* v. *Mackay*, 1932 S.C. 505; *Aiken's Exrs.* v. *Aiken*, 1937 S.C. 678.

[29] *Crosbie's Trs.* v. *Wright* (1880) 7 R. 823; *Aiken's Exrs.* v. *Aiken*, 1937 S.C. 678; *per* Lord President Clyde in *Graham's Trs.* v. *Gillies*, 1956 S.C. 437 at p. 449; but it must be clear that the deceased intended to make a present gift: *Taggart* v. *Cochrane* (1900) 8 S.L.T. 139; (1900) 37 S.L.R. 843.

[30] *Graham's Trs.* v. *Gillies*, 1956 S.C. 437.

[31] *Gibson* v. *Hutchison* (1872) 10 M. 923; *Macpherson's Exx.* v. *Mackay*, 1932 S.C. 505; *Aiken's Exrs.* v. *Aiken*, 1937 S.C. 678.

[32] *Ross* v. *Mellis* (1871) 10 M. 197; *Crosbie's Trs.* v. *Wright* (1880) 7 R. 823.

[33] *Crosbie's Trs.* v. *Wright* (1880) 7 R. 823; *Scott's Trs.* v. *Macmillan* (1905) 8 F. 214.

intention) may be relevant, and a motive only to save tax payable on the donor's death is not compatible with *animus donandi*.[34]

12.16   The three essentials are so interrelated that weak evidence in support of one may be eked out by strong evidence in support of one or both of the others.[35]

12.17   A donation *mortis causa* must be to an individual personally, and not to an individual as a trustee.[36]

12.18   "When the mortis causa donor predeceases the donee without having revoked, nothing passes by succession or otherwise to the donee; he is then (as he has been all along) owner of the property by virtue of the *de praesenti* donation."[37] Consequently, where it is established that a donation *mortis causa* has been made, and legal title is in name of the donee, the gifted property need not be disclosed in the inventory of A's estate, though it must be reported at page 3 and in Section 3 of the account as a "gift with reservation." If legal title remained in the name of the deceased, the gifted property should be appended to the inventory as "property held in trust by the deceased for the donee," and should also be reported at page 3 and in Section 3 of the account as a "gift with reservation." It has been suggested that a gift *mortis causa* cannot qualify for any of the lifetime exemptions, but will qualify for the exemptions on death.[37a]

Proof of donation

12.19   In all cases, it is difficult to overcome the presumption against donation, which is stronger in the case of *inter vivos* gifts than in the case of those *mortis causa*.[38] Proof of *animus donandi* can be difficult, since the transfer could have been made merely to give the alleged donee control of the property for administrative purposes only.

12.20   The evidence of the alleged donee alone is not sufficient, and must be corroborated by real evidence from any documents of gift or, preferably, by the parole evidence of a third party as

---

[34] *Miller* v. *Miller* (1874) 1 R. 1107; *Rose* v. *Cameron's Exr.* (1901) 3 F. 337; *Forrest-Hamilton's Tr.* v. *Forrest-Hamilton*, 1970 S.L.T. 338; cf. *Lord Advocate* v. *Galloway* (1884) 11 R. 541.

[35] *Per* Lord President Clyde in *Macpherson's Exx.* v. *Mackay*, 1932 S.C. 505 at pp. 514–515.

[36] *Thomson* v. *Dunlop* (1884) 11 R. 453.

[37] *Per* Lord President Clyde in *Macpherson's Exx.* v. *Mackay*, 1932 S.C. 505 at p. 513.

[37a] Dymond, *Capital Taxes*, 13.110–119.

[38] *Sharp* v. *Paton* (1883) 10 R. 1000; *per* Lord President Normand in *North of Scotland Bank* v. *Cumming*, 1939 S.L.T. 391 at p. 394; but cf. Lord President Clyde in *Macpherson's Exx.* v. *Mackay*, 1932 S.C. 505 at p. 513.

to the donor's conduct and the circumstances surrounding the transfer.[39]

12.21 Particular care should be taken where the alleged gift is of a deposit receipt or bank account opened with the deceased's money, where the account is in the names of the deceased and another. In such a case, the names in the account title do not prove who owned the money invested beneficially, and readers are referred to the established texts on this subject.

Separate schedule showing the lifetime transfers

12.22 Where the donor has made a number of lifetime gifts, the normal practice is to prepare a separate schedule setting out all relevant details of all the lifetime gifts, and to refer to this schedule in the answers to questions 1 and 2 on page 3 and in completing section 3 on page 9. In respect of each gift, the schedule should set out:

1. the property gifted;

2. the identity of the donee;

3. the date of the gift;

4. the value (or estimated value) transferred at the time of the gift, or the time when the reservation ceased (whichever is appropriate): where an estimated value is given, it should be clearly marked as an estimate;

5. in the case of an immediately chargeable lifetime transfer (a "non-PET"), whether the deceased undertook to pay the inheritance tax on the gift: if so, the gift must be grossed-up when calculating the inheritance tax due on it[40];

Any reliefs or exemptions which may be appropriate should be deducted at page 10 of CAP Form A-3 under the heading "Deduct the amount of any exemption or relief" in arriving at the "Net total of chargeable transfers". The exemptions and reliefs include:

---

[39] Donation *inter vivos*: *Thomson's Exr.* v. *Thomson* (1882) 9 R. 911; *Sharp* v. *Paton* (1883) 10 R. 1000; *McNicol* v. *McDougall* (1889) 17 R. 25; *Dawson* v. *McKenzie* (1891) 19 R. 261; *Brownlee's Exx.* v. *Brownlee*, 1908 S.C. 232; *Grant's Trs.* v. *McDonald*, 1939 S.C. 448. Donation *mortis causa*: *Crosbie's Trs.* v. *Wright* (1880) 7 R. 823; *Macpherson's Exx.* v. *Mackay*, 1932 S.C. 505.

[40] IHTA 1984 (c. 51), ss. 3(1) and 5(4).

(a) annual exemption (both for the tax year of the gift/cessation of the reservation, and for the previous tax year, if not already used)[41];

(b) small gift exemption[42];

(c) normal expenditure out of income[43];

(d) gifts in consideration of marriage[44];

(e) spouse exemption[45];

(f) payments for the maintenance of the donor's spouse, child or dependant relative[46];

(g) charitable exemption[47];

(h) political parties exemption[48];

(i) gift for national purposes (*e.g.* to a national museum, National Trust for Scotland, local authority, university, etc.)[49];

(j) gift for public benefit (*e.g.* land or buildings of scenic, historic, or scientific interest)[50];

(k) gift to a housing association[51];

(l) business relief[52];

(m) agricultural relief[53];

(n) relief where quoted stocks or shares or land or buildings gifted by the deceased are worth less at the time of the donor's death than when gifted — or where such property was sold before the donor's death for less than its value when gifted.[54]

Question 1: Life Policies

12.23 The deceased may have paid premiums on life policies taken out on his own life or on the life of someone else.

12.24 Where a life policy is payable on the deceased's death to his heirs, executors or assignees, the executors will confirm to it. If

---

[41] IHTA 1984 (c. 51), s. 19 as amended by Finance Act 1986 (c. 41), s. 101(1), Sched. 19, para. 5.

[42] *Ibid.*, s. 20.

[43] *Ibid.*, s. 21 as amended by ICTA 1988 (c. 1), s. 844, Sched. 29, para. 32.

[44] *Ibid.*, s. 22.

[45] *Ibid.*, s. 18.

[46] *Ibid.*, s. 11.

[47] *Ibid.*, s. 23 as amended by Finance Act 1989 (c. 26), s. 171.

[48] *Ibid.*, s. 24 as amended by Finance Act 1988 (c. 39), s. 137.

[49] *Ibid.*, s. 25 and Sched. 3.

[50] *Ibid.*, ss. 26 and 26A (inserted by Finance Act 1986 (c. 41), s. 101(3) and Sched. 19, para. 6).

[51] *Ibid.*, s. 24A (inserted by Finance Act 1989 (c. 26), s. 171(1)).

[52] *Ibid.*, ss. 103–114, as amended, especially ss. 113A and 113B, (inserted by Finance Act 1986 (c. 41), s. 101(3), Sched. 19, para. 21 as amended).

[53] *Ibid.*, ss. 115–124B as amended, especially ss. 124A and 124B (inserted by Finance Act 1986 (c. 41), Sched. 19, para. 22 as amended).

[54] *Ibid.*, ss. 131–140 as amended.

the policy has, for instance, been written under the Married Women's Policies of Assurance Acts 1880 and 1980 (see paras. 10.161–10.162), transferred into a trust (see paras. 10.163–10.164), or assigned in security of a debt or by way of gift (see paras. 10.165–10.270), it may be uplifted without being confirmed to.

12.25 Where the deceased has paid premiums on a life policy which is not included in the inventory, any premiums which the deceased paid within seven years of his death will be treated as lifetime transfers of value, but will often result in a "nil" chargeable transfer due to the application of the inheritance tax exemption for "normal expenditure out of income."[55] This exemption requires to be claimed, however, and is not automatically available.

12.26 Where, within seven years of his death, the deceased had gifted the right to a life policy by way of an assignation, or had transferred the policy into a trust, he made a lifetime chargeable transfer, which will be valued in terms of the rules outlined at paragraphs 12.84–12.86.

Question 2: Gifts with reservation

12.27 This question seeks to ascertain whether the deceased had, on or after March 18, 1986, gifted property, but yet continued to enjoy a benefit from the property. If the reservation ceased before the deceased died, it is taxed as a gift made at the time the reservation ceased.[56] If the deceased still enjoyed the benefit of the property at the time of his death, it bears tax as if it were part of his estate for inheritance tax purposes.[57]

Question 3: Settled property

12.28 This question seeks to ascertain whether the deceased had, within the seven years before his death or at the time of his death, been entitled to either

1. a life interest of a trust (*e.g.* a liferent); or

2. an annuity; or

3. any other "interest in possession" of a trust (*e.g.* a right of occupancy).

---

[55] IHTA 1984 (c. 51), s. 21 as amended by ICTA 1988 (c. 1), s. 844, Sched. 29, para. 32.
[56] Finance Act 1986 (c. 41), s. 102(4).
[57] *Ibid.*, s. 102(3).

12.29 Subject to certain exceptions, when an "interest in possession" in a trust comes to an end on death, inheritance tax is calculated on the capital value of the trust property at that time.[58] If the "interest in possession" comes to an end during the lifetime of the beneficiary and another individual benefits thereby, it is treated for inheritance tax purposes as a potentially exempt transfer by that beneficiary of the capital value of the trust property.[58a]

Question 4: Joint property

12.30 Under Scots law, the issue is not one of joint property, but of property owned in common. These questions are designed to ascertain whether the deceased had donated part of the property to the owner in common (see paras. 12.10–12.21). If the account in question is derived from funds provided only by the deceased on or after March 18, 1986, it may be caught by the "gift with reservation" rules (see para. 12.27).

Question 4: Property passing under a special destination

12.31 Where property passes under a special destination (see 10.109 *et seq.*), it is not necessary to include the item in the inventory of the deceased's estate, though inheritance tax is payable on the value transferred. Details of the property and the special destination should be set out here, and the estimated value of the item carried to page 9, Section 3 of the CAP Form A-3 under the heading "Other Property". If the destination passes the property to the deceased's surviving spouse, the surviving spouse exemption[59] should be deducted at page 10 of CAP Form A-3.

Question 5: Nominations

12.32 Since a nomination will take effect irrespective of the deceased's testamentary writings, or the rules of intestate succession which would otherwise apply,[60] the CTO must be advised of the property nominated, its value and the nominee—in order to apply, for instance, the surviving spouse exemption[61] correctly. The property itself requires to be returned in Account No. 3 of the CAP Form A-3.

---

[58] IHTA 1984 (c. 51), s. 52(1).
[58a] IHTA 1984 (c. 51), s. 3A (inserted by Finance Act 1986 (c. 41), s. 101 and Sched. 9, para. 1 as amended by Finance Act (No. 2) 1987 (c. 51), s. 96).
[59] *Ibid.*, s. 18.
[60] See paras. 13.10–13.18.
[61] IHTA 1984 (c. 51), s. 18.

Question 6: Deduction of liabilities

12.33   This question is directed to ascertaining whether the anti-avoidance provision contained in section 103 of the Finance Act 1986 (discussed at para. 12.92) might be applicable.

Question 7: Details of the deceased's family

12.34   The answers to these questions are important. The questions are designed to ascertain whether any person is entitled to claim legal rights on the deceased's estate,[62] and, where the deceased died intestate, to whom his estate passes. Estate passing to the deceased's surviving spouse will normally be exempt from inheritance tax.[63]

12.35   If the deceased was a widow or widower, details of his or her spouse's name and date of death will enable the CTO to locate the file for the spouse, which may contain details relevant to

1.   claims for business or agricultural relief on the deceased's estate, based on the predeceasing spouse's occupation or ownership.

2.   claims for relief from tax on the capital value of a trust fund liferented by the deceased which had been set up on the death of his or her spouse before November 13, 1974, estate duty having been paid on the first death.[64]

3.   claims for tax on the capital value of a trust fund liferented by the deceased which had been "spouse exempt" from inheritance tax when it was set up.

COMPLETION OF THE INVENTORY: VALUATION OF THE ESTATE

Valuation

12.36   Except where indicated, the rules set out at paragraphs 12.41–12.89 apply equally to the valuation of lifetime transfers, to the valuation of a trust fund liferented by the deceased, and to the valuation of estate included in the inventory.

Valuation: lifetime gifts

12.37   The measure of a transfer of value is the loss to the donor's

---

[62] See paras. 6.51–6.54.
[63] IHTA 1984 (c. 51), s. 18.
[64] *Ibid.*, s. 273, Sched. 6, para. 2.

estate.[65] This will normally be the open market value of the actual item gifted (see paras. 12.41 *et seq.*), but if the item is more valuable to the donor than to the donee, the value of the transfer is ascertained by deducting the value of the donor's estate after the gift, from its value before the gift. Examples where this approach would be necessary include

1. where the gift was of one of a pair of antique candlesticks; and

2. where the gift was of 2 per cent of the issued share capital of a company, which brought down the donor's holding from 51 per cent to 49 per cent.

Liabilities of the donor

12.38   If the donor undertook to pay the inheritance tax on a chargeable lifetime gift, this must be taken into account in calculating the "loss to the donor,"[66] and grossing-up will be necessary.[66a]

12.39   No allowance can be made for any of the following payments made by the donor:

1. capital gains tax or other taxes paid in consequence of the gift[67]; and

2. the expenses of effecting the transfer.[68]

---

[65] *Ibid.*, s. 3(1).

[66] *Ibid.*, s. 5(4).

[66a] *Example* Mr A has already made lifetime chargeable transfers within the previous seven years which, in aggregate, exceed the nil rate band for inheritance tax. He now puts £60,000 into a discretionary trust (a lifetime chargeable transfer) and undertakes to pay any inheritance tax thereon. The tax bill is then calculated as follows:-

$$£60,000 \times \frac{100}{100 - x} \quad \text{(where x is the marginal rate of IHT, say 40\%)}$$

$$- £60,000$$

$$= £60,000 \times \frac{100}{60} - £60,000$$

$$= £100,000 - £60,000 = £40,000$$

The total loss to the donor is £60,000 (the gift) and £40,000 (the IHT). The net position for the trustees is the same as if the donor had given £100,000 on the understanding that the trustees would pay the inheritance tax due on it of £40,000 (£100,000 at 40%).

[67] IHTA 1984 (c.51), s. 5(4).

[68] *Ibid.*, s. 164(*a*).

Liabilities of the donee

12.40   In calculating the value transferred, any of the following payments can be deducted if paid by the donee:

> 1.   where the gift was the disposal of an asset for capital
>   gains tax purposes and a chargeable gain or a develop-
>   ment gain arose, any capital gains tax or income tax
>   paid[69]; and

> 2.   the expenses of effecting the transfer.[70]

The general valuation rule: open market value

12.41   In the account, the executors must specify all property which
formed part of the deceased's estate immediately before his
death,[71] valuing such property to the best of their knowledge
and belief.[72] If an exact value cannot be placed on an item, it is
permissible to estimate its value, provided that this is clearly
stated.[73]

12.42   Normally, the market value of the item must be used—that is:

> "the price which the property might reasonably be expected
> to fetch if sold in the open market at that time; but that
> price shall not be assumed to be reduced on the ground
> that the whole property is to be placed on the market at
> one and the same time."[74]

Hypothetical sale:

12.43   The statutory provision postulates a hypothetical open market
sale. It is irrelevant that a prudent owner would not have sold
at the time of the transfer,[75] that the donor (or deceased) had
no intention to sell, or that he had no power of sale. If there
are in reality restrictions on the owner selling the asset on the
open market,[76] the item is valued as if the restrictions do not

---

[69] IHTA 1984 (c.51), s. 165 as amended by TCGA 1992 (c. 12), Sched. 10, para.
8(1) and (8).

[70] *Ibid.*, s. 164(*b*).

[71] The duty to report does not extend to property treated as part of the deceased's estate for inheritance tax purposes by virtue of the "gift with reservation"
rules. (IHTA 1984 (c. 51), s. 216(3) as amended by Finance Act 1986 (c. 41),
s. 101(3), Sched. 19, para. 29(2)).

[72] IHTA 1984 (c. 51), s. 216(1) and (3) as amended by Finance (No. 2) Act 1987
(c. 51), Sched. 7, para. 4(2); Finance Act 1986 (c. 41), Sched. 19, para. 29(1).

[73] IHTA 1984 (c. 51), s. 216(3)(*a*).

[74] *Ibid.*, s. 160; this provision is almost identical to that under estate duty, and
accordingly, the relevant estate duty cases are cited.

[75] *Per* Lord Reid in *Duke of Buccleuch* v. *I.R.C.* [1967] 1 A.C. 506 at p. 525A.

[76] *e.g.* the Articles of Association of a private company may provide that shares
may only be sold to existing shareholders at a stated price.

impede the hypothetical purchaser's purchase, but any sale by him would be subject to these restrictions.[77]

The parties:

12.44 In the open market sale, it is presumed that there is a willing (but not anxious[78]) seller and a willing purchaser.[79] The purchaser is presumed to have access to all publicly published information, but to no other information.[80]

12.45 Where there is a special purchaser willing to pay over the odds for an item of property, his existence cannot be disregarded,[81] although it cannot be assumed that he will in fact pay his highest price.[82]

The property:

12.46 "A person's estate is the aggregate of all the property to which he is beneficially entitled, except that the estate of a person immediately before his death does not include excluded property[83]."[84] Thus, if a deceased person had liferented some property, and personally owned other property, which, if taken with the liferented property, would be more valuable, both properties must be valued together, and the total value then apportioned.

12.47 Further, the "related property" rules[85] require that if an item of the deceased's estate would be more valuable if it were sold along with either:

(a) property belonging to the deceased's spouse; or

(b) property which is, or within the previous five years, was the property of a charity, political party, national or public body or registered housing association, or is held in trust for charitable purposes only, following a gift by the deceased or the deceased's spouse

---

[77] *I.R.C.* v. *Crossman* [1937] A.C. 26; confirmed *Lynall & Anor.* v. *I.R.C.* [1972] A.C. 680; applied in IHT cases *Alexander* v. *I.R.C.* [1991] S.T.C. 112, and *Baird's Exrs.* v. *I.R.C.*, 1991 S.L.T. (Lands Tr.) 9.

[78] *Per* Pickford L.J. in *I.R.C.* v. *Clay* [1914] 3 K.B. 466 at p. 478.

[79] *Per* Lord Guest in *Winter* v. *I.R.C.* [1963] A.C. 235 at p. 262.

[80] *Lynall & Anor.* v. *I.R.C.* [1972] A.C. 680 (when valuing shares in a private company, this decision has been superseded by IHTA 1984 (c. 51), s. 168: see paras. 12.77–12.81).

[81] *I.R.C.* v. *Crossman* [1937] A.C. 26.

[82] *I.R.C.* v. *Clay* [1914] 3 K.B. 466.

[83] As defined in IHTA 1984 (c. 51), s. 6 as amended by ICTA 1988 (c. 1), s. 844(1), Sched. 29, para. 32.

[84] IHTA 1984 (c. 51), s. 5(1).

[85] *Ibid.*, s. 161 as amended by Finance Act 1989 (c. 26), s. 171.

then the value of the item of estate is the appropriate proportion of the combined values of the two properties.

12.48 For stocks, shares, debentures, etc., of one class, this calculation is done on the basis of the number of shares, etc., held,[86] and in all other cases, on the basis of the relative value of the related property.[87]

Example:

> If the deceased owned an antique chair individually worth £5,000, and his wife owned five identical chairs, the whole set of chairs together being worth £50,000, under the related property rules, the deceased's chair is worth

$$£50,000 \quad \times \quad \frac{£5,000}{£5,000 \quad + \quad £25,000} \quad = \quad £8,333$$

The mode of sale:

12.49 The hypothetical sale is to be carried out in the way which will realise the best price: it may be in the market place, in a place to which buyers resort, by auction, by inviting tenders, etc.[88] Depending on the nature of the property to be valued, the hypothetical sale can either be on the basis of the sale of the property as one lot, or with the property lotted in a number of natural units[89]: it should not be part of the hypothetical sale to postulate an elaborate and expensive subdivision of the whole.[90]

12.50 It is assumed that the seller will take "such steps as are reasonable to attract as much competition as possible for the particular piece of property which is to be sold."[91] There must be adequate publicity, the nature of the property determining what is adequate.[92]

Time of sale:

12.51 The sale is presumed to have taken place at the time when the property has to be valued—be this immediately before the death,[93] in the case of a gift with reservation, when the reservation ceased[94] or, in the case of an outright gift, at the time of the gift.

---

[86] IHTA 1984 (c. 51), s. 161(4) and (5).
[87] *Ibid.*, s. 161(3).
[88] *Per* Lord Reid in *Lynall & Anor.* v. *I.R.C.* [1972] A.C. 680 at p. 695E.
[89] *Earl of Ellesmere* v. *I.R.C.* [1918] 2 K.B. 735; *Duke of Buccleuch* v. *I.R.C.* [1967] 1 A.C. 506.
[90] *Per* Lord Reid in *Duke of Buccleuch* v. *I.R.C.* [1967] 1 A.C. 506 at p. 524F.
[91] *Ibid.*, at p. 524F–G.
[92] *Per* Lord Reid in *Lynall & Anor.* v. *I.R.C.* [1972] A.C. 680 at p. 695D.
[93] IHTA 1984 (c. 51), s. 4(1).
[94] Finance Act 1986 (c. 41), s. 102(4).

Price:

12.52 The price is what the hypothetical purchaser is prepared to pay, on the basis of the information then available to him, and not the item's intrinsic value.[95] It is presumed that the sale will be for the best price that can be obtained—that is, without deduction of the expenses of sale (but compare the rules for property abroad, outlined at para. 12.98).[96]

Evidence of an actual sale at the time:

12.53 If an actual open market sale happened about the time of the hypothetical sale, the evidence of the actual sale price obtained will be persuasive, unless there had been a material change of circumstances between the valuation date and the date of the sale.[97] But if it should be shown that a higher price would have been obtained, if another method of sale had been adopted, the higher price will be adopted as the open market value.[98]

12.54 If the actual sale was not at arm's length, the sale price will not be a true reflection of the open market value, and for this reason will normally be ignored.

12.55 If the deceased's testamentary writing had given someone an option to purchase an asset on favourable terms, this has no special effect on the date of death open market value.

Special valuation rules: restriction on freedom to dispose

12.56 Where the right to dispose of property has been excluded or restricted by contract, on the first inheritance tax transfer of the property thereafter, the property is valued ignoring the exclusion or restriction—except to the extent that consideration in money (or money's worth) was given for it.[99]

VALUATION OF SPECIFIC ASSETS

(A) Heritage

Property registered in the names of the deceased and others in pro indiviso *shares*

12.57 Where title to the property is taken in *pro indiviso* shares, the

---

[95] *Per* Plowman J. in *Re Lynall dec'd.* [1969] 1 Ch. 421 at p. 436C.

[96] *Per* Lord Reid in *Duke of Buccleuch* v. *I.R.C.* [1967] 1 A.C. 506 at p. 525B.

[97] *I.R.C.* v. *Marr's Trs.* (1906) 44 S.L.R. 647 (where a herd of prize shorthorn cattle was valued at the date of death (June) and sold the following October: the enhanced value at the time of the sale was due to the nature of the subject and the special circumstances of the market at the time of the sale).

[98] *Earl of Ellesmere* v. *I.R.C.* [1918] 2 K.B. 735 (where after the death, an estate was sold in one lot, and the purchaser resold in lots shortly thereafter at a substantial profit).

[99] IHTA 1984 (c. 51), s. 163.

value of the deceased's interest in the property is computed by taking the proportionate share of the value of the whole property calculated at the date of death, and, where the owners are not spouses,[99a] claiming a discount to reflect the disadvantages of ownership in common, such as the expenses of an action of division and sale required before a *pro indiviso* proprietor may realise the value of his investment.[1] In the case of jointly owned property in England and Wales the discount available is normally 10 per cent,[2] but although it has been suggested that no discount is allowed if the property is property owned in common and in Scotland,[3] in practice the district valuer will allow a small discount, normally no more than five per cent.

Example: Deceased owned a one-quarter *pro indiviso* share in a house. At the date of his death, the whole house is valued at £100,000. The item should be shown in the inventory as follows:

Value of 1 High Street, Anytown	£ 100,000	
Deceased's one-quarter interest therein		25,000
Less: Discount (5%)		1,250
		23,750

12.58 The discount will not apply where the *pro indiviso* shares are caught by the related property rules (see paragraphs 12.47–12.48).

Property bought at a discount in terms of the "tenant's right to buy"

12.59 Where the deceased had purchased a property at a discount in terms of a tenant's right to buy under the Housing Acts, and was taken bound to repay a percentage of the discount on a sale within the following five years, the value of the property on his death within the five-year period is calculated on the basis of a hypothetical sale to a purchaser who would become obliged to repay the discount if he sold (the sale to the hypothetical purchaser not triggering the repayment obligation)[4]: in other words, the open market value of the property is *not* found by deducting from the property's value the amount repayable if the property had been sold on the day the deceased died.

[99a] IHTA 1984 (c. 51), s. 161.

[1] Cf. the English joint property cases of *Cust* v. *I.R.C.* (1917) 91 E.G. 11; *Wight and Anor.* v. *C.I.R.* (1982) 264 E.G. 935.

[2] In *Cust* v. *I.R.C.* (1917) 91 E.G. 11, the discount was 5 per cent of the value of a town house, and 10 per cent in the case of country estate. In *Wight and Anor.* v. *C.I.R.* [1982] 264 E.G. 935; [1984] 24 R.U.R. 163 a discount of 15 per cent was given where the co-owners had the right to occupy domestic property jointly.

[3] Cf. Foster's *Inheritance Tax* at para. F3.78 which is wrong on this point.

[4] *Alexander* v. *I.R.C.* [1991] S.T.C. 112.

Property owned by the deceased subject to a lease

12.60   Where land owned by the deceased is subject to a tenancy, the method of valuation depends upon the balance of the term for which the lease has to run, taking into account any security of tenure which the tenant may have under, for instance, the Agricultural Holdings Act.

12.61   Where only a few years of the lease are left to run, the land may be valued at a percentage of its vacant possession value.

12.62   If possession cannot be recovered for many years, the appropriate approach is to capitalise the net rent (that is, the gross rent after deduction of the landlord's reasonable outgoings).

12.63   It would appear that if the tenant had been a partnership in which the deceased landlord had had a substantial involvement as one of the partners, the Revenue may seek to lot the land and the partnership interest together for valuation purposes.[5]

Leases for life

12.64   Unless granted for full consideration, a lease for life (or lives), or for a period ascertainable only by reference to a death, or which is terminable on a death, or at a date ascertainable only by reference to a death, shall be treated as a settlement.[6] The value of the landlord's interest in the property is calculated as follows[7]:

$$\frac{\text{consideration actually paid when lease granted}}{\text{full consideration when lease granted}} \times \frac{\text{value}}{\text{of property}}$$

12.65   The tenant's interest is calculated as follows[8]:

value of property − value of landlord's interest (calculated as above)

Tenancy held by deceased

12.66   Except in the case of certain agricultural tenancies referred to below, a tenancy held by the deceased falls to be valued for inheritance tax purposes when it is transferred[9]—whether on the death of the tenant, or during the tenant's life. In one case, the tenancy was valued at 25 per cent of the farm's vacant possession value,[10] but the appropriate percentage will vary (in the

---

[5] *Gray* v. *I.R.C.* [1994] S.T.C. 360 (where the deceased landlord of a farm was entitled to 92.5 per cent of the profits of the partnership which leased the farm, and had power to dissolve the partnership).

[6] IHTA 1984 (c. 51), s. 43(3).

[7] *Ibid.*, s. 170.

[8] *Ibid.*, s. 50(6).

[9] *Baird's Exrs.* v. *I.R.C.*, 1991 S.L.T. (Lands Tr.) 9.

[10] *Baird's Exrs.* v. *I.R.C.*, 1991 S.L.T. (Lands Tr.) 9.

range of between five per cent and 50 per cent), depending on the benefits of the particular tenancy.[11] The more favourable the terms, the higher the percentage will be. It is relevant to consider the following evidence of transactions contemporaneous with the transfer:

1.   "golden handshakes" paid by landlords to tenants in exchange for them surrendering their tenancies;

2.   from "sale and leaseback transactions," the amount by which the sale price is reduced on account of the tenant being granted a leaseback; and

3.   payments of compensation to tenants following compulsory purchases.

12.67   In another case, where it was unrealistic to expect that the parties would realise the vacant possession premium, the tenancy was valued on the basis of the profit to the tenant plus the compensation for tenant's improvements less delapidations.[11a] It would therefore appear that the question of whether a tenancy should be valued as a percentage of vacant possession value, or on the capitalised profits, depends on the particular tenancy arrangement. Each case must be considered on its own merits.

12.68   It would therefore appear that whether the tenancy should be valued as a percentage of the vacant possession value or on the capitalised profits, depends on the particular tenancy arrangement. Each case must be considered on its own merits.

12.68A   Agricultural tenancies The following provisions apply when the deceased had been the tenant of agricultural property in Scotland continuously for at least two years immediately preceding his death, or had inherited such a tenancy[12]:

1.   where the tenancy was for a fixed term which had not expired at the time of the tenant's death, the prospect of the lease being renewed by tacit relocation is to be ignored in valuing the deceased's estate[13]; and

2.   where at the time of the tenant's death, the lease was held by tacit relocation, and the lease is acquired by a new tenant, the value of the deceased tenant's interest

---

[11] For examples see "Summary of Meeting between the Representatives of the Law Societies of England and Wales and of Scotland, and the Inland Revenue" reproducd in Foster's *Inheritance Tax* at para. X6.50.
[11a] *Walton's Exrs.* v. *I.R.C.* (1994) 1 C.T.C. 584.
[12] IHTA 1984 (c. 51), s. 177(3).
[13] *Ibid.*, s. 177(1).

under the lease is to be ignored in valuing the deceased's estate.[14] The value attributable to tenant's improvements is, however, taxable,[15] and must be valued.

12.69 Where agricultural property is leased to a partnership, the provisions outlined in para. 12.68A do not apply, and the tenancy falls to be valued as an asset of the partnership, in which the deceased partner had a share.

Crofting Tenancies

12.70 It is submitted that the provisions discussed above with regard to the valuation of leased property are not appropriate in the particular circumstances of crofting tenure, and that the value to be placed on a croft should include the permanent improvements provided by the deceased, and any grassum which a third party might offer for the crofting tenancy.[16]

Farm properties

12.71 Where any cottage on the farm is occupied by persons employed solely for agricultural purposes in connection with the farm, the cottage is to be valued effectively as a tied cottage, "no account . . . (being) taken of any value attributable to the fact that the cottage . . . (is) suitable for the residential purposes of persons not so employed."[17]

12.72 The valuation rules relevant when the deceased held an agricultural tenancy are set out at paragraphs 12.66–12.69.

(B) Moveable property

Quoted shares and securities

12.73 The CTO will accept as the market value of any shares or securities listed in The Stock Exchange Daily Official List any price within the range for the day in question, though the normal practice is to adopt the capital gains tax valuation rules, that is to use the lesser of:

1. a quarter up from the lower to the higher limits of the stock market quotation for the day in question; and

2. the price midway between the lowest and highest recorded bargains of the day.[18]

12.74 Where no stock exchange quotation is available for the day in

---

[14] IHTA 1984 (c. 51), s. 177(2).
[15] *Ibid.*, s. 177(4).
[16] Donald J. MacCuish and Derek Flyn, *Crofting Law* (1990), para. 7.05.
[17] IHTA 1984 (c. 51), s. 169.
[18] TCGA 1992 (c. 12), s. 272 (3).

question, the price used is for the first available day either before or after the transfer.

12.75 Where the price of one of the deceased's shareholdings moved upwards dramatically on the date of death because of the release of a special piece of news after the death, it is possible to argue that the opening price is the market value of that shareholding.

Special markings

"*xd*" (or ex dividend) requires the net dividend (or interest) to be added to the price quoted.
"*ex-captn*" means that there has been a bonus issue, and the new shares should be included as part of the original holding and valued accordingly.
"*ex-rights*" means that there has been a rights issue, and the value of the rights should be included with the original shareholding.
"*1k*" (or market shorts plus interest) means that the gross accrued interest should be added to the bargain price.
"*ex interest*" means that the amount of the gross interest accrued from the date the last interest was paid to the date the bargain was done should be deducted from the bargain price.
"*1K xd*" (market shorts minus interest) means that the gross accrued interest from the date of death to the date of payment should be deducted, and the net amount of the interest added, to the bargain price.

Shares and securities dealt with on the Unlisted Securities Market
12.76 Shares and securities dealt with on the Unlisted Securities Market are treated as "quoted shares" for valuation purposes.[19] Details of the bargains done at or near the relevant date are but one of the relevant factors.[20]

Unquoted shares and securities
12.77 The principles of valuing unquoted shares and securities are complex, and outwith the scope of this work. If the share holding is taxable, specialist professional advice should be obtained.

12.78 The general valuation principles set out at paragraphs 12.41–12.55 apply: the value of shares in a private company is the best price obtainable on a hypothetical sale on the open market, but it is to be assumed that any prospective purchaser has available to him "all the information which a prudent prospective purchaser might reasonably require if he were proposing to purchase them from a willing vendor by private treaty and at arm's

[19] Finance Act 1987 (c. 16), s. 58, Sched. 8, para. 17.
[20] SP 18/80.

length."[21] The amount of the information which the prudent purchaser would require will depend on the size of the holding and the overall value of the proposed investment. Evidence of actual sales (or agreements to sell)—whether or not open market sales—and even of agreements as to the valuation of the shares for tax purposes may be taken into account.[22]

12.79 Factors which affect the value of a share-holding, include:

the size of the holding
the dividend record of the company
the profit cover for dividends paid
the earnings yield and price/earnings ratio
asset value[23] per share
comparison with quoted companies
any restrictions in the Articles of Association affecting the transfer of the shares[24]

12.80 The relative importance of these factors depends on the size of the holding to be valued. Thus asset value is very significant in the case of a holding of more than 75 per cent of the issued share capital, and dividend record when the holding is less than 25 per cent. Since preference shares are normally repayable at par, their value is unlikely to be in excess of par.

12.81 The related property rules (see paragraphs 12.47–12.48) can be of particular significance in valuing the deceased's interest in a private company.

Unit trusts
12.82 The Revenue will normally accept the manager's buying price (the lower price quoted) for the date in question, or the nearest date for which a price is available.

National Savings Certificates
12.83 A letter from the Director of Savings, Savings Certificates and SAYE office, Lytham St Annes, Lancashire FY0 1YN determines the value of National Savings Certificates.

Life policies
12.84 A life policy on the deceased's own life, which is payable to his or her executors, is valued at maturity value (including bonuses).[25]

---

[21] IHTA 1984 (c. 51), s. 168 as amended by Finance Act 1987 (c. 16), s. 72, Sched. 8, para. 12, Sched. 16, Pt. IX.
[22] *I.R.C.* v. *Stenhouse's Trs.* [1992] S.T.C. 103; 1993 S.L.T 248.
[23] After allowing for any tax liabilities incurred if the company were wound up.
[24] *I.R.C.* v. *Crossman* [1937] A.C. 26; *Lynall & Anor.* v. *I.R.C.* [1972] A.C. 680.
[25] IHTA 1984 (c. 51), s. 171(1) and (2).

12.85   Where a life policy was taken out on the life of a third party who was still alive at the time of the deceased's death, and the policy is payable to the deceased or his heirs or executors, the policy must be included in the inventory to the deceased's estate, the value shown being the policy's saleable value (not its surrender value), at the date of the deceased's death.

12.86   If the deceased transferred a policy (other than an ordinary term policy) during his life, the value at the time of the transfer is the greater of

(a)   the policy's open market value at the time of the transfer; and

(b)   the total of the premiums or other consideration already paid on the policy, less any sum already paid out under the policy. If the life policy is linked to units in a unit trust, the value based on the premiums or other consideration is reduced by any depreciation in the value of the underlying units after they have been allocated to the policy.[26]

Foreign property

12.87   Foreign property is normally valued in the local currency, which is then converted into sterling at the London buying rate.[26a] An exception to this rule is a shareholding in a company with a dual register: it is valued at the price quoted on the (London) Stock Exchange Official List, rather than the foreign quotation.

12.88   If, because of exchange control or other regulations, it is not possible for the executors to remit the foreign estate to this country, a discount on the value may be negotiated. Alternatively, if substantial assets are involved, the tax may be deferred.[27]

Valuation of debts owed to the deceased

12.89   Where the deceased is owed a debt, the debt is to be valued at its full face value, except to the extent that recovery has become impossible or is not reasonably practicable for reasons outside the deceased's control.[28]

---

[26] IHTA 1984 (c. 51), s. 167 as amended by Finance Act 1986 (c. 41), Sched. 23, Pt. X.

[26a] As shown in the *Financial Times* (in the case of major foreign currencies) or in the *"F.T.Guide to World Currencies"* published weekly in the *Financial Times* (in the case of less common currencies) (IHT 210, Feb., 1993, para. 35).

[27] ESC F. 6.

[28] IHTA 1984 (c. 51), s. 166.

COMPLETION OF PAGE 8–9 OF CAP FORM A-3

Section 1: Estate in the United Kingdom

12.90 The total United Kingdom estate as shown on pages 5 *et seq.* of the inventory is brought forward to Section 1 on page 8 of CAP Form A-3 and split between the headings of "Non-instalment option property" and "Instalment option property." The item number from the inventory and a brief description should identify the estate which makes up the instalment option property. Property qualifying for the instalment option on death transfers comprises:

(a) land;[29]

(b) shares or securities which gave the deceased control of the company[30];

(c) certain unquoted shares[31]; and

(d) a business or an interest in a business.[32]

Debts: general

12.91 The deceased's debts and reasonable funeral expenses[33–34] may generally be deducted[35] at their value at the date of death. If liability for a particular debt does not fall to be discharged until a future time, the value of this debt falls to be discounted to take account of the delay in payment and any contingency affecting the liability.[36]

12.92 The following anti-avoidance provisions should be borne in mind:

1. Debts which are not legally enforceable may not be deducted, even if a moral obligation exists: a liability to make future payments under a voluntary covenant is not deductible.[37]

2. Debts incurred or incumbrances created by the deceased

---

[29] IHTA 1984 (c. 51), s. 227 as amended.

[30] *Ibid.*, ss. 227–228 as amended.

[31] *Ibid.*

[32] *Ibid.*, s. 227 as amended.

[33–34] Including the costs of a gravestone (SP 7/87).

[35] IHTA 1984 (c. 51), s. 5(3).

[36] *Ibid.*, s. 162(2).

[37] *Ibid.*, s. 5(5).

are not deductible unless they were incurred "for a consideration in money or money's worth."[38]

3. Deduction of a debt or incumbrance may be subject to abatement if the value of any consideration given therefor consisted of (a) property derived from the deceased or (b) consideration given by any person who had at any time derived property from the deceased.[39]

4. No deduction shall be made for any debt in respect of which there is a right of reimbursement from any other estate or person (such as where the deceased had stood as guarantor), unless such reimbursement cannot be obtained.[40]

5. A liability which is an incumbrance on a particular property shall, so far as possible, be taken to reduce the value of that property.[41]

6. Where the debt is owed to a person resident outside the United Kingdom which neither (a) falls to be discharged in the United Kingdom nor (b) is an incumbrance on property in the United Kingdom, it is taken, so far as possible, to reduce the value of property outside the United Kingdom.[42]

12.93   It should be remembered that if it is clear that the deceased's estate is absolutely insolvent (*i.e.* the liabilities are greater than the assets[43]), an executor should not confirm to the estate, but must petition for the sequestration of the deceased's estate in terms of section 5(3)(*a*) of the Bankruptcy (Scotland) Act 1985 or for the appointment of a judicial factor.[44] If the executor continues to act for some time after it should have been clear to him that the estate was absolutely insolvent, he will be denied the protection of the confirmation in his favour, and will be treated as a vitious intromitter.[45]

Debts secured over deceased's property
12.94   Where a debt has been secured over the deceased's property (whether heritable or moveable), the normal practice — which is the approach preferred by the Capital Taxes Office — is that the amount of the loan outstanding at the date of the deceased's

---

[38] IHTA 1984 (c. 51), s. 5(5).
[39] Finance Act 1986 (c. 41), s. 103.
[40] IHTA 1984 (c. 51), s. 162(1).
[41] *Ibid.*, s. 162(4).
[42] *Ibid.*, s. 162(5).
[43] Bankruptcy (Scotland) Act 1985 (c. 66), s. 73(2).
[44] *Ibid.*, s. 8(4).
[45] *Ibid.*, s. 8(4); see further paras. 1.49–1.56.

death is deducted as a debt (at page 8 of the CAP Form A-3) and set against the value of the item over which it is secured.

12.94A   In certain circumstances (such as where it is desired to reduce the dues of confirmation or the amount of the bond of caution required[45a]), the alternative approach may be adopted, of deducting in the body of the inventory the amount of the debt from the value of the item over which it is secured.[46] If this approach is adopted, a note should be annexed to the list of debts on page 8 of the CAP Form A-3 to the following effect:

NOTE: A debt of £60,000 has been deducted from item 1 of the inventory.

The figure of £60,000 must not be carried into the effective total of debts listed on page 8.

12.95   The following are examples of property over which a debt is secured:

  1. an interest in land over which a standard security has been registered;

  2. a corporeal moveable pledged in security of a debt;

  3. an incorporeal moveable assigned[47] in security of a debt;

  4. a registered ship mortgaged in security of a debt, where the mortgage has been registered by the registrar of the ship's port registry[48];

  5. a registered fishing vessel (or a share therein) mortgaged in security of a debt, where the mortgage has been registered by the Secretary of State[49]; and

  6. an aircraft and its spare parts,[50] mortgaged in security of a debt, where the mortgage has been entered in the Register of Aircraft Mortgages kept by the Civil Aviation Authority.

[45a] See paras. 9.11–9.14.

[46] IHTA 1984 (c. 51), s. 162(4). See example at para. 10.104 *et seq.*

[47] An assignation will be binding on the deceased's executors, even if it has not been intimated—see *Brownlee* v. *Robb*, 1907 S.C. 1302; *Strawbridge's Trs.* v. *Bank of Scotland*, 1935 S.L.T. 568.

[48] Merchant Shipping Act 1894 (57 & 58 Vict. c. 60), s. 31 as substituted by Merchant Shipping Act 1988 (c. 12), s. 10, Sched. 1, para. 21.

[49] Merchant Shipping Act 1988 (c. 12), s. 21, Sched. 3 and S.I. 1988 No. 1926, esp. paras. 39–47.

[50] S.I. 1972 No. 1268, arts. 3, 4.

Section 2: Estate outside the United Kingdom

12.96   The total estate outside the United Kingdom as listed below the summary for confirmation is brought forward to Section 2 on page 8 of the CAP Form A-3, and split between the headings of "Non-instalment option property" and "Instalment option property" (see para. 12.90 above).

12.97   Where a debt is due to a person resident outside the United Kingdom which neither falls to be discharged in the United Kingdom nor is secured over property in the United Kingdom, the debt is to be deducted so far as possible from the value of the deceased's foreign property.[51]

12.98   A deduction may also be claimed for the additional expenses[51a] incurred in administering or realising the overseas estate, up to a limit of five per cent of the property's gross value.[52]

Section 3: Property on which tax is payable not included in Sections 1 and 2 (page 9 CAP Form A-3)

12.99   The details of the settled property, gifts with reservation, lifetime chargeable transfers, and other relevant property (including property passing under a special destination which has not been evacuated by the deceased) should be brought forward to page 9 from page 3 of the account. Such property must be split between "Non-instalment option property" and "Instalment option property." Any reliefs or exemptions should be deducted from page 10.

The declaration

12.100   Since the CAP Form A-3 doubles as the Inland Revenue Account, the executor must declare at the foot of page 9 that "to the best of his knowledge and belief pages 5 to 9 of the account specify all appropriate property and its value."[53] Where the value of property included in the account has been estimated, the declaration should be amended to read:

> "after making the fullest enquiries that are reasonably practicable in the circumstances, the executor is unable to ascertain the exact value of this item of estate. The executor

---

[51] IHTA 1984 (c. 51), s. 162(5).

[51a] That is, those over and above the expenses which would have been incurred had the property been situated in the U.K.

[52] IHTA 1984 (c.51), s. 173.

[53] *Ibid.*, s. 216(1).

undertakes to deliver a further account of this item as soon as its value is ascertained."[54]

12.100A Beside the declaration is a warning in the following terms:

"You may be liable to penalties or prosecution if you fail to make full enquiries and include all property on which Inheritance Tax is payable".

12.100B The purpose of this warning is to remind each deponent of the provisions of section 247 of the Inheritance Tax Act 1984 which narrates:

"(1) If any person liable for any tax on the value transferred by a chargeable transfer fraudulently or negligently delivers, furnishes or produces to the Board any incorrect account, information or document, he shall be liable, in the case of fraud, to a penalty not exceeding the aggregate of £50 and twice the difference mentioned in subsection (2) below and, in the case of negligence, to a penalty not exceeding the aggregate of £50 and that difference.

(2) The difference referred to in subsection (1) above is the amount by which the tax for which that person is liable exceeds what would be the amount of that tax if the facts were as shown in the account, information or document.

(3) Any person not liable for tax on the value transferred by a chargeable transfer who fraudulently or negligently furnishes or produces to the Board any incorrect information or document in connection with the transfer shall be liable, in the case of fraud, to a penalty not exceeding £500, and in the case of negligence, to a penalty not exceeding £250.

(4) Any person who assists in or induces the delivery, furnishing or production in pursuance of this Part of this Act of any account, information or document which he knows to be incorrect shall be liable to a penalty not exceeding £500."

The Board's current practice is to consider charging penalties in all such cases.

---

[54] IHTA 1984 (c. 51), s. 216(3).

COMPLETION OF PAGES 10 TO 12 OF CAP FORM A3

Section A: Summary of chargeable transfers

12.101   After bringing forward the totals of Sections 1, 2 and 3 from pages 8 and 9, any reliefs and exemptions appropriate to the property included in Sections 1, 2 and 3 are deducted. These may include:

    (a)   spouse exemption[55] which applies where in terms of a nomination, a destination, a provision in the deceased's will or in a "deed of family arrangement," or in satisfaction of prior or legal rights or the intestate succession rules, estate passes to the deceased's surviving spouse;

    (b)   charitable exemption[56];

    (c)   political parties exemption[57];

    (d)   bequest for national purposes (*e.g.* to a national museum, National Trust, local authority, university, etc.)[58];

    (e)   bequest for public benefit (*e.g.* land or buildings of scenic, historic, or scientific interst)[59];

    (f)   bequest to a housing association[60];

    (g)   business relief[61];

    (h)   agricultural relief[62];

    (i)   woodlands relief.[63]

Section B: Calculation of tax due on the death estate

12.102   Inheritance Tax is calculated on the net total of chargeable trans-

---

[55] IHTA 1984 (c. 51), s. 18.
[56] *Ibid.*, s. 23 as amended by Finance Act 1989 (c. 26), s. 171.
[57] *Ibid.*, s. 24 as amended by Finance Act 1988 (c. 39), s. 137.
[58] *Ibid.*, s. 25 and Sched. 3.
[59] *Ibid.*, ss. 26 and 26A (inserted by Finance Act 1986 (c.41), s. 101(3) and Sched. 19, para. 6).
[60] *Ibid.*, s. 24A (inserted by Finance Act 1989 (c. 26), s. 171(1)).
[61] *Ibid.*, ss. 103–114, as amended, especially ss. 113A and 113B (inserted by Finance Act 1986 (c. 41), s. 101(3), Sched. 19, para. 21 and Finance Act 1992 (c.48), Sched. 14, para. 1).
[62] *Ibid.*, ss. 115–124B as amended, especially ss. 124A and 124B (inserted by Finance Act 1986 (c. 41), Sched. 19, para. 22 and Finance Act 1992 (c. 48), Sched. 14, para. 4).
[63] *Ibid.*, ss. 125–130.

fers brought out in Section A, at the rates of tax applicable at the date of death.

12.103   Where part of the death estate is exempt, the completion of Sections A and B may not be straightforward.[64] There is generally no difficulty where a specific bequest is exempt (the value of the bequest would form a deduction in the exemptions and reliefs box), or if the whole of the residue is exempt and all the non-exempt legacies bear their own tax (in Section A, the value of the residue would be deducted in the exemptions and reliefs box, bringing forward as the "net total of chargeable transfers" the value of all non-exempt legacies). The following notes may be of general guidance for the more complex cases:

(a)   *Specific legacy does not bear its own tax and the whole residue is exempt*
Here the legacy requires to be grossed-up,[65] and that figure which is the grossed-up equivalent of the tax-free legacy is then deducted from the total of A1 and A2 to give the net amount of the exempt residue: the resulting figure is then deducted in the exemptions and reliefs box.

(b)   *Exempt legacies and part only of residue is taxable*
The residue is found by deducting the amount of the exempt legacies, and is then divided between the residuary beneficiaries. In Section A, the value of the exempt legacies and the exempt share(s) of residue are deducted in the exemptions and reliefs box.

(c)   *Specific legacy does not bear its own tax, another specific legacy bears its own tax, and/or part of residue is exempt*
Here it is necessary to effect double grossing-up of the legacies which do not bear their own tax,[66] the calculation of the "net tax due on death estate" (end of Section B) being on a separate schedule. Accordingly, in the inventory, Section A from the "gross total of chargeable transfers" and the whole of Section B will not be completed.

(d)   *A legal rights claim where only part of the estate is taxable*
Provided that the deceased's moveable estate was realised in ordinary course and without undue delay, the amount of a claim to the legal rights of *jus relicti, jus relictae* or legitim is the appropriate fraction (one-third or one-half) of the deceased's net moveable estate, quantified at the date of his death.[67] Further, the amount of inheritance tax

---

[64] IHTA 1984 (c. 51), Pt. II, Chap. III.
[65] *Ibid.*, s. 38(3).
[66] *Ibid.*, s. 38(4) and (5).
[67] *Alexander* v. *Alexander's Trs.*, 1954 S.L.T. 342.

due on the estate is ignored in computing the amount of
the legal rights claim, but once the amount of the claim
has been computed, the inheritance tax on the executry
estate is calculated on the basis that the legal rights claim
is treated as a legacy which bears its own tax.[68] Where
the amount of the legal rights claim is relevant to the
inheritance tax due on the death,[69] a separate schedule
computing the legal rights claim is normally attached to
the inventory.

(e) *Partly exempt estate with property qualifying for business or
agricultural relief*[70]
Specific gifts of agricultural or business property are to be
taxed at their value net of agricultural or business relief.
Other specific gifts have attributed to them only a share
of the agricultural or business relief:

$$\text{value of gift} \quad \times \quad \frac{\text{value of estate after relief} - \text{value of specific gift after relief}}{\text{value of estate before relief} - \text{value of specific gift before relief.}}$$

Section B: Deduction of tax on lifetime transfers including failed PETs

12.104   If the deceased had made lifetime chargeable transfers or failed
PETs, there falls to be deducted the notional amount of inheritance tax which would be paid on them, calculated at the rates
of tax applicable at the date of death.

Section B: Quick succession relief and double taxation relief

12.105   Where appropriate, there then falls to be deducted:

1. Quick succession relief[71]

12.106   Where within five years of his death, the deceased's estate had
been increased by a chargeable transfer on which inheritance
tax had been paid, the inheritance tax payable on his death
estate may be reduced by a percentage of the tax paid on the
earlier transfer, the percentage being
100% if the two transfers   40% if the two transfers

---

[68] IHTA 1984 (c. 51), s. 42(4).
[69] *e.g.* where the deceased's widow claims legal rights and the rest of the estate
is taxable, or the deceased's children claim legal rights and (part of) the rest of
the estate passes to the widow.
[70] IHTA 1984 (c. 51), s. 39A (inserted by Finance Act 1986 (c. 41), s. 105).
[71] *Ibid.*, s. 141.

were less than a year apart 80% if the two transfers were between one and two years apart 60% if the two transfers were between two and three years apart	were between three and four years apart 20% if the two transfers were between four and five years apart

2. Double taxation relief (i.e. relief from liability to United Kingdom inheritance tax and a similar foreign duty)

12.107   If the deceased's estate is liable to United Kingdom inheritance tax and to a death or similar duty in another state, then relief from double taxation will be given by means either of:

1.   a Double Taxation Convention[72]—where the terms of the particular convention are applied; or

2.   where no Double Taxation Convention applies, or if greater tax relief will be afforded, unilateral relief—by setting the foreign tax paid on a particular asset against the United Kingdom inheritance tax liability on it.[73]

12.108   In such cases, the tax paid overseas is converted into sterling using the London selling rate in force at the date the foreign tax was paid.[73a]

Section C: Death Estate on which tax is to be paid on this form

12.109   It is necessary to pay on the CAP Form A-3:

1.   the inheritance tax due on the non-instalment option property of which the deceased was competent to dispose (the "free estate"); and

2.   the instalments already due on the instalment option property of which the deceased was competent to dispose.

12.110   It may not be convenient to pay inheritance tax on the other items on which inheritance tax is payable in consequence of the death, and the value of such items may be deducted at Section C.

[72] IHTA 1984 (c. 51), s. 158 as amended by Finance Act 1987 (c. 16), s. 70(2) (at the time of writing, the only double taxation agreements on IHT are with France, Ireland, India, Italy, the Netherlands, Pakistan, South Africa, Sweden, Switzerland, USA).

[73] *Ibid.*, s. 159.

[73a] Dymond, *Capital Taxes*, para. 51.

Section D: Payment by instalments

12.111   Inheritance tax can be paid in 10 equal annual instalments (the first falling due at the end of the month six months after the death) on certain property. The property qualifying for the instalment option comprises:

(a) land[74];

(b) shares or securities which gave the deceased control of the company[75];

(c) certain unquoted shares[76]; and

(d) a business or an interest in a business.[77]

12.112   Where it has been decided that inheritance tax should be paid by instalments on part or the whole of the instalment option property included in the estate, the property in respect of which the option is made should be indicated.

Section E: Assessment

12.113   The executors or their agents should complete pages 10–12 of the inventory CAP Form A-3, showing the inheritance tax provisionally self-assessed. Before the executors can apply for confirmation, they must pay to the Inland Revenue Cashier the inheritance tax so calculated. Where the instalment option has been claimed, this will comprise the tax due on the deceased's ordinary moveable estate, and the appropriate instalment(s) of tax due on the deceased's instalment option property. When the tax is being paid more than six months after the end of the month in which the death occurred, interest will also be due,[78–79] calculated at the rates applicable from time to time.

The role of the sheriff clerks in the tax collection process

12.114   It has been seen that once confirmation has been granted, the sheriff clerk must transmit most inventories to the CTO. Even before confirmation is granted, the clerk will carry out certain checks which have more to do with ensuring that inheritance tax is paid timeously, than with ensuring that the commissary technicalities are complied with.

---

[74] IHTA 1984 (c.51), s. 227 as amended.
[75] *Ibid.*, ss. 227–228 as amended.
[76] *Ibid.*
[77] *Ibid.*, s. 227 as amended.
[78–79] *Ibid.*, s. 226(1) amended.

12.115   Presently, sheriff clerks are instructed not to grant confirmation on an inventory unless either:

1. the inventory is receipted by the Capital Taxes Office, showing that all inheritance tax provisionally assessed has been paid, or that, provisionally, no tax is payable[80]; or

2. where the deceased was domiciled in the United Kingdom on his death, page 10 of the CAP Form A-3 has been completed, and the estate is less than the taxable threshold ruling at the date of the deceased's death, or is so after deduction of the inheritance tax exemptions and reliefs on page 10; or

3. where the deceased was not domiciled in the United Kingdom on his death, the gross estate in the United Kingdom does not exceed £5,000.

12.116   Confirmation will also not be granted if the inventory is not completed on the official accounts (CAP Form A-3, CAP Form B-3 or CAP Form B-4) or on an approved substitute form.

12.117   Where an inventory does not meet such criteria, confirmation will not be granted, and the inventory will be returned to the agent.

Excepted estates

12.118   The financial limits for "excepted estates" are periodically updated by statutory instrument. At the time of writing, "excepted estates" are those which meet all the following conditions:

1. the deceased died domiciled in the United Kingdom on or after April 6, 1995;[81]

2. the deceased had not made any lifetime gifts chargeable to inheritance tax or capital transfer tax[82] nor had he been entitled to an interest in possession in trust property;

---

[80] Probate and Legacy Duties Act 1808 (4 Geo. 3, c. 149), s. 42, as amended by Statute Law Revision Act 1888 and Finance Act 1975 (c. 7), s. 19(2) and Sched. 4, para. 38(2).

[81] Customs, Inland Revenue and Savings Banks Act 1877 (40 & 41 Vict. c. 13), s. 12, as amended by Statute Law Revision Act 1894 (55 & 56 Vict. c. 56), Finance Act 1980 (c. 48), s. 94(7) and Law Reform (Miscellaneous Provisions) (Scotland) Act 1980 (c. 55), s. 9.

[82] That is, excluding exempt gifts such as those within the annual exemption limit or the spouse or charitable exemption.

3. the gross value of the estate for tax purposes (*i.e.* the "Total for Confirmation" plus the total of any "Estate Abroad") does not exceed £145,000;

4. the estate comprises only property passing under the deceased's will,[83] or under the rules of intestate succession, or by nomination or by a survivorship destination[84]; and

5. not more than £15,000 consists of property situated outside the United Kingdom.[85]

12.119 When the estate is an "excepted estate," the CAP Form B-4 may be used—unless the value of the estate is such that the small estates procedure is applicable.[86]

12.120 If the executors subsequently discover that the estate should not have been classified as an excepted estate, then, within six months of the discovery, they must deliver to the CTO an account of all the property comprised in the estate: a Form D-1 should accordingly be completed.

12.121 If the CTO do not examine the inventory and raise observations within the prescribed period of 60 days from the issue of confirmation, then the executors are automatically discharged from any claim for inheritance tax in respect of the deceased's estate.

Financing the payment of inheritance tax

12.122 Where tax is due, the executors will normally require to obtain a bank loan, since they have no title to uplift the executry

---

[83] For the purposes of these rules, this includes a testate estate subject to a claim for legal rights.

[84] In applying the £145,000 limit to property passing under a survivorship destination, only the value of the deceased's interest in the property has to be taken into account.

[85] S.I. 1995 No. 1459. The previous limits are as follows:

Date of death	Gross estate limit	Foreign estate limit
1.4.91–5.4.95	£125,000	£15,000 (S.I. 1991 No. 1249)
1.4.90–30.3.91	£115,000	£15,000 (S.I. 1990 No. 1111)
1.4.89–30.3.90	£100,000	£15,000 (S.I. 1989 No. 1079)
1.4.87–30.3.89	£70,000	£10,000 (S.I. 1987 No. 1128)
1.4.83–30.3.87	£40,000	Higher of £2,000 or 10% of gross value (S.I. 1983 No. 1040)
1.4.81–30.3.83	£25,000	Higher of £1,000 or 10% of gross value (S.I. 1981 No. 881)

[86] See Chap. 11.

funds until they obtain confirmation.[87] Unless the testamentary writing expressly prohibits borrowing, the executors have power to borrow money on the security of the estate.[88]

12.123 If, prior to confirmation being granted, a bank loan is taken out to pay inheritance tax on moveable property,[89] the executors can obtain income tax relief on any interest which they pay within one year of obtaining the loan.[90] If the loan is used for other purposes (such as meeting the expenses of the funeral, or the costs of applying for confirmation), the interest should be apportioned between that incurred for the qualifying purpose (paying inheritance tax) and that incurred for the other non-qualifying purposes.

12.124 Inheritance tax may be paid by a Certificate of Tax Deposit or by encashment of the deceased's National Savings Investments.[90a]

12.125 The Registrar of the CTO is now permitted to destroy any inventory.[91]

---

[87] Succession (Scotland) Act 1964 (c. 41), s. 14; Administration of Estates Act 1971 (c. 25), s. 6(2).

[88] Trusts (Scotland) Act 1921 (c. 58), ss. 2 and 4(1)(*d*).

[89] It is possible to elect to pay inheritance tax on heritable property over 10 years by equal annual instalments (IHTA 1984 (c. 51), s. 227(1) and (2)). Consequently, if confirmation is applied for before the "Due date" (*i.e.* six months after the end of the month in which the deceased died—IHTA 1984 (c. 51), s. 226(1)), no inheritance tax need be paid on the heritage, provided that the instalment option has been claimed. It is for this reason that income tax relief is restricted to interest on loans to pay IHT on moveable property.

[90] ICTA 1988 (c. 1), s. 364.

[90a] See Form IHT 11S.

[91] Law Reform (Miscellaneous Provisions) (Scotland) Act 1980 (c. 55), s. 9 amending Customs, Inland Revenue and Savings Banks Act 1877 (40 & 41 Vict. c. 13), s. 12.

CHAPTER 13

PAYMENTS WITHOUT EXHIBITING CONFIRMATION

Introduction

13.01   In order to ingather the estate and transfer it to the deceased's heirs, the executors do not need to obtain confirmation provided that all the assets in the deceased's estate are either

1. of such value that the particular investment body will pay out without requiring to have confirmation exhibited to them (see paras. 13.05–13.09);

2. the subject of a nomination which the deceased had not revoked (see paras. 13.10–13.18);

3. the subject of a special destination which the deceased had not revoked (see paras. 13.19–13.26); or

4. the proceeds of a life assurance policy taken out by a person who dies domiciled outside the United Kingdom (see para. 13.27).

13.02   In such cases, the executor is still under a duty to lodge an account with (a) the sheriff court and (b) the Capital Taxes Office and, as he will intromit with the deceased's estate without being confirmed, may be found to be a vitious intromitter.

Inheritance tax where estate is realised without confirmation

13.03   In such cases, although the estate is realised without obtaining confirmation, the executors must still consider whether they require to deliver an account to the Inland Revenue for inheritance tax purposes.[1] The Capital Taxes Office *may* be prepared to give an assurance that no liability to inheritance tax arises—where the applicant has completed the Form 20 (which may be obtained on application from the Capital Taxes Office at 16 Picardy Place, Edinburgh), there are no suspicious or unsatisfactory circumstances and the estate is less than £25,000. However, the Capital Taxes Office cannot dispense with the

---

[1] See para. 12.03.

statutory requirement that the executors lodge an account with the sheriff court.

13.04   Where inheritance tax is due in consequence of a death, the Capital Taxes Office may recover the tax either from the executors or from the persons to whom the deceased's property has passed.[2]

PAYMENT WITHOUT CONFIRMATION PERMITTED BY STATUTE

13.05   A number of investment bodies are enabled by statute to pay out a deceased person's investment without confirmation being exhibited. A financial limit is set on the amount of any one investment which can be uplifted in this way. The limit is updated by statutory instrument[3] and, at the time of writing, is £5,000.[4]

13.06   The rules applying to the different kinds of investment vary, both as to the circumstances in which payment can be made without confirmation being exhibited, and as to the potential payees. However, there is one feature common to all the provisions—the controller of the funds is given a discretion as to whether payment should be made without confirmation being produced, and he cannot be compelled by court action to exercise that discretion.[5]

13.07   A number of the rules provide for payment to be made to "those entitled by law to receive" the payment. Payments must then be made to all the heirs of the deceased, and the controller of the funds cannot pick and choose among those known to be the legal successors of the deceased.[6]

13.08   Set out below are the main investments which can be paid out without confirmation being exhibited. The current enabling legislation is shown in the footnotes.

Building society funds, where the member or depositor was

---

[2] Inheritance Tax Act 1984 (c.51), s. 200(1) (*a*) and (*c*) and s. 199(4).

[3] As provided generally by Administration of Estates (Small Payments) Act 1965 (c.32), s. 6(1); and for the various National Savings products, by updating the regulations.

[4] Generally, see Administration of Estates (Small Payments) (Increase of Limit) Order 1984 (S.I. 1984 No. 539), applying to deaths after May 11, 1984; for savings certificates, S.I. 1991 No. 1031, reg. 15; National Savings Bank accounts, S.I. 1984 No. 602; Premium Savings Bonds, S.I. 1984 No. 601; Stock on the National Savings Register, S.I. 1984 No. 600; and savings contracts, S.I. 1984 No. 599.

[5] *Escritt* v. *Todmorden Co-operative Society* [1896] 1 Q.B. 461.

[6] *Per* Lord President Robertson in *Symington's Exr.* v. *Galashiels Co-operative Store Co. Ltd.* (1894) 21 R. 371 at p. 376.

domiciled in the United Kingdom; payment only to the heir
(whether under a will or on intestacy)[7]

Friendly society policies[8]

Government stock[9]

Industrial and provident society (which includes property in a
housing association)[10]

National Savings Bank accounts[11]

National Savings Certificates[12]

Stock held on National Savings Stock Register[13]

Pensions, etc., for local government employees, teachers, health
service workers, police and firemen[14]

Premium Savings Bonds[15]

Salary and superannuation benefits due to civil servants, and
employees of public bodies[16]

Salary due to local government officers[17]

Salary due to Members of Parliament, Ministers and other office
holders[18]

Savings contracts[19]

Social security payments due to the deceased—for which there
is no statutory maximum, although in practice the payments will be considerably less than £5,000[20]

TSB accounts[21]

Wages, etc., due to personnel in the armed forces[22]

---

[7] Building Societies Act 1986 (c.53), s. 32 and Sched. 7, para. 1.

[8] Friendly Societies Act 1992 (c.40), s. 18 & Sched. 9, para. 3.

[9] National Debt Act 1972 (c.65), s. 6(1); S.I. 1965 No. 1420, reg. 6(3), inserted
by S.I. 1990 No. 2253, applicable where the total value of the deceased's holdings
of all stocks is less than the financial limit.

[10] Industrial and Provident Societies Act 1965 (c.12), s. 25, as amended by
Family Law Reform Act 1969 (c.46), s. 19.

[11] National Savings Bank Act 1971 (c.29), ss. 2 and 9(1); S.I. 1972 No. 764, reg.
40 and S.I. 1991 No. 72.

[12] National Debt Act 1972 (c.65), s. 11; generally, S.I. 1991 No. 1031, regs. 15
and 33; if acquired under a yearly plan, S.I. 1984 No. 779, reg. 15; and if children's bonus bonds, S.I. 1991 No. 1407, regs. 13 and 29.

[13] National Debt Act 1972 (c.65), s. 3; S.I. 1976 No. 2012, reg. 41.

[14] Various regulations under Superannuation Act 1972 (c.11), ss. 7, 9, 10 and
24 (amended by Police Pension Act 1976 (c.35), s. 13(1) and Sched. 2, para. 10)
and Sched. 3, para. 8.

[15] National Debt Act 1972 (c.65), s. 11; S.I. 1972 No. 765, reg. 13.

[16] Superannuation Act 1972 (c.11), ss. 1 and 4(1).

[17] Local Government Act 1972 (c.70), s. 119.

[18] Parliamentary and Other Pensions Act 1987 (c.45), s. 2 and Sched. 1, para.
8 enables the passing of regulations, including power to pay out without confirmation.

[19] National Debt Act 1972 (c.65), s. 11; S.I. 1969 No. 1342, reg. 10.

[20] Social Security Administration Act 1992 (c.5), s. 5(1) (*g*) and (*q*).

[21] Trustee Savings Banks Act 1981 (c.65), ss. 27(1) and 28; Trustee Savings
Banks Act 1985 (c.58), s. 4(3) and (5), and S.I. 1986 No. 1223, para. 9.

[22] Navy and Marines (Property of Deceased) Act 1865 (28 & 29 Vict. c.111),
ss. 5–8 (sale of effects, wages, etc., due to naval officer, seaman or marine);
Pensions and Yeomanry Pay Act 1884 (47 & 48 Vict. c.55), s. 4 (pensions paid

Non-statutory payments without confirmation

13.09   A number of other institutions will pay out estate without requiring sight of confirmation or a grant of probate or letters of administration from England and Wales, or Northern Ireland. For instance, a number of registrars of public limited companies will dispense with the need for confirmation, etc., where the total estate is less than a given figure, often £5,000.[23]

NOMINATIONS

13.10   Under statute, the holder of certain investments is able to nominate an individual or individuals to inherit the particular investments on the holder's death. Thus, a nomination is a document of a testamentary nature,[24] which has the character of a special destination contained in a share certificate.[25] When the nominator dies, the nominee is entitled to the payment without confirmation being exhibited.

Standard formalities for nominations

13.11   Although a nomination is testamentary in character,[26] the Scots law rules regarding the execution of testamentary writings do not apply. To be validly constituted, the nomination must meet the rules prescribed for the particular investment. The normal rules are as follows:

1.   The nominator must have attained 16 years of age when he signs the nomination.

to officers, soldiers, etc., and their surviving spouse or relative)—extended to Air Force personnel by S.R.& O. 1918 No. 548; Regimental Debts Act 1893 (56 & 57 Vict. c.5), s. 7, 8 and 16 (as amended) (arrears of pay due to officer or soldier)—extended to Air Force personnel by S.R.& O. 1918 No.548.

[23] *e.g.* Abbey National plc, British Gas plc, Scottish Hydro-Electric plc, Scottish Power plc (all where holding is valued up to £5,000); British Telecom plc (where U.K. estate is up to £5,000); British Petroleum plc (where holding is valued up to £5,000, unless passing to deceased's spouse, when limit is £10,000).

[24] *Gill* v. *Gill*, 1938 S.C. 65. See also Collins L.J. in *Bennett* v. *Slater* [1899] 1 Q.B. 45 at p. 53; *per* Farwell J. *Re Barnes, Ashenden and Heath* [1940] Ch. 267 at p. 273 and Megarry J. *Re Danish Bacon Staff Pension Fund Christensen & Others* v. *Arnett & Others* [1971] 1 All E.R. 486 at pp. 493–494. *Cf.* Phillimore J. in *Caddick* v. *Highton and Others* (1901) 68 L.J.Q.B. 281 at p. 282.

[25] *Per* Lord President Normand in *Ford's Trustees* v. *Ford*, 1940 S.C. 426 at p. 431, a view not supported by Lord Carmont in *Clark's Exrs.* v. *Macaulay and Others*, 1961 S.L.T. 109 at p. 113 (see also Lord Guthrie at p. 114). On special destination to share certificates, see further para. 13.26.

[26] *Per* Lord Justice-Clerk Macdonald in *Morton* v. *French*, 1908 S.C. 171 at p. 173; *Gill* v. *Gill*, 1938 S.C. 65.

2. The nominator must sign the nomination in the presence of one witness, who attests the nominator's subscription.

3. A nominee cannot act as witness.

4. The nomination must be sent to the administrator of the particular investment during the nominator's life.

13.12 A nomination authenticated by the nominator's mark, and by the signature of two witnesses did not meet regulations which permitted a nomination "by writing under [the member's] hand."[27]

Revocation of the nomination

13.13 The nomination will receive effect on the nominator's death, unless it has earlier been revoked in the way authorised by the enabling statute. The normal prescribed methods of revoking a nomination are as follows:

1. The marriage of the nominator.

2. A subsequent nomination of the same asset.

3. A written notice of revocation, signed by the nominator in the presence of one attesting witness, which is duly intimated to the administrator of the particular investment during the nominator's life.

13.14 In the case of National Savings products, it is specifically provided that the death of the nominee will also revoke the nomination.[28] In an English case,[29] where there was no specific regulation covering the point, it was held on general principles that the death of the nominee revoked the nomination.

13.15 In the case of most investments which can be nominated, it is now expressly provided that a nomination will not be revoked by a subsequently executed testamentary writing or codicil[30] and

---

[27] *Morton* v. *French*, 1908 S.C. 171.

[28] National Savings Bank accounts (S.I. 1972 No. 764, reg. 35(1)); savings certificates (S.I. 1991 No. 1031, reg. 37, Sched. 2, para. 4); stock on National Savings Stock Register (S.I. 1976 No. 2012, reg. 36(1)).

[29] *Re Barnes, Ashenden* v. *Heath* [1940] Ch. 267 (*Caddick* v. *Highton and Others* (1901) 68 L.J.Q.B. 281 not followed).

[30] Expressly for National Savings Bank deposit accounts (S.I. 1972 No. 764, reg. 35(1)) and funds with an industrial and provident society (Industrial and Provident Societies Act 1965 (c.12), s. 23(4)); and by implication for National Savings certificates (S.I. 1991 No. 1031, reg. 37, Sched. 2, para. 4(1)) and stock on the National Savings Stock Register (S.I. 1976 No. 2012, reg. 36(1)(*a*)).

this approach is also revealed in case reports.[31] At variance with this approach is the *obiter dictum* in the Inner House decision of *Clark's Executors* v. *Macaulay and Others*,[32] where the court indicated that, in respect that a nomination is a special destination, it would be revoked in circumstances where a special destination would be revoked—*e.g.* by a subsequent testamentary writing which revokes the destination either expressly or by necessary implication. It was suggested that where the testamentary writing contained a clause disposing of the entire means and estate over which the testator "might have power of disposal by will or otherwise" and a clause expressly revoking all former testamentary writings executed by her, the nomination would be revoked.[33]

Financial limit for nominations

13.16 A financial limit is set on the value of an investment which can be nominated and this limit is updated by statutory instrument.[34] The limit applies on the basis of when the nomination was delivered to the administrator. Thus, a nomination delivered between August 6, 1965 and August 10, 1975 is an effective nomination of £500[35]; if between August 11, 1975 and May 11, 1984, of £1,500[36]; and if on or after May 12, 1984, of £5,000.[37] Where the value of the investment at the time of the nominator's death exceeds the prescribed financial limit, the nominee receives only the value of the investment up to the limit, and the excess is administered under the general law.[38]

Investments which can be nominated

13.17 The investment bodies whose investments can be nominated are as follows:

---

[31] *Bennett* v. *Slater* [1899] 1 Q.B. 45; (1899) 68 L.J.O.B. 45; *Ford's Trs.* v. *Ford*, 1940 S.C. 426.

[32] 1961 S.L.T. 109.

[33] See, for instance, Lord Guthrie at p. 114, who reserved his opinion on the question.

[34] Administration of Estates (Small Payments) Act 1965 (c.32), ss. 2 and 6 and Sched. 2.

[35] *Ibid,*, s. 2 and Sched. 2.

[36] S.I. 1975 No. 1137, though this provision would appear to have been revoked by S.I. 1984 No. 539, s. 4.

[37] S.I. 1984 No. 539.

[38] *Bennett* v. *Slater* [1899] 1 Q.B. 45; *cf. Re Baxter* [1903] P. 12, where the Act permitting the nomination was worded more strictly.

Friendly societies	A member can, by a writing under his hand,[39] nominate any sum payable on his death by any friendly society (excluding a benevolent society, a working men's club or an old people's home); an officer or member of the society cannot be the nominee, unless he is the spouse, parent, child, sibling, nephew or niece of the nominator.[40]
Industrial and provident societies (shares, loans, deposits, etc.)	The nomination must be by a written statement signed by the nominator; an officer or servant of the society cannot be the nominee, unless he is the spouse, parent, child, sibling, nephew or niece of the nominator.[41]
National Savings accounts, Savings Certificates, and Stock on Register	Since May 1, 1981, it has not been competent to make a nomination, but one made earlier will remain operative until revoked.[42] In addition to the normal methods of revoking a nomination (see paras. 13.13–13.15), the death of the nominee will revoke the nomination.
TSB accounts	Since May 1, 1979, it has not been possible to make a nomination.[43] Nominations under the previous regulations will continue to be recognised by the TSB plc.[44]

[39] Which excludes authentication by the member's mark (*Morton* v. *French*, 1908 S.C. 171).

[40] Friendly Societies Act 1992 (c.40), s. 18 and Sched. 9, paras. 1 & 2.

[41] Industrial and Provident Societies Act 1965 (c.12), s. 23.

[42] For National Savings Bank accounts, S.I. 1972 No. 764, regs. 33–38, as amended by S.I. 1981 No. 484; for National Savings certificates, S.I. 1991 No. 1031, reg. 37 and Sched. 2 (or if acquired under a yearly plan, S.I. 1984 No. 779, reg. 13); and for stock on National Savings Stock Register, S.I. 1976 No. 2012, regs. 32–39, as amended by S.I. 1981 No. 485.

[43] S.I. 1979 No. 259, s. 2(*d*) and (*e*).

[44] S.I. 1986 No. 1223, s. 7.

13.18 It should be noted that it is perfectly possible for the regulations of other investment bodies to provide for investors making nominations, in which case the particular rules of the scheme (rather than the detailed rules outlined above) will apply. Thus, in *Young* v. *Waterson*,[45] the rules of an unregistered mutual assurance association enabled members to make nominations but, on an analysis of the rules, the court held that the nominee had title to collect the money, but had to account to the deceased's executors for the benefits he received. Thus, this particular nomination did not operate as a testamentary provision.

"JOINTLY" HELD PROPERTY

13.19 Individuals frequently refer to themselves colloquially as being the "joint owners" of an item of property. The ownership of such property following the death of one of the holders is a complex issue, depending in part on the nature of the property held, in part on where the property is situated, and in part on how the property was acquired. The principles are set out at 13.20–13.26.

Heritage in Scotland—ownership in common

13.20 Heritage held by two or more persons in common is frequently subject to a contractual destination, as where the disposition narrates that "the price was paid by A and B in equal shares" and the property is disponed "to and in favour of the said A and B and the survivor of them and to their respective assignees and disponees and to the executors of the survivor whomsoever". From the registration of the deed in the Sasine or Land Register on behalf of the disponees, the law infers that they have contracted that, on the first death, the property will devolve on the survivor or survivors[46]—even although they may never have expressly authorised their agents to prepare the deed in such terms. Consequently, on the first death, provided that the disponee had not revoked the contractual destination, the heritage will pass under the destination to the survivor or survivors[47] who will take the property subject to any secured debts. In an Outer House decision, it was held that the property passed under the destination free of the deceased's unsecured

---

[45] 1918 S.C. 9.

[46] *Per* Lord Morison in *Gordon-Rogers* v. *Thomson's Exrs.*, 1988 S.L.T. 618 at p. 620L; Conveyancing (Scotland) Act 1924 (c.27), s. 10(3).

[47] *Bisset* v. *Walker* (1799) Mor. App. No. 2 "Deathbed," where destination was "to A and B and the longest liver of them two."

debts,[48] but this decision has been doubted.[48a] In such cases, it is not necessary to disclose the deceased's interest in the heritage in the inventory of his estate for confirmation purposes,[49] though it must be shown in the Form A–3 at part 4 on page 3 and in Section 3, "Other Property" at page 9.

13.21   Even where the title to a property was originally taken in the names of A and B, with a survivorship destination, and A has conveyed his interest in the property to B, on B's death his original one-half interest in the property will pass to A under the destination, and will be disclosed only at part 4 on page 3 and at Section 3, "Other Property" on page 9 of the Form A–3. Only the one-half interest which B acquired from A will require to be confirmed to, and will pass under B's testamentary writing or under the rules of intestate succession.[50]

Revocation of a contractual destination

13.22   The rules relating to the revocation of a contractual destination are discussed at paragraph 10.113 *et seq*. Where the destination has been revoked, confirmation must be obtained to the deceased's *pro indiviso* interest in the heritage.

Destination to heritage: "to A and then to B"

13.23   Where the destination is in the form "to A and then to B", although the property will pass to B on A's death, it is always necessary to include the property in the confirmation to A's estate, in order that a good title may be given to B.[51]

Leasehold property in Scotland—held in common

13.24   Where leasehold property is held by two or more individuals under a contractual destination "to A and B and the longest

[48] *Barclays Bank Ltd.* v. *McGreish*, 1983 S.L.T. 344.

[48a] Cusine (1984) 29 J.L.S. 154; Morton, 1984 S.L.T. (News) 133; Halliday, 1984 S.L.T. (News) 180; Gretton, 1984 S.L.T. (News) 299 and Halliday, *Conveyancing Law and Practice in Scotland*, Vol. IV, para. 49–18. It should be noted that the Scottish Law Commission *Report on Succession* (Scot. Law Com. No. 124) recommends that the destinee should be personally liable for the debts of the deceased owner up to the value inherited (paras. 6.15 to 6.16, recommendation 29 and cl. 29(6)).

[49] Succession (Scotland) Act 1964 (c.41), s. 36(2)(*a*); A.J. McDonald (1965) 10 J.L.S. 73; M.C. Meston, *The Succession (Scotland) Act 1964* (4th ed.), p. 87.

[50] See letter by D.A. Johnstone, 1985 S.L.T. (News) 18; Professor M.C. Meston, "Special Destinations" in *A Scots Conveyancing Miscellany*, at p. 65.

[51] Succession (Scotland) Act 1964 (c. 41), s. 18(2); Halliday, *Conveyancing Law and Practice in Scotland*, Vol. IV, para. 49–27.

liver and their heirs", the destination cannot normally be altered either by *inter vivos* or testamentary deed[52] and the property will always pass to the survivor.

13.25　It has been suggested that there will not be an automatic destination of a lease to the survivor of tenants in common, where the tenants hold under an assignation, rather than under the original lease.[52a]

Moveable property—held in common

13.26　Items of moveable property such as stocks and shares, and bonds and other documents of debt, are frequently registered in the names of two or more parties. Sometimes, though not always, the registration includes a survivorship destination. Where one of the registered holders dies, such investments are frequently transferred into the name of the survivor or survivors, simply on the production of the death certificate.[53] Such a transfer should be viewed primarily as an administrative arrangement of the particular investment body, and, where the transferee is not the legal owner, he may be called upon to account to the legal owner for the value so transferred. The proprietorial rights of holders in common of moveable property is considered more fully at paragraphs 10.176–10.177. The following paragraphs describe only those circumstances in which an investment is registered automatically in the name of the surviving registered holders on the death of one of their number, and where this is the case, confirmation to the particular asset is not required, though the asset should be reported on the Form A–3 at page 3, part 4, and at page 9, section 3, "Other property".

> 1. Where Scots law is the proper law of the debt, an asset (not being a bank or building society account or bank deposit receipt[54]) which is registered in the names of "A and B and the survivor of them" will, on A's death, pass

---

[52] *Lidderdale* (June 22, 1627) Mor. 4247; *Macalister* v. *Macalister* (1859) 21 D. 560; *Robertson's Tr.* v. *Roberts*, 1982 S.L.T. 22; for fuller discussion see Halliday: *Conveyancing Law and Practice in Scotland*, Vol. IV, para. 49–16.; Rankine, *Law of Leases in Scotland*, at p. 76; Bell, *Leases* (1825), pp. 147–148; and Paton and Cameron, *Landlord and Tenant* (1967) at p. 62.

[52a] G.L. Gretton, Destinations and Leases, 1982 S.L.T. (News) 213. See *Walker* v. *Galbraith* (1895) 23 R. 347.

[53] For example, if the operating instruction on a bank account in Scotland permits signatures by "A or B or survivor," on the death of A, B can still withdraw all the funds. If the authority of both holders is required to a withdrawal, on A's death, the account becomes inoperable until confirmation to A's estate is exhibited.

[54] *Connell's Trs.* v. *Connell's Trs.* (1886) 13 R. 1175.

automatically to B[55], unless the destination had been revoked by A's testamentary writings.[56] A party who did not contribute to the purchase price is unable to revoke the destination by testamentary provision.[57]

Where government stock is held by investors who are domiciled Scots, the destination to the stock will be construed according to Scots law.[58]

2. Where the proper law of the debt is not Scots law, the court will presume, until the contrary is shown, that the principles applicable are the same as those under Scots law.[59]

3. Under English law, where an asset is registered in the names of A and B (joint tenancy), survivorship is always presumed, and on B's death, the asset passes automatically to A.[60] Indeed, the joint tenancy could not be severed by B's testamentary writings.

Life assurance policies

13.27 A United Kingdom insurance company may pay out a policy of life assurance effected by a person who died domiciled elsewhere than the United Kingdom without having sight of a grant of confirmation, probate or letters of administration to establish the right of the payee to receive the policy proceeds.[61] The person who effected the policy need not be either the life assured or the owner of the policy.

[55] *Cunningham's Trs.* v. *Cunningham*, 1924 S.C. 581.
[56] For a more comprehensive discussion see para. 10.177, para. 3.
[57] *Taylor's Exrs.* v. *Brunton*, 1939 S.C. 444, following *Renouf's Trs.* v. *Haining*, 1919 S.C. 497 (destination in title to heritage).
[58] *Cunningham's Trs.* v. *Cunningham*, 1924 S.C. 581.
[59] For a more comprehensive discussion see para. 10.177, para. 6.
[60] *Re Bishop, National Provincial Bank Ltd.* v. *Bishop* [1965] Ch. 450; *Connell's Trs.* v. *Connell's Trs.* (1886) 13 R. 1175.
[61] Revenue Act 1884 (47 & 48 Vict. c.62), s. 11, as amended by Revenue Act 1889 (52 & 53 Vict. c.42), s. 19.

CHAPTER 14

THE EFFECT OF (A) CONFIRMATIONS AND (B) GRANTS OF PROBATE OR ADMINISTRATION

Introduction

14.01   Before estate situated in the United Kingdom can be uplifted, it is, in general,[1] necessary to produce a grant of probate, letters of administration or confirmation:

> "Notwithstanding any provision to the contrary contained in any local or private Act of Parliament, the production of a grant of representation from a court in the United Kingdom by probate or letters of administration or confirmation shall be necessary to establish the right to recover or receive any part of the personal and heritable estate and effects of any deceased person situated in the United Kingdom."[2]

This chapter explores the circumstances in which it is appropriate to apply for confirmation, or a grant of probate, or letters of administration. It also describes the effect of such grants within the United Kingdom.

A. THE EFFECT OF CONFIRMATION AND THE CIRCUMSTANCES WHERE CONFIRMATION WILL BE GRANTED

Confirmation and the executor's powers of administration

14.02   Every part of the deceased's estate—whether heritable or moveable—which falls to be administered under the law of Scotland and to which confirmation has been obtained, vests for the purposes of administration in the executor thereby confirmed.[3] The confirmation confers upon the executor full power to take possession of, make up title to, uplift or receive the estate and effects to which he obtains confirmation,[4] and to administer and

---

[1] For circumstances where estate in Scotland can be ingathered without producing confirmation see Chap. 13.

[2] Revenue Act 1884 (47 & 48 Vict. c.62), s. 11, as amended by Revenue Act 1889 (52 & 53 Vict. c.42), s. 19 and Succession (Scotland) Act 1964 (c.41), s. 14(1).

[3] Succession (Scotland) Act 1964 (c.41), s. 14(1).

[4] Revenue Act 1884 (47 & 48 Vict. c.62), s. 11, as amended by Revenue Act 1889 (52 & 53 Vict. c. 42), s. 19 and Succession (Scotland) Act 1964 (c. 41), s. 14(1).

dispose of the same,[5] grant discharges thereof, pursue therefor where necessary and generally everything concerning the estate which belongs to the office of executor-dative or executor-nominate as appropriate—subject to the provision that the executor shall render just count and reckoning for his intromissions with the executry estate when legally required.

The powers of an executor are more fully set out at paragraphs 1.33–1.45.

Validation by subsequent confirmation

14.03   If the executors purport to deal with or transfer the deceased's estate before they are confirmed, confirmation granted subsequently will validate the purported dealing or transfer retrospectively[6]:

> "No doubt confirmation was required in order that [the trustees] might secure an active title to intromit with and administer the estate, but it seems to me to be perfectly clear that if they subsequently obtained confirmation the defect in their title could be effectively cured, and the cure could draw back to the date of the assignation."[7]

Parties intromitting with the executor are protected

14.04   Any person or body may rely on a confirmation granted under the Confirmation of Executors (Scotland) Act 1858[8] in making any payment or bona fide transfer upon such confirmation and shall be indemnified and protected in so doing, notwithstanding any defect or circumstance whatsoever affecting the validity of such confirmation.[9] This rule originally applied to moveable estate in Scotland only, but has since been extended to cover heritable securities and debts secured by heritable securities[10] and any interest in heritable property held by the deceased and described in the confirmation.[11] Where a person has acquired,

---

[5] *e.g. Rotherwick's Trs.* v. *Hope and Others*, 1975 S.L.T. 187.

[6] *Mackay* v. *Mackay*, 1914 S.C. 200 (assignation of copyright); *Garvie's Trs.* v. *Garvie's Tutors*, 1975 S.L.T. 94 (transfer of lease); *Chalmers' Trs.* v. *Watson* (1860) 22 D. 1060 (unconfirmed trustee voted at a meeting regarding a composition offer in a sequestration).

[7] *Per* Lord President Strathclyde in *Mackay* v. *Mackay*, 1914 S.C. 200 at p. 203.

[8] (21 & 22 Vict. c.56), s. 8.

[9] Confirmation and Probate Amendment Act 1859 (22 Vict. c.30), s. 1.

[10] Conveyancing (Scotland) Act 1924 (14 & 15 Geo. c.27), s. 5(2).

[11] Succession (Scotland) Act 1964 (c.41), s. 15(1), as amended by Law Reform (Miscellaneous Provisions) (Scotland) Act 1968 (c. 70), s. 19 and Act of Sederunt (Confirmation of Executors) 1964, s.1 (S.I. 1964 No. 1143), as amended by Act of Sederunt (Confirmation of Executors Amendment) 1966, s. 1 (S.I. 1966 No. 593).

in good faith and for value, title to heritable property or a security over heritable property which has vested in an executor, the title will not be challengeable on the ground that the confirmation was reducible or has been reduced.[12]

Executor suing the deceased's debtors

14.05   Even before confirmation is obtained, an executor (whether nominate or dative) is entitled to sue for the estate,[13] but he must confirm the debt before extract.[14] In the case of an executor-dative, it is his appointment which gives him the title to sue: a person eligible to be decerned executor-dative, but who has not yet been decerned, has no title to sue.[15]

14.06   Probate or letters of administration from a foreign court are sufficient title to sue, but their authenticity must be attested by the signature of a notary,[16] or, where the country concerned is a signatory to the 1961 Hague Convention Abolishing the Requirement of Legalisation of Foreign Public Documents,[16a] by an apostille which certifies them as authentic (see Style 3.04), duly issued by the Foreign and Commonwealth Office. However, without confirmation, an executor can neither enforce payment[17] nor grant a discharge.

14.07   Similarly, an unconfirmed executor may claim in a sequestration.[18] However, no executor can enforce payment or grant an effectual transfer or discharge until he has obtained confirmation.[19]

14.08   The distinction between suing and extracting decree was revealed in a case[20] brought by a person to whom the unconfirmed executor had passed an item of the deceased's estate. The deceased's trustees had assigned copyright owned by the deceased before they obtained confirmation to it. It has been

---

[12] Succession (Scotland) Act 1964 (c.41), s. 17.
[13] See *obiter dicta* of Lord Adam in *Symington* v. *Campbell* (1894) 21 R. 434 at p. 437; and Lord President Clyde in *Bentley* v. *Macfarlane*, 1964 S.C. 76 at p. 79.
[14] McLaren, *Wills and Succession* (3rd ed.), Vol. 2, p.878, para. 1616; *Stevenson* v. *Maclaren* (1800) Hume 171; *Reid* v. *Turner* (1830) 8 S. 960; *Chalmers' Trs.* v. *Watson* (1860) 22 D. 1060;*Bones* v. *Morrison* (1866) 5 M. 240; *Mackay* v. *Mackay*, 1914 S.C. 200.
[15] *Malcolm* v. *Dick* (1866) 5 M. 18.
[16] *Disbrow* v. *Mackintosh* (1852) 15 D. 123.
[16a] Cmnd. 2617 (1965).
[17] Revenue Act 1884 (47 & 48 Vict. c.62), s. 11, as amended by Revenue Act 1889 (52 & 53 Vict. c.42), s. 19 and Succession (Scotland) Act 1964 (c.41), s. 14(1).
[18] *Chalmers' Trs.* v. *Watson* (1860) 22 D. 1060.
[19] Ersk., III.ix.39; Maclaren, *Wills and Succession* (3rd ed.) pp. 878–879.
[20] *Mackay* v. *Mackay*, 1914 S.C. 200.

seen at paragraph 14.03 that such an assignation will be validated by the subsequent grant of confirmation. The court further
held that the assignee had a good title to sue for breach of the
copyright but he could not extract decree for payment until the
trustees had been confirmed.

Executors and vitious intromissions

14.09   A vitious intromitter[21] is someone who takes possession of or
uses any moveables belonging to the deceased without legal
right to do so. It is open to the deceased's creditors (but not his
legatees) to plead vitious intromission. A vitious intromitter by
intromitting becomes liable for all the debts of the deceased,[22]
including liability for inheritance tax on the deceased's estate.[23]
Confirmation operates as a complete protection from liability
for the penalty of vitious intromission, and vitious intromissions
may generally be purged by a subsequent confirmation expede
within a year of the death.

Estate to be administered under the law of Scotland

14.10   Confirmation will be granted to any estate which will be completely administered under the law of Scotland, and to that part
of an estate which falls to be administered under the law of
Scotland. Thus, where the deceased died domiciled in Scotland,
Scots law will determine the succession to his worldwide moveable estate and to his heritable estate in Scotland, and confirmation will be granted to his estate in Scotland, England and
Wales and Northern Ireland, with a note of the foreign estate
appended. Where the deceased died domiciled somewhere
other than Scotland, Scots law will determine the succession to
his heritable estate in Scotland, and in order to make up title
to this, and to moveable estate in Scotland,[24] either Scottish
confirmation or something recognised as equivalent to confirmation must be obtained.

Scottish confirmation where deceased died domiciled in Scotland

14.11   This is the normal Scottish confirmation, and is dealt with generally in Chapter 13.

---

[21] Ersk., III.ix.49–56; Bell, *Prin.*, §1921; Bell, *Comm.*, II.xii.5.
[22] Vitious Intromitters Act 1696 (c.20).
[23] Inheritance Tax Act 1984 (c.51), s. 199(1)(c) and (4)(a).
[24] *Smith's Trs.* v. *Grant* (1862) 24 D. 1142.

Scottish confirmation where deceased died domiciled outside the United Kingdom

14.12   Since probate or letters of administration, etc., granted by a foreign court will not give the executor the right to administer the Scottish estate,[25] it therefore follows that where a deceased person who had been domiciled outside the United Kingdom leaves property situated in Scotland, it is necessary to obtain Scottish confirmation to his estate.[26] As this is a case where the deceased died domiciled outside of Scotland, it is competent to confirm to the deceased's Scottish estate only. Such a Scottish confirmation will be additional to any grants of probate or letters of administration taken out in other countries where the deceased held property.

14.13   Where the deceased died domiciled outside Scotland, his only United Kingdom estate being in Scotland, and Scottish confirmation is required:

1.   the right of the executor to administer by the laws of the country of the deceased's domicile must be proved— either by the production of a grant of probate or letters of administration issued from a court of the deceased's domicile, or the opinion of a person versed in the laws of the deceased's domicile;[27-28] and

2.   the Inland Revenue Form A-3 must be lodged, disclosing the estate wheresoever situated, and inheritance tax on the estate in Scotland[29] must be accounted for to the Capital Taxes Office in Scotland. The practice is that if the gross estate in Scotland exceeds £5,000, the inventory must be sent to the Capital Taxes Office for examination, before it can be forwarded to the sheriff clerk for confirmation.[30]

Resealing as an alternative

14.14   Irrespective of where the deceased was domiciled on death, where a grant of probate or of letters of administration has been obtained in a Commonwealth country or South Africa, it is pos-

---

[25] *Ibid.*

[26] Revenue Act 1884 (47 & 48 Vict. c.62), s. 11, as amended by Revenue Act 1889 (52 & 53 Vict. c.42), s.19 and Succession (Scotland) Act 1964 (c.41), s. 14(1).

[27-28] See, further, paras. 2.62 *et seq.* and Styles 3.01 and 3.04.

[29] Excluding, in the case of a member of a visiting armed force, his tangible moveable property and any emoluments due on death (IHTA 1984 (c.51), ss. 5(4) and 155).

[30] See *Instructions for the Completion of Inland Revenue Inventory Forms Cap A-3 (1986):* Cap Form A-5 (1986), p. 1.

sible that the grant can be resealed under the Colonial Probates Act 1892.[31] A grant resealed in Scotland is treated as equivalent to a Scottish confirmation—so that, in such circumstances, a separate Scottish confirmation is unnecessary.[32]

Scottish confirmation where deceased domiciled in England and Wales or Northern Ireland

14.15   Normally, when a person dies domiciled in England and Wales or in Northern Ireland, a grant of probate or letters of administration will be obtained there, which will cover estate in Scotland. Occasionally, the commissary court has issued confirmations to the estates of persons who have died domiciled in England and Wales or in Northern Ireland, but this usually only occurs where either the deceased left only estate in Scotland, or the executor does not require to administer estate in the other parts of the United Kingdom. As this is a case where the deceased died domiciled outside of Scotland, only the estate in Scotland may be confirmed to.

14.16   The right of the executor to administer by the laws of the country of the deceased's domicile must be proved, by the opinion of a person versed in the laws of the domicile.[33] In testate cases, it may be necessary to found on the Wills Act 1963.

14.17   For inheritance tax purposes the inventory must disclose estate wheresoever situated, the non-Scottish estate being appended after the inventory of the Scottish estate and the total for confirmation, and inheritance tax accounted for to the Capital Taxes Office in Scotland.

Deceased domiciled in Scotland: Estate in England and Wales or Northern Ireland

14.18   Provided that the deceased died domiciled in Scotland, confirmation may be granted to any of the deceased's estate—whether personal or real[34]—which is situated in England and Wales or Northern Ireland. In the case of real estate, the short

[31] See, further, Chap. 15.
[32] Colonial Probates Act 1892 (55 & 56 Vict. c.6), s. 2(1), as amended by Finance Act 1975 (c. 7), s. 52 and Sched. 12, para. 4.
[33] See paras. 2.62 *et seq.* and Style 3.02.
[34] Confirmation of Executors (Scotland) Act 1858 (21 & 22 Vict. c.56), s. 9, as amended by Statute Law Revision Act 1892 (55 & 56 Vict. c.19), Administration of Estates Act 1971 (c.25), ss. 6(1) and 7 and Sched. 2 and Finance Act 1975 (c.7), ss. 52 (2), 59 and Sched. 13.

description may be used.[35] The estate in England and Wales and that in Northern Ireland should be shown separately.[36]

14.19 Provided that the confirmation discloses that the deceased died domiciled in Scotland, the confirmation is automatically treated as equivalent to letters of representation (in the case of confirmation-dative) or to a grant of probate (in the case of confirmation-nominate) for the purposes of the laws of England and Wales[37] and of Northern Ireland.[38] Thus, estate in England and Wales or in Northern Ireland may be paid out to the executor confirmed by a Scottish court on the basis of the confirmation alone or on the basis of an individual certificate of confirmation.[39]

14.20 This statutory rule of automatic recognition applies equally to additional confirmations, such as eiks, confirmations *ad omissa* and confirmations *ad non executa*.[40]

Evidence of confirmations in England and Wales and Northern Ireland

14.21 In England, Wales and Northern Ireland, a document purporting to be a confirmation, additional confirmation or certificate of confirmation, or a duplicate thereof, given under the seal of office of any commissariot in Scotland, shall, until the contrary is proved, be taken to be such confirmation, additional confirmation or certificate of confirmation without further proof.[41]

B. The Effect of Grants from England and Wales or Northern Ireland

Outline of executry administration in England and Wales and Northern Ireland

14.22 The process known in Scotland as obtaining confirmation is, in

---

[35] Administration of Estates Act 1971 (c.25), s. 6(2) and Act of Sederunt (Confirmation of Executors) 1964, s. 1, as amended by Act of Sederunt (Confirmation of Executors Amendment) 1966, s. 1.

[36] Confirmation of Executors (Scotland) Act 1858 (21 and 22 Vict. c.56), s. 9, as amended by Statute Law Revision Act 1892 (55 & 56 Vict. c.19), Administration of Estates Act 1971 (c.25), ss. 6(1) and 7 and Sched. 2 and Finance Act 1975 (c.7), ss.52(2), 59 and Sched. 13.

[37] Administration of Estates Act 1971 (c.25), s. 1(1) and (2).

[38] *Ibid.*, s. 2(2) and (3).

[39] *Ibid.*, ss. 1(1) and 2(2).

[40] *Ibid.*, ss. 1(7) and 2(6).

[41] *Ibid.*, s. 4(1)(*a*) and (*b*).

England and Wales and in Northern Ireland, known either as obtaining a grant of probate, or obtaining a grant of letters of administration.

Outline of procedure for obtaining a grant

14.23   In order to obtain a grant, the executor[42] or the administrator[43] must lodge

1.   an oath;

2.   the will (if there is one) and any codicils; and

3.   except in the case of an "excepted estate,"[44] an Inland Revenue account, which does not require to be sworn, provided that the deceased died after March 12, 1975. If the account shows that the deceased's gross estate exceeds the current tax threshold, the account must first be forwarded to the Capital Taxes Office, and any inheritance tax due must be paid, or a certificate annexed to the account showing that no tax is payable.[45] It is only possible to delay payment of inheritance tax until the grant is issued if there is property in respect of which the instalment option applies, or the Inland Revenue permits postponement because it would cause excessive hardship to raise the full amount of tax.

Thus, the oath and account correspond generally to the inventory and relative oath upon which confirmation proceeds.

14.24   Thereafter, the executors may apply to the High Court[46] for a grant of probate or administration. Such an application will be made to either

1.   the Principal Registry of the Family Division of the High Court (commonly referred to as the Principal Probate Registry)[47]; or

2.   a District Probate Registry[48]; or

---

[42] This office corresponds to that of the executor-nominate. See Halsbury, Vol. 17, para. 702.

[43] This office corresponds largely to that of the Scottish executor-dative. See Halsbury, Vol. 17, para. 703.

[44] See paras. 12.118–12.119.

[45] Supreme Court Act 1981 (c.54), s. 109, as amended by Inheritance Tax Act 1984 (c.51), s. 276 and Sched. 8, para. 20(a).

[46] Supreme Court Act 1981 (c.54), s. 25(1).

[47] *Ibid.*, s. 105.

[48] *Ibid.*

3. in the case of a contentious estate, the Chancery Division.[49]

Probate

14.25   Probate corresponds generally to confirmation of an executor-nominate in Scotland, with the difference that, under the law in England and Wales, an executor derives his title from the will, so that before the grant, he is able to ingather the estate and give receipts, pay debts, and assign the estate.[50] Probate is categorised either as non-contentious (where either there is no dispute, or the dispute has been resolved) or as contentious.

(a) Probate in common form: non-contentious business
14.26   In a non-contentious case, an application for probate in common form is made to the Family Division of the High Court or to the District Probate Registry. Probate in common form is, like confirmation, granted on an *ex parte* application and without any formal procedure in court.

14.27   Like confirmation, probate in common form is revocable on cause shown[51]; but, until revoked, it is conclusive evidence of the executor's title to receive the estate and grant discharges. Probate in common form can be revoked in the court that granted it,[52] whereas it is to be remembered that, in Scotland, the reduction of a confirmation or of the testamentary writing upon which it has proceeded, is competent only in the Court of Session.[53]

(b) Probate in solemn form
14.28   Contentious probate proceedings, otherwise known as probate in solemn form, fall within the jurisdiction of the Chancery Division of the High Court.[54] A probate action is defined as

> "an action for the grant of probate of the will, or letters of administration of the estate of a deceased person or for the revocation of such a grant or for a decree pronouncing for or against the validity of an alleged will, not being an action which is non-contentious or common form probate business."[55]

Thus, probate in solemn form (in contrast to confirmation-nominate) may involve a judicial determination as to the validity of a will.

---

[49] *Ibid.*, s. 61(1) and Sched. 1.
[50] Halsbury, Vol. 17, para. 730.
[51] Supreme Court Act 1981 (c. 54), s. 121.
[52] *Ibid.*, ss. 105 and 121.
[53] Ersk. I.ii.6; I.v.28.
[54] Supreme Court Act 1981 (c.54), s. 61(1) and Sched. 1.
[55] R.S.C., Ord. 76, r.1.

14.29   A grant of probate in solemn form refers to every part of the testamentary writing or writings on which it is granted, and the validity of the whole contents of each and every testamentary writing included in the probate (whether it relates to the nomination of executors or not) is held to be proved, the judgment being binding on everyone who has had notice of the action.[56] In contrast, a confirmation refers only to the appointment of executors, and it is only the nomination of executors that is confirmed, any judgment upon the documents being limited to the validity of that nomination, although for the purpose of determining entitlement to property bequeathed in a testamentary writing, the writing will be treated as valid in respect of the formalities of execution once confirmation has been granted.[57] Confirmation gives the executors merely a right of administration—and they may find that an action of reduction of the deed is subsequently raised.[58]

Letters of administration

14.30   Letters of administration correspond roughly to confirmation-dative. Letters of administration are granted where the deceased died intestate, whether wholly or partially, and until the grant is made, such part of the deceased's estate as is undisposed of by will vests in the President of the Family Division of the High Court. Letters of administration with the will annexed are granted where the will is proved by someone other than the executor as where no executor is appointed, or where the executor has died during the testator's lifetime, or before the issue of the grant, or where the executor renounces.[59] Where there is a will, it is proved by the administrator, and a copy thereof is annexed to his title.[60]

14.31   An application for letters of administration will be made to the Family Division of the High Court or to the District Probate Registry.

14.32   Formerly all administrators were required to give a bond as security for due administration of the estate but this requirement was abolished with effect from January 1, 1972,[61] although the High Court retains the discretion to require one or more

---

[56] Halsbury, Vol. 17, para. 888.
[57] Succession (Scotland) Act 1964 (c.41), s. 32(1)(2) and (3)(e) (as substituted by the Requirements of Writing (Scotland) Act 1995 (c.7), s.14(1) and Sched. 4, para. 40.
[58] *Per* Lord Shand in *Hamilton* v. *Hardie* (1888) 16 R. 192 at p. 198. See, further, paras. 19.72–19.86.
[59] Supreme Court Act 1981 (c.54), s. 119.
[60] *Ibid.*; see Halsbury, Vol. 17, paras. 978–980.
[61] Administration of Estates Act 1971 (c.25), s. 8 and s. 14(2).

sureties to guarantee any loss which any person interested in the administration of the deceased's estate may suffer in consequence of the administrator breaching his duties.[62] Sureties are not required in routine cases. Sureties are the equivalent of the caution which executors-dative must find in Scotland.

Further differences between the grant and confirmation

14.33   Probate and letters of administration differ from confirmation in the following main respects:

1.   They do not contain any particulars of the estate in respect of which they are granted—only the total value of the estate in the account is stated on the grant. Therefore, no person to whom they are presented as a title has any means of knowing whether the claim made against him has been included, or at what amount it may have been valued. Indeed, no debtor or other party is entitled to concern himself with any such question, for it is not a good objection against either an executor or administrator that the marking of the gross value of the estate amounts to, say, £10,000, while the debt or debenture or mortgage proposed to be dealt with amounts by itself to, say, £12,000.

2.   The account of the estate is not available to the public—indeed, even if the executor or administrator loses his own copy, he cannot obtain a new copy without the leave of the appropriate Inland Revenue department.

3.   The original copies of the wills and other documents are kept under the control of the High Court in the Principal Registry or in the District Probate Registry from which the grant was issued.[63] The executor or administrator may obtain an office copy or a sealed or certified copy from the registry which issued the grant.[64]

Additional estate discovered after grant has been issued

14.34   If it is discovered that estate has been omitted from the original Inland Revenue account, a corrective account may be given up in the country from which the grant issued for inheritance tax purposes. An Inland Revenue docket may be endorsed on the grant to the effect that a corrective account has been filed, but

---

[62] Supreme Court Act 1981 (c.54), s. 120.
[63] *Ibid.*, s. 124.
[64] *Ibid.*, s. 125.

the amount in the act of probate or letters of administration is not amended by the probate registrar.

Grants from England and Wales or Northern Ireland may carry estate in Scotland

14.35   Provided that the deceased died domiciled in England and Wales or in Northern Ireland, grants of probate or letters of administration granted from, respectively, the High Court or the District Probate Registry[65] in England and Wales, or the High Court in Northern Ireland, are, in relation to property situated in Scotland, equivalent to a confirmation given under the seal of the office of the Commissariot of Edinburgh.[66] Such grants, therefore, automatically give the executor or administrator a good title to estate in Scotland, both moveable and heritable,[67] and including heritable securities and debts secured by heritable securities (even if there is no description).[68]

Grants where deceased did not die domiciled in England and Wales or Northern Ireland

14.36   However, if the deceased did not die domiciled in England and Wales or in Northern Ireland, there is no statutory rule enabling Scottish estate to be carried by the grant of probate or letters of administration issued by the courts of these jurisdictions. Thus, if the deceased died domiciled outside the United Kingdom, it will be necessary to obtain a Scottish confirmation to estate in Scotland, and a grant of probate or letters of administration in England and Wales, or in Northern Ireland, to the estate there.

Grants where deceased died domiciled in Scotland

14.37   Indeed, while it is competent to obtain a grant of probate or letters of administration to the estate situated in England and Wales or in Northern Ireland of a person who died domiciled in Scotland, it is not competent to include Scottish estate in such a grant. Paragraphs 14.40–14.49 set out the procedure to be adopted where the deceased was domiciled in Scotland and, after a grant was obtained, it is discovered that estate in Scotland has to be ingathered.

---

[65] These are made in the name of the High Court under the seal used in the registry: Supreme Court Act 1981 (c.54), s. 106(1).
[66] Administration of Estates Act 1971 (c.25), s. 3(1).
[67] Succession (Scotland) Act 1964 (c.41), s. 15(1), as amended by Law Reform (Miscellaneous Provisions) (Scotland) Act 1968 (c.70), s. 19.
[68] Conveyancing (Scotland) Act 1924 (c.27), s. 5(2), as amended by Succession (Scotland) Act 1964 (c.41), ss. 15(1), 34(2) and Sched. 3 and Administration of Estates Act 1971 (c.25), Sched. 1, para. 3.

Evidence of grants of probate and letters of administration

14.38   The Supreme Court Act 1981 provides that every document purporting to be sealed or stamped with the seal or stamp of the
Supreme Court or of any office thereof[69] shall be received in
evidence in all parts of the United Kingdom without further
proof.[70]

Estate in Scotland not fully administered

14.39   If the deceased died domiciled in England and Wales or in
Northern Ireland, and the sole or last surviving executor in
whose favour the original grant was issued has died leaving
estate in Scotland which was not fully administered, a title to
this estate may be obtained as follows:

1. If the estate is registered in the name of the deceased
    executor as an individual without reference to the trust
    then it may be treated as it appears, and the appropriate
    grant of probate or letters of administration in favour of
    his executor or administrator may be founded on as a
    title.

    In practice, this is perhaps the least satisfactory option,
    since the grant bears to be an absolute (rather than a
    fiduciary) title.

2. If the deceased died domiciled in England and Wales or
    Northern Ireland, the chain of executorship may not be
    broken, as where the sole or last surviving executor him-
    self nominated an executor.[71-73] If this new executor
    proves the will of the deceased executor in England and
    Wales or in Northern Ireland, then this grant is a good
    title to the unadministered estate in Scotland, provided
    that the grant discloses that the deceased executor died
    domiciled in England and Wales or in Northern Ireland.

3. If the deceased died domiciled in England and Wales or
    in Northern Ireland, and the chain of executorship has
    been broken by the sole or last surviving executor dying
    without nominating an executor, a *de bonis non* grant
    (which is similar to the Scottish *ad non executa*
    confirmation) in respect of the original deceased may
    have been issued in the country of the deceased's domi-

---

[69] *i.e.* including grants of probate and letters of administration issued by the
High Court Divisions of the Family Division and Chancery Division and the
District Probate Registry: Supreme Court Act 1981 (c.54), ss. 1, 5 and 99.

[70] Supreme Court Act 1981 (c.54), s. 132 which extends to Scotland (s.
153(4)(c)).

[71-73] Halsbury, Vol. 17, paras. 747–750.

cile[74]; this grant is a good title to the unadministered estate in Scotland, provided that the grant contains a statement of the deceased's domicile.[75]

4. If section 6 of the Executors (Scotland) Act 1900 can be applied, then probate granted in England and Wales or in Northern Ireland in favour of the executor-nominate of the deceased executor, or a Scottish confirmation (with a note of the trust property appended), is effectual for the executor of the deceased executor to intromit with the trust property.

    See further paragraph 16.10 (on the procedure for "quasi-probate") and paragraphs 16.07–16.09 (on the procedure for "quasi-confirmation"). In the case of a probate, the deceased executor must have been domiciled in England and Wales or Northern Ireland. It should be remembered that section 6 only gives power to recover such trust property, and to assign and transfer it to such person or persons as may be legally authorised to continue the administration thereof, or, where no other act of administration remains to be performed, directly to the beneficiaries entitled thereto, or to any person or persons whom the beneficiaries may appoint to receive and discharge, realise and distribute the same.

    It must be borne in mind that section 6 does not apply where a grant of letters of administration has been obtained in England and Wales or Northern Ireland.

5. An *ad non executa* confirmation, using Form X-1,[76] may be taken out. The completed *ad non executa* inventory must be lodged in the Edinburgh Commissary Court along with:
    (1) in all cases,
        (a) an opinion by a solicitor or other person versant in the law of the country in which the original deceased died domiciled, which narrates briefly the facts of the case and states specifically who is now entitled to carry on the administration of the unadministered estate (Style 3.03); and
        (b) any documents referred to in the opinion;
    (2) in a dative application,
        (a) an executor-dative petition (based on Styles 6.46 and 6.47 (reference being made to the grant produced, instead of to the recording of the inventory and confirmation in condescendence 2, and to the opinion in condescendence 3));

---

[74] *Op. cit.*, paras. 984–987.
[75] Administration of Estates Act 1971 (c.25), s. 3(1).
[76] Obtainable from the sheriff clerk's office.

  (b) caution for the *ad non executa* estate; and

  (c) where a will was annexed to a grant of representation, the will;

 (3) in a nominate application (*i.e.* the executor-nominate of the last surviving executor-nominate is applying), all the grants, etc., referred to in the opinion must be referred to in the deposition and be produced with the inventory for recording, and docketed and signed with reference thereto. It is exceptional for caution to be required in such circumstances.

Domicile in Scotland, but original grant issued in England and Wales or Northern Ireland

General

14.40 Although the normal practice where the deceased died domiciled in Scotland is to obtain confirmation in Scotland to his estate in Scotland, England and Wales and Northern Ireland, on occasion a grant may be taken out in the first instance in either England and Wales or in Northern Ireland to estate in that country. Such could happen if the deceased died while living in England, but without having lost his Scottish domicile and it appeared that all his estate was situated in England. Subsequently, it may be discovered that the deceased left estate in Scotland. A grant from a court in England and Wales or in Northern Ireland, in respect of the estate of a person domiciled in Scotland, cannot extend to the deceased's Scottish estate, for the grant is a title to estate only in the country from which it is issued.[77] Instead, confirmation will be required to the Scottish estate.

14.41 While obtaining a grant in England and Wales or in Northern Ireland to the estate there, followed by obtaining confirmation in Scotland to the Scottish estate, will delay the administration of the estate and is not an economical procedure, it is, however, competent.[78] The Confirmation of Executors (Scotland) Act 1858[79] (which enabled a Scottish confirmation to be resealed in an English or Irish probate court, and to be thereafter treated as a grant of probate or letters of administration) and now the Administration of Estates Act 1971 merely provide a convenient method of an executor (to a person who died domiciled in Scotland) obtaining title to English, Welsh and Irish estate, and do not replace the older more cumbersome process of obtaining confirmation to the Scottish estate, and separate probate or let-

---

[77] See paras. 14.35 and 14.36.

[78] *Kennion's Exrs.*, 1939 S.L.T. (Sh. Ct.) 5.

[79] (21 & 22 Vict. c.56), ss. 12 and 13 (now repealed by Supreme Court of Judicature (Consolidation) Act 1925 (c.49), s.226 and Sched. 6 and Administration of Estates Act 1971 (c.25), s.12(1) and Sched. 2, Part I, respectively).

428   *Confirmation of Executors*

ters of administration to the estate in England and Wales and in Northern Ireland.[80] In such circumstances, obtaining confirmation to the Scottish estate only is not partial confirmation.[81]

Choice of court in Scotland

14.42   If the deceased had no fixed or known domicile save that it was in Scotland, the application for confirmation must be made in the court in Edinburgh. Otherwise, the application must be made in the sheriffdom in Scotland where the deceased was last domiciled, the sheriff court being that for the district where the deceased last resided.

Confirmation-nominate

14.43   One difficulty frequently encountered in testate estates is that it may not be possible to determine from the copy of the will attached to the grant whether the will is validly executed by the law of Scotland. The grant of probate is acceptable only in so far as it sets up the annexed copy will as a good copy and except in the case of a probate in solemn form, does not validate the will. For this purpose it may be possible to found on the grant to set up the validity of the will under the Wills Act 1963,[82] but if this procedure is not applicable and the will is not *ex facie* validly executed then a proof of due execution or an action under section 4 of the Requirements of Writing (Scotland) Act 1995 may be required. The will in fact may be signed on each sheet or separate page but this may not be patent from the face of the copy will attached to the grant; in these circumstances it may be possible to obtain a certificate to that effect from the registrar of the court which issued the grant. Similarly, if the will is holograph and affidavits setting up the handwriting and signature have been lodged in the probate court, it may be possible to obtain certified copies of those affidavits from the registrar.

Confirmation-dative

14.44   If the deceased died intestate, or died testate and executors-nominate are not applying for confirmation, then it is necessary to adopt the usual first step in Scotland of lodging a dative petition to have an executor decerned; if intestate, the grant of letters of administration need not be produced.

14.45   Caution must be obtained to the gross estate in Scotland only,[83] unless it all passes to the deceased's surviving spouse in satisfaction of his or her prior rights.

---

[80] *Kennion's Exrs.*, 1939 S.L.T. (Sh. Ct.) 5.

[81] *Ibid.*, at p. 7, para. 4.

[82] See, further, paras. 3.06 *et seq.*

[83] The administrator may have been required to produce sureties in respect of the estate in England and Wales or Northern Ireland, as appropriate: see para. 14.32.

Drafting the inventory

14.46 Where the deceased died domiciled in Scotland, and the original grant was obtained in England and Wales or in Northern Ireland and was limited "until representation be granted in Scotland" (which is now standard practice), the entire estate—including that to which the grant was obtained—will require to be confirmed.

14.47 Where the deceased died domiciled in Scotland but the original grant obtained in England and Wales or in Northern Ireland was not limited, the estate in that jurisdiction to which a title has already been obtained should be shown in the inventory of estate as a lump sum under declaration that a grant of probate or letters of administration has already been obtained to it in the country where it is situated. Because the deceased was domiciled in Scotland, it is competent to seek confirmation to estate in England and Wales or in Northern Ireland, which was not included in the original grant obtained in those jurisdictions, by including it in the confirmation.[84]

Formalities in so far as United Kingdom inheritance tax is concerned

14.48 Where the grant has been taken out in England and Wales or in Northern Ireland, the usual Scottish Inland Revenue inventory must be deponed to, and stamped inheritance tax "paid" or "nil" by the Inland Revenue authorities in the other jurisdiction, before confirmation may be applied for.[85]

Confirmation

14.49 Confirmation fees are charged only on the estate being confirmed.[86] Confirmation will be issued on lodging the inventory (in testate cases along with the grant or a sealed copy thereof) at the appropriate court.

---

[84] Administration of Estates Act 1971 (c.25), ss. 1(1) and 6(1).

[85] Probate and Legacy Duties Act 1808 (48 Geo. 3, c.149), s.42, as amended by Finance Act 1975 (c.7), s.19 and Sched. 4, para. 38(2).

[86] *Kennion's Exrs.*, 1939 S.L.T. (Sh.Ct.) 5.

CHAPTER 15

RESEALING UNDER COLONIAL PROBATES ACT 1892

Introduction

15.01 Where a person dies domiciled abroad leaving estate in Scotland, it will be necessary to consider how title can be made up to such estate. Exceptionally, no special legal process is necessary,[1] the most commonly occurring instance being where a person who died domiciled abroad left a life assurance policy taken out with a United Kingdom company.[2] Apart from such specialities, it was formerly always necessary to obtain confirmation to the deceased's estate in Scotland (see, further, paras. 10.79 and 14.12–14.13), as well as going through an equivalent process in the country either of the deceased's domicile or where the bulk of the estate was held. However, the Colonial Probates Act 1892 now enables a grant of probate, letters of representation or whatever, granted by a court of a Commonwealth country,[3] to be resealed in the Sheriff Court of Lothian and Borders in Edinburgh. The estate in Scotland can then be uplifted on the basis of the resealed grant. It should be noted that resealing a Commonwealth grant is not always to be recommended—see paragraph 15.02.

Corresponding arrangements have been set up in other Commonwealth countries which enable a Scottish confirmation to be resealed in the Commonwealth country—so dispensing with the need to obtain a separate grant in that country (see para. 15.26 *et seq.*).

Confirmation as an alternative to resealing

15.02 Instead of resealing a Commonwealth grant, it is equally competent for the grantee(s) to be confirmed to the Scottish estate (see paras. 10.79 and 14.12–14.13 for details of the process in such circumstances). The advantages of obtaining a Scottish confirmation, rather than resealing a Commonwealth grant, are as follows:

---

[1] See Chap. 13 for details.
[2] Revenue Act 1884 (47 & 48 Vict. c.62), s. 11, as amended by Revenue Act 1889 (52 & 53 Vict. c.42), s. 19.
[3] Colonial Probates (Protected States and Mandated Territories) Act 1927 (c.43) extended the 1892 Act to protected and mandated territories.

1. Certificates to individual items of estate may be obtained, where confirmation has been granted, but not where a grant has been resealed.

2. With the appropriate drafting of the inventory, a confirmation will contain a description of heritable property in Scotland which is sufficient to identify the property for conveyancing purposes.[4] Such a description may not have been included in the grant since it is not, strictly speaking, necessary.[4a]

3. If a resealed grant is lost, it is necessary to raise an action in the Court of Session to prove the tenor of the lost deed,[4b] whereas if a Scottish confirmation is lost, a duplicate confirmation or individual certificates may be obtained.

4. Where a bond of caution is required before a grant may be resealed, a special form of bond must be obtained— see Styles 9.03 and 9.04.

5   Since resealing only operates in favour of the executors named in the original grant, it may not be appropriate.[5]

The only disadvantage of seeking confirmation is that, because the deceased died domiciled outside of Scotland, a special petition is required. The fees charged for resealing are the same as those for confirmation. In view of the factors listed above, the resealing procedure is now very rarely used.

Resealing of Commonwealth Grants

Countries to which the Colonial Probates Act 1892 applies

15.03   Those countries whose grants may be resealed under the Colonial Probates Act 1892[6] are normally fixed by Order in Council,[7]

---

[4] Succession (Scotland) Act 1964 (c.41), s. 15(1), as amended by Law Reform (Miscellaneous Provisions) (Scotland) Act 1968 (c.70), s. 19, and Act of Sederunt (Confirmation of Executors) 1964, s.1 (S.I. 1964 No. 1143), as amended by Act of Sederunt (Confirmation of Executors Amendment) 1966, s. 1.

[4a] Law Reform (Miscellaneous Provisions) (Scotland) Act 1968 (c.70), s.19 enabled probates or grants of administration sealed under the Colonial Probates Act 1892 to be a link in title, even if it did not contain a description of the property.

[4b] It may be possible to have a duplicate grant of probate or letters of administration resealed (as if the earlier resealing had not taken place).

[5] See paras. 15.16–15.18.

[6] Colonial Probates Act 1892 (55 & 56 Vict. c.6), s. 1.

[7] S.I. 1965 No. 1530 unless otherwise stated.

but occasionally the operational ambit of the 1892 Act has been extended by Act of Parliament. Resealing presently applies to grants made in the following Commonwealth countries:

Aden (if grant made before November 1, 1967)
Alberta
Antigua
Australian Capital Territory
Bahamas
Barbados
Basutoland (now Lesotho)
Bechuanaland Protectorate (now Botswana)
Belize (formerly British Honduras)
Bermuda
Botswana (formerly Bechuanaland Protectorate)
British Antarctic Territory
British Columbia
British Guiana (now Guyana)
British Honduras (now Belize)
British Solomon Islands Protectorate
British Sovereign Base Areas in Cyprus
Brunei
Cayman Islands
Ceylon (now Sri Lanka)
Christmas Island (Australia)
Cocos (Keeling) Islands
Cyprus (Republic)
Dominica
Falkland Islands
Fiji
Gambia
Ghana
Gibraltar
Gilbert and Ellice Islands
Grenada
Guyana (formerly British Guiana)
Hong Kong[18]

Jamaica
Kenya
Lesotho (formerly Basutoland)
Malawi
Malaysia
Manitoba
Montserrat
New Brunswick
New Guinea (Trust Territory)
New Hebrides[8]
New South Wales
New Zealand
Newfoundland
Nigeria
Norfolk Island
Northern Territory of Australia
North-West Territories of Canada
Nova Scotia
Ontario
Papua
Prince Edward Island
Queensland
St Christopher, Nevis and Anguilla
St Helena
St Lucia
St Vincent
Saskatchewan
Seychelles
Sierra Leone
Singapore[9]
South Australia
Southern Rhodesia
Sri Lanka (formerly Ceylon)
Swaziland Protectorate
Tanzania
Tasmania
Trinidad and Tobago

---

[8] It is likely that it will not be competent to reseal a Hong Kong grant after July 1, 1997, when sovereignty and jurisdiction over Hong Kong return to China.
[9] S.I. 1976 No. 579.
[10] Singapore Act 1966 (c.29), s. 1.

Turks and Caicos Islands   Western Australia
Uganda   Zambia
Victoria   Zimbabwe[11]
Virgin Islands

15.04   Although outside the Commonwealth, grants from South Africa[12] may be resealed.

15.05   Section 3 of the Colonial Probates Act 1892 also enables the resealing of a grant of probate or of letters of administration granted by a British court in a foreign country.[13]

15.06   It should be noted that grants from the Isle of Man or Channel Islands cannot be resealed, and Scottish confirmation must be obtained.

When resealing in Scotland is competent

15.07   The Colonial Probates Act 1892 provides that any grant of probate or letters of administration by a court in one of the countries listed in paragraph 15.03–15.04 may, on certain conditions, be resealed in the "Sheriff Court" of Lothian and Borders in Edinburgh.[14] The 1892 Act is merely an enabling provision, and the court accordingly has a discretion whether to reseal or not. Before resealing a Commonwealth grant:

> 1.   Where letters of administration have to be resealed, the court must be satisfied that there is sufficient caution to cover the property in the United Kingdom, without deduction of debts.[15]
>
> 2.   The court may require caution to be obtained to cover the payment of debts due from the estate to creditors residing in the United Kingdom.[16] The court will only consider whether to exercise this discretion if one of the creditors makes application, by way of a petition, to the sheriff.[17]

15.08   The court is empowered to take evidence as to the domicile of the deceased person.[18] There is a number of reasons why the

---

[11] Zimbabwe Act 1979 (c.60), s. 6(1) and Sched. 2, para. 2.

[12] South Africa Act 1962 (c.23), s. 2(1) Sched. 2, para. 1.

[13] Defined as any British court having jurisdiction out of the Queen's Dominions in pursuance of an Order in Council (Colonial Probates Act 1892 (55 & 56 Vict. c.6), s. 6).

[14] Colonial Probates Act 1892 (55 & 56 Vict. c.6), ss. 2(1) and 6.

[15] *Ibid.*, s. 2(2)(*b*).

[16] *Ibid.*, s. 2(3).

[17] Rules of Court made by the Sheriff of Lothians and Peebles for applying the Act—see Appendix to this Chapter.

[18] Colonial Probates Act 1892 (55 & 56 Vict. c.6), s. 2(2).

deceased's domicile is sigificant in resealing cases. First, although the 1892 Act does not expressly restrict the resealing process to grants where the deceased died domiciled overseas, commissary practice is to refuse to reseal a foreign grant where the deceased died domiciled in Scotland.

15.09   Secondly, before a grant will be resealed in Scotland, it is necessary to show that the persons in whose favour the grant was issued would have been entitled to confirmation in Scotland — that is, it must be shown that the persons in whose favour the grant was issued would have been entitled to office under the law of the country or of the state or province[19] where the deceased was domiciled at the time of his death.[20] This requirement will not cause a problem where the grant bears that when the deceased died he was domiciled in the country (or in the state or province) which issued the grant, since it is then axiomatic that the grantee was entitled to office under the law of his domicile. In other cases, it will be necessary to put to the court the opinion of a person versed in the laws of the deceased's domicile, confirming who, under those laws, is entitled to office.[21]

15.10   Thirdly, if, in terms of the general law, the deceased was domiciled in the United Kingdom, he would also have been domiciled there for inheritance tax purposes, and United Kingdom inheritance tax will be payable on his world-wide estate.[22]

Procedure for resealing in Scotland

15.11   The Rules of Court in connection with the resealing of a Commonwealth grant of probate or letters of administration are set out in the Appendix to this Chapter. The following are brief notes of what must be put up to the sheriff before a Commonwealth grant can be resealed:

1.   The original grant of probate or letters of administration,[23] or alternatively, a duplicate of the grant, sealed with the seal of the court granting it, or a copy thereof (which must contain a complete copy of the grant) certified as correct by and under authority of the court.[24]

The name and address of the Scottish agents presenting the inventory should be shown on the copies.

---

[19] In some countries — for instance, Australia and Canada — the law varies from state to state, or province to province.
[20] See, further, paras. 2.62 *et seq.*
[21] See, Styles 3.01, 3.02 and 3.04.
[22] Inheritance Tax Act 1984 (c.51), ss. 5(1) and 6(1).
[23] Colonial Probates Act 1892 (55 & 56 Vict. c.6), s. 2(1).
[24] *Ibid.*, s. 2(4).

2. Where a testamentary writing is annexed to the grant, a certified copy of it, or an exemplification, provided that it contains a full copy of the original grant with a copy of the will annexed (if appropriate).

    The name and address of the Scottish agents presenting the inventory should be shown on the copies.

3. The appropriate Scottish Inland Revenue inventory— either a Form A-3, Form D-1, or Form X-1—with the declaration amended for resealing (see Style 8.13) by deleting from the crave references to "confirmation" and substituting therefor "resealing."

    Overseas estate. Provided that the deceased was not domiciled in the United Kingdom for inheritance tax purposes within the meaning of section 267 of the Inheritance Tax Act 1984, property situated outside the United Kingdom need not be detailed, since no inheritance tax is payable on such estate.[25] Accordingly, the inventory need contain only a statement that "The deceased left estate in [*name country or countries*], which is being administered there," without specifying any value or details.

    First United Kingdom resealing in Scotland. Where the grant is being resealed in Scotland, before being resealed elsewhere in the United Kingdom, all the British estate should be detailed in the inventory (even although the Scottish estate alone is being resealed). Where the deceased died domiciled outside the United Kingdom, leaving estate in the United Kingdom in excess of £5,000,[26] the inventory must be forwarded to the Capital Taxes Office in Edinburgh before the grant can be resealed, and payment of any inheritance tax due on the United Kingdom estate[27] must be made. If the deceased was domiciled in the United Kingdom for inheritance tax purposes,[28] inheritance tax falls to be calculated on the United Kingdom estate[29] and any property situated outside the United

---

[25] Inheritance Tax Act 1984 (c.51), ss. 3(2) and 6(1).

[26] See *Inland Revenue Cap Form A-5 (1986)*, p. 1, arrangements permitted by Probate and Legacy Duties Act 1808 (48 Geo. 3, c.149), s.42, as amended by Inheritance Tax Act 1984 (c.51), s.256.

[27] Excluding, in the case of a member of a visiting armed force, his tangible moveable property and any emoluments due on death (Inheritance Tax Act 1984 (c.51), ss. 6(4) and 155), as amended by S.I. 1986 No. 948.

[28] Inheritance Tax Act 1984 (c.51), s. 267.

[29] Excluding where, in terms of the general law, the deceased was domiciled in the Channel Isles or the Isle of Man, war savings certificates, national savings certificates, premium savings bonds, deposits with the National Savings Bank and certified contractual savings schemes within the meaning of s. 326 of the Income and Corporation Taxes Act 1988 (c.1) (Inheritance Tax Act 1984 (c.51),

Kingdom. The inventory will then be returned, bearing an inheritance tax "paid" or "nil" stamp, and will be acceptable for submission for resealing.[29a]

Resealing has already taken place in England and Wales. If the grant has already been resealed in England and Wales, only the estate in Scotland need be shown in detail. A lump sum total, or a nil return as appropriate, should be shown for each of the estate in England and Wales, the estate in Northern Ireland and any taxable estate situated outside the United Kingdom.[30] The inventory should then be presented to the Capital Taxes Office in England which dealt with the case, in order that it can be stamped inheritance tax "paid" or "nil." Resealing may then be applied for.

Declaration made by attorney. In order to simplify the administration where the executor or administrator is abroad, the declaration in the inventory is almost always taken by an attorney or mandatory to the executor or administrator under the necessary power. The power of attorney should be in the form set out at Style 7.04 and it is advisable to have it executed in Scottish form—before one witness with the usual testing clause. Such a power of attorney should be referred to in the declaration to the inventory and docketed and signed with reference thereto.

4. Where necessary,[31] a bond of caution to the required amount: the bond is in a special form (see Styles 9.03 and 9.04).

5. The fees for resealing, based on the gross estate in Scotland.

Notes on Scottish practice on resealing

15.12 Sometimes, some of the executors nominated in a will are not included in the grant.

(a) Office declined or renounced before grant

15.13 If such an executor is referred to in the grant as having declined or renounced his rights to office, no further evidence of the

---

s. 6(3)), as amended by Income and Corporation Taxes Act 1988 (c.1), s.844 and Sched. 29, para. 32.).

[29a] Probate and Legacy Duties Act 1808 (48 Geo. 3, c. 149), s.42, as amended by Financee Act 1975 (c.7), s.19 and Sched. 4, para. 38(2).

[30] No detail need be given of the non-taxable estate: see *supra*.

[31] See Chap. 9.

declinature or renunciation is required. However, if there is no such reference, the executor who was not named in the grant must be cleared off in the normal way in the oath, and the original declinature or a certified copy thereof from the issuing court must be produced.

(b) Executor dies before grant issued

15.14   Similarly, if a nominated executor died *before* the grant was issued, and the grant issued was in favour of the survivors, then resealing will operate in favour of the survivors, the predeceasing executor being cleared off in the oath in normal course.

(c) Executor originally did not claim office, but grant reserved a power to him to claim office subsequently

15.15   Occasionally, the disparity between the nominated executors and those named in the grant can occur because a nominated executor did not claim the office in the court of the domicile, and the grant was issued in favour of the remaining executors with power being reserved to the other to claim the office at a later date if he so wished. A qualified declinature is not normally acceptable in a Scottish court, but if the deceased's domicile is abroad, then the Scottish court has no jurisdiction or concern with a title to any estate except that in Scotland and, in these circumstances, such a declinature is acceptable. In such cases, the grant may be resealed in favour of the persons in whose favour it was issued, the other being described and referred to in the oath as "not claiming the office."

15.16   It may, however, be that the persons who did not claim the office did so because they were resident in the United Kingdom, and they may now desire to act. In such a case, resealing is not appropriate, in that the 1892 Act merely permits the original grant to be resealed without modification. Instead, confirmation must be applied for.

(d) Executor in whose favour grant was issued dies

15.17   Where a person in whose favour the grant was issued has died since the date of issue, it is not competent to seek to have the grant resealed since, under the 1892 Act, resealing operates only in favour of the executors named in the original grant, without modification. Instead, Scottish confirmation should be applied for.

(e) Executor in whose favour grant was issued does not wish to continue to act in Scottish estate

15.18   An executor in whose favour the grant was issued may not wish to act in relation to the Scottish estate, perhaps because he is overseas. In such a case, resealing is not appropriate and, as confirmation cannot be granted here with a reservation of power to the executor who does not wish to act, he must decline the office of executor to the estate in Scotland, and the declinature must be produced before confirmation can be granted.

Form of resealing docket

15.19   The resealing docket takes the following form:

"Edinburgh, [*date*].

Sealed under and in terms of the Colonial Probates Act 1892. Amount of Estate in Scotland £   ."

Effect of resealing

15.20   Once the grant has been resealed, it has the like force and effect in the United Kingdom as if granted by the resealing court.[32] Thus, in the case of a probate, it will be equivalent to a confirmation-nominate and, in the case of a grant of letters of administration, it will be equivalent to a confirmation-dative.

Estate in Scotland and in other parts of the United Kingdom

15.21   A resealed grant is only effective in so far as moveable or heritable estate in Scotland is concerned. Consequently, if the deceased also held property in England and Wales or in Northern Ireland to which title is required, the grant must also be resealed in those countries. Where a grant has to be resealed in Scotland, and in England and Wales or Northern Ireland, all United Kingdom inheritance tax must be paid when resealing is first applied for.

15.22   In England a limited grant—that is, a grant to certain items of English estate only—has been resealed under the Colonial Probates Act 1892.[33]

Additional resealing

15.23   Where additional estate has been discovered since the grant was resealed, it is competent to have an additional resealing in respect of this estate, provided that all the executors in whose favour the original resealing was granted are still acting. An additional or corrective Inland Revenue inventory (Form D-1) is used, with the variation that in the oath, "resealing" is substituted for "confirmation," and in the crave, "resealing in respect of the additional estate [in the same terms as in the original inventory]," is substituted for "confirmation."

15.24   If a power of attorney was used in the original resealing, and it

---

[32] Colonial Probates Act 1892 (55 & 56 Vict. c.6), s. 2(1).
[33] *Smith* [1904] P. 114.

is still in force, then it may again be used to sign the additional inventory.

Ad omissa and ad non executa estate

15.25   If the executors in whose favour the original resealing was granted are dead or otherwise incapacitated from acting, it may be possible to obtain a title to administer any estate which was not included in the original resealing, or any estate included in the original resealing which has not been fully administered. The form required depends on the circumstances:

1.   If a *de bonis non* grant[34] has been made in the court which issued the original grant, then this grant may be resealed here in respect of the *ad omissa* or *ad non executa* estate, subject to the same rules and qualifications applicable to the original resealing.

   The fees payable are the resealing fees based on the gross estate in Scotland.

2.   If a *de bonis non* grant has not been issued then an *ad omissa* or *ad non executa* confirmation must be applied for. If an attorney is to sign the inventory, the power of attorney set out at Style 7.04, suitably amplified and amended for confirmation, should be used.

   In addition, there must be obtained an opinion by a person versant in the law of the place of the deceased's domicile[35] (*e.g.* a judge, solicitor, notary, etc., who is not connected with the solicitors acting in the deceased's estate) briefly narrating the history of the case in hand, and stating specifically who is now entitled to carry on the administration of the unadministered estate. If more than one person is so entitled, and all are not acting, the opinion must state whether or not it is necessary to obtain the consents of the others. It should be noted that general references to sections in statutes, etc., are not acceptable. The opinion may be based on Style 3.04.

   If the inventory contains any *ad omissa* estate, it must be assessed to inheritance tax, and bear an inheritance "tax paid" or "nil" stamp.

   The fees payable are the usual confirmation fees based on the estate in Scotland only.

---

[34] The equivalent of the Scottish *ad omissa* or *ad non executa* confirmation.
[35] Rather than the law of the place from which the grant was issued.

RESEALING OF SCOTTISH CONFIRMATIONS

Resealing of Scottish confirmations in a Commonwealth country

15.26   The Commonwealth and other countries listed at 15.03–15.04 have all set up arrangements corresponding to those set out in the Colonial Probates Act 1892, which enable a Scottish confirmation to be resealed in the Commonwealth or other country. Indeed, before a particular country can be included in the Order of Council, it must be shown that adequate provision for this has been made.[36] The Acts of the various Commonwealth countries concerned are in similar terms to the 1892 Act.

Requirements to be met before a Scottish confirmation can be resealed

15.27   In order for a Scottish confirmation to be resealed in any court where resealing is competent, there must be produced in that court

1.   the confirmation itself, or a certified extract thereof; and

2.   a certified extract of any testamentary writing.[37]

15.28   The certified copies must be signed by the clerk of the issuing court under the court seal, with the signature authenticated by the sheriff (see Style 5.01).

15.29   No other authentication is normally required before a Scottish confirmation will be resealed by a Commonwealth court although, of course, the local Revenue affidavits, etc., must be lodged in the court abroad. Sometimes evidence is required that the United Kingdom inheritance tax has been paid on the estate. The foreign court is normally satisfied by a full copy of the Inland Revenue inventory, including all accounts, etc., prepared by the agent and certified by the Capital Taxes Office, or alternatively by a certificate of discharge, in respect of the whole death estate, issued in terms of section 239(2) of the Inheritance Tax Act 1984.

---

[36] Colonial Probates Act 1892 (55 & 56 Vict. c.6), s. 1.

[37] In the case of grants of probate or letters of administration, any testamentary writing is normally annexed thereto. Therefore, while a testamentary writing does not form part of a confirmation, it is generally considered safer if an authenticated copy of the testamentary writing is put up with the confirmation for resealing—lest the Commonwealth court refuse to reseal until the testamentary writing is produced.

APPENDIX
RULES OF COURT MADE BY THE SHERIFF OF THE LOTHIANS AND
PEEBLES FOR REGULATING THE PROCEDURE AND PRACTICE IN
THE SHERIFF COURT OF EDINBURGH IN CONNECTION WITH THE
COLONIAL PROBATES ACT 1892 c.6
(EDINBURGH, June 9, 1893)

Whereas by the said Act, entitled "An Act to provide for the recognition in the United Kingdom of Probates and Letters of Administration granted in British Possessions" (May 20, 1892), it is enacted, Section 2(5), that "Rules of the Court may be made for regulating the procedure and practice, including fees and costs in Courts of the United Kingdom on and incidental to an application for sealing a Probate or Letters of Administration granted in a British Possession to which this Act applies,"—the Sheriff enacts and ordains as follows:

1. When any Probate or Letters of Administration granted by a Court of Probate in any [country] to which this Act applies is produced along with a copy thereof in the Sheriff Court of Edinburgh, it shall be sealed by the Commissary Clerk with the Seal of Office of the Commissariot of Edinburgh. Provided—
    (1) That a duly stamped Inventory, with relative oath in the ordinary form modified to suit the circumstances, has been exhibited in said Court, which Inventory, after being recorded, shall be transmitted to the Commissioners of Inland Revenue: but it shall not be necessary to record along with said Inventory any Testamentary Writings of which a copy is deposited in terms of the Act.
    (2) That in the case of Letters of Administration, Caution has been found to cover the Estate in Scotland given up in such Inventory, and that such Caution shall be subject to the same rules as regards restriction thereof, the terms of the bond and otherwise, as are applicable to caution for Executors-dative.
    (3) That no application has been made under subsection 3 of section 2 of the Act, or that such application has been disposed of, and that any such application shall be by Petition to the Sheriff.

2. The oath to the Inventory shall set forth the domicile of the deceased at the time of his death; and where, on any ground, it may appear doubtful whether the person or persons in whose favour the grant of Probate or Letters of Administration has been made, would be entitled to confirmation in Scotland, such grant shall not be sealed without the special authority of the Sheriff.

3. The Commissary Clerk shall, by note on the document sealed, set forth that it is sealed under and in terms of

the Colonial Probates Act 1892, and the amount of the Estate in Scotland, and such note shall be dated and signed by him.

4. The ordinary fees shall be charged for examining and recording the Inventory and oath.

ALEXR. BLAIR

CHAPTER 16

TRANSMISSION OF TRUST AND EXECUTRY PROPERTY

Introduction

16.01   Where a trustee or executor holding trust or executry property dies, the question arises as to how the title to the property can be transferred. If the trustee or executor who has died is but one of a number of trustees or executors who are all registered holders, the title to the asset will (except in the case of a "joint appointment") accresce to the surviving trustees and executors. However, where the trustee or executor who dies is the sole or last surviving trustee registered as holder, or the sole or last surviving executor confirmed, the matter is more complex. Clearly, there will be no surviving trustee or executor able to give a good title to the property and instead a variety of legal processes have been developed to resolve the problem (see paras. 16.02 to 16.17). Similar difficulties can arise where a sole trustee has become insane or incapable of acting, for which other solutions have been devised (see paras. 16.18 to 16.20).

Sole trustee or executor has inmixed funds with his own estate

16.02   Where the sole trustee or executor has so inmixed the funds with his own estate that it cannot be separately identified, the funds cannot be dealt with as trust property. Instead, it is necessary to confirm all the extant estate as belonging to the deceased trustee or executor, and then to deduct the trust or executry claim as a debt.

16.03   In the case of a sole trustee, there is a particular problem in this connection with investments in companies registered under the laws of England and Wales, in that such companies will not recognise a trust,[1] and share certificates will be issued showing the name of the trustee as the registered holder, without any qualification as to his capacity being noted. Where it is possible to identify the asset as a trust investment nevertheless, there would seem to be no objection to adopting the quasi-confirmation or quasi-probate or confirmation *ad non executa* procedures outlined below.

---

[1] Companies Act 1985 (c.6), s. 360.

443

Quasi-confirmation

(a) To trust and executry property in Scotland: section 6 of the Executors (Scotland) Act 1900[2]

16.04 Where, on or after September 10, 1964,[3] a sole or last surviving trustee[4] or executor (A) has died with any property (whether heritable or moveable) situated in Scotland vested[5] in him as trustee or executor, A's executors (whether nominate or dative) may[6] append to the inventory (or additional inventory) to his estate a note or statement of such property.[7] The inventory must disclose estate in Scotland—which may be fictitious, and of nominal value. The note or statement appended must include

1. a reference to the deed, confirmation or other document whereby any property, referred to in the note or statement and not standing or vested in the name of the deceased trustee or executor or to which he had not completed title, became vested in him[8];

2. any moveable property held by the deceased in trust; and

3. a description of any heritable property or interest therein held by the deceased in trust, the description to be sufficient to identify the heritable property as a separate item.[9]

While there is no statutory requirement that such trust property is valued in the inventory, it can be of assistance to the Capital

---

[2] (63 & 64 Vict. c.65), as amended by Succession (Scotland) Act 1964 (c.41), Sched. 2, para. 13; Administration of Estates Act 1971 (c.25), Sched. 1, para. 2 and Statute Law (Repeals) Act 1974 (c.22).

[3] Where the deceased trustee or executor died before Sept. 10, 1964, reference should be made to the 7th edition of this work at pp. 248–250.

[4] "Trustee" is assumed to include not just testamentary trustees but anyone who holds property in trust for another, whether there is a written constitution of trust or not. It clearly covers curators and judicial factors.

[5] In the case of an executor, this includes property which he has confirmed to, even if he has not made up title in his own name as executor (Succession (Scotland) Act 1964 (c.41), s. 14(1)).

[6] It should be noted that the executors of the deceased trustee or executor cannot be forced to make up title to the trust property in this way (Executors (Scotland) Act 1900 (63 & 64 Vict. c.55), s. 6, as amended by Succession (Scotland) Act 1964 (c.41), Sched. 2, para. 13; Administration of Estates Act 1971 (c.25), Sched. 1, para. 2 and Statute Law (Repeals) Act 1974 (c.22), Sched.).

[7] Executors (Scotland) Act 1900 (63 & 64 Vict. c.55), s. 6, as amended by Succession (Scotland) Act 1964 (c.41), Sched. 2, para. 13; Administration of Estates Act 1971 (c.25), Sched. 1, para. 2 and Statute Law (Repeals) Act 1974 (c.22), Sched.

[8] Act of Sederunt (Confirmation of Executors) 1964, s. 2(1)(a) (S.I. 1964 No. 1143).

[9] Act of Sederunt (Confirmation of Executors) 1964, s. 1 (as amended by Act of Sederunt (Confirmation of Executors Amendment) Act 1966, s. 1) and s. 2(1) (S.I. 1966 No. 593).

Taxes Office if values are shown. The note or statement may be appended on a Form A-3, B-3 or B-4 (see style of note in Style 10.03). See summary of procedure at paragraph 16.21.

16.05   The confirmation granted in favour of A's executors will then repeat the note or statement.[10] This enables A's executors to recover such property, and either

1.   assign and transfer it to such person or persons as may be legally authorised to continue to administer it; or

2.   where administration is complete, transfer it directly to the beneficiaries entitled to it; or

3.   transfer it to any person or persons whom the beneficiaries may appoint to receive and discharge, realise and distribute the property.[11]

Under this procedure, A's executors cannot continue to administer the estate as if they were the executors of the original deceased.

16.06   If, after confirmation has been obtained to the estate of the deceased trustee or executor, it is discovered that trust or executry property was vested in him alone, it will be necessary to give up an additional inventory or Form D-1 (to which the note of the trust or executry property may be appended) and to expede an eik to the confirmation. In such cases, it may be necessary to restate at a nominal increase of value some item of estate previously confirmed, or to confirm to a fictitious asset in Scotland[12] (see Style 10.04).

(b) To trust and executry property situated in England and Wales or Northern Ireland

16.07   Where the deceased trustee or executor died domiciled in Scotland, and confirmation or additional confirmation, which notes that domicile, is granted in respect of property situated in Scotland, the note or statement appended to the inventory may include property situated in England and Wales or in Northern Ireland held by the deceased in trust,[13] and such a note or statement will be recognised in England and Wales and Northern

---

[10] Act of Sederunt (Confirmation of Executors Amendment) 1966, s. 2(2) (S.I. 1966 No. 593).

[11] Executors (Scotland) Act 1900 (63 & 64 Vict. c.55), s. 6, as amended by Succession (Scotland) Act 1964 (c.41), Sched. 2, para. 13, Administration of Estates Act 1971 (c.25), Sched. 1, para. 2 and Statute Law (Repeals) Act 1974 (c.22), Sched.

[12] It is necessary to have an additional inventory to which the note is to be appended (see s. 6 of the 1900 Act).

[13] Administration of Estates Act 1971 (c.25), s. 5(1).

Ireland.[14] The note or statement may be appended on a Form
A-3, B-3 or B-4.

16.08   It will be noted that, unlike the remedy described in paragraphs
16.04–16.06, this remedy only applies if the deceased trustee or
executor died domiciled in Scotland.

16.09   If the deceased trustee or executor died while domiciled in Scotland, but personally held no estate in Scotland to which his
executors require to confirm, it will be necessary to confirm to
a fictitious asset in Scotland[15] (see Style 10.03). See summary of
procedure at paragraph 16.21.

Quasi-probate: section 6 of the Executors (Scotland) Act 1900

16.10   Where the sole or last surviving trustee or executor (A) died
domiciled in England and Wales or in Northern Ireland, probate
granted there, which notes A's domicile therein, gives the executors a similar right to make up title to the trust or executry
property.[16] It should be noted that since section 6 is limited to
cases where probate was granted, it does not provide a remedy
where A died domiciled in England and Wales or in Northern
Ireland, and letters of administration have been issued. In such
a case, the only way in which section 6 can provide a remedy
is if confirmation-dative can be obtained in Scotland to A's
Scottish estate, with a note of the trust property being
appended.[17] However, it should be remembered that title
cannot be made up in this way to trust property situated in
England and Wales or Northern Ireland since A died domiciled
outwith Scotland.[18]

Confirmation *ad non executa*: section 7 of the Executors (Scotland) Act 1900[19]

16.11   Where confirmation has become inoperative because of the
death or incapacity of all the executors (whether dative or
nominate) in whose favour it was granted, confirmation *ad non
executa* may be granted to any estate contained in the original
confirmation which has not been uplifted or transferred to the

---

[14] *Ibid.*, s. 5(2).

[15] It is necessary to have an additional inventory to which the note is to be
appended (see s. 6 of the 1900 Act).

[16] See Executors (Scotland) Act 1900 (63 & 64 Vict. c.55), s.6 as amended by
Administration of Estates Act 1971 (c.25), Sched. 1, para. 2.

[17] See para. 16.04.

[18] See para. 16.07.

[19] (63 & 64 Vict. c.55), as amended by Succession (Scotland) Act 1964 (c.41),
Sched. 2, para. 14.

persons entitled thereto[20] (see Style 10.05). The executors confirmed *ad non executa* have sufficient title to continue and complete the administration of the estate[21]: unlike the quasi-confirmation and quasi-probate processes described at paragraphs 16.04 and 16.10 above, they do not require to denude in favour of trustees or beneficiaries. It is expressly provided that the rights and preferences conferred by confirmation on executors-creditor are not to be affected.

16.12   Where the failure of the executry administration is due to the incapacity of an executor, a medical certificate certifying the original executor's incapacity to act must be produced.

16.13   The persons entitled to confirmation *ad non executa* are those entitled to confirmation *ad omissa*, the rules being the same[22] (see paras. 17.17 *et seq.*). Where they are to be confirmed as executors-dative, they first require to petition to be decerned as executors-dative (see Style 6.35).

16.14   As confirmation *ad non executa* is viewed as an additional confirmation, it would therefore seem that in addition to confirmation *ad non executa* applying to estate in Scotland, it will also apply to estate in England and Wales or in Northern Ireland, provided that the confirmation notes that the deceased was domiciled in Scotland.[23]

16.15   See paragraph 15.25 on procedure where there is *ad non executa* estate which has to be resealed.

The inventory
16.16   The executor applying for confirmation *ad non executa* must complete the Form X-1, which can be obtained from the sheriff clerk's office. It is important to ensure that the narrative of the items of estate shown in the *ad non executa* inventory mirrors the entries in the original confirmation, in order to show that it is estate *ad non executa* (on which no further inheritance tax is payable) as opposed to estate *ad omissa* (on which further inheritance tax must be paid). Usually, the items will simply be re-listed. Sometimes, however, this is not possible. For instance, the original executor may have uplifted or realised the asset originally confirmed to and reinvested it: in that case, the narrative of the reinvestment in the *ad non executa* inventory should state that it "represents the [*identify original asset*] contained in the original confirmation." Again, the description of a shareholding may have been altered, perhaps by the company

---

[20] Executors (Scotland) Act 1900 (63 & 64 Vict. c.55), s. 7, as amended by Succession (Scotland) Act 1964 (c.41), Sched. 2, para. 14.
[21] *Ibid.*
[22] *Ibid.*
[23] Administration of Estates Act 1971 (c.25), ss. 1(1) and (7) and 2(1) and (6).

changing its name, or by conversion: in this case, the asset should be described in the *ad non executa* inventory by its original description as in the confirmation, and thereafter stated to be "now represented by [*new description*]."

16.17   Confirmation *ad non executa* is a competent midcouple or link in title for the purposes of any deduction of title in relation to the estate from the former executors.[24-25]

It is also competent for an executor to be confirmed *ad non executa et ad omissa.*

Appointment of new trustees or executors-nominate by the court

16.18   Under section 22 of the Trusts (Scotland) Act 1921, where a "sole trustee" is or has become insane, or is or has become incapable of acting because of physical or mental disability appointed in or acting under any trust, the Court of Session or an appropriate sheriff court may appoint a trustee or trustees. The court may grant warrant to the new trustees to complete title to any heritable property forming part of the trust estate and specify the moveable or personal property, which shall operate as an assignation thereof in favour of the new trustees.

Completion of title in lapsed trust

16.19   As an alternative to having new trustees or executors appointed where the previous ones have died or become incapable of acting, it is possible for the beneficiary who is entitled to the possession of any heritable, moveable or personal property for his own absolute use to apply to the court for authority to make up title to such property in his own name. Such a petition is raised in the Court of Session or an appropriate sheriff court. Decree is equivalent to a conveyance of heritage to the petitioner, and an assignation to him of the moveable and personal estate.[26]

16.20   The procedure may also be used by any person deriving right from the deceased trustee or executor, who can show that he is entitled to possession "for his own absolute use." The consequence is that the procedure cannot be adopted by the testamentary trustees or executors of such a beneficiary,[27] and in

---

[24-25] Executors (Scotland)Act 1900 (63 & 64 Vict. c.55), s. 7, as amended by Succession (Scotland) Act 1964 (c.41), Sched. 2, para. 14.

[26] Trusts (Scotland) Act 1921 (11 & 12 Geo. 5, c.58), s. 24, as amended by Law Reform (Miscellaneous Provisions) (Scotland) Act 1980 (c.55), s. 13.

[27] *McClymont's Trs., Petrs.*, 1922 S.L.T. 379; *Scott's Trs., Petrs.*, 1957 S.L.T. (Notes) 45; *cf. Paisley Cemetery Co. Ltd., Petrs.*, 1933 S.L.T. 415.

such cases it would be appropriate to petition the court under section 22 of the Trusts (Scotland) Act 1921 for the appointment of new trustees (or executors).

SUMMARY OF PROCEDURE UNDER SECTION 6 OF THE EXECUTORS (SCOTLAND) ACT 1900

16.21 Where it is desired to adopt the procedure which is set out in section 6 of the Executors (Scotland) Act 1900 for making up title to trust property in a lapsed trust:

1. Append to the inventory or corrective inventory, after the summary for confirmation, a note of the trust property;

2. Include in the note a statement containing the following details:
    (a) a statement that the deceased was the "last surviving" or "sole" trustee or executor, and
    (b) a statement that the property referred to in the note stands in the name of the deceased; and
    (c) the deed, confirmation or other document whereby the property referred to in the note became vested in the deceased;

3. Where the trust property includes estate in Scotland (whether heritable or moveable)
    (a) Ensure that estate in Scotland is being confirmed to, in the normal way, whether it is real, or a fictitious "nominal sum";
    (b) Set out in the note, a list, under a heading "Estate in Scotland," of the items situated in Scotland (whether heritable or moveable), giving full details of such property, and its value at the time of the death of the last surviving or sole trustee or executor;

4. Where the trust property includes estate in England and Wales or Northern Ireland (whether heritable or moveable) the procedure is *only* competent if the deceased trustee or executor died domiciled in Scotland. Therefore
    (a) Ensure that estate in Scotland is being confirmed to, in the normal way, whether it is real, or a fictitious "nominal sum";
    (b) List, under a heading "Estate in England and Wales" or "Estate in Northern Ireland", the items situated there (whether real or personal), giving full details of such property, and its value at the time of the death of the last surviving or sole trustee or executor.

CHAPTER 17

ADDITIONAL INVENTORIES AND CONFIRMATIONS

Introduction

17.01 If, after recording the original inventory, the executors discover additional estate, they must, within two calendar months of the discovery, exhibit in the proper sheriff or commissary court, an additional inventory of the discovered estate, in which the amount of the original inventory is specified,[1] and they may obtain an eik to the original confirmation in respect of the discovered estate, both heritable and moveable.[2]

CORRECTIVE INVENTORIES

17.02 Where no additional estate has to be given up or confirmed to, but the amount of inheritance tax payable falls to be adjusted, a corrective inventory (Form D-1) may have to be prepared, though the matter may also be dealt with by informal letters. The following notes may be of assistance.

   1.   The deposition should be made by the executor personally.[3]

   2.   In cases where too little tax has been paid because the original account was "defective in a material respect by reason of anything contained in or omitted from it," the corrective inventory must be delivered within six calendar months after the discovery of the mistake, for payment of the deficient tax and interest.[4] Before calculating the amount of the additional tax, correction can be made of an insufficient deduction in respect of debts and funeral expenses.

   3.   Where the corrective inventory has been duly assessed

---

[1] The Probate and Legacy Duties Act 1808 (48 Geo. 3, c.149) s. 38 (repealed 12–14 Geo.VI, c.47 (Scheds. I, IV and V); Finance Act 1975 (c.7), Sched. 13).
[2] Confirmation of Executors (Scotland) Act 1823 (4 Geo. 4; c.98), s. 3 as amended by Succession (Scotland) Act 1964 (c.41), (4 Geo. 4, c.98), s. 14(1).
[3] Inheritance Tax Act 1984 (c.51), s. 216(1).
[4] *Ibid.*, s. 217.

by the Capital Taxes Office and the tax paid, it should be lodged at once with the commissary or sheriff clerk, if it contains any additional executry estate in respect of which confirmation is or may be required. Where confirmation is not required, the fact that confirmation is not required can be stated on the Form D-1 at page 1, and a request may be placed thereon that the corrective inventory, after being stamped, be passed direct to the registrar for the purpose of filing in the Capital Taxes Office. In this case, once the corrective inventory has been duly assessed, and tax paid as necessary, the Capital Taxes Office, Edinburgh, may file it without it being recorded.

4. "Delivery" takes place only when the inventory is delivered for recording in the court books or for filing at the Capital Taxes Office.

5. Where too much inheritance tax has been paid, the corrective inventory (duly deponed to) should be sent to the registrar of the Capital Taxes Office with a written application explaining the circumstances.

EIKS TO THE CONFIRMATION

General

17.03   The Confirmation of Executors (Scotland) Act 1823 (which abolished partial confirmation) provided that it was still competent to eik to the original confirmation any estate discovered after the original confirmation was granted, but the eik must contain the whole of the additional estate. The relevant form is the Form D-1. Though a separate document, it is really an addition to the original confirmation—the sum confirmed in the eik and the title granted by it are limited to the additional estate. The first eik applied for is so named, but there may be a second and a third eik, and more if required.

17.04   Provided that the deceased was domiciled in Scotland, the confirmation will give title to the executors to estate in Scotland, England and Wales[5] or Northern Ireland.[6] An eik may be resealed under the Colonial Probates Act 1892, giving title to the estate in the Commonwealth country where the resealing takes place.

17.05   Where the deceased was domiciled abroad, and Commonwealth

---

[5] Administration of Estates Act 1971 (c.25), s. 1(1) and (7).
[6] *Ibid*, s. 2(2) and (6).

letters of administration or grant of probate have been resealed in Scotland, it may be possible to use the *ad omissa* procedure,[7] but errors in the confirmation cannot be corrected.

What appears in the eik

17.06 An eik—unless confirmed by an executor-creditor, which may be limited to the amount of the creditor's debt[8]—must contain the whole of the deceased's estate not already confirmed.[9]

17.07 The eik will not always show additional value—it may contain only one item (shares saleable only at a discount), stated to be of "no value" and an eik to the confirmation will be issued accordingly.[10]

17.08 An eik may also correct any error that may have been made in the original inventory. Thus, estate which has been over-estimated may be set out at its true value, and the difference deducted. If any item has been wrongly included, it may also be deducted. The schedule of debts may also be amended, either by addition or deduction. If any item contained in the original inventory and confirmation has been so inaccurately entered or described that it cannot be uplifted by the executors, the remedy is to lodge a corrective additional inventory, in which, after setting out the amount in the original inventory, and deducting the value of the item incorrectly entered, the item is correctly set out as new or additional estate under the head of effects omitted (Style 10.02). There will be no additional tax payable, if the estate (though wrongly described) was correctly valued in the original inventory.

Original executors had been confirmed

17.09 Additional estate may be confirmed in the form of an eik by the executors currently acting—the executors already confirmed, with the exception of any who have since died or resigned office, and with the addition of any executors assumed by executors-nominate or appointed by the court. Where an executor has resigned or been assumed, the relative deed of resignation or deed of assumption must be produced, referred to in the oath, and docketed and signed as relative thereto.

---

[7] See para. 15.25.

[8] Confirmation of Executors (Scotland) Act 1823 (4 Geo. 4, c.98), s. 4.

[9] *Ibid.*, s. 3 as amended by Succession (Scotland) Act 1964 (c.41), s. 14(1).

[10] *Wilson*, Sept. 22, 1905, unreported.

Original executors had not been confirmed

17.10   If confirmation of the additional estate is required, and no part of the estate has been previously confirmed, although the inventory has been recorded in the commissary court books, then, as there can be no partial confirmation, the whole must be included in the confirmation craved.[11] The grant is in that case the principal confirmation, though proceeding on an additional inventory, and the fee payable is the difference between the total confirmation fee on the whole confirmable estate, less the recording fee already paid.

Substitute executors to those originally confirmed

17.11   Where the original testamentary writing provided for a substitute executor on, say, the death of the original executors, the substitute executor has in some cases expeded an eik,[12] but a confirmation *ad omissa* (see paras. 17.17 et seq.) appears to be the more correct form.

Confirmed executor is now insane

17.12   Where one of a number of confirmed executors has become insane, and has been removed by court decree in terms of section 23 of the Trusts (Scotland) Act 1921,[13] if additional estate is thereafter discovered, an eik to the confirmation will be issued in favour of the remaining executors, the fact that one of the confirmed executors has been removed by court decree being referred to in the eik.[14]

17.13   If, after confirmation has been issued, the sole executor becomes insane, an eik to the confirmation may be expede on the application of his *curator bonis*.[15] It should, however, be noted that the curator's right to sign on behalf of the executor may not be recognised outside Scotland, which may cause a problem if the deceased held estate outside Scotland which has to be confirmed to. In such a case, the appointment of a new executor under section 22 of the Trusts (Scotland) Act 1921[16] may be the preferable course, with the new executor thereafter expeding the eik.

---

[11] Confirmation of Executors (Scotland) Act 1823 (4 Geo, 4, c.98), s. 3 as amended by Succession (Scotland) Act 1964 (c41), s. 14(1).

[12] *Murray*, Feb. 1, 1886, unreported.

[13] (11 & 12 Geo. 5, c.58) as amended by Law Reform (Miscellaneous Provisions) (Scotland) Act 1980 (c.55) s. 13.

[14] *Stewart*, Nov. 8, 1945, unreported.

[15] *Mailer*, Nov. 1, 1888, unreported.

[16] as amended by Law Reform (Miscellaneous Provisions) (Scotland) Act 1980 (11 & 12 Geo. 5, c.58), (c.55), s. 13(a).

Eiks and bonds of caution

17.14   Where executors-dative seek an eik to the confirmation in their favour, if there is any increase in the value of the gross amount of the estate situated in the United Kingdom, a bond of caution must be obtained to cover the excess over the original bond. If, however, there is no net increase in the gross estate, no further caution will be required.[17] Caution will also not be required if the executor-dative is the deceased's surviving spouse who has right to the whole of the deceased's intestate estate (including the estate shown in the additional inventory) in terms of section 9(2) of the Succession (Scotland) Act 1964.[18]

Eiks and inheritance tax

17.15   The Form O-1 should be submitted for assessment and stamping at the Capital Taxes Office before it is lodged with the sheriff clerk for confirmation, whether or not inheritance tax is payable. Where, in the interval between lodging the original and additional inventories, there has been a refund or an additional payment of inheritance tax, such refunds or payments must be taken into account in adjusting the tax due on the form.

17.16   If additional or corrective inventories containing estate for which an eik was not required have been lodged at the Capital Taxes Office for adjustment of tax only, then, if additional estate is thereafter discovered to which an eik is required, these intermediate inventories must be lodged for recording in the commissary court books. If any of the intermediate inventories contain confirmable estate, then, since a partial confirmation is incompetent, the confirmable estate must be included in the eik and either of two alternative courses may be adopted:

1.   the oath to the intermediate inventory may be amended to crave an eik, but it should be remembered that if the date of the original oath is more than six months past, the crave is held to be abandoned and the inventory must be re-sworn—if this course of action is followed, the intermediate inventory is treated as a separate additional inventory, and two eiks (one in respect of each additional inventory) are issued, confirmation fees being charged on the face value of each in normal course; or

2.   the intermediate inventory or inventories may be com-

---

[17] *Wilson*, Sept. 22, 1905, unreported.
[18] Confirmation of Executors (Scotland) Act 1823 (4 Geo. 4, c.98), s. 2 as amended by Statute Law Revision Act 1888, (51 Vict. c.3) Sched., Pt. I, Statute Law Revision (No. 2) Act 1890 (53 & 54 Vict. c.51). Sched., Pt. II and Law Reform (Miscellaneous Provisions) (Scotland) Act 1980 (c.5), s. 5.

bined with the additional inventory now being lodged and one eik issued to the whole estate, one fee only being payable.

CONFIRMATION *AD OMISSA* AND CONFIRMATION *AD OMISSA VEL MALE APPRETIATA*

Confirmation *ad omissa* or confirmation *ad omissa vel male appretiata*

17.17   Confirmation *ad omissa* is the competent form of title, where an eik cannot be obtained, because all the executors originally confirmed have resigned or died, but it is necessary to obtain title to some item of estate which was omitted in the original confirmation, and which therefore still remains *in bonis* of the deceased.[19] It is also an appropriate procedure where the original executor declines to act.[20] If, in addition to estate being omitted from the original confirmation, some estate has been undervalued, then confirmation *ad omissa vel male appretiata* is the competent form of title.

17.18   There is one case where confirmation *ad omissa* (or *ad omissa vel male appretiata*) will be granted in favour of an executor who has already been confirmed—that is an executry where the original confirmation had been granted under the Small Estates Acts and the additional estate brings the estate above the small estates limit (see, further, para. 11.21).

Who are to be confirmed *ad omissa* or *ad omissa vel male appretiata*

17.19   The question of who is to be confirmed *ad omissa* (or *ad omissa vel male appretiata*) is decided as if the persons confirmed had not taken up office—as if they had survived the deceased but had all declined to act or had died before expeding confirmation. Thus, where a testator had appointed A, whom failing, B, to be his executor, B would be entitled to be confirmed *ad omissa* (or *ad omissa vel male appretiata*). If confirmation cannot be made in a nominate capacity, an executor dative appointment must be made. If the original appointment had been of a person (E) as executor because of his rights to succeed to the estate, since the succession to the estate of the original deceased opens at the moment of his natural death, when the characters of his heirs

---

[19] *Atkinson* v. *Learmonth*, Jan. 14, 1808 F.C.; *Warrender*, Jan. 11, 1884, unreported); *Jazdowski*, Mar. 19, 1889, unreported.

[20] *Darling*, June 15, 1906, unreported.

are irrevocably fixed,[21] it is not possible to confirm *ad omissa* (or *ad omissa vel male appretiata*) *qua* beneficiaries those who would have been entitled to share in the deceased's estate only if one of the actual beneficiaries (such as E) had predeceased (but see also para. 17.21).

17.20   The present commissary practice is to confirm as executor *ad omissa* (or *ad omissa vel male appretiata*) in the following order:

1.   the executor specifically nominated under the testamentary writing of the deceased, that is, persons nominated (failing the originally appointed executors) as substitute executors[22]: they will be confirmed as executors-nominate;

2.   In terms of section 3 of the Executors (Scotland) Act 1900, the persons nominated as substitute testamentary trustees: they will be confirmed as executors–nominate.

3.   in terms of section 3 of the Executors (Scotland) Act 1900, the general disponee, universal legatory or residuary legatee[23]: if all are able to take office, they will be confirmed as executors-nominate, otherwise one or more will be confirmed as executor(s)-dative; and

4.   those who would have been originally entitled to be confirmed as executor-dative, whether as heir under the Succession (Scotland) Act 1964, as creditor, or whatever[24]: they will be confirmed as executors-dative.

17.21   If any person within categories 3 and 4 above has died, then his executors will be entitled to be confirmed *ad omissa* (or *ad omissa vel male appretiata*) as executors-dative[25] *qua* representatives of the deceased beneficiary,[26] but only after they have confirmed to the deceased beneficiary's estate, including therein his interest in the estate of the original deceased[27] (see Styles 6.02 and 6.06 for dative petition and 8.15 and 8.16 for the oath).

17.22   Example:

A died intestate on June 1, 1990, survived by his widow, B, and uncles and aunts. If by virtue of her prior rights

---

[21] Except in exceptional cases such as where a nearer heir is *in utero* at the death of the predecessor, and is born alive.

[22] See 5.28–5.32.

[23] See 5.50–5.85.

[24] See Chap. 6.

[25] Representatives are always confirmed as executors-dative, and are not entitled to the office of executor-nominate.

[26] *Webster* v. *Shiress* (1878) 6 R. 102; *Chrystal* v. *Chrystal*, 1923 S.L.T. (Sh. Ct.) 69.

[27] Bell, *Prin.*, para. 1896.

under the Succession (Scotland) Act 1964, B takes A's whole estate, B is entitled to be appointed executrix, and is so confirmed. B dies without having completed the administration of the estate and additional estate is thereafter found[28] of such an amount that it will all pass to B by virtue of her prior rights. A's uncles and aunts have no beneficial interest in the estate.[29] It is therefore B's executors (whether nominate or dative) who will be confirmed *ad omissa* (or *ad omissa vel ad non executa*) *qua* representative of the surviving spouse to A's estate having indicated in the confirmation to A's estate the sum due to her from B's estate.

Procedure where the original executor declines to act

17.23 Where the original executor-nominate declines to act, and a substitute executor seeks to be confirmed, it is sufficient for the original executor to sign a letter of declinature, which will then be referred to in the deposition, and produced and docketed as relative thereto. In other cases the petition for confirmation *ad omissa* (or *ad omissa vel male appretiata*) but the petition must be served on any executor confirmed[30] who is still alive and is not *incapax*.

17.23B If there are grounds to presume fraud, confirmation *ad omissa* (or *ad omissa vel male appretiata*) will be granted to the exclusion of the principal executors.[31] But if it appears that the executor has neither left out nor understated any item *dolose*, the items omitted, or the difference between the estimations in the principal confirmation and the true value will be added to the eik to the confirmation in favour of the principal executors,[32] and only if the principal executors do not confirm will confirmation *ad omissa* (or *ad omissa vel male appretiata*) be granted.

17.24 Where the principal executor is an executor-creditor, he is not entitled to prevent another creditor being decerned and confirmed *ad omissa* (or *ad omissa vel male appretiata*); but he may be conjoined with him.[33]

---

[28] If no additional estate is found, title to the unadministered estate will be made up in terms of the procedures discussed in Chap. 16.

[29] Some (but not all) of them may be entitled to be decerned executors-dative *qua* next-of-kin to the deceased.

[30] *Duff* v. *Alves*, 1631, Mor. 2188.

[31] *Robertson* v. *Robertson* (Feb. 16, 1703), Mor. 3498.

[32] Erskine, III.ix, 36,37; *Norris* v. *Law* (1738) Elchies Executor No. 6.

[33] *Lee* v. *Donald*, May 17, 1816, F.C.; *Smith's Trs.* v. *Grant* (1862) 24 D. 1142.

Unreported cases

17.25 Where one next-of-kin had been confirmed, and another applied to be decerned *ad omissa*, and claimed to be a creditor on the executry estate, alleging that the executor had omitted a debt due by himself, which, however, the executor did not admit, both were decerned executors-dative *ad omissa*.[34]

17.26 Where a next-of-kin applied for appointment as executor-dative *ad omissa*, either alone or along with another next-of-kin already decerned and confirmed, the application was refused, no sufficient ground being set forth why the executor already confirmed should not be allowed to expede the eik, which he was willing to do and to continue the administration.[35]

The inventory

17.27 The inventory will be completed on the Form X-1 (obtainable from the sheriff clerk's office) and must contain the whole of the estate not already confirmed.

Inheritance tax

17.28 In all *ad omissa* cases, the inventory must be submitted to the Capital Taxes Office prior to applying for confirmation, and inheritance tax must be paid on the additional estate.

Small estates

17.29 There is a type of confirmation *ad omissa* which may be issued to an executor who has already been confirmed. This occurs when confirmation has been issued under the Small Estates Acts and additional estate is discovered which brings the total value of the estate above the small estates limits. Although the original executor is still acting, an eik to the confirmation cannot competently be issued, and the procedure is to take out an *ad omissa* confirmation for the additional estate (see, further, para. 11.21).

General

17.30 Confirmation *ad omissa* is a good title to call upon the represent-

---

[34] *Campbell* Oct. 13, 1879, unreported. However, as they could not agree as to the estate to be given up, confirmation could not be proceeded with, and a judicial factor was appointed.
[35] *Turnbull*, March 13, 1885, unreported.

atives of any previous executors to account for such portions of the estate as they may have intromitted with or included in their inventory but not confirmed to.[36] It is not necessary for a creditor[37] or heir on intestacy[38] to be confirmed *ad omissa* in order to call upon the original executor to account for funds in his possession, though not included in his confirmation.[39]

[36] *Nicol and Carney* v. *Wilson* (1856) 18 D. 1000.
[37] *Torrance* v. *Bryson* (1841) 4 D. 71.
[38] *Smith* v. *Smith* (1880) 7 R. 1013.
[39] Erskine, III.ix.36.

CHAPTER 18

RECORDS—EXTRACTS—CALENDARS

Records

18.01   The earliest records of all the commissary courts in Scotland are now deposited in the Scottish Record Office, H.M. General Register House, Edinburgh. They comprise

1.   the records of the old inferior commissary courts up to the abolition of these courts in 1823; and

2.   all commissary records for the following courts:-

Aberdeen (to 1980)	Inverness (to 1979)
Airdrie (to 1984)	Jedburgh (to 1984)
Alloa (to 1984)	Kilmarnock (to 1981)
Arbroath (to 1981)	Kinross (to 1975)
Ayr (to 1981)	Kirkcaldy (to 1977)
Banff (to 1980)	Kirkcudbright (to 1975)
Cupar (to 1972)	Kirkwall (to 1980)
Dingwall (to 1970)	Lanark (to 1968)
Dornoch (to 1971)	Lerwick (to 1978)
Dumbarton (to 1981)	Linlithgow (to 1980)
Dumfries (to 1980)	Nairn (to 1976)
Dunblane (to 1975)	Paisley (to 1980)
Dundee (to 1975)	Peebles (to 1984)
Dunfermline (to 1971)	Perth (to 1981)
Dunoon (to 1977)	Peterhead (to 1980)
Duns (to 1984)	Rothesay (to 1959)
Edinburgh (to 1984)	Selkirk (to 1984)
Elgin (to 1984)	Stirling (to 1973)
Falkirk (to 1980)	Stonehaven (to 1972)
Forfar (to 1981)	Stornoway (to 1847)
Glasgow (to 1984)	Stranraer (to 1976)
Greenock (to 1984)	Tain (to 1868)
Haddington (to 1979)	Wick (to 1971)
Hamilton (to 1981)	Wigtown (to 1975)

18.02   The records for Kirkwall are now held at the Orkney Library, Kirkwall and for Lerwick at Shetland Archives, Lerwick. Since 1985 all commissary records are held by the Commissary Records Unit in Edinburgh (see paras. 18.07 and 18.10). Where a record is sought which was recorded before January 1, 1985 but is not held by the Scottish Record Office (see list at para. 18.01), application should be made to the appropriate court circuit.

18.03 The commissary court books were at one time a competent record for all deeds with a clause of registration, probative deeds registered under the Act of 1698, and for protested bills and promissory notes under the Act of 1681. However, the Public Records (Scotland) Act 1809[1] declared unlawful the recording of all such writs in the commissary courts after the expiration of six months from the passing of the Act.

18.04 The proper commissary records relating to the confirmation of executors originally consisted of a register of decrees-dative and a register of testaments or confirmations, both testamentary and dative. Before 1804, there was no separate register of inventories and testamentary writs, these documents having been recorded only along with the confirmation in which, according to the forms then in use, both were engrossed. By the Stamp Act 1804,[2] it became necessary to record inventories and relative testamentary writs, whether confirmation was required or not. Accordingly, a special register was then instituted in which were recorded all inventories and writs exhibited under that Act, relating to estates of persons dying before October 10, 1808. A new register of inventories and testamentary writs, relating to the estates of persons dying after October 10, 1808, was begun under the Probate and Legacy Duties Act 1808[3] and has been carried on continuously to the present time. The inventories and confirmations and the writs constitute one register although, for convenience, they were formerly often kept in separate series of volumes.[4] It is incompetent to record any testamentary writing except as an adjunct to an inventory.

18.05 Notwithstanding the amalgamation of the commissary courts and sheriff courts in 1876, the records of the commissariot are still distinct from those of the sheriffdom. Inventories and relative testamentary writings are not recorded in the ordinary sheriff court books but in the register of inventories and writs instituted as above mentioned. They are described in the confirmation as being recorded, not in the sheriff court books, but in the court books of the commissariot. There is a practical difference. Inventories are recorded for revenue purposes, and the relative writs as the grounds upon which confirmation may be issued. After they have been recorded they are given up—the inventory to the Capital Taxes Office, and the relative writs to

---

[1] (49 Geo. 3, c.42), s. 2 repealed by Public Records (Scotland) Act 1937 (1 Edw. 8 & Geo. 6, c. 43), s. 15.

[2] (44 Geo. 3, c.98), s. 23, repealed Statute Law Reform Act 1872 (35 and 36 Vict. c.63).

[3] (48 Geo. 3, c.149), s. 38 (amended by Finance Act 1949 (c.47), s. 52 (10) and Sched. 11, Pt. IV; Finance Act 1975 (c.7), s. 52 and Sched. 13 and Law Reform (Miscellaneous Provisions) (Scotland) Act 1990 (c.40), s. 74 and Scheds. 8 and 9).

[4] Since 1985, all have been kept together.

the ingiver.[5] In contrast, where a deed is recorded in the sheriff court books, it is registered for preservation, is retained in the custody of the court, and an extract is issued.

18.06 The Registrar of the Capital Taxes Office, who was originally required to keep all inventories without limit of time,[6] is now permitted to require that only certain inventories be delivered to him[6a] and may, after examination, destroy them,[7] although a copy is recorded in the commissary court books.

Documents relating to confirmation which are available to the public

18.07 The commissary records now comprise:

1. initial writs for appointment as executors-dative, and various other applications to the sheriff in commissary matters described elsewhere in this book, together with the decrees pronounced thereon;

2. copies of inventories of estate lodged for recording, where no confirmation has been issued (excluding the schedule of debts and funeral expenses, and the parts of the inventory which disclose lifetime gifts, estate held in trust, etc., which are not recorded);

3. bonds of caution;

4. copies of confirmations;

5. copies of testamentary writings and other documents referred to in the oath to the inventory;

6. copies of documents sealed in Scotland under the Colonial Probates Act 1892 and copies of inventories recorded under that Act;

7. minute book of inventories; and

8. register of petitions and other applications.

From January 1, 1985, records in respect of items 2, 4, 5 and 6 above are kept by the Commissary Clerk in Edinburgh.[8] The

---

[5] Customs, Inland Revenue and Savings Banks Act 1877 (40 & 41 Vict. c.13), s. 12.

[6] *Ibid.*

[6a] Finance Act 1980 (c. 48). s. 94(7).

[7] Law Reform (Miscellaneous Provisions) (Scotland) Act 1980 (c.55), s. 9(*b*) and Sched. 3.

[8] S.I. 1992 No. 3256, ss. 4(3) and 5.

length of time the remaining records are held, and their location, are prescribed from time to time by the Keeper of the Records of Scotland.[9]

18.08 The Commissary Clerk in Edinburgh holds the original wills of soldiers and airmen of Scottish domicile whose wills have been filed under the Regimental Debts Acts[10] since 1971. Where confirmation is to be obtained to executors named in such wills, the sheriff clerk may apply for it to be delivered to him, and must give the commissary clerk a receipt for it.[11] Solicitors were also permitted to make similar application—but only for the purpose of making up title to heritage on behalf of a client named in the will.[12] The testamentary writing of a seaman or marine who dies in service is held by the Admiralty, who will release it in order that confirmation may be obtained.[12a]

18.09 All the documents listed at paragraph 18.08 may be examined by the public at the place where they are held, on payment of the appropriate fee. Copies, extracts, etc., may be obtained as noted below.

18.10 With effect from January 11, 1993, all commissary records have been centralised at the Commissary Records Unit (CRU), H.M. Commissary Office, in Edinburgh. Where a copy of a record which was recorded on or after January 1, 1985 is required once confirmation has been granted, application must be made direct to the CRU,[13] supplying (where possible) the full name and address of the deceased, the date of death, and the court which issued confirmation. The requisite fee must be paid in advance. The charges for copies obtained through the CRU is regulated by the Sheriff Court Fees Amendment Order 1992.[14]

18.11 The CRU will issue a plain unsigned and uncertified copy of the document, but if it requires certification, it will be returned to the court of origin for this purpose, before being issued to the applicant.

Types of copies which can be issued from the commissary records

(1) Plain copies
18.12 These are straightforward copies without certifying signatures

---

[9] S.I. 1990 No. 106, s. 8.
[10] Regimental Debts Act 1863 (26 & 27 Vict. c.57), s. 26 and Regimental Debts Act 1893 (56 & 57 Vict. c.5), s. 21(1)(*a*) and S. R. & O. 1918 No. 548.
[11] Regimental Debts (Deposit of Wills) (Scotland) Act 1919 (9 & 10 Geo. 5), (c.89), s. 1 and S. R. & O. 1918 No. 1367.
[12] *Ibid.*
[12a] S.I. 1956 No. 1217.
[13] S.I. 1992 No. 3256, (s. 263).
[14] S.I. 1992 No. 413.

or extracting clauses. They are neither authenticated nor certified as true copies.[15] Plain copies may be requested by anyone.[16]
They are now normally only requested by individuals carrying
out family history research, having been superseded for legal
purposes by "certificates of confirmation."

(2) Extracts

18.13   From the records in the commissariot books, the following
extracts will be made, signed by the clerk of court and sealed
with the seal of the commissariot, and issued:

> any decree-dative;
> a confirmation and relative testamentary writings;
> where no confirmation has been issued, the inventory
> alone; and
> the testamentary writings alone.

18.14   Commissary practice is to treat such extracts as not having the
same effect as extracts from a register of probative writs, but
only as certified or authenticated copies.[17] In extracting testamentary writings alone, they are always described in the preamble as having been exhibited along with an inventory of the
estate, and the whole writings are included in the extract as
together constituting the will.

(3) Certified extracts: for use abroad

18.15   Extracts for use abroad are more formal than the ordinary ones
which are to be used in Great Britain in that, in addition to the
extracting clause, they have a certificate of authentication signed
by the sheriff (see Style 5.01) whereas the ordinary extract is
signed by the sheriff clerk.

18.16   A foreign court will usually ask for a "grant of probate" or
"letters of probate" in nominate cases, or a "grant of letters
of administration" in dative cases, or exemplifications of those
documents. The comparable documents from our courts are a
certified extract of the confirmation along with a certified extract
of the will. If the period from the date of confirmation exceeds
six months, certain states demand a certificate that confirmation
has not been revoked and is still in full force and effect (see
Style 5.02).

18.17   Occasionally, a certified copy of the whole Inland Revenue
form, including the accounts, is asked for. This is sometimes
required where the United Kingdom inheritance tax is to be set
off against the duty paid in the country abroad. This copy
cannot be given from commissary records, and the practice is

---

[15] See, further, Lord Mackay in *Watt*, 1942 S.C. 214 at p. 219.
[16] *Per* Lord Mackay in *Watt, supra,* at p. 219.
[17] *Ibid.,* at p. 218.

that the solicitor in the executry prepares a complete copy of the inventory and accounts, etc., and sends it to the Capital Taxes Office for certification.

18.18   A few foreign (though not Commonwealth) countries require the extracts to be further authenticated or, where the country concerned is a signatory to the 1961 Hague Convention Abolishing the Requirement of Legislation for Foreign Public Documents,[18] by an apostille, which certifies them as authentic (see Style 3.05), duly issued by the Foreign and Commonwealth Office.

Duplicate confirmations

18.19   A duplicate confirmation is an exact facsimile of the original confirmation, including the date of issue, without extracting or certifying clauses of any kind. Its format varies from court to court, but in Edinburgh it is headed and backed "Duplicate," and a note is put in the left-hand margin of the first page— "Duplicate issued [*date*]."

18.20   A duplicate confirmation may be issued only to the executor or his agent.

Certificates of confirmation

18.21   A certificate of confirmation is a supplementary document certifying that confirmation has been issued and that the estate included, *inter alia*, the single item of estate which is specified on the certificate. For this purpose, several items in one company or government holdings are reckoned as one item. A certificate can be issued in respect of moveable[19] and heritable[20] property situated in Scotland and, where the deceased died domiciled in Scotland, real and personal estate in England and Wales[21] and in Northern Ireland.[22]

---

[18] Cmnd. 2617 (1965).
[19] Act of Sederunt anent certain Forms of Procedure in the Sheriff's Ordinary and Small Debt Courts, etc. (S.I. 1933 No. 48), s. 5.
[20] Succession (Scotland) Act 1964 (c.41), s. 14(2); Act of Sederunt (Confirmation of Executors) 1964 (S.I. 1964 No. 1143) and Act of Sederunt (Confirmation of Executors Amendment) 1971 (S.I. 1971 No. 1164).
[21] Administration of Estates Act 1971 (c.25), ss. 1(1) and 6(1) and (2); and Act of Sederunt (Confirmation of Executors Amendment) 1971 (S.I. 1971 No. 1164).
[22] Administration of Estates Act 1971 (c.25), ss. 2(2) and 6(1) and (2); and Act of Sederunt (Confirmation of Executors Amendment) 1971 (S.I. 1971 No. 1164).

18.22   The Act of Sederunt (Confirmation of Executors) 1964, section 5 provides that "A certificate in the form set out in Schedule D of the Act of Sederunt of February 1933 may be issued in terms of section 3 of that Act of Sederunt."[22a] The practice is that anyone—not just the executors of the deceased and those acting on their behalf—may obtain such a certificate.[23]

18.23   The form of the certificate (to be adapted when issued by the Commissariot of Edinburgh) is as follows[24]:

SHERIFF COURT OF
at

Confirmation was issued from the Commissariot of   on   19   , in favour of (here describe executors) as Executors (insert any qualification in the appointment of executors, *e.g.* executor-nominate, executor-dative, *sine qua non*, or that a majority is a quorum) of A.B. (Describe deceased)
who died on   19   DOMICILED IN SCOTLAND

It is hereby certified that the said confirmation contained, *inter alia*, the following item of estate situated in (Insert Scotland, England and Wales or Northern Ireland as appropriate)

(Here state in each Certificate such item as may be desired by the person requesting the certificate)

Given under the Seal of Office of the Commissariot of   , and signed by the Clerk of Court
at   the   day of   ,
Nineteen Hundred and

Sheriff Clerk of

18.24   The certificates of confirmation are used to expedite the process of uplifting the estate, and *quoad* the item in the certificate, are as valid and effectual as if the confirmation itself had been exhibited. If ordered when the inventory is lodged, each certificate

---

[22a] S.I. 1964 No. 1143.

[23] *Cf. Watt*, 1942 S.C. 214 in connection with the interpretation of the comparable earlier provision contained in the Act of Sederunt Feb. 3, 1933, s. 5, which provided that the "clerk shall, on request, issue Certificates."

[24] Act of Sederunt anent certain Forms of Procedure in the Sheriff's Ordinary and Small Debt Courts and for the Confirmation of Executors dated Feb. 3, 1933 (S.I. 1933 No. 48), s. 5 and Sched. D), as amended by Act of Sederunt (Confirmation of Executors Amendment) 1971 (S.I. 1971 No. 1164) and Act of Sederunt (Confirmation of Executors Amendment No. 2) 1971 (S.I. 1971 No. 1655).

presently costs £3.00. Any certificates required later must be ordered from the CRU—the first certificate then costing £9.00 and each additional certificate £3.00.

Calendar

18.25 The Commissary Clerk of Edinburgh maintains a calendar of all confirmations granted, inventories recorded and grants resealed in Scotland, specifying in each case the surname, forenames and addresses of the deceased, as shown in the inventory, whether he or she died testate or intestate, and where and on what date confirmation was granted or the inventory was recorded.[25] The records date from 1876.

18.26 A copy of the calendar for the years 1876 to 1984 is also available for inspection in H.M. General Register House, Edinburgh.

[25] Sheriff Courts (Scotland) Act 1876 (39 & 40 Vict. c.70), s. 45, as repealed by Statute Law Revision Act 1894 (57 & 58 Vict. c.56), Sched. and amended by (Calendar of Confirmations and Inventories) Order 1968 (S.I. 1968 No. 140) in terms of Sheriff Courts and Legal Officers (Scotland) Act 1927 (c.35), s. 19.

CHAPTER 19

JUDICIAL PROCEEDINGS

Introduction

Sheriff court proceedings

19.01 Although all confirmations proceed in name of the sheriff, in most cases no special reference is made to him, the proceedings being conducted in the office of the clerk of court. The sheriff will only intervene directly in the following applications:

1. For appointment of an executor-dative (see paras. 19.07–19.14);

2. For recall of the appointment of an executor-dative (see paras. 19.15–19.17A);

3. For restriction of caution (see paras. 19.18–19.27);

4. For special warrant to issue confirmation, or where there is any speciality or cause of doubt in respect of which the clerk of court declines to proceed without the authority of the court (see paras. 19.28–19.34);

5. For a proof of due execution of a testamentary writing under section 39 of the Conveyancing Act 1874 (see paras. 19.35–19.53);

6. For warrant to seal or examine the repositories of a deceased person (see paras. 19.54–19.61);

7. For commissions to take an oath or to take evidence (see para. 19.62); and

8. Where a caveat has been entered (see further paras. 19.63–19.71) and objections have been lodged.

In most of these applications, there is no defender or respondent. Each case is considered on its merits. The sheriff may *ex proprio motu* refuse the application if he considers that there is proper ground for doing so—even if there is no objector or if the objector's case has failed, either on the merits or because he has no title.

Court of Session proceedings

19.02/3 An action of reduction of a testamentary writing, or of a decree of appointment of an executor, or of a confirmation of an executor (see paras. 19.72–19.89) must be brought in the Court of Session. An action of reduction generally involves two parties— the challenger, and the party (or parties) benefiting under the deed which the challenger seeks to reduce. In such cases, the challenger must prove his case.

SHERIFF COURT PROCEEDINGS

General: form and procedure in commissary cases

19.04   The form and procedure in commissary cases is the same as in ordinary actions in the sheriff court. The form of the writ is normally as set out in Form G1 of the Ordinary Cause Rules 1993,[1] and must be written, typed or printed on A-4 sized paper of durable quality. It must not be backed.[2]

General: appeals

19.05   Initial writs are submitted in the first instance to the sheriff, from whose judgment an appeal lies either to the sheriff principal and then, if desired, to the Court of Session, or directly to the Court of Session. The ultimate appeal is to the House of Lords.

19.06   The procedure in a commissary appeal is the same as in an appeal in an ordinary sheriff court action, with one difference. If the Court of Session comes to a decision which requires an appointment or confirmation of an executor other than the executor appointed or confirmed by the sheriff, the Court of Session will itself recall the appointment or confirmation made or granted by the sheriff, but will not appoint or confirm. Instead, it will remit the matter to the sheriff with directions.[3] A similar approach is taken when a sheriff has refused to appoint or confirm and the Court of Session remits the matter back to the sheriff with directions to appoint or confirm a named person or persons.

APPOINTMENT OF THE EXECUTOR-DATIVE

Petition for the appointment of executor

19.07   A petition for appointment (or decerniture) of an executor

---

[1] Sheriff Courts (Scotland) Act 1907 (7 Edw. 7, c. 51) First Sched., rule 3.1. (1) (as substituted by S.I. 1993 No. 1956).

[2] *Ibid.*, rule 3.1. (2) (as substituted by S.I. 1993 No. 1956).

[3] *Denman v. Torry* (1899) 1 F. 881.

should conform to the style set out in Schedule 2 to the Act of Sederunt (Confirmation of Executors) 1964 (see Styles in section 6).[4] The petition shall be intimated by the sheriff clerk affixing a full copy of the petition on the door of the sheriff court house, or in some conspicuous place of the court, or of the office of the sheriff clerk, in such manner as the sheriff has directed.[5] In addition, special intimation must be made to all executors already decerned or confirmed to the deceased person,[6] and to any party who has already presented a petition in respect of the same estate[7] which may be effected by first class recorded delivery,[8] with a notice to the following effect printed on the envelope:

> "This envelope contains a citation to or intimation from [*specify the court*]. If delivery cannot be made at the address shown it is to be returned immediately to:- The Sheriff Clerk [*insert address of sheriff clerk's office*]".[9]

Thereafter, the sheriff clerk shall certify on the petition "Intimated in terms of the statute", date it and sign it.[10]

Petition not opposed

19.08   Once nine clear days have elapsed[11] since the date of the sheriff clerk's certificate without a competing petition or caveat being lodged, the normal practice is that the petition is laid by the sheriff clerk before the sheriff in chambers. Provided that the sheriff is satisfied that the petition is in proper form, and that the proceedings have been regular, he will decern the petitioner as executor, without hearing any party.[12] If there is something unusual or special in the petition, the current commissary practice is that the clerk will approach the petitioner's agent, and

---

[4] S.I. 1964 No. 1143, s. 6(1).

[5] Act of Sederunt (Edictal Citations, Commissary Petitions and Petitions of Service) 1971 (S.I. 1971 No. 1165), s. 2(2).

[6] Sheriff Courts (Scotland) Act 1876 (39 & 40 Vict. c. 70), s. 44 as amended by Act of Sederunt (Confirmation of Executors Amendment No. 2) 1971 (S.I. 1971 No. 1655), s. 2.

[7] Confirmation of Executors (Scotland) Act 1858 (21 & 22 Vict. c. 56), s. 5 as amended by S.I. 1964 No. 1143.

[8] Sheriff Courts (Scotland) Act 1907 (7 Edw. 7 c. 51), First Sched., rule 5.3. (1) (as substituted by S.I. 1993 No. 1956).

[9] Sheriff Courts (Scotland) Act 1907 (7 Edw. 7 c. 51) First Sched., rule 5.3. (3) (as substituted by S.I. 1993 No. 1956).

[10] Sheriff Courts (Scotland) Act 1876 (39 & 40 Vict. c. 70), s. 44 as amended by Act of Sederunt (Confirmation of Executors Amendment No. 2) 1971, s. 2 (S.I. 1971 No. 1655).

[11] Where the *induciae* expire on a Sunday or public holiday, a notice or appearance may be timeously lodged on the first day following on which the court is open for business: MacPhail, *Sheriff Court Practice* (1988), para. 8–02.

[12] Act of Sederunt (Unopposed Executry Petitions) 1948 (S.I. 1948 No. 621).

seek to have the petition adjusted. It is now very unusual for the sheriff to direct that the petition be called and heard in court; if there is a hearing, it is usually now in chambers.

19.09 The form of the extract of a decree-dative is prescribed by section 6 of the Act of Sederunt (Confirmation of Executors) 1964.[13]

Petition is opposed

19.10 Where the objector does not wish to compete for the office of executor, but simply opposes the pursuer's application, he must lodge objections before the expiry of the nine day *induciae*.

19.11 If the objector opposes the pursuer's application and also intends to compete for the office of executor, or to apply to be conjoined as executor, he must lodge a writ. Nothing is done until the expiry of the *induciae* in the later writ, after which both applications will be considered together.

19.12 If the question is simply one of law, the sheriff may conjoin the processes, hear the parties, and decide the case; or he may appoint a diet of debate, and thereafter pronounce judgment.

19.13 Where the objector avers that the petitioner is applying to be decerned as executor in the wrong capacity, amendment may be allowed.[14]

19.14 Where the facts are in dispute, the practice is to allow a record to be made up in one of the applications, and the case proceeds in the same manner as an ordinary sheriff court action, except that the term "answers" is used instead of "defences", and the term "respondent" instead of "defender". The other initial writ is continued until the question has been decided, when both writs are disposed of together.

RECALL OF THE APPOINTMENT OF AN EXECUTOR

Applications for the recall of appointment of executor

19.15 Where an executor has been decerned but not confirmed, it is normally competent for another party to seek to have the appointment recalled (and a new executor substituted and conjoined), without bringing an action of reduction of the original decree.[15] However, an action of reduction will be necessary

---

[13] S.I. 1964 No. 1143.
[14] *Muir, Petr.* (1876) 4 R. 74.
[15] *Webster* v. *Shiress* (1878) 6 R. 102.

if part of the case is that decree was erroneously granted by the wrong sheriff, on the basis of a false averment as to the place of the deceased's domicile,[16] for the sheriff in one jurisdiction has no authority to recall a decerniture granted in another sheriffdom.

19.16   A writ (see Style 6.39) to recall the previous decerniture, and to conjoin or substitute the new pursuer as executor is lodged in court and court dues (currently of £10)[17] paid. Where the new pursuer seeks to be appointed executor, the petition must be intimated "by the Sheriff Clerk affixing a full copy of the petition on the door of the Sheriff Court House, or in some conspicuous place of the Court, or of the office of the Sheriff Clerk", in such manner as the sheriff has directed,[18] and special intimation must be made to the decerned executor. The special intimation may be effected by first class recorded delivery,[19] with a notice to the following effect printed on the envelope:

> "This envelope contains a citation to or intimation from [*specify the court*]. If delivery cannot be made at the address shown it is to be returned immediately to: The Sheriff Clerk [*insert address of sheriff clerk's office*]".[20]

The executor who has been decerned must enter appearance if he wishes to oppose the application.

19.17   In the case of an unopposed application for the recall of the appointment of an executor, the application will not call in court. Instead, the application will be laid before the sheriff in chambers. If the sheriff is satisfied that the application is in proper form, and that the proceedings have been regular, he may recall the appointment without hearing any party. Alternatively, he may direct that the application be called and heard in court.

19.17A   It is also competent for an executor-dative himself to minute for recall of his appointment on the initial writ, provided that he has not been confirmed (see Styles 6.40–6.44).

RESTRICTION OF CAUTION

The amount of caution

19.18   Caution must be found by an executor-dative, and is normally

---

[16] See Sheriff Lee's *obiter* observations in *Webster* v. *Shiress, supra* at p. 103 on *Dowie* v. *Barclay* (1871) 9 M. 726.

[17] S.I. 1993 No. 2957.

[18] Act of Sederunt (Edictal Citations, Commissary Petitions and Petitions of Service) 1971, s. 2(2) (S.I. 1971 No. 1165).

[19] Sheriff Courts (Scotland) Act 1907 (7 Edw. 7 c. 51), First Schedule, rule 5.3. (1) (as substituted by S.I. 1993 No. 1956).

[20] Sheriff Courts (Scotland) Act 1907 (7 Edw. 7 c. 51), First Schedule, rule 5.3. (3) (as substituted by S.I. 1993 No. 1956).

for the full gross amount of the estate shown in the inventory (*i.e.*, the "Total for Confirmation"), without deduction of the debts and funeral expenses of the deceased,[21] although a debt which is secured over an item of the deceased's estate may be deducted from the item of estate over which it is secured,[22] so reducing the amount of the "Total for Confirmation", and the amount of the caution.

19.19 An executor-dative may seek to have the amount of the caution reduced.[23] The reported cases on this topic date from the nineteenth century, when the reason for making the application was the executors' inability to find an individual to act as cautioner who was able (or prepared) to grant caution for the full amount of the gross estate. Once insurance companies entered into the field of acting as cautioners, anyone could obtain caution to any amount, and the applications for restriction of caution ceased. There is, however, no reason why an application to restrict the amount of caution should not be granted in other circumstances, though the expenses of the application will now often exceed any possible saving from the reduced premium charged for the bond of caution.

Application to restrict caution

19.20 An application for restriction of caution may not be included in the petition for the appointment of an executor-dative, but must be made separately.[24] The "executor must present a written application, stating shortly the extent of the inventory to be confirmed, the amount to which he wishes the caution be limited, and the grounds on which his demand is founded".[25] The form of the initial writ is set out at Style 1.01. The court dues for the application are £10.[25a]

Consents to application to restrict caution

19.21 Prior to raising the application, the executor-dative should obtain the consent of all of the deceased's heirs on intestacy. Written evidence of such consent must be produced as part of

---

[21] Confirmation of Executors (Scotland) Act 1823 (4 Geo. 4 c. 98), s. 2 as amended by Statute Law Revision Act 1888 (51 & 52 Vict. c. 3), Sched. Pt I and Law Reform (Miscellaneous Provisions) (Scotland) Act 1980 (c. 55), s. 5.

[22] See paras. 9.12–9.14.

[23] Confirmation of Executors (Scotland) Act 1823 (4 Geo. 4, c. 98), s. 2 as amended by Statute Law Revision Act 1888 (51 & 52 Vict. c. 3) Sched., Pt I and Law Reform (Miscellaneous Provisions) (Scotland) Act 1980 (c. 55) s. 5.

[24] *Girdwood, Petr.*, 46 Sh. Ct. Rep. 115.

[25] Instructions by Commissaries of Edinburgh dated December 31, 1823, para. 4.

[25a] S.I. 1993 No. 2957.

the court process,[26] though if the consenter is unable to write, a verbal statement made to the clerk of court, and certified by him, has been accepted.[27] The consent must be by the individual himself, and not his agent,[28] or attorney, unless specially authorised to grant it.[29] Consent by a *curator bonis* or other legal guardian is sufficient.[30] Where the beneficiary is domiciled in Scotland and is under the age of 16 years, he cannot himself give consent,[31] but his guardian may give consent for the beneficiary,[32] and it would be safe only to accept the beneficiary's own consent once he is over 18 years,[33] though a court may ratify the consent of a beneficiary who is aged over 16 but under 18 years.[33a]

Procedure in an application to restrict caution

19.22 The first interlocutor is one ordering advertisement in appropriate papers, and allowing objections within 10 days or such other appropriate period, after the advertisement. The advertisement (see Style 1.01) must state

1. the name and designation of the deceased;

2. the name and designation of the executor;

3. the character in which the executor has been decerned; and

4. the amount of the restricted caution proposed by the executor.[34]

19.23 The application is disposed of by the court in a summary manner with due regard to the circumstances of the case.[35] When the 10 day or other period has expired, the pursuer lodges the advertisements and any other productions. The initial writ and productions are laid before the sheriff, who either

---

[26] This rule was introduced by Order by the Commissary dated March 13, 1862 and appears still to be applied.
[27] *Durward*, Nov. 9, 1885, unreported; *Thorburn*, Dec. 27, 1886, unreported.
[28] *Scott*, Feb. 28, 1879, unreported.
[29] *Stewart*, Nov. 25, 1885, unreported.
[30] *Szillassy*, Nov. 12, 1886, unreported.
[31] Age of Legal Capacity (Scotland) Act 1991 (c. 50), s. 1(1) (a) and 9(d).
[32] *Ibid.*, s. 5(1).
[33] *Ibid.*, s. 3(1) permits the child to set aside a prejudicial transaction which he entered into between 16 and 18.
[33a] *Ibid.*, s. 4.
[34] Commissary's Order, Sept. 26, 1870.
[35] Instructions by Commissaries of Edinburgh dated December 31, 1823, para. 4.

grants the petition, or appoints a hearing. It should be noted that even if there are no objections, the amount of the restriction asked for will not be granted automatically.[36]

Objections to an application to restrict caution

19.24 Any objector must lodge written objections (see Style 1.02) stating his interest and the ground of his objection. He is not required to state what the amount of caution should be. His claim must be relevant, but he is not required to prove it.[37]

19.25 Where objections are lodged, they are transmitted with the application to the sheriff, who, either at once, or after hearing the parties, fixes the amount of caution. Should the application be refused or withdrawn, the objector may be entitled to expenses.[38]

Practice on the amount of the restricted caution

19.26 Where no objections have been lodged, the general rule is that where the debts have been paid, and all the beneficiaries are of age and represented either as pursuers or consenters, it is sufficient if the amount of caution is fixed at a figure between five and 10 per cent of the estate to be confirmed. If these conditions are not fulfilled, the amount of caution will not be reduced below the total of the claims of the creditors and of those beneficiaries whose consents have not been obtained. In this connection, it should be noted that even if there is no evidence that the deceased had issue (whether illegitimate or not), the court is likely to require caution of an amount to cover the claim of any illegitimate children on the estate,[39] and section 7 of the Law Reform (Miscellaneous Provisions) (Scotland) Act 1968[40] has no application.

19.27 In the event of their being a claim against the cautioner, it should be noted that the non-consenters would not appear to have any preference on the cautionary fund.

Examples

    1.   All of the deceased's next-of-kin, except two who were insane, had been decerned as executors-dative, but were

---

[36] *Nicolson*, Nov. 9, 1871, unreported.
[37] See para. 19.27 example 2.
[38] *Peacock*, Mar. 8, 1889, unreported.
[39] *Wishart*, Sept. 16, 1994, unreported.
[40] (c. 70), as amended by the Law Reform (Parent and Child) (Scotland) Act 1986 (c. 9), s. 10, Sched. 1, para. 10 and Sched. 2.

unable to find caution for the full amount. The Court of Session remitted to the sheriff to confirm the persons decerned on their finding caution to the extent of two-twenty-fifth parts of the amount of the inventory, this being the amount of the shares of those next-of-kin who were not to be confirmed.[41]

2.   Where the whole estate was £15,000, and restriction to £300 was craved, an objector alleged that he had a claim for £5,000 under a will which the executor did not admit was valid. Caution was fixed at £5,000, but the objector appealed on the ground that under the will there were other legatees who would have an equal claim on the caution, and that his interest could only be secured by caution for the full amount. The appeal was sustained, and the restriction refused,[42] though when the will was subsequently reduced, the caution was ultimately fixed at £300, as originally craved.[43]

3.   An eik included estate which had been wrongly described in the original confirmation. A restriction of caution which had been granted in respect of the original confirmation was held to apply also to the eik.[44]

4.   In the case of a French administrator, where there were no debts or legatees in this country, and the estate in France was sufficient to meet all claims there, on evidence that the law of the domicile did not require security from the administrator, caution was restricted to £5, though the estate to be confirmed in Scotland was very considerable.[45]

5.   The deceased's husband, who had been decerned as her executor, averred that he was beneficially entitled to her whole moveable estate under English law—the law of her domicile. The inventory included a heritable bond, and the quesion was raised as to whether he or his wife's heir on intestacy under Scots law was entitled to the bond. Caution was restricted to the amount of the bond.[46]

6.   Where an objector alleged that the deceased had not fully accounted for certain funds which he had held as a trustee, restriction was refused.[47]

---

[41] *Bell* v. *Glen*, June 28, 1883, unreported.
[42] *Morison*, Nov. 13, 1873, unreported.
[43] *Morison*, June 23, 1874, unreported.
[44] *Burns*, Dec. 24, 1885, unreported.
[45] *De la Lastra*, Oct. 21, 1889, unreported; *De la Torre*, Oct. 21, 1889, unreported.
[46] *Mayhew*, Mar. 14, 1887, unreported.
[47] *Wilson*, May 13, 1875, unreported.

SPECIAL WARRANT FOR CONFIRMATION

Circumstances giving rise to a need for a special warrant for confirmation

19.28   On occasion, the language of a testamentary writing is such that it is not clear whom the deceased appointed to act as executor. In such a case, the sheriff clerk will not confirm on his own initiative, and it will be necessary to apply to the sheriff for special warrant to issue confirmation. A writ for special warrant will be necessary in the following cases:

1.   The writing founded on is not clearly testamentary.[48]

2.   There is an irregularity in the terms of the appointment of the executors (see paras. 5.45–5.48 for implied appointment).

3.   There is an irregularity in the terms of the execution of the deed appointing the executors—*e.g.* in a deed executed prior to August 1, 1995, the notarial execution may bear to have been effected by someone with an interest in the estate, or the testaator may have executed by mark (see para. 3.137).[49]

4.   An executor is wrongly named; or is named, but is not designed, or is not designed sufficiently to identify him (see paras. 5.03–5.04); or is not named, but is designed sufficiently to identify him (see paras. 5.06 and 5.10–5.14).

5.   The declinature or acceptance of any executor has not been ascertained (perhaps because he is abroad or cannot be found) and it is necessary to proceed with the confirmation.

6.   There is a conditional appointment of an executor (see paras. 5.33–5.35).

7.   The general disponee, universal legatory or residuary legatee seeks appointment as executor-nominate in terms of section 3 of the Executors (Scotland) Act 1900 (see paras. 5.49 *et seq.*). If the terms of the testamentary writing are such that it is clear that a particular person has the character of general disponee, universal legatory or residuary legatee, special warrant may not be required. If, however,

---

[48] *Ayrshire Hospice, Petrs.*, 1993 S.L.T. (Sh. Ct.) 75.
[49] *e.g. Fraser's Exr., Petr.*, 1955 S.L.T. (Sh. Ct.) 35; *Paterson's Exr. Petrs.*, 1956 S.L.T. (Sh. Ct.) 44; *Aitken, Petr.*, 1965 S.L.T. (Sh. Ct.) 15.

the residuary bequest is to a class (*e.g.* "my children"), or to substitute beneficiaries (*e.g.* "to A" (who predeceased the testator) "his executors and representatives whomsoever"), a special warrant must be obtained. A good example of a case where special warrant was necessary before the general disponees could be confirmed in terms of section 3 of the 1900 Act is *Miller, Petitioners,*[50] where the bequest to the general disponees was subject to the proviso that "they shall have always provided a home for me". A special petition should not be necessary in the case of a straightforward will, leaving, for instance "my whole estate to my sister Jean Smith". In such a case the want of the full designation could be made up for in page 2 of the inventory.

8.   The petitioners found on a writing which is not clearly testamentary.[51]

9.   The executors are a class and it is necessary to ascertain who are members of that class (see paras. 5.10–5.11).

10. In a nominate case, the deceased's address set out in the inventory does not support the declared domicile.

11. There is a substantial informality in the inventory or the oath (though it is normally easier for a fresh inventory to be prepared and executed).

Court writs and other papers

19.29   The writ to be used will depend on the circumstances giving rise to the application—see Styles in section 4. The dues of the petition for special warrant are currently £10.[51a]

19.30   Where the writ is in respect of an executor who has been wrongly named, or who had not been designed, or had been insufficiently designed, affidavits setting up the identity of the executor are required (see Style 2.03). Where the applicants are seeking appointment as general disponees, universal legatories or residuary legatees and the testamentary provision was, for instance, "to my children" (without naming them or further designing them), some courts require affidavits setting up the identity of the legatee, while others do not. The person before

---

[50] 1977 S.L.T. (Sh. Ct.) 67.

[51] *Ayrshire Hospice, Petrs.*, 1993 S.L.T. (Sh. Ct.) 75.

[51a] S.I. 1993 No. 2957.

whom the affidavits are sworn must not be the agent of the person whose identity is being set up.[52]

Procedure

19.31   Where a caveat has already been entered (see paras. 19.63–19.64) and objections lodged, there will be a special hearing.

19.32   In other cases, the sheriff may require that the petition be intimated to interested parties—for instance, when the validity of a testamentary writing is in question, he will order that the petition is intimated to those who would share the estate under the intestacy rules.[53] If appearance is then entered, there will be a special hearing.

19.33   Where no intimation is made, or if intimation is made, but no appearance is entered, the sheriff will either grant the prayer of the writ at once, or, where necessary, he will either order a proof before answer, or appoint the party to be heard before giving judgment.

19.34   It is not a valid ground of objection to the appointment of an executor-nominate that he intends to claim legal rights (rather than accept the testamentary provisions),[54] especially if the testator had foreseen the possibility.[55]

PROOF OF DUE EXECUTION OF TESTAMENTARY WRITING: CONVEYANCING (SCOTLAND) ACT 1874, SECTION 39[56]

Proof of due execution of a testamentary writing executed prior to August 1, 1995 under section 39 of the Conveyancing (Scotland) Act 1874[57]

19.35   A testamentary writing executed in Scotland prior to August 1, 1995 is treated as probative if the testator subscribed it on each page, in the presence of two subscribing witnesses, whose names and designations are inserted in the testing clause or appended to their subscriptions:[58] alternatively, the testator may

---

[52] *Barr, Petr.*, 1960 S.L.T. (Sh. Ct.) 7 (where the testator appointed his mistress as sole executrix, and designed her as if she was his wife).

[53] *Russell*, Nov. 30, 1871, unreported.

[54] *Smart* v. *Smart*, 1926 S.C. 392.

[55] *Anderson* v. *Hare*, 1952 S.L.T. (Sh. Ct.) 40.

[56] (37 & 38 Vict. c. 94) as amended by Conveyancing (Scotland) Act 1924 (14 & 15 Geo. 5 c. 27), s. 18 and Succession (Scotland) Act 1964 (c. 41), s. 21.

[57] *Ibid.*

[58] Conveyancing (Scotland) Act 1874 (37 & 38 Vict. c. 94), s. 38.

have acknowledged his signature to the two subscribing witnesses. If there is any irregularity in the execution, the testamentary writing may still be held to be valid provided that it was subscribed by the granter and bears to be attested by two witnesses subscribing and it can be shown that the testamentary writing was subscribed by the granter and attested by two subscribing witnesses. The burden of proof is on the person who seeks to found on the testamentary writing for confirmation as part of the commissary process.[59]

19.36 It is competent to make a special application for proof of due execution—either to the Court of Session or to the sheriff court within whose jurisdiction the defender resides.[60] but, in practice, proof of due execution of a testamentary writing always occurs as part of the commissary process, the application being made to the court where confirmation will be obtained.

Application for proof in the sheriff court

19.37 The application will be by way of an initial writ. It is normally presented at the instance of the person(s) appointed as executor(s) in the testamentary writing whose execution is in question, and will normally be combined with an application for warrant to issue confirmation nominate[61]—see Styles 4.12–4.14.

19.38 Where the initial writ has to be presented at the instance of an executor-dative,[62] the application will be combined with the petition for the appointment as executor-dative.

19.39 The initial writ should contain averments as to:

1. The defect in the testamentary writing giving rise to the application.

2. Any details missing from the testamentary writing.

3. The fact that the testamentary writing is subscribed by the granter and bears to be attested by two witnesses.

4. The fact that the subscriptions to the testamentary writing are the genuine subscriptions of the testator and of both witnesses.

[59] Conveyancing (Scotland) Act 1874 (37 & 38 Vict c. 94), s. 39 as amended by Conveyancing (Scotland) Act 1924 (14 & 15 Geo. 5 c. 27) s. 18 and Succession (Scotland) Act 1964 c. 41 s. 21. A separate action may also be brought.
[60] *Ibid.* For a style, see Dobie, *Sheriff Court Styles* (1951), p. 115.
[61] *e.g. Sheils, Petr.*, 1951 S.L.T. (Sh. Ct.) 36.
[62] See paras. 6.14 *et seq.* for the circumstances in which an executor-dative may be appointed, even although the deceased left a valid testamentary writing.

19.40   The initial writ will be lodged in court with the testamentary writing, affidavits, draft inventory[63] and the appropriate fee. The papers will then be examined, and the sheriff may order service or intimation on such persons as he deems appropriate, having regard to the papers before him.

19.41   The proof is normally by affidavit evidence alone, decree being granted *de plano*, but, in difficult cases or where the application is opposed, proof at large will be required.

> "Wherever there is room for suspicion or doubt as to what really was the deed or the sheets which the testator really intended to subscribe, the Court will refuse to sustain the deed. The Court will always, and rightly, exact the clearest proof on this point".[64]

Where proof has to be led, it should not be limited to the bare fact that the subscriptions were genuine—but proof of all surrounding facts and circumstances attending the subscription of the granter and witnesses should be led.[65]

19.42   The sheriff will either refuse the application (where either the irregularity of execution is more than an "informality", or proof of the required facts is not led), dismiss it as unnecessary (where the irregularity is trivial), or grant it. Examples of trivial irregularities include an error of a single letter in the surname of a witness,[66] the designation of a witness as "their" servant instead of "our" servant,[67] the testator's signature being written on erasure,[68] the signature of a party to a deed including the initial of her maiden name,[69] and the signature of a party to a deed including the initial of her middle name which had not been specified in the testing clause.[70]

Affidavit evidence

19.43   Affidavit evidence will be taken in relatively straightforward cases—as where the testator subscribed the last page only but there is a catch word linking the foot of each previous page with the top of the following page. An indication of the material to

---

[63] Some sheriff clerks will accept the completed inventory with the initial writ—so speeding the issue of confirmation once decree is granted.

[64] *Per* Lord Gifford in *McLaren* v. *Menzies* (1876) 3 R. 1151 at p. 1170 (in considering the possibility of sheets being inserted which the granter had not intended to form part of the deed).

[65] *Per* Lord Deas, *ibid.* at p. 1158.

[66] *Dickson's Trs.* v. *Goodall* (1820) Hume 925.

[67] *Speirs* v. *Speirs' Trs.* (1878) 5 R. 923.

[68] *Brown* v. *Duncan* (1888) 15 R. 511.

[69] *Grieve's Trs.* v. *Japp's Trs.*, 1917 1 S.L.T. 70.

[70] *Ibid.*

be contained in an affidavit is set out at Styles 2.04–2.08. The following affidavits should be obtained and lodged:

1.   Affidavits by the subscribing witnesses;

2.   Affidavits by any other person present at the execution; and

3.   In the case of a testamentary writing written on more than one sheet but subscribed on the last sheet only, an affidavit by the person who found it or who had it in his custody.

Affidavits from anyone else who has something to add may be lodged as well. The affidavits should be sworn before a notary public, a justice of the peace, or some person authorised by the law of the place where the affidavits are sworn.

Cases where section 39 has been successfully invoked

19.44   Provided that the burden of proof under section 39 can be discharged, the following mistakes in the execution of a testamentary writing effected prior to August, 1995 may be ignored:

1.   The testator subscribed the testamentary writing on the last page only;[71]

2.   The testamentary writing is on one page and execution is on the next page, but there is a link between the two pages;[72]

3.   The designations of the witnesses are not set out in the deed, or in the testing clause, or added after their signatures;[73]

4.   The testing clause contains errors of description, such as

---

[71] *McLaren* v. *Menzies* (1876) 3 R. 1151 (Case B at para. 19.49); followed in cases where it was less clear that the testator intended the unsigned page(s) to be joined to the signed one—*Brown, Petr.* (1883) 11 R. 400; *Inglis' Trs.* v. *Inglis* (1901) 4 F. 365; *Sheill, Petr.*, 1936 S.L.T. 317 (Case C at para. 19.50); *Manson* v. *Campbell* (1948) 64 Sh. Ct. Rep. 28; *Bogie's Exs.* v. *Bogie*, 1953 S.L.T. (Sh. Ct.) 32; and *Bisset*, 1961 S.L.T. (Sh. Ct.) 19, (1960) 76 Sh. Ct. Rep. 173.

[72] *McNeill* v. *McNeill*, 1973 S.L.T. (Sh. Ct.) 16; *Ferguson, Petr.*, 1959 S.C. 56; *cf. Baird's Trs.* v. *Baird*, 1955 S.C. 286 (where there were no linking words between the pages of the will and the subscription).

[73] *Addison, Petr.* (1875) 2 R. 457 (Case E at para. 19.52); *Nisbet* (1897) 24 R. 411; *Garrett* (1883) 20 S.L.R. 756; *Thomson's Trs.* v. *Easson* (1878) 6 R. 141 (Case D at para. 19.51) and *Elliot's Exs.*, 1939 S.L.T. 69.

an error in a witness's name, or an incomplete or wrong designation;[74]

5. There are unauthenticated interlineations or deletions in the testamentary writing;[75]

6. Part of the notarial docket has been omitted;[76]

7. A witness included a title such as "Miss" in her signature;[77] and

8. Probably, a signature or signatures on erasure.[78]

19.45 It is no bar to a petition under section 39 being granted that the "mistake"—for instance, the omission of a witness's designation—could have been made good under section 38 of the Conveyancing (Scotland) Act 1874,[79] before the testamentary writing was founded on in court or registered for preservation.[80]

19.46 A petition under section 39 can never validate any of the following testamentary writings executed prior to August 1, 1995:

1. A testamentary writing which the deceased did not subscribe;[81]

2. A testamentary writing signed by one witness only—perhaps where the testator had acted as a witness to his own signature[82] or, the writing bearing to be notarially executed, the "notary" acted as witness;[83]

3. A testamentary writing where an attesting witness adhibited his signature after the testator's death;[84]

4. A testamentary writing where a witness adhibited his signature before the testator signed;[85]

---

[74] *Richardson's Trs.* (1891) 18 R. 1131; *cf. Dickson's Trs.* v. *Goodall* (1820) Hume 925.

[75] *Elliot's Exrs.*, 1939 S.L.T. 69 (Case F at para. 19.53).

[76] *Shiels*, 1951 S.L.T. (Sh. Ct.) 36, see also Conveyancing (Scotland) Act 1924 (14 & 15 Geo. 5 c. 27), s. 18(2).

[77] *Per* Sheriff Berry in *McGurk* v. *Leydon*, 1937 53 Sh. Ct. Rep. 307.

[78] *Per* Lord Shaw of Dunfermline in *Walker* v. *Whitwell*, 1916 S.C. (H.L.) 75 at p. 87.

[79] (37 & 38 Vict. c. 94).

[80] *Thomson's Trs.* v. *Easson* (1878) 6 R. 141.

[81] *Baird's Trs.* v. *Baird*, 1955 S.C. 286.

[82] *Terret* v. *Frew*, 1951 S.L.T. (Sh. Ct.) 29.

[83] *Cameron* v. *Holman*, 1951 S.L.C.R. 14.

[84] *Walker* v. *Whitwell*, 1916 S.C. (H.L.) 75.

[85] *Cf. Smyth* v. *Smyth* (1876) 3 R. 573 (action relating to an assignation).

> 5. A testamentary writing where a witness did not sign his or her name;[86] and
>
> 6. A testamentary writing where a witness neither saw the testator sign nor heard him acknowledge his signature.[87]

19.47 The following cases are illustrative of the operation of section 39:

Case A

19.48 Where a will had been registered in the Books of Council and Session, without the designation of the witnesses being added, and an extract was exhibited along with the inventory for confirmation, the sheriff allowed a proof of due execution. On the evidence of the witnesses, whose signatures were appended, the sheriff held that the will had been duly executed for the purpose of confirmation, and granted authority to issue confirmation in favour of the executor named therein.[88]

Case B

19.49 A will was written on two sheets, which were stitched together, the ends of the thread being sealed with the testator's seal. It was signed only at the end by the testator and three witnesses who were not designed. On application to the Court of Session, and after proof, the will was found to be duly subscribed by the testator and witnesses, the designations of the latter being given in the interlocutor.[89] An extract of the finding was produced in the commissary court along with the will, and founded on in the application for confirmation.

Case C

19.50 A solicitor sent to a married couple for approval a draft of their mutual trust disposition and settlement. The draft consisted of two separate sheets of paper, fastened together with a brass paper-fastener or clip and was backed as "draft". The spouses subscribed on the second sheet only before two witnesses who also signed on that sheet, and returned it to the solicitor. An engrossment was prepared, but the husband died before signing it. The Lord Ordinary, after proof, granted declarator that the mutual settlement was a deed or writing subscribed by the petitioner and her deceased husband as makers thereof, and by the two named persons as witnesses, and that it was to be deemed valid notwithstanding the failure to sign the first sheet.

---

[86] *Allan* and *Crichton, Petrs.*, 1933 S.L.T. (Sh. Ct.) 2 (where the words "Mrs Bernhard" were held not to constitute the signature of a witness)—but see discussion at para. 3.99.

[87] *Forrest* v. *Low's Trs.*, 1907 S.C. 1240.

[88] *Young*, May 7, 1920, unreported.

[89] *McLaren* v. *Menzies* (1876) 3 R. 1151 (*per* Lords Neaves, Ormidale and Curriehill in a majority decision).

He further directed the clerk of court to delete the word "draft" on the back and to docket each page of the settlement as being the document to which the decree applied.[90]

Case D

19.51 After proof, an undated codicil, which bore to be subscribed by the testator and by two witnesses whose designations had not been added before it had been exhibited and recorded with the inventory, and founded on in numerous court actions, was held to be validly executed.[91]

Case E

19.52 The deceased and two witnesses subscribed a testamentary writing, but the testing clause was not filled up and, and at the time of the death, could not be filled up since the precise date of signing was unknown. After proof the writing was held to be validly executed.[92]

Case F

19.53 A testator, shortly before her death, dictated to her solicitor a codicil to her testamentary writing which he read back to her. She instructed certain alterations, and the solicitor deleted and interlined, as required. The deed was then signed by the testator, in the presence of two witnesses, who had been present throughout the whole proceedings, and who signed as witnesses. The testator did not authenticate the deletions and interlineations, no testing clause was inserted, and the witnesses did not add their designations (probably because of insufficient space to do so). After proof, it was held that the deed, subsequent to the deletions and interlineations being made, was validly executed.[93]

SEALING THE DECEASED'S REPOSITORIES

Warrant to open, examine and seal the deceased's repositories etc

19.54 Although the procedure is now seldom used, it is competent for any person with an interest in a deceased person's estate — such as the deceased's heir or a creditor — to apply to the sheriff for warrant to examine and seal the deceased's repositories, to

---

[90] *Sheill, Petr.*, 1936 S.L.T. 317. For a further case of a draft testamentary writing signed on the last of several sheets see *Inglis' Trs. v. Inglis* (1901) 4 F. 365.

[91] *Thomson's Trs. v. Easson* (1878) 6 R. 141.

[92] *Addison, Petr.*, (1875) 2 R. 457, Lord President Inglis observing (at p. 45) that the s. 39 petition might not have been appropriate if it had still been possible to fill up the testing clause.

[93] *Elliot's Exrs.*, 1939 S.L.T. 69.

inspect his papers, and to secure his effects, until it appears who is entitled to take charge of his affairs.[94] The application may also be made by anyone (for instance, a landlord or housekeeper), who wishes to be relieved of the responsibility of intermeddling with the deceased's papers or valuables which are in his possession, or which he has access to, while the amount or disposition of the deceased's property is unknown: such a person could otherwise be held to be a vitious intromitter.

19.55   The procedure has also been used by a person decerned as executor, but not yet confirmed, in order to break open lockfast places which are believed to contain property belonging to the deceased;[95] or to get access to the deceased's effects which had been refused by the person in whose custody the deceased had left them;[96] or to examine on oath a person employed by the deceased to manage his affairs.[97]

19.56   The procedure appears to have developed from the Act of Sederunt of February 23, 1692, which applied only where the heir of the deceased was a pupil, minor, idiot or furious person. It is designed to preserve the estate: it does not operate as a way of settling competing claims for the custody of the effects.[98]

Procedure

19.57   The application must set out the whole circumstances which give rise to the need for the court to intervene (see Styles 1.03 and 1.04). The court dues for the petition are currently £10, and if repositories are to be sealed up, an additional charge currently of £15 per hour is made. The sheriff may order intimation to interested parties—such as a person who has presented a petition for appointment as executor.[99]

19.58   The warrant, when granted, is in favour of the clerk of court and his assistants, and is executed by them, possibly in the presence of the interested parties. They take possession of any testamentary writing, money, documents of debts, and articles of value and remove them for safe custody to the sheriff clerk's office where the repositories are sealed. The premises are then

---

[94] Erskine, *Inst.* III.ix.56; Cameron, *Summary of the Law of Intestate Succession in Scotland* (2nd ed.), pp. 156–157; 15 McGlashan, *Practical Notes on the Jurisdiction and Forms of Process in Civil Causes of the Sheriff Courts of Scotland*, para. 262.

[95] *Balgarnie*, Mar. 4, 1866, unreported.

[96] *Mather*, Nov. 6, 1864, unreported.

[97] *Henderson v. Reid* (1832) 10 S. 632.

[98] *Milligan v. Milligan* (1827) 5 S. 206.

[99] *Thick*, Oct. 15, 1867, unreported.

secured. A report of the proceedings is made to the sheriff and lodged in process.

Recovering the papers

Deceased had nominated executors

19.59 If a testamentary writing is discovered containing a nomination of executors, the named executors may apply by minute to the sheriff for an order for the testamentary writing and any property in the possession of the clerk of court to be delivered to them. Where a will was found naming four executors, three of them (being a majority), were held entitled to delivery of the will, although the fourth, who had been with the deceased when he died abroad, had written to request that nothing should be done until he returned.[1]

Deceased did not nominate executors

19.60 If no appointment of executors is discovered, the whole effects remain in the custody of the clerk of court until an executor-dative has been appointed. The executor-dative will, on his decerniture, obtain access to the papers to enable the inventory to be prepared, but the papers will normally only be delivered to him once confirmation has been granted.[2] Exceptionally, where the effects were of trifling value, authority was granted to deliver them to the agent of the heir on intestacy even before he was decerned as executor,[3] and in another case, the *curator bonis* of a general legatee who had been decerned but not confirmed was held to be entitled to delivery of the property in the custody of the clerk.[4]

19.61 If the deceased, although he did not nominate executors, left a testamentary writing, the general disponee, universal legatory or residuary legatee may be confirmed as executor-nominate in terms of section 3 of the Executors (Scotland) Act 1900 (see further paras. 5.49–5.96 and paras. 19.28–19.34). On an averment that he is the general disponee, universal legatory or residuary legatee, or once the sheriff has granted a special warrant that he is entitled to be confirmed as executor-nominate in that capacity (where there is doubt), he may apply by minute to the sheriff

---

[1] *Littlejohn*, April 1861, unreported.

[2] The unreported decision of *Macdonald* (June 6, 1865) appears to be slightly anomalous. In that case, the deceased left a holograph writing naming a residuary legatee but no executors or trustees. The heir on intestacy was decerned executor. Warrant was granted to the clerk of court to record the writing in the Books of Council and Session, and to deliver an extract to the executor-dative, apparently before the executor-dative was confirmed.

[3] *Macpherson*, June 30, 1880, unreported.

[4] *Shand*, June 9, 1870, unreported.

for an order for the testamentary writing and any property in the possession of the clerk of court to be delivered to him.

EVIDENCE TO BE TAKEN ON COMMISSION

Commissions to take oath or evidence.

19.62 Evidence may be taken on commission where a witness resides beyond the jurisdiction of the court, or is unable to attend because of illness, age, infirmity or other sufficient cause. The evidence may either be taken to lie *in retentis* (where there is a risk that the evidence of a witness may be lost before a hearing as by a witness dying), or after proof has been allowed. Where it is believed that part of the deceased's estate is held by another the procedure can be used to find out the extent of the deceased's estate for inclusion in the confirmation.[4a] The topic is dealt with at length in the textbooks on evidence,[5] and will not be considered further in this work.

CAVEATS

A caveat: the protective step

19.63 Any person may lodge a caveat in order that he will receive intimation if someone seeks to be appointed executor to a particular deceased, or applies for confirmation to his estate (see style 6.44), or seeks to reduce the amount of caution. The fee for lodging a caveat is currently £16.00.[6] The caveat will expire after 12 months,[7] but, before it expires, it may be renewed for a further 12 months[7a] on payment of renewal fees currently of £16.00.

19.64 By lodging a caveat in one court in a sheriffdom, the person can be assured that he will be advised of any action in *any* court within the same sheriffdom.[8] However, a caveat does not itself bar any proceeding.

[4a] *Henderson* v. *Reid*, June 9, 1832, Fac. Dec.
[5] Macphail, *Sheriff Court Practice* (1988), para. 5–115 *et seq.*; Walker and Walker, *Law of Evidence in Scotland* (1964), pp. 422–427; Dickson, *Evidence* 1708, 1727 *et seq.*; *Stair Memorial Encyclopedia*, Vol. 17, paras. 1153–1156.
[6] S.I. 1993 No. 2957.
[7] Macphail, *Sheriff Court Practice* (1988), para. 21–76. Sheriff Courts (Scotland) Act 1907 (7 Edw. 7) c. 51 First Schedule rule 4.2. (2) (as substituted by S.I. 1993 No. 1956).
[7a] Sheriff Courts (Scotland) Act 1907 (7 Edw. 7, c. 51), First Sched., rule 4.2.(1) (as substituted by S.I. 1993 No. 1956).
[8] Codifying Act of Sederunt 1913, Sched., Book L, Chap. 5, s. 4.

Action following a caveat

19.65   Where the caveat is directed against the appointment of an executor-dative, once the petition is lodged in court, decree will be granted on the expiry of the *induciae* unless the party who has lodged the caveat, on receiving intimation, enters appearance and lodges answers or submits a competing writ.

19.66   Where the caveat is directed against the issue of confirmation, once the petition is lodged in court, confirmation will be issued unless the party who has lodged the caveat, on receiving intimation, lodges a note of his objections. This is treated as a notice of appearance, for which the appropriate court fee, presently £42, is paid. The sheriff or commissary clerk must then intimate to the person applying for for confirmation that confirmation can be proceeded with only under the authority of the sheriff. Unless the objector withdraws, the person applying for confirmation must present a writ answering the objections, and praying for authority to the clerk to issue confirmation (see style). The sheriff may appoint the parties to be heard, and thereafter decide; or he may order intimation to the objector, and ordain him to answer the writ as respondent, and the case will proceed as an ordinary sheriff court action.

19.67   Where it is averred that there is a serious risk that the estate might be dissipated or lost if left in the hands of an executor-nominate, the court may sist the process, and instead of confirming the executor-nominate, appoint a judicial factor.[9]

19.68   If the caveat is against restriction of caution, objections must be lodged when the application is intimated (see paras. 19.24–19.27).

When a caveat and consequent action is not enough

19.69   While a caveat can be used successfully in commissary cases in adding an executor, who has a claim on the deceased's estate which is equal to or better than that of the petitioner, a caveat alone will not lead to an appropriate remedy in all commissary cases where there is thought to be an irregularity in the procedure. For instance, a testamentary writing which is *ex facie* valid will be treated as valid until it has been reduced (see para. 19.72 *et seq.*). As Lord Shand opined:[10]

> "the effect of confirmation is merely to give a title to the executors to administer the estate of the deceased, and . . .

---

[9] *Campbell* v. *Barber* (1895) 23 R. 90; *Simpson's Ex.* v. *Simpson's Trs.* 1912 S.C. 418.

[10] *Hamilton* v. *Hardie* (1888) 16 R. 192 at p. 198.

they are liable to an action . . . to have the deed set aside
. . . the practice is to give confirmation—subject to any challenge of the will at a future time".

Hence, where the party who lodged the caveat is alleging that
the testamentary writing is invalid, confirmation will be granted
in favour of the executors nominated under the challenged
deed, unless the challenger has in fact had the testamentary
writing reduced.[11] The court may sist the case in order to allow
the objector to bring an action of reduction.[12] If the action of
reduction has been raised, and there is reason to believe that
the executors-nominate might dissipate the estate, the court
may refuse to confirm them.[13]

19.70/71 The position is however different when the testamentary writing under consideration was executed prior to August 1, 1995
and is not probative but holograph. The onus is then on the
party who is seeking to be confirmed on the basis of the testamentary writing to prove that it was in fact holograph of, and
signed by the deceased.[14] If the proof is not satisfactory, confirmation will be refused.[15-18] Where the testamentary writing
was executed (or is presumed to have been executed) on or after
August 1, 1995, but is not self-proving, a similar action must be
raised (see further paras. 4.92–4.94).

COURT OF SESSION PROCEEDINGS
ACTIONS OF REDUCTION

Actions of reduction

19.72 An action of reduction—whether of a testamentary writing, of

---

[11] *Hamilton* v. *Hardie, supra.*

[12] *Munro,* June 3 and July 19, 1889, unreported, where the sheriff sisted the
case for a month to allow the objector to bring an action of reduction, and on
the action being commenced, continued the sist until the action was determined.
When the will was reduced, the petition for warrant to issue confirmation was
refused, and a warrant was granted to issue confirmation under a will of a prior
date (*Munro,* June 20, 1890, unreported).

[13] *Hamilton* v. *Hardie* (1888) 16 R. 192, *per* Lord President Inglis at p. 196 and
Lord Shand at p. 198. But *cf.* the earlier decision of *Graham* v. *Bannerman* (1822)
1 S. 362 where even although it was alleged that an action had been raised to
reduce the will which was being challenged (on the ground that it was fraudu-
lent and *ultra vires* of the testator), confirmation was granted in favour of the
executors-nominate, in preference to heirs on intestacy, until the deed was
reduced.

[14] See further paras. 3.120 *et seq.*

[15-18] *Anderson* v. *Gill* (1858) 3 Macq. 180; *cf.* the notarial execution in *Henry* v.
Reid (1871) 9 M. 503.

a decree of appointment of executor,[19] or of a confirmation of executors—is competent only in the Court of Session.[19a] If the court is to grant decree, the pursuer must be able to show that he has title to pursue the action, and to prove a valid ground of challenge.

Reduction of a testamentary writing

Title

19.73 The parties who have title to raise an action of reduction of a testamentary writing are the heirs on intestacy,[20] and the beneficiaries under a prior testamentary writing, provided that they can lodge it in Court.[21] A person having a *ius crediti* under a marriage contract entered into by the deceased has no title to reduce the deceased's testamentary writing.[22]

19.74 If the prior testamentary writing has been mislaid, an action must be brought to prove the tenor of the lost deed, before the heirs under the lost deed can raise an action of reduction of the later deed.[23]

Grounds of Challenge:

19.75 The grounds on which a testamentary writing may be reduced can be summarised as follows:

1. The testamentary writing was void from uncertainty.[23a]

2. Forgery: it was not subscribed by the testator.

3. "Facility and circumvention" or "incapacity and undue influence of the testator".[24]

4. Essential error caused by misrepresentation.[25]

5. Insanity of testator: evidence of deteriorating powers is insufficient to establish mental incapacity.[26]

---

[19] Where confirmation has not yet been granted in favour of the executor dative, it is competent to petition for the recall of the appointment, rather than to have the appointment reduced. See para. 19.15.

[19a] *Blair* v. *Duncan* (1901) 4 F. (H.L.) 1.

[20] *Crichton* v. *Crichton's Trs.* (1874) 1 R. 688; *Gilchrist* v. *Morrison* (1891) 18 R. 599.

[21] *Gilchrist* v. *Morrison, supra.*

[22] *Smith* v. *Smith's Trs.* (1905) 12 S.L.T. 782; cf. *Mackie* v. *Gloag's Trs.* (1884) 11 R. 10.

[23] Cf. *Gilchrist* v. *Morrison* (1891) 18 R. 599.

[23a] Ersk. I. iv. 18 (Note (c)) 18 (Note (c)) (Nicholson ed., 1871).

[24] See para. 3.15.

[25] *Munro* v. *Strain* (1874) 1 R. 522.

[26] See para. 3.15.

6. The proper formalities of execution have not been met. The onus of proof is heavy, for the courts are reluctant to prefer the oral evidence of a witness that he did not see the testator sign, or hear him acknowledge his signature, in the face of the evidence of the witness's signature on the deed.[27]

"it has always been recognised that such evidence [*i.e.* of instrumentary witnesses] requires to be scrutinised with very special anxiety and care. Where the signature of a deed is admitted . . . to be genuine and bears to be attested, every legal presumption tells in favour of the validity of the deed. To set such a deed aside upon the sole evidence of the testimony of the instrumentary witnesses would indeed appear to afford a solitary example of the preference of oral over written evidence.

"There is authority for the view that such evidence should be disregarded unless there is other evidence to corroborate it (see Dickson on Evidence, section 904 and also section 698) . . . .

"If the evidence of the instrumentary witnesses may in law be accepted as sufficient without corroboration, it has at least been recognised that the witnesses must themselves be regarded as entirely trustworthy".[28-29]

7. In the case of a notarial execution prior to August 1, 1995, the notary by whom the will was executed did not write out the docket.[30]

Reduction of a decree appointing an executor

19.76   As discussed at para. 19.15, where it is desired to remove an executor-dative from office, it is not normally necessary to raise a Court of Session action of reduction of the decerniture of the executor. It is submitted that the only instance when such an action of reduction is appropriate is where it is argued that the decerniture was on the basis of a false averment as to the place of the deceased's domicile[31-33]—whether the false averment was as to the sheriffdom[34] or as to the country[35] in which the deceased was domiciled.

---

[27] Burns, *Conveyancing Practice According to the Law of Scotland* (4th ed.) pp. 5 and 6; Halliday, *Conveyancing Law and Practice in Scotland*, para. 3–16; Walker and Walker, *The Law of Evidence in Scotland*, para. 182(a).

[28-29] *Per*, Lord Moncrieff in *McArthur* v. *McArthur's Trs.*, 1931 S.L.T. 463.

[30] *Henry* v. *Reid* (1871) 9 M. 503.

[31-33] See Sheriff Lee's *obiter* observation in *Webster* v. *Shiress* (1878) 6 R. 102 at p. 103 on *Dowie* v. *Barclay* (1871) 9 M. 726.

[34] *e.g. Dowie* v. *Barclay, supra.*

[35] *Cf. Baine's Ex.* v. *Clark*, 1957 S.C. 342.

19.77 A person who has a prior or equal claim to be appointed executor-dative or who was nominated executor in the deceased's final testamentary writing, has title to raise an action of reduction of a decree of appointment of an executor.

Reduction of a decree decerning an executor and confirmation thereon

19.78 A person who has a prior or equal claim to the deceased's estate under the laws of intestacy, or who was nominated executor in the deceased's last testamentary writing, has title to raise an action of reduction of a decree of appointment of an executor and the confirmation thereon.

19.79 The ground on which such a decree and confirmation may be reduced is of essential invalidity: that an averment in the petition, on the basis of which decree was granted, was false. Possible grounds of challenge include:

1. A false averment as to the domicile of the deceased— either as to the sheriffdom[36] or as to the country[37] in which the deceased was domiciled.

2. An error as to the relationship of the petitioner to the deceased.[38]

3. Failure to narrate the existence of a relative with a prior claim on the intestate's estate.

4. The existence of an unrevoked testamentary writing.

19.80 The fact that the date of a decree was written on erasure is not a valid objection.[39]

Reduction of the confirmation

19.81 A person who has a preferable claim to be confirmed as executor (*e.g.* the person nominated executor in a subsequent testamentary writing to that referred to in the confirmation) has title to raise the action of reduction.

---

[36] *e.g. Dowie* v. *Barclay, supra.*

[37] *Cf. Baine's Exr.* v. *Clark, supra.*

[38] However, in the pre-1964 succession case of *Dowie* v. *Barclay, supra.* the court was prepared to ignore the fact that the petitioner had described herself as "one of the next-of-kin" of the deceased, whereas she was in fact the representative of a pre-deceasing next-of-kin, in which capacity, in any event, she would have been entitled to the appointment. See also *Bones* v. *Morrison* (1866) 5 M. 240.

[39] *Dowie* v. *Barclay* (1871) 9 M. 726.

19.82 The ground on which confirmation of an executor may be reduced is that an averment in the inventory was false. Possible grounds of challenge include:

1. An error in the stated domicile of the deceased—both as to the sheriffdom[40] and as to the country[41] in which the deceased was domiciled.

2. The testamentary writing founded on had been revoked (see paras. 3.154–3.176).

3. There is a subsequent testamentary writing appointing an executor.

Commissary consequences: amending the records

19.83 Once decree has been granted in an action of reduction of a testamentary writing on which confirmation has been issued, or of the confirmation itself, the appropriate sheriff clerk or commissary clerk at Edinburgh must have express authority from the court in order to make the appropriate amendments to the commissary records.

19.84 The simplest method of achieving this is if the Court of Session summons includes a conclusion for warrant and authority for the commissary records to be amended.[42] The amendments will then be made on production of the certified copy interlocutor, or an extract of the Court of Session decree.

19.85 If the summons does not contain such a conclusion, it is necessary to adopt the more complicated procedure of presenting a petition to the commissary office craving authority for the necessary amendments to be made.[43]

19.86 When the confirmation is reduced, the following records are noted by the sheriff clerk of the appropriate sheriff court with the date etc of the decree of reduction:

1. Index of dative decrees (if appropriate)

2. Minute book of court

3. Petition for decerniture (if appropriate)

---

[40] Cf. *Dowie* v. *Barclay, supra.*
[41] Cf. *Baine's Exr.* v. *Clark,* 1957 S.C. 342.
[42] See Note to Style 4.15.
[43] See Style 4.15.

4. Bond (which may be returned to the cautioner if this is requested)

5. Day book

6. Confirmation itself, which must be returned by the agent and is retained by the sheriff clerk

The commissary clerk in Edinburgh notes the copy of the confirmation and (if appropriate) the testamentary writing held in the Commissary Records Unit, making the appropriate deletions. The sheriff clerk will put a note on the confirmation and records in the following terms:

Cancelled by Order of the Lords of Council and Session (*or* the Sheriff) conform to decree dated (*or* interlocutor dated)

(signed)

Sheriff Clerk

The new confirmation

19.87 Once the confirmation has been reduced, a new inventory must be lodged. If the same agents are involved, the old fee stands as a credit against the fee payable on the new inventory, with the appropriate payment or repayment being made. If different agents are involved, the old agents will reclaim the fee paid, and the new agents will pay the confirmation dues in normal course.

19.88 This approach is revealed in a number of old cases:

1. An application for confirmation by an executor-nominate was opposed by the heir-on-intestacy, who stated that an action had been commenced to reduce the will on the ground of incapacity and impetration. The sheriff sisted the process. The petitioner appealed to the Court of Session, where because there was added specific averments impeaching the conduct and intentions of the executrix-nominate and alleging danger to the estate, the court dismissed the petition for confirmation and appointed a judicial factor on the executry estate, reserving the right to the petitioner to apply again in the event of the reduction failing and the factory being recalled.[44]

2. In a petition for warrant to issue confirmation, the executor-nominate averred that the deceased died domiciled

---

[44] *Campbell* v. *Barber* (1895) 23 R. 90; followed in *Simpson's Ex.* v. *Simpson's Trs.*, 1912 S.C. 418.

in Scotland, by the law of which the will founded on was validly executed. The objector averred that the deceased died domiciled in England, by the laws of which the will was invalid, and further that at the time of making it, the testator was not responsible for his actions. The sheriff sisted the case for a month to allow the objector to bring an action of reduction, and on the action being commenced, continued the sist until the action should be determined.[45] Once the will was reduced, the petition for warrant to issue confirmation was refused, and a warrant was granted to issue confirmation under a will of a prior date.[46]

[45] *Munro*, June 3 and July 19, 1889, unreported.
[46] *Munro*, June 20, 1890, unreported.

INDEX

References are to paragraph numbers.

INDEX

References are to paragraph numbers.